W9-DHL-689

THE PRACTICAL IMAGINATION

THE
PRACTICAL IMAGINATION
The German Sciences of State
in the Nineteenth Century

DAVID F. LINDENFELD

THE UNIVERSITY OF CHICAGO PRESS
Chicago and London

DAVID F. LINDENFELD is professor of history at Louisiana State University and the author of *The Transformation of Positivism: Alexius Meinong and European Thought, 1880–1920.*

THE UNIVERSITY OF CHICAGO PRESS, CHICAGO 60637
THE UNIVERSITY OF CHICAGO PRESS, LTD., LONDON

© 1997 by The University of Chicago
All rights reserved. Published 1997

Printed in the United States of America

06 05 04 03 02 01 99 98 97   1 2 3 4 5
ISBN: 0–226–48241–3 (cloth)
ISBN: 0–226–48242–1 (paper)

Library of Congress Cataloging-in-Publication Data

Lindenfeld, David F.
    The practical imagination : the German sciences of state in the
nineteenth century / David F. Lindenfeld.
        p.   cm.
    Includes bibliographical references and index.
    ISBN 0-226-48241-3 (alk. paper).—ISBN 0-226-48242-1 (pbk. :
alk. paper)
    1. Social sciences—Germany—History—19th century. 2. Public
administration—Germany—History—19th century. 3. Policy sciences—
History—19th century. 4. Germany—Intellectual life—19th
century.   I. Title.
H53.G4L56   1997
320.943—dc20   96-43699
                                                                                    CIP

⊗The paper used in this publication meets the minimum requirements of the American National Standard for Information Sciences—Permanence of Paper for Printed Library Materials, ANSI Z39.48-1984.

Contents

Tables and Figures

Acknowledgments

THIS WORK has been long in preparation, and the debts incurred along the way have been many. Foremost among them are to my sources of funding. The Deutscher Akademischer Austauschdienst provided two three-month fellowships for study in the Federal Republic at the beginning and end of my research. The International Research and Exchanges Board (IREX) supported a four-month stay in the former German Democratic Republic in 1984. The American Philosophical Society enabled me to travel to Vienna in the summer of 1987. Finally, a grant from the National Science Foundation's program in the history and philosophy of science enabled me to make full use of a 1989 sabbatical.

The librarians and archivists who have assisted me are too numerous to mention, but some stand out: Dr. Jürgen Zander at the Schleswig-Holsteinische Landesbibliothek in Kiel and Dr. Volker Schäfer at the Universitätsarchiv in Tübingen. The staff at the Universitätsbibliothek in Heidelberg kept up with my immoderate demands for dusty old university catalogues for two summers running, while that of the Louisiana State University interlibrary loan office performed similarly heroic feats. The staff at the Zentrales Staatsarchiv Merseburg were also exceptionally cooperative.

Of the individuals who gave me encouragement and constructive criticism, I should mention Bernhard vom Brocke, Rüdiger vom Bruch, Dirk Käsler, Anthony LaVopa, M. Rainer Lepsius, Paul Paskoff, Fritz Ringer, the late Siegfried Richter, Wolfram Siemann, Peter Thal, and Keith Tribe. I am also grateful to Erk Volkmar Heyen and Hans Erich Bödeker for providing me the opportunities to present some preliminary findings at three colloquia at the Werner-Reimers-Stiftung in Bad Homburg. In the United States, the German Studies Association, the Southern Historical Association, the Consortium on Revolutionary Europe, and the LSU History Department's Works-in-Progress seminar afforded similar occasions for testing my ideas. In Baton Rouge, Rudolf Heberle and Franziska Tönnies Heberle shared their book collection, their personal reminiscences, and many hours of good fellowship. My colleagues Dena Goodman and John Henderson read portions of the manuscript—in Henderson's case, most of it—acting as lenses to focus on the forest rather than the trees. Two undergraduate student workers, Christopher Pope and Karen Holt, cheerfully helped with the more tedious tasks of data entry and compilation of tables.

Finally, a special note of acknowledgment should go to someone I never met: the former president of Louisiana State University, James Monroe Smith. I am told that Smith, before going to prison for embezzlement and forgery in 1939, personally wrote a check for the purchase of the nineteenth-century economist Richard T. Ely's papers and book collection—a deed which made Louisiana State a preeminent site for writing a book on the German sciences of state.

Baton Rouge, September 1995

Introduction: A Theoretical Framework

This book is a study of practical reasoning. It traces a discourse of thinking about politics, economy, and society in Germany that came to be known as the sciences of state (*Staatswissenschaften*). The term implied not simply that the state was the object of this discourse, but also its subject: the sciences of state originated as a curriculum to train administrators in the skills and knowledge they would need to do their jobs well.

The sort of practical reasoning described here is to be distinguished from two other approaches which modern Western societies have employed to guide action by the state. The first of these may be called the Machiavellian, which treated politics basically as an art based on interpersonal, intuitive knowledge. The maxims of governing were learned by studying concrete cases of interactions and struggles among princes, or between princes and their subjects. The basic elements of such interactions were mostly personal virtues and vices: whether one exercised one's power through fear or love, using generosity or cruelty, honesty or duplicity, and so forth. Although impersonal circumstances could not entirely be ignored, they lent themselves to anthropomorphizing, as in Machiavelli's depiction of fortune as a woman. This art of governing was summed up in the term *cleverness* (*Klugheit*). Thus a German dictionary of 1732 gave one meaning of politics as "a particular cleverness, to contrive the advantages of a prince or a state, to seek [these] through hidden paths, and to attain them by all manner of means."[1]

In contrast, the discourse to be treated here tended to view governing as more impersonal, an administration of a population which consisted of an ensemble of people and things.[2] It was concerned with domestic affairs rather than with diplomacy or the military. Moreover, the maxims of administration could be systematized and made into a science, appropriate to an academic setting. Admittedly, the educational curricula for officials which included the sciences of state were rarely exclusively academic; they included an apprenticeship in the field. But insofar as book learning was also considered valid, the

---

1. *Zedlers Universal-Lexikon* (1732), quoted in Brückner, *Staatswissenschaften*, 92.
2. For a fuller development of this contrast, see Foucault, "Governmentality," 89–92.

1

impetus existed for a systematic treatment of such knowledge; hence the growth of a constellation of sciences in the seventeenth and eighteenth centuries, partly rooted in the medieval disciplines of ethics, politics, and economy, but soon acquiring a life of their own.

A second, contrasting, approach may be called the utopian, which came to predominate in the nineteenth century. Stemming from the ideals of the French Revolution, it tended to view political action in terms of future goals: the realization of freedom, equality, and the community of shared goods. Although the literature based upon these assumptions was rich and varied, it is safe to say it was relatively less concerned with practical reasoning, that is, with discussing in detail exactly *how* such goals were to be implemented. The reason for this lack is well known: the implementation was to be carried out by the progressive movement of history, which sooner or later, somehow or other, would arrive at the desired destination. This is not to say that the intellectual leaders of these movements believed that human subjects were automatons, or that the movements themselves had little or no practical effect: the followers of St.-Simon and Marx demonstrate the contrary. But it is to say that the project of a systematic science of practice, of weighing alternative choices of action and formulating criteria for deciding among them, was not their prime concern. In contrast, the sciences of state were less concerned with articulating the goals or ends of action and were more concerned with the techniques of implementation. This did not mean that practical reasoning took place in a moral vacuum. On the contrary, the theme of the moral and ethical purpose of government and administration was reiterated time and time again, usually expressed in the phrase "the general welfare" of the population. But the writers in this tradition tended to assume that this general welfare would result from well-considered action itself, rather than consisting of a lofty or distant goal to be realized in a remote continent or at the end of a historical process. The mind-set was neither exclusively one of calculating, instrumental rationality, nor of substantive, value-oriented rationality, but of both at once. This notion of ethically directed practical reason was derived from Aristotle, whose *Nicomachean Ethics* began with just this idea: "It is thought that every activity, artistic or scientific, in fact every deliberate action or pursuit, has for its object the attainment of some good."[3]

One reason for writing this book is my admittedly impressionistic belief that there is a relative dearth of models for practical reasoning in the United States. The religious and enlightenment traditions which shaped this country have tended to pitch the level of public discussion, for conservatives and liberals

---

3. Aristotle, *Nicomachean Ethics*, 1.1. For a discussion of the Aristotelian basis of early modern political thought, see Hennis, *Politik und praktische Philosophie*, chap. 2.

alike, at the utopian heights, focusing on the idealistic ends of policy rather than asking how they are to be attained. And while there are certainly counterinstances to this assertion, such as the constitutional principle of checks and balances or the well-developed art of balancing conflicting interest groups through compromise in Congress, these techniques are more applicable to the activity of legislation than to administration. Add to this a well-founded democratic distrust of bureaucracy with its hierarchical structure, and of the authority of experts. But bureaucracy cannot simply be wished away: administrative tasks and turfs continue to sprout unexpectedly in response to unforseen problems and crises of great complexity and magnitude, as they have in all industrialized societies since the beginning of the twentieth century. Bureaucracy and its discontents are an expression of the dissonance between the egalitarian ideals of democracies and the hierarchical realities of their industrial economies and societies, based as these are on elaborate divisions of labor. In plainer terms, we may not like elites or bureaucracies, but they are likely to be with us for some time to come. Thus we still need their histories. The issues which the *Staatswissenschaftler* grappled with, such as the best form of taxation or how to give aid to the poor, are still with us today. The study of bureaucratic mind-sets in the past may provide us with a greater sense of alternatives on how to live with them and make the best of them.

The attempt to systematize practical knowledge in the service of bureaucratic education at the university level occurred in Germany, a country not known for its egalitarian tendencies in the nineteenth century. The growth of the Prussian bureaucracy, its social composition, and its role in politics have all been amply studied; the predominance of the aristocracy in its upper ranks, particularly in the Wilhelminian era, is a matter of record; the subsequent acquiescence and support of the civil service in the Nazi regime cannot be denied.[4] What struck me, however, as I began work on this study, was the refreshingly un-Teutonic nature of much of the writing in the sciences of state, at least in the eighteenth and early nineteenth centuries. It was during this period that the bureaucracies of the German states were leading forces for change in matters such as peasant emancipation and the dismantling of guild privileges. Here, it seemed, was a discourse that was sober, empirical, and utilitarian in its

---

4. Studies include Muncy, *The Junker in the Prussian Administration;* Preradovich, *Führungsschichten in Österreich und Preussen;* Morsey, *Oberste Reichsverwaltung unter Bismarck;* Gillis, *Prussian Bureaucracy in Crisis;* Röhl, "Higher Civil Servants in Germany," 129–51; Caplan, "Bureaucracy, Politics and the National Socialist State," 234–56; Caplan, "'The Imaginary Universality of Particular Interests,'" 299–317. The bureaucracies of the other German states have been less thoroughly studied, although this has been remedied somewhat by the multivolume *Deutsche Verwaltungsgeschichte,* 6 vols., ed. Kurt G. A. Jeserich, Hans Pohl, and Georg-Christoph von Unruh. Also Bernd Wunder, *Geschichte der Bürokratie in Deutschland,* provides a balanced treatment.

conception of the general welfare. It appeared far removed from the metaphysical language of Fichte or Hegel and from the unending appeals to *Geist* and *Kultur* that characterized so much of German thought—and might well be-called the German variant of utopian thinking. As my research continued, however, the links between this practical discourse and the other, better-studied, sectors of German learning became clearer. A case in point was the connection between the sciences of state in the early nineteenth century and the emerging social sciences which partially replaced them in the late nineteenth and early twentieth centuries—where nationalistic and imperialistic themes were more prominent, and the sobriety of tone was undermined. This gradual dissipation of practical reasoning became one of the major themes of the book.

Another major theme is the breadth of knowledge which was part of this tradition. The notion that professors should be comprehensive in their knowledge rather than specialists was widespread in German universities before the nineteenth century, when original research came to be the standard by which academic excellence was judged. The decisive shift to this standard occurred for the sciences of state in the 1860s and 1870s, that is, somewhat later than for other disciplines. And even as it occurred, many leading practitioners sought to maintain a degree of breadth by maintaining close ties between the social sciences and such fields as history, law, philosophy, and (to a lesser extent) the natural sciences. All of this may have a certain contemporary relevance and appeal to those who are disillusioned with the highly quantified and specialized approaches of some contemporary social sciences (such as economics) in addressing complex social issues. This brings me to the methodological and theoretical assumptions underlying this study.

The history of the *Staatswissenschaften* affords a case study of the multiple relationships between knowledge and power—both in the straightforward sense of knowledge in the service of power, that is, the training of administrators to do the bidding of the sovereign state, and in the sense developed by Michel Foucault, who viewed systems of knowledge as themselves instruments of specific forms of domination that are suffused throughout a society.[5] The latter occurs in a number of ways: (1) through a specific set of institutions (e.g., universities, their professorial chairs and research institutes), which participate in the creation of social differences by elevating some and excluding others, thereby forming part of an apparatus by which power is distributed; (2) through the very content of knowledge, by the drawing of boundaries which define the material to be covered and the material to be excluded by a given science, and by the establishment of hierarchical distinctions within the science itself. Foucault was admittedly less interested in applying this approach to the domi-

5. See Foucault, *Power/Knowledge*, 92–133.

nant elites than to the dominated subjects,[6] but it is also proving fruitful for the study of elites as well, specifically by posing new ways of looking at their roles in the larger societies to which they belong.

The portrayal of such relationships between knowledge and power inevitably hinges on some type of spatial analogy. Foucault's language sometimes suggests an organic circulatory system, and more often an electrical grid:

> Power must be analysed as something which circulates, or rather as something which only functions in the form of a chain. It is never localised here or there, never in anybody's hands, never appropriated as a commodity or piece of wealth. Power is employed and exercised through a net-like organzation.[7]

Pierre Bourdieu employs the more explicit concept of an intellectual *field*, a term which suggests an arena for the play of intellectual forces and power relationships, such as those between orthodox and heterodox positions, within it.[8] One can thus picture elitist thought and its changes as taking place within a delimited *area* within a larger space occupied by the culture as a whole (which of course may contain a multitude of other discourses or subcultures). The delimited area will contain some ideas or meanings which are esoteric to it and will share others with the space of the larger culture. For Bourdieu, power draws on various forms of "capital"—not only economic, but also cultural and symbolic. Symbolic capital consists, for example, of the prestige and power that come with holding an advanced degree. The conflicts between mainstream and marginal discourses within a field are struggles over such symbolic power.[9] I have elsewhere used the term *system* to convey a similar notion, namely that the basic "units" of discourse are complex configurations of ideas and practices.[10]

Whatever the label, these spatial metaphors share several common features. (1) They refer to complex wholes, in which the meaning of any single element is distorted if taken in isolation; rather they are characterized by the relationships and positions of ideas and practices with respect to each other. (2) They reject a dichotomy between thought and action. The area is composed of theo-

---

6. Ibid., 96–98, although *The Order of Things* constitutes an exception to this in Foucault's work as a whole.

7. Ibid., 98. Cf. 142; also *The Order of Things*, xx, xxii, 63, 346; "Politics and the Study of Discourse," 54.

8. Bourdieu, "The Intellectual Field: A World Apart," 140–49; see also Fritz Ringer, *Fields of Knowledge*, chap. 1.

9. Bourdieu, "Social Space," 135–36; "Intellectual Field," 143, 145.

10. Lindenfeld, "On Systems and Embodiments," 36–38. *System* admittedly has a different set of connotations than *field*, implying a a relatively stable and insulated body of ideas that are clearly set apart from a surrounding milieu (e.g, law, medicine, physics); hence it is more applicable to specialized disciplines that gradually emerge out of a broader field. But in terms of the discourse we will be studying, these distinctions are relative.

ries and discoveries expressed not only in lectures and publications, but also in the institutional structures and practices. Thus a field or system has a politics of its own and a process of socialization by which people become members of its elite. (3) They involve a set of boundaries by which some ideas, practices, people, or places are included, and others are excluded or marginalized.[11] None of these features are static. Taken together, they afford a means by which a field may be viewed as an arena of struggle and negotiation, or alternatively as one of meanings and ideas misunderstood and understood—and of translating one perspective into the other.

The German sciences of state constituted an empirically accessible instance of such a field, one characterized by a distinctive body of knowledge based on practical criteria. This can be seen by opening any German university catalogue from the nineteenth century, where the heading "sciences of state" (or "state and cameral sciences") appeared alongside history, philosophy, the natural sciences, philology, law, and medicine. Depending on the decade and the locale, one would find under that heading lectures in economics, statistics, finance, politics, "police science" (*Polizeiwissenschaft*, meaning roughly "public administration"), agriculture, forestry, mining, "technology," social policy, and sociology. Other lectures in state and administrative law would more likely, but not invariably, be found in the listings for the juristic faculty—an instance of a partial overlap of fields. Thus one important aspect of this history is to trace the shifts within this intellectual field by which some disciplines became extinct, new ones came into existence, others migrated to different subject areas, and still others were transformed in content or method. By drawing boundaries which defined the material covered—and excluded—by the sciences of state, the practitioners of these disciplines created a sphere of authority for themselves, which in turn lent legitimacy to their specific practical prescriptions. As the boundaries changed, so did the nature of that authority—as happened, for example, when social science emerged from the broader category of state science after 1870.

Moreover, the history of the sciences of state is full of struggles for symbolic power—between advocates of academic or practical field-training as the main component of bureaucratic education, or, more pervasively, between partisans of the sciences of state versus those of civil law as the dominant element in university study. As we shall see, these struggles were clearly expressions of conflicts among social groups for access to prestigious administrative positions. They thus reflected the broader changes in German politics, economy, and society.

A second theoretical concept that elucidates the relations between knowl-

11. See Luhmann, *Soziale Systeme*, chap. 2 ("System und Umwelt").

edge and power is that of *embodiment*.[12] Embodiments may be thought of as foils to fields or systems. Their primary characteristic is that of simplicity. Embodiments are unit-ideas or symbols which serve to condense or fixate a variety of meanings or shades of meaning into a single unit. Think, for example, of a national flag, a physical embodiment of patriotism. The values and assumptions associated with the meaning of patriotism will be different to different people. These values could easily be spun into a system, or even contrasting systems. The purpose of a flag, however, is not to articulate these values, but to collapse them into a unifying meaning. By virtue of their simplicity, embodiments can be apprehended quickly and shared by diverse groups within a culture. They thus transgress the boundaries established by systems and the hierarchical distinctions within them. They communicate on an emotional as well as a cognitive plane. Moreover, words, even in the absence of physical symbols or images, can perform the same function. Words like *Geist* and *Kultur* in nineteenth-century Germany, or *democracy* or *freedom* in the United States, carry with them a multitude of connotations and elicit a variety of thoughts and emotions which do not need to be spelled out in order to be effective. And while the history of the sciences of state in nineteenth-century Germany is primarily the history of a constellation of systems, embodiments enter into that history at crucial points. Words like *Volk, nation, organic,* or *society* may be said to be among the major "actors" in the story, serving, so to speak, as points of gravitation within the intellectual and cultural fields at once. In addition to physical and verbal symbols, people can serve as embodiments. Charismatic leaders may be said to embody the ideas and values they represent by expressing the identity of their persons with the higher truths they expound. In secular cultures, intellectuals frequently claim to have a unique grasp of the totality of truth that eludes lesser mortals; they fashion themselves as the vessels of that totality.[13] Fritz Ringer's ideal type of the German mandarin exemplifies this: a figure who personifies *Geist* and *Kultur.* As Ringer put it, "The state lives neither for the ruler nor for the ruled as a whole; it lives for and through the 'men of culture' and their learning."[14] As the sciences of state devolved into the social sciences in the late nineteenth century, the appearance of such figures who explicitly invoked such unit-ideas became increasingly conspicuous.

Taken together, the notions of systems and embodiments provide a way of giving more precise meaning to the term *ideology.* Certain bodies of ideas have exerted a hold on people's minds for long periods of time because they have communicated at a variety of levels: simple and complex, logical and emo-

---

12. Lindenfeld, "Systems and Embodiments," 38–42.
13. See, for example, Jay, *Marxism and Totality,* 11–13, 529–30.
14. Ringer, *Decline of the German Mandarins,* 11.

tional. Ideologies such as nationalism or socialism generally consist of an elaborately developed system or systems, created by and for elites; but part and parcel of these systems are the concrete and verbal symbols that are shared by much larger groups of people (e.g. "bourgeois" and "proletariat" in the case of Marxism). This helps to explain why intellectuals who operate within such ideologies can become powerful influences on public opinion—as happened in the case of the *Staatswissenschaften* at the turn of the twentieth century.

This brings me to a final category in this theoretical arsenal: that of intellectual *strategies*. I mean by this the thought processes which shape the various features of an intellectual space—mainstream and marginal positions, systems and embodiments—into a coherent pattern. Such strategies help explain why some disciplines waxed as others waned at various times within the canon of the sciences of state, or why the boundaries between the sciences of state and other fields changed as they did. Strategies are rarely consciously articulated, but they can be discovered as common underlying traits among a variety of thinkers and writers. One can think of strategies as roughly analogous to linguistic rules: the principles which govern the positions and relations of elements.[15] For example, I shall argue in the first chapter that mid-to-late-eighteenth century cameralism, particularly as taught in Göttingen, was characterized by the strategy of classification, of finding the right order of its constituent elements. Classification represents a distinct synthesis of systematization and simplification: it sees in the proper subsumption of individualities under common labels the key to understanding complexity. In the course of writing this book, I found new strategies emerging with a certain regularity every twenty-five years. These were of course determined in part by the changes that were taking place in Germany at the time; but the pattern suggested a generational rhythm which underlay these factors. One can discern, from one generation to the next, a swing of the pendulum between love of systematization and disillusionment with it. But neither the love nor the disillusionment were repeated in the same way twice; rather, they were shaped by differing strategies. The individual chapter headings give the names of these strategies (assimilation, deliberation, variation, organized research and charisma, specialization and clarification)—perhaps at the expense of a certain overformalization. The narrative, I hope, will provide enough detail to offset the impression that these are simplistic formulas.

I do believe that, by the use of these categories, it is possible to construct a narrative of a tradition. Certainly it was the intent of Foucault and other structuralist and poststructuralist critics to call such grand narratives into question.

---

15. Cf. Foucault's "rules of formation" as a defining element of a discourse, "Politics," 54; *The Archaeology of Knowledge*, 38.

The tools which they fashioned, however, can be used to give the narrative form a greater precision than it had in the past. As Foucault himself admitted when asked, the issue is not one of choice between continuity and discontinuity per se, but rather the mapping of the plurality of elements and relationships that constitute a discourse—"to give the monotonous and empty concept of 'change' a content, that of the play of specified modifications."[16] Such modifications—or strategies—become part of a tradition, superimposing new patterns upon old ones without completely obliterating them. In the sciences of state, the institutional patterns of examination requirements, established professorial chairs, and lecture courses provided an inertia to these academic disciplines, perpetuating accepted strategies over long periods of time. The newer strategies which came with generational changes and with the political, economic, and social upheavals between 1789 and 1914 transformed the old pattern, but less radically than is often thought. Thus my reading of the overall history of these disciplines stresses continuity as often as not. For example, the advent of liberalism in the early nineteenth century was not as sharp a break with the past as is usually portrayed. The same applies to the growth of historical economics in the 1850s and 1860s. Likewise, the points of continuity between the *Sozialpolitik* of the Second Empire and the earlier *Polizeiwissenschaft* are emphasized. Indeed, it is the persistence of the sciences of state and their practical reason well into the nineteenth century, rather than their sudden shrinkage in the face of Humboldtian ideals of *Bildung*, that constitutes an underlying theme of the book.

16. Foucault, "Politics," 58, nn.

✢ 1 ✢

The Seventeenth- and Eighteenth-Century
Background: Classification

THE BACKGROUND OF CAMERALISM

The nineteenth-century sciences of state represented an outgrowth of an earlier curriculum known as cameralism, which arose in the century following the Peace of Westphalia in 1648. We may view it as an example of what Gerhard Oestreich has called "the establishment of social discipline"—a campaign to restrain the destructive passions unleashed in the previous century by religious fanaticism and civil war. Discipline was seen as an alternative to cruelty.[1] Symptoms of this attitude were as diverse as the new military drill, the ideal of the *honnête homme*, the deliberate artificiality of baroque aesthetics, the elaborate court rituals of Louis XIV, and the regulation of merrymaking during religious festivals in Germany, which had led to such excesses of gluttony and alcoholism as satirized by Grimmelshausen in *Simplicissimus*.

Such social discipline was a widespread European phenomenon associated with absolutism, but it had some specifically German variations. One was the fact that princes and kings who aspired to absolute rule had to contend with the constitutional structure of the Holy Roman Empire. The period 1648–1750 witnessed many attempts to make the Empire a viable political entity; this gave rise to the efflorescence of public law as the arena in which conflicts between the constitution and the claims of princes could be resolved. Another was the smaller scale of many of the German principalities, which enabled the rulers to present themselves as paternalistic figures, managing their country as a lord would run his estate. The analogy was made countless times between the prince and the head of a household—as formulated by Aristotle in his *Oikonomie* (*Oikos* means "household").[2] The theory of the well-run household em-

---

1. Oestreich, *Neostoicism*, 265, 267; See also Rabb, *Struggle for Stability*, esp. 118–19. Oestreich first formulated this notion of social discipline in 1962, thirteen years before the appearance of Foucault's *Discipline and Punish*. Oestreich further rejects the sharp dichotomy which Foucault posits between centralized state power in the form of sovreignty on the one hand, and "discipline" in the sense of total control and surveillance on the other. One has power over goods and wealth, the other over time and labor. See Foucault, *Power/Knowledge*, 97, 104–8.

2. Tribe, *Governing Economy*, 23, 27; Brückner, *Staatswissenschaften*, 55; Krauth, *Wirtschaftstruktur*, 96–97.

braced not just allocation of resources, but the proper relation of the master to his family, workers, and slaves; it was thus a social and ethical doctrine as well. The persistence of such views in Germany perhaps explains why Hobbes's argument for absolutism, based on more cynical and impersonal considerations, never found the reception in Germany that it did elsewhere.[3]

This paternalistic view can be seen in a work that gained some popularity, the *Teutscher Fürsten Stat* (1665) of Veit Ludwig von Seckendorff, an official to the court of Gotha. In addition to the specific administrative duties of a prince, Seckendorff emphasized the need to maintain high standards of personal conduct.[4] As befitted a small-scale principality in the scarce years following the Thirty Years' War, Seckendorff's emphasis was less on expanding internal trade and manufactures and more on sound fiscal management.[5] The *Teutscher Fürsten Stat* may be viewed as an early version of cameralism.

Cameralism has been called the German version of mercantilism—an appropriate label only if one can disregard the layers of polemical connotations which have been attached to it since the days of Adam Smith.[6] Mercantilism was in the first instance a body of practices, formulated in response to specific situations, rather than a coherent body of thought. Just as the absolute monarchs frequently found themselves working through and with the aristocracy as a matter of pragmatic necessity, rather than simply imposing their will, so did their mercantilist advisers recognize the need to work with private economic initiative rather than simply impose state control. Their writings thus involved conceptions of society as well as of economics and politics.[7] Writers such as Johann Joachim Becher, a trusted official of Emperor Leopold I, had a concept

3. Stolleis, *Geschichte des öffentlichen Rechts*, 1: 281.

4. Seckendorff, *Teutscher Fürsten Stat*, 139–205.

5. Ibid., Part 3, esp. 368.

6. Smith identified mercantilism with certain theories of commerce and the role of money therein: for example, the assumption that wealth is ultimately representable in terms of money alone, hence enabling wealth to be exchanged. Smith used the concept as the target of an extended polemic against the attempt to regulate such commerce. This negative version of mercantilism thus became part of classical economic thought and the historiography attached to it. A very different version gained prominence through the nineteenth-century historical school which sought to oppose the liberalism of Smith. According to one of its founders, Gustav Schmoller, mercantilism was a political as well as an economic doctrine; it had as its goal the formation of a strong, unified state. Centrally directed economic policy was a means for building a powerful administrative apparatus at the expense of traditional local powers and estates. It was, in other words, an expression of absolutism. Schmoller's portrayal carried a clearly nationalistic message. Nevertheless, this political-cum-economic definition also found acceptance among subsequent historians both inside and outside Germany. Both the Smithian and Schmollerian interpretations of mercantilism are now recognized to have imputed more system and rationality to mercantilism than was actually there. See Smith, *Wealth of Nations*, 1: 450–73; Schmoller, *Mercantile System*, 50–51, 76; Heckscher, *Mercantilism*, 1: 21–22; Coleman, "Heckscher," 52, 66; Schumpeter, *History of Economic Analysis*, 336.

7. Heckscher, *Mercantilism*, 2: 269, 271–75, 337–38.

of an autonomous social order—a "civil society" which was as much a part of their overall scheme as their economic or political prescriptions.

It is worth dwelling on the details of Becher's social classification, since it contains the first formulation of a scheme that was replicated frequently in eighteenth-century cameralism and in the nineteenth-century sciences of state. In his best-known work, the *Political Discourse* of 1668, Becher divides the people in a community into two groups. The first comprises authorities, whom he calls "servants . . . because the community is not there for the sake of the authorities, but the authorities for the sake of the community."[8] The second group is the community itself. For Becher, the authorities include rulers, clergy, academicians, doctors, pharmacists, barbers, bathers, and soldiers. The community is divided into three classes, based on their economic activities:

> The people who essentially constitute civil society . . . may be divided into three orders [*Stände*]. The first order is the largest, namely the farmers; the second, the craftsmen; the third, the merchants. . . . The farmers' order is the first and largest, also the most necessary . . . it gives the raw materials which the craftsman processes [*verarbeitet*] and the merchant sells.[9]

Becher goes on to urge that these three orders should be kept separate and in proper proportion, since each group depends on the previous one. Craftsmen should be more numerous than merchants, and farmers more numerous than craftsmen. Thus in this area too, the purpose of public policy was to maintain a balance—in this case a balance of different occupations. Although Becher displayed an animus against merchants who profited excessively from foreign trade, he nevertheless emphasized the importance of commerce within a country: it was the circulation of goods which allowed farmers to prosper and manufacturing to take place.[10] This concept of a proper balance may be seen as a further example of the mentality of social discipline.

A further German peculiarity was the rooting of these notions of discipline in academia. As is well known, certain universities became the seats of enlightened reform movements—notably Halle and later Göttingen. At Halle, Christian Thomasius was recognized as an outstanding systematizer and educational reformer who succeeded in making Halle a magnet for young nobles throughout Germany. His efforts were directed against pedantry and in favor of practical knowledge. He formulated a curriculum, centered in the law faculty, designed to make nobles both cosmopolitan and competent to rule. Thomasius

8. Johann Becher, *Discurs*, 4. This is a change from the scheme that one finds in Luther's writings and which goes back to Plato—a division of society into three groups: the soldiers, scholars, and those who provide material goods (*Wehrstand, Lehrstand, Nährstand;* see Sommer, *Kameralisten,* 2: 33).

9. Johann Becher, *Discurs*, 4–9.

10. Ibid., 101–3.

was but one of several professors and officials who began calling for a vitalized teaching of economics and administration, going beyond the traditional "practical philosophy."[11]

This social role that universities played helped to form a particular notion of science that was purveyed there. The emphasis was not on a "scientific method" or even an in-depth investigation of a particular subject, but on comprehensiveness and systematic knowledge. An educated person was to draw on a common stock of knowledge, including the classics and the scriptures; specialization was not a priority.[12] Even within a given area, such as law or medicine, the efforts of professors were aimed at conveying an overview. This approach to knowledge helps to explain the popularity in the first half of the eighteenth century of Christian Wolff, whose strong point was the ability to subsume all aspects of knowledge in a single comprehensive system. For cameralism, his seminal work was *Reasonable Thoughts on the Social Life of Man, Particularly the Commonwealth, for Furthering the Happiness of the Human Race*, first published in 1721. The work is divided into two parts, the first of which treats the domestic polity—that is, the marital state, the paternal family (*die väterliche Gesellschaft*), the relation of master and servant (*die herrschaftliche Gesellschaft*), and finally the house, which combines the first two. The second part concerns the commonwealth (*gemeinen Wesen*), its various types (the Aristotelian notion of types of government), its institutions (the police regulations and ordinances), its laws, its power and how it should be exercised, and its warfare.

Cameralism, as it developed at such innovative institutions, was thus both practical and systematic. Therein lies its fascination and its enduring interest, for it was an attempt to formulate a *science of praxis*, in which various types of public activity formed the basis for its categories. Its history provides a test case as to the viability of such an attempt.

CAMERAL SCIENCE DEFINED

By the middle of the eighteenth century, the term "Cameral Science" (*Kameralwissenschaft*) had acquired two senses: a narrow one and a broad one.

In the narrow sense, *Kameralwissenschaft* meant public finance, that is, managing the princely budget. The need to systematize such knowledge had already arisen before the Thirty Years War, when the need for revenues led the princes to try to husband their resources and to rely on learned officials—at first law professors—to advise and supervise tax collection and render it more consistent. This was the task of the *Kammer*, and in this connection arose a litera-

---

11. Stieda, *Nationalökonomie*, 3 ff; Feist, *Geschichte*, 15; Tribe, *Governing Economy*, 35–39; Brückner, *Staatswissenschaften*, 60–61. On Göttingen, see McClelland, *State, Society, and University*, 46–47.

12. Turner, "Prussian Professoriate," 112–14.

ture (*economia satrapica*).[13] The importance of keeping good records was stressed early on, and the bureacratic control of taxation meant that the practice of tax farming never reached such proportions as it did in France, nor did the sale of offices ever wreak such havoc.[14]

In addition to taxes, the cameral officials gradually acquired control of the two other major sources of state income: that of the princes' own lands (*Domänen*) and of government monopolies and privileges (so-called *Regalien*). The extension of powers of the *Kammer* into these areas thus marked the consolidation of the private and public incomes of the princes under one agency. This can be seen most graphically in the case of the *regalia*. As in English, the term originally meant any right reserved for royalty; in the context of German cameralism, the usage evolved to cover only those rights which involved payment. Originally the *Regalien* had been divided into "high" and "low," that is, those rights which the prince exercised for the public good versus those which he exercised for his own maintenance. The former included the issuing of coins, maintaining a postal service, and upkeep of roads, for which tolls could be charged; the latter included income from mines, forests, and fisheries.[15] As the categories of cameral science became fixed, this distinction disappeared, and seven or eight *Regalien* emerged to remain a staple of the textbooks of public finance: (1) mining and salt springs; (2) coinage; (3) customs and tolls; (4) granting of fiefs and titles (*Lehen*); (5) granting of hunting and fishing privileges; (6) granting of woodgathering privileges in the princely forests; (7) control of waterways; and (8) postal service.[16]

The most famous practitioner of such fiscal consolidation—both for his contemporaries and for such later ponderers of bureaucratic authority as Max Weber—was Prussia's soldier-king, Friedrich Wilhelm I. Faced with two collection agencies, one for taxes and the other for domains and regalia, which were beginning to quarrel with each other, Friedrich Wilhelm combined them in 1713. Fourteen years later, he established the first professorships in *Kameralwissenschaften* at the universities of Halle and Frankfurt/Oder. The king came to Halle to give the inaugural lecture himself. According to the newly appointed Halle professor, Simon Peter Gasser, the king had complained that the law students were getting inadequate training in economics and finance.[17]

This brings us to the broader meaning of *Kameralwissenschaften*. When the word was used in the plural, it referred to the field of several sciences that were

13. Krauth, *Wirtschaftstruktur*, 114–26.
14. Kindleberger, *Financial History*, 168–73.
15. Gasser, *Einleitung*, 254–58.
16. Seckendorff, *Fürsten Stat*, 314–491, 511–12; Gasser, *Einleitung*, 248–305, 315–33; Justi, *Staatswirtschaft*, 2: 144–305.
17. Gasser, *Einleitung*, 9–10.

useful in training administrators. These included *Oekomomie* and *Polizei*, terms that are not precisely translatable. Gasser's appointment was in these two plus cameral science in the narrow sense. Both *Oekonomie* and *Polizei* had a history dating back to Aristotle. Together with ethics, Aristotelian economics and politics had found their way into the medieval canon of university subjects under the name of practical philosophy. In practice, economics was often neglected, since it did not lend itself easily to scholastic disputation.[18] During the Reformation, however, Melanchthon found it useful to promote Aristotelian philosophy in the Protestant universities, since it fit the paternalistic views of the family and the state held by Luther.[19] In Catholic universities, practical philosophy in general was relegated to a modest place in the fifteenth and sixteenth centuries, and the Jesuit curriculum did nothing to revive it.[20]

In any event, Aristotelian practical philosophy did not provide the technical knowledge needed by farmers and craftsmen. This need came to be filled by a popular genre known as *Hausväterliteratur.* Aimed primarily at noble farmers in the years following the Thirty Years' War, these books of practical advice contained information on growing crops, veterinary medicine, the construction of farm houses, the relations of husband and wife, religious and moral obligations, household industries, the interpretation of dreams, and astrology.[21] By the early eighteenth century, the usefulness of some of this material for administrative officials—and hence its appropriateness for university training—came to be recognized. Johann Peter Ludewig, the rector at Halle at the time of Gasser's installation, expressed the dissatisfaction with the previous teaching of *Oekonomie* in his inaugural address:

> How it stands with the farms, meadows, ponds, forests, gardens, and plants; . . . how to increase the manure on the farm; how to brew and sell the grain; what a landlord needs to do and leave undone each day of the year; what provisions are needed for the chimney, the food vault, and the cheese basket; how to provide these economically, to preserve them and give them out: of this there is not a syllable in Aristotle. Therefore also his creatures, the previous professors of economics, have not given it any effort or trouble.[22]

Ludewig was equally critical of the unsystematic nature of the *Hausväterliteratur,* since these works "have no foundation in the causes which lie in nature and reason." A student of this economics needed a firm grounding in theoreti-

18. Brückner, *Staatswissenschaften,* 51; Maier, "Lehre der Politik," 62.
19. Brückner, *Staatswissenschaften,* 150–1; Maier, "Lehre der Politik," 78, 86–87.
20. Maier, "Lehre der Politik," 63, 84–85.
21. Brückner, *Staatswissenschaften,* 53. Also Brunner, "'Ganze Haus,'" 34–35. There were frequently chapters devoted to the *Hausmutter* and her duties; by the late eighteenth century, *Hausmutterliteratur* had become a separate genre. See Gray, "Prescriptions," 413–26.
22. Ludewig, *Profession,* 142–3.

cal and practical or experimental physics.[23] Thus cameralism would be seen as a part of the system of "science."

Although the new teaching of *Oekonomie* was directed primarily at royal officials, its relevance to the private sector was not overlooked. Friedrich Wilhelm I claimed that the new professorship would be just as beneficial to the management of private estates as to his own. Many young nobles also ran their estates into debt and did not form capital.[24] If the task of the cameralists was to educate the bureaucracy, the task of the bureaucracy was also to educate the private farmer.[25] However often the cameralists invoked the analogy between the household patriarch and the prince, they did not suggest that the former should be merely the passive object of the latter's will. Good household management should rather apply to both private and public spheres. The subject matter of *Oekonomie* comprised material which could apply equally to a private subject or to the prince as a private landowner (e.g., the assessment, leasing, and sale of property, and the rudiments of agriculture). To quote Ludewig:

> We call a prince who increases the income of his country through trade and traffic, and who takes in more than he spends, a good *Wirt* . . . it follows that just as the art of making a livelihood belongs to the lot of the common man, the townsmen and the farmers, so also for the prince and the whole country; so also may the word *Wirtschaft* be taken and used for all of these.[26]

The German term *Wirtschaft*, which Ludewig preferred to *Oekonomie*, also expressed the common characteristic of economics and public finance as the German writers viewed it: the key activity was neither exchange nor production, but management and allocation of resources. As such its meaning was soon extended to cover the economy of towns as well as farms.

The third science of the cameralist triad, "police science" (*Polizeiwissenschaft*), also had its roots in Aristotle, although the line of filiation was by no means direct and has been the subject of scholarly controversy.[27] *Polizei* derived from the latin *Politeia*, which corresponded to one of the Aristotelian forms of government, namely, rule by the many.[28] This was obviously distinct from his

23. Ibid., 149–50.

24. Gasser, *Einleitung*, 8–9

25. Brückner, *Staatswissenschaften*, 74.

26. Ludewig, *Profession*, 146. Further examples of the state's regard for private property rights can be found in the police regulations of the early eighteenth century. To promote productivity, the states renounced their right to claim property on the death of subjects when they had no direct heirs. See Raeff, *Police State*, 75–76.

27. Maier, *Verwaltungslehre*, 99–100, 116; on the controversy over the role of Aristotelian university philosophy in Germany versus that of Dutch neo-Stoicism—and of a German "peculiarity" versus a European-wide movement—see Bruch, "Wissenschaftliche, institutionelle oder politische Innovation?," in Waszek, ed. *LNDU*, 102–4.

28. Aristotle, *Politics*, 3.7.

Politics, which was the science of government as a whole. The German word appeared in the fifteenth century, at first in the context of a well-run civic government, but it was soon transferred to a territorial context. In 1530, the Holy Roman Emperor issued a *Polizei* ordinance for the entire Reich. The impetus behind this use of *Polizei*—manifested in an increasing stream of ordinances— was the assertion of the will of the ruler over the estates in the name of the common good. Most frequently the ordinances had to do with curbing luxury, regulating dress, enforcing religious observance, and generally stamping out immorality in all areas, from marital relations to money-lending.[29] In Protestant Germany, *Polizei* filled the vacuum created by the absence of church regulation of schools, marriage, and the other sacraments. In places like Catholic Bavaria, it was the church itself, and its rights and obligations, that were subject to increased regulation.[30]

None of this appears to have had an impact on the teaching or the study of politics within practical philosophy during the sixteenth century. Only in the seventeenth century did politics begin to appear beside ethics in the designations of professorial chairs.[31] The decisive change came in the years following the Thirty Years' War, as the process of social discipline was reinforced in the universities through a revival of politics and natural law. The intellectual impetus came partly from a revived interest in Aristotle and partly from the influence of Neostoicism emanating from Holland. The key figure in the latter movement was Justus Lipsius (1547–1606), a professor at Leiden. His *Six Books of Politics*, published in 1589, went through ninety-six editions in all, including translations, in virtually every country in Europe by 1751.[32] Lipsius produced in essence a program for absolutism: he urged an active government and a strong bureaucracy and army (one of his pupils was the famous military reformer Maurice of Orange). Although similar to Machiavelli in placing high value on *raison d'état*, Lipsius's doctrine was based on a very different view of human nature and ethics. Duty, self-control, moderation, and constancy all played important roles in motivating a prince. Thus his doctrines could inspire the work of Grotius in natural and international law. German students flocked to the Dutch universities in the seventeenth century; among them were the Great Elector of Prussia, the neo-Aristotelian philosopher Hermann Conring, and the natural law philosopher Samuel Pufendorf.[33]

Aside from Lipsius, Pufendorf was the most prolific conduit of European

29. Maier, *Verwaltungslehre*, 82–83; Raeff, *Police State*, 43, 54, passim.

30. Raeff, *Police State*, 59.

31. See the lists of such titles in Denzer, *Moralphilosophie*, 300–307.

32. Oestreich, *Neostoicism*, 57–58. By contrast, Bodin's *Six livres de la république* was reprinted seventeen times.

33. Oestreich, *Neostoicism*, 96–101, 118–31.

political thought into Germany. Like Grotius, he believed in the inherent sociability of human nature, rooted in human appetite, impulse, and reason (in the latter he differed from Grotius). He was critical of Hobbes's individualistic state of nature. Social contracts were the expression of mutual obligations among people in communities (his "state of nature") and states.[34] Given the rationality of human beings and of nature itself, the study of natural law was a science. Pufendorf occupied the first chair of natural and international law at Heidelberg in 1661. Under his influence, natural law supplanted Aristotelian practical philosophy in the philosophical faculties of German universities, and politics now became part of natural law.[35]

The effect of this transformation was to create a two-tiered system of politics that was not to be found in Aristotle. Politics as scientific natural law dealt with the nature of states, types of government, constitutions, and other general issues. This subject matter would eventually find its way into the sciences of state. Such a level of generality created, however, a space for a second tier, that of particular states, their laws and administration. The former set the norms and limits; the latter developed the means for their implementation.[36] The second tier could be filled in various ways. In Halle, for example, it was done as *politica specialis,* which treated the positive law of the Holy Roman Empire.[37] For other writers, it was a way of granting permission to justify a Machiavellian *raison d'état:* numerous treatises and dissertations appeared on the subject in the late seventeenth century, concerned with distinguishing between "good" and "bad" *raison d'état.*[38] For still others, it suggested the systematization of *Polizei* as a science, the practical science of administration. This evolved gradually, for the notion of administration as a separate governmental function, distinct from the dispensation of justice and the management of public finance, did not emerge at one stroke.[39] In general, however, *Polizei* was limited to domestic administration; military and foreign affairs were considered the personal prerogative of the prince.[40]

Police science thus represented the application of absolutist social discipline in the name of a secularized natural law, which provided the ends to which

34. Denzer, *Moralphilosophie,* 92–96, 103, 142; Tuck, "'Modern' Theory of Natural Law," 105.

35. Brückner, *Staatswissenschaften,* 157; Denzer, *Moralphilosophie,* 318–19; Kähler, "Entwicklung," 118–26.

36. Thus Pufendorf distinguished between natural and positive law; the neo-Aristotelians distinguished *scientia* from *prudentia,* whereas Aristotle himself had characterized this practical discipline as *prudentia* exclusively. See Denzer, *Moralphilosophie,* 221 ff, 320–21; Brückner, *Staatswissenschaften,* 154–63.

37. Kähler, "Entwicklung," 124.

38. Meinecke, *Machiavellism,* 127–45.

39. Preu, *Polizeibegriff,* 43–45; Maier, *Verwaltungslehre,* 152–64.

40. Maier, *Verwaltungslehre,* 153 n.

such discipline was directed. In the hands of Thomasius and Wolff, these ends were increasingly articulated in terms of happiness, and the corresponding emphasis of *Polizeiwissenschaft* was on the welfare and prosperity of the state and its subjects.[41] It thus overlapped with *Oekonomie*, but with a more technocratic emphasis: in *Polizeiwissenschaft*, the state tended to be the active subject, the people the passive objects. Nevertheless, *Polizeiwissenschaft* shared with the other two cameralist disciplines the assumption that the science of government should be that of sound management. Whether in the balancing of accounts in public finance, or in trying to make a profit as a landowner, or in trying to promote happiness as an administrator, the emphasis was on the optimum adjustment of means to ends. Thus economics and administration were not opposed, but were two sides of the same technocratic coin.

STATISTICS AND STATE LAW

Before leaving the late seventeenth century, we turn to two other disciplines that were not considered to be part of cameralism at the time, but formed powerful tributaries to the stream of the sciences of state which emerged in the second half of the eighteenth century.

The first of these was the comparative empirical description of individual states—their territories, governments, economies, and peoples—known as *Notitia rerum publicarum*, or *Staatenkunde*, later *Statistik*. This was utterly different from the mathematical forerunner of modern statistics which was developing in England under the name of "political arithmetic." The first to announce academic lectures on *Statistik* was Hermann Conring at Helmstedt in 1660, based on Aristotle's project of the description of 158 individual polities.[42] By bringing this empirical material together in one place, one could infer structural similarities and future developments among states. Conring's lectures provided needed information on states other than one's own, and the subject spread quickly to other universities.[43]

From Conring onward, statistics was closely intertwined with certain types of history. Conring already distinguished political history as a distinct literary genre—though not necessarily in the form of a narrative of events—which provided the source material for statistics.[44] Conring's contemporary at Jena,

41. Ibid., 161–62.

42. Brückner, *Staatswissenschaften*, 34–35; Horvath, "Statistische Deskription," 40–41. Conring's classification followed Aristotle's system of four causes: (1) *causa materialis:* population and economic aspects; (2) *causa formalis:* juridical and constitutional aspects; (3) *causa finalis:* purpose of states; (4) *causa efficiens:* administration (i.e., finances, army, and fleet).

43. Brückner, *Staatswissenschaften*, 40–41.

44. Seifert, "Staatenkunde," 226–27, 245–46; Pasquino, "Politisches und Historisches Interesse," in Bödeker et al., eds., *Aufklärung und Geschichte*, 156–57.

Johann Andreas Bose, included history as the first section of his description of each state.[45] This association lasted well into the nineteenth century and gave German statistics a very different emphasis from the quantitative science that was developing in England.

The second new discipline was what today would be called constitutional law, but was then known as state or public law (*Jus Publicum, Publizistik, Staatsrecht*). It too had an empirical emphasis and owed much to Conring. Conring opposed the strictly deductive approach to the law of the Holy Roman Empire that began with Roman law, regarding the imperial office as the center of authority. Instead he achieved a more realistic description of the roles of the territorial princes vis-à-vis the emperor. This involved an acknowledgment of the peculiarities of the German case, including the fact that the Holy Roman Empire did not fit the accepted classification of forms of government.[46] Although this study of positive imperial law did not spread as quickly as *Statistik*, it finally came into its own under Thomasius at Halle. He combined natural law derived from Pufendorf with positive state law, a combination which was soon widely imitated.[47]

Here too, history played a crucial role. The very illogicality of the Empire meant that the only way of explaining its structure was to explain how it developed. Thus Thomasius made "doctrina historica" and "doctrina systematica" the two parts of his course in state law.[48] Under his successor, Ludewig, imperial history became a separate offering, not limited to the legal aspects, but including the customs and usages of Germany as well. Ludewig was more willing than Thomasius to turn these lectures into defenses of Prussian state policy.[49] A further step in the development of history from state law was taken by Ludewig's colleague and rival, Nicolaus Hieronymus Gundling, who, in the interests of cosmopolitanism, instituted lectures in the history of the European state system.[50]

These, then, were the building blocks of the *Staatswissenschaften*. In fact, during the first half of the eighteenth century, the empirical-political disciplines flourished at the expense of the cameralistic ones.[51] Only one additional chair in *Kameralwissenschaft* was created, although several special academies for train-

---

45. Valera, "Statistik, Staatengeschichte, Geschichte im 18. Jahrhundert," in Bödeker et al., eds., *Aufklärung und Geschichte*, 124–25.

46. Hammerstein, *Jus und Historie*, 32–33, 38–39.

47. Ibid., 92, 110; McClelland, *State, Society, and University*, 34–35.

48. Hammerstein, *Jus und Historie*, 113, 118.

49. Ibid., 177–204; Hammerstein, "Reichs-Historie," in Bödeker et al., eds., *Auklärung und Geschichte*, 85; Hentschel, "Staatswissenschaften," 184. Ludewig's inaugural address for the chair of cameralism was mostly a long panegyric in praise of the soldier-king.

50. Hentschel, "Staatswissenschaften," 185; Hammerstein, *Jus und Historie*, 234–35, 241–42.

51. Hentschel, "Staatswissenschaften," 182.

ing officials were launched without much success.[52] The hope of spreading rational agriculture through university teaching in Prussia was disappointed, as Gasser complained in 1739. During his last years he neglected the subjects entirely. The situation got no support from Frederick the Great, who generally neglected the universities in favor of furthering French culture. His opinion of *Oekonomie* was especially low. "One learns *Oekonomie* from the farmers, not in the universities," he is reported to have said.[53] As successor to Gasser, he appointed someone trained in Hebrew theology, and relegated the chair from the law faculty to the less prestigious philosophical faculty.[54]

Part of the difficulty for cameralism was in finding qualified pedagogues for a new subject, and part was the very unwieldiness of the cameral disciplines themselves. The combination of *Oekonomie, Polizei,* and finance led to much duplication: discussion of postal service and maintaining roads could—and did— occur in both Finance and *Polizei;* drainage control could be—and was—part of both *Oekonomie* and *Polizei.* On the extent and boundaries of *Polizeiwissenschaft,* it was generally agreed that there was no agreement.[55]

THE EXPANSION OF CAMERALISM AFTER 1750

Despite these obstacles, cameral science proliferated in the second half of the century. The 1760s saw the establishment of nine university chairs, and about sixty general texts appeared between 1760 and 1790.[56] This is all the more remarkable in view of the continuing overall decline in university enrollments during this period.[57] The initiative for these changes often came from the enlightened princes and their advisers, sometimes in cooperation with the professors, but as often as not against them.[58] And even in Prussia, one of Frederick's advisers managed in 1770 to incorporate the cameral subjects into the curricular requirements for officials in justice and administration, despite the monarch's indifference.[59] All this activity met with mixed results as far as effective education was concerned; reports of announced lectures which never took

52. Stieda, *Nationalökonomie,* 38–46.

53. Quoted in Schrader, *Geschichte,* 1: 362.

54. Feist, *Geschichte,* 45–47.

55. Zincke, *Cameralisten-Bibliothek,* 1: 310; Justi, *Polizeiwissenschaft,* Vorrede zur ersten Ausgabe (n.p.).

56. Bruch, "Wissenschaftliche, institutionelle oder politische Innovation?," in Waszek, ed. *INDU,* 87n; Tribe, *Governing Economy,* 91.

57. McClelland, *State, Society, and University,* 63–65.

58. For a positive case, see Osterloh, *Sonnenfels,* 31 (Vienna); for negative cases, Hennings, "Wirtschaftswissenschaften an der Universität Leipzig," in Waszek, ed. *INDU,* 124 (Leipzig); Biesenbach, *Entwicklung,* 13 (Freiburg).

59. Bleek, *Juristenprivileg,* 76–78.

place, or of those with three or four students, were numerous.[60] There were some successes, however, which set the tone for the subsequent generation. Moreover, cameralist ideas were being taken seriously as guidelines for policy-making, as recent studies of such diverse states as Hesse-Cassel and Hamburg have shown.[61]

What led to this expansion? Part of the impetus came from the spread of enlightenment pedagogical ideas from Protestant to Catholic Germany, where the expansion was connected with the diminution of the Jesuits' role. The ideas of Thomasius and Wolff were imitated explicitly in the Bishopric of Würzburg and in Bavaria, while Mainz adopted the model of nearby Göttingen.[62] In the Habsburg lands, cameralism was associated with the Theresian domestic reforms following the War of Austrian Succession. In Austria particularly, the Habsburgs adhered to the absolutist model of social discipline through centralization of authority.[63]

The expansion, however, was not limited to Catholic territories; the broader phenomenon may be explained as a response to a more profound tendency that was challenging the *dirigisme* of the absolutist policy itself—and would change the notion of discipline as well. This was the increasing role of a civil society that defined itself outside the bounds of state activity, whether in the form of a private sector of the economy, or of an independent reading public.[64] Agriculture, manufacturing, and commerce were becoming less dependent on the state; the limits of state activity were becoming increasingly evident to the cameralists themselves.[65] This is most dramatically illustrated by a study of the German book market for the years 1740, 1770, and 1800. It shows the relative decline of traditional academic subjects such as theology and law, the increase of books in *Staatswissenschaften*, and a much sharper increase in those dealing with the private economic sphere (see table 1).

The increased book trade was also reflected in the explosion of independent

60. Tribe, *Governing Economy*, 114; Stieda, *Nationalökonomie*, 223; Feist, *Geschichte*, 67. On the general state of the universities, see McClelland, *State, Society, and University*, 63–65.

61. Ingrao, *Hessian Mercenary State*, 10, 31–32; Lindemann, *Patriots and Paupers*, 21, 74–78.

62. Hammerstein, *Aufklärung*, chs. 2–4. See also Blanning, "Enlightenment," 119–26.

63. Hammerstein, *Aufklärung*, chap. 6, esp. 184.

64. Neither the terms *private* nor *public* do full justice to this social phenomenon. Jürgen Habermas expressed the overlapping notions of bourgeois society, public opinion, and the private sphere in tabular form in *Strukturwandel der Öffentlichkeit*, 41. Reinhart Koselleck has connected his sphere with the rise of political utopianism and freemasonry, and with the development of an apolitical "inner space" in *Kritik und Krise*, 60, while Ursula R. Becher has—correctly, I think—questioned whether this was the sole result of bourgeois autonomy; she sees the development of a "political society" that was willing to countenance resistance to established authority. See Ursula Becher, *Politische Gesellschaft*, 26.

65. Osterloh, *Sonnenfels*, 96; Preu, *Polizeibegriff*, 193.

Table 1 *German Book Market, Selected Categories*

	1740		1780		1800	
	No.	Percent	No.	Percent	No.	Percent
Theology	291	38.6	280	24.5	348	13.7
Jurisprudence	97	12.9	61	5.3	129	5.1
Sciences of State	10	1.3	32	2.8	93	3.6
Agriculture, Manufacturing	8	1.0	59	5.2	220	8.6
Agriculture	2		29		106	
Military science	2		10		12	
Manufacturing	3		16		63	
Commerce	1		4		20	
General					19	
TOTAL SAMPLE	754		1144		2544	

Source: Rudolph Jentzsch, *Der deutsch-lateinische Büchermarkt* (Leipzig: Voigtländer, 1912), tables 1–3.

reading societies, especially after 1770. Analyses of the books owned by these societies have revealed an emphasis on general education and useful knowledge rather than belles lettres.[66]

If the constituencies of the reading societies are any indication, this independent reading public appears to have been largely university-educated. Membership consisted mostly of officials, doctors, clergy, officers, and academics, rather than merchants or farmers.[67] Many of these were employees of the state. This meant not merely that these independent societies could not be too pointedly critical of the established order, but also that their members had already been subject to the social discipline that came with their education. As James Melton has shown, the project of compulsory education which was attempted in the mid-eighteenth century in Prussia and Austria demonstrated the state's conscious commitment to extend this discipline.[68] Now, however, the recognition of the limits of the state vis-à-vis the public altered its emphasis: the goal was not to enforce blind obedience, but rather to instill a sense of self-discipline whereby that obedience would be freely rendered.[69] The mentality was thus neither that of classical liberalism, in which the freedom of the individual took precedence over that bestowed by a state, nor the "discipline" of the prison and the barracks described by Foucault, in which the actions of individuals or groups are controlled down to the last detail; rather, it was something in between that was particularly suited to German circumstances. This mentality may be summarily described as one which insisted on a clear and strict boundary between the autonomous sphere of self-discipline and that imposed by the

66. Stützel-Prüsener, "Lesegesellschaften," 74, 80; Koptizsch, "Lesegesellschaften," 92.

67. Cf. Stützel-Prüsener, "Lesegesellschaften," 78; Blanning, "Enlightenment," 124.

68. Melton, *Absolutism,* xix–xxii. Melton argues convincingly that the results of this project were anything but completely successful.

69. Ibid., xxii.

state. Such a boundary certainly made sense in Prussia, which had built up its population through a policy of religious toleration—a policy that necessarily presupposed a limit to state authority in matters of conscience. Such clearly circumscribed spheres would also be most useful for a civil servant who wished to participate in a discussion group. In any case, the fuller meaning of this formula may be explicated by turning to the changes in the resurgent cameral sciences, which were symptomatic of this state of affairs.

The writer who best expressed these crosscurrents was Johann Heinrich Gottlob von Justi. Justi taught briefly at Vienna and Göttingen before becoming minister of mines in the Prussian state service. He was prolific and well known: some of his works went through several editions, and he was the only eighteenth-century German economist to have two works translated into French.[70] Although a supporter of absolutism, he was critical of many institutions of his day, including the granting of feudal privileges, hereditary judicial powers, and compulsory labor service on the land.[71] Justi consciously identified himself with "the enlightenment of reason and the extension of human knowledge": as an official of the Austrian censorship commission, he battled the Jesuits to approve Montesquieu's *Spirit of the Laws* and Voltaire's *Age of Louis XIV;* at the same time he disapproved of low comedy.[72] With respect to the teaching of the cameral sciences, he was one of the first to urge a separate faculty with several professors, including auxiliary personnel from the natural sciences. Only in this way could a higher degree of sophistication and coherence be achieved. As an introduction to this program, Justi proposed an encyclopedic survey; the book he wrote in 1755 to cover this field he called *Staatswirtschaft* (state economy).[73] The book is an attempt at a comprehensive science of state, as it goes beyond the material of the cameralist triad to include politics as well. Yet the title of the work was more than coincidental. It reflected the centrality of the concept of wealth to Justi's thinking. "The highest power," he wrote, "consists in the use of the total wealth and powers of the state to achieve its ultimate goals, namely the attainment of common happiness." His word for "wealth" was *Vermögen,* with its connotation of potential, rather than the more tangible "riches" (*Reichtum*), and he explicitly stated that wealth includes not only goods, "but also all the capacities and skills of the . . . persons, indeed the persons themselves."[74] This notion of wealth as the totality of potential re-

---

70. Carpenter, *Dialogue in Political Economy,* 17–18. The author speculates that one translation may have been intended for a German market.

71. Frensdorff, *Justi,* 124–25.

72. Justi, *Staatswirtschaft,* 1: 127n, 131–32n.

73. Ibid., 1: xxxv.

74. Ibid., 1: 48. Justi was not the first to use the word *Vermögen* in this way; he probably derived it from the *Cameralisten-Bibliothek* of G.H. Zincke in 1751.

sources that can be tapped and developed by the state corresponded on the economic plane to the notion of a pool of "talent" that pedagogues were coming to recognize in the same period as the object of their efforts.[75] In his later writings, Justi took increasing pains to emphasize the importance of this active private sphere. For example, in the second edition of *Staatswirtschaft*, he added,

> The freedom of the subjects is indispensably necessary to their happiness. Freedom, secure property, and flourishing trades, so that each can attain the comforts of life by his own industry, there are the three chief pieces on which the happiness of the state and the subjects depend.[76]

Justi recognized that wealth was a manifestation of nature and, as such, existed prior to the state. This was evident in his *Polizeiwissenschaft*, which he claimed was the "basis for a genuine cameral science."[77] The organization of that science progressed from interactions between the state and nature to those between the state and specifically human activities. It began with "the cultivation of the country," that is, the winning over of land from a state of nature (*Wildheit*) and making it fit for human purposes. This involved both "external cultivation" (e.g., clearing forests, draining swamps, making rivers navigable, building roads and bridges, establishing sanitation and lighting in towns, not to mention beautification), and "internal cultivation," that is, increasing and maintaining the population. There followed the "measures to encourage a prosperous level of sustenance," which were divided into the winning of products from the land (agriculture, forestry, mining), the elaboration of these products (manufacturing, crafts), and trade and circulation—the same scheme as in Becher. The third section had to do with "the ethical state of the subjects" (i.e., the supervision of religion, morality, and schooling), as well as the prevention of idleness and begging. The final sections dealt with the internal security of the state and with police laws and their enforcement. This organization was to become paradigmatic for many subsequent works of *Polizeiwissenschaft*.[78]

Justi's work on public finance exerted a seminal influence as well, and it was based on the concept of *Vermögen*. If economics was the science of the preservation and increase of this wealth, then finance was the science of the state's *use* of wealth to meet its own expenses.[79] It followed that a state should not seek to deplete its wealth to the advantage of the ruler or the court, and that a flourishing private sector was the best means to a full treasury.[80] Justi devoted much

---

75. LaVopa, *Grace, Talent, and Merit*, 51, 173.
76. Justi, *Staatswirtschaft*, 1: 66 n; see also 51 n.
77. Justi, *Policeywissenschaft*, "Vorrede zur ersten Ausgabe" (n.p.)
78. Lindenfeld, "Decline of Polizeiwissenschaft," 165.
79. Justi, *Staatswirtschaft*, 2: 3–4, 19.
80. Ibid., 2: 25, 63, 81.

attention to questions of the technique of tax collection: the relative efficiency, ease, and justice of one type of taxation compared to another. This led him to oppose the excise tax of his day, an internal duty on moveable goods, often collected at the gates of a town. Anticipating Turgot, Justi argued that such a tax hampered internal trade, required a lot of officials, and was easily subject to fraud.[81] Elimination of the excise later became one of the goals of the Prussian reformers at the turn of the century.

The cameralist writings of the 1750s formed part of an international interest in political economy.[82] Three years before the appearance of Justi's work, Adam Smith began to lecture in moral philosophy at Glasgow. His lectures on justice, police, revenue, and arms bear a family resemblance to the cameralist systems, but Smith used these lectures to develop the arguments of *The Wealth of Nations*—a theory of growth based on the division of labor and the human propensity to exchange.[83] During the same years, the French physiocrats developed a third version, deriving a theory of economic equilibrium based on the primacy of land as the source of all wealth. This they perceived to be "the natural order of things."[84]

Once again, however, we find a particularly German variation on this European theme, for *The Wealth of Nations* did not make a strong impact on German cameralism when it first appeared in 1776; that came only around 1800. And although physiocracy attracted a number of German disciples, its impact was also limited. The tendency was to regard it as unfruitful: "Physiocracy," wrote Johann Heinrich Jung-Stilling in 1787, "is an angelically beautiful girl, but unhappily a vestal, who is incapable of making an honorable man happy."[85] The German objections centered less on the role of *laissez-faire* versus the state than on the physiocrats' premise that land was the single source of wealth.[86]

81. Ibid., 2: 357–64; cf. Turgot, "Plan for a Paper on Taxation . . . " [1763], 100–101.

82. In this I take exception to Foucault, who in *The Order of Things* (166) claims that political economy did not exist in the eighteenth century because the concept of production had not yet surfaced. Instead, Foucault finds a fully developed "analysis of wealth" in the mercantilist writers and the physiocrats. I would argue that, in addition to the analysis of wealth, there existed a science of management and allocation of resources, and that this constituted political economy.

83. Adam Smith, *Lectures*. Smith's discussion of "Police" has two divisions, (1) "of cleanliness and security," which he dispenses with in two pages, and (2) "of cheapness or plenty," which goes on for 103 pages! It begins with the observation that nature provides basic needs for all animals; only man is dissatisfied with what nature alone provides (157–58).

84. Spiegel, *Growth of Economic Thought*, 185 ff. See Hentschel, "Zwecksetzungen," 113–17, for an insightful comparison of these three doctrines. Hentschel correctly observes that they arose concurrently, not successively as is often portrayed.

85. Jung-Stilling, *Jubelrede*, 18. On the reception of physiocracy in Germany, see Tribe, *Governing Economy*, chap. 6. Tribe states that the main impact of physiocracy occurred outside academic circles (119).

86. Blaich, "Beitrag der deutschen Physiokraten," 15, 19 ff.

The cameralists, with their typically academic concern for comprehensiveness, resisted the notion that wealth could be traced back to a single source. In fact, cameralism found more inspiration in natural history than in political economy during the second half of the century.

The Cameralist System and Natural History

If the cameralists produced nothing comparable to the ideas of Smith and the physiocrats in order to explain how wealth was created or increased, it was because their primary concern remained one of classifying rather than explaining. The model they found most congenial came not from an economist but from a natural philosopher, Linnaeus. Linnaeus's conception of "natural history," with its postulates of an unchanging natural order marked by miniscule gradations in a continuous "chain of being," appealed to the cameralists. They sought to extend the chain from the natural to the human and practical realms. Unlike Smith, they felt the need to cover their subject comprehensively and evenhandedly. They channeled their literary efforts into ordering and making sense of the sprawling subject matter attached to their professorial chairs. They were no less concerned than the physiocrats to adapt their political program to "the natural order of things," but their academic backgrounds and roles as state officials led them to seek a static representation of the continuity of natural and social phenomena that would help ground the social equilibrium that they sought to maintain. It is no coincidence that, as a group, the cameralists continued to decry the easy access of poor students to the universities, which would upset that equilibrium; the recognition of an autonomous society based on talent did not translate into an argument for social mobility.[87] The emphasis on ordering the subject matter was, in short, a way in which state officials could continue to order society in their minds—maintaining a sovereign grasp on it while acknowledging its increasing autonomy. In this sense it served a similar function to the codification of civil law, which both established and limited the rights of individuals.[88] It provides an elegant illustration of Bourdieu's theory of how elite groups construct a symbolic system homologous with the social system in which they are dominant.[89]

Thus in the second half of the eighteenth century there emerged among the cameralists a shared classificatory scheme for the interaction between human beings and their materials, which was applied both to private individuals and groups, and to the state and its regulations. The scheme followed Becher's

---

87. LaVopa, *Grace, Talent, and Merit*, 49–52. It is also no coincidence that Linnaeus himself included racial distinctions of superiority and inferiority in his taxonomy.

88. Cf. Habermas, *Strukturwandel*, 88–89.

89. Bourdieu, "Social Space," 131–32.

division of society into three basic occupational groups of agriculture, manufacture, and commerce, to which a service sector was frequently added.

The decisive turn which entrenched this threefold classification came in Göttingen in the 1770s at the hands of Johann Beckmann (1739–1811). Göttingen's increasing reputation as the university of choice for the nobility in the smaller German states enhanced his influence. Beckmann had studied the natural sciences at Göttingen from 1759 to 1762; he then traveled to Holland, Russia (where he taught for two years in a German school in St. Petersburg), and Sweden, where he worked for a year with Linnaeus on the classification of plants. In 1766 he completed *Fundamental Principles of Natural History*, which he claimed was the first German compendium on the subject.[90] In the same year, he began teaching at Göttingen, where his initial subjects were natural history, *Oekonomie*, and mathematics. In later years he added the other cameralist disciplines, such as *Polizei* and finance. He maintained throughout his life that good administration required a knowledge of the natural sciences, which were propaedeutic to cameralism proper.

In essence, Beckmann found in the threefold classification a basis for anchoring the cameralist disciplines in the natural sciences. The categories of agriculture, manufacturing, and commerce were ways of ordering human interactions with nature; in this way the continuum of scientific classification could be extended from the natural to the human realm. Beckmann's major publications followed just this pattern. In 1769 he published *Principles of German Agriculture*, which claimed to be a break from the previous *Hausväterliteratur;* it was "philosophical" rather than "practical."[91] In 1777 appeared *Guide to Technology, or On the Knowledge of Handcrafts, Factories, and Manufactures*. Both this and the *Agriculture* went through five editions by 1806. In 1789 appeared *Guide to Commercial Science (Handlungswissenschaft)*. What Beckmann had done was to split *Oekonomie* into three specialties, each taught separately. His other activities included a journal, a popular history of inventions, and the inclusion of excursions to nearby manufacturing sites as part of his teaching—a practice that was to remain a staple of German economics until the First World War.[92]

Beckmann's work on agriculture exemplified the attempt to impose an order on the swirling tide of innovation and invention going on around him—

90. Beckert, *Beckmann*, 68. Another German pupil of Linnaeus, Johann Christian Daniel Schreber, taught economics, technology, and *Kameralistik* in his capacity as professor of medicine at Erlangen; his inaugural lecture there in 1770 was on the relationship between medicine and economics. See Goerke, "Linnaeus' German Pupils," 231.

91. Beckert, *Beckmann*, 73–75. Beckmann's criticism of *Hausväterliteratur* as a genre did not preclude his praising individual works in that genre, such as those of Otto von Münchhausen or Christian Friedrich Germershausen's work on the *Hausmutter* (Gray, "Hausmütterliteratur," 417).

92. Beckert, *Beckmann*, 84.

and the difficulties inherent in such a project. Germany participated in the international fascination with agriculture in the mid-eighteenth century, of which French physiocracy was but one reflection. German writers—and not just cameralists—were going well beyond the traditional homilies of the *Hausväterliteratur;* more and more they were criticizing the practice of letting fields lie fallow, for example.[93] A number of agricultural societies were formed which offered prizes for essays on new techniques, as did many of the learned academies at the time.[94] Both the French and the Germans acknowledged the leadership of England in these new techniques and practices, and the English publications were soon translated. But the dissemination of these changes through the print media did not necessarily mean that they reached the farmers themselves, who, as we have seen, did not tend to belong to the reading public. In Hannover, George III established one of the first agricultural societies in 1764, which the Hannoverian nobility visited regularly, but the attempts of Frederick the Great to convert the Prussian nobles through a model farm were less successful.[95] While some cameralists such as Justi urged that Germany imitate English methods wholesale, others were skeptical of such an "Anglomania." For example, many reacted to Jethro Tull's revolutionary seed drill in the same way they had reacted to physiocracy: Tull's claims for the utility of his method were extravagant to the point of denying the further need for fertilizer![96] This was too simplistic. Beckmann mentioned Tull's drill as one of seventeen similar inventions, and concluded that no one of them was so decisively superior as to warrant his endorsement.[97]

Nevertheless, cameralistic agriculture was part of a broader movement of reform that was beginning to show results by the end of the century. Crop rotation was introduced in some places to replace the three-field system, which brought with it a change to feeding cattle in stalls.[98] Elsewhere, fallow fields were gradually replaced by winter crops for fodder, such as clover; this in turn expanded cattle production, which provided more manure for fertilizer, bringing higher yields. Later, potatoes replaced clover as a crop that could feed both animals and humans.[99] Beckmann noted a consequence of these changes that was becoming obvious to the landowners themselves: the new techniques could not spread sufficiently because of the hereditary rights and obligations of the

93. Fraas, *Geschichte der Landbau-und Forstwissenschaft,* 140–45.
94. Tribe, *Governing Economy,* 99.
95. Schröder-Lembke, "Englische Einflüsse," 30, 33.
96. Ibid., 30, 32.
97. Beckmann, *Grundsätze der deutschen Landwirtschaft,* 100.
98. In Hesse-Cassel, for example. See Ingrao, *Hessian Mercenary State,* 100–101.
99. Berdahl, *Politics of Prussian Nobility,* 87; Gagliardo, *Pariah to Patriot,* 9.

peasants, such as the scattered holdings of strips in different fields, and these could only change through "the higher power of the *Polizei*."[100]

Beckmann is best remembered for having founded *Technologie* as a university-level discipline. In the mid-eighteenth century, there arose a fascination with machines which paralleled that with farming, though in lesser degree (see table 1). Thus Beckmann encountered a situation here that was not unlike that of agriculture, but one on which the cameralists had had a greater impact. Instruction in certain manufacturing processes had been interspersed throughout the *Hausväterliteratur*, which was appropriate insofar as some processing of raw materials took place on the farms, such as distilling and grinding of grain. But the notion of separate instruction in crafts and manufactures had been gaining ground in the early eighteenth century. It conveniently fit the projects of social discipline and care for the indigent, such as the workhouses; the Pietists had also made it a central part of their practical involvement in the world. This had led to a fruitful exchange of ideas between cameralists such as Seckendorff and Pietists such as Philip Spener and August Hermann Francke in Halle.[101] The result was a series of trade schools (*Realschulen*) in Halle, Berlin, Magdeburg, and Braunschweig.[102] When Beckmann's book appeared, it spread quickly to these schools as well.[103]

In the work, Beckmann wrestled with finding a "natural order of crafts and arts" which would have the same appropriateness to its subject matter as the Linnaean taxonomy did to plants and animals, but admitted that he could find no decisive ordering criterion. Ordering by materials used (e.g., stone, metal) would not work because of certain processes that used combinations of these; also, he found that arrangement by use (food, clothing) was unsatisfactory, as was the traditional order of guilds.[104] He tentatively offered a classification based on the processes themselves, from the simple to the more complex (e.g., from weaving, dying, and bleaching to ceramics, metallurgy, and refining). There were 51 categories encompassing 324 different crafts. The body of the text is a selection of 32 of these crafts, in which their location, raw materials, favorable conditions, and the processes and machines are described. Despite the impact of the *Technologie*, it ultimately foundered on the same problems

100. Beckmann, *Grundsätze der deutschen Landwirtschaft*, 81–82. Cf. Berdahl, *Politics of Prussian Nobility*, 86.

101. Timm, *Kleine Geschichte*, 34. Timm's account of eighteenth-century technical education helps correct the impression that German technical higher education stemmed exclusively from the French model of the *École Polytechnique*.

102. Ibid., 34–36; Troitzsch, *Ansätze technologischen Denkens*, 143–49.

103. Troitzsch, *Ansätze technologischen Denkens*, 144.

104. Beckmann, *Anleitung zur Technologie*, 21–22.

as his book on agriculture: the inability of such a classificatory approach to accomodate change, in this case the new technologies of the industrial revolution. There was no room in Beckmann's scheme for the steam engine, and even in textiles, such basic machines as the spinning jenny escaped his attention.[105] The whole approach provided a graphic contrast to that of the French *Encyclopédie,* which renounced the possibility of a natural order of classification and turned to an alphabetical one, precisely so that changes could be accommodated.

Beckmann's classificatory impulses extended also to commercial science, where he was best known not for a comprehensive treatment of the whole, but for the "science of commodities" (*Waarenkunde*). This involved a listing of major products from abroad and their characteristics—information invaluable to a merchant who had to distinguish genuine goods from fraudulent ones, and superior from inferior quality. His work in this area was, however, eclipsed by a nonacademic from Hamburg, whose publications on the subject became widespread in universities: Johann Georg Büsch (1728–1800). Prospective merchants were not good candidates for university study, because their apprenticeship began at age fourteen or fifteen; Büsch's alternative was a boarding school, or commercial academy, which he ran for thirty years with considerable success: among his 360-odd students were 80 Englishmen and 30 Russians. He soon found imitators in Vienna and—unsuccessfully—in Berlin.[106] Like the Hamburg merchants he taught, Büsch was cosmopolitan: he cited more English and French writers than German ones in his books. He had few kind things to say about the economic theory of his day, claiming that insight came from practical experience. Even Adam Smith elicited his skepticism. Among the objects of his attack were the mercantilist notions that money was the index of prosperity and that one should try to accumulate it at the expense of one's neighbors.[107] He did, however, recommend technology, geography, and parts of natural history as useful background for a merchant.[108]

The system of cameral sciences thus formed the link between the sciences of nature on the one hand and those of the state proper (e.g., *Polizei* and finance) on the other. In so doing, it also contained a formulation of the boundary between the private and the public spheres. This could be seen in the static vision of Justi and Beckmann and their notion of social equilibrium, expressed in the metaphor of the state as machine. To quote Beckmann, from the introduction to his *Technologie:*

105. Beckert, *Beckmann,* 88.
106. Redlich, "Academic Education for Business," 205–12; on the student figures, see Wilhelm Roscher, "Zur Erinnerung von Johann Georg Büsch," 219.
107. Büsch, *Sämtliche Schriften,* 14: 22.
108. Ibid., 1: 141.

Farmers, handworkers, and merchants in their trades look after their private interest. *Polizei* directs them for the best of the whole state, that is, it commands and forbids, if the advantage of the individual citizen is not the advantage of the whole society. . . . May the citizen thus look after his private interest! That is why he lives in a state, and contributes his part to its tasks—in order to learn a trade, not what belongs to the general good, and pursue the former, without having to spend time in caring for the latter. Only he should obey when the authorities command, and they should understand and observe their duties. Then is the state the most artificial machine that men have ever produced, in which a countless number of large and small wheels and drives intermesh.[109]

Here Beckmann uses the mechanistic metaphor of the state in a way similar to that in which other writers after him used the organic metaphor: to convey an internal differentiation of parts which function harmoniously together. How different is this ideal machine from that which Foucault described in *Discipline and Punish!* Instead of a "microphysics of power," in which every bodily motion is subject to scrutiny and rendered homogenous, to the exclusion of spontaneity and caprice, we have here a taxonomy which takes as its starting point the heterogeneity of occupations and seeks an equilibrium among them; control is exercised in the form of regulation, of correcting imbalances, of seeing that the wheels and drives "intermesh."[110]

CAMERALISM AND THE SCIENCES OF STATE

In the late eighteenth century, the cameralist sciences drifted in two diverging directions: either they elaborated the description of the private economic sector and its connection to natural science (i.e., agriculture, manufacturing, commerce), paying less attention to public policy, or they continued to view the state as the unifying point of reference, but enlarged the scope to include other subjects such as law, politics, statistics, and history. From this emerged the field of the sciences of state. Despite the divergence, however, the two directions never completely separated; at the very least, *Polizei* constituted an area of overlap. We will examine each of these tendencies in turn.

The first can be seen in the rise of a number of special cameralist faculties

109. Beckmann, *Anleitung zur Technologie*, "Vorrede zur ersten Ausgabe" (n.p.). For references of other writers to the state as a machine, see Timm, *Kleine Geschichte*, 42–43; LaVopa, *Grace, Talent, and Merit*, 171 n; Ursula Becher, *Politische Gesellschaft*, 87.

110. Cf. Foucault, *Surveiller et Punir*, 138–40. Foucault acknowledges that the surface resemblance between taxonomy and this sort of discipline may be deceptive: taxonomies in natural history were used to categorize individual differences rather than eliminate them (151). Furthermore, in his lectures at the Collège de France in 1978, Foucault differentiated a sphere of "security" from that of "discipline" as a type of governmental activity. Security and liberty were equally indispensable in guaranteeing a certain level of prosperity of a state. See Colin Gordon, "Governmental Rationality," 19–20; Foucault, "Governmentality," 102.

in the universities. They addressed the problem of the complexity of the subject and acknowledged the need for an entire curriculum to cover it. They were for the most part based on the model of the Cameral Institute of Lautern (Kaiserslautern), founded in 1774 by an independent agricultural society, the Physical-Economic Society of the Palatinate (originally the Physical-Economic Bee Society).[111] Realizing that its program of awarding prizes and influencing local agriculture directly was not working, the members directed their efforts to training officials. Their institute, with three full-time faculty members, gained official recognition from the Elector Palatine in 1777; to his irritation, however, the school tended to attract more students from other German states than from his own, and even from Sweden and Poland.[112] In 1784, the institute moved to Heidelberg, where enrollments had declined drastically; one observer in 1789 noted that the institute was the most active part of the university.[113] Other such institutes were established as faculties of universities at Giessen in 1777, Mainz in 1782, Rinteln and Marburg in 1789, and Landshut in 1804, in addition to the famous Karlsschule in Stuttgart in 1781 (see table 2). The curricula in each were remarkably uniform, and the emphasis on the natural sciences was clear.

These institutes by no means resolved all the problems facing the cameral sciences. Enrollments were frequently spotty, and curricular questions continued to cause trouble.[114] But there were cases of penetrating work within these fields. The director of the Lautern institute could claim, for example, that its work in economic botany had superseded Beckmann's compendium.[115]

The professor of political economy at Lautern, later at Heidelberg and Marburg, was Johann Heinrich Jung-Stilling, whose work may be considered representative of cameralism at this stage. Jung-Stilling was a figure of great renown, as an eye surgeon and even more as a Pietist writer, whose autobiography was published in 1774 by his friend Goethe.[116] An autodidact in the cameral sciences, he was doubtless a spirited teacher.

Jung-Stilling's system (as of 1792) reflected a cursory reading of Wolff and the same sense of harmony between religious and enlightenment tenets. It also reflected the tendency to classify public policy and government as posterior to

111. Tribe, *Governing Economy*, 98–101. On agricultural societies, see also Stieda, *Nationalökonomie*, 46–50.

112. Tribe, "Die kameral Hohe Schule zu Lautern," in Waszek, ed. *INDU*, 177.

113. Tribe, *Governing Economy*, 109–10.

114. At Lautern, 103 students entered the institute between 1774 and 1784; 117 entered in the following decade (Tribe, *Governing Economy*, 111); at Stuttgart, there were 37 cameralists out of 287 in 1781, 22 out of 414 in 1791 (Stieda, *Nationalökonomie*, 151); at Giessen, there were only 3 students in 1787, though this rose to 30 under a new professor (ibid., 185).

115. Stieda, *Nationalökonomie*, 319.

116. Buchholz, "Nachwort" to *Jung-Stillings Lebensgeschichte*, 222–24.

Table 2 *The Cameral Academies*

	Lautern	Stuttgart	Giessen	Mainz	Ingolstadt
Encyclopedia					x
Physics (*Naturlehre*)	x		x	x	x
Natural history, botany	x	x	x	x(2)	x
Zoology		x	x	x	x
Mineralogy		x	x		
Chemistry	x	x	x	x	x
Pure mathematics	x		x(2)		x
Applied mathematics	x		x	x	x
Mining	x	x	x	x	x
Architecture, civil engineering	x	x	x	x	x
Agriculture	x	x(2)	x	x	x
Forestry		x	x	x	x
Veterinary medicine			x	x	x
Technology	x	x	x	x	x
Commercial Science	x	x	x	x	x
Accounting		x	x	x	x
Polizeiwissenschaft	x	x		x	x
Political economy	x			x	
Finance	x	x	x		x
Natural law	x	x	x	x	x
Cameral law		x		x	x

Source: Wilhelm Stieda, *Die Nationalökonomie als Universitätswissenschaft* (Leipzig: Teubner, 1906), 116, 149, 174, 192, 243. Lectures offered in one institution only are not listed.

private economics. Part 1 of the work comprised the threefold classification, namely production, fabrication, and commerce, which he collectively called the industrial sciences (*Gewerbswissenschaften*). These were followed by the sciences of government (*Regierungswissenschaften*), namely *Polizei*, finance, and a new "science of legislation" (*Nomocratie*). Jung-Stilling introduced a psychological dimension, that of need (*Bedürfnis*), which he defined as the lack of something required for happiness. The industrial sciences dealt with acquiring from nature the means for satisfying physical needs, while *Polizei* was the legislation concerning the satisfaction of individual needs and the general good of the subjects.[117] In his own words,

> True enlightenment is the recognition of the means for satisfying all needs of
> the individual and the general good. . . . The realization of the individual

117. Jung-Stilling, *Grundlehre der Staatswirtschaft*, 52, 79.

good takes precedence over that of the general. . . . True religion can be discovered by true enlightenment.[118]

This notion of *Bedürfnis* was to become a staple in the conceptual framework of nineteenth-century German economics.

The second tendency, to broaden the cameralist curriculum to a more comprehensive system of state sciences, emanated from two centers: Vienna and Göttingen. Given the centralizing efforts of the Habsburgs, the innovations at Vienna became standard for universities throughout Austria. The central figure in this process was the first professor of *Polizei* and cameralism at the University of Vienna, Joseph von Sonnenfels. Sonnenfels's accomplishments as teacher and reformer merited a street being named for him in the old quarter of the city. He contributed to the reform of the Austrian police and the codification of criminal, civil, and administrative law, including the abolition of torture. He had a clear plan for training civil servants in the "political sciences," as he increasingly called them; he argued that the proper study of politics was based on a study of law, and that this in turn was anchored in ethics and natural law. In practical terms, this meant transferring his chair from the philosophical to the law faculty, prescribing a five-year curriculum combining law and political science, and requiring that officials be certified as having attended these courses.[119] His textbook remained the required work for students of law and administration in the Austrian lands until 1848. It found much resonance in the other German states as well before the turn of the century.[120]

Sonnenfels clearly saw the need for greater parsimony and theoretical rigor in his subject. In his inaugural lecture, he severely censured the earlier cameralists such as Gasser, Dithmar, Zincke, and Darjes. "What do they contain?" he said, "what else, but mainly practical instruction for a future farmer, for a future official of domain land, for a supervisor of a forestry office, for the lessee of a ruler's lands."[121] His accomplishment was to excise the entire *Oekonomie* and to divide the old *Polizei* in two parts: one to deal with order and internal security, and the other with managing the economy. Sonnenfels reserved the name *Polizei* for the former, and chose the term *Handlungswissenschaft* for the latter. Finance remained the concluding part. Together with the doctrine of

118. Ibid., 30, 41, 48.
119. Osterloh, *Sonnenfels,* 242–47. In addition, Sonnenfels instituted a course for proper writing style for officials, which also became part of the presecribed curriculum; in this capacity, he reviewed practically all the legislation in the first years of Joseph II's reign (ibid., 237).
120. Ibid., 122. Despite the fact that Jung drew on Sonnenfels for parts of his works, I find the differences between them more striking than the similarities. See Roscher, *Geschichte der Nationalökonomik* (554), who after pointing out agreements on numerous individual points, admits that Jung was more influenced by the idea of freedom than was Sonnenfels.
121. Quoted in Tribe, *Governing Economy,* 84.

external security (i.e., defense and diplomacy), these made up the sciences of state.[122] Sonnenfels was also concerned with founding these sciences on firm principles, not merely on collected practical experience. He rejected as too general Justi's principle of happiness as the goal of state activity.[123] Instead, he proposed to find such goals in the things society provides to individuals which they cannot provide for themselves: (1) security; (2) satisfaction of basic needs for subsistence; (3) leisure and comfort. He concluded that the best means of providing these is to increase the population of the society. The more people, the greater the potential resistance to attack from without or rebellion from within, and the greater the diversity of their products, which would better meet their needs for subsistence and comfort. Finally, the more citizens, the less each has to contribute to public expenditure—the basic principle of the science of finance.[124]

Sonnenfels was the first in Germany to develop in detail the functions of *Polizei* in preserving security and order. The earlier cameralists had treated local and central police functions indifferently; Sonnenfels was interested in the latter as an arm of absolutism; he drew more on French than on German models.[125] Certainly anyone looking for justification of subsequent police spying and censorship in Austria will find it in Sonnenfels.[126] Like Justi, he had a low opinion of low comedy, and was responsible for banning the popular Punch and Judy shows under Maria Theresa's reign.[127] At the same time, he was concerned to separate legislation and police activity, and to use police power to encourage obedience to the laws as well as to command and punish. Thus supervision of education and the church, both of which improved the ethical level of the population, came under *Polizei* as well as law enforcement. Sonnenfels preserved the separation between the public and private spheres that had been evolving under cameralism: he divided security into that of the state and that of its citizens. *Polizei* had the duty to protect both. Under the latter, Sonnenfels discussed public health, and the extensive system of public health commissions in Austria was in large part his achievement. From this developed a separate science of public health: *Medicinische Polizei*.[128] The role of police in

122. His concern with security was manifest in his also using the term *Staatswissenschaft* in the narrower sense to refer to the doctrine of external security. See Sonnenfels, *Policey, Handlung, und Finanz,* 1: 20.

123. Ibid. 1: 24–25.

124. Ibid., 1: 25–33.

125. Osterloh, *Sonnenfels,* 45–46, 49–50.

126. Sonnenfels, *Policey, Handlung, und Finanz,* 1: 189, 211.

127. Kann, *History of the Habsburg Empire,* 374; Melton, *Absolutism,* 86–89.

128. Osterloh, *Sonnenfels,* 60–63. The major author in this area was Johann Peter Frank, who worked in the Habsburg service for a number of years. His six-volume *System of a Complete Medical Police* appeared between 1778 and 1817. He classified the aspects of public health by the various

acting both for the protection of the state and the private citizen tended in practice to widen the scope of state activity rather than narrow it.[129]

When it came to the state's regulation of the economy, however, Sonnenfels was current with the thinking of his generation in distrusting overzealous state activity. As with *Polizei*, Sonnenfels was receptive to French influences here: the basic definitions of *Handlungswissenschaft* come from a French neomercantilist, Forbonnais.[130] The framework which Sonnenfels thus established represented a break with the older notion of management in favor of that of exchange and commerce: the multiplication of wealth comes as people exchange goods with each other—a very Smithian idea.[131] His recommendations were similar to those of Justi in matters of land policy and guild regulation: large estates should be broken up, and compulsory labor service abolished; guilds should be preserved but made open.[132]

In finance, Sonnenfels went beyond the traditional goal of simply raising as much revenue as possible to that of increasing the wealth of the individual citizen.[133] He also emphasized taxes as a source of revenue rather than the *Regalien*, and his writing on taxation reveals a sophisticated level of economic thinking, honed in part by his encounter with the physiocrats. In rejecting their proposal for a single tax, he pointed out the multiplicity of needs (*Bedürfnisse*) and the effect of fluctuating conditions on them in a way that anticipated the idea of a demand curve:

> [Suppose] I need four casks of wine, which I get for 100 pounds. . . . It may be that in years of surplus I will be stimulated by the cheapness to consume more; but will I drink so much as to consume eight casks [if they go for the same price]?[134]

Sonnenfels proposed grouping taxable objects according to four levels of need, from the necessary to the luxurious. By so simplifying the classification scheme, he believed the excise tax could be made workable. If each group of objects was to yield an equal amount to the total tax burden, the higher groups would

---

stages of the life-cycle: reproduction (i.e., population and marriage), birth (e.g., midwifery), childhood (foundlings), adulthood (supervision of clothing, housing, food), and death. His basic definition of *Polizei* as directed towards security followed that of Sonnenfels, and in volumes 4 and 5 he explored the effect of various disturbances of the peace on public health.

129. Brückner, *Staatswissenschaften*, 257.

130. See Tribe, *Governing Economy*, 80–82.

131. Sonnenfels, *Policey, Handlung, und Finanz*, 2: 2–6; cf. Brückner, *Staatswissenschaften*, 255.

132. Sonnenfels, *Policey, Handlung, und Finanz*, 2: 121–25, 179–85. Cf. Justi, *Policeywissenschaft*, 111, 160.

133. Osterloh, *Sonnenfels*, 108.

134. Sonnenfels, *Policey, Handlung, und Finanz*, 3: 310–11.

be paid by the more affluent taxpayers, who would thereby contribute a higher portion of their income, thus making the tax progressive.[135]

In Protestant northern Germany, meanwhile, a new empirical-historical approach was gaining ground which differed markedly from Sonnenfels's deductive system—although the differences were ones of emphasis rather than of totally different content.[136] The reasons for these differences may be stated as follows. In Catholic territories, philosophical natural law served as a tool with which rulers could limit the power of the church—a tool which Protestant rulers did not need, since they had controlled their churches since Luther's time.[137] On the other hand, Protestant rulers in small states did seek legitimation through the peculiar constitutional law of the Holy Roman Empire, which, as we have noted, was justified by its history. Thus it is not surprising that an alternative curriculum of the sciences of state came out of Protestant Göttingen, one that did not merge cameralism with legal studies in their entirety, but combined portions thereof with history and statistics. This was an outgrowth of the curriculum that had been pioneered at Halle in the early part of the century.

This outlook by no means involved a radical break with natural law; rather, it reflected a changing conception of natural law itself, one which recognized limits to state activity and established standards by which state actions could be criticized and reformed.[138] This attitude could lead to the affirmation of individual rights; in the German case, it could and did also lead to the belief that humans were "naturally" social beings, and that the autonomy of society vis-à-vis the state had to be protected. This belief in autonomy was closely connected to a belief in diversity: the notion that each society was a unique product of definite historical conditions. Thus Montesquieu's treatment of the diversity

<hr/>

135. Ibid., 3: 356–63. Sonnenfels deserves to be included in the long list of forerunners of Austrian marginal utility theory. Not only did Sonnenfels clearly formulate the notion of descending orders of needs in language similar to Menger's; he also developed a notion of approaching a quantitative limit for each order as a means of determining the tax rate: "The needs of the first and second class can be taxed to the point that the increase in prices produced thereby does not lead to the fear that occupations will be reduced, [and] the needs of pleasure in all levels should only be taxed to the point that . . . the use of the same is not limited." (361) He further identified, as Menger did later, the corresponding scale of *goods* with a causal process which ultimately led to the satisfaction of basic needs: "For the gold of the artist who makes me a watch, the wage of the servants in the anteroom, etc. goes through a path, sometimes direct, sometimes circuitous, always into the hands of someone who uses it on a basic need." (358).

136. There were defenders of the historical subjects in the emperor's circle who convinced Joseph II to mandate an empirical survey of Austrian political law over Sonnenfels' objections (Osterloh, *Sonnenfels*, 247–52).

137. Hammerstein, *Aufklärung*, 254.

138. On changing conceptions of natural law, see Stolleis, *Geschichte des öffentlichen Rechts*, 1: 269; Preu, *Polizeibegriff*, 194.

of human societies based on natural factors such as soil and climate had a great impact in Germany.[139] Moreover, the professors of state law could also invoke Montesquieu to sanction the separation of powers, which translated into the powers of the territorial princes within the Empire. For example, the jurists emphasized increasingly the separation between the governmental functions of (1) justice, which could be appealed to the imperial court, and (2) *Polizei,* which rested at the princely level.[140]

A related trend was the development of police law as distinct from police science in the second half of the eighteenth century. The increasing awareness that the powers of the prince were not unlimited or arbitrary led to the recognition of police law as a way of setting boundaries to that power. The emphasis shifted from techniques of administration to rules thereof. Emerging first within the framework of Wolffian state law, police law gradually became more empirical and historical, based on the positive laws of the various German states.[141]

The main protagonists of the empirical-historical approach at Göttingen were Johann Stephen Pütter (1725–1807), Gottfried Achenwall (1719–1772), and his successor, August Ludwig von Schlözer (1735–1808). Pütter arrived at Göttingen in 1746; his friend Achenwall came two years later. Pütter soon submitted a plan for a curriculum for training administrators and jurists.[142] The plan combined German state law with history that included European as well as German history, plus statistics, geography, heraldry, numismatics, and diplomacy—as well as a newly defined science of politics (*Politik*).[143] The latter, which was Achenwall's contribution, purported to treat states "as they really are" rather than beginning with idealized precepts.[144] *Politik* at Göttingen in fact encompassed a wide range of material, from the Aristotelian forms of government to *Polizei* and finance.

Göttingen was remarkable in that a student could be both exposed to the historical-statistical sciences of state, Beckmann's cameralism, and the new

139. Iggers, "European Context of Eighteenth-Century German Enlightenment Historiography," in Bödeker et al., eds., *Aufklärung und Geschichte,* 228.

140. Preu, *Polizeibegriff,* 42–44, 68.

141. Reiner Schulze, "Polizeirecht im 18. Jahrhundert," 208, 210–11.

142. The university's chancellor Münchhausen brought Pütter's proposal to the attention of Johann Jakob Moser, the most famous writer on state law at the time. Moser found it too historical; he soon issued a counterproposal to establish a separate academy at Göttingen, which Pütter declined. See Walker, *Moser,* 177–80. Moser went on to establish his own short-lived academy at Hanau; his daughter married Achenwall.

143. Bödeker, "Staatswissenschaftliche Fächersystem," 153–54; Pütter, *Academischen Gelehrten-Geschichte,* 1: 285. See Mohnhaupt, "Vorstufen der Wissenschaften von 'Verwaltung' und 'Verwaltungsrecht' an der Universität Göttingen (1750–1830)," in Heyen, ed., *Formation,* 82–84. Mohnhaupt stresses Pütter's ties to *Oekonomie* in his other writings (84).

144. Achenwall, *Staatsklugheit,* "Vorrede," no. 5 (n.p.).

classical philology under Christian G. Heyne that was being developed at the same time. As many of the subsequent generation of government officials studied at Göttingen, this helps explain how later reformers, such as Karl August Hardenberg, could combine a bureaucratic and utilitarian attitude towards public policy with a respect for the humanities. Pütter considered Hardenberg one of his prize pupils.[145]

In his own work, Pütter succeeded in fusing systematic and historical concepts; he did so to portray the law of the Holy Roman Empire in all its peculiarities—a hybrid of Roman and Germanic law.[146] He began his text on German state law with the geography of the Holy Roman Empire and its historical ties with Italy.[147] By spelling out in detail the respective rights and powers of the emperor, the territorial princes, the free cities, and the other components of the Empire, he provided a model which was attractive to nobles from the smaller German states, who flocked to Göttingen.[148] Pütter's work reflected the gradual changes of emphasis—and the built-in tensions—that characterized German state law at mid-century: the affirmation of natural freedom, and the suspicion of excessive paternalism in the name of welfare, while still legitimizing the police powers of the princes. For example, Pütter circumscribed the definition of *Polizei*, limiting it to the prevention of danger to the state, rather than the positive function of providing for the general good. Pütter did not deny the princes this positive role; he merely reclassified it as an "accidental" function of government as distinguished from the "essential" function of providing security.[149] These definitions still allowed the prince at least as much latitude in exercising positive functions as with Sonnenfels, if not more.[150] Nevertheless, his systematic works contributed to the clarification of legal limits to power, such as the division between constitutional and administrative law, though he did not use these terms himself.[151]

If Achenwall and Pütter were contemporaries of one generation, Beckmann and Schlözer were of the next. Both studied at Göttingen at the same time and

---

145. Hausherr, *Hardenberg*, 39, 40–45. The other leading figure of the Prussian reform period, Karl von Stein, also studied at Göttingen, but had little interest in literature or philology. See Ritter, *Stein*, 29.

146. Stinzing and Landsberg, *Geschichte der deutschen Rechtswissenschaft* 3.1, 337, 341, 350–51; On the fusion of natural and positive law, see Link, "Pütter," 316.

147. Pütter, *Teutschen Staatsrechte*, "Auszug aus der Vorrede zur ersten Edition" (n.p.). On Pütter's relation to Achenwall, see Mahoney, *Good Constitution*, 158–60.

148. Brückner, *Staatswissenschaften*, 264.

149. Pütter, *Teutschen Staatsrechte*, "Vorrede zur ersten Edition" (n.p.); 246–47; Link, "Pütter," 319, 323–24, 326.

150. Preu, *Polizeibegriff*, 184.

151. Stinzing and Landsberg, *Geschichte*, 3.1: 347.

became friends in St. Petersburg. Schlözer also went to Uppsala to study with Linnaeus, but was unsuccessful; he studied with one of his students instead.[152] When Achenwall died unexpectedly in 1773, Schlözer was given his lectures in statistics and political history, through Pütter's intercession.[153] His ability to stimulate independent thought from the lecture platform was widely noted; it is estimated that he lectured to 700–900 students in the last third of the century.[154] In Schlözer, moreover, we find an attempt to take the sciences of state beyond the static classifications that had previously characterized them.

Schlözer's work reflected the influence of Linnaeus, as Herder pointed out in his famous criticism.[155] In his *Universal History*, he began with a register of all the known peoples inhabiting the earth at a particular time; this was followed by a method for determining their order of importance. The result he called an "aggregate," which accomplished for history what the system of nature has already achieved for mechanical events.[156] Schlözer was clear, however, on the need to go beyond such an aggregate to a "system," that is, to take causes into account and to arrive at the real or natural coherence of events. This necessitated combining a chronological dimension with a synchronic one—however these may be at odds with each other—through proper periodization.[157] As Peter H. Reill has suggested, this more dynamic analogy with natural processes probably had sources other than Linnaeus, such as Buffon.[158] Nevertheless, the classificatory mentality was still evident in the final product: each period was broken down into such categories as length, subdivisions, main peoples and subsidiary peoples, sources and monuments, and a summary of events.

The same concern for integrating static and dynamic aspects ultimately defined for Schlözer the proper relation of history and statistics. History did not consist merely of the biographies of kings or the chronicles of battles, but also their agriculture, commerce, legal systems, and so on—the very subject matter of statistics. "History is continuous statistics," he wrote, "and statistics is static history."[159] In another formulation, he wrote, "Statistics teaches how they [states] really are; political history teaches how they became what they really are."[160]

Schlözer was also conscious of the methodological problems of statistics. He

152. Karle, *Schlözer*, 26.

153. Ibid., 92.

154. Ursula Becher, "August Ludwig v. Schlözer," *DH*, 7: 10.

155. Ursula Becher, "Schlözer," *DH*, 7: 18; Horvath, "Statistische Deskription," 41, 44.

156. Schlözer, *Weltgeschichte*, "Vorrede zur zweiten älteren Ausgabe," 1775, n.p.

157. Ibid., 5, 7, 77–80, 90.

158. Reill, "Science and the Science of History in the Spätaufklärung," in Bödeker et al., eds., *Aufklärung und Geschichte*, 436–38, 440–43.

159. Schlözer, *Statistik*, 86.

160. Ibid., 94–95.

stressed the difficulty of collecting reliable data and the need for putting these in numerical terms—although he could not bring himself to endorse political arithmetic.[161] He taught his students how to observe better when traveling and when reading the newspaper. He also recognized the unreliability of many statistics and underscored the need for the state to take responsibility for collecting them. He viewed openness and accuracy in statistical reporting as a force of liberation:

> Statistics and despotism are incompatible. Countless defects of the country are errors of the state administration: the statistics reveal them, thereby exercising a check on the government, even becoming a prosecutor: the despot does not take this gracefully. . . . Open statistics on the other hand, collected year in and year out, is a barometer of civil freedom, and thus also the least suspect and well documented eulogy of a wise government.[162]

Here too, the contrast with Foucault's use of "surveillance" is striking: rather than seeing statistics as a means to greater control of individual action on the part of the state, the Göttingen *Staatswissenschaftler* saw it as a means of keeping the power of the state in check.

As the years went on, Schlözer became increasingly concerned with developing a well-informed reading public, as a means of keeping government within its proper limits. His famous journal, the *Staatsanzeigen,* espoused various causes such as ecclesiastical, penal, and judicial reform; free speech and press; and improvements in agriculture, industry, and commerce. It achieved a circulation of 4,000 and was read by Joseph II, among others.[163] Schlözer also built upon Achenwall's conception of a science of politics, and it was in this form that the concept of the "entire sciences of state" was passed on to the nineteenth century. Schlözer deliberately sought a terminological reform, and was critical of such overlapping terms as *cameral sciences* and *Polizeiwissenschaft,* replacing them with compounds of the word *state.*[164] In his terminology, cameralism became *state administration* (see table 3).

Schlözer's conception of the sciences of state, in contrast to the older notion of cameralism, expressed a broadened mission for the enlightened reformer: from classifying and ordering society to helping mobilize it as a political force. As reading clubs were gradually supplemented by patriotic societies, the public, with direction from the press, was gradually being transformed into a voice

161. Horvath, "Statistische Deskription," 43.

162. Schlözer, *Statistik,* 51–52.

163. Karle, *Schlözer,* 125, 130–31, 183; Melton, "Enlightenment to Revolution," 109.

164. Mohnhaupt, "Vorstufen der Wissenschaften," 93. Thus Schlözer did not, as Hentschel maintains, seek to expunge political economy from the sciences of state, but only to subsume it under adminstration (see Henstchel, "Staatswissenschaften," 186). This is clear if one views his state administration as a continuation of Achenwall's *Staatsklugheit.*

Table 3 *Schlözer's Science of Politics*

Part 1: Historical
A. Statistics: How states really are
B. History of states: How they came to be what they really are
Part 2: Philosophical
A. Metapolitics (an abstract of natural law, a segment of anthropology): Humanity prior to the state
B. State law: Demonstration of mutual compulsory duties and rights with the state contract
C. State constitution, forms of government: Partly historical—descriptive of real or possible forms of government; partly philosophical in that it seeks to determine the advantages and dangers of each . . .
D. State administration, science of government, practical politics: The business of government and the means by which it can be achieved

Source: August Ludwig von Schlözer, *Theorie der Statistik nebst Ideen über das Studium der Politik überhaupt* (Göttingen: Vandenhoeck & Ruprecht, 1804), 94–96.

critical of established institutions.[165] The contentious tone of Schlözer's journalism paralleled the increasingly oppositional stance of the French press in France. The rulers feared "coming in the Schlözer [i.e., the *Staatsanzeigen*]," to use the expression of the time.[166] Freedom of the press became a central demand, expressing the notion of public opinion as a tribunal for governmental policies.[167] Schlözer of course never went so far as to advocate overthrow of existing regimes; he favored constitutional monarchy as the type of government most open to gradual reform.

Schlözer's curriculum, like Achenwall's before him, reflected these priorities. History stressed the dynamic aspects of society and predisposed his audience to accept change. Statistics, like the press, helped dissolve the provincial ties to principality or hometown; it was at once an agent of cosmopolitanization and nationalization. Finally, the inclusion in the curriculum of politics, along with history and statistics, encouraged officials to think of the state as an *object* of study and critique. This was the main innovation of the sciences of state vis-à-vis cameralism, which still conceptualized the state as the *subject* of administrative activity.

The coexistence of cameralism and the sciences of state in different universities at the end of the eighteenth century exemplified the contradictory tendencies in German society and politics. Cameralism was effective in practice—sometimes too effective in its overzealous regulation: in Hesse-Cassel, for example, the increasingly liberal trend of cameralist thought had not penetrated

165. Sheehan, *German History,* 191–93; Gerth, *Bürgerliche Intelligenz,* 69–71; Bödeker, "Prozesse und Strukturen," 10–31.

166. Habermas, *Strukturwandel,* 85. For the French scene, see Baker, "Politics and Public Opinion," 208–14.

167. Bödeker, "Prozesse und Strukturen," 21, 24–25.

to the practicing state officials.[168] There as elsewhere, commitment to enlightened reform coexisted with personal extravagance, sometimes in the same person.[169] Economically, a market economy flourished in the Rhineland and in East Prussia; elsewhere, farms and towns were still self-sufficient to a great degree.[170] Germany's political fragmentation imposed limits to economic expansion and reform, which could only be achieved by breaking down the barriers to trade and general human interchange.

In a sense, the mechanistic analogy of the state, to which Schlözer still adhered, expressed this fragmentation.[171] It portrayed the state as a complex with clear lines of authority from the top down, combined with room for a certain amount of autonomous activity of individual parts. But the channels of public participation and authoritarian command were fixed in place, as were the boundaries between the parts themselves (e.g., the constitutions and corporations of the German principalities within the Empire). And classification as the primary mode of knowledge of state and society was particularly well-adapted to this mentality of stasis—even if it did not possess the characteristics of regimentation which Foucault ascribed to the notion of discipline. In any case, both the political reality and the intellectual construct were soon to be shaken by the French Revolution.

168. Ingrao, *Hessian Mercenary State*, 50–51.

169. Ibid., 164. Other examples would include Baron von Erthal, the last bishop of Mainz, Duke Karl Eugen of Württemberg, both of whom founded cameral faculties or institutes, and Karl Theodore of Bavaria. See Gooch, *Germany and the French Revolution*, 9–10, 14.

170. Lütge, *Sozial-und Wirtschaftsgeschichte*, 370. Contrast the descriptions of Mainz in Blanning, *Reform and Revolution in Mainz*, with that of East Prussia in Berdahl, *Politics of Prussian Nobility*, 77 ff, or of Weimar in Richard Friedenthal, *Goethe*, 180.

171. Krieger, *German Idea of Freedom*, 77–79; Schlözer, *Statistik*, 27 nn.

🎋2🎋

The French Revolutionary and

Napoleonic Era, 1789–1815:

Assimilation

GERMAN RESPONSES TO THE REVOLUTION
Bildung and the Critique of the Mechanical Metaphor of the State

The assumptions of static equilibrium shared by the sciences of state were to be severely challenged in the late eighteenth and early nineteenth centuries, both at the political and intellectual levels. The French Revolution made Schlözer's shrill criticism coupled with gradual reform increasingly untenable; the end of the Holy Roman Empire rendered Pütter's state law obsolete. The new stirrings in German letters and philosophy which led to romanticism were often directed against the utilitarian assumptions on which the sciences of state were based. And Adam Smith's *Wealth of Nations* was about to take German cameralism by storm.

Under these circumstances it might seem surprising that the cameralist-state science field survived at all. In particular, the revolution in learning that one associates with such names as Wilhelm von Humboldt and Fichte—and with such universities as Jena and Berlin—appears to be at odds with the practical orientation of the sciences of state. One thinks of the cultivation of spiritual values, of the close ties between philosophy and the arts stemming from the court of Weimar, of the emphasis on self-cultivation and spontaneity associated with Humboldt's idea of *Bildung*, and of his notion of universities as research-cum-teaching institutions—all this seems worlds apart from the commitment to order and fixed classification, enshrined in textbooks, that characterized the sciences of state. Yet the latter were not swept aside by these changes, nor (in my view) even fundamentally transformed.[1] Rather, they had already acquired

---

1. In this I differ from Keith Tribe's interpretation of this period. According to Tribe, cameralism gave way to economics, which served as an expression of emancipation as opposed to regulation. "The subject of the territorial ruler, governed by the regulations and directives of a sovereign whose purpose was to make his subjects happy and (thereby) his states powerful, was set free and, at the same time, presented with a new field of action for the exercise of this freedom." (*Governing Economy*, 149). This rests on a different reading both of the late eighteenth and early nineteenth centuries; in my view, the recognition of an autonomous sphere of human action had already progressed considerably under cameralism, and the economic subject of the new thinking was not the individual but the nation.

a sufficient degree of institutional stability in terms of curricula and teaching positions to retain their identity. And there was enough diversity among the German universities to allow for places like Jena, where the sciences of state had a minimal presence, and places like Halle and Göttingen, where they revived or remained strong. More important, however, the field itself, for all its emphasis on static states, was sufficiently flexible to be able to assimilate certain features of the new learning. This was facilitated by certain embodiment-type ideas whose connotations reached beyond any one particular social or intellectual group. Thus the discourse of the sciences of state was not as hostile to the notion of *Bildung* as might first appear. As one would expect, however, this was not uniformly true of all the disciplines; those most prone to atrophy were the technical ones, especially technology and commerce. This chapter will trace these various changes.

To begin, a few preliminary remarks on *Bildung* are in order. This notion did not originate with Humboldt, but was dear to the philosophers of the Enlightenment such as Kant and Moses Mendelssohn as well. Like most terms of embodiment, it meant different things to different people.[2] In Prussia, *Bildung* had already become a value for many officials in the days of Frederick the Great, where it served as a foil to the harsh rule of the monarch: officials had to obey outwardly but could maintain a sense of superiority and status through cultivation in their private lives. After the death of Frederick, administrators felt freer to express their beliefs, and when they did so, it was with a political emphasis.[3] Indeed, *Bildung* had become central to the Germans' notion of public opinion: it denoted a level of general education and training of the mind that would lay the foundation for the use of reason and thereby for the exercise of free thought and expression.[4] "I understand the public use of reason," wrote Kant in his famous essay, "What Is Enlightenment?" of 1784, "as that which someone makes of it as a *learned person* [*Gelehrter*] before the whole public of *readers*."[5] This notion of public cultivation was also important to a *Staatswissenschaftler* like Schlözer, who saw it as a dimension of political education that would lead to a very different revolution in Germany from that of France, one based on reform rather than violent overthrow:

> The revolution will happen slowly to be sure, but it happens. The Enlightenment rises, as in France, from below; but it also bumps against Enlightenment on high. Where are there more cultivated sovereigns than in Germany? . . . And that it happens gradually, without mischief, without anarchy, is to all ap-

2. Sheehan, *German History*, 204.
3. Rosenberg, *Bureaucracy, Aristocracy, and Autocracy*, 188–90, 198.
4. Habermas, *Strukturwandel*, 84. For similar notions of public opinion as a forum and tribunal for reason in France, see Baker, "Politics and Public Opinion," 233–34, 243–46.
5. Kant, "Was ist Aufklärung?" *GS*, 8: 37.

pearances more the work of writers than of cabinets. Princes will remain princes, and all German persons will become free persons.[6]

In many ways, then, the year 1789 did not mark a new beginning in Germany, but an intensification of developments that had been taking shape for some time in the public sphere. If most of the educated public in Germany were able to greet the opening weeks of the French Revolution with enthusiasm, it was because the notion of freedom had already been a topic for public discussion. Ernst Moritz Arndt could write in his autobiography, "Even in the narrow circle of our home [in Pomerania], despite the conservative habits of my parents, this new epoch made its influence felt. Political interest grew from year to year. I, too, took my share, and for several years I had not only read the papers aloud, but also to myself."[7] The interest continued: between 1790 and 1796, some nine humdred writings appeared on the theme of freedom and equality, and over eighty journals devoted to history and politics appeared in the decade.[8]

If this interest did not always translate directly into the demand for political representation or the overthrow of tyrants, it did at the very least betoken a disillusionment with state authority that was exercised in a "mechanical" manner. The words *machine* and *mechanical* came to serve as embodiments for all that was evil in government: rigidity, coldness, and impersonality. A critique of mechanistic rule had been central to the Storm and Stress movement of the 1770s and 1780s, and the notion of *Bildung* was in part a response to it.[9] Schlözer, in the passage quoted above, also employed *Bildung* in a new, antimechanistic way: rather than seeing it as belonging to a public sphere rigidly separated from the state, as Beckmann had done, he saw it as spreading to the state's leaders, thus quietly revolutionizing the state itself.

Others were more skeptical. Humboldt, in his essay *On the Limits of State Action* of 1792, defended individuality against the encroachments of the state. He claimed,

> As State interference increases, the agents to which it is applied come to resemble each other, as do all the results of their activity. And this is the very design which States have in view. They desire comfort, ease, tranquillity; and these are most readily secured to the extent that there is no clash of individualities. But what man does and must have in view is something quite different—

6. Schlözer, *Staatsanzeigen* 16 (1791), 96 n; quoted in Bödeker, "Prozesse." 28–29. Schlözer welcomed the French Revolution at first, but began to deplore its excesses by the end of the summer of 1789. See Gooch, *French Revolution*, 74–78.

7. Arndt, *Autobiography*, quoted in Gooch, *French Revolution*, 38.

8. Stolleis, "Verwaltungslehre," *DV,* 2: 58.; Moran, *Toward the Century of Words*, 41 n.

9. For a recent treatment of this much-discussed topic, see LaVopa, *Grace, Talent, and Merit*, 256–57, 264 ff.

it is variety and activity. . . . [Those who do not understand this] may justly be suspected of misunderstanding human nature, and of wishing to make men into machines.[10]

Humboldt concluded that any state activity in the name of the welfare or happiness of its citizens is illegitimate.

The antimechanistic rhetoric of such intellectuals certainly bespoke a willingness to question the established system of government; in actuality, the system that had governed Germany as a whole was breaking down. The Revolution exposed the glaring weaknesses of the Holy Roman Empire. The French occupation of Speyer, Worms, and Mainz in 1792 made this customary defense of the Empire as preserving the freedom and diversity of the small territories increasingly untenable. Furthermore, both critics and defenders of the Empire agreed that its decentralized structure severely hampered economic growth.[11]

Another established institutional system that came under critical scrutiny was that of the universities. It was not uncommon for enlightened officials to view universities as vestiges of a medieval past, as corporations of professors who conferred privilege regardless of merit, and who were being rendered obsolete by the new independent reading public and by the learned academies as centers of scholarship. Universities also seemed outdated as teaching institutions, emphasizing rote learning and finished systems, which were out of step with the latest pedagogical theories of J. H. Pestalozzi and J. B. Basedow. Certainly the financial state of the universities was not conducive to innovation. The salaries of most professors were inadequate, which led them to supplement their incomes by holding more than one chair or to divide their time between academic and nonacademic careers. Declining enrollments and the great number of small universities only exacerbated the problem. In the absence of financial rewards, professors did hold on to traditional privileges, such as control over certain ecclesiastical posts, or the right to own beer and wine cellars.[12] The tendency for young academics to gain access to a position by marrying into a professor's family was well known.[13] By the 1790s, criticism of these practices was so extensive that a few enlightened administrators began to question the need for universities at all—as opposed to some sort of practical vocational higher education.[14] At the same time, these criticisms were offset by the continuing example set by Göttingen, or by the revival of humanistic learning that was taking place at Jena.

The call for an increased pace of reform, whether within each state or

10. Humboldt, *The Limits of State Action*, 24.
11. Gagliardo, *Reich and Nation*, 130.
12. Turner, "University Reformers and Professorial Scholarship," 2: 508.
13. Ibid., 513; Gerth, *Bürgerliche Intelligenz*, 35–36.
14. McClelland, *State, Society, and University*, 76–77.

within the Empire, was not the only response of German intellectuals and political leaders to the French Revolution. There was also a more conservative one, which had already taken shape by the 1790s in the form of a reaction to the Enlightenment. At first, it was the enlightened reformers' skepticism of traditional religion which aroused protest, and defenders of the latter began to establish journals to fight the Enlightenment on its own ground around 1780.[15] When it came to political views, conservatives also attacked the mechanistic model of the state, but from the opposite perspective of Humboldt. Whereas the latter did so in the name of preserving individual freedom, the former did so in the name of an organic state which absorbed the individual. In this they could look to Justus Möser (1720–1794). Möser had been an articulate spokesman for the rights of the local community, expressed in a history of his native Osnabrück. His protest was against those who attempted to tamper with such local traditions from outside (i.e., from a centralized administration), as they tended "to reduce everything to simple principles . . . to let the state be ruled by academic theories and a general plan . . . to make the art of government easier for themselves and to make of themselves the mainspring of the whole state machine."[16]

It was Möser who was primarily responsible for introducing the organic metaphor of the state as an alternative to the mechanistic one. Generally, this metaphor likened the body politic to a natural state or process such as the human body. As Möser developed it, the organic metaphor expressed two aspects of society which the mechanical one did not. First, its members were interdependent, and this could only be seen by looking at the whole rather than at the isolated parts. The mechanistic picture of the state as a complex of intermeshing wheels and drives was inadequate to convey this interdependency. Second, the organism was not static, but developed and grew.[17] During the Revolution, the main spokesman for the conservative position was Adam Müller, who wrote on a great variety of topics, among them politics and economics. He painted previous systems of political economy in broad swaths as mechanistic, and modeled his idea of the state on that of the family.[18]

Party lines between enlightened reformers and conservative opponents were already taking shape in the 1780s. In 1788, the Prussian minister in charge of education, Johann Christoph Wöllner, deliberately sought to remove enlightenment influences in favor of religious mysticism. Needless to say, the increasingly violent course of the French Revolution bolstered the conservative cause in Germany and made the appeal to enlightened public opinion more

15. Epstein, *Genesis of German Conservatism*, 81.
16. Quoted in Walker, *German Home Towns*, 177.
17. Epstein, *Genesis*, 322.
18. Müller, *Nationalökonomische Schriften*, 2, 6.

difficult to maintain. Schlözer, despite his opposition to the excesses of the Revolution, was forced to suspend publication of his *Staatsanzeigen* in February, 1794. The same fate befell the initial efforts of another famous publisher, Johann Friedrich Cotta, whose *Europäische Annalen* and *Neueste Weltkunde* were modeled on Schlözer's papers.[19] In places where bureaucratic reform had already gained momentum, conservatives were able to slow the process without stopping it entirely. A good example was the promulgation of the legal code (*Allgemeine Landrecht*) for Prussia in 1794. A product of late enlightened absolutism, and begun during the reign of Frederick the Great, its original draft incorporateda preliminary section that its authors viewed as a surrogate constitution. It articulated the basis and the limits of monarchical power and prohibited royal decrees except those approved by a legislative commission.[20] The final version was ready in 1792, but under the influence of events in France and his own conservative advisers, King Frederick William II suspended it. After a two-year struggle, it finally took effect, but with the "constitutional paragraphs" omitted.[21]

The Bureaucratic Counteroffensive in Bavaria and Prussia

The challenges to bureaucratic reform did not necessarily result in a flagging of effort on the part of administrators; on the contrary, in some cases it led to renewed efforts. These had the effect of strengthening the institutional bases for the sciences of state. The most graphic example was Bavaria, where a new prince, Max Joseph, installed Count Maximilian Montgelas as the dominant minister in 1799. Educated in France, Montgelas is commonly acknowledged as being a product of the Enlightenment.[22] He had seen that the weakness of Bavaria under the previous ruler, Karl Theodor, had led to pressures from France for territory and from Austria for annexation; he was determined to strengthen the state both internally and externally. This involved the integration of Bavaria's different provinces into a single, centralized administrative system as well as the elimination of corruption. Montgelas immediately instituted a set of rigorous curricular requirements and examinations to improve the caliber of administrators. His conception of bureaucratic reform, while making entry more difficult, contributed to the self-image of bureaucrats as professionals.[23]

19. Moran, *Toward the Century of Words*, 59, 101. Moran shows how Cotta's survival as a publisher depended on the protection of the princes, and was thus subject to the shifting diplomatic and military situaion of these years.

20. Epstein, *Genesis*, 377.

21. Ibid., 385.

22. Knemeyer, *Regierungs-und Verwaltungsreformen*, 160; Weis, *Montgelas*, 1: 283.

23. Wunder, *Privilegierung und Disciplinierung*, 198–99, 204–7.

Montgelas had pointed to the need for reforming the universities and improving their quality before he took office. His imagination was practical rather than humanistic: his own interests ran to politics, state and church law, history, and economics rather than religion or art.[24] Accordingly, he made cameralist training prominent. From 1799, theology students were required to hear lectures in agriculture and in pedagogy; jurists were required to take forensic medicine, medical *Polizei*, and the basic cameral sciences (agriculture, police science, finance, and political economy).[25] In the same year, a cameral institute was created at the University of Ingolstadt, consisting of members of the faculties of law, medicine, and philosophy. Prospective adminstrators were required to take a broad range of subjects, from law to natural sciences—although the emphasis was on the natural sciences, following the Lautern-Heidelberg pattern. A year later, the entire university was moved from the "Jesuit cage" of Ingolstadt to Landshut.[26] The cameral institute remained intact and later became a separate faculty when the university was again moved to Munich in 1826; it remained in this form throughout the nineteenth century. When Bavaria acquired the University of Würzburg in 1803 after the bishopric there was dissolved, it established another cameral faculty.[27]

The mere existence of cameralist institutes, in this case as in subsequent ones, did not mean that they had the unequivocal support of the faculty or the bureaucracy. In particular, the law faculties were to be the source of much criticism of the cameralist curricula throughout the century. It was universally acknowledged that administrators needed training in the law, regardless of whatever additional demands a cameralist curriculum might make on them, but in the opinion of many law professors, an attempt to graft juristic studies to cameralism would only dilute the rigor of the former and spread the student too thin. Thus the influential law professor Anselm Feuerbach, who was one of Montgelas's closest advisors, thought the program contained too many lectures, many of them unneccessary.[28] In Bavaria as elsewhere, the cameralist faculties had a precarious claim on the training of officials.

Prussia also witnessed a spate of reforms in a variety of areas before 1806, although no single figure dominated the process as in Bavaria. Here economic conditions provided the background: the Revolution had accelerated the trend

24. Weis, *Montgelas*, 1: 463.

25. Permaneder, *Annales Almae Literarum Universitatis Ingolstadii*, 508.

26. Dickerhof, "Kameralstudium und Bildungssystematik in Bayern," in Waszek, ed., *LNDU*, 246–47; Pechmann, "Geschichte der Staatswirtschaftlichen Fakultät," 135.

27. Schanz, "Die Staatswirtschaftliche Fakultät der Universität Würzburg," 8–10. The university flourished for three years until Würzburg became independent in 1806, to return again to Bavaria in 1815.

28. Pechmann, "Staatswirtschaftliche Fakultät," 136.

towards a market economy in a variety of ways. Agricultural prices had been rising since 1790, due partly to increased demand from England's industrial cities and partly to the decline of trade between England and France during the revolutionary wars. Prussia's neutrality between 1798 and 1806 redounded to her profit, and the prosperity of farms spread to the towns (grain exports from Danzig, for example, increased fourfold from 1790 to 1801).[29] The amount of metal money in circulation increased in North Germany, leading to quick fortunes being made. This only increased the fragility of the manorial system: more and more bourgeois were in a position to buy aristocratic estates; at the same time, the demand for greater productivity on the part of the land-owners made the peasants themselves increasingly restive.[30] As in Bavaria, a new ruler was the triggering factor for change. If Frederick the Great's successor, Frederick William II, had been conservatively oriented in reaction to the Revolution, the next king, Frederick William III, who came to power in 1797, was genuinely interested in reform. Given the increased rumblings from the peasantry, he opened the discussion of ending the feudal system on the land.[31] Although many members of the bureaucracy were not yet ready for such a step, the king went ahead with eliminating serfdom from the royal domains, beginning in 1799—an act which in fact freed more serfs than Stein's more famous edict of 1807.[32] While the king himself was irresolute when it came to further measures, his cabinet prepared the way for significant economic reforms, such as the elimination of internal tariff barriers, which was completed in 1805.[33] Furthermore, a beginning was made on the reform of the bureaucracy itself, although there were serious splits among the officials as to how this should be done. The lines of division between reformers and conservatives were already clear. Hardenberg, a product of Göttingen, favored administrative centralization, while Otto Karl Voss, who represented the interests of the Junkers, favored the devolving of authority more on local powers.[34] These divisions were to persist into the post-Napoleonic period.

The status of cameralism in Prussia reflected this situation. The cameralist professors at Halle developed plans for a separate institute in 1804, and al-

---

29. Hasek, *Introduction of Adam Smith's Doctrines into Germany*, 54–55 and n.

30. Berdahl, *Politics of Prussian Nobility*, 78–84, 115; Schissler, *Preussische Agrargesellschaft im Wandel*, 59 ff; Hagen, "The Junkers' Faithless Servants," 75–77.

31. Harnisch, "Peasants and Markets," 62–63; Schissler, *Preussische Agrargesellschaft im Wandel*, 54–56; Ernst Rudolf Huber, *Deutsche Verfassungsgeschichte*, 1: 185.

32. Hintze, "Prussian Reform Movements Before 1806," 71, 459. According to Georg Friedrich Knapp, the 1799 edict freed 50,000 serfs; that of 1807 freed 45,000.

33. Ritter, *Stein*, 131.

34. Hintze, "Prussian Reform Movements Before 1806," 80–83; Knemayer, *Regierungs-und Verwaltungsreformen*, 85–87, 192–94. The king accepted Voss's version. This plan did, however, separate the bureaus of justice and administration, fulfilling one of Hardenberg's goals.

though the rest of the philosophical faculty did not encourage it, a pamphlet by one of the professors, Ludwig Heinrich Jakob, by chance fell into the hands of the king. The king ordered that no one be admitted to the administration who had not passed a rigorous examination, and directed his minister in charge of education to report back to him with a new curricular plan.[35] Although the Battle of Jena prevented its implementation, this plan eventually became a major reference point in the ongoing debate over proper policy in the decades following.[36] Its stated purpose at the time was to "disabuse [the student] of the unfortunate delusion that the study of the cameral sciences demanded any less exertion of intellectual powers than that of theology, medicine, etc."[37]

Here too the tensions and controversies between jurists and cameralists revealed themselves. The director of the University of Frankfurt/Oder responded to the plan as follows:

> It is more possible that a member of the royal war and domains chamber not know how windmills and water mills are constructed, . . . not know that splenic fever is a special disease of sheep, how lacemakers and buttonmakers are different from each other, than that he ignore the legal bases of all these objects.[38]

In time, the opposing sides in this controversy would become aligned with the reformist and conservative factions in the bureaucracy, with the reformers urging the importance of cameralist studies and the conservatives arguing for the predominance of law.[39]

A secondary controversy centered on whether curricular plans should be required courses of study or merely suggested guidelines that would leave students free to follow their own lights according to principle of *Bildung*. One professor of cameralism at Halle remonstrated as follows against requirements: "The disadvantage of such mechanical things is that they narrow a good head . . . and spoil it completely into a machine."[40] The attitude, however, of most of these utilitarian reformers toward the new emphasis on *Bildung* was pragmatic rather than rigid. Thus Montgelas was willing to allow the turn from enlightenment to romanticism at Landshut and to approve an honorary doc-

35. Muth, "Preussische Kameralstudienpläne," 292–93. The cameral institute was first conceived as a separate faculty, but met with strong objections from the philosophical faculty (ibid., 286–87). See also Lehmann, "Halle," 32–44.

36. Muth, "Preussische Kameralstudienpläne," 305; Bleek, *Juristenprivileg*, 100–101.

37. Directive of 7 Feb. 1806, quoted in Muth, "Preussische Kameralstudienpläne," 297; Bleek, *Juristenprivileg*, 100.

38. Muth, "Preussische Kameralstudienpläne," 302.

39. Bleek, *Juristenprivileg*, 89.

40. Lehmann, "Nationalökonomie in Halle," 44–45.

torate for the romantic philosopher Schelling.[41] In Prussia, the conflict between utilitarian and humanistic education would result in both being taken into account in the wave of reforms that followed the military defeat of 1806.

THE ASSIMILATION OF KANT AND SMITH

The sciences of state, then, continued to be associated with the need for reform from above as an alternative to revolution. At the same time, their practitioners were not impervious to the discontent with the prevailing political order implied in the critiques of the mechanical metaphor of the state. Their openness to revising the corresponding conceptual order of their disciplines can be seen in their interrelated encounters with the ideas of Kant and Smith.

Kant had reached the height of his fame during the 1790s. Given the revolutionary turmoil abroad and the increased fragility of the Empire at home, all eyes looked to Königsberg for philosophical guidance. After his *Metaphysical Foundations of Law* was published in 1797, six compendia explaining the work appeared in the next three years.[42] In this systematic work, Kant sanctioned reform and representational government, not violent revolution.[43] But he also held that there was no *ultimate* legal basis for any intermediate corporations or orders (such as a nobility, an established church, or a guild) that stood between the individual and the the state as part of a God-given "nature of things." Such orders may be needed in specific times and places, and may be legalized by specific statutes, but these could as easily become obsolete.[44] The same argument applied to the concept of the ruler as landowner and to the whole set of manorial obligations that revolved around it.[45] Kant based these arguments on the principles of practical reason, which he had presented in his second critique nine years before. The historically conditioned arrangements which led to specific political orders were for Kant relationships of cause and effect, which he had categorized as the realm of pure reason; jurisprudence, on the other hand, dealt with actions and relationships of free human beings, who were not governed solely by laws of nature, but by the moral categories of practical reason. "Law," according to Kant, "is thus the essence of the conditions under which the will of one can be united together with the will of another according to a general law of freedom."[46] The purpose of law was thus to allow maximal free-

---

41. Dickerhof, "Kameralstudium und Bildungssystematik in Bayern," in Waszek, ed., *INDU*, 249.

42. Ludwig, "Einleitung" to Kant, *Metaphysische Anfangsgründe der Rechtslehre*, xxiv–xxv.

43. Kant, *Metaphysische Anfangsgründe der Rechtslehre*, *GS*, 6: 340–41, 319.

44. Ibid., 324. See also Radbruch, *Rechtsphilosophie*, 107; Tuck, "'Modern' Theory of Natural Law," 99.

45. Kant, *Metaphysische Anfangsgründe der Rechtslehre*, *GS*, 6: 323–24.

46. Ibid., 230.

dom of the individual without infringing on that of another, rather than to provide for the individual's happiness or welfare. According to Kant, "[The latter] could perhaps happen much more easily and comfortably in a state of nature (as Rousseau claims), or also under a despotic government."[47]

Kant's philosophy thus presented a fundamental challenge to the utilitarian assumptions of the sciences of state. He explicitly attacked Achenwall's foundation of law on this basis.[48] Moreover, the administrative apparatus and functions of the state—including managing the economy, *Polizei*, and finance—were all merely historically contingent institutions, like the estates, operating on the principles of cause and effect. Kant mentioned them merely in passing.[49] Similarly, the sciences of state themselves could be justified as studies of contingent "technical-practical rules" that ensure the happiness of citizens, but not as consistent workings-out of the fundamental moral principles underlying law. To know whether such rules were effective required knowledge of cause and effect, which made such studies the corollaries of natural rather than moral science.[50] They therefore had no place in the law faculty of the university. Kant certainly recognized that lawyers had to be in part technicians, that as practitioners they could not afford to ruminate continually on the philosophical bases of their deliberations. But the proper technical-practical discipline for such people was legal exegetics, not a science of administration.[51]

If the sciences of state did not belong in the law faculty, they did not have a prominent role in Kant's vision of the philosophical faculty either. Kant devoted an essay to the question of the competence of the different university faculties in 1798. The occasion was Wöllner's attempt to censor Kant's own writings on religion, which raised the question of the duties of a university professor to the state as a civil servant. Kant claimed that the state could command such unquestioning obedience from the theological, law, and medical faculties, for they had the function of practical training of candidates for state positions. The philosophical faculty, however, had a higher goal, that of the search for truth through critical scrutiny in the light of pure and practical reason.[52] Thus practical-technical subjects were out of place, and *The Conflict of Faculties* made no mention of the sciences of state. The philosophical faculty contained two departments, one for historical knowledge (history, geography, philology, hu-

---

47. Ibid., 318.
48. Kant, "Über den Gemeinspruch: Das Mag in der Theorie Richtig Sein, Taugt aber nicht für die Praxis," *GS*, 8: 301–2.
49. Ibid., 325.
50. Kant, *Kritik der Urteilskraft*, *GS*, 5: 172–73.
51. Kant, *Streit der Fakultäten*, *GS*, 7: 24–25.
52. Ibid., 22, 27–28.

manities, and empirical natural science), and the other for knowledge of pure reason (pure mathematics, philosophy, metaphysics of nature and morals).[53]

Evidence for Kant's low opinion of the sciences of state may be found in a recommendation on the cameralist curriculum from the University of Königsberg in 1794 in response to a request from Wöllner, which Kant cosigned. The document outlined no specific curriculum for administrators and contained no reference to the sciences of state. Rather, it included the plan of the entire philosophical faculty, in which cameralism was incorporated along with philosophy, philology, mathematics, and the fine arts. Within this, the cameral sciences had the goal of making students into "useful citizens . . . [and] to acquire, preserve, and make use of a temporal fortune, in order to take care of the need, comfort and welfare of human life."[54] It further recommended that the survey lecture, "Encyclopedia of Cameral Sciences," should not be taught as a public lecture: the sciences which qualified for public lectures should meet the needs of different classes of students; cameral science was too specialized.[55]

Kant's popularity forced most of his contemporaries to reflect on the disciplinary boundaries between philosophy, law, and the sciences of state, though the outcome of such reflections was by no means unanimous—nor in agreement with Kant's own position. On the one hand, the disjunction of philosophical and positive law opened the door to the historical school, which sought to develop positive law based on inductive rather than deductive methods.[56] On the other, it also led to a revival of philosophical natural law itself as a study of norms and human rights. The fact that no less than 103 books on natural law appeared between 1790 and 1831 is an indication of the strength of this trend.[57] Natural law included much of what today would be called political theory: the origins of the state, the concept of sovereignty, the various "powers" of the state (e.g., legislative, executive, etc.), and the forms of the state (e.g., monarchy, aristocracy, democracy). Many writers accepted Kant's notion that the purpose of the state was to protect individual freedom rather than to promote happiness and welfare.[58] Thus the limitation of the state's power was a

53. Ibid., 28. Kant does, however, mention medical police, that is, the provision of public comfort and security, as a central purpose of the medical faculty (26–27).

54. Muth, "Preussische Kameralstudienpläne," 265–66.

55. Ibid., 266; Bleek, *Juristenprivileg*, 98.

56. The pivotal figure in this process was Gustav Hugo, a Göttingen professor who developed a system of natural civil law that was free of deductions from first principles in the manner of Thomasius and Wolff. See Stinzing and Landsberg, *Geschichte der deutschen Rechtswissenschaft*, 3.2: 18–19; on Hugo's assimilation of Kant, 32, 37–41.

57. Klippel, "Naturrecht als politische Theorie," 268 n, 273–76.

58. For example, see Bauer, *Lehrbuch des Naturrechts*, 265; Gros *Lehrbuch des philosophischen Rechtswissenschaft*, 215. The first editions of these works appeared in 1807 and 1802 respectively.

major concern, and the doctrine of the separation of powers to prevent abuse assumed a central place. The enumeration of distinct powers of government stemmed not only from Montesquieu, but also from the discussion of different rights of sovereignty (*Hoheitsrechte*) in German state law as developed by Pütter and others.[59] There was much disagreement on how many distinct powers of the state there were. Some asserted a unitary power; others discerned as many as five.[60] Insofar as opinion on the proper limits of these spheres was divided, it affected the coherence of the sciences of state themselves, particularly that of police science.

Indeed, police science was the discipline among the sciences of state most directly disturbed by Kant's reformulation, for a variety of reasons. If happiness and welfare were no longer the goals of state activity, the importance of police science would be drastically reduced. And even Pütter's definition, which had defined *Polizei* as providing security for the state and its subjects, was undermined. For if the purpose of laws *as a whole* was such security (i.e., to protect citizens from infringing on the freedom of others), what special role was left for police? Kant himself had defined *Polizei* rather narrowly, as serving "public security, comfort, and respectability"; police functions were subordinate to the maintenance of law. By maintaining an atmosphere of public peace and decency—Kant specifically mentioned the prevention of begging, street noise and odors, and public vulgarity—they made the government's task of maintaining the laws easier.[61] In any event, the 1800s witnessed a flurry of publications over the definition and scope of police science, with issues so complex that no clear regional or ideological groupings emerged.[62]

Given Kant's neglect of the sciences of state per se, his followers took considerable latitude in drawing out the implications of his individual ideas and language for the area, often finding stimulation in one or two works to the neglect of others, and usually arriving at conclusions that were very different from Kant's own. Thus Wilhelm Josef Behr, newly appointed at age twenty-two to a chair of state law in Würzburg in 1799, after a year of study in Göttingen, presented in the following year a system of politics which proclaimed law rather than happiness as the supreme end of the state, and then presented the sciences of state—largely following Schlözer—as a means to this end.[63]

59. Böckenförde, *Gesetz und gesetzgebende Gewalt*, 63–65.

60. Klüber, *Öffentliches Recht des teutschen Bundes*, 165–66 n. The question of whether the judicial power should be included under the executive or not was one such bone of contention. Further subdivisions of the executive power generally included justice and *Polizei*.

61. Kant, *Metaphysische Anfangsgründe der Rechtslehre, GS*, 9: 325.

62. For a masterful summary, see Preu, *Polizeibegriff*, 224–73; also Maier, *Staats-und Verwaltungslehre*, 193–94.

63. Behr, *Notwendigkeit des Studiums der Staatslehre*, 13, 16, 66, 77. Behr's texts were later used in Freiburg and Greifswald as well.

Another self-styled disciple, the former priest Johann Paul Harl, was also adept at clothing older ideas in Kantian terminology. Newly appointed at Erlangen in 1805, he claimed in his systematic work of that year that the sciences of state were badly in need of first principles, a "metaphysics of the state." His newly discovered "principle" for economics was a paraphrase of the categorical imperative: "Seek that all actual and attainable bodily and spiritual capacities of the members of a state are employed to further the well-being of the entire society of the state."[64] Needless to say, such formulas usually reestablished the utilitarian basis of administration that Kant had so clearly rejected.

The jargon notwithstanding, it can be said that writers in the sciences of state, as a result of their encounter with Kant, were more conscious of the need to base their systems on fundamental principles. In this way, they were able to fashion a response to the antibureaucratic strand of public opinion and defend the state as more than a mere bureaucratic machine. It is in this context that the reception of Smith may also be understood.

The Wealth of Nations had been translated into German in 1777, but for almost two decades it had attracted little notice. Academic cameralists had tended to lump Smith with the physiocrats, and approached his work with their usual condescension as one source among many.[65] This situation changed in the mid–1790s. In 1794, a new translation appeared by Christian Garve, a "popular philosopher" who consciously strove to transmit the Scotch enlightenment to a broad reading public.[66] Garve's translation went through two more editions by 1810; during the same years, more and more professors began to give Smith's ideas a central place in their lectures and textbooks. Among those who thoroughly assimilated *The Wealth of Nations* were the leaders of the later Prussian reform movement, Karl von Stein and Hardenberg.[67]

It would be too simple to characterize this "discovery" of Smithian free market principles as an economic counterpart to the realm of inner freedom nurtured by *Bildung*—though both were indeed conceived as existing beyond state control. As we have seen, the cameralists had long since acknowledged a free sphere of economic activity, if only to classify it. What Smith now offered them was a means of going beyond static classification by providing principles that could explain the causal processes by which wealth was acquired and transmuted. Given such a foundation, economics could become a true science of first principles in Kantian terms rather than a mere set of technical direc-

64. Harl, *Grundlinien einer Theorie des Staates,* i, xii, 1–17. For other examples of Kant's influence on cameralist writers, see Tribe, *Governing Economy,* 158–60.

65. Tribe, *Governing Economy,* 143–46.

66. Hasek, *Introduction of Smith's Doctrines into Germany,* 68.

67. Treue, "Adam Smith in Deutschland," 108–9. Stein's principal encounter with Smith occurred in 1809, after his great reform ministry.

tives. For some of these writers, the turn from classification to explanation coincided with their abandonment of the mechanical metaphor to describe the state in favor of the organic one. This metaphor conveyed, as did the Smithian system in their hands, the interdependence of parts of the economy—both private and public—as opposed to the compartmentalization implied by the mechanical one. It is no coincidence that the young Adam Müller, who was a conservative even as a student, nevertheless came away from his Göttingen years an admirer of Smith—even though his admiration was too unsystematic to win him acceptance among the professors.[68]

The occurrence of the word *nation* in the title of Smith's book played no small role in the timing of its reception, for *nation* had become a term of embodiment for patriotic sentiments, thanks to the example of the French Revolution. While German publicists reported on the national assembly and the attempts to find the appropriate constitution for the French nation, and French patriotism inspired its armies to military victory and occupation, *The Wealth of Nations* pointed to the economic power and potential of the nation as distinct from that of the state. The phrase summarized the complex of activities in the private sector which the cameralists had long since sought to liberate. Smith's title now gave them a common term with the romantic thinkers of their day such as Fichte and Savigny. Thus Smith's ideal became incorporated into the cameralist system under the name *Nationalökonomie*—although some writers preferred the native German term *Volk* to embody the same complex—hence the synonym *Volkswirtschaft*.[69]

The two universities which first served as points for the entry of Smithian ideas were Göttingen and Königsberg. Göttingen, as usual, was in advance of other universities, and its connection to England meant that Smith's views were probably discussed there informally before they attained formal recognition in texts and lectures. The first person to publish an adaptation of Smith for classroom use was Georg Sartorius, a Göttingen product. He had studied theology and history there in the 1780s and began to lecture in 1792; he became full professor in 1802 and in 1814 was named Schlözer's successor as professor of Politics. Following Schlözer, he claimed that "history is inseparable from politics," and taught and published in both areas throughout his career.[70] His well-roundedness attracted him to Goethe, who became a lifelong friend after they

68. Berdahl, *Politics of Prussian Nobility*, 165, 168.
69. On the first uses of these, see Burkhardt, "Begriff des Ökonomischen," in Waszek, ed., *INDU*, 67–69.
70. Sartorius, *Einladungs-Blätter zu Vorlesungen über die Politik*, 21. His best-known historical work was *The History of the Hanseatic League*, 1802–8. His regular lectures included the general history of Europe, statistics, politics, and economics.

met in 1801.[71] His gifts as a teacher inspired one of his students, Heinrich Heine, to write a sonnet in his praise.[72] His delicate temperament and carefully controlled passion found expression in his political views, which consistently advocated moderation and opposed revolutionary enthusiasm.[73]

Sartorius's writings exemplified the mix of tradition and innovation that characterized the sciences of state at this time, as well as a distrust of overly rigid systems. His *Handbook of Political Economy for Use in Academic Lectures According to Adam Smith's Principles* (1796) was at once a vehicle of clarification and critique. He proposed to present Smith in a more readily accessible form, while also noting that the time was ripe "to test the fundamental principles of science."[74] Ten years later, a revised version appeared, but with the critical commentary reserved for a separate volume. The organization suffered somewhat as a result, but Sartorius now believed that a book which was too neat and followed the opinions of a professor too closely discouraged students from thinking for themselves and promoted rote memorization.[75]

The integration of theoretical, cameralist, and historical perspectives is especially evident in the critical volume. For example, in the essay "On the Collaboration of the Supreme Power of the State in the Furthering of National Wealth," Sartorius supported moderate state intervention in the economy. He argued both against excessive intervention and against the view that individual self-aggrandizement would automatically lead to the common good in all cases.[76] When a few individuals acquired too great a proportion of wealth, then the mechanism of competition as Smith outlined it could not properly operate—as Smith himself had maintained. Sartorius applied this both to international and domestic situations. When one country monopolized too great a proportion of trade or production, other countries were justified in protecting their industries.[77] In domestic policy, Sartorius argued that some of Smith's recommendations had reflected peculiarly English circumstances. For example, Smith advocated the privatization of canals, highways, and bridges, as well as banks—but there was a great need for state support of these in Germany, where the fortune and expertise for such operations was lacking.[78] One could also justify government regulation of corporate (e.g., ecclesiastical) property, of

---

71. Goethe, *Goethes Briefwechsel mit Georg und Caroline Sartorius*, x. Sartorius was one of the few professors in Göttingen who was willing to discuss Goethe's theory of colors with him.

72. Ibid., xviii.

73. Ibid., xvii–xviii; Sartorius, *Einladungs-Blätter zu Vorlesungen über Politik*, 7.

74. Sartorius, *Handbuch der Staatswirtschaft*, xlii–xliii.

75. Sartorius, *Elementen des National-Reichthums*, ix–xi.

76. Sartorius, *Abhandlungen*, 212–13.

77. Ibid., 247–49, 265–71.

78. Ibid., 498–506.

forests, mines, and land division, not to mention state sponsorship of education, or of grain distribution to the poor in times of crop failure—in short, much of the program of police science.[79] In sum, Sartorius was far from a mindless follower of Smith, but reflected an awareness of the specific circumstances of Germany.

The second major center of Smithian influence was Königsberg. The economic conditions there provided an ideal soil for doctrines of free trade: noble and bourgeois landowners in East Prussia were geared to the Baltic grain trade with Poland, Russia, and England, and thus shared a common interest with the merchants of the city. Both groups were receptive to the ideas of Christian Jakob Kraus, a paradigmatic case of a "political professor."[80]

Kraus was born in Königsberg and studied there under Kant, who was struck by his intelligence and encouraged him. He went to Göttingen for a year in 1779, where he heard Schlözer and Heyne. On returning to Königsberg, he was made full professor of practical philosophy at the age of twenty-seven. He lectured on a great variety of subjects, including the Greek classics, history, and mathematics. Although he made no claim to originality in these subjects—nor in economics—he was regarded as a spirited teacher. He had many acquaintances among landowners and merchants, and spent time observing their operations. For a time he was among Kant's closest intimates and a regular guest at his dinner table. At some point, however, a falling-out occurred at Kraus's initiative for reasons unknown.[81] Certainly the two differed in philosophical approach, and not the least of their differences was their estimate of cameralism. It was Kraus's proposal for a cameralist curriculum that carried the greatest weight in Berlin in the discussions of 1805–06, eleven years after the memo signed by Kant which rejected such a project.[82]

Kraus came to economics gradually, through the prompting of state officials. When the minister of finance, Johann von Struensee, visited Königsberg in 1789, he suggested to Kraus that he influence the landowners in the doctrines of Smith, so that they might be weaned away from their attachment to serfdom.[83] In 1794 the president of the provincial government, Leopold von Schrötter, mandated a plan for the study of cameralism in Königsberg; Kraus met this need with such success that Schrötter issued an order in 1800 requiring that future East Prussian administrators hear lectures by Kraus.[84] By 1806, his lectures drew as many as 105 students out of 333 registered in the entire univer-

79. Ibid., 298, 322, 351–52, 465, 515.
80. Treue, "Adam Smith in Deutschland," 110–12.
81. Stuckenberg, *The Life of Immanuel Kant*, 213–14.
82. Muth, "Preussische Kameralstudienpläne," 295–96.
83. Treue, "Adam Smith in Deutschland," 113.
84. Ibid., 114–15.

sity for that year.[85] Stein paid Kraus the following tribute: "The whole province has gained in light and culture through him, his views forced their way into all parts of life, into the government and legislation."[86] He died at age 54 in 1807.

Like Sartorius, Kraus distrusted closed systems and textbooks; he preferred oral communication to writing and was reluctant to publish his lectures, which appeared only posthumously. They were for the most part translations of the *Wealth of Nations*. Nevertheless, his deviations from Smith's text, minute as they were, appropriated the language of German thought in the early 1800s. Here, for example, is his use of the word *nation* and the organic analogy in his paraphrase of Smith's definition of political economy:

> Political economy [*Staatswirtschaft*], considered as a branch of the science of a statesman or legislator, proposes two distinct objects: first, to provide the nation a plentiful income [Smith: to provide a plentiful revenue or subsistence for the people], or more properly, to enable them to provide this for themselves; and secondly, to supply the government [Smith: state or commonwealth] with a revenue sufficient to cover public needs [Smith: sufficient for the public services]. It proposes to enrich the nation and the state, [Smith: it proposes to enrich both the people and the sovereign].

Kraus then added a passage of his own:

> This involves seeing that the state is like a living body, where no alteration of the smallest part can take place without the effect being more or less transmitted to the whole.[87]

Kraus's conception of political economy was couched in the language of Kantian principles. The first task of political economy was to determine the "necessary and general conditions" of income and wealth (*Vermögen*) of a nation. This was not to be done merely by developing concepts, but "primarily by the discovery of natural laws (if one can call them that), which govern the different processes of national economy." These must be able to explain events in the real world, just as abstract laws of motion can illumate real motion.[88] In treating the division of labor, Kraus omitted Smith's formulation, which presented it as the result of a "certain propensity in human nature . . . to truck, barter, and exchange one thing for another." Kraus preferred a Kantian terminology: "In any case, the division of labor is the general and necessary condition, with-

---

85. Vopelius, *Altliberalen Ökonomen*, 25.
86. K. A. Varnhagen von Ense, *Denkwürdigkeiten des eignen Lebens* (Leipzig, 1871), 176–77, cited in Hasek, *Introduction of Adam Smith's Doctrines into Germany*, 93.
87. Kraus, *Staatswirtschaft*, 1: 1–2.
88. Ibid., 1: 4–5.

out which the different inborn gifts that different persons might have could never purposefully express themselves."[89]

Kraus's adapatation of Smith showed that he had not broken with the cameralist tradition any more than had Sartorius. This was particularly evident in the fifth book of his political economy, which was not a paraphrase and dealt with practical applications. It was organized by the threefold classification and dealt with the ways in which government can help or hinder agriculture, manufacturing, and commerce. It was tailor-made to conditions in East Prussia, dealing extensively with landed domains, types of leasing and assessments on them, the elimination of serfdom, credit institutions for agriculture, the dissemination of information on farm techniques, the guilds as counterproductive organizations, grain trade, and tariff policy. In all these areas, Kraus's pragmatic sense asserted itself: he argued for minimal state intervention, but justified it when needed. Tariffs, for example, were necessary, but should be moderate and well publicized. They should not be levied on basic foodstuffs, but were permissible on manufactured goods as long as there was no substitute for them.[90]

While numerous other writers took up Smith's ideas in the 1800s, two deserve particular mention here: Count Julius von Soden, a retired official, and Ludwig Heinrich Jakob, professor at Halle. Their influence consisted of combining, via the medium of compendious textbooks, the older *esprit de systeme* with the new emphasis on causal laws—somewhat to the detriment of the open-endedness that Sartorius and Kraus valued. Soden and Jakob also both independently coined the term *Nationalökonomie* in the same year, 1805.

Soden provides a good illustration of how ideas from *The Wealth of Nations* could be adapted to the priorities of the German nation—well in advance of Friedrich List. His nine volumes on economics, which appeared between 1805 and 1824, were the work of an independent scholar who was not always a precise thinker. Central to the sprawling edifice, however, was the distinction between state and nation. A state was an expression of the rights and duties of people in society; a nation was an expression of their individuality and their ethical relations to one another, independent of the legal framework.[91] Soden emphasized that these ethical bonds were cosmopolitan, and that the striving of a nation for its own prosperity should not break the "tender, invisible bond of the great world-family."[92] Doing so involved a nation's developing its individual productive materials and powers, and finding the proper balance between domestic production and foreign commerce. Soden was sharply critical of British commercial policy in this respect, which stifled productive development in

89. Ibid., 1: 51. Smith's formulation is in book I, chap. 2 of the *Wealth of Nations*.
90. Ibid., 5: 258–60. For Kraus's ideas on agrarian reform, see Vopelius, *Altliberalen*, 25 ff.
91. Soden, *Nationalöknomie*, 1: 10.
92. Ibid., 2: 12, 1: 14.

other countries by selling manufactured goods below their value.[93] Soden employed the notion of "productive power" (*Productiv-Kraft*) to describe the collective and individuual wealth of a nation and its members.[94]

While Soden was widely quoted among subsequent economists, the work of Jakob was still more influential. His textbooks were clear, well-organized, and easily accessible. His *Principles of Economics* went through three editions by 1814; his various texts were used at Erlangen, Heidelberg, Munich, Marburg, and Würzburg following the Napoleonic wars; his influence can be detected in at least eight other economics texts.[95]

Jakob began his academic career as a zealous disciple of Kant. He turned out popularizations of Kant's philosophy at the rate of one or two a year in the 1790s, and at one point urged Kant to modify his terminology in order to win more adherents.[96] From 1795 to 1797 he edited a journal entitled *Annals of Philosophy and the Philosophical Spirit*.[97] It was in this capacity that he became repulsed by the excesses of romantic *Naturphilosophie* and turned away from philosophy to the sciences of state. He began lecturing on Smith, using Sartorius's text, around 1799.[98]

It was clarity and accessibility that characterized Jakob's economics text and which he had found wanting in Sartorius. In this he was aided considerably by the appearance of Jean-Baptiste Say's *Traité d'économie politique* in 1803, which Jakob himself was later to translate into German. Say organized Smith's ideas into the topics which became standard in German economics textbooks: the acquisition, distribution, and consumption of wealth. Say emphasized that these processes occurred according to fundamental scientific laws. He was also responsible for the labels "land," "labor," and "capital" as subdivisions of the section on the acquisition of wealth. Jakob appropriated all of these. The following passage indicates how he combined this new language with eighteenth-century utilitarian goals and the new emphasis on the nation:

> The main final goal that everyone has in uniting into a civil society is: to lead a more secure, comfortable, and happier life. The means to a happy life, insofar as they are given to the power of persons, lie partly in the private energies of the individual members, partly in the public, united energies of the state. A happy life depends first on the availability of the necessary means to still the needs [*Bedürfnisse*] that one has. These means must be brought forth or acquired for the most part by the members of the nation; their essence is

93. Ibid., 2: 34–35, 72–74; Roscher, *Geschichte der Nationalökonomik*, 681–82.
94. Soden, *Nationalökonomie*, 1: 24.
95. Tribe, *Governing Economy*, 174 n.
96. Jakob to Kant, 15 April 1790, Kant, *GS*, 11: 164–67.
97. Lehmann, "Halle," 91. His criticisms of the Schiller-Goethean periodical *Xenien* won a harsh satire from the Weimar circle in return, for which Goethe later apologized (ibid., 104).
98. Jakob, *Grundsätze der National-Oekonomie*, v.

called the national wealth [*National-Vermögen*], or, insofar as a surplus is available, the national riches [*National-Reichtum*]. The first condition of this is security of persons and of property. This is given by the state. . . . Thus it follows that all of the means to be employed by the state must be subordinated to the higher goals of the nation and may never contradict these. The science of the means whereby the state or the government can attain its goal is called state or government politics. . . . The means whereby the people, under protection of the government, fulfills its goal—the acquisition, increase, and enjoyment of wealth—is economics.[99]

Jakob's career at Halle was interrupted by the defeat at Jena, which led to the closing of the university. He spent the following years in Russia, where he served on an imperial commission to reform the currency and taught at the university of Kharkov. His works were translated into Russian. He returned to Halle in 1816, where he once again became active in university administration and lectured not only on political economy, but on the sciences of state as a whole. His extremely broad interpretation of the sciences of state as a curriculum, encompassing natural science, law, and the Schlözerian canon, was indicative of how Smithian currents were being integrated into the older comprehensive systems from the eighteenth century.[100]

The net effect of writers like Soden and Jakob was to absorb the dynamic approach that Smith represented into the older classificatory scheme of cameralism: theoretical economics—comprising the causal processes of acquisition, distribution, and consumption of wealth—could be fit neatly between the static descriptions of concrete economic activities in the private sector on the on hand and the treatment of state economic policy on the other. Thus the professor of cameralism at Tübingen, Friedrich Karl Fulda, expanded his systematic outline from two parts to three, which he labeled "private economy" (the threefold classification of agriculture, technology, commerce), "national economy" (the Smithian material), and "state economy" (economic *Polizei* plus finance).[101] The same structure characterized the Prussian curricular plan of 1805, which followed Kraus's recommendation. In it, the old cameralist disciplines which dealt with the private sector were renamed as "sciences of trades" (*Gewerbekunde*), "which primarily serve the transmission of factual knowledge," and were to be compressed into a single lecture course. It was to be followed by political economy, "which concerns itself extensively with economic theory based on

99. Ibid., 1–4.
100. Cf. Tribe, *Governing Economy*, 182.
101. Fulda, *Grundsätze der . . . Kameralwissenschaften*, iii. Cf. Fulda's earlier *Systematische Abriss der sogenannten Kameralwissenschaften*, whose two parts are labeled "theory of production" (*Produktionslehre*) and "trades police" (*Gewerbspolizei*) and are equivalent to parts 1 and 3 of the later scheme.

the system of Adam Smith." The third course was to be finance and police science, "as a sort of practical application of the economic constitution."[102] Thus the classificatory strategy, with its emphasis on comprehensiveness, proved to be remarkably adaptive in incorporating the innovations of *National-ökonomie*, even though these represented a significant departure from the static assumptions of the cameralist system.

THE NAPOLEONIC PERIOD

During the early nineteenth century, important differences emerged between north and south Germany in the institutionalization of the sciences of state and the development of their ideas. These differences can largely be traced to the territorial changes that marked the end of the Holy Roman Empire between 1803 and 1806. As his armies moved into Germany, Napoleon's goal was to create a chain of medium-sized states that would be more efficient than the patchwork of the Empire, yet not so large as to threaten France. This was accomplished first by the dissolution in 1803 of the ecclesiastical territories and imperial cities as "compensations" to the most important German princes for their lost territory west of the Rhine; then by the creation the the Rhenish Confederation in 1806, which effectively ended the Empire; and finally by loss of Prussian territory at the Treaty of Tilsit in 1807. As a result, the number of German states was reduced from 317 to 36; in the process, the number of universities was reduced from 44 to 22.[103] These changes affected German society at the grass roots more profoundly than all the enlightened reforms of the previous century: the Napoleonic Wars disrupted the civilian population more than any series of wars since the Thirty Years War.[104] The effect of the continual shifting of battle lines, alliances, territories, trade and manufacturing patterns alike was one of uncertainty: one never knew what tomorrow would bring. Mack Walker's chronicle of Weissenberg, a town in Franconia which

102. Muth, "Preussische Kameralstudienpläne," 295–96. To this were added the elements of the Schlözerian canon: statistics and natural law, as well as positive law, history of the fatherland (i.e., Prussia), and a lecture on general court procedure.

103. The close connection between territorial consolidation, the survival of universities, and the prominence of the sciences of state is illustrated by the case of Giessen, the state university for the Grand Duchy of Hesse-Darmstadt, which appeared to by dying with a total student enrollment of twenty-five in 1797. But the Duchy was enlarged as part of the Rhenish confederation and survived with further alterations (including the area around Mainz) into the German Confederation after 1815. The University became indispensable as a training center for officials, and the cameralist Friedrich Wilhelm Crome—a supporter of Napoleon—played a prominent role in university affairs during the occupation; during the Wars of Liberation he was driven out of town, but was allowed to return in 1814. See Moraw, *Kleine Geschichte der Universität Giessen*, 95–101.

104. Blessing, "Der Geist der Zeit hat die Menschen sehr verdorben . . .," 234; Walker, *German Home Towns*, 194–96, 198.

changed territorial hands five times between 1796 and 1806, brings the point home graphically.[105]

No less disruptive than these changes were the legal and administrative ones. Napoleon introduced the *Code Civil* in the occupied Rhineland and in the northern Rhenish states, which were reserved for his relatives, but the effects of similar changes were more thorough in Baden, Württemberg, and Bavaria, where the sovereigns were German.[106] Baden's territory had increased fourfold, Württemberg's had doubled, and both were now mixed Catholic and Protestant. The Grand Duke of Baden and the new King of Württemberg had a vested interest in holding on to their newly enlarged states; they thus both instituted strong centralizing bureaucracies similar to the one that Montgelas had already started in Bavaria. Baden's new legal code was very close to the Napoleonic one; like the Bavarian reform, it sought to undermine the local authorities in town government and in guilds by submitting these to state approval. While neither government felt strong enough to institute land reform, they did attack the judicial and police powers of the local nobility and placed these in the hands of the bureaucracy.[107]

These centralizing impulses contributed powerfully to the entrenchment of the sciences of state in South Germany. A uniform administration meant uniform qualifications, examinations, and university curricula; the curricular reforms featured the integration of state law, administration, and economics. This is not to say that these attempts were uniformly successful: just as the attempts to ride roughshod over local powers and traditions often alienated the bureaucracy from large portions of the population, so did curricular reforms encounter opposition from the older faculties.

In Württemberg, for example, students of law were required to attend lectures in state science and finance in 1811. This, however, did not remove the major traditional obstacle to administrative reform there. Württemberg harbored a distinctive institution of "scribes": administrative officials who had no university education and were acknowledged to be "arbitrary, pedantic, greedy, and corrupt." Their income was calculated by the number of pages written, so it was not uncommon for them to add long legal-historical prefaces to their financial statements.[108] These abuses eventually led to the founding of a separate cameral faculty at Tübingen, but this did not occur until 1817.

In Baden, by contrast, the conditions for curricular reform were more favorable. The testing of officials had been in place since 1789, but the state

105. Walker, *German Home Towns*, 234–43.
106. Heffter, *Deutsche Selbstverwaltung*, 106.
107. Hippel, "Zum Problem der Agrarreformen in Baden und Württemberg," 137–38.
108. Bleek, *Juristenprivileg*, 195 and n.

possessed no university until 1803, when it acquired Heidelberg.[109] The Baden-ese rewrote the statutes for the impoverished university and revitalized it. Their success in establishing Heidelberg as a center for the training of officials was probably due to their regard for the traditional structure of the university. Thus it was decided to integrate the cameral institute into the philosophical faculty, but only when the majority of cameral professors had retired.[110] Training for officials was centered in the law faculty, where two eminent professors of state law were hired: Johann Ludwig Klüber and Karl Salomo Zachariae. At first, however, it was not clear what state law there was to teach.[111] Within a few years, however, both Klüber and Zachariae had produced constitutional law-books for the Rhenish Confederation which artfully dodged the embarassing circumstances of its origin.[112] It was also a Heidelberg professor, Anton Thibaut, who proposed a codification of civil law for all of Germany along the lines of Napoleon's *Code Civil*. Despite the extinction of the cameral faculty, the tie between law and economics remained strong in Baden in the succeeding period, and Heidelberg replaced Göttingen as the preferred university for officials from the smaller German states.

In Austria, the renunciation of the Roman imperial crown in 1806 led to a curricular reform in 1810, in which German state law and history were eliminated in favor of their purely Austrian counterparts. The architect of this plan, F. Zeiller, found state law to be superfluous, for "the few remining fundamental laws of the German Austrian states do not form a whole . . . they can be conveniently taught partly in Austrian history, which is taught in philosophy [faculty] . . . partly in statistics, and partly in political statutes [*politische Gesetz-eskunde*]."[113] Zeiller's overall plan retained the disciplinary constellation initiated by Sonnenfels: law and the sciences of state combined in a single curriculum and faculty. Despite his concern for meeting internal Austrian needs, Zeiller was not closed to intellectual currents from the rest of Germany: unlike Sonnenfels, he made history an obligatory part of the curriculum and incorporated Kantian principles into his own work on natural law.[114] Nevertheless, the

109. Lee, *Politics of Harmony*, 71, 84. Baden acquired Freiburg in 1806, but did not lavish the same attention on it.

110. Keller, *Geschichte der Universität Heidelberg*, 166–67.

111. Ibid., 188–89. On the atmosphere at Heidelberg, see Stolleis, *Geschichte des öffentlichen Rechts*, 2: 69.

112. On Klüber, see Stinzing and Landsberg, *Geschichte der deutschen Rechtswissenschaft* 2.1: 171; on Zachariae, see Mohl, *Geschichte und Literatur der Staatswissenschaften*, 2: 520–21.

113. Kink, *Geschichte der kaiserliche Universität Wien*, 617 n. On the origins of this course in the Austrian curriculum, see Osterloh, *Sonnenfels*, 247–52.

114. Ebert, *Grazer Juristenfakultät im Vormärz*, 39, 48–49. Ebert offers a corrective to Kink's over-drawn portrayal of the differences between Austrian and German thought (35).

Humboldtian ideal of universities did not transfer to Austria; universities there remained centers of purely practical training in the first half of the nineteenth century, without a commitment to general education.

In northern Germany, it was loss of territory rather than consolidation which shaped the subsequent contours of the sciences of state. Hannover was absorbed into the Kingdom of Westphalia, where Napoleon imposed a purely French administrative model. Under these conditions, Göttingen lost much of its preeminence; official documents subseqently referred to the period as the "Westphalian Usurpation."[115]

In Prussia, territorial losses during the Napoleonic wars were tremendous: she lost more than half her territory and half her population at the Treaty of Tilsit and was reduced from a major power to a medium-sized German state. In addition, the French exacted a tribute: Prussian state debt increased from 53 million Thaler in 1806 to approximately 100 million in 1810, and to 206 million in 1815.[116] The defeat was perceived as more than merely military, but as a defeat of the Prussian polity: the inability of the government to call forth "all the energies of the nation," as the reorganization edict of 1808 referred to it.[117] In the crucial test, the mechanical state had failed; the alternative was not to be liberal democracy, but some version of an organic state: still hierarchical, but with a greater degree of interaction between local and central authority. The question was, Who should provide the leadership for such a state, the traditional nobility or the enlightened officials? For the moment, the latter group had the king's ear, and with this the sciences of state—particularly as developed at Göttingen—gained influence.

The reforms themselves were the product of several thinkers. One of them was Hardenberg, whom Pütter had praised as one of "most noble and talented youths" he had ever encountered. Hardenberg generally advocated administrative centralization and rationalization. In this respect, the other great reformer, Baron Karl von Stein, acted as a foil. Stein came from a family of imperial knights; he was also a Göttingen product, where he had read widely in German and English state law and history, economics, and finance. Schlözer was probably his most influential teacher.[118] Despite the acknowledged influence of Montesquieu, Burke, and later Smith on his thinking, Stein was not doctrinaire; his views evolved with practical experience as an administrator. His way of revitalizing the energies of the people was to institute self-administration at the municipal level and to create the office of provincial *Oberpräsident*

115. For example, memo of 14 Sept. 1814, UA Göttingen, PA 4 V b/62 Sartorius.
116. Schissler, "Einleitung: Preussische Finanzpolitik 1806–1820," 37.
117. Huber, *Verfassungsgeschichte*, 1: 149.
118. Ritter, *Stein*, 28–29.

that would serve as a liason between the local region and the central administration.[119]

The reformers' views on the training of officials reflected the antagonism between administrators and Junkers, as expressed in the rivalry between cameralists and jurists. In the eyes of Hardenberg and others, legal training bred resistance to change, so that the study of law was downplayed. The set of regulations for testing administrators in 1808 was one of the few in the entire century in which law was excluded entirely from curricular requirements.[120] One of the reformers, Karl von Altenstein, went so far as to claim that administrators rather than jurists should be the primary legislators because of their breadth of vision; the function of jurists was merely to interpret the laws.[121]

At the same time, the reformers emphasized the importance of general education as part of the training of officials: they thought of themselves as men of "Geist" who represented the interest of the state as a whole above any particular class. They did not see a conflict between *Bildung* and practical education, and clearly recognized the universities as serving both functions. The appointment of Humboldt in 1808 as head of the educational division of the ministry of the interior shows the high priority of education in the reformers' agenda of awakening the powers of the nation. The 1808 regulations also spelled out for the first time the requirement of university education for administrators.[122] Equally striking was the decision to establish a new university at Berlin, despite Prussia's economic weakness and indebtedness.

It is overly simplistic to characterize Humboldt's views on university education as "nonutilitarian."[123] Humboldt acknowledged that universities had to serve the practical needs of the state. For this reason, there was also a need for an academy of sciences that would be solely devoted to research; the state had the right to appoint university professors, while the academy was self-selecting.[124] He did argue, however, against what he believed to be a false or

119. Muncy, *Junker in the Prussian Administration*, 160. Muncy's book contains a comprehensive survey of the Prussian administration.

120. Bleek, *Juristenprivileg*, 103–4. The required subjects included political economy, police science, technology, statistics, experimental physics and chemistry, botany and agriculture.

121. Ibid., 89–90.

122. This point, often overlooked, is stressed by Mueller, *Bureaucracy, Education, and Monopoly*, 158.

123. As does Peter Lundgreen, "Organization of Science and Technology in France: A German Perspective," 311–12. For a more accurate portrayal, including the views of Schelling and Schleiermacher, see Manegold, *Universität, Technische Hochschule und Industrie*, 27–31, and Sweet, *Humboldt: A Biography*, 2: 43–44.

124. Humboldt, "Über die innere und äussere Organisation der höheren wissenschaftlichen Anstalten in Berlin," *GS*, 10: 259. Humboldt did not favor the complete separation of law and sciences of state in the training of lawyers and administrators (Bleek, *Juristenprivileg*, 93).

shortsighted utilitarianism: one that focused on immediate results as opposed to one derived from the general, unitary principles that general education provided. Humboldt repeatedly emphasized that neither science nor the humanities were to be presented at the level of higher education as a set of finished, collected results, but as a "problem which is not yet quite solved."[125] Consequently, it was general and special education which should not be mixed, rather than utilitarian and nonutilitarian education. The special schools and institutes which had a narrow, vocational focus should as a rule be separated from the institutions of general education such as *Gymnasien* or universities.[126] The institutional separation of universities and special schools did not preclude students' taking advantage of both if it suited their needs. This applied particularly to the training of administrators, and Humboldt viewed Berlin as especially favorable for the study of cameralism because of the many other related institutes in the city.[127]

The leading figure in the sciences of state at Berlin until the 1840s was a man who spent most of his career as an official and simultaneously as an academic: Johann Gottfried Hoffmann. Hoffmann was already serving in the bureaucracy when he was named Kraus's successor at Königsberg in 1807; among his many positions was head of the Prussian statistical bureau after 1810. In 1810, Humboldt called on Hoffmann to make specific recommendations on the teaching of the sciences of state at the new university. Hoffmann's proposal of 25 May reflected the idealism of the reformers and envisaged a broad role for these sciences in general education. Their purpose was not only to train officials, but to awaken the powers of the nation via public opinion:

> The more the public service vacillates between schematism and arbitrariness, the more indispensable is a well-founded public opinion [*öffentliche Meinung*], expressed through a legal organ, to orient it. It is perhaps indifferent whether this organ be an efficiently composed national representation, or freedom of the press, or both: the question is rather that the government assist in conveying the living conviction that it methodically organizes its own decline if it shuts off the treasure of instruction and reprimands that could come from the mass of the nation, when the latter is roused to a consistent investigation of its own interests.
>
> The civil servant will be the more skilled to the degree which he avoids that unspeakable and unfortunate one-sidedness which splits the government

125. Humboldt, "Innere und äussere Organisation," *GS*, 10: 251.

126. Ibid., 10: 260; "Bericht der Sektion des Kultus und Unterrichts," *GS*, 10: 206. Humboldt's pragmatism as an administrator can be seen in his report on the *Ritterakademie* in Liegnitz of 7 Sept. 1809, which he recommended should continue as an institution of general instruction and of agriculture ("Über die Liegnitzer Ritterakademie," *GS*, 10: 160–61).

127. Humboldt,"Generalbericht an den König, 23 Mai 1810," *GS*, 10: 280.

into individual hostile offices, . . . [to the degree] which he is habituated through his entire training to view the state as an organic whole.[128]

Hoffmann's specific proposals combined Schlözerian ideas with Krausian ones. One can see in them also the distrust of overly rigid systems. There were three major divisions, the "publicistic, the economic, and *Polizei*." The first conveyed the general purpose of the state and was based on history and statistics. The economic division treated the sources of national wealth and what the government should do to increase it. While these sources were classifiable into production, manufacturing, and commerce, Hoffmann did not recommend professorships for each of these: this knowledge could be acquired in the special institutes or by special lectures by people involved in the trades themselves. In political economy, "there is now so much experimentation . . . that I would wish for the university a man who would be more a critic than a systematician."[129] As for the *Polizei*, Hoffmann confessed that "what is usually taught under police [*Polizeikunde*] appears to me . . . unworthy, trivial, and one-sided." Accordingly, he recommended that police science be taught by the professor of political economy.[130] It was Hoffmann himself who assumed the professorship (after its having been offered to Sartorius, who refused it—partly on Goethe's advice).[131] Hoffmann thus held the dual positions of professor and statistician for most of his career. While this arrangement did combine theory and practice, it did not allow Hoffmann to devote as much time to teaching and research as his ambitious program demanded.[132] Nevertheless, his joint activities as statistician and professor of sciences of state set a precedent for Berlin that was to last through the 1860s.

Notably absent from Hoffmann's curricular proposals was positive state law. This reflected the different experience of North Germany from the South in the Napoleonic wars; for the loss of territory in Prussia did not occasion the need for codification that the southern rulers experienced with their territorial gains. As with the administrative reforms, the dominant emphasis in Prussian juristic thinking was against centralization. Thus the Heidelberg professor Thibaut's proposal for codifying civil law gave rise to the famous controversy with Friedrich Karl von Savigny, who argued that such codification would be pre-

128. J. G. Hoffmann, "Gutachten," 25 May 1810, quoted in Köpke, *Gründung der königlichen Friedrich-Wilhelms-Universität*, 209.

129. Ibid., 211. Hoffmann mentioned Adam Müller by name as unsuitable for the post.

130. Ibid.

131. Lenz, *Friedrich-Wilhelms-Universität*, 1: 255; Goethe, *Goethes Briefwechsel*, 101–2, 106, 110–11.

132. Lenz, *Friedrich-Wilhelms-Universität*, 1: 256. Hoffmann's appointment gave rise to one of the few controversies in the press over the reform movement: an attack by Adam Müller in Kleist's *Berliner Abendblätter* on the late Kraus. Hoffmann responded with a defense of his teacher, See Treue, "Adam Smith in Deutschland," 127–29.

mature. For Savigny, law was an outgrowth of the history of a nation, which—in Germany's case—no longer coincided with a state. The distrust of codification in North Germany extended to state law as well. The classic example was Karl Friedrich Eichhorn, Savigny's colleague at Berlin and later Professor at Göttingen. Son of a Göttingen orientalist, Eichhorn had studied under Pütter and Hugo, and was determined to make a career as professor of state law.[133] The Napoleonic era called forth his patriotism and changed his intellectual project to writing a history of German law as a whole, in which state law was but a part. Although he lectured on state law per se, he never published a systematic compendium on it. He later wrote, in 1829,

> The present circumstances make it very difficult to acquire a more exact practical acquaintance with state law . . . to lecture on state law requires much more circumspection and purposive connection of the historical and philosophical dimensions of individual theories; hence the great lack of state law professors [*Publicisten*] who really deserve the name.[134]

Thus in northern Germany, state law receded from the canon of sciences of state.

As Hoffmann's reference to public opnion indicates, the possibility of mobilizing a broad spectrum of opinion was never far from the reformers' minds. For fear of Napoleon's reprisals, however, they did not seek to create a popular basis for their program through pamphlets or newspapers.[135] Still, they toyed repeatedly with the idea of a representative assembly—to involve the people and to guide public opinion—an idea which encountered resistance from the nobility.[136] When Napoleonic occupation gave way to the Wars of Liberation, however, the reformers did not hesitate to stir patriotic sentiments through journalism.

SHIFTS WITHIN THE FIELD

If the field defined by cameralism and the sciences of state remained intact, it was not without significant internal modifications. It remains to trace the impact of these turbulent years on the individual disciplines.

Finance

As we have seen, the Napoleonic wars confronted the German states with staggering problems of debt, which made Smith's cautions about excessive debts—

---

133. Frensdorff, "Karl Friedrich Eichhorn," *ADB*, 6: 469.
134. Quoted ibid., 480 (original source not given).
135. Moran, *Toward the Century of Words*, 110.
136. Koselleck, *Preussen*, 186–88, 193, 211–15.

along with those of Hume and Montesquieu—seem irrelevant.[137] Whereas some of the South German states were relatively insulated from having to think through these problems by the availability of Jewish lenders, the Prussian and Bavarian reformers did a lot of dilettantish floundering in their desperate straits following 1806.[138] Austrians and Prussians alike had resorted to the issuance of paper money, and questions of finance thus became questions of monetary theory, on which the German economists wrote much. A prominent issue was whether money was a merely a medium of exchange, or itself a commodity with a value. If the former were the case, the amount of money in circulation could depend on the demand, and in times of increased demand such as wartime, the amount could increase. It further did not matter what material was used for money, and paper could be justified. If the latter were true, money required backing in hard currency, and issuance of paper was suspect. In general, German writers were about evenly divided on this issue, but had little to offer by way of new insight.[139] One gets the impression that the magnitude of the debt problem momentarily stunned their practical imagination.

A general trend in the theory and practice of finance during the period was to give greater prominence to taxation as a source of revenue vis-à-vis the domains and regalia. There was general agreement that domains were uneconomical if administered directly by the state; the attachment to the land by those who worked it was a powerful incentive to increased productivity. Therefore domains should either be sold, as Smith had recommended, or subject to hereditary lease.[140] Although regalia were generally viewed as antiquated, they were usually treated individually, with some—such as mines and waterways—acknowledged as profitable. There was less agreement on what type of taxation was best, although there was a general consensus that an income tax was intrusive and impractical: to try and assess the wealth of private citizens was more than the state should undertake.[141] Hardenberg's edict of 1810 reflected these priorities: he promised that the domains would be sold to pay off the state debt, and an income tax was not included. Nevertheless, he introduced it two years

137. Smith, *Wealth*, bk. 5, chap. 3; Georg Schanz, "Öffentliches Schuldenwesen," *ENTW,* no. 40: 3.

138. Mosse, *Jews in the German Economy,* 67–68; Schissler, "Einleitung: Preussische Finanzpolitik," 43–49; on Montgelas's abilities, his wife once commented, "As foreign minister one could find none better, as interior minister he is adequate, but as finance minister he deserves to be hanged." Quoted in Demel, *Bayerische Staatsabsolutismus,* 192.

139. For a survey, see Altmann, "Zur deutschen Geldlehre des 19. Jahrhunderts," *ENTW,* no. 6: 6–12, 34–35.

140. See for example Kraus, *Staatswirtschaft,* 5: 13, 19–20; Lotz, *Revision der Grundbegriffe,* 4: 134; Schmalz, *Handbuch der Staatswirtschaft,* 302.

141. Sonnenfels, *Policey, Handlung, und Finanz,* 3: 329; Lotz, *Revision der Grundbegriffe,* 4: 213; Fulda, *Grundsätze der . . . Kameralwissenschaften,* 291; Schmalz, *Handbuch der Staatswirtschaft,* 319.

later, when the estates' protest against his consumption tax on grain caused him to withdraw the latter.[142] Aside from the excise, extensive taxation was still relatively new, and theoreticians and practitioners were learning together. There was general agreement, however, that the system of tax collection should be simplified and made more equitable, with fewer inconsistencies and exemptions—as Smith, the cameralists, and the physiocrats had all urged.[143]

In any event, the financial exigencies of Prussia and Bavaria forced them to sell large portions of their domains.[144] This was an event of considerable importance for the subsequent role of cameralism in the state, because these sales not only shifted the basis of state revenues in the direction of taxes, but also removed one of the original practical grounds for cameralism: to train state economic managers. Thus it is not surprising that cameralism gradually made way for legal training in the course of the nineteenth century, and that the broader subject matter of the sciences of the state eventually supplanted the more technically oriented cameralist curriculum. But this was a slow and uneven process.

The Sciences of Trades: Agriculture, Forestry, Technology, Commerce

During this period, the three components of the older cameralist curriculum evolved in separate directions. In South Germany, they remained an integral part of the university curriculum. In Prussia, however, Humboldt's and Hoffmann's desire to separate special education from general education created a situation which tended to favor the pursuit of these subjects in institutes outside the university.

Of these three fields, agriculture took the path of specialization as an independent discipline, while continuing to draw on the innovative ideas of political economy. Its impact was considerable. This was due to the presence of a strong personality, Albrecht Daniel Thaer, whose *Principles of Rational Agriculture* (1809–1812) went through thirty-seven editions in various languages by 1880.[145] Thaer was a Hannoverian who was involved in an active exchange of ideas with British agriculturalists. The result of this was his first major work, *Introduction to the Knowledge of English Agriculture and its Recent Practical and Theoretical Advances,*

142. Schmoller, "Epochen der preussischen Finanzpolitik," 84–86; Thielen, *Hardenberg,* 269–70.

143. Cf. Smith, *Wealth of Nations,* bk. 5, chap. 2, pt. 2; Justi, *Staatswirtschaft,* 2: 478; Sonnenfels, *Policey, Handlung, und Finanz,* 3: 46–47. On Prussian reforms, see Huber, *Verfassungsgeschichte,* 1: 211; on Bavaria, see Wilhelm Volkert, "Bayern," *DV,* 2: 534.

144. Demel, *Bayerische Staatsabsolutismus,* 204–5; Koselleck, *Preussen zwischen Reform und Revolution,* 325–26.

145. Klemm, "Agrarwissenschaftlichen Schule A. D. Thaers," 121 n. Klemm mentions publications in Denmark, England, the United States, Italy, Russia, Poland, and Sweden.

with Respect to the Improvement of German Agriculture, for Thinking Farmers and Cameralists (1798). This work drew the attention of the Prussian reformers, who invited him in 1804 to establish an experimental farm and teaching institute at Möglin, seven miles east of Berlin. The Napoleonic occupation of Hannover clinched his decision to accept. The institute opened in the inauspicious year 1806, and its fortunes varied with the patterns of war and peace in the years following, but by 1815 its reputation was secure.[146] Thaer also participated in drafting the reform legislation under Hardenberg to implement the serfdom emancipation edict of 1807.[147]

Thaer's contribution to scientific agriculture lay less in any single original insight or finding than in his overall conception of method and the intensity and consistency with which he pursued it. This conception involved two main components. First, Thaer broke with the classificatory approach in favor of an explanatory one. He distrusted all-encompassing systems "that everyone only needs to imitate mechanically."[148] In the *English Agriculture* he was sharply critical of most German writers as taking too piecemeal an approach to the subject, rather than an exact investigation of cause and effect. "I found practically nowhere," he wrote, "correctly established experiments, in order to demonstrate that this [particular] effect stemmed from that cause and no other. . . . Even more I missed exact economic calculations."[149] Scientific agriculture was not a matter of a collection of rules for specific situtions, but of arriving at basic principles from which these rules could be derived. Thaer was aware of the parallel with Smithian economics and had high praise for Kraus's work.[150] Second, Thaer combined this rigorous approach to research with a mode of teaching that emphasized direct experience rather than book learning alone. Universities were not the best places to teach agriculture; Thaer rejected the ideal of encyclopedic knowledge that had prevailed there. Rather, the basic sciences that a farmer needed were best taught on site, where the general content could be illustrated by the experiential material at hand. He did not conceive of his experimental farm as an optimum situation applicable to all locales, but as a test of what could be accomplished given the specific, even adverse conditions at hand—the unfavorable sandy soil of Brandenburg.[151] Thus he realized in a practical context the unity of teaching and research that Humboldt had envisioned.

146. Meyer and Klemm, *Thaer*, 35–75.
147. Ibid., 85–87.
148. Thaer, *Englischen Landwirtschaft*, 3: x.
149. Ibid., 1: 8.
150. Thaer, *Rationellen Landwirtschaft*, 1: 15–16; Treue, "Adam Smith in Deutschland," 130–31.
151. Thaer, *Geschichte meiner Wirtschaft*, 3–4; *Rationellen Landwirtschaft*, 1: 14.

Despite Thaer's criticisms of cameralist agriculture, his ties to that tradition were stronger than might appear at first glance. For example, despite his emphasis on the natural sciences, he did not break with the notion that agriculture was fundamentally a type of economic management:

> Agriculture is a trade [*Gewerbe*] whose purpose is to earn a profit through the production of vegetables and livestock. The greater the profit, the more completely is its purpose fulfilled.[152]

Thaer acknowledged that the other sciences of state were relevant to agriculture and needed to be taught in conjunction with it, and that agricultural economics was an important subject for the administrator as well as the farmer. Thus when Humboldt offered him a professorship at Berlin in 1810—which on Schleiermacher's vote was demoted to an associate professorship—Thaer accepted, despite his mixed feelings about universities.[153] At Berlin, Thaer remained true to his principles of shaping his material to his particular audience, in this case teaching agriculture in the context of politics, finance, and *Polizei*.[154] Thaer eventually found this arrangement unsatisfactory and gave up his post in 1819, but students from Berlin could thenceforth receive credit for courses at Möglin, so the connection between cameralist training and agriculture was not severed.[155] Nevertheless, the precedent of teaching agriculture as a subject apart from the university was set, and Thaer was not replaced.[156]

Thaer's rationalism and commitment to free-market principles won him the opposition of the conservative party and of Adam Müller.[157] His policies did indeed betray a certain obliviousness to the social and human consequences of agricultural reform.[158] Notably absent in the *Principles* is a discussion of agricultural credit, which other writers such as Kraus had already recognized as a

152. Thaer, *Rationellen Landwirtschaft*, 1: 3.

153. Humboldt, "An . . . Dohna," *GS*, 13: 316–18; Meyer and Klemm, *Thaer*, 90; Lenz, *Friedrich-Wilhelms-Universität*, 1: 256–57. Despite the title, Thaer asked for and got a full professor's salary. He restricted teaching to the winter semester; his courses there became part of the two-year curriculum at Möglin, although the university refused to recognize the institute as an affiliated body. This recognition eventually came in 1819 (Meyer and Klemm, *Thaer*, 156). Thaer's lecture on individual branches of agriculture in 1811–12 drew 46 students, compared to 65 students in Savigny's, and 61 and 36 students in Fichte's two lectures respectively. (Universität Berlin, *Verzeichnis von den zustandegekommenen Vorlesungen*, GPSA Dahlem, Rep. 76 Va Sect. 2 Tit. XIII, vol. 1: 1).

154. Thaer, *Geschichte meiner Wirtschaft*, 347.

155. Meyer and Klemm, *Thaer*, 156.

156. Memo of 6 April 1820, GPSA Dahlem, Rep. 76 Va Sect. 2 Tit. IV no. 5, vol. 6: 209–10. The chemist Hermbstädt took over the subject of agriculture.

157. Schnabel, *Deutsche Geschichte im neunzehnten Jahrhundert*, 1: 468; Müller, *Nationalökonomische Schriften*, 309–21.

158. Heuss, *Deutsche Gestalten*, 86; more recently, Marion W. Gray has pointed to the demotion of women in supervisory positions in Thaer's schemes as compared to those of the older *Hausväterliteratur*, in "From the Household Economy to 'Rational Agriculture,'" 52–53.

crucial element in the transition from feudal to market agriculture. Kraus had recognized the destructive potential in the Prussian credit institutes, which granted generous terms to wealthy landowners and shut off access to smaller farmers, thereby encouraging speculation and rural poverty at the same time.[159] But Kraus was no longer alive to promulgate his views, and the adverse consequences he predicted became true in the years that followed.

Despite the adverse criticism from conservatives, Thaer was honored in his own day as a reformer—his fiftieth doctoral anniversary even elicited a sonnet from Goethe—and his ideas spread, albeit slowly, to other parts of Germany.[160] The older term *Ökonomie* came increasingly to mean agricultural economics exclusively, as distinct from *Nationalökonomie*.

By 1815, a further specialized discipline had emerged out of agriculture: forestry. While the need to regulate forests dated back to the time of Charlemagne, the first academic works devoted to forestry alone appeared in the early eighteenth century. The cameralist enterprise of classifying different types of trees dominated the field from the 1760s through the 1780s—often to the disgruntlement of foresters themselves, who knew far more about the subject than did the professors.[161] By the 1780s, however, the usefulness of a scientific classification of trees was becoming evident, and three forestry academies were established during the decade, plus a short-lived professorship at Freiburg.[162] By 1791 it was possible to write a book which applied principles of botany to the cultivation of trees—not only the classification of different types, but a knowledge of their growth and productivity. A system of assessing the economic value of a forest in terms of its yield over time had also emerged. The leading innovator in the field was Georg Ludwig Hartig, whose impact on forestry has been compared to Thaer's in agriculture.[163] As with agriculture under Thaer, the primary locus of such instruction was not the universities but the separate forestry institutes.

If agriculture and forestry became specialized systems during this period, technology and commerce went in the opposite direction of dissipation. This was not for lack of recognition of their practical importance. Stein saw indus-

---

159. Kraus, *Staatswirtschaft*, 5: 93–95, 106–9; see also Lotz, *Revision der Grundbegriffe*, 2: 274 f. For a thorough discussion of these and other plans, see Vopelius, *Altliberalen Ökonomen*, 70–80.

160. Frauendorfer, *Ideengeschichte der Agrarwirtschaft*, 1: 227. On the slowness, see Vopelius, *Altliberalen Ökonomen*, 50.

161. Fraas, *Geschichte der Landbau-und Forstwissenschaft*, 514, 535, 547.

162. Ibid., 553.

163. Hartig also sought affiliation with the University of Berlin, but did not get a professorship (Lenz, *Friedrich-Wilhelms-Universität*, 1: 257; *ADB*, 10: 665). But Hartig was only one of a number of effective teachers of forestry, who enabled it to spread throughout Germany during this period. For example, Heinrich von Cotta (1763–1844; see *ADB*, 4: 521–26); Johann Matthäus Bechstein (ibid., 2: 205–6), and Johann Christian von Hundeshagen (ibid., 13: 401–6).

trial education as essential to the awakening of the powers of the nation and wanted it integrated with a general education for craftsmen and workers.[164] He created a special business department (*Gewerbedepartment*) in 1808 as well as a central clearing house for technical and commercial information (*Technische Gewerbe-und Handels Deputation*)[165]. But the Prussian reformers were by no means agreed on its implementation or even its relative importance. As usual, there were factions arguing for traditional and innovative approaches, in this case a neomercantilist policy of state-sponsored industries, like those that had existed under Frederick the Great, versus a free-market approach. Hardenberg leaned towards the latter; moreover, he favored small-scale manufacturing in rural settings over urban-based factories.[166] In his opinion, the people who most needed technical education were the potential manufacturers rather than officials. Thus when one of his assistants, Peter Christian Beuth, proposed a grandiose educational scheme for training technical advisors to be placed throughout the administration, Hardenberg did not endorse it.[167] His skepticism was reinforced by that of Humboldt and Hoffmann, who saw no reason in this case to override the division of general and special higher education. For this reason, neither favored a full professorship of technology at Berlin.[168] In general, the debate over technical education was focused more at the secondary rather than the university level.

If there was no counterpart to Thaer or Hartig to forge technology into a coherent system, it was due in large measure to the intractability of the subject matter itself. Technology was too heterogenous: the processes of transforming raw materials into finished ones were based on no single set of principles, nor could they be seen as variations of a single process, as was the case with planting and harvesting. Beckmann, admittedly, had made a belated attempt to arrive at a new classification to hold these divergent strands together, which he called "general technology," as distinguished from the special technology of individual processes. His highly abstract categories referred to various ways in which the substances of raw materials were transformed (i.e., splitting apart, loosening, uniting, condensing, and giving form), regardless of what the raw materials or manufacturing processes were. [169] One of his students, Johann Poppe at Tübingen, heroically elaborated this scheme by finding examples from chemistry

164. Gispen, *New Profession, Old Order*, 18–20.

165. Brose, *The Politics of Technological Change*, 9; Gispen, *New Profession, Old Order*, 20.

166. Brose, *Politics of Technological Change*, 33–39.

167. Ibid., 101–2.

168. Humboldt, "Generalbericht an den König," *GS*, 10: 280; Hoffmann, "Gutachten," 210.

169. Beckert, *Beckmann*, 86; Poppe, *Studium der Technologie*, 6; Karmarsch, *Geschichte der Technologie*, 866–67.

and physics which applied to each of these categories.[170] The result was still static, however, and did not lead to an awareness of problems to be solved by research in individual areas. Fruitful interaction of theory and practice was not to be found at this level of generality, but in individual activities such as mining and metallurgy, for which several schools had been founded in the eighteenth century. One of them, at Freiberg in Saxony, won an international reputation and was the home of the Neptunist theory of the the origins of the earth; many of its students found their way into the elite Prussian Mining Corps.[171] After the turn of the century, the field of technology was increasingly acknowledged to be divided into mechanical or chemical parts.[172] Nevertheless, lectures on these subjects continued to be given in the universities as surveys for officials, betokening a continuing commitment to comprehensiveness.

As for commercial science, its institutional hold in the universities had been so fragile that the borders between it and technology became increasingly indistinct in this period. One can see this in the titles of administrative offices which dealt with this area and were frequently labeled offices of manufacturing and commerce (*Gewerbe und Handel*), such as Stein's Deputation. In fact, *Handlungswissenschaft* was never taught at Berlin, although it continued to remain prominent in the southern universities. As with technology, the emphasis on commercial education was at the secondary level, with Büsch's academy in Hamburg as the most important model. Thus Beuth, having failed to establish a network of cameralist technical officials, went on in the 1820s to instigate a network of trade schools and a separate technical institute at Berlin.[173]

To summarize, one can say that the *spirit* of a newly dynamic cameralism, namely to bring the energies of the state to bear on economic and social change, flourished with the Prussian reforms, even if its modes of implementation evolved away from the university curriculum as its starting point. Men like Thaer, Hartig, and Beuth went on to exercise a considerable influence on practical reasoning in Prussia and the rest of Germany after 1815.

Police Science

As we have mentioned, the Kantian critique of happiness and welfare as the ends of government created problems for police science during this period. The

170. Poppe, *Allgemeinen Technologie*.

171. Manegold, *Universität, Technische Hochschule und Industrie*, 24–25; Brose, *Politics of Technological Change*, 134–35.

172. Jung-Stilling, *Staatswirtschaft*, 556–57; Hoffmann, "Gutachten," 210; Poppe, *Allgemeinen Technologie*, 3–4.

173. Lundgreen, *Techniker in Preussen*, chap. 2; Mieck, *Preussische Gewerbepolitik*, 29 ff. On Beuth's combination of technical zeal, aesthetic neoclassicism, and anti-Semitism, see Brose, *Politics of Technological Change*, chap. 3.

solution which Pütter had previously provided—that of retaining the traditional taxonomy of police activities, and simply redefining the ends which they served as security or legality rather than happiness—was satisfying to some, but proved difficult to apply to the description of actual practice.[174] Too many state activities—such as education and recreation—could not be treated as merely ancillary to security without obvious distortion. Stein, for example, used the term *Polizei* in his memoranda to cover a variety of activities, including care for the poor, workhouses, hospitals, recreation, and the post.[175] The dilemma was clear in the most ambitious work of the period: the seven-volume *Handbook of German Police Law* (1802–1808) by Günther Heinrich von Berg, a colleague of Pütter at Göttingen. This was a grand attempt at codification. Berg began with the security criterion, but by volume 4 he had changed his mind: welfare and happiness could not be excluded.[176]

One reason for the persistence of welfare was the increased attention which officials were forced to pay to problems of poverty and vagabondage—an obvious response to the economic dislocations of the period.[177] There was still a certain tendency to see these as moral rather than economic problems, that is, as rooted in the laziness or weakness of individuals rather than in the shifting patterns of trade and manufacture. Thus one common solution was the regulation of gambling and curbing of luxury.[178] The possibility that the increase in beggars and vagabonds was due to an increase in population went against one of the basic axioms of police science heretofore: that a numerous population is the sign of an internally healthy state. Another traditional attitude was that poverty was strictly a local matter, to be regulated by each town, which had the power to expel outsiders who were a burden on the community. This attitude persisted in South Germany, where in 1807, for example, all Württembergers had to be registered as residing in a specific locale.[179] In Prussia, on the other hand, the responsibility of the state to provide for those who were not locally registered was affirmed in the *Allgemeines Landrecht*.[180] For some writers, the influence of Smithian ideas aided their recognition that poverty was not a local problem, and that guild restrictions on trade made it difficult for the unem-

174. Preu, *Polizeibegriff,* 257; Stolleis, "Verwaltungslehre und Verwaltungswissenschaft," *DV,* 2: 84.
175. Schilly, "Nachrichtenwesen," *DV,* 2: 267. For similar use in Bavaria, cf. Volkert, "Bayern," ibid., 2: 529–30.
176. Preu, *Polizeibegriff,* 258–59, 267.
177. For a vivid description of conditions, see Brunschwig, *Enlightenment and Romanticism,* 106–18, who nevertheless exaggerates their significance.
178. Endres, "Armenproblem," 224.
179. Ibid., 230; Sachsse und Tennstedt, *Armenfürsorge,* 196.
180. Sachsse und Tennstedt, *Armenfürsorge,* 196, 275–76.

ployed to find jobs elsewhere. Jakob in particular incorporated these ideas into his work on police science in 1809.[181]

If the tumultuous changes of the period put a premium on the welfare functions of *Polizei*, they simultaneously intensified the pressures to use it as an instrument of repression (e.g., of spying on secret societies or on percieved enemies of the regime). The first instance of such a "political police" preceded the French Revolution: it appeared in Austria in 1786 under Joseph II, and stemmed from his personal distrust of his own officials and of public opinion; it was to be secret and to operate under cover of the official police organization.[182] Montgelas experimented with similar measures, one of which operated through the post, but these were disbanded after his fall.[183] Undoubtedly the main impetus came not from Germany but from France, in that Napoleon established a spy network in the Kingdom of Westphalia to check on subversion. When Napoleon's secret police denounced Stein as an enemy of France and the Rhenish Confederation in 1808, Prussia decided it was time to imitate the French example.[184] An efficient secret police was established, directed against external enemies. In 1812, as the notion of national liberation gained momentum, its competence was extended to internal enemies by none other than Hardenberg.[185] None of these rulers thought of *Polizei* as exclusively repressive or secret; it was merely an additional function among many to protect the security of the state and its subjects. They did not see a "police state" and a "legal state" as disjunctive categories, as later generations were to do,[186] but it clearly went against the claims of the state to further individual freedom, and this contradiction became increasingly obvious after 1815.

For the *Staatswissenschaftler*, one way of cutting through this thicket of different usages was to shift from defining *Polizei* in terms of purposes and goals (e.g., happiness, security) to those of activities and functions (e.g., compulsion, persuasion).[187] It was generally agreed that compulsion was one legitimate police activity that might more frequently be used in preventing danger to the state, while encouragement and persuasion were more appropriate to promoting happiness or prosperity. But method and aim did not coincide in all cases: it could be argued, for example, that the state had the right to use force to promote welfare in compelling children to go to school, or compelling the poor

181. Jakob, *Policeygesetzgebung*, no. 232.
182. Siemann, "*Deutschlands Ruhe, Sicherheit, und Ordnung*," 42–47.
183. Ibid., 48–57.
184. Ibid., 63–65.
185. Ibid., 69.
186. Stolleis, "Anmerkungen zum Verhältnis von 'echtem Recht' und 'Polizeirecht,'" 190–91.
187. For example, see Lotz, *Begriff der Polizei*, 27. See also Preu, *Polizeibegriff*, 233.

to work. These and other specific cases were matters of debate.[188] However inconclusive these discussions were, the subject matter of police science retained its importance in the education of officials. The challenges of the era were not strong enough to dislodge it from the curriculum or even yet to suggest that it be broken down into its constituent parts. The latter trend did occur, however, after 1815.

Statistics

If Kantianism had helped to undermine *Polizeiwissenschaft*, the rising nationalism helps to explain a brief but impassioned protest against numerical statistics that emanated from Göttingen during the Napoleonic occupation. This temporarily undermined the close association of history and statistics that Achenwall and Schlözer had forged.[189] The protest occurred in the face of an increasing zealousness in tabulation in the late eighteenth century, occasioned in part by the greater freedom of the press, which made more data available; Napoleon's liking for statistics was also well known.[190] To the young historian Adolf Heeren, however, collecting such numbers was an instance of despotic state control. "There are no columns," wrote Heeren in the *Göttingische Gelehrte Anzeigen*, "for national spirit, love of freedom, the genius and character of great or small men at the top."[191] Heeren's colleague August Ferdinand Lueder mounted a more thorough methodological critique, questioning the accuracy of statistical data as they were then collected. Moreover, Lueder claimed that numbers convey a false sense of objectivity. "There is not a single result to be drawn from statistical data," he wrote, ". . . which does not proclaim one thing to one person, another thing to another."[192]

Although such sentiments probably helped to keep German writers at a safe distance from English political arithmetic, they failed to stem the tide of statistical compendia in Germany—or the use of statistics by administrative bureaus. Hoffmann's activities as head of the Prussian statistical bureau succeeded in allaying much of the skepticism regarding the reliability of statistics by improving its presentation.[193] The changes he introduced were propelled by

188. Preu, *Polizeibegriff*, 230–31, 248–55.

189. Schlözer himself was favorable to numbers: in his view they could reveal the significance of facts which would otherwise go unrecognized (for example, that there were some 25,000 deafmutes in Germany). See Schlözer, *Statistik*, 47.

190. Kern, *Empirische Sozialforschung*, 25; Meusel, *Lehrbuch der Statistik*, vi, 6.; Schlözer, *Statistik*, 42.

191. Heeren, Review of Conrad Mannert, *Statistik der europäischen Staaten*, 834. The author was identified by August Ferdinand Lueder in his *Kritische Geschichte der Statistik*, 230. Lueder had taught statistics at Göttingen, and he portrayed his critique as a refutation of his life's work (vi–vii).

192. Lueder, *Kritische Geschichte der Statistik*, 181.

193. Hanssen, "Statistische Büreau," 333.

logistical considerations rather than theory. When he took over, Hoffmann found records spread out among 625 columns on sheets 16 meters long, which he began to organize topically into such categories as population, health facilities, churches and schools, and businesses.[194] These efforts gradually did much to allay the criticism coming from Göttingen.

German Theoretical Economics

The penchant for systematic completeness that we have seen in the economics of Soden and Jakob did not occur entirely to the exclusion of original thought or critical reflection. The assimilation of Smithian ideas spurred an increased interest in economic theory; German writers grappled with the notions of value and price during the same years that Malthus and Ricardo were engaged in similar pursuits in England. Naturally the Germans' treatment of these concepts were filtered through German conditions and traditions, which included the dramatic fluctuations in prices of the Napoleonic era as well as post-Kantian idealism in thought. An equally powerful legacy was the classificatory strategy of cameralism itself, which continued to give the German theoretical discussion a distinctive shape and content in the course of the nineteenth century. The theoretical and practical imaginations were linked.

In general, German writers from Sartorius to Adam Müller were quick to focus on the intangible, nonmaterialistic aspects of economic concepts. They had long been sympathetic to the idea that the resources of a nation included its intellectual skills and services as well as material goods—an idea found in Becher, Justi, and Say. The influence of Kant only reinforced this tendency. Gottlieb Hufeland, professor of civil law at Jena and later at Landshut, was one of the first to appropriate Kantian legal theory, and his treatise on economics in 1807 reflected the same mentality. He defined goods as "every means to an end of a human being . . . all goods are only goods by virtue of the representation that human beings make of them."[195] Goods thus included land and soil, talents and spiritual capacities. Although he criticized the organic metaphor as being overused, Hufeland affirmed its basic conception of the interdependence of goods. This constituted the subject matter of economics as a separate sphere of human activity from that of the state.[196]

Regarding the concept of value, the German economists inherited from cameralism a skepticism of any single definition of value or of any single criterion for measuring it. They tended to be critical of the labor theory of value from the outset, partly because it was too simplistic, partly because it was in-

194. Seibt, "Statistik," *ENTW,* 2: no. 37: 7–8; Hanssen, "Statistische Büreau," 336.
195. Hufeland, *Grundlegung der Staatswirtschaftskunst,* 1: 17–18, 20.
196. Ibid., 1: 113–16.

sufficiently subjective.[197] For the same reasons, they emphasized the notion of "use value" as being equal in importance to "exchange value."[198] Smith had little to say further about use value; his labor theory treated labor as an exchangeable commodity. Sartorius, the historian-economist, not only criticized Smith's neglect of use value, but claimed that all determination of value varied with time and place, with geographical and social conditions.[199]

The cameralist penchant for taxonomical completeness was evident also. Soden postulated all sorts of types and subtypes of value with scholastic zeal: value was absolute or relative, positive or compared, direct or indirect, existing in different degrees, and so on. [200] Hufeland discerned a similar plethora for prices, which could be inner or outer, real or arbitrary, one-sided or double-sided.[201]

The person who most successfully wielded the subjective and taxonomic approaches in the analysis of a contemporary economic problem was Johann Friedrich Eusebius Lotz, an official in the service of the house of Saxony-Gotha. Lotz was one of the most perceptive writers in both police science and economics; it is notable that he never held an academic position and even rejected the prospect.[202] Lotz had noted the agricultural prosperity engendered by the early years of the revolutionary era and the sudden fall in prices after the onset of the Continental System.[203] His *Revision of Basic Concepts of Economic Theory* (1811) began with the question of what causes prices to fluctuate, or what leads to "expense and cheapness" (*Teuerung und Wohlfeilheit*).[204] His analysis is worth some attention, for it helped establish the terms of theoretical discourse which continued throughout the century.

Lotz began his investigation of these fluctuations by defining value and

197. Sartorius, *Abhandlungen*, 25–29; Hufeland, *Grundlegung der Staatswirtschaftskunst*, 1: 39; Lotz, *Revision der Grundbegriffe*, 1: 99–102.

198. The difference between the two—to use an example from Smith himself—is illustrated by the contrast between water on the one hand, which is extremely useful, but because of its abundance has little or no value in exchange, and diamonds on the other, which have little use, but have high exchange value because of their scarcity. See Smith, *Wealth of Nations*, bk. 1, chap. 4.

199. Sartorius, *Abhandlungen*, 29–30; see also Hufeland, *Grundlegung der Staatswirtschaftskunst*, 1: 156 ff; Lotz, *Revision der Grundbegriffe*, 1: 99 ff. Jakob was an exception here (*National-Oekonomie*, 7).

200. Soden, *Nationalökonomie*, 1: 34–37.

201. Hufeland, *Grundlegung der Staatswirtschaftskunst*, 1: 132ff.

202. Lotz had academic aspirations as a young man, but left his studies at the University of Jena, probably for financial reasons (the stated reason was the death of his father). Lotz held a variety of positions as an official, including a post in the police department, on the debt commission, and as administrator of a territory awarded to Sachsen-Gotha at the Congress of Vienna. Despite his refusal of a professorship at Bonn in 1819, he served on editorial boards of several journals in the sciences of state. See *ADB*, 19: 285–87.

203. Lotz, *Revision der Grundbegriffe*, 1: 529–32.

204. Ibid., 1: xi, 1.

price. Building on Soden's and Hufeland's work, he held that value was based on subjective evaluation; value was to be distinguished from price, which was the good or mass of goods that were actually exchanged, that is, agreed to by the exchanging parties.[205] The price was thus the outcome of a bargaining process which involved both objective and subjective factors, which Lotz enumerated as follows:

1. the greater or lesser dispensability of the good on the one hand, the greater or lesser necessity of the same on the other;
2. the greater or lesser readiness of one side or the other to exchange;
3. the representation (*Vorstellung*) that each side forms of the ease or difficulty of obtaining a good . . . by other means;
4. the representation that each side forms of the degree of effectiveness of the motives by which the opponent may be brought to exchange;
5. the greater or lesser competition of buyers and sellers who want to exchange.[206]

In this formulation, the variables of supply (item 1) and demand (item 2) are placed within a larger matrix which implies subjective choices and judgments (items 3 and 4). It marks a distinct contrast to Smith's and Ricardo's discussion of price fluctuations, which focussed more narrowly on the production costs as prime determinants of the "natural price."[207]

Lotz concluded that the "expense or cheapness" of a good is determined by the discrepancy between price and value, that is, when the exchanging parties fail to agree on the above matters, causing the price to rise above or fall below the value.[208] This disagreement could in turn be prompted by such factors as scarcity, discrepancy of wealth between buyer and seller, unfair trade advantages, restrictions on trade, and of course production costs. Like Sartorius, Lotz chose to emphasize the variability of conditions that could affect the market equilibrium; he also criticized Smith for writing from an English perspective, particularly for his neglect of immaterial goods and their use-value.[209]

By taking such a multicausal view, Lotz was less inclined to emphasize the self-correcting mechanism of the market than were Smith or Ricardo: since, in the classical view, it was production costs—including the cost of labor—that ultimately brought buyers and sellers into line, the emphasis on other factors undermined the belief in such a relatively easy adjustment. Lotz's subsequent volumes spelled out how such discrepancies could be minimized by state administrative policies—the familiar material of police science and finance.

205. Ibid., 1: 67.
206. Ibid., 1: nos. 33–42. The phrases are taken from the table of contents.
207. Cf. Ricardo, *Principles of Political Economy and Taxation*, chap. 4.
208. Lotz, *Revision der Grundbegriffe*, 1: nos. 76–80.
209. Ibid., 3: 3, 431–32.

In sum, many of the features that are normally associated with German economic thought of the middle and late nineteenth century—the awareness of varying historical and geographical conditions, the emphasis on the subjective factors, the critique of the English writers as too reductionistic, the positive view of the state—were all present to a significant degree in the first generation of Smithians.

∴

THE FINAL YEARS of the Napoleonic era witnessed a combination of the trends that had alternated throughout the period. The appeal to the nation took concrete form in the call to arms. In the face of a retreating Bonaparte, the Prussian officials encouraged popular journalism; the ensuing patriotic zeal heartened the generals more than the reformers.[210] Hardenberg once more brought out plans for representative government. At the same time, the nobles' opposition to the reform program grew in strength and confidence. In southern Germany, the uncompleted attempt to centralize the administration elicited a similar reaction from local government: the hometownsmen now knew who their enemies were.[211] There was diversity also in attitudes on how to educate and train public officials: the conservative reaction in Prussia was in part a reaction against reform-oriented *Staatswissenschaften* in favor of legal training. And divergence persisted within the sciences of state themselves: cameralism still tended to be more narrowly associated with the practical training of officials, while the notion of the sciences of state as a whole, with their inclusion of history, statistics, and politics, was directed to the broader political education of a cultivated and informed public. But despite these divergences, the bureaucratic ethos remained strong, as did the optimism that reform from above could be harmonized with individual and collective initiative from below. The challenges of the years of upheaval had tempered and refined this belief, which emerged as more realistic and flexible than before. The sciences of state were about to enter a new, creative period.

210. Moran, *Toward the Century of Words*, 112–14; Sheehan, *German History*, 375–87.
211. Walker, *Hometowns*, 211–13, 216 nn.

❧ 3 ❧

The Sciences of State at Their Height,

1815–1840: Deliberation

The "Entire Sciences of State" and Their Institutional Background

The features of the period 1815–40 are familiar to most students of German history. Economically, the post-Napoleonic years brought continued hard times, with the crop failures of 1816–17 followed by a collapse of prices due to renewed English competition. By the mid–1820s, however, stability had returned. Politically, Napoleon's territorial settlement held to a great degree in the form of the German Confederation; once the French had departed, the South German rulers quickly granted constitutions as a means of creating unity and loyalty within their fragile new states. These constitutions offered obvious challenges to the powers of the traditional estates, and the outcome of this conflict varied from one state to another. In Prussia, by contrast, the reformers failed to deliver a constitution they had promised because of the increased power of the reactionaries. Nevertheless, the idealism and nationalism of the Wars of Liberation continued to find outlets such as the *Burschenschaften*, until the Karlsbad Decrees of 1819 ushered in a decade of censorship. The 1830 revolution in France sparked further protest and another round of constitutions in states such as Saxony and Hannover—coupled with further repression and conflict. Under these circumstances, the growth of the press was uneven compared to that of the late eighteenth century; the term *Biedermeier* expressed the corresponding growth of the private sphere, that is, of sociability centered in the home.[1]

If political liberalism—a term which arrived in Germany in the 1820s—was thus often suspect, economic liberalism gained ground. English competition notwithstanding, German industrial growth was impressive, though reflected in the proliferation of handcrafts rather than in factories. Pressure for the free movement of goods and labor increased. The German Customs Union, established in 1834 on Prussia's initiative, marked a turning point in opening up attitudes as well as markets. Karl Biedermann, a leading liberal

---

1. Sheehan, *German History,* 535–42; on the press, see Wehler, *Deutsche Gesellschaftsgeschichte,* 2: 526.

politician in Saxony, noted in his memoirs that this event, combined with the new railroad from Leipzig to Dresden in the same year, had the effect of turning many people—including himself—in a more practical direction.[2] In both the political and economic arenas, the bureaucracy continued to play a crucial role. Officials continued to make advances in gaining job security and other accoutrements of professionalization.[3] As loyal servants of their respective monarchs, officials viewed themselves as agents of restoration. Yet their commitment to orderly reform from above continued from the previous century, adjusting itself to the new legacies of the revolutionary era.[4] The exception was Austria, where power remained centered in the court, and police supervision was sufficiently strong to stamp out most innovation in the bureaucracy. Elsewhere in Germany, however, officials generally accepted constitutional government where it existed and were frequently elected to the representative assemblies. In Württemberg, for example, officials regularly comprised over half the members of the legislature.[5] Even in the period of reaction following the Karlsbad Decrees, they continued to work for change behind the scenes.[6] On economic issues, they continued to work for the abolition of feudal obligations on the land and of guild monopolies in the towns. The prestige of the bureaucratic career was in part reflected in the dramatic increases in the number of law students between 1815 and 1830 (attorneys were still considered state officials).[7] These increases were part of a big increase in all fields—an 89.4 percent increase in Prussia—so that the student population in 1830 was higher than at any subsequent time before the 1870s.[8] In any case, the number of new graduates greatly exceeded the number of positions available.[9] Nevertheless, the ideology of officials bespoke a high degree of optimism and confidence. "The general striving of the human spirit," wrote one official in 1817 in a memorandum recommending the establishment of a political faculty at Tübingen, "which can

2. Biedermann, *Mein Leben*, 51–55.

3. Sheehan, *German History*, 426–28. On Württemberg, see Wunder, *Priviligierung und Disciplinierung*, 297 ff.

4. The continuities between the late eighteenth century and the postrevolutionary period have been stressed by a number of scholars, including Vierhaus, "Aufklärung und Reformzeit," 288; Weis, "Enlightenment and Absolutism," 196; Stolleis, "Verwaltungslehre," *DV*, 2: 61.

5. Langewiesche, *Württemberg zwischen Revolution und Reichsgründung*, 72.

6. Walker, *German Home Towns*, 283–87.

7. In Prussia, the number of law students increased from 974 to 1603, by 64.6 percent; at Heidelberg, the figures were 223 to 496, by 122.4 percent. See Titze, *Hochschulstudium*, 94; Weisert, *Verfassung der Universität Heidelberg*, 152–53. The figures are for winter semesters.

8. Titze, *Hochschulstudium*, 94; McClelland, *State, Society, and University*, 156. The figures for Germany as a whole are sketchy before 1830.

9. Bleek, *Juristenprivileg*, 139–40 on Prussia; Lee, *Politics of Harmony*, 80 on Baden. Cf. O'Boyle, "Problem of an Excess of Educated Men," 473–78.

Table 4 *Lectures and Enrollments 1820–1840*

	Total Lectures	Lectures: Prussia	Lectures: South	Law Students: Germany (Avg.)	Law Students: Prussia (Avg.)
1820–25	1468	349	656	—	1161
1825–30	1591	430	697	—	1584
1830–35	1634	453	752	3950	1425
1835–40	1403	472	607	3130	1039

Sources: 1. Lectures: university catalogues. Figures do not include lectures in state law except when listed under the heading of state sciences. See appendix.

2. Enrollments: Hartzmut Titze, ed. *Das Hochschulstudium in Preussen und Deutschland, 1820–1944*, vol. 1 of *Datenhanbuch zur deutschen Bildungsgeschichte* (Göttingen: Vandenhoeck & Ruprecht, 1987), 86, 94.

escape no attentive observer of the events of our day, can no more be nullified than the law of gravity."[10]

On the whole, the sciences of state mirrored the confidence of the bureaucracy. In purely numerical terms, the number of lectures increased—as did the number of students—until the 1830s, when both began to decline sharply (see table 4).

In substantive terms, professors of the sciences of state generally held liberal views, such as beliefs in rule of law, a limited degree of popular representation, a free press, and a vital public opinion. This was the period when the term *Rechtstaat* was introduced into public discourse. In essence it represented a re-formulation, in Kantian terms, of the cameralists' desire to combine guarantees of individual and social autonomy with a strong and vigorous government.[11] In the words of the liberal law professor, Karl Theodor Welcker, "The final goal of the state is: the greatest possible attainment of the virtue and humanity and thus of the happiness [*Glückseligkeit*] of all, through and in the form of objective law."[12] The notion of law as the instrument of such aims preserved the preference for clear distinctions and boundary lines between the state and the citizen that had been at the heart of the earlier mechanical analogy: law set the boundaries within which administrative activity could take place. While the tendency to think of the citizen is part of an organic state was by no means absent during this period, the notion of the *Rechtstaat* provided a powerful foil to it.[13] One has the impression that conservative treatises such as Haller's *Restauration der Staatswissenschaften* or Adam Müller's work found little resonance in the treatises and textooks of the *Staatswissenschaftler* at this time.

10. Gehring, *List*, 407.

11. Krieger, *German Idea*, 252–61; Böckenförde, *State, Society, and Liberty*, 48–53.

12. Welcker, *Letzte Gründe von Recht, Staat, und Strafe*, quoted in Krieger, *German Idea*, 255.

13. See, for example, Krieger, *German Idea*, 258.

There has nevertheless been a tendency, particularly among American historians, to emphasize as peculiarly German the characteristics of subservience to the state and distrust of popular rule among the liberals.[14] But more German writers than not endorsed the right to resist state orders when these were unlawful or unjust; many professors themselves were arrested or deprived of their positions for speaking their convictions.[15] Furthermore, a comparison with French political thought of the same period undermines this interpretation. Writers such as Benjamin Constant and François Guizot shared the same distrust of the plebs and sought to achieve change within the framework of constitutional monarchy. Like their German contemporaries, they sought to make sense of their current situation, rather than simply propounding liberal ideals in the abstract.[16] It is that realistic tendency of the sciences of state during this period that has been least appreciated, perhaps because it did not occur to the exclusion of philosophical speculation or the monarchical principle, but in combination with them.

At a more subtle level, the discourse of the sciences of state reflected the ambivalence of the authorities with respect to order and change. On the one hand, ordering and classifying remained central concerns. In this respect, the sciences of state witnessed an intellectual "restoration" which paralleled the political one. This was the great age of comprehensive classificatory systems, encompassing everything from natural law to economics and political history. Of the two subfields of cameralism and Schlözer's broader sciences of state, the latter became increasingly the focus of attention. This was reflected in the titles of the encyclopedic survey lectures in the universities, where the label "sciences of state" gradually took its place beside "cameralism" (see figure 1).

Just as Hegel's grand philosophical system sought to find the rational in the real, so did that of state science seek to overcome any antinomies between norms and practices by establishing a series of gradations from one to the other. To this end, classification still served a useful purpose: by an appropriate order-

14. Ibid., 3, 6, 293; Sheehan, *German Liberalism*, 45–48.

15. Mohl, *Geschichte und Literatur* 1: 330. Sheehan estimates that over one-sixth of the delegates to the Frankfurt parliament had been in prison (*German Liberalism*, 37); of the nineteen universities, at least five could count a professor of *Staatswissenschaft* who had been arrested or removed from his post (Rotteck at Freiburg, Dahlmann at Göttingen, Jordan at Marburg, Mohl at Tübingen, and Behr at Würzburg).

16. See Johnson, *Guizot*, 25, 43, 58, 63–65; Gall, *Benjamin Constant*. Gall's rich comparative study underscores the differences between Constant's liberalism and that of the German writers, but he cites enough variation among the latter to undermine that judgment. Thus he views Constant's treatment of natural law as more down-to-earth than that of Rotteck, Jordan, Pfizer, and Murhard (56), yet elsewhere points to the similarity of Zachariae and Mohl to Constant on this point (108); Although some Germans disputed Constant's version of the monarchical principle as based on the separation of powers rather than the unity of the state (183), Constant in fact ascribed more power to the monarch than did Hegel (202).

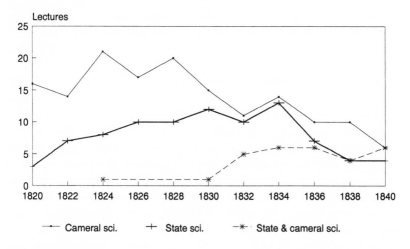

Source: University catalogues.
See appendix for details.

Fig. 1. Survey Lectures in Cameral and State Sciences, 1820–1840

ing of the component disciplines, the continuities rather than the conflicts between theory and practice could be displayed.

At the same time, the *Staatswissenschaftler* did not ignore the inescapable changes in the politico-economic world that had occurred since the eighteenth century—any more than did Hegel. And if classification was a more limited means of accounting for change than was dialectic, the *Staatswissenschaftler* at least developed a healthy distance from too rigid an adherence to a single, unalterable classificatory scheme.[17] There was no longer the expectation that the order of thought appropriate to the moment would reflect the natural order of things for all time. In the words of one of the most influential professors of the sciences of state, Carl Rotteck,

> It is unavoidable that with the ongoing development of constitutional and governmental systems and with changing relations of time and place . . . doctrines will sometimes be treated as main parts of state science or elevated to the status of a discipline, sometimes treated merely as special topics of existing disciplines, and that sciences formerly foreign to those of the state will be drawn into its circle.[18]

I will argue that this tension between conceptual order and real flux was a healthy one for the intellectual enterprise of the sciences of state, for what

17. Pölitz, *Staatswissenschaften*, 1: 19; Rotteck, *Lehrbuch des Vernunftrechts*, 2: 8; Mohl, *Geschichte und Literatur*, 1: 4–7.

18. Rotteck, *Lehrbuch des Vernunftrechts*, 2: 8.

emerged in the works of the most distinguished classifiers was a new style which one might call *deliberative*. Instead of a mere enumeration of constitutions, administrative activities, types of production, and so on, there was a tendency to treat each of these spheres as consisting of a range of choices, which could serve as the basis of argument over the best policy. This mode of academic activity still contrasted sharply with the Humboldtian idea of research that was being developed in other areas such as philology, history, and the natural sciences; its means of communication was still the lecture and the textbook rather than the seminar or the laboratory. But this did not mean that the sciences of state were moribund; rather they developed a type of innovation that was appropriate to their subject matter: classificatory schemes matured from being mere catalogs toward being frameworks for arguments over specific policies. The deliberative style also left its mark on those works which went beyond classification, such as Friedrich Dahlmann's *Politics*, Friedrich Hermann's *Investigations in Political Economy*, and Johann von Thünen's *Isolated State*. In this sense, the period witnessed a flowering of the practical imagination.[19]

South Germany and Saxony

The bulk of the contributions to this systematic approach came from South Germany, where constitutional monarchies were in place, and the need for consolidation of administration persisted from the Napoleonic era. This can most clearly be seen in the case of Württemberg, where the conflicts between officials and estates had been a fact of life for centuries.[20] That atmosphere of conflict seems to have provided a fertile ground for practical science: it is perhaps more than coincidental that Württemberg produced so many innovators in the sciences of state—Hegel, Friedrich List, Robert von Mohl, and later Gustav Schmoller.

In October of 1817, the new king, Wilhelm I, endorsed a plan for a new faculty of political economy (*Staatswirtschaft*) at Tübingen, following the Bavarian precedent. The plan itself reflected a certain tension between the conceptions of cameralism and the sciences of state. The first was represented by Fulda, the professor of cameral sciences; the second by a young finance official, Friedrich List.[21] List had not yet achieved national fame, but his writing was no less impassioned at age twenty-eight than later. List viewed the need for scientific training of officials as grounded in the changing times—the destruction of

19. My interpretation thus differs sharply from that of Volker Hentschel, "Staatswissenschaften" (189), who claims that the system of *Staatswissenschaften* was already obsolete in 1820, having only symbolic value; his main examples come from Prussia and Hanover, where this fragmentation did indeed occur.

20. See Vann, *The Making of a State*, chaps. 3–5, 295.

21. Gehring, *List*, 163–64; Born, *Geschichte der Wirtschaftswissenschaften*, 12–13.

the old empire and the coming of representative government. He urged a "political faculty," which would comprehend both law and the sciences of state. This would give the student "a philosophical view of the whole structure of the state."[22] List managed to gain the ear of Karl August von Wangenheim, who drafted the plan and incorporated List's language—minus the crusading tone—into his recommendation. In addition, he urged that List himself be appointed professor of state administrative practice. The king approved the plan and established the faculty without the consent of the faculty senate and despite Fulda's reservations.[23] List's two years as university professor were full of conflicts with colleagues and warnings from Stuttgart not to be too critical of established institutions. The suspicion of the *Burschenschaften* and the events leading to the Karlsbad Decrees only worsened the situation, and in May of 1819 he asked to be released from his post. In 1823 he was banished from Württemberg and emigrated to the United States.

At Tübingen, List's difficulties meant that Fulda's cameralist conception of the faculty triumphed: positions were established for economics (Fulda himself), agriculture, forestry, and technology. The curricular guidelines were heavily weighted towards the natural sciences rather than law or philosophy, including lectures in botany, zoology, and chemistry—although courses from the law faculty in state law were also included.[24] The faculty led a precarious existence at first: the fact of its establishment did not guarantee its acceptance or respect by other colleagues or by the bureaucracy itself. The continuing influence of the scribes meant that no examinations or requirements for the upper administration were enacted until 1837—many of the scribes lacked the knowledge of Latin required for the university—and the university refused to allow the new faculty to grant doctorates.[25] Low enrollments were the result, with barely forty students on the average, even as the university itself was growing.[26]

This situation was reversed largely by the efforts of a single person: Robert von Mohl, who joined the faculty in 1828. Mohl did more to revitalize the

22. List, "Gutachten," in *Schriften, Reden, Briefe*, 1: 344. See also Gehring, *List*, 164–65.

23. Gehring, *List*, 166–77; Born, *Geschichte der Wirtschaftswissenschaften*, 20–21. Wangenheim's recommendation is reprinted in Gehring (406–15). Gehring erroneously states that this was the first faculty of political economy, given the Bavarian one at Ingolstadt, later moved to Landshut and Munich.

24. Jolly, "Staatswissenschaftlichen Fakultät," 163. Examination questions for 1823 included describing glassmaking, identifying a machine to lift a heavy object 20–60 feet, describing the physiocratic system, giving the general principles of taxation, discussing the effect of introducing foreign grains onto native soil, determining the conditions in which press censorship is justified, and identifying which selling prices should not be used as a basis for assessing the value of a piece of land (165).

25. Born, *Geschichte der Wirtschaftswissenschaften*, 29–30; Bleek, *Juristenprivileg*, 206–8.

26. Jolly, "Staatswissenschaftlichen Fakultät," 165.

sciences of state than any other individual—not only in Tübingen, but in Germany as a whole. His first two major works helped to revive two sciences that had been in crisis, namely state law and police science. He was one of the first in Germany to write on the "social question," that is, the status of the proletariat; later he was one of the first to point to the need for a science of society to complement the sciences of state.[27] His mind was definitely of a classificatory bent: he excelled at ordering vast amounts of material rather than in providing developmental schemata or causal explanations, but he was free of the pedantry and dullness that so often characterized his contemporaries. This was in no small part due to his personal engagement with his material: he never left any doubt as to what he liked or disliked, and his prose was full of enthusiastic praise and scathing condemnation in rather unequal measure (weighted towards the latter). His conception of the sciences of state had its own dynamic, which he recognized as different from that of the natural sciences: its material was closer to human reality, and its growth mirrored the changes in that reality. This meant a series of discrete deliberations of policy problems rather than the testing of hypotheses and conducting of experiments.[28] In this way, Mohl helped transform the classificatory approach from mere ordering to argument.

Under Mohl's influence, the center of gravity in the faculty shifted from natural science and technology to law, history, and politics.[29] The purpose of such a faculty—he deliberately preferred *staatswissenschaftlich* to *staatswirtschaftlich*—was to provide a general theoretical framework for officials, rather than training them to be technicians.[30] He oversaw the creation of two new chairs, one in finance, *Polizei*, and interior law, the other in political history and statistics; meanwhile, the agriculture and forestry chairs were combined into one.[31]

27. Mohl's two works: *Staatsrecht des Königreiches Württemberg* (1829–31); *Die Polizeiwissenschaft nach den Grundsätzen des Rechtstaates* (1832–33); on factory conditions, "Über die Nachteilen, welche sowohl den Arbeitern selbst, als dem Wohlstande und der Sicherheit der gesamten bürgerlichen Gesellschaft von dem fabrikmässigen Betriebe der Industrie zugehen" (1835); on science of society, "Gesellschafts-Wissenschaften und Staats-Wissenschaften."

28. Mohl, *Geschichte und Literatur,* 1: 4–7. Mohl worked hard to keep his lectures up to date in terms of legislation and literature. See his *Lebenserinnerungen* 1: 147.

29. Strictly speaking, theoretical economics was not part of the sciences of state, according to Mohl, but because of its closeness to subjects that were (including economic police and finance), it was included. See *Geschichte und Literatur,* 3: 293; "Literarhistorische Übersicht über die Encyklopädien der Staatswissenschaften," 427.

30. Mohl, "Errichtung eigener staatswissenschaftlicher Fakultäten," 228–29.

31. Memo of political economy faculty to senate, 6 Nov. 1835, UA Tübingen 127/34 (Personalia, Nationalökonomie . . .), file 2 (Mohl); senate to faculty, 3 Nov. 1836, file 3 (Fallati); ministry to senate, 9 Feb. 1837, file 4 (Hoffmann); faculty, 2 March 1840; ministry to senate, 10 April 1840, 127/41 (Personalia, Land-und Forstwirtschaft), file 2 (Knaus). See also Born, *Geschichte der Wirtschaftswissenschaften,* 38.

Mohl also helped secure the right for the faculty to grant doctorates in 1830; in 1837, the ministry of churches and schools finally approved a series of state examinations which emphasized the faculty's curriculum—with the expected tonic effect on enrollments. Württemberg became the only German state to have separate examinations for officials in the interior and finance departments, the former weighted more towards law.[32]

Despite Mohl's influence, the appeal of the sciences of state in Tübingen remained limited: the students as a whole were drawn more to philosophy and the theological criticism of David Friedrich Strauss.[33] Moreover, Mohl's views did not go unopposed. The minister of the interior, Johannes Schleyer, took the view that only training in civil law was the proper qualification for the administration, and flouted the new regulations by admitting law graduates to the bureaucracy. Mohl opposed this view strenuously, but without success.[34] His letters revealed his growing impatience and frustration at the continued narrowness of vision and unneccessary paperwork of officials; finally, in 1845, one of these letters became public, and Mohl was relieved of his professorship.[35] For all his status as an insider, the outcome was little different than it was for List.

Mohl spent the rest of his academic career as professor of administrative law at Heidelberg. His acceptance there—the faculty recommended him "urgently and exclusively"—was indicative of the support which the sciences of state found in Baden.[36] The position of the bureaucracy vis-à-vis the estates was much stronger there than in Württemberg; as a consequence, officials had judiciary as well as administrative power. Thus legal training was essential for many civil servants, though a separate curriculum existed for financial officials.[37] At Heidelberg, paradoxically, the absence of a separate faculty in the sciences of state was a sign of relative harmony between the advocates of legal and administrative training in Baden; given the broad acceptance of both types, there was no need to rely on additional institutional measures to bolster the administrative side.

Baden's constitution was a product of official predominance and was the most liberal in Germany. At the same time, it created an anomalous situation: the diet provided a forum for increasingly vocal opposition to the government's

32. Born, *Geschichte der Wirtschaftswissenschaften*, 35–38; Bleek, *Juristenprivileg*, 213–19.

33. Klüpfel, "Aus Johannes Fallatis Tagebüchern," 2.

34. Mohl, *Lebenserinnerungen*, 1: 171; "Wissenschaftliche Bildung der Beamten," 129–84; Angermann, *Mohl*, 47.

35. Angermann, *Mohl*, 50–52.

36. Memo, law faculty, 10 May 1843, GLA, Abt. 235/3117, (Kultusministerium, Heidelberg, juristische Fakultät . . .), 113.

37. Ott, "Baden," *DV,* 2: 596–97; Bleek, *Juristenprivileg*, 263–64. On the cameralist curriculum, see Lee, *Politics of Harmony*, 72, 74.

avowedly liberal policies by people who called themselves liberal as well. Baden's educated elite was struggling with the notion of loyal opposition: it sensed that the interests of the government and the people were at some level in conflict and sought to find appropriate channels for it—without changing the fundamental structure of the state or unleashing popular revolution.[38]

The spokesman for this oppositional stance, in all its ambiguity, was Carl Rotteck, professor of the sciences of state at Freiburg and member of the lower house. Rotteck had initially attained popularity as the author of a multivolume general history, which went through twenty-five printings by 1867.[39] The height of his fame came in the wake of the revolutions of 1830, when the federal diet in Frankfurt overrode the Badenese liberals by demanding a strict censorship law and depriving Rotteck of his professorship—whereupon he was elected mayor of Freiburg.

Rotteck's comprehensive traversal of the sciences of state appeared during these years in his four-volume *Textbook of Rational Law and the Sciences of State* (1829–35). The work did not match his history in popularity, however, being too dry for popular taste and too general for scholarly consumption.[40] Rotteck soon found another medium which was more suitable for his concerns: the *Staatslexikon,* an encyclopedia of the state, in collaboration with another law professor, Theodor Welcker, who had been dismissed at the same time.[41] The impulse for the work had come from List, who had returned from America and was still seeking ways of communicating his views to a larger public. It was billed as a "handbook for civil servants of all grades and subjects, members of the estate assemblies, landowners, renters, merchants and industrialists, and for the educated [*Gebildete*] of all classes."[42] It was recognized as a mouthpiece for the liberal viewpoint and enjoyed great success in the 1840s.[43]

In Bavaria, the political economy faculties were subject to a number of vicissitudes after Montgelas' departure in 1817. Cameralism was suspect among some conservative opponents of Montgelas as being a product of the enlightenment.[44] In addition, officials were responsible for both justice and administra-

38. On liberal ambivalence, see Sheehan, *German Liberalism,* 39–40; Lee, *Politics of Harmony,* 168–72.

39. Rohr, *Origins of Social Liberalism,* 109 n.

40. Zehntner, *Staatslexikon,* 9.

41. Welcker's views were considerably more conciliatory than Rotteck's, emphasizing the need to harmonize conflicting forces. See his "Allgemeine encyklopädische Uebersicht der Staatswissenschaft und ihrer Teile," in Rotteck and Welcker, eds., *Staatslexikon* 1: 5, 11. For a full discussion of Rotteck's and Welcker's contrasting views, see Zehntner, *Staatslexikon,* 61–79.

42. Zehntner, *Staatslexikon,* 11.

43. Ibid., 93–94.

44. Dickerhof, "Kameralstudium und Bildungssystematik," in Waszek, ed., *INDU,* 255; Pechmann, "Staatswirtschaftliche Fakultät," 139–40.

tion at the local level—as in Baden—necessitating training in both fields. Officials were tested in private and public law, political economy, police science, finance, and agriculture.[45] This assured a clientele for courses in these subjects, but left unclear the status of the faculty of political economy itself, which had been reduced to three professors in the early 1820s. Who should be its clientele, if the majority of its students were enrolled in the law faculty?[46] Nevertheless, the new king, Ludwig I, decided to retain the faculty—his penchant for conservative philosophy notwithstanding. Ludwig, who had studied under Sartorius at Göttingen, was sympathetic to liberal economic programs at first, including the customs union; he insisted, for example, that students for the priesthood also be versed in agriculture.[47] But his own erratic nature made it relatively easy for conservative ministers to circumvent him.

An example of this inconsistency was the attempt to turn the political economy faculty into a technical institute, which reached its climax during the mid–1830s. In the wake of increasingly radical political opposition from the parliament following the July revolution, Ludwig had turned to an interior minister, Prince Oettingen-Wallerstein, whose policy was to ameliorate social discontent through economic development. His ambitious plans included canals, railroads, steamships, and a system of technical schools, culminating in a *Technische Hochschule* concentrated in the Munich political economy faculty.[48] True to the spirit of extensive regulation, the plans spelled out separate curricular requirements for forestry, agriculture, industry, and civil engineering. A total of ten professorships was envisaged, ranging from police science to "higher mechanics."[49] These plans were never implemented. Ultimately, Oettingen-Wallerstein was unable to stem the parliamentary criticism and was replaced with a reactionary interior minister, Carl Abel, who did nothing to implement the plan.[50]

45. Bleek, *Juristenprivileg*, 262; Schanz, "Staatswirtschaftliche Fakultät," 56; On attempts to separate justice and administration, see Volkert, "Bayern," *DV,* 2: 519, 529.

46. Dickerhof, "Kameralstudium und Bildungssystematik," *LNDU,* 250–54; Schanz, "Staatswirtschaftliche Fakultät," 13–15.

47. Dickerhof, "Kameralstudium und Bildungssystematik," *LNDU,* 258–59; Schanz, "Staatswirtschaftliche Fakultät," 56.

48. *Bayrischer Intelligenzblatt,* 20 April 1836, 510; Ursula Huber, *Universität und Ministerialverwaltung,* 151–66; Dickerhof, "Kameralstudium und Bildungssystematik," *LNDU,* 263. On Oettingen-Wallerstein's policies, see Spindler, "Die Regierungszeit Ludwigs I (1825–1848)," in Spindler, ed., *Bayerischen Geschichte,* 2.1: 186, 188.

49. *Bayrischer Intelligenzblatt,* 510. Specifically: two positions for forestry, one for higher mechanics, two for mechanical and chemical technology, one for agriculture, one for pharmacy, one for political economy, one for mining, and one for police science and law.

50. U. Huber, *Universität u. Ministerialverwaltung,* 158; 326–29. The one remaining source of students for the faculty was foresters, since the government had closed the separate forestry school at Aschaffenburg in 1832—only to reopen it in 1843 (Pechmann, "Staatswirtschaftliche Fakultät," 143).

Nevertheless, the faculty continued to serve as a center not only of economics but of applied science, with continuing appointments in chemistry and mining as well as agriculture and forestry.

An exception to the concentration of the sciences of state in South Germany was Saxony. This was due to the presence of a well-known popularizer in Leipzig, Karl Heinrich Ludwig Pölitz, professor of political economy and politics from 1820 to 1838. Pölitz was something of a holdover from the eighteenth century: a true polymath and systematizer, he published 184 works in philosophy, history, and linguistics, as well as the sciences of state. He was an outstanding lecturer, and his students numbered some sixty-three hundred.[51] He was an uncompromising advocate of the enlightenment. "Mysticism," he wrote in his work on police science, "is the religious plague of our days and should be treated as emphatically as . . . pox or yellow fever."[52] He was best known for his history of the European state system and for his work on comparative constitutions. Given the variety of constitutional states that had arisen in Europe and America since 1789, his work in this area filled a genuine need. The industrialist Gustav Mevissen, who as a young man could not attend university, especially valued Pölitz's work in this area.[53] His system, *The Sciences of State in the Light of Our Time*, went through two editions by 1827. As with Rotteck, Pölitz's surveylike works rendered him vulnerable to the charge of superficiality; his aim, however, was not originality, but dissemination to a wide audience. He was most concerned with defining the boundaries of the individual sciences of state with respect to one another and establishing a reasonable ordering of them. He grouped them in ascending order of complexity, as Auguste Comte was doing for the sciences as a whole in France. Unlike Comte, however, he denied that this taxonomy was based on a historical law of development: the individual sciences of state were in different stages of maturity, and as they developed, the taxonomy might change.[54] The simplest were those directly based on the ideal notion of the *Rechtstaat* (the law of nature and of peoples); next came those normative sciences which also took into account the empirical fact of force or compulsion (the law of the state or of states); those which added the purpose of serving material welfare within the limits set by law (politics, theoretical economics, state economics and finance, police science); and finally, those which added historical knowledge to these (history of state systems, statistics, positive [comparative] constitutional law, positive international law, diplomacy, and state practice).[55]

51. Lippert, "Pölitz," *HDS*, 5: 157.
52. Pölitz, *Staatswissenschaften*, 1: 503.
53. Hansen, *Mevissen*, 65; Stieda, *Nationalökonomie*, 279.
54. Pölitz, *Staatswissenschaften*, 1: 18–20.
55. Ibid., 1: 6–21.

The Fragmentation of the Sciences of State in North Germany

In Prussia and in northern Germany, by contrast, no single vision of the sciences of state prevailed. While the number of lectures in the sciences of state grew modestly, some of the material found its way into Hegelian philosophy, and some into political history. The commitment to a comprehensive treatment was notably lacking, as was a systematic account of Prussian state law. Once again this situation was a reflection of political circumstances.

Superficially, Prussia in 1815 was in a situation similar to that of the South German states in 1805: as a result of the peace settlement, her population more than doubled from that of 1814; her territory now included the Rhineland, which had been under French occupation since the 1790s. The government was confronted with the task of administering these heterogeneous territories; but unlike the situation in the south, the attempt to impose the least bit of uniformity was thwarted by the demands for local and regional self-government which the Prussian reformers themselves had promoted after 1806. Superimposed on these conflicts were rivalries among different bureaucratic offices and their opposing economic approaches—between the liberalism of Hardenberg on the one hand and the neomercantilism of the mining corps and the *Seehandlung*, a government investment corporation, on the other.[56] In addition there were the familiar tensions between aristocracy and bourgeoisie, sometimes reinforcing the regional issues and bureaucratic factions, sometimes intersecting them. These various interests were often able to hold each other in check between 1815 and 1840.[57]

The effect of this situation was to create a discrepancy between the self-image of the bureaucracy and its actual power. Its prestige remained high in the 1820s, as indicated by the swelling number of young men who aspired to enter it. It could think of itself as the "universal class," as Hegel was proclaiming from the lectern in Berlin, dedicated to the twin goals of security and welfare, which both he and Hardenberg espoused. In fact, however, the increased repressiveness of police power meant that the power of the state was increasingly used against its own officials, who could be removed from office at will, and whose initiative was throttled by censorship.[58] It is true that some bureaucrats channeled their idealism into such reforms as the customs union, the spread of technical schools, and state-sponsored enterprises.[59] But here also it is easy to overestimate the impact of the bureaucracy: some of the most effec-

56. For a masterful portrait of these factions, see Brose, *Politics of Technological Change*, esp. 36–37, chaps. 4, 6.

57. Ibid., 9–10, 18, 263.

58. Koselleck, *Preussen*, 407–10, 433; Raumer, *Lebenserinnerungen*, 2: 112.

59. Henderson, *Zollverein*, chaps. 2, 3; Mieck, *Preussische Gewerbepolitik;* Lundgren, *Techniker in Preussen;* Brose, *Politics of Technological Change.*

tive reforms were made by provincial governors in opposition to the policies emanating from Berlin.[60] In areas such as banking and railway construction, administrative policies were conservative compared to those of other states.[61] When the Rhenish businessman Ludolf Campenhausen came to Berlin to promote a railroad between Cologne and Antwerp, he met with indifference and delay.[62]

The discrepancy between intent and practice also characterized the training of officials. After 1815, the reformers' commitment to cameralist as opposed to legal training waned as other battles became more important. As in Baden and Bavaria, officials were found to require legal knowledge if they were to effectively strengthen the state against traditional privileges. Thus Hardenberg's regulations of 23 October 1817 specified that, as part of the training process, a practicum with a court would be desirable in addition to one in agriculture or business; one year later, this judicial apprenticeship became mandatory. Such a practicum required a legal education, and thus it reintroduced—in unwritten form—the juristic requirement into the curriculum.[63] The major difference between this situation and that of Baden and Bavaria was that it was unregulated: rather than following a prescribed combination of law and state science, a prospective official was expected on paper to pursue both separately. This led in practice to a decline of the bureaucratic career track per se. The career track of an administrator compared to that of a jurist involved an additional burden of study and financial sacrifice—so much so that a certificate of sufficient means was required for entry.[64] Given the pressures of the examinations, the sciences of state were increasingly neglected. When professors such as Jakob petitioned the ministry of culture to stiffen requirements in the sciences of state to boost their sagging enrollments, they met with half-hearted response.[65] In Bonn, the professorship in the sciences of state was left

60. For example, on Theodor von Schön in East Prussia, see Berdahl, *Politics of Prussian Nobility,* 272–73; on Theodor Sack in the Rhineland, see Diefendorf, *Businessmen and Politics,* 238–39. On recent opinion on the *Zollverein,* see Sheehan, *German History,* 503–4; on economic policy, see Rüfner, "Verwaltungstätigkeit," *DV,* 2: 476.

61. Tilly, "Political Economy of Public Finance," 487; Berdahl, *Politics of Prussian Nobility,* 312.

62. Caspary, *Campenhausen's Leben,* 35–38.

63. Bleek, *Juristenprivileg,* 105–6.

64. Ibid., 111–12; Koselleck, *Preussen,* 246.

65. For petitions, see Jakob to ministry, 22 Oct. 1822, GPSA Dahlem, Rep. 76 Va Sect. 1 Tit. VII no. 11, vol. 1: 105–11; F. B. Weber (Breslau) to ministry 29 August 1822, ibid., 112–19. On responses, see Altenstein to ministries interior, police [*sic*], and finance 15 March 1824, ibid., 1: 128–30, which proposed certification; Ministry of Interior to Altenstein, 4 June 1824, ibid., 131, which concurred; justice ministry 14 March 1824, ibid., 132–33, which dissented. Weber complained on 29 Jan. 1827 that the situation had not changed (ibid., 166–69). On a subsequent attempt, see Brose, *Politics of Technological Change,* 125–26.

unfilled from 1826 to 1842.[66] The conservatives undoubtedly used the juristic emphasis to further their cause, and the number of nobles in the upper echelons increased from one-quarter to one-third between 1820 and 1845.[67] Finally, a new set of regulations was enacted in 1846, which spelled out what had already become practice: it required a common juristic examination for administrators and judges upon completion of study and eliminated the written entrance exam for the bureaucracy proper in the sciences of state. All that remained was an oral exam, which required familiarity with the sciences of state (*Nationalökonomie*, police science, and finance) plus general knowledge of auxiliary sciences, mainly agriculture.[68]

Not all the difficulties of the *Staatswissenschaften* in Prussia were political. The teaching and literature of the disciplines frequently suffered in comparison to the brilliant innovations in other fields such as philosophy, philology, and history. The Humboldtian ideal of research was taking hold in these areas in a way that would not penetrate to the sciences of state until the later nineteenth century.[69] As one professor in Breslau noted, "superficial lack of content was the basic tone of most writings and lectures in the cameral sciences, and it became a kind of curse among the students to belong to the cameralists."[70] Moreover, the historical school of law, as taught by Savigny in Berlin, was more easily identified with the ideals of *Bildung:* its emphasis on Roman law established a continuity—at least in the minds of the professors—with the classical education of the *Gymnasium.*[71] As a result, student interest generally declined, despite the efforts of some spirited professors. According to one official who left his memoirs, one rarely attended lectures, and those who took conscientious notes were mocked by their contemporaries.[72] Another official who contributed much to trade legislation in later years, Rudolf von Delbrück, confessed that history rather than state science was his main interest during his student days.[73]

The retreat can be further documented in the writings of Hoffmann at Berlin. He continued to play a variety of roles in the upper administration and to direct the statistical bureau, where his work on income and tax statistics won him the respect of later generations.[74] He nevertheless saw his professorship as

---

66. Bezold, *Rheinischen Friedrich-Wilhelms-Universität,* 351.

67. Bleek, *Juristenprivileg,* 125, 145–47, 157; Koselleck, *Preussen,* 245.

68. Bleek, *Juristenprivileg,* 136.

69. Steven Turner, "Prussian Professoriate," 112.

70. GPSA Dahlem, Rep. 76 Va Sect. 1 Tit. VII no. 11, vol. 2: 2 (Eiselen to ministry, 24 Nov. 1828).

71. Bleek, *Juristenprivileg,* 110; GPSA Dahlem, Rep. 76 Va Sect. 1 Tit. VII no. 11, vol. 1: 128–30 (Altenstein to Ministry of Interior, 15 March 1824).

72. Diest, *Leben eines Glücklichen,* 63–64.

73. Delbrück, *Lebenserinnerungen,* 1: 70.

74. Inama-Sternegg, "Hoffmann," *ADB,* 12: 602.

his main calling, where he was highly respected as a teacher, as his enrollments testify (see table 5).[75] As a scholar he was unenterprising, and his multiple commitments undoubtedly contributed to this: he never wrote the comprehensive statistical work on Prussia that he aspired to.[76]

Hoffmann's views on the sciences of state changed significantly after 1815. He no longer viewed them as vehicles for the education of public opinion; there was no room for them as part of general education.[77] In a veiled reference to the *Burschenschaften*, Hoffmann defended classical education as teaching political restraint to the student: "The jewel of youthful life—modesty—. . . the feeling of lack of knowledge and experience rightly restrains him from expressing opinions on public matters."[78] The sciences of state themselves had originated as practical disciplines for the administration of domains. Only as these tasks became more complex did they become university subjects, for which most administrators lacked the necessary classical schooling:

> Little of benefit could come about when the least prepared of all the students at that time, the so-called cameralists, occupied themselves with speculations that belonged to the highest . . . [of] the human spirit. . . . The cameralist curriculum in this sense is not to be preserved, and it is one of the positive signs of the times that it declines.[79]

As income from domains represented a diminishing proportion of the state's revenues, there was no reason for an exclusively cameralist curriculum.[80]

On the contrary, Hoffmann came to endorse legal studies as important for the official as well as the judge. In flowery terms, Hoffmann praised the legal expert as the mediator of special-interest groups within society:

> The feudal landowner, the tenant and free farmer, the merchant, the factory owner, the artisan, appear only to speak in the interest of their class and business. . . . The jurist appears as defender of the right of each class against unjust claims of the others . . . the jurist, like the cleric and the doctor, knows the needs and attitudes of the middle and lower classes, but stands more generally than they closer to the higher and highest classes.[81]

75. Hoffmann, memo 20 January 1825, GPSA Dahlem, Rep. 92 Altenstein A V I a, no. 28: 6–8; Waszek, "Staatswissenschaften an der Universität Berlin," in Waszek, ed., *LNDU,* 279.

76. Hoffmann, *Lehre vom Gelde,* iv–v.

77. Hoffmann, *Nachricht von dem Zwecke und der Anordnung der Vorträge,* 11.

78. Ibid.

79. Hoffmann, memo of 21 Nov. 1822, GPSA Dahlem, Rep. 76 Va Sect. 1 Tit. VII no. 11, vol. 1: 101.

80. On the sale of domains to extinguish debt, see Koselleck, *Preussen,* 329. The figure of 45 million Thaler represented about one-fourth of the debt of 1820. The government resorted to such measures partly to avoid a loan, which would have raised the call for a constitution, since Hardenberg had explicitly linked these issues as late as 1820 (E. R. Huber, *Verfassungsgeschichte,* 1: 311).

81. Hoffmann, *Nachricht von dem Zwecke und der Anordnung der Vorträge,* 15–16.

Table 5 *Enrollments in Philosophy of Law, State Law, and Cameralism
University of Berlin, 1819–1840*

Year	Natural Law (Hegelians)	State Law and Politics	Police Science	Cameral Encyclopedia
1819	53 (Hegel)	—	21	82 (Schmalz)
1820	—	30 (Raumer)	12 (Eiselen)	83 (Schmalz, Eiselen)
1821	56 (Hegel)	36 ″	—	38 (Schmalz)
1822	20 (Hegel) 12 (Henning)	37 ″	18 (Hoffman)	44 ″
1823	12 (Henning)	26 ″	21 ″	50 ″
1824	57 (Hegel) 25 (Henning)	75 ″	26 ″	65 ″
1825	29 (Henning)	80 ″	10 ″	53 ″
1826	9 (Michelet)	68 ″	8 ″	47 ″
1827	35 (Henning)	37 ″	25 ″	52 ″
1828	35 (Henning) 184 (Gans)	32 ″	78 ″	47 ″
1829	10 (Henning) 13 (Michelet) 207 (Gans)	341 (Gans)	80 ″	52 ″
1830	6 (Michelet) 108 (Gans)	331 (Gans) 71 (Raumer)	74 ″	—
1831	20 (Michelet)	57 (Raumer) 143 (Gans)[a]	115 ″	—
1832	22 (Michelet) 135 (Gans)	30 (Raumer) 122 (Gans)	79 ″	—
1833	12 (Michelet) 167 (Gans)	54 (Raumer) 101 (Gans)	124 ″	45 (Riedel)[b]
1834	32 (Henning) 122 (Gans)	39 (Raumer) 127 (Gans)	102 ″	72 (Riedel)
1835	28 (Henning) 147 (Gans)	28 (Raumer) 152 (Gans)	10 (Helwing)	34 (Riedel) 93 (Henning) 10 (Helwing)
1836	34 (Henning) 189 (Gans)	46 (Raumer) 172 (Gans)	32 (Dieterici) 15 (Helwing)	17 (Helwing) 27 (Riedel)
1837	28 (Henning) 134 (Gans)	35 (Raumer) 165 (Gans)	8 (Dieterici) 15 (Helwing)	33 (Helwing) 121 (Riedel)
1838	51 (Klenze) 166 (Gans)	158 (Gans)	22 (Dieterici) 9 (Helwing)	23 (Helwing) 28 (Riedel)
1839	10 (Benecke) 32 (Henning) 27 (Michelet)	38 (Raumer)	28 (Dieterici) 15 (Helwing)	68 (Helwing) 54 (Riedel)

Source: Universität Berlin, Verzeichnis von den zustandegekommenen Vorlesungen, GPSA Dahlem, Rep. 76 Va Sect. 2 Tit. XIII, vols. 1–11.

Each year includes summer semester, followed by appropriate winter semester. (e.g., 1819, 1819–20).

[a]European, especially German state law

[b]Several sections, including "Introduction to study of state and cameral science" and "Cameral science"

Thus for Hoffmann it was the jurist, rather than merely the administrator, who fit the description of the "universal class."

This did not mean that Hoffmann wanted to extinguish his own discipline completely. It was important for law students to have training in statistics, economics, and finance. In addition, Hoffmann reintroduced police science, which portrayed the "principles of the [police] laws"—in contrast to his memo of 1810.[82] What was missing was any consideration of the state as a whole or of comparative forms of government, which might raise the troublesome issue of constitutions. In the self-deprecating words of Hoffmann's successor, Carl F. W. Dieterici, these lectures constituted the *Brotstudium* for administrators.[83] Dieterici continued the lecture subjects set by Hoffmann and explicitly defended them on the grounds that they excluded the issue of constitutions. Police science was the "genuine science of government," and conscientious study would convince the student that "unity and order in the administration under a benevolent and energetic monarchy" is preferable to representative governments, "where many are called together to speak of matters that must be more deeply thought through."[84]

Hoffmann's writings on economics itself showed an adherence to the status quo and a certain lack of practicality.[85] A case in point was his tax policy. Hoffmann disapproved of an income tax: the state could not determine fairly "what proportion of each person's income would be better utilized through public channels than by the person himself."[86] Instead, he proposed a head tax, to fall on rich and poor alike, adjusted so as not to be burdensome on the latter. The adjustment was not to be made on income, but on one's "position in external life."[87] The result was the class tax of 1820, which divided society

82. Ibid., 25; see above, p. 73.
83. Dieterici, memo of 7 March 1838, GPSA Dahlem, Rep. 76 Va Sect. 1 Tit. VII no. 11, vol. 2: 44.
84. Ibid, 45–46, 47. Dieterici's proposed curriculum for combining law and sciences of state in six semesters was as follows (ibid., 50):

I.	II.	III.
1. logic	1. practical philosophy	1. physics
2. botany	2. chemistry	2. mineralogy
3. natural law	3. institutions	3. Pandekten
4. history of Roman law	4. German law	4. Prussian statistics

IV.	V.	VI.
1. canon law	1. construction law	1. international law
2. technology	2. criminal law	2. trial law
3. economics	3. agriculture	3. forestry
4. state law	4. finance	4. police science

85. Schmoller, "Epochen der preussischen Finanzpolitik," 94.
86. Hoffmann, *Lehre von den Steuern*, 38–40.
87. Ibid., 163, 146–47.

into four classes: in the towns, these were the patricians, upper and lower middle classes (*Grossbürger, Kleinbürger*), and resident aliens (*Beisassen*); in the country, they were the aristocracy, large and small farmers, and day-laborers and servants.[88] In practice, the code was a disaster from the beginning. According to Koselleck, complaints about it "run almost like a red thread through the government reports."[89] It was a regressive tax in the extreme, with the lowest category paying 46 percent of the total, while the first payed only 4 percent. Local officials could only plead for exemptions for increasing numbers of urban and rural poor; by 1837, the population increase of 22 percent yielded an increase of only 6 percent.[90]

Hoffmann consistently clothed his pragmatic arguments in high-minded ethical pronouncements. One reason why taxing the poor was permissible was because material goods themselves were no decisive indication of a person's inner riches, regardless of class.[91] He repeatedly stressed the importance of *Bildung* as a factor in economics, which he rated higher than physical resources and goods in determining the strength of a state.[92] The factor of education entered into his thoughts on such diverse subjects as paper money and population. On the former, he held that "the trust on which the possibility of paper money actually rests is only the fruit of progressive general education and public morality."[93] On the latter, his disagreement with Malthus's theory was based on the premise that "the power of the human race over nature increases not only extensively with the population, but also intensively with its education."[94]

The uninspired level of the sciences of state in Berlin was acknowledged at the time.[95] But if students at Berlin were not finding a systematic overview of politics in the sciences of the state, they could readily find it as part of Hegel's philosophy. His contribution to the sciences of state can be found in the *Elements of the Philosophy of Right* (subtitled *Outline of Natural Law and State Science*) (1820), based on his political lectures. The subtitle reveals its derivation as a variation

---

88. Ibid., 164–65. Hoffmann admitted that some occupations would be difficult to classify and warned against too great a multiplication of categories.

89. Koselleck, *Preussen*, 536. Schmoller agreed in "Epochen der preussischen Finanzpolitik," 95.

90. Koselleck, *Preussen*, 534–38. Only in 1851 was the class system revised to encompass thirty brackets. This was not based on a declaration, but on the assessment of officials. See Rüfner, "Verwaltungstätigkeit," *DV*, 2: 499.

91. Hoffmann, *Lehre von den Steuern*, 144–45.

92. Hoffmann, *Sammlung kleiner Schriften*, 144–45.

93. Hoffmann, *Lehre vom Gelde*, 198.

94. Hoffmann, *Sammlung kleiner Schriften*, 43.

95. The Minister of Instruction in Saxony reported this recognition by Eichhorn, the minister of culture, in the early 1840s (Stieda, *Nationalökonomie*, 294).

of the lectures on natural law that had become widespread since Kant. The standard format of such lectures was to begin with private property, proceed to family, and then go on to the state. Into this order, Hegel inserted the famous section on civil society, in which individuals and families satisfy their needs through relations of social interdependence. That section incorporated current economic thought (the "System of Needs"), which seemed to Hegel a good example of reason working through particular needs and desires. By this he meant that the pursuit of individual gain could nevertheless benefit society as a whole.[96] Yet for Hegel, the Smithian postulate was only half true: the multiplication of needs and desires necessarily led to inequalities of wealth and mass poverty; this could be modified by public regulation: the administration of justice and *Polizei*. These functions obviously presupposed the state, and in contrast to Kant, Hegel did not exclude happiness as a legitimate goal of the state; he defined more broadly the regulation of public life by *Polizei*.[97] Hegel also placed great emphasis on *Bildung* in the *Philosophy of Right*. By instilling habits of reflection, general education sublimated the desires and mediated the natural and the rational, thus contributing to the smooth working of the state.[98] Like Kant, Hegel was skeptical of a too technically oriented curriculum for administrators at the expense of general education.[99]

The initial effect of Hegel's lectures should not be overestimated: although he was a popular professor, with an influence in Berlin society as well, his lectures on philosophy of law were modestly attended (see table 5); his lectures on logic and metaphysics, aesthetics, and philosophy of history regularly drew larger numbers. Hegel only offered the lecture four times, and his discontinuing it after 1824 may have been in response to the cultural ministry's circular of the same year, which stated that "the political and revolutionary upheavals and confusions of our time [have stemmed] in large part from perverse notions of general state law."[100] In any case, Hegel turned away from politics to art and religion in the mid–1820s; he was also satisfied that his general philosophical approach had been accepted by the Prussian educational authorities. His close friend, Johannes Schulze, was in charge of administering the secondary schools and universities.[101] As for the philosophy of law, it was only under his student Eduard Gans that this material gained a large following of students. Gans also

---

96. Avinieri, *Hegel's Theory*, 126–27. On Hegel's assimilation of economics as contributing to this separation of state and society, see Riedel, *Studien zur Hegel's Rechtsphilosophie*, 86–89.

97. Hegel, *Philosophy of Right*, 83, 145–49.

98. Ibid., 29, 124–26.

99. Ibid., 193.

100. Bleek, *Juristenprivileg*, 115.

101. Toews, *Hegelianism*, 86, 113. See also Friedrich Paulsen, *Geschichte des gelehrten Unterrichts*, 2: bk. 5, chap. 5.

had to restrain his support for enlightenment reforms in public lectures in exchange for the ministry's protection.[102]

While Hegel subordinated the sciences of state to his overall philosophical scheme, the philosophical faculty at Berlin was also concerned to preserve the connection between the sciences of state and empirical history in the manner initiated by Schlözer. To this end they petitioned the Ministry of Education in 1818 to appoint the professor of *Staatswissenschaften* at Breslau, Friedrich von Raumer, to Berlin, where he came and taught until 1859.[103] Raumer's lectures in "State law and politics" rivaled those of Hegel and his disciples in popularity—at least until Gans's arrival (see table 5). Among his qualifications was his practical experience: during the reform era, he had been Hardenberg's closest associate, nicknamed "the little chancellor."[104] After his arrival at Berlin, Raumer became a sharp critic of the reaction on issues such as freedom of speech, religious toleration, and municipal voting rights. He refused to clothe his criticisms in high-flown language and was reprimanded on several occasions, despite his popularity.[105] As an academic, Raumer did little to further the sciences of state. His interests turned increasingly away from politics and statistics to history: he was the principal lecturer in European history before Ranke's arrival. In addition, several other *Privatdozenten* combined state science and history during these years.[106] Thus the tie between history and the sciences of state established by Schlözer and Sartorius was strengthened.

The most famous representative of the historical sciences of state during this period was Friedrich Christoph Dahlmann, who held posts in Schleswig-Holstein and Hannover. Dahlmann's journey was the reverse of Raumer's: he was trained in philology and turned to the sciences of state only in his thirties. Dahlmann's background was that of German romanticism and nationalism, but he did not take these ideas in a conservative direction, nor did he focus his immediate hopes on a unified Germany. He applied them rather to the cause of an autonomous Schleswig-Holstein, a cause which he largely created.[107] The slogan "forever undivided," a watchword of the Schleswig-Holstein

102. Knudsen, "Liberal Politics," 130–31; on Gans's arduous road to success as a converted Jew, see Toews, *Hegelianism*, 108–11.

103. Lenz, *Friedrich-Wilhelms-Universität* 2.1: 249–50; Wegele, "Raumer," *ADB*, 27: 412.

104. "Raumer," *ADB*, 27: 405.

105. Knudsen, "Liberal Politics," 124; Raumer, *Lebenserinnerungen*, 2: 116, 255–67; the file in GPSA Dahlem, Rep. 76 Va Sect. 2 Tit. IV no. 39, vol. 1 (Der Regierungs-Rath und Professor . . . von Raumer, 1822–1833).

106. Lenz, *Friedrich-Wilhelms-Universität* 2.1: 253; Raumer, 2: 100. The others included Ernst Helwing (1803–1875), Adolph Riedel (1809–1872), and Wilhelm von Doenniges (1814–1872). See Lenz, 2.1: 505–6; Waszek, "Staatswissenschaften an der Universität Berlin," in Waszek, ed., *INDU*, 286–88.

107. Carr, *Schleswig-Holstein 1815–48*, 48–49.

movement through the 1860s, originated with him. These activities won him fame throughout Germany in the 1820s.[108]

Dahlmann's transition to teaching the sciences of state came about somewhat by chance. His agitation in Schleswig-Holstein limited his chances for advancement to full professor under the Danish crown. When the offer came from Göttingen in 1829 to be Sartorius's successor, Dahlmann eagerly accepted, thus assuming the duties of teaching economics, police science, and finance, as well as politics and history.[109] The latter two disciplines remained his passion, however, and he soon narrowed the scope of the survey lectures on the entire sciences of state to politics and police science, based on contemporary history.[110]

Dahlmann published his *Politics*, based on his lectures, in 1835. He had hesitated to do so because he feared nothing would come of it, given the isolation of his approach from the mainstream.[111] Nevertheless, the first edition sold out within a year; along with the *Staatslexikon* of Rotteck and Welcker, it became the most influential book on politics in the pre–1848 period.[112] Dahlmann directed it to the middle class, which he identified as the present "nucleus of the population . . . the center of gravity of the state," who were in need of political education.[113]

Dahlmann's tenure at Göttingen was to be short. In 1837 the "Göttingen Seven" affair took place: when the new Duke of Hannover suspended the recent constitution, Dahlmann drafted a protest, signed as well by six other professors. By the end of the year, they were relieved of their posts. Only in 1842 did Dahlmann obtain another position, this time in the service of Prussia at the University of Bonn.

Although the sciences of state developed in different directions in North and South Germany, these differences should not be exaggerated. Communication among scholars was sufficiently advanced so that they formed a single national network. This can be seen in the records of appointments to professorial chairs: South Germans like Rau, Mohl, and Hermann were in demand in Hannover and Prussia, while Dahlmann was the Tübingen faculty's first choice as Mohl's replacement. When he refused, they nominated three other North Germans.[114] Thematically, the concern with classificatory systems in the South

---

108. Ibid., 48–56.

109. Springer, *Dahlmann*, 1: 260; anonymous letter [presumably Archivrath Pertz] 15 Feb. 1829, UA Göttingen PA 4 V b 90 Dahlmann.

110. Universität Göttingen, *Index Lectionum*, 1830–31, 1831–32.

111. Beseler, *Erlebtes und Erstrebtes*, 27.

112. Springer, *Dahlmann*, 1: 385 n; Riedel, "Einleitung," in Dahlmann, *Politik*, 8–9.

113. Dahlmann, *Politik*, 207, 182–83.

114. On Rau, see below, p. 119; on Mohl, see anon., "Skizzen der Personal der juristischen Fakultäten, Südwestdeutschland betreffend," n.d., GPSA Merseburg, Rep. 92 Altenstein V Vi b

was not completely isolated from the concern with philosophy and history in the North. The problem of reconciling order and change was common to both, and the individual sciences of state resolved it with varying degrees of success.

THE SHAPE OF THE FIELD
State Law and Politics

State law and politics offered a rich field for classification and deliberation during this period. The new constitutions had to be meshed with existing laws and practices; the formula of the *Rechtstaat* had to be translated into a set of concrete guidelines for legislation and administration. It was uniformly recognized that the German states were still governed by the "monarchical principle," but the questions of how to harmonize this with the demands for representation in the political process remained to be worked out.[115] Although academics were by no means the only voices to be heard on these subjects, their prestige was widely recognized, and their opinions carried great weight. State law was an interdisciplinary pursuit during this period, studied by jurists, philosophers, and *Staatswissenschaftler* alike. For example, the number of lectures in state law that were listed under the sciences of state increased during these years—from 80 in the 1820s to 123 in the 1830s. This development peaked in the 1840s at 201, dropping to 128 in the 1850s.[116]

The belief that the sciences of state should be based on a theory of the *purposes* of the state, as expressed in the norms of natural law, was still widespread. At the same time, there was a growing awareness that the Kantian version of the *Rechtstaat* was too restrictive a formulation: it failed to do justice to the variety of norms and purposes that actually occurred.[117] We have already noted the restoration of happiness and welfare in addition to the rule of law in the work of Mohl, Pölitz, and Hegel. Furthermore, Kant had regarded the different traditions and forms of government as historical accidents and therefore irrelevant to understanding the purpose of the state; for the generation of 1815, however, that very variety of forms was essential to such understanding. Thus, although Rotteck and Dahlmann acknowledged a set of universal ethical norms and goals, they denied that the sciences of state should simply proceed deductively from them. For Rotteck, the "metapolitics" of state law included both a "state metaphysics," which treated the origin and purposes of the state,

---

no. 14: 81–83; on Hermann, see Lenz, *Friedrich-Wilhelms-Universität*, 2.2: 12; on Dahlmann, see Dahlmann to faculty 31 Dec. 1845, UA Tübingen 127/34, no. 6 (Helferich); faculty memo 18 August 1846 (ibid). The candidates were Georg Hanssen, Lorenz von Stein, and Franz Dönniges. On the general point, see Moraw, *Kleine Geschichte der Universität Giessen*, 110.

115. Boldt, "Zwischen Patrimonialismus und Parlamentarismus, 80–82.

116. Source: university catalogues. See appendix, especially paragraph 3.

117. Böckenförde, *Gesetz und gesetzgebende Gewalt*, 112.

and a "state physics" which treated its material bases and needs (e.g., climate, geography, economy). State law was a product of both the ideal unity and the natural diversity.[118] For Dahlmann, a common goal of humanity was a matter of faith, but not a matter of investigation for the sciences of state, which had to recognize the frequent conflicts between the ethically good and the legally correct. It followed that the rule of law was one concern of the state, but not its ultimate purpose; it also followed that the state was not simply a manifestation of a divine order—although Dahlmann asserted that it was the closest thing on earth to such an order.[119] Mohl went the furthest in the direction of relativism, advocating what he called the "anthropological" approach:

> The state is the essence of those arrangements which are relevant to the ordered coexistence of a certain group of persons (a people) in a given territory. The purpose which a people should and want to attain through such a sum of institutions may not be determined in general nor with a priori necessity. This is not to say that a state has no definite purpose, [or] that the spirit which animates a state is left up to chance; only that human nature is much too rich and diverse . . . thus there exist different purposes of states. They are perhaps not all equally noble or equally lofty, but they are . . . equally true.[120]

The interest of the *Staatswissenschaftler* in natural law also extended to international law. The two had long been closely associated, as the Latin title of the first professorial chairs (*Jus Naturae et Gentium*) had indicated; the connection remained through the Kantian school. Like state law, international law had a philosophical and a positive dimension: the former dealt with the conditions of peaceful coexistence, given the assumption of a common humanity; the latter dealt the actual relations between states (treaties, diplomacy, rules of trade, rules of war, etc). Only in the eighteenth century at Göttingen did international law begin to receive separate treatment, and only after 1830 did an extensive monographic literature arise—which Mohl highly praised for its quality.[121] Undoubtedly the conference diplomacy in the years following the Congress of Vienna contributed to this interest, as did the absence of international wars. Pölitz gave international law a prominent place in his system, and Hegel assigned it a crucial role in his dialectic: it was through international relations that states were thrust into the stream of world history, by which their successes and failures would ultimately be judged.

The question of how to translate such general norms into actual legislation which reflected social and political realities was approached from several directions. One was to draw from the past—to salvage what one could from the

118. Rotteck, *Lehrbuch des Vernunftrechts*, 2: 11.
119. Dahlmann, *Politik*, 39–40.
120. Mohl, *Staatsrecht Württembergs*, 1: 3–4.
121. Mohl, *Geschichte und Literatur*, 1: 45, 337–38, 404–54. See also Martitz, "Völkerrecht," 375.

jurisprudence of the Holy Roman Empire and, more important, to render explicit the customs and traditions of the individual states. The historical school of law contributed much to this work in North Germany, and it was complemented by the more systematic approach in the South. The general description of the powers and obligations of different branches of government in a *Rechtstaat* could serve as a measuring rod for the treatment of particular constitutions, which was the task of positive state law. Once again, Mohl set the standard: his first major work was a two-volume *State Law of the Kingdom of Württemberg*, which attested to his powers of clear ordering. Mohl took pains in this work to be evaluative, not simply descriptive.[122] He was well aware of the excesses of legalistic formalism as a way of ignoring injustice or of legitimizing the status quo.[123] In addition to expostulating the rights and powers of government, he included an extensive section on the rights of citizens. It was one of the first works to make explicit the division between constitutional and administrative law and to give the latter its due. Mohl's project did not find equal acceptance throughout Germany, however, given the distrust of codification on the part of the historical school.[124]

In addition to the study of laws of individual states, there was an intense interest in the law of Germany as a whole—either in the form of the German Confederation, or more frequently in the practices and traditions which the various individual state laws might share in common (see figure 2).[125] The main representative of this trend was Johann Heinrich Klüber, who first published a *Staatsrecht* of the Confederation a mere two years after its founding, dedicated to "the fatherland." Klüber was able to incorporate precedents from both the Napoleonic confederation and the Holy Roman Empire, thus establishing a certain continuity with the past—and continuing the tradition of historicity of state law established by Pütter in the eighteenth century.[126] The attention which legal scholars lavished on the Confederation was far out of proportion to its effectiveness and was undoubtedly an expression of nationalism. This could and did clash with the dynastic interest of particular states; symptomatically, Klüber's book was banned from use for lectures at the University of Berlin in the 1820s.[127] As the figures indicate, however, interest in German state law increased in Prussia also as Germany moved towards revolution in the 1840s.

122. Mohl, *Staatsrecht Württembergs*, 1: vii; Angermann, *Mohl*, 35.

123. Mohl, *Lebenserinnerungen*, 1: 132; *Geschichte und Literatur* 2: 393–94.

124. Bleek, *Juristenprivileg*, 112–13; Lenz, *Friedrich-Wilhelms-Universität*, 2.1: 214. Mohl surveyed the literature, state by state, in *Geschichte und Literatur* 2: 334–94.

125. Stolleis, *Geschichte des öffentlichen Rechts*, 2: 99.

126. Klüber, *Öffentliches Recht des teutschen Bundes*, viii–ix; Smend, "Einfluss der deutschen Staats- und Verwaltungsrechtslehre," 328.

127. Smend, "Einfluss der deutschen Staats-und Verwaltungsrechtslehre," 331.

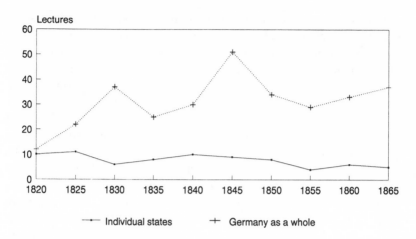

Fig 2. Lectures in German Positive State Law at Five-Year Intervals, 1820–1865

The interest in *Politik*, or *Staatskunst*, followed roughly the same trajectory as in state law during this period (see figure 3). In fact the conceptual line between politics and general state law was anything but clear. In theory, all were agreed on a definition of *Politik*, which could be traced back to the older notion of *Klugheitslehre:* the study of the means which were best suited to achieving the ends and purposes set out by the normative disciplines.[128] But were constitutional arrangements to be considered as means to the fulfillment of the precepts of natural law, or as legal norms in their own right? As the notion of the plurality and historicity of forms of government took hold, so did the tendency to treat such forms as pragmatic arrangements rather than as derivatives of natural law. The terms *general theory of state* (*Allgemeine Staatslehre*) and *Politik* came increasingly to refer to the division of powers and various forms of government.[129] In most cases, these forms consisted of the traditional categories of monarchy, aristocracy, democracy, and mixed forms; Mohl added the patriarchal and the theocratic.[130] Pölitz saw the different forms as appropriate to different stages of cultural maturity.[131]

128. For example, Gros, *Lehrbuch des philosophischen Rechtswissenschaft*, 33; Mohl, *Geschichte und Literatur*, 3: 339; *Encyclopädie der Staatswissenschaften*, 543n; Rotteck, *Lehrbuch des Vernunftrechts*, 2: 12; Pölitz, *Staatswissenschaften*, 1: 7–8, 336–37.

129. For example, Rotteck, *Lehrbuch des Vernunftrechts*, 2: 171 ff; Pölitz, *Staatswissenschaften*, 1: 335 ff. See also Stolleis, *Geschichte des öffentlichen Rechts*, 2: 122–23.

130. Mohl, *Staatsrecht Württembergs*, 1: 6–12; Rotteck, *Lehrbuch des Vernunftrechts*, 2: 176–201.

131. Pölitz, *Staatswissenschaften*, 1: 366, 474–75.

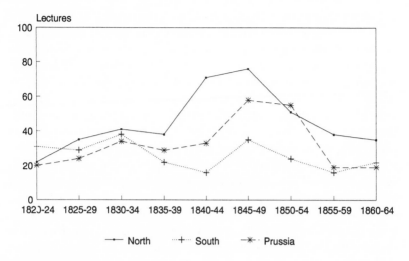

Source: University catalogues.
See appendix for details.

Fig. 3. Lectures in Politics, 1820–1865

In such questions of definition, Mohl again stood out as having the clearest grasp of the theoretical issues. *Politik* needed to be rigorously separated from state law and from a comparative description of constitutions: not all states were based on the rule of law, and the type of politics depended on the type of state and its purpose.[132] A true science of the means to achieve an end presupposed a different set of questions entirely. How are the consequences of actions to be evaluated? How are alternative means to achieve a given end to be compared to one another? If rigorous experiments cannot be conducted, how firm can the findings be? All these questions pointed to the need for a logic of politics—an inductive logic based on probabilities. Mohl looked to England as the place where such efforts were furthest developed and praised the work of Bentham and Mill.[133]

If Mohl's analysis was the most searching, Dahlmann's was the most influential. He accepted the Aristotelian notion of humankind as a political species.[134] This did not imply that the state was always right: there was an ethical dimension to human existence which the state could only appproximate, never fulfill. The purpose of the study of politics was to know those approximations, so that one could do better: "Politics," he wrote, "is a theory of health, not because it can give health, but because it can discover the causes of sickness

132. Mohl, *Geschichte und Literatur,* 3: 344.
133. Ibid., 3: 363–66.
134. Dahlmann, *Politik,* 37.

and often reduce them." [135] As a textbook, his *Politics* marked a clean break with the classificatory tradition. This is evident from the full title: *Politics, Reduced to the Ground and Measure of Existing Conditions.* It alternated sweeping historical surveys with in-depth discussions of particular topics—without any claim to comprehensiveness. Dahlmann drew his material from memoranda and newspaper articles he was writing at the time; his book remained a fragment of a larger work which was never completed. [136] British parliamentary practice, which Dahlmann admired, was treated extensively, while French constitutional arrangements, which he disliked, were barely mentioned. Consistent with his emphasis on political education of the bourgeoisie, Dahlmann treated the regulations for municipal governments in the various German states at great length, seeing these as the best experiential school for broader participation; he treated formal education as well, emphasizing the importance of academic freedom. In sum, Dahlmann remained true to Schlözer's project of using comparative empirical data to measure the achievements and the shortcomings of the present. It represented a route beyond mere classification to deliberation.

One issue which demanded such deliberation was the applicability of the doctrine of separation of powers to the new constitutional monarchies. The neat division of legislative, executive, and judicial branches did not easily fit the German cases. There was much disagreement on how many distinct powers of the state there were. Some asserted a unitary power; others discerned as many as five. [137] Did the bureaucracy constitute a separate power from the sovereign and his court? Should it be separate from the judicial? What power did the police serve? Given such difficulties, as well as the increasing recognition of the historical elasticity of governmental forms, there came to be less reliance on clear delineation of the separate branches of government as a guarantee of legal protection. Instead, there was a trend towards emphasizing the indivisibility of state power at the metapolitical level, that is, to argue that the legitimacy of government rested on a single ground, whether it be divine-right monarchy or popular sovereignty. The task of *Politik* then became to elucidate the pragmatic relationships between that power and the diverse claims and rights of constituent groups that were represented within the state. Since most of the German states were still monarchies, this took the form of a practical dualism in which the king and his ministers were arrayed against the estates or parliament as representatives of the people. [138]

135. Ibid., 41.
136. Springer, *Dahlmann,* 1: 385–86, 389.
137. Mohl, *Geschichte und Literatur,* 1: 273; Klüber, *Öffentliches Recht des teutschen Bundes,* 165–66n.
138. Mohl, *Geschichte und Literatur,* 1: 282; Rotteck, *Lehrbuch des Vernunftrechts,* 2: 212–13; Rotteck, "Constitution," *Staatslexikon,* 2: 776.

Given this inherently adversarial structure, the question of how to adjudicate conflicts between the two sides soon became central. It was discussed in terms of the issue of ministerial responsibility to parliament or to the estates. Responsibility was not precisely defined at first, and was more or less synonymous with accountability. According to Mohl, this "appeared to most as the keystone of the constitutional state edifice."[139] Given Mohl's liberalism and his distrust of popular sovereignty, he could not at first accept the notion of a vote of parliamentary nonconfidence. And given his penchant for clarity, he could not accept the vagueness of the term itself, for a loosely defined ministerial responsibility could open the door to endless conflict, or—prophetically—to manipulation by exceedingly clever ministers who could rule in defiance of the representatives' wishes.[140] Mohl's solution, true to the character of the *Rechtstaat*, was a judicial arbitration commission to settle such conflicts.[141] Only later, after a trip to England in the 1840s, did Mohl's advocacy of the parliamentary system increase.[142]

Like Mohl, Hegel was also opposed to a rigid and mechanical separation of powers and viewed the organic metaphor of the state as a truer expression of reason's work.[143] Hegel explicitly chose the old word *estate* (*Stand*) to describe both the social classes and the proper functioning of the legislative power of government, thus fusing his social classification with his political one. The agricultural estate was to comprise the upper house and was based on inheritance; the business estate (encompassing both manufacturing and commerce), or lower house, was to be elected, while members of the civil service, with their practical experience and supposed impartiality, should also sit in the legislature—a view that was shared by Rotteck.[144] Dahlmann, in contrast, viewed ministerial responsibility as operating through public opinion and the press as well as through legislation.[145] In this way as well, a strict notion of the separation of powers was overcome.

139. Mohl, *Verantwortlichkeit der Minister*, v; cf. Pflanze, "Juridical and Political Responsibility," 167. Pflanze's treatment of this important issue begins with the 1848 revolution.

140. Mohl, *Verantwortlichkeit der Minister*, 12–13. In Mohl's own words, "[It could happen] that a man of great boldness or strong conviction could wage a bitter parliamentary war . . . without being deflected from his unconstitutional behavior" (12).

141. Ibid., 17.

142. For a thorough analysis of this change, see Angermann, *Mohl*, 56–57, 401–26; see also Boldt, "Zwischen Patrimonialismus und Parlamentarismus," 95–97.

143. Hegel, *Philosophy of Right*, 164, 175–78, 197, 292.

144. Ibid., 197–201; Rotteck, *Lehrbuch des Vernunftrechts*, 2: 218. Knox uses the word *class* as a translation for *Stand*, which misleads insofar as Hegel uses the same term to refer to the social groups and the representative bodies—even though the word *Klasse* had already been introduced into the Prussian *Allgemeines Landrecht* (Koselleck, *Preussen*, 75).

145. Dahlmann, *Politik*, 115.

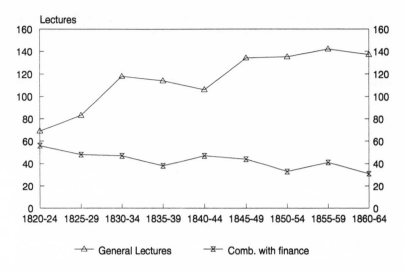

Fig. 4. Lectures in Economics, 1820–1865

Cameralism Transformed: Continuity and Discontinuity in Economics

Interest in economics continued to grow during this period: even as university enrollments fell in the early 1830s, the number of lectures in economics increased in absolute terms, declining only gradually thereafter (see figure 4). In the mid–1830s, economic questions began to eclipse political ones as Germany approached the "takeoff" period of the 1840s.[146] Although economics in Germany had been rooted in cameralism, "the daughter has grown and puts the mother in the shade," according to Friedrich Bülau of Leipzig.[147] In northern Germany, the term *cameralist* came to be less and less frequently used; by the 1840s in Prussian university statistics, it came to mean a student of agriculture. In Baden and Württemberg, however, it still retained its original meaning of a finance official. It was in South Germany that the continuity between cameralism and Smithian economics could best be seen. The two major actors in this process were Karl Heinrich Rau at Heidelberg and Friedrich Benedikt Hermann at Munich.

Rau and Hermann both began their careers at Erlangen in Bavaria, at the time a rather unpromising place for intellectual innovation. Rau himself began to study there in 1808. He was dissatisfied with the cameralistic instruction,

146. Wehler, *Gesellschaftsgeschichte*, 2: 94; Rau, "Nutzen," 10.
147. Bülau, "Über das Formelle in den Staatswissenschaften," 2.

but was encouraged to pursue the subject by his brother-in-law, a professor of cameralism at Würzburg, and by Soden, who lived in the area.[148] Rau began teaching at Erlangen in 1812; his first ten years were highly productive ones, with original publications on a variety of topics, both theoretical and practical. They included essays on the role of location and transportation in the economy, the optimal size of farms, the question of the abolition of guilds, luxury, and the balance of trade.[149] By 1818 his reputation was sufficient to warrant an offer from Berlin (as *Privatdozent*) and a professorship at Erlangen. In 1822, he accepted a professorship at Heidelberg, where the cameral school had been dissolved two years before and where he was to remain. From this point on, he began publishing systematic works: *Über die Kameralwissenschaft* in 1825, and in 1826 the first volume of the *Lehrbuch der politischen Oekonomie*. This work went through eight editions in his lifetime and became the standard work in German political economy for a generation.[150]

There is some disagreement on the degree of continuity which Rau exhibited with the past. According to some, he was the last cameralist, with all the lack of analytical rigor which the term implied; to others, he succeeded in breaking with cameralist assumptions significantly.[151] Rau stated his own view on this issue in his book on cameralism of 1825:

> Cameralism can no longer remain what it was in the previous century, [but] the necessity of its decline does not yet follow; there is a third [option]—it can go forth rejuvenated, purified, and strengthened from the test.[152]

148. Roscher, *Geschichte der Nationalökonomik*, 847; Neumann, *Lehren K. H. Rau's*, 7.

149. Rau, *Ueber das Zunftwesen und die Folgen seiner Aufhebung* (1816); *Ueber den Luxus* (1817); *Ansichten der Volkswirtschaft* (1821). In addition, Rau worked through the Smithian legacy by translating the latest systematic presentation of economics by Heinrich Friedrich von Storch, the economist at the imperial court at St. Petersburg. Rau added some two hundred pages of commentary to relate Storch's text to German conditions and to point out where Smith's propositions needed revision. See Storch, *Handbuch der National-Wirtschaftslehre*, xii–xiii.

150. Even in Austria, where Sonnenfels was still the required textbook, professors began to deviate from it—"not without the silent consent of the government," according to Joseph Kudler, professor of economics at Vienna. When Kudler eventually published his own text in 1846, it followed Rau's organization. See Kudler, *Grundlehren der Volkswirtschaft*, 1: iv.

151. For the first view, Neumann, *Lehre K. H. Rau's*, 101, 103; and Hentschel, "Die Wirtschaftswissenschaften als akademische Disiziplin an der Universität Heidelberg 1822–1924," in Waszek, ed., *INDU*, 195–96; for the second, Winkel, *Deutsche Nationalökonomie*, 21–22, and Tribe, *Governing Economy*, chap. 9, 197–98. According to Tribe, Rau viewed "the activity of the state . . . as supplementary to, and not constitutive of, individual welfare"; this set him apart from previous writers as recent as Fulda. My view is that this change came much earlier.

152. Rau, *Kameralwissenschaft*, 2. Towards the end of his career, he reflected on his own contribution as that of transmitting the legacy of the first generation of Smithians to a younger generation (Rau to the Würzburg political economy faculty 1 May 1862, in Schanz, "Staatswirtschaftliche Fakultät," 74).

This commitment was reflected in his teaching career: during his early years he taught the full complement of cameralist lectures; while he eventually dropped some of them to concentrate on economics, he continued to teach agriculture, commerce, and police science throughout his career.[153]

Rau's conceptual clarification of cameralism consisted in taking the cameralists' assimilation of Smith—as articulated, for example, by Fulda, whose text he used at first—and fashioning from it a new, tripartite sequence of political economy. Fulda had begun with the sciences of trades (*Privatökonomie*), proceeded to the Smithian laws (*Nationalökonomie*), and concluded with the role of the state in economics (*Staatsökonomie*), the latter consisting of the economic parts of police science and finance. While Rau adhered to this plan in his survey lectures on cameralism, he abridged it in his system of political economy. This consisted of the second and third parts of Fulda's scheme: *Nationalökonomie* became the theoretical part, though Rau preferred the more German-sounding synonym *Volkswirtschaftslehre*.[154] *Staatsökonomie* became the practical part, with economic policy (*Volkswirtschaftspolitik*) and finance serving as two independent subdivisions. Strictly speaking, Rau maintained, only these practical disciplines were part of the sciences of state. Shifting some of the material away from police science into *Volkswirtschaftspolitik* made the teaching of the former more manageable.[155] *Volkswirtschaftspolitik* did not imply an endorsement of ubiquitous government regulation, but a discussion of the circumstances in which such regulation was or was not appropriate. This inclusion of *Volkswirtschaftspolitik* set off German economics from its British or French counterparts.[156] The three economics lectures then became the standard offering in German universities in the latter part of the nineteenth century.

Part of Rau's cameralist heritage had been a certain preference for concreteness, that is, taking specific occupations as one's fundamental categories rather than abstract concepts such as value and price.[157] As he shifted from cameralism to political economy, this preference was suppressed but not eliminated—as can be seen in his treatment of the sciences of trades: rather than discarding the material of Fulda's *Privatökonomie*, he reinserted it into his theo-

153. For more detail, see Hentschel, "Wirtschaftswissenschaften," in Waszek, ed., *LNDU,* 197–98.

154. On the origin and use of such overlapping terms, see Burkhardt, "Der Begriff des Ökonomischen in wissenschaftsgeschichtlicher Perspektive," in Waszek, ed., *LNDU,* 66–72. Particularly confusing is *Staatswirtschaft,* which could alternatively mean finance, or finance plus economic sections of *Polizei,* or these plus theoretical economics. Rau was one of the first to point to this confusion.

155. Rau, *Kameralwissenschaft,* 10, 13; "Begriff und Wesen der Polizei," 605–25.

156. Rau, *Lehrbuch,* 5–8th eds., 1.1: 16 n. Rau criticized Say for leaving such matters to the science of legislation; the British writers McCulloch and Senior had no such applied sections.

157. Rau, *Kameralwissenschaft,* 24–25, 42; *Ansichten der Volkswirtschaft,* 37–38.

retical economics. Thus after a lengthy treatment of the essence, production, distribution, and consumption of material goods in the manner of Smith and Say, Rau turned to a description of "the productive trades," from mining to agriculture, manufacturing, and commerce. "The special treatment of trades in their political-economic relations," he wrote, "serves not only to illustrate the general laws of economics, but also makes its structure more vivid and gives the necessary prior knowledge for the effect of the government on economic activity."[158] The *Volkswirtschaftspolitik* combined these two organizational principles: it treated government policy with respect to the production, distribution, and consumption of wealth, but it was primarily concerned with the individual branches of production—agricultural policy, guild policy, commercial policy, and so on.

From the generation that preceded him, Rau also inherited the belief that *Volkswirtschaft* was the economy of the people or the nation rather than the individual. He insisted that this economy was greater than the sum of its individual parts, and it was at the collective level that the laws of economics operated. In his first essay on the subject, he prescribed two directions for the future course of economics: (1) to tie it more firmly to the principles of the sciences of state, that is, of the general welfare, and (2) to connect the general and the individual; the opening three pages of that essay on the subject contain the words *organic, organ*, and *organism* four times.[159] Thus economics was a discipline in which the boundaries between state and citizen tended to be blurred rather than clarified. All of this seemed to run squarely counter to the trend of economic analysis, which helps explain Joseph Schumpeter's relegation of Rau to a footnote in his history thereof.[160] But to dismiss him as superficial would be an injustice: Rau could argue in depth about the pros and cons of practical proposals, e.g., land reform or the regulation of guilds. In this respect, he contributed, as did Mohl, to the deliberative style of presentation. And if his penchant for completeness led him to be less than consistent, he did not shy away from theoretical analysis when the occasion warranted. He saw, for example, that supply and demand factors lent themselves to graphic representation.[161] He was also one of the first to discuss the notion of an aggregate net national income and how it might be calculated—a project consonant with his collectivistic preference.[162]

An important part of Rau's self-image was as a disseminator of ideas to a larger audience—through which he also contributed to the spread of a civic-

158. Rau, *Lehrbuch*, 1.2: 151.
159. Rau, *Ansichten der Volkswirtschaft*, 22–24, 39. See also *Kameralwissenschaft*, 26–28.
160. Schumpeter, *History of Economic Analysis*, 503 n.
161. Rau, *Lehrbuch*, 1.1: 196–99, 368–70; Neumann, *Lehren K. H. Rau's*, 50–53.
162. Rau, *Lehrbuch* 1.1: 359–66; Winkel, *Deutsche Nationalökonomie*, 21–22.

minded economic liberalism. Rau served in the Badenese parliament and on a number of commissions, ranging from the customs union to railroads.[163] He sought to further the study of economics for more than financial officials and, like Mohl, combatted the dominance of legal studies for administrators.[164] He did not view his position as antagonistic to the other sciences of state, but supported the teaching of the entire curriculum at Heidelberg on the model of Tübingen, though he did not go so far as to urge a separate faculty.[165] He worked for the appointment of Mohl and held his work in high esteem, an opinion which Mohl characteristically did not reciprocate. "Surely righteous and honorable, industrious and erudite, but of moderate gifts, pedantic and stodgy in life and in science," was Mohl's evaluation.[166]

This opinion, uncharitable as it was, contained more than a grain of truth with regard to Rau's later years. For Rau, once established, did not avoid the besetting sin of the classificatory approach: stasis. This was already evident in 1842, when the finance ministry complained of the mediocre quality of the examinations, due to a preparation "based more on memory than on understanding."[167] Unlike Mohl himself, Rau adapted his textbook to the changes in his field through agglutination rather than revision. This can be demonstrated by the sheer increase in weight of the successive editions of his text: the volume on theoretical economics increased from 368 to 580 pages between 1826 and 1847—although it remained constant thereafter—while the one on economic policy grew from 436 to 897 pages between 1828 and 1862. Volume 1 of Mohl's police science, in contrast, went from 619 to 688 pages between 1844 and 1866.

That this sin was not inevitable for someone of cameralist training can be seen from the life and work of Hermann. Hermann came from a family of officials from the former free imperial city of Dinkelsbühl who were transferred to Erlangen in 1812.[168] He entered the university as a student of cameralism and mathematics the year after Rau began teaching there and heard his lectures. His early career was divided between these two fields, with a *Habilitation*

163. Neumann, *Lehre K. H. Rau's*, 8.

164. Rau, "Gedanken über die wissenschaftliche Vorbereitung," 85–88.

165. Rau, memo, 27 Oct. 1845, GLA, Abt. 235/3140, (Kultusministerium, Heidelberg, Lehrkanzel der Staatswirtschaft . . .).

166. Mohl, *Lebenserinnerungen,* 1: 245. On Rau's attitude, see Rau to Mohl, 6 Nov. 1845, 14 Nov. 1845, UB Tübingen, Md 613, Nachlass Mohl.

167. Hentschel, "Wirtschaftswissenschaften," in Waszek, ed., *INDU,* 199 n. The Prussian official Gustav von Diest listed Rau in his memoirs as one of the professors he heard while at Heidelberg in 1847, but not as one of the professors who attracted him. See Diest, *Leben eines Glücklichen,* 62.

168. On this and following see Eisenhart, "Hermann," *ADB,* 12: 170–74; Wernitz, "Hermann," 26–37.

at Erlangen in cameralism in 1821 and a position as professor of mathematics at a Nuremberg gymnasium and polytechnical school in 1825. In 1827 he was appointed as *Extraordinarius* in technology, political arithmetic, and political economy at the University of Munich, which had just been moved from Landshut the year before under the auspices of the new king, Ludwig I.[169]

Hermann's appointment appeared to be entirely consistent with the cameralist mission of the political economy faculty that Montgelas had established at the turn of the century. But once arrived, Hermann felt under no particular compulsion to continue that mission: he discarded technology, teaching it only three times in the next seven years, while economics, finance, commerce, and political arithmetic remained staples in his repertory through the 1830s. Unlike Rau, he became more of a specialist in the economic and statistical subjects.

Under these circumstances, it is not surprising that Hermann's main scholarly work, *Investigations in Political Economy*, which appeared in 1832, marked a sharp break with the cameralist tradition. Unlike Rau, Hermann made no claims to systematic completeness, although he adopted Rau's tripartite division for teaching purposes.[170] His his aim was analytical: to concentrate on a few concepts that were in need of further clarification, although he criticized Ricardo for going too far in this direction.[171] The *Investigations* thus consisted of eight discreet chapters, each addressed to a specific topic: political economy itself, productivity, two on capital, price, profit, income, and use (consumption). The quality of Hermann's analysis won him recognition both in Germany and England, where Alfred Marshall referred to his "brilliant genius."[172] This penchant for analysis did not mean, however, that Hermann forsook the holistic assumptions of German economics. On the contrary, he insisted that self-interest was an insufficient motive to explain economic behavior; equally important was a sense of common interest (*Gemeinsinn*).[173] The agents of such common interest were not limited to the state, but also included family and community institutions. For Hermann, it was the study of such collectively oriented activity that distinguished the second, practical part of economics from the first, theoretical part. He preferred the term *economic maintenance* (*Volks-*

169. Wernitz, "Hermann," 27.

170. Hermann, *Nationalökonomie und Finanzwissenschaft*. [Lecture notes for winter semester 1856/57], Lousiana State University rare book collection.

171. Hermann, *Staatswirtschaftliche Untersuchungen*, iv, v.

172. Marshall, *Principles of Economics*, 68. Marshall studied in Germany in 1868 and 1870–71, just at the time Hermann's second edition appeared. On his indebtedness to German authors, including Hermann, see Streissler, "Influence of German Economics," in Caldwell, ed., *Menger*, 55–58.

173. Hermann, *Staatswirtschaftliche Untersuchungen*, 14–15.

wirtschaftspflege) rather than *Volkswirtschaftspolitik* to describe it, implying that such maintenance was not the exclusive responsibility of the state.[174]

The content of Hermann's analysis reflected the German economists' concern for completeness and taking all factors into consideration. The deliberative style could be felt here too, in that the emphasis on completeness translated into a range of choices available to the economic actor. This type of thinking was largely at odds with the predominant mode of theorizing in Britain, namely that of Ricardo and his followers, whose *modus operandi* was to simplify and mine the implications of a few propositions.[175] The contrast is perhaps clearest in the treatment of value and price, in which Hermann built on the work of Hufeland and Lotz from the previous generation. This stressed both the interests of the buyer and seller rather than focusing, as Ricardo did, on the costs of production as determining price. Hermann classified the factors affecting price on both sides of the bargaining table. On the supply side, there were of course (1) the production costs, but also (2) the costs of competing goods, and finally, (3) the exchange value of the medium of payment, for example, currency fluctuations.[176] On the demand side, there was (1) the use-value for the buyer, (2) the buyer's ability to pay, and (3) the incidental costs (such as transportation, taxes, etc.). Both the second and third factors automatically forced the buyer to make comparisons between the good in question and other goods: affordability, obviously, forced the buyer to make choices between necessities and luxuries. Incidental costs, for example, could put the product at a disadvantage compared to other goods that met the same need.[177] Hermann concluded that, Ricardo notwithstanding, the demand factors were more crucial in determining price.[178] He went on to apply this analysis of price to wages and interest, which he defined as the prices of labor and capital respectively.[179] The drift of this approach—that the cost or price of a given unit of a commodity was determined by that of other units or the same or a comparable

174. Ibid., 18–19.

175. Schumpeter, *History of Economic Analysis,* 472; Hermann, *Staatswirtschaftliche Untersuchungen,* v. Neither German nor British economics was a monolith: Rau and Hermann, in their quest for completeness, both learned from Ricardo. The Oxford professor Nassau Senior, for one, found Ricardo's definitions too restrictive, and, in Hermann's opinion, came to conclusions that had been common knowledge to German economists for some time. Senior later modified his definition of capital in response to Hermann's criticism. See Bowley, *Nassau Senior,* 97, 101, 112, 156; Rau, *Lehrbuch,* 2d ed., 1: ix; Hennings, *Austrian Theory of Value and Capital,* 56.

176. Hermann, *Staatswirtschaftliche Untersuchungen,* 76–93.

177. Ibid., 67–76.

178. Ibid., 95

179. Hermann, *Staatswirtschaftliche Untersuchungen,* 2d ed., 460, 534. Hermann contested vigorously the "wage-fund" theory of capital, which stated that the amount of capital determines the level of wages and thus regulates demand (406).

product—was precisely the assumption of the later marginal revolution.[180] It implied that allocation rather than growth was the central concern of economics—a premise rooted in the cameralist tradition.

Hermann did not publish another major work on economics after the *Investigations*. His failure to do so pointed up a problem that was to confront many other *Staatswissenschaftler:* the conflicting pulls of academia and involvement in practical affairs of state. Hermann's services to the Bavarian government included heading the statistical bureau from its founding in 1839 (which involved editing its reports), participating in the board of churches and schools, representing Bavaria in various industrial exhibitions, heading the state mining commission, and tutoring the crown prince (though his closeness to the king cooled somewhat after he refused a royal order to tutor Lola Montez as well). During the revolution of 1848, he was second vice president of the national assembly and served in the Bavarian parliament thereafter.[181] It was only after his retirement from active political life that he returned to a revision of the *Investigations*. He did not live to complete the project, but a second edition, partially revised, was published posthumously in 1870.

Police Science

The number of lectures in police science shows most clearly the differences between North and South Germany, though these narrowed after 1835 (see figure 5). The definitions still tended to vary: some emphasized the goals of *Polizei* as limited to attaining security for individuals and for the state, while others continued to see it as contributing positively to social welfare. As Hegel perceptively put it, the limits of police activities "are determined by custom, the spirit of the rest of the constitution, contemporary conditions, the crisis of the hour, and so forth."[182] But the scope of police functions remained largely the same, regardless of definition. In the minds of police officials themselves, the formula of "security and welfare" was generally accepted without undue concern for its limits or precise content.[183] In the understanding of academics, the term *Polizei* continued to be associated not only with repressive measures against dissidents, but also with addressing the staggering social and economic problems that Germany faced: population growth, consequences of land re-

---

180. Spiegel, *Growth of Economic Thought*, 505; Blaug, *Economic Theory in Retrospect*, 310. On Hermann's anticipations of that theory, see Hennings, *Austrian Theory of Value*, 49–50; Bowley, *Nassau Senior*, 180 n; Streissler, "Influence of German Economics," in Caldwell, ed., *Menger*, 41–42. See also Rau, *Lehrbuch*, 8th ed., 1.1: 90.

181. Wernitz, "Hermann," passim.

182. Hegel, *Philosophy of Right*, 146.

183. Lüdtke, *"Gemeinwohl," Polizei und "Festungspraxis,"* 73–75.

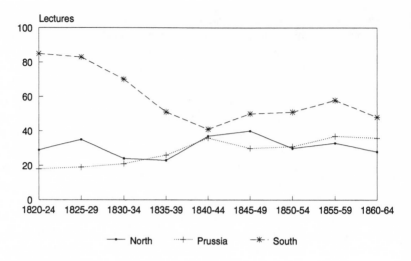

Source: University catalogues.
See appendix for details.

Fig 5. Lectures in *Polizeiwissenschaft*, 1820–1865

form, poverty in the cities, and so on, as well as policies for furthering economic growth. Like politics, it offered ample room for deliberation.

Once again, the central contribution to the revival of police science came from Mohl. His *Police Science According to the Principles of the Legal State* of 1832 brought administrative science into line with the standards of individual liberty guaranteed by the *Rechtstaat*. Police activities served to remove obstacles to the free development of individuals. Anything which individuals or groups could not do for themselves became a legitimate sphere of police activity; whatever individuals or groups could do independently was beyond the bounds of proper police intervention.[184] This still left considerable scope for state administration: it could include negative activities such as preventing danger from natural disasters or epidemics, or positive ones such as supporting education or boosting the economy.

The main divisions of Mohl's work included care for the physical welfare of the people (population policy, public health, and poverty), their spiritual welfare (education and culture), and their wealth. Indeed, the entire second volume was devoted to economic police, and covered much the same area as Rau's *Volkswirtschaftspolitik* (see table 6). Both incorporated the traditional threefold classification of cameralism: state responsibility for the winning of raw materials (agriculture, forestry, mining), manufacturing, and commerce. In these sec-

184. Mohl, *Polizeiwissenschaft*, 1: 10–11, 17, 20.

Table 6 Polizeiwissenschaft *and* Volkswirtschaftspolitik

Mohl	Rau

State concern for the wealth of citizens

Mohl	Rau

1. General favoring the acquisition of property
  a. Lifting of personal disabilities (slavery, serfdom)
  b. Easing the acquisition of landed property
  c. Favoring the acquisition of capital
 	
2. Securing previously acquired property from destruction by acts of nature
 	
3. Encouraging enterprise
  a. Encouraging production of raw materials
    1. Agriculture
    2. Mining
  b. Encouraging trades
  c. Encouraging commerce
    1. Free trade
    2. Easing communication
    3. Encouraging circulation
 	
4. Measures concerning the enjoyment of wealth
	1. Directly productive activity
	  a. General conditions of production
	    1. Work
	    2. Capital
	  b. Individual classes of work
	    1. Mining
	    2. Agriculture
	    3. Trades
	
	2. Distribution of products
	  a. Exchange
	    1. General (incl. weights and measures, money)
	    2. Trade
	  b. Credit
	  c. Effect of state power on prices
	  d. The poor
	
	3. Consumption of goods

Sources: Mohl, *Polizeiwissenschaft,* vol. 2; Rau, *Lehrbuch,* vol. 2.
Mohl treats state policy on poverty along with public health and population in vol. 1 under "Care of physical person".

tions particularly, one can see in both Mohl and Rau the evolution from classification to deliberation: the listing of all the points for or against an issue, from which the author then drew his recommendation.

In the area of agricultural policy, the disastrous consequences of land reform for the small farmer had become known, and by the 1830s and 1840s, discussion centered increasingly on the proper size of farms.[185] Liberals like Rau, Mohl, Rotteck, and Welcker vied with conservatives in glorifying the independent peasant proprietor.[186] Rau sought to demonstrate that small plots were not inherently inefficient; although he admitted a minimum size was necessary, he claimed that this minimum would be difficult to enforce and could not be uniform from one area of the country to another.[187] Mohl stressed the ethical desirability of private ownership of small farms and claimed that this

185. See Kolb, "Theilbarkeit des Grundeigentums," 84–116; Rau, "Verkleinerung der Landgüter," 116–23; cf. Vopelius, *Altliberalen Ökonomen,* 52–70.
186. Gagliardo, *Pariah to Patriot,* 235–50.
187. Rau, *Lehrbuch,* 2d ed. (1839–1841), 2: 127, 130.

could outweigh the economic advantages of large estates. This was not an absolute, however, and more damage was done by improper division of large estates than by the act of division itself.[188]

Another area of lively debate in the early nineteenth century was that of privatization of state-owned lands and enterprises, particularly forests and mines. On these issues, Mohl leaned towards state activity, while Rau leaned in the other direction. Mohl sided against privatization of forests, since the temptation to harvest wood prematurely for profit contradicted the public good that would come from allowing the trees to mature. Extensive regulation of wood production was essential to ensure an adequate supply.[189] Similarly, he argued for state-owned mines and railroads, since both are most efficient when pursued on a scale beyond the means of most private entrepreneurs—though this could be decided on a case-by-case basis.[190] Rau opted for opening forests and mines to private enterprise, but with stringent regulation. He agreed with Mohl on railroads, however.[191]

In the area of industrial and trade policy, Mohl and Rau shared in the general consensus that guild monopolies should be abolished, but that immediate abolition of guilds themselves would be disastrous. The question was not one of complete freedom or complete control of manufacturing, but of how deregulation should take place with a minimum of disruption. Even Rotteck, a doctrinaire on so many issues, took this position.[192] Rau and Mohl took a similarly undogmatic position on free trade versus protective tariffs: there were situations where protection was justified.[193]

Both writers devoted considerable attention to the problem of poverty. With their customary attention to completeness, they enumerated the different types of poverty (from individual laziness to disability to lack of employment) and the contempoary remedies for it. Rau's discussion of welfare for the able-bodied unemployed may serve as a paradigmatic instance of the deliberative style.[194] He listed five possible solutions: (1) establishing employment agencies; (2) state-created jobs, for example, public works projects; (3) workhouses, where the unemployed are given room and board but no wages; (4) worker colonies to cultivate land, like those in Holland and Belgium; (5) encouraging emigration. Rau noted that employment agencies, like the public works projects, competed with

188. Mohl, *Polizeiwissenschaft*, 2d ed., 2: 19–31.
189. Ibid., 2: 232–37, 247–48.
190. Ibid., 2: 270, 425–26.
191. Rau, *Lehrbuch*, 2d ed., 2: 63 (on mines), 232–33 (forests); 445–46 (railroads).
192. Vopelius, *Altliberalen Ökonomen*, 100–21 (115–16 on Rotteck). Vopelius points to Hoffmann's influential writings on this question. See also Rau, *Lehrbuch*, 2d ed., 2: 300; Mohl, *Polizeiwissenschaft*, 2d ed., 2: 289.
193. Rau, *Lehrbuch* 2nd ed., 2: 338–39; Mohl, *Polizeiwissenschaft*, 2d ed., 2: 367.
194. Rau, *Lehrbuch*, 5–8th eds., 2.2: 451–74.

the normal functioning of the private sector. These agencies were valuable, however, if they served more than one community, so that a labor surplus in one locality could relieve a shortage in another. On workhouses, he first listed the arguments against them: (1) the cost to the state; (2) the competition with the private sector; (3) the undermining of family life. His response was: (1) housing and feeding all the inhabitants under one roof would minimize the cost; except for large cities, they could be established at the regional rather than the local level; (2) they would be only for people temporarily out of work or the disabled; (3) they would maintain strict rules for order, peace, respectability, and industriousness. Although similar advantages obtained for worker colonies, experiments in this type of welfare had not proved successful. On emigration, Rau was also lukewarm, since it did not address the temporary nature of much unemployment. Emigration was costly for the state and could rob a country of human resources which would be needed in more prosperous times.[195]

Mohl and Rau shared in a growing perception that poverty was taking on a new urgency during this period and was related to the growth of factories.[196] As early as 1817, the Prussian reformers had noted with alarm the growth of child labor, but hesitated to intervene on Smithian grounds.[197] Rau at first was skeptical about factories: he linked the increase in poverty to the concentration of workers in cities and urged a dispersal of factories throughout the country-side. The best solution would be to attain a proper balance between manufac-turing and agriculture, and to avoid overdependence on foreign markets and their vicissitudes—a conviction he shared with Soden and Rotteck.[198] Only gradually did Rau come to accept the reality of the Industrial Revolution, as revealed in successive editions of the *Lehrbuch*.[199] Mohl also came to the issue gradually—he passed over it in the first edition of the *Police Science* in 1832— but when he did so, he made it a central issue.[200] In an 1835 article in Rau's *Archive* entitled "On the Disadvantages Which Come from a Factory-Type of Industrial Enterprise, Both for the Workers Themselves and for the Well-Being and Security of the Entire Civil Society," he clearly pointed to a new sort of poverty that was a mass phenomenon, one which robbed the factory worker of any hope for the future.[201] He tended to view the problem as a social-

195. In the fifth edition of 1862, Rau was more positive about worker colonies and was willing to admit that state-sponsored emigration, though not a good solution, was sometimes necessary (2: 461–62, 469–70).

196. See Vopelius, *Altliberalen Ökonomen* (121–33) for a survey of these views.

197. Koselleck, *Preussen*, 625–26.

198. Rau, *Ansichten der Volkswirtschaft*, 117; *Lehrbuch*, 1st ed., 2: 376; Rotteck, *Lehrbuch des Vernunf-trechts*, 4: 186; Soden, *Nationalökonomie*, 2: 72–74.

199. Vopelius, *Altliberalen Ökonomen*, 124.

200. Angermann, *Mohl*, 222, 213–14.

201. *APO* 2 (1835): 141–203. See Angermann, *Mohl* (224–306) for a full discussion.

psychological one, calling for an improvement in employer-employee relations, giving the workers a greater sense of opportunity—without this, an increase in wages would only lead to increased dissatisfaction—and for improving their physical and mental condition. He was willing to go further than Rau in advocating state intervention.[202] Going considerably beyond the *juste milieu*, he advocated profit sharing as one solution to the problem—a solution he later came to regard as problematical, but which he could not part with entirely.[203]

Finance and Monetary Policy

In the science of finance, there were also signs of the deliberative style, but not to the same extent as in the previously discussed disciplines. As with police science, the post-Napoleonic period was one of consolidation in finance. A number of new systematic treatises appeared with the intent of digesting the experience of the previous upheavals. Indeed, some of the leading authors were officials rather than professors: Carl Freiherr von Malchus, who had served Napoleon in the Rhenish confederation and in Württemberg thereafter, and Friedrich Nebenius, one of the pivotal leaders of Badenese liberalism. These writers were generally suspicious of too great a reliance on theory and stressed the need to take the circumstances of individual states into account.[204] The organization of these systems followed the traditional division of revenues into domains, regalia, and taxes, but these formed the framework for the discussion of controversial issues and causal relationships rather than the mere enumeration of revenues. With respect to domains and regalia, the issues were those of state monopolies versus privatization from a fiscal perspective. With respect to taxes, writers had assimilated the Ricardian notion that certain taxes enabled the payers to shift the burden from themselves to other groups (e.g., a tax on land from the owner to the tenant). Even the most doctrinaire (such as Rotteck) did not subscribe to any simple method of spreading the tax burden; the consensus was that a variety of taxes were necessary, both direct and indirect.[205] Of this generation, Rau was the most successful at integrating the theoretical and practical dimensions: he insisted that net income should be the major general criterion by which the level of taxation was determined, without sacrificing the variety of methods and types of taxes that practical necessity dictated.[206]

The discussion of state debt had become an integral part of finance, and

202. Mohl, "Nachteilen," 173; Angermann, *Mohl*, 278.

203. Angermann, *Mohl*, 281–89.

204. Jakob, *Staatsfinanzwissenschaft*, 1: v–x; Malchus, *Handbuch der Finanzwissenschaft*, 1: viii; Rau, *Lehrbuch*, 8th ed., 3.1: 14–15.

205. Rotteck, *Lehrbuch des Vernunftrechts*, 4: 304–5; Malchus, *Handbuch der Finanzwissenschaft*, 1: 361.

206. Rau, *Lehrbuch*, 8th ed., 3.1: 400–5.

with it came issues of monetary policy. The writers of this period gradually increased their acceptance of paper money. Even opponents of the easy issue of money such as Jakob recognized that the evil was not issuing money itself, but rather the fluctuations in value of money and goods that could result from it.[207] The most thorough investigation came from Nebenius, who explored the effects of state borrowing not only on money but on interest rates and the availability of capital as well. While he recognized that such borrowing could have a tonic effect on the economy even in a noncrisis situation, he concluded that the disadvantages were much more significant when the level of debt was high. In this way he did not go beyond the orthodox thinking of the period.[208] This attitude was reflected in the cautious policies of the state ministries of finance regarding expansion of the money supply.[209] Certainly the idea of fostering the "economic powers" of the nation was still present, but it did not necessarily translate into the furthering of industrial growth in a way that seems obvious only with hindsight. Thus the Prussian government saw itself as a prime backer of credit institutions for agriculture, particularly the *Junkers,* but discouraged the creation of too many joint-stock companies, which might channel investment away from agriculture—and from the government's treasury bills.[210] Meanwhile, the private merchants and bankers developed their own methods of accumulating capital, relying frequently on family connections and extending easy credit to those within that network via bills of exchange; these practices constituted a fund of experience from which the great investment banks of the later nineteenth century could draw.[211] That this pool of knowledge developed independently of the sciences of state is an indication that for the latter, fiscal considerations of balancing the budget could often outweigh the notion of state credit as a motor of economic growth. Given the choice between considerations of finance and economic *Polizei,* finance frequently won out.

Statistics

Statistics, or *Staatenkunde,* as it was still called, continued to follow the pattern set by Achenwall and Schlözer; the leading textbook of the period was a description of the principal political, geographical, economic, and social features

207. Jakob, *Staatsfinanzwissenschaft,* 2: 54; Malchus, *Handbuch der Finanzwissenschaft,* 1: 414.

208. Nebenius, *Öffentliche Credit,* 683–84; Schanz, "Öffentliches Staatsschuldwesen," *ENTW,* no. 40, 9. Only Zachariae took a more positive view of borrowing; he saw it as a type of tax (ibid., 12).

209. Tilly, "Germany, 1815–1870," 156–57, 181.

210. Ibid., 154–55.

211. Ibid., 174–75, 178. According to Wehler, there was no dearth of capital in pre–1848 Germany (*Gesellschaftsgeschichte* 2: 95).

of major European states.[212] The discipline had survived the critique of numbers during the Napoleonic years, in that tables were regularly used.[213] But numbers were still seen as illustrative of verbal descriptions of these features rather than as the essence of statistics. In the words of Berlin's leading statistician, Dieterici,

> Statistics [as a discipline] is dead, an unfruitful, mostly mindless and often empty compilation, when it is limited to the naked stringing together of facts and figures, without comparison to other relationships, without a retrospective view of the development of circumstances as they have been *historically* formed.[214]

In this respect, German statistics as a university discipline distanced itself from developments in France and England, where the enthusiasm for complilation was rife.[215] Whereas French statisticians came to the subject largely out of concern for public health, Germans viewed it as linked to geography and history. Of the eighty professors of all ranks who taught the subject in German universities from 1820 to 1840, roughly the same number came from these fields as from the sciences of state.[216] And the notion of statistics as a technique of calculating probabilities regarding human behavior was even more remote. Although political arithmetic was a recognized subject, the *Staatslexikon* of Rotteck and Welcker treated political arithmetic as an auxiliary to statistics rather than statistics itself.[217] Statistics was viewed rather as an instrument of *Bildung*: it encompassed the study of all major European nations, not just one's own state, and thus contributed to the general knowledge and cosmopolitanism of students—although this trend declined after 1835 (see figure 6).

The persistence of the Achenwall-Schlözer model in the universities did not mean that scientists of state were impervious to the benefit of central statistical bureaus as aids to government legislation and administration. The professor of statistics and history at Tübingen, Johannes Fallati, pointed out how Germany lagged behind France, England, and Belgium in this respect.[218] In addition to

---

212. Hassel, *Lehrbuch der Statistik der Europäischen Staaten fur höhere Lerhanstalten, zugleich als Handbuch zur Selbstbelehrung* (1822).

213. Wagner, "Statistik," *DS*, 10: 423.

214. Dieterici, review of *Handbuch der allgemeinen Staatskunde von Europa* by F. W. Schubert, quoted in Kurt Braunreuther, "Die Staatswissenschaften von 1810–1860 an der Humboldt-Universität," 1618.

215. Porter, *Rise of Statistical Thinking*, 27, 35–36.

216. The exact numbers are 23 who taught primarily history or geography, 26 who taught sciences of state, 13 who taught both, and 18 who could not be determined. Source: the university catalogues.

217. Rotteck and Welcker, eds., "Politische Arithmetik," *Staatslexikon*, 12: 588.

218. Fallati, "Gedanken über Mittel und Wege zu Hebung der praktischen Statistik," 496.

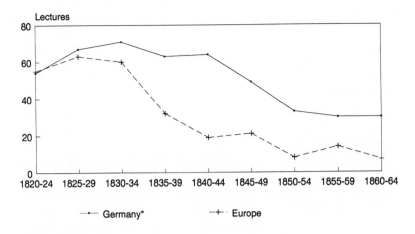

Source: University catalogues.
See appendix for details.
*Includes individual states.

Fig. 6. Lectures in Statistics of Germany and Europe, 1820–1865

the centralized bureaus, Fallati praised the involvement of lay persons in the English commissions of inquiry as part of the process of gathering data. "Statistical activity," Fallati claimed, "is always the greatest in those areas in which the principle of 'self-government' [Fallati used the English phrase] is allowed the greatest soil, i.e., in commerce, manufacturing, and agriculture, and in the numerous and varied domains of non-political associations."[219] He thus called both for greater specialization within the bureaucracy and for increasing the involvement of private citizens.

In fact, statistical bureaus existed in Prussia, Austria, Bavaria, and Württemberg during this period. The Prussian bureau in particular under Hoffmann's direction distinguished itself for the general reliability of its figures; under der Dieterici it began to publish regular figures on population, institutions, and occupations.[220]

Cross-Fertilizations: Agriculture, Economics, and History

During this period, agriculture and technology were undergoing a transition from the fields of cameral to natural science. True, lectures in these subjects continued to be offered under the rubric of *Staats-und Kameralwissenschaften*. A decline set in only after 1835 (see figure 7). These disciplines remained a part

219. Ibid., 501.
220. Hanssen, "Statistische Büreau," 333, 336.

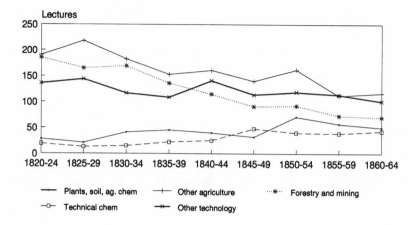

Lectures

1820-24 1825-29 1830-34 1835-39 1840-44 1845-49 1850-54 1855-59 1860-64

——— Plants, soil, ag. chem   —+— Other agriculture   ···*··· Forestry and mining

—□— Technical chem   —×— Other technology

Source: University catalogues. Does not
include lectures in agr. institutes,
even if affiliated with a university.

Fig. 7. Lectures in Agriculture, Forestry, and Technology, 1820–1865

of the required curriculum for officials in Baden and Württemberg.[221] But the innovative work was being done elsewhere.

By 1850 there were a dozen agricultural academies modeled on Möglin, founded in large part by Thaer's students.[222] These played no small part in the striking success of German agriculture after 1826, as production doubled over the next fifty years.[223] A turning point was Justus von Liebig's epoch-making work at the University of Giessen, which offered an explanation of crop fertility in terms of a unified chemical science.[224] The eventual result was to preserve the universities as legitimate institutions for agricultural research—though outside the cameral sciences.[225] Technology was also developing its own set of institutions, the polytechnic schools, of which eight were founded between 1815

221. On examination requirements, see Bleek, *Juristenprivileg*, 214 (Württemberg, 1837); *Grossherzogliches Badisches Staats-und Regierungsblatt*, 1838: 194 (for finance officials).

222. 1806: Möglin; 1811: Tharand in Saxony; 1819: Hohenheim in Württemberg; 1822 Schleissheim in Bavaria, with the help of Thaer's student Max Schönleutner; 1826 Jena; 1827 Greifswald-Eldena in Prussia; 1835: Geisberg near Wiesbaden; 1835 Braunschweig; 1842, 1846, 1847: Regenwald, Ragnit, and Proskau in Prussia; 1848: Bonn-Poppelsdorf, founded by Schweitzer, another student of Thaer.

223. Wehler, *Gesellschaftsgeschichte*, 2: 32, 43, 51.

224. Fraas, *Geschichte der Landbau-und Forstwissenschaft*, 241, 337, 340–41, 350–51.

225. Giessen also became the home of a forestry institute, under the codirection of Johann Christian Hundeshagen, whose *Encyclopedia of Forest Science* incorporated more current natural science than any previous work. See Schott, "Hundeshagen," *ADB*, 13: 403.

and 1840.[226] These schools often contained traces of the cameralist curriculum, such as programs in agriculture and commerce, which set them apart from pure engineering schools modeled on the French *École Polytechnique.*[227]

Although these former cameralist sciences were now on the periphery of the field we have been discussing, they nevertheless continued to exert an influence on its content. This was particularly true of agriculture, in which the connections to other disciplines remained alive through three leading personalities.

One of these was Friedrich Gottlob Schulze, who founded an agricultural institute at Jena which continued to straddle agriculture and economics. As a teacher, Schulze was undoubtedly effective, for the Prussian Minister of Culture, Altenstein, sought to win him for Prussia. In 1834 he was successful, and Schulze moved to the university of Greifswald to establish another agricultural institute there.[228] Five years later, however, Schulze returned to Jena, where he published a polemic against Liebig in 1846.[229] Schulze held that farmers should attend a university to give them "autonomy of thinking and willing," to wean them away from the exclusive pursuit of profit and towards the "higher tasks of life," and to expose them to a "national school for the German people."[230] He nevertheless subscribed to Smithian principles and to natural scientific training for farmers. Through him, the romantic idealism of Jena entered into the history of economics and agriculture: he has been aptly called the economist of the *Burschenschaften.*[231]

A more profound connection was made by the great theorist Johann Heinrich von Thünen. Historians of economics have high regard for him, but their treatment masks the fact that he was as much an agriculturalist as an economist: he named Smith and Thaer as his two great teachers.[232] Thünen made his living not as a professor or official, but as a farmer. In 1810 he was able to purchase a large estate in the relatively isolated state of Mecklenburg; for the

226. Wehler, *Gesellschaftsgeschichte,* 2: 499–504. These were Vienna, 1815; Karlsruhe, 1825; Dresden, 1826; Berlin and Munich, 1827; Stuttgart, 1829; Hannover, 1831; Braunschweig, 1835.

227. Hermann, *Polytechnischen Institute,* 155–56; Nebenius, *Technische Lehranstalten,* 139–56 (Nebenius also advocated teaching of economics at the school); *Deutschen technischen Hochschulen,* 52, 126.

228. Schulze, *Geschichtliche Mitteilung,* 8–13. This was part of Altenstein's plan to upgrade that university. See Beseler, *Erlebtes,* 41.

229. Frauendorfer, *Ideengeschichte der Agrarwirtschaft,* 249. The work was entitled *Thaer oder Liebig?*

230. Schulze, *Geschichtliche Mitteilung,* vi–viii. Schulze believed that university teachers needed philosophical training, which he himself had received from Johann Jakob Fries, who supported the *Burschenschaft* movement. Not surprisingly, Schulze was rediscovered by the Nazis (Frauendorfer, *Ideengeschichte der Agrarwirtschaft,* 246).

231. Roscher, *Geschichte der Nationalökonomik,* 224.

232. Thünen, *Isolierte Staat,* 401. On economists' praise, see Schumpeter, *History of Economic Analysis,* 466, who places him above Ricardo; Blaug, "Economics of Johann von Thünen," 1–2.

next five years he kept scrupulous records of expenses and crop yields in the manner established by Thaer. By 1819 he was ready to write down his findings in the first draft of his magnum opus, *The Isolated State*. It was first published in 1826 and revised in 1842. Thünen continued to expand the work, leading to further installments which were published posthumously in 1863.[233]

Thünen's clear idea of experimental agriculture was one powerful component of his scientific prowess; what made him outstanding was his combination of this empirical bent with a talent for model-building and deductive reasoning. Thünen got the idea for an ideal-typical model in his youth; he described it in the opening pages of *The Isolated State:*

> Let one imagine a very large town situated in the middle of a fertile plain, with no navigable streams or canals flowing through it. The plain itself consists of thoroughly uniform soil which is everywhere capable of cultivation. At a great distance from the town, the plain ends in an uncultivated wilderness which completely cuts off this state from the rest of the world. The plain contains no other towns besides the single large one. . . .
>
> There now arises the question: how will agriculture take shape under these conditions, and how will the greater or lesser distance from the town affect cultivation if the latter is pursued with maximum consistency?[234]

Specifically, Thünen asked how transportation costs would affect food prices and hence what could be grown where. Perishable or bulky products, such as produce or firewood, would be most economically grown close to town, while grain and dairy products could come from farther away. The result was a picture of concentric circles of different agricultural products. Thünen verified these hypotheses with data from his own estate, paying careful attention to the ways in which conditions there deviated from the model. In order to sift out what could be generalized, he resorted to algebraic equations based on his data—and was again one of the first to do so.[235]

Thünen's equations were capable of being worked in two ways: to determine how location affected the behavior of prices—an economic question—or how it affected different sorts of cultivation—an agricultural question. The emphasis in the first two editions of *The Isolated State* was clearly on the latter. Thünen factored in not only the transportation costs, but the yields from different types of crop rotation, fertilizer, and so on. He was aware of the dawning science of organic chemistry but claimed that it had not yet "found its Euclid." Justus von Liebig's early work in this area met with his criticism.[236]

233. For biography see Blaug, "Economics of Johann von Thünen," 4–7; Waentig, "Thünen," in *Isolierte Staat*, iii–v.

234. Thünen, *Isolierte Staat*, 11–12.

235. Ibid., 44–49.

236. Ibid., 77, 85–87.

Nevertheless, the work contained important side-glances at economic and social questions. Agricultural prices could help determine the location not only of farms but of factories, as food prices as well as production costs could affect wages. Thus potatoes could allow for lower wages and hence a greater concentration of workers in the city than more expensive grain products.[237] And the marginal principle was already there: the greater the distance from the town, or the less fertile the soil, the more expensive it would be to farm (Thünen arrived at this conclusion before reading Ricardo). The price of grain must therefore be at least so high as to compensate sufficiently the most remote or the least fertile farmer who could satisfy the demand of the town-dweller.[238] It was this marginal farmer who determined the level of price as a whole.

Thünen's approach was not as isolated from the trends of his own day as is often thought. If Hermann, Rau, and Roscher did not adopt Thünen's approach lock, stock, and barrel, they integrated his ideas on crucial points.[239] The importance of location as an economic variable was also grasped by Rau in his more creative years, and he published three articles on the subject in his collection of essays in 1821.[240] Rau's approach admittedly contrasted sharply with Thünen's and was closer to that of German statistics: economists should begin with the given geographical conditions of particular locations rather than with abstract formulas.[241] As transportation developed, the importance of these particularities diminished; nevertheless, where such contact was still sparse, the variables affecting production were sufficiently few as to be mathematically treatable; formulas could be used, for example, to help clarify the proper proportion of rural and urban workers that such a locale could support.[242] Thus the more interdependent Germany became, the less relevant was mathematical analysis. For Rau, the relevance of such analyses to the economic diversity and *Kleinstaaterei* of Germany was clear: individual principalities which were too small to be self-supporting had to rely on improvements in trade and transportation—the same mind-set that led to the customs union.[243] In any case, Thü-

237. Ibid., 220–21, 316. In the later edition, Thünen included "a dream with serious content, written in 1826: on the lot of the workers" (440).

238. Ibid., 45, 226. See also Blaug, "Economics of Johann von Thünen," 11–12.

239. Hennings, *Austrian Theory of Value*, 65. Dickinson, in "Von Thünen's Economics" (898), claims that Thünen was virtually unread because he was a liberal, a theorist, and a nonacademic. This is more applicable to the late nineteenth century than to the early, when liberalism predominated and nonacademics such as Lotz and Nebenius were widely read.

240. Rau, "Einfluss der Oertlichkeit auf die ursprüngliche Gestalt der Volkswirtschaft"; "Weitere Entwicklung der Volkswirtschaft durch Lebendigkeit des Verkehres"; "Folgen für die Staatsverwaltung," *Ansichten der Volkswirtschaft*, 41–142.

241. Ibid., 41.

242. Ibid., 96–98.

243. Ibid., 96.

nen's work eventually led to a branch of economics known as *location theory*. This field was cultivated mostly by Germans beginning in the late nineteenth century—in striking contrast to the predominantly historical analysis which had taken over by then.[244]

A third figure who synthesized a variety of disciplinary trends was Georg Hanssen. Hanssen was one of the first to fuse economic and historical argument, as opposed to the mere juxtaposition of these disciplines in a taxonomic order. He was thus crucial in giving subsequent German economics its distinctive stamp as a venue for historical research. For Hanssen, agriculture was the catalyst in this fusion.

Unlike Thünen, Hanssen was very much in the academic mainstream. He held professorships in Leipzig (1841–48), Göttingen (1848–1860, 1869–1884), and Berlin (1860–1869), and had offers from Erlangen, Rostock, Munich, and Vienna.[245] A favored student of Rau in the 1820s, he decided to spend his summers on a farm in Württemberg to gain practical experience—much to his teacher's dismay; he later established an agricultural institute with a model farm near Göttingen.[246] He soon joined this to an interest in statistics: returning to northern Germany, he matriculated at Kiel in 1829, where he eventually taught statistics of the fatherland—that is, Schleswig-Holstein; he was part of the liberal Schleswig-Holstein movement at the same time. Hanssen's love for the particular, concrete locale was already evident: he had already "grasped the walking stick from town to town and from village to village to satisfy the need for his own economic views."[247] His first major publication was a historical-statistical portrait of the Island of Fehmarn. From the materials he discovered here and on other farms in Schleswig-Holstein (such as land surveys), Hanssen was able to reconstruct, for the first time, the development of land patterns and methods of crop rotation in the area from the time of Tacitus onwards, and it was this work in agricultural history for which he became most famous.[248] This project was already formulated in the 1830s. Moreover, this interest was never purely antiquarian; Hanssen used it to train students to see the specific conditions around them in pursuit of their administrative tasks.[249] Hanssen was not, however, given to methdological pronouncements and fan-

244. Blaug, "Economics of Johann von Thünen," 1–2; Blaug, "German Hegemony of Location Theory," 23.

245. UB Göttingen, Handschriftenabteilung, Cod Ms Hanssen, file 136 (Anstellungen).

246. Hanssen, "Lebenserinnerungen," 27, 116–19; Cohn, *Hanssen,* 6.

247. Quoted in A. von Miaskowski, "Hanssen," 850. On his activity at Kiel, see "Lebenserinnerungen," 61; Pusback, "Kameral-und Staatswissenschaften an der Universität Kiel," *INDU,* 327–28. Hanssen's patriotic activities lost him his post in Kiel and took him to Leipzig.

248. Cohn, *Hanssen,* 6, 8; Miaskowski, "Hanssen," 838–40; Beseler, *Erlebtes,* 12–13; Meitzen, "Hanssen als Agrar-Historiker," 379, 411.

249. Cohn, *Hanssen,* 7, 14; Schumpeter, *History of Economic Analysis,* 810 n.

fare. This may account for his relative obscurity compared to the members of the so-called historical school.

THE EFFECTIVENESS OF THE SCIENCES OF STATE IN ECONOMIC AND SOCIAL POLICY

The existence of an academic discourse directed at ameliorating social ills leads one to raise the question of its effectiveness—a question at once inevitable, controversial, and unanswerable by any simple formula. There was great variation from state to state and no clearcut causal relationship between the sciences of state and specific reform programs. The case of Bavaria shows that a strong institutional basis for the sciences of state did not necessarily translate into a quick pace of reform.[250] The case of Hannover shows the converse: the enlightened and effective land reform bills of 1831 and 1833 came from the pen of Carl Bertram Stüve, a product not of the sciences of state, but of the historical school of Savigny and Eichhorn.[251] As with most initiatives in social and economic reform, the results were rarely commensurate with the will or intent. Nevertheless, the persistence of bureaucratic initiative in land reform, manufacturing, and trade policy throughout Germany is undeniable, and the results were impressive. We have already noted the increase in agricultural productivity, and the story of the customs union hardly needs retelling.

In any case, academic training was but one factor in a complex picture of social and economic change. Thus in Württemberg and Baden, where police science was most innovative, the very heterogeneity of the territories acquired in the Napoleonic era was at once the major impetus to administrative centralization and the major obstacle to an easy resolution of land-tenure disputes. In both states, population was dense, the number of small holdings was great, the variety of feudal obligations was staggering, and the resistance of the nobility was considerable.[252] The ordinances of the 1830s saw a strong role for the state in both cases: the treasury was to provide compensation for the extinguished dues and services when the farmers could not afford it. But since the state itself was often the landlord (Württemberg drew 19.7 percent of its revenues from such dues in 1823–24), it is not surprising that such reforms were implemented slowly, and that the lot of the small farmer often remained precarious.[253] A similar situation prevailed with respect to manufacturing, where small farmers frequently turned to cottage industry to keep themselves alive, thereby impeding the growth of factories. In one sense, Mohl's and Rau's concern with factor-

---

250. Dipper, *Bauernbefreiung*, 91, on agriculture; Spindler, *Bayerische Geschichte*, vol. 4, bk. 2, 795.
251. Dipper, *Bauernbefreiung*, 75; G. Stüve, "Stüve," *ADB*, 37: 84.
252. Dipper, *Bauernbefreiung*, 82–87.
253. Ibid., 114. This percentage only dropped to 15.9 percent by 1846–47.

ies deflected their attention from the more pervasive misery of the artisans involved in the putting-out system.[254]

Moreover, the population growth increased the size of the small towns, and the constitutions gave them a political voice with which to oppose change. Thus industrial freedom was acknowledged in principle but implemented slowly in practice; the officials found that it was easier not to confront the guilds with detailed legislation, but to gradually apply pressure behind the scenes.[255] Such a commitment to slow change also went hand-in-hand with the traditional treatment of poverty and welfare as a local problem.[256]

In many of these cases, the effectiveness of administrative measures devolved on a political issue: whether municipal citizenship should be determined by the local authorities or by the central government.[257] Such control of citizenship was the most effective means whereby local powers could resist the reforms from above, for it involved the power of determining who should be excluded from industrial and welfare measures. It was also an issue that was largely ignored in the books on police science. To this extent, academic discourse was out of touch with reality—although it was to catch up by 1848.

In Prussia, where the commitment to training officials in the sciences of state had dwindled, the practicioners themselves were not always equal to carrying out their appointed tasks. It seems probable that Prussian officials tended to be more dogmatic and visionary than their South German counterparts—although by no means in agreement with one another. For some, the vision was that of laissez-faire. Thus in trade policy, the architects of the customs union insisted on a low external tariff despite the desire of the Rhenish industrialists for protection. A reluctance to intervene in industrial issues led to the hesitation in enacting a child-labor law: though the need was recognized as early as 1817, a law was passed only in 1839.[258] For others, the vision was one of neomercantilism, as with Rother's *Seehandlung;* as Rother's influence increased in the 1830s, the share of state-run enterprises increased from 4–5 percent to 11–12 percent.[259]

254. Ibid., 214. By the mid-1840s and the revolt of the Silesian weavers, this problem could no longer be ignored, as Hoffmann noted in his essay on pauperism of 1845 (Hoffmann, *Kleine Schriften,* 220–23).

255. Walker, *German Hometowns,* 293; on Baden, see Lee, *Politics of Harmony,* 124, 149–50; on Württemberg, see Bernhard Mann and Gerhard F. Nüske, "Württemberg," *DV,* 2: 573.

256. Sachsse and Tennstedt, *Armenfürsorge,* 1: 196–97. Only in the 1840s did this attitude change in Württemberg. Prussia's approach to legislation on poverty was the opposite of that of the South German states in recognizing the obligation of the state (operating through regional associations) over and above the local communities in the face of an increasingly mobile labor force (ibid., 196, 226–28).

257. See, for example, Lee, *Politics of Harmony,* 140–45; Koselleck, *Preussen,* 563, 572–82.

258. Koselleck, *Preussen,* 624–26; Wehler, *Gesellschaftsgeschichte,* 2: 293.

259. Brose, *Politics of Technological Change,* 207.

Whatever the vision, Prussian officials found themselves increasingly at odds with the private sector after 1830 and unwilling to adapt to the changing demands of the business class. We have already noted the caution of the officials over innovative monetary policies and new forms of investment; both Peter Beuth and Christian Rother were cautious about railway investment in the face of popular enthusiasm.[260] Thus the stage was set for the increased alienation of public opinion from the bureaucracy that was noticeable in the 1840s and led up to the Revolution of 1848.

260. Ibid., 217–20 nn.

§4

A Period of Transition, 1840–1866:

Variation

The middle years of the nineteenth century marked Germany's "double revolution": the economic transition to an industrialized society on the one hand and the political transition to a unified nation-state on the other. Neither of these transitions was smooth, as both the "hungry forties" and the failed Revolution of 1848 attest. Nor did the subsequent two decades lend themselves to consensus on how to deal with these changes.

Needless to say, these transformations also affected the sciences of state— more profoundly than the disruptions of the French Revolutionary years. As in that period, there was a deep-seated disillusionment with overly rigid systems, which the classificatory approach seemed to represent. This can be seen in the decline of encyclopedic survey lectures, a pattern which contrasts sharply with the patterns of university enrollment overall (see figure 8).

Yet, in contrast to the French Revolutionary years, no coherent alternative to the classificatory approach emerged immediately: there was no coherent body of ideas such as those of Adam Smith that could be assimilated. Moreover, the model of specialized "scientific" research that had spread to other German academic disciplines such as philology, history, and the natural sciences did not really yet take hold in the *Staatswissenschaften*. Instead one finds a period of groping, in which the discourse was no longer delimited by a common system of knowledge, but by a set of unit-ideas, or embodiments, imprecisely defined but rich in connotation. They found expression in such key words or phrases as *social question* or *society, historical method,* or the already familiar *state-as-organism.* Such phrases frequently had uses and connotations outside the academic community and could easily merge with the ideological rhetoric of the right or the left. This is not to say that scholars and intellectuals suddenly renounced their elaborate systematizations in favor of propaganda. On the contrary, they maintained their identity as scholars, committed to the elucidation of complexities and the elaboration of detail—even when they actively participated in other forums of expression such as journalism or parliaments. But the style of elaboration and explication in their scholarship was different from the categorizing impulse of the eighteenth century or the deliberative one of the early nine-

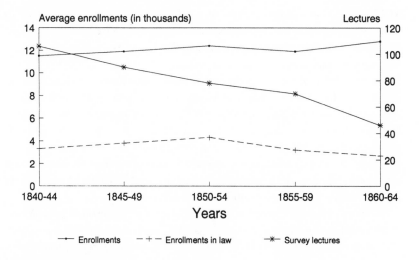

Sources: Titze, ed., Hochschulstudium
(enrollments)--see Table 4;
university catalogues (lectures).

Fig. 8. Enrollments and Survey Lectures, 1840–1865

teenth. Rather than claiming complete coverage of their subjects, the scientists of state of this period tended to proceed associatively, exploring different implications of the basic embodiments. One could say that their organizing principle shifted from the Linnean to the Wagnerian: from enunciation of an articulated order to variation on a few recurring *Leitmotive*. This principle of variation was perhaps appropriate to an age of transition, in which too stable a set of intellectual structures would have misrepresented the shifting political and economic realities of the period. Out of these variations, newly articulated patterns of scholarship and practical engagement eventually emerged, but this happened for the most part after 1866. Thus the quarter century following 1840 can be characterized as a period of transition for the sciences of state as well.

For purposes of presentation, the process will be broken down into two periods: pre- and post-1848.

THE 1840s
Bureaucracy and the Social Question

The decade of the 1840s brought a new air of impatience to German economy, society, politics, and thought. A prominent target of this discontent was the bureaucracy. Indeed, the word became a pejorative term for the first time, as

Mohl pointed out.[1] However reformist in intent, the administrators came to represent intrusiveness, high-handedness, and paternalism to a variety of groups for a variety of reasons. In Baden, the home towns protested the attempts of the bureaucrats to dictate residency requirements; in the Rhineland, industrialists viewed them as tools of the conservative Junkers; in East Prussia, the Junkers saw them as tools of the king. The accession of Fredrick William IV to the Prussian throne raised hopes for a more responsive bureaucracy, but these hopes were short-lived. From all this, there arose a cry for "self-government" and an admiration for British politics as the model to follow.[2] Certainly the antibureaucratic sentiment was an expression of increased popular involvement in politics that accompanied the multiplication of newspapers and the demands for greater political representation.[3]

Naturally, this mood could not help but affect the *Staatswissenschaften*. Many of the established professors found themselves confronted by a new generation. "It is striking," wrote Bruno Hildebrand in his *Economics of the Present and Future* on the eve of the 1848 Revolution, "that the men who are normally regarded as the leading voices in the science of economics, men like Hermann, Rau, Nebenius, are silent . . . and the practical men of the people, who stand in the midst of business life, or the new generation of political literati, have seized the arena."[4] In Saxony, where the impatience with the earlier gradual reformism was clearly felt, it was not Friedrich Bülau, the professor of *Staatswissenschaften*, censor, and editor of the semiofficial newspaper who was the main spokesman of liberalism, but Karl Biedermann, a *Dozent* in philosophy who was forsaking apolitical scholarship for journalism.[5] Another of these literati was of course Karl Marx; rather than rehearse again the familiar story of Marx's development in the 1840s, our task is to show how frequently his ideas were anticipated and echoed by others.

One manifestation of this impatience was a reaction against the liberal economists of the previous generation. The word *school* entered the vocabulary of the sciences of state for the first time—also as a pejorative term to describe the German followers of Adam Smith. The main agent in this was List, whose

1. Mohl, "Über Bureaukratie," 330.
2. Heffter, *Deutsche Selbstverwaltung*, 256–61. On Baden, see also Lee, *Politics of Harmony*, 216–17; on Prussia, Koselleck, *Preussen*, chap. 3.2; and Berdahl, *Politics of Prussian Nobility*, 311–26.
3. Wehler, *Gesellschaftsgeschichte*, 2: 526.
4. Hildebrand, *Nationalökonomie der Gegenwart und Zukunft*, 3. Hildebrand was probably referring to businessmen like David Hanesmann, Gustav Mevissen, and Friedrich Harkort. See Rohr, *Origins of Social Liberalism*, chaps. 3, 5.
5. Bazillion, *Modernizing Germany*, 82–84. On Bülau, see Hennings, "Wirtschaftswissenschaften an der Universität Leipzig," *LNDU*, 144; Stieda, *Nationalökonomie*, 300–2; anon., "Bülau," *ADB*, 3: 512–13.

National System of Political Economy appeared in 1841 and was an immediate success. List argued that the alleged dogmatism and rigidity of academic economics prevented it from serving Germany's national interest, which consisted of developing domestic industry and a protectionist trade policy. List's animus against the academic economists masked a deeper ambivalence towards authority, which led him both to shun the established structure and to seek a secure place within it. Thus despite his sustained polemics against the Smithian economists, List sought to ingratiate himself with Rau in order further to promote his protectionist program.[6] For its part, the establishment did not remain impervious to List's critique: Rau reviewed List's book with his customary scrupulousness and fairness, taking it apart point by point. Rau was the first of a long line of commentators—soon to include Marx—who characterized List's portrayal of the "school" as a caricature.[7] Indeed, a professor at Giessen, Friedrich Schmitthenner, accused List of plagiarism, an attack which played a role in List's suicide in 1846.[8]

In police science, a similar phenomenon occurred in 1845: a disillusioned Hannoverian official named Gustav Zimmermann published *The German Police in the Nineteenth Century,* in which he claimed that "the present textbooks have everything except what one needs in the service." Zimmermann fully exploited the ambiguities of the term *Polizei,* claiming that police in practice was an institution devoted to preserving the state by "observation, prevention, repression, and discovery," rather than by benevolent welfare measures. Yet his book was reviewed favorably in several scholarly books and journals.[9]

Robert von Mohl, who despised Zimmermann's work, nevertheless took a more radical turn himself, announcing in the 1844 preface to his new journal—the *Zeitschrift für die gesamte Staatswissenschaft* (*Journal for the Entire Sciences of State*)—an emphasis on "pauperism, proletariat, organization of labor, association, and commerce among peoples."[10] His subsequent dismissal for criticizing the bureaucracy did not subdue the mood of the faculty, who wrote in a memorandum regarding his replacement, "It lies in the essence of this faculty not only [to convey] knowledge of the prevailing public law, but also the critique of the same from the standpoint of the sciences of state, and not to remove from

6. Fallati to Mohl, 10 Oct. 1842, UB Tübingen, Nachlass Mohl, Md 613. For a similar encounter between List and Mohl, see Mohl, *Lebenserinnerungen,* 2: 8.

7. Rau, review of List's *Nationales System, APO* 5 (1843): 256; Marx, "Über Friedrich Lists Buch," 453; Szporluk, *Communism and Nationalism,* 135.

8. Friedrich Lenz, *List,* 340.

9. Zimmermann, *Deutsche Polizei,* 1: 21–22. On reviews, see Lüdtke, "Polizeiverständnis preussicher Polizeihandbücher," 337; Brater, "Neueren Bearbeitungen der Polizeiwissenschaft," 78.

10. Mohl, "Vorwort," *ZGS,* 1: 6.

view the indications of its possible improvements."[11] Mohl's friend and colleague, Fallati, who remained, was an even more self-consciously political professor.[12]

In Prussia, the policies of the new king also affected the sciences of state. The new minister of culture was Eichhorn, the historical jurist. He sought to remove the influence of the Hegelians from the universities, and appointed to Hegel's old chair the conservative Friedrich Julius Stahl. Stahl's philosophy of law allowed at least for an accommodation with the liberal viewpoint. He accepted the concept of the *Rechtstaat* and the limitation of the state's powers over the individual, but his indifference to economic issues limited his effectiveness in the 1840s.[13] More spectacular was Eichhorn's rehabilitation of professors who had lost their positions in the previous years—among them Dahlmann. His appointment to the long-vacant professorship at Bonn was regarded as atonement for the injustice of the Göttingen Seven affair. When Dahlmann arrived at Bonn by steamboat, "the ship's cannon thundered as with a reception of a prince."[14] However, Eichhorn's high-handed policy of regulating the universities too minutely led to protests, and he soon succeeded in alienating his potential supporters.[15]

The political atmosphere manifested itself in the revived interest in state law and politics (for the latter, see figure 3). Ever since the appearance of the *Staatslexikon* in 1834, there had been a tendency to question the applicability of the historical school of law to this area and to return to the timeless principles of natural law.[16] At Bonn, Dahlmann's main passions continued to be history and politics: his next two publications were histories of the British and French Revolutions. His younger colleagues, Heinrich von Sybel at Bonn and Johann Gustav Droysen at Kiel, combined liberalism with an emphasis on national unification, following Dahlmann's example in bringing history together with current political concerns.[17]

In the 1840s, however, the national question was equaled in public atten-

11. Staatswirtschaftliche Fakultät, 6 July 1846, UA Tübingen, 127/34, 1 (1835–72): no. 6 (Helferich).

12. Sieber, "Politische Professor," 293. Fallati rejected the idea of Wilhelm Roscher's coming to Göttingen, because he was Dahlmann's replacement after the Göttingen Seven incident (ibid., 287).

13. Berdahl, *Politics of Prussian Nobility,* 367, 373.

14. Bezold, *Rheinischen Friedrich-Wilhelms-Universität,* 357.

15. Ibid., 359; Max Lenz, *Friedrich-Wilhelms-Universität,* 2.2: 103–4. See also Paulsen, *Geschichte des gelehrten Unterrichts,* 2: 461–73.

16. Siemann, *Frankfurter Nationalversammlung,* 42–43.

17. Gooch, *History and Historians,* chap. 8; Jörn Rüsen, "Johann Gustav Droysen," *DH,* 2: 7; Hellmut Seier, "Heinrich von Sybel," ibid., 2: 25. Seier states incorrectly that Gervinus and Droysen lectured both on politics and history (33).

tion—if not overshadowed—by the social question: the problem of poverty and the threat of a revolutionary proletariat. Marx was not exaggerating when he claimed that the specter of such a worker's uprising was haunting Europe, nor were Marx and Engels alone in their thinking. The number of publications on the social question increased dramatically in the early 1840s, and the need for programs to help the poor was widely recognized.[18] "Nothing is more conservative than the principle of reform, and nothing abets revolutionary efforts more than blindly holding fast to the old," according to the *Deutsche Vierteljahrs Schrift* in 1844.[19] Rau wrote to Mohl in 1844, "It is odd that these days this part of our science becomes the fashion."[20] Many entrepreneurs recognized the danger and, far from holding to a mindless laissez-faire, advocated savings and credit programs for the workers.[21] Frederick William IV of Prussia advocated a lay order of social helpers—derisively called the "swan order" by some. Although it never was established, it did lead indirectly to the founding of the Central Organization for the Welfare of the Working Classes in Berlin in 1844, which the king generously supported. This was to be a coordinating organization for various charitable societies. The founders included eleven entrepreneurs and eight higher officials.[22] In Baden, a professor of law and sciences of state at Freiburg, Franz Josef Buss, drew initial attention to the social question in the diet in 1837, in a speech lifted almost verbatim from Mohl's article of two years before.[23] Buss was active in formulating a Catholic response to the problem, which led to its own network of charitable organizations.[24]

The awareness of the social question led mainstream academics to take socialism seriously as an expression of a genuine need. The principal mediators in this process were Lorenz Stein and Bruno Hildebrand. Both began their academic careers in the 1840s and went on to achieve fame in the subsequent quarter century. Stein was born in Schleswig-Holstein in 1815, the illegitimate son of an army officer. He studied law in Kiel, Jena, and Berlin, and came in contact with the left Hegelians through Arnold Ruge.[25] Two years in advance of Marx, he went to Paris, not as a political exile but on a royal Danish scholarship. There he wrote the book that was to gain him national attention, *The Socialism and Communism of Contemporary France* (1842). In addition to a historical

18. Reulecke,"Anfänge der organisierten Sozialreform," 22–23.

19. "Pauperismus und dessen Bekämpfung," *Deutsche Vierteljahrs Schrift* 1844, 3.Heft, 323, quoted in Reulecke, "Anfänge der organisierten Sozialreform," 23.

20. Rau to Mohl, 10 Sept. 1844, UB Tübingen, Nachlass R. v. Mohl, Md 613. Rau had seen the conditions himself in a visit to Münster.

21. Heffter, *Deutsche Selbstverwaltung*, 276; Rohr, *Origins of Social Liberalism*, 98, chap. 5.

22. Reulecke, "Anfänge der organisierten Sozialreform," 28–30.

23. Angermann, *Mohl*, 312; Rohr, *Origins of Social Liberalism*, 160.

24. Dornreich, *Badische Politiker,* 82, 108, 123.

25. Werner Schmidt, *Stein*, 25–29, 144–49.

sketch of the rise of the principle of equality during the French Revolution, and a detailed portrayal of the ideas of St.-Simon, Fourier, Proudhon, Louis Blanc, and others, Stein predicted that such principles and movements would come to Germany before long.[26] He couched their significance in terms of the rise of the industrial proletariat, which was distinct from other varieties of paupers by virtue of its labor power.[27] Moreover, the proletariat had a dialectical role to play in the history of civilization, which was approaching a crucial impasse. The West had developed a set of self-contradictory values, embracing the universal idea of personal worth on the one hand and the selfish attachment to private property on the other. The new consciousness of the proletariat would be the means for overcoming this contradiction:

> The question whether there can be a reconciliation between the idea of absolute personality and personal property begins to become clear to the non-possessing mass of the people, and gradually there emerges in them the ever growing part that answers it with a fanatical *no*.[28]

Whereas the French Revolution was a movement of the people against the state, the coming revolution would be a movement of a class against society.[29] This revolution would assume different forms in different countries, depending on their national character: in France, it was taking place in the material realm, while in Germany it was transmuted into ethical and philosophical ideas.[30]

In all these respects, Stein was typical of the left Hegelians' mode of basing a philosophy of history on human agency rather than divine spirit; in these respects also he may be said to have anticipated Marx.[31] But the conclusions he drew were those of a "bourgeois socialist." The future held the prospect of reconciliation through the state:

> In this idea of the state, the personality is not cancelled [*aufgehoben*], but only its standing alone. [Only] in this unity of all individuals can the latter attain its true perfection.[32]

This commitment to the state as the unity of opposites made it possible for Stein to write for newspapers that were banned by the Prussian government

26. Stein, *Socialismus und Communismus*, iv.
27. Ibid., 13.
28. Ibid., 28.
29. Ibid., iii.
30. Ibid., 135–36.
31. Marx's notebooks that have been published to date do not contain notes on Stein; Engels had a few uncomplimentary references to him but did not subject Stein's work to any extensive critique. In *The German Ideology*, Marx and Engels quoted Stein's work frequently to show how Karl Grün had derived his ideas on St. Simon from Stein rather than from the original. See Marx and Engels, *Marx-Engels Werke*, 3: 480–99. See also Blasius and Pankoke, *Stein*, 34.
32. Stein, *Socialismus und Communismus*, 117.

(such as Marx's own *Rheinische Zeitung*) and simultaneously serve as a secret agent for the Prussian government while in Paris.[33] Stein's esteem for the state also suited him to a career in the *Staatswissenschaften:* in 1843, he published an article on the need for training in the sciences of state in Schleswig-Holstein; in the same year, he came to Kiel as a *Privatdozent* in law and was named extraordinary professor of *Staatswissenschaft* in 1846.[34]

Stein brought with him a neo-Hegelian perspective on the sciences of state: they were to be studied in connection with law and philosophy.[35] This commitment did not prevent him from making an important break with past tradition: he announced the need for a science of society intended to complement the sciences of state and to understand the revolution of the future, for in the future society would shape the state rather than vice versa.[36] Although far from fully worked out, the notion of a new science of society was to provide a rallying point for a number of diverse thinkers in the 1850s and 60s.

While Stein made room for socialism in the sciences of state, Hildebrand assimilated it within the narrower framework of economics. Hildebrand approximated the archetype of the political professor of the 1840s: a participant in the Hambach festival as a student, he began his academic career as a historian but switched to economics. A study trip to England in 1846 took him to the meetings of the Communist League there, and the newspapers he brought back with him were sufficient to get him arrested and dismissed from his professorship at Marburg.[37] It was in these circumstances that he wrote *The Economics of the Present and Future*, which appeared in 1848. As Hildebrand played a prominent role in the events of that year, the book had an appreciable impact.[38]

Like Stein, Hildebrand heralded a reform of the discipline: the work was to be the first in a series which would establish economics as a historical science based on the laws of development of peoples.[39] As with Stein's social science, this notion of a new historical economics was little more than a phrase: the other volumes never appeared, and there was scarcely a trace of history in the

33. Blasius and Pankoke, *Stein*, 23, 28.

34. Schmidt, *Stein*, 33–35, 150–57. Stein petitioned for the position in 1844 but was refused twice, once—ostensibly—for budgetary reasons, once because of his dubious politics. Stein had lectured on German state law and philosophy of law, which appeared risky as the movement for independence of Schleswig and Holstein gained momentum in the 1840s (156).

35. Ibid., 28, 77–79. Stein originally petitioned for a position in public law and sciences of state (150). Nevertheless, the synthesis of these disciplines could not take place in the same way as Hegel's (28).

36. Stein, *Socialismus und Communismus*, v, 446–47.

37. Eisermann, *Grundlagen des Historismus*, 160–63; Hildebrand, *Nationalökonomie der Gegenwart und Zukunft*, vi–vii.

38. Eisermann, *Grundlagen des Historismus*, 163–64.

39. Hildebrand, *Nationalökonomie der Gegenwart und Zukunft*, v.

book itself. Hildebrand had a more immediate agenda: a critique of the existing theories of economics. Hildebrand dealt with Smith, Müller, List, and the socialist theories; the latter occupied over half the book. He devoted special attention to Engels's *The Condition of the Working Classes in England* and to the writings of Proudhon. Hildebrand was much less of an apologist for socialism than Stein, but he did acknowledge its role in unmasking the contingency of Smithian economics. He concluded that each economic system is a product of a certain stage of development—a point already implicit in Stein's work and explicit in Marx's dialectical materialism.[40] Hildebrand's positive convictions were nationalistic: it was up to the moral energy of each individual people to solve its economic problems in its own way.[41]

Meanwhile, Thünen was contemplating the turbulent 1840s from the relative seclusion of his Mecklenburg estate. He was moved to write a second volume to *The Isolated State* that analyzed the central variables of economic theory—capital, rent, interest, and wages—within the framework of the social question. The 278-page discussion centered on the question, "Is the small wage, which the normal handworker earns almost everywhere, a natural wage, or does it arise through usurpation which the worker cannot evade?"[42] Not the experience of history, but the tools of reason would deliver the answer.[43] From a quantitative treatment of these variables, Thünen concluded that the natural wage of labor was not a function of its supply and demand, but of the worker's subsistence and productivity—in other words, his or her use-value as opposed to exchange value.[44] When the goods which workers produced were in the hands of the capitalist rather than their own, Thünen concluded, then wages could be kept artifically low. "In the separation of the worker from his product lies the root of the evil," he wrote.[45] His remedy was for capitalist economics to incorporate the principle of socialism through schemes such as profit-sharing, which he actually applied at his estate in Tellow.[46]

At the same time, on an estate in neighboring Pomerania, another independent landowner-scholar was beginning to ruminate on economics and the so-

40. Ibid., 275, 282, 325–26.
41. Ibid., 94, 282.
42. Thünen, *Isolierte Staat*, 435.
43. Ibid., 440.
44. Ibid., 475–77; 549–50. Specifically, Thünen derived the formula that the "natural" (i.e., optimum) wage was given by $\sqrt{ap}$, where a was the quantity of goods necessary to keep a worker alive, and p was the quantity of goods he or she produced that exceeded the cost of subsistence. Thünen derived this formula in several different ways, altering each variable one at a time while holding the others constant.
45. Ibid., 598–600.
46. Ibid., 583–84, 604 ff.

cial question: Johann Karl Rodbertus. Although Rodbertus had studied law and economics at Göttingen, Berlin, and Heidelberg, his thinking was far removed from the deliberative style of the academic sciences of state. He preferred to proceed axiomatically. This drew him to Ricardo, and he was one of the few Germans to accept the labor theory of value as his starting point.[47] Through a series of ingenious deductions concerning the relations of wages, profits, and rent—pitched at a high level of abstraction—he convinced himself that the fundamental cause of the poverty and commercial crises of his day was the declining share of wages in the total national income under free market conditions.[48] He viewed capitalism as a transitory stage to socialism, although this would not occur in the immediate future.[49] Meanwhile, the state could take steps to ameliorate the situation by regulating wages and working hours.[50] In advocating eventual "state socialism" as an alternative to revolution, Rodbertus reached the same conclusion as Stein, though by a very different route. Although he took pains to buttress his arguments with empirical and historical data, he seemed most comfortable when arguing at length with other theoreticians in print. As a result, his writings were not widely read; it was only in the 1870s that he became recognized as an important thinker—thanks to the attention of the socialist Ferdinand Lassalle and the conservative reformer Adolph Wagner.

The Concern with Stages of Economic Growth

If the interest in socialism and the call for a social science were variations on the theme of the social question, they were also closely linked to an interest in history as a series of lawful stages. As we noted in the cases of Stein and Hildebrand (not to mention Marx and Engels), their sympathy for socialism engendered an awareness of the ideological aspect of economic theories and raised the possibility that laissez-faire doctrine was thereby the expression of a particular class at a particular stage of history. It was this insight into the relativity of beliefs and institutions that was perceived at the time as shared, under a very different ideological banner, with the historical school of law. This in turn gave

47. Rodbertus, "Erkenntnis unserer staatswirtschaftlichen Zustände," 41–102. The French socialists also played an important formative role in Rodbertus's thought. See Gide and Rist, *History of Economic Doctrines*, 415.

48. Rodbertus, "Zweiter und dritter Brief an von Kirchmann," 379. Historians of economic thought are divided on the merits of Rodbertus's arguments. Rist finds his theory "nearer the facts as judged by statistics." See Gide and Rist, *History of Economic Doctrines*, 427; Schumpeter, by contrast, finds it "factually and theoretically equally indefensible" (Schumpeter, *History of Economic Analysis*, 507).

49. Rodbertus, "Zweiter und dritter Brief an von Kirchmann," 671.

50. Stavenhagen, *Geschichte der Wirtschaftstheorie*, 60.

rise to the perception that a historical school also developed in economics in the 1840s.

As far as the first generation of this "school" is concerned (customarily including Wilhelm Roscher, Hildebrand, and Karl Knies), the label is more misleading than helpful. The figures involved no more constituted a school than did the targets of List's polemic: they neither collaborated in disseminating their ideas nor shared a commonality of viewpoint on what was meant by historical method.[51] Nor did they have a monopoly on a historical approach to economics or on a concern with laws of development.[52] The phrase *historical method* signified an embodiment rather than a school, expressing a generalized awareness of the historical contingency of one's own time. One of the principal variations associated with it was the notion of stages. For this generation, the new interest in historical stages expressed an appreciation of the epochal nature of the changes that were taking place in Europe before their eyes and which today go by the general label of modernization. The combination of growing nationalism and industrial development during the period reinforced this interest in stages, for it raised in the same breath the questions of the role of economics as ideology and of the comparative economic growth of different nations. Once again, the case of Marx and Engels is an obvious illustration that does not need elaboration here.

Admittedly, the notion of economic development by stages was far from original. Such schemas had also played a prominent role in the eighteenth century—Smith had entitled Book 3 of the *Wealth of Nations* "Of the Different Progress of Opulence in Different Nations."[53] He had postulated there a natural progression from agriculture to manufacturing to commerce; elsewhere in the work he also referred to hunting and shepherding as two more primitive states.[54] But this approach had become submerged in the nineteenth century both by Ricardian analysis and German classification. True, the notion that different nations developed in similar stages at different times could not completely escape the scientists of state—particularly the followers of Hegel, or those who emphasized comparative empirical studies, such as the much-

51. Bruch, "Zur Historisierung der Staatswissenschaften," 135–36; Schumpeter, *History of Economic Analysis*, 507; for further elaboration, see Lindenfeld, "Myth of the Older Historical School."

52. Other writers of the 1840s who shared this interest were Johann Friedrich Eiselen at Halle (*Lehre von der Volkswirtschaft . . . in ihrer Besonderen Entwicklung*, 1843), and Karl W. C. Schüz at Tübingen ("Das politische Moment in der Volkswirtschaft," 1844).

53. Meek, *Social Science and the Ignoble Savage*, esp. 109–25 on Smith's early moral philosophy, and 219–22 on economics.

54. Adam Smith, *Wealth of Nations*, 1: 405; 2: 213. According to Smith, this natural order was distorted in medieval Europe by the rise of cities, which emphasized commerce to the detriment of agriculture (405–6). In his discussion, however, Smith treated manufacturing and commerce as one (433).

maligned Pölitz,[55] but it was not until the 1840s that it became the focus of attention. When it did so, the threefold classification of agriculture, manufacture, and commerce provided ready-made categories for the stages.

This was in part the significance of List's *National System*. It is most famous for having advocated a protectionist tariff policy to promote domestic manufacturing and thereby giving economic expression to nationalism. List had already espoused such policies by 1820; according to his own account, he developed the notion of stages while in America.[56] It is nonetheless difficult to trace the specific influences that shaped List's thinking, since he drew on so many sources, from Charles Dupin to Alexander Hamilton to Schlözer and Soden.[57] Only the lack of influence of Adam Müller and the romantics has been well established.[58] Suffice it to say that many of List's ideas sound familiar to anyone who knows the cameralist tradition: the notion of "productive forces" as being the true sources of wealth, including people's mental capacities as well as their labor or capital, or the importance of the state in formulating sound economic policy (which List identified with police science).[59] List's contribution was to concretize these ideas in a new way: in the context of the specific historical situations of different nations. He thus began the book with a survey of the economic history of nine countries. His conclusion was similar to the ideological critique of Marx: that economic doctrines and policies are themselves expressions of collective material interests and situations and must be interpreted as such. In List's case, however, the actors were nations rather than classes.[60]

The type of economics appropriate to a given nation depended more specifically, according to List, on the stage of economic development that nation had reached. List's stages represented a combination of the older four-stage theory and the threefold classification: "hunting stage, pastoral stage, agricultural stage, agricultural-manufacturing stage, agricultural-manufacturing-commercial stage."[61] List's distinctive contribution was the clear delineation of how, in the last three stages, each new activity had a retroactive influence upon the others. Thus, for example, a nation that remained at the agricultural stage

55. Pölitz, *Staatswissenschaften*, 2: 146. For other examples, see Winkel, *Deutsche Nationalökonomie*, 89–92. The tendency to criticize Pölitz as superficial was a good indication of the sea change that occurred after 1840. See Roscher, *Geschichte der Nationalökonomik*, 841–43; Lippert, "Pölitz," *HDS*, 5: 157.

56. List, *Nationales System*, xi, xvii. For a biographical account, see Henderson, *List*, 48, 154–55.

57. On Dupin, see List, *Schriften*, 4: 56–57; on Hamilton, see Henderson, *List*, 155; on Soden, F. Lenz, *List*, 24–25, and his "Friedrich List und der Liberalismus." 419.

58. List, *Schriften*, 4: 54.

59. List, *Nationales System*, xxxviii. See also F. Lenz, *List's Staats-und Gesellschaftslehre*, chap. 1. Szporluk neglects these cameralist roots.

60. List, *Nationales System*, 132.

61. List, *Nationales System*, 13.

when experiencing a growth in population was condemned to provincialism and poverty. Only the mobilization of productive powers through manufacturing would improve agricultural productivity. Likewise, manufacturing interests were to be distinguished from commercial interests. According to List, England achieved her dominance in trade because of her achievements in the arts, sciences, and manufacturing, not vice versa.[62] List distrusted an overdeveloped commercial economy if it was not based on sound agriculture and manufacturing. It discouraged well-rounded national development by making one country the exclusive source of raw materials or manufactured goods for others. This was misplaced cosmopolitanism. List concluded,

> Therefore, every nation which values independence and preservation must strive to move as soon as possible from a low cultural state to a higher one, as soon as possible to unite agriculture, manufactures, shipping and commerce in its own territory.[63]

Only England had thus far achieved this integration and could thus afford the "cosmopolitan" ideology of free trade; only when all nations which were capable of reaching this stage had done so could they move from a "political" economy to a "cosmopolitan" one (List believed that only nations in the temperate zone were so capable, and that tropical nations were condemned to dependence on those in the temperate zone).

In 1843, a textbook appeared which propounded a theory of stages: Wilhelm Roscher's *Outline of Lectures on Political Economy by the Historical Method*. The book, which invoked the method of Savigny and Eichhorn as its model, is generally heralded as marking the beginning of the historical school, which set German economic thought apart from the classical mainstream. In Roscher's case, the approach to history grew out of his association with Göttingen, where the combination of history and sciences of state had already been established by Schlözer and Sartorius.[64] The son of a Hannoverian official, Roscher studied in Göttingen from 1835 to 1838 under Heeren, Dahlmann, and Georg Gervinus. His early focus was on political history rather than economics or the sciences of state: he traveled to Berlin to attend Ranke's seminar, and his first publication was on Thucydides. But by the time he returned to Göttingen in 1840 as a *Privatdozent* in history and the sciences of state—in effect to replace Dahlmann—he had already resolved to concentrate on economics. Evidently,

---

62. Ibid., 69, 295; Szporluk, *Communism and Nationalism*, 141.

63. List, *Nationales System*, 13.

64. Schmoller noted this in 1888. See his *Litteraturgeschichte der Staats-und Sozialwissenschaften*, 151–52.

he had originally intended to lecture on history as well, but gave up this idea in 1843.[65] He stated his project clearly in the preface to his textbook:

> The question of how best to further national wealth is admittedly also a major question for us; but it is by no means our authentic goal. Political economy is not merely a chrematistics, an art of becoming rich, but a political science, where it is a matter of judging people and controlling people. Our goal is to depict what peoples have thought, willed, and sensed in economic matters, what they have sought and attained, why they have sought it and why they have attained it. Such a depiction is only possible in the closest alliance with the other sciences of the life of peoples, particularly of legal, political, and cultural history.[66]

The means to this end of putting economics in human context was to understand how it developed. Ideas in the abstract meant little divorced from the political reality which they mirrored.[67] This reality had a lawfulness given in the theory of stages. "The difficulty of discovering the essential and the lawful in the great mass of phenomena," he wrote, "requires us urgently to compare all peoples . . . with one another."[68] Roscher presented this comparative approach as similar to that of the natural scientist, as doing for the human sciences what histology and zoochemistry had done for natural history.[69]

This version of historical method was clearly far removed from Ranke's critique of sources and had little in common with the Savigny-Eichhorn approach, despite Roscher's reference to it.[70] In the same passage, he also invoked Malthus and Rau—as opposed to Ricardo—and in a letter to Gervinus also mentioned Smith as model. According to Roscher, it was Gervinus himself who provided him with the idea of argument by comparative analogy from one culture to another.[71]

If Gervinus provided the strategy, cameralism and Smithian economics provided the categories. Roscher organized his text and his lectures according to the scheme established by Rau.[72] Beginning with the abstract categories of pro-

---

65. Roscher to Gervinus, 5 June 1840, quoted in Gottfried Eisermann, *Grundlagen des Historismus*, 130; Roscher to Cabinettsrath [Hoppenstadt], 13 March 1843, UA Göttingen, P.A 4 V b 113 Roscher.

66. Roscher, *Grundriss*, iv.

67. Ibid., 1.

68. Ibid., iv.

69. Ibid., v, 2.

70. It is true that recent scholarship on Savigny has stressed the metaphysical and naturalistic assumptions underlying the historical school of law, which were similar to Roscher's view. Böckenförde, *State, Society and Liberty*, 7–11, esp. n. 32. Nevertheless, one finds even in Savigny's systematic works a far greater degree of attention to the sources than in Roscher.

71. Roscher, *Grundriss*, v; Eisermann, *Grundlagen des Historismus*, 130, 136.

72. See Schmoller, *Litteraturgeschichte*, 153–54.

duction, distribution, and consumption of goods, he proceeded to the cameralist threefold classification of agriculture, manufacturing, and commerce, to which he added a section on population; public finance followed, as usual. The historical dimension in all of this consisted of two strategies. First, he simply inserted sections on the history of a particular concept or doctrine in the appropriate section of theoretical or practical economics (as in price theory, for example). The results were often forced and artificial for theoretical economics—"historical sauce on a classical dish," in the words of one commentator.[73] Second, Roscher sometimes treated the categories themselves as chronologically successive stages. This worked best with the threefold classification, which he genuinely transformed. Thus agriculture became a chronological treatment from primitive farming through the three-field system to the abolition of feudal dues; manufacturing went from the rise of medieval towns to the dissolution of guild monopolies; commerce also traversed the period from the middle ages to current banking policy. In finance, the three types of income—domains, regalia, and taxes—lent themselves nicely to treatment as successive stages.

Although Roscher's system was clearly derived from the cameralist classificatory system, he did not forget the ties to the sciences of state that had been strong in his youth. He continued to hold that economics was a part of political science, which portrayed the laws of development of the state in general; he published his *Politics: Historical Natural Theory of Monarchy, Aristocracy, and Democracy* in 1892, based on lectures he had given since the 1840s.[74]

Roscher's developmental schemes fell far short of their promise as objective cross-cultural comparisions, much less as detailed historical-empirical research. In their Whiggishness and all-inclusiveness, they were akin to the schemes of Comte in France and Spencer in England of the same era. Yet Roscher did open up a wider horizon to his students than Rau had provided.[75] His ability to integrate the appeal to change with the classificatory tradition undoubtedly accounted for his success in the ensuing years.

In sum, the 1840s was a decade of innovativeness within the sciences of state. The commitment to comprehensive systems diminished, but did not die out completely. Marx and Engels, Stein, and Roscher all presented sketches of works they were later to elaborate (as did Richard Wagner in another medium with his outline of the *Ring of the Nibelungen*). In each case, systematizing meant accounting for change rather than static classification. For Marx and Engels

73. The commentator was Robert Wilbrandt, quoted in Bruch, "Historisierung," 136; cf. Schmoller, *Litteraturgeschichte*, 157.

74. Roscher, *Naturgeschichte der Monarchie, Aristokatie, Demokratie* (1892). On his early definition, see *Grundriss*, 4.

75. Schmoller, *Litteraturgeschichte*, 154.

and for Stein, it was Hegelian philosophy which provided the necessary infusion of vitality; for Roscher, it was a loose invocation of historical and scientific method. In these ways the sciences of state drew allusively from the main currents of German intellectual history of the previous period. The experiences of revolution from 1848 to 1850 were to give these ideas a more definite coloring in the years that followed.

1848 AND AFTER: INSTITUTIONS AND ACTORS

The cliché that the Frankfurt Assembly of 1848–49 was a "parliament of professors" has long since been refuted in terms of the occupational makeup of that body: of 812 members, only 49 were university professors. The assembly included 56 businessmen and 20 writers and journalists, some of whom also played prominent roles both as speakers and in the provisional government; nevertheless, the assembly did have a predominance of officials and other highly educated men: 600 had attended university, 491 of them in law.[76] Thus we may assume that many had been exposed to the sciences of state as part of their training.

Although outnumbered by jurists and historians, the *Staatswissenschaftler* played a conspicuous role, as might be expected. Dahlmann had prepared a preliminary draft of a constitution which was widely discussed in the press and had drawn the attention of King Maximilian of Bavaria, Frederick William of Prussia, and Prince Albert of England among others.[77] Mohl drafted the rules of procedure; later he was named minister of justice in the provisional government. Fallati, who had been a prominent figure in the early days of the revolution in Tübingen, served in the provisional ministry of trade, handling consular affairs and statistical projects. Hermann was twice elected second vice president of the assembly and served with Fallati and Hildebrand on the economic committee. Hermann's student, Wilhelm Stahl (brother of the Berlin law professor) was also a prominent speaker on this committee.[78] The very conspicu-

---

76. Siemann, *Deutsche Revolution*, 126. The notion of the "parliament of professors" dates back to the Revolution itself, an expression of the disillusionment of the left. In the 1850s, writers such as Biedermann and Rochau attributed the failure of the parliament to its excessively theoretical orientation, thus reinforcing the legend. See Lees, *Revolution and Reflection*, 79. Lees uses the label "intelligentsia" to describe the assembly; this is misleading in that it usually implies a group whose primary loyalty is to ideas and ideals. Most of the educated representatives at Frankfurt were employees of the state with considerable experience in administration. See Noyes, *Organization and Revolution*, 224–25.

77. Springer, *Dahlmann*, 2: 224–26.

78. E. R. Huber, *Verfassungsgeschichte*, 2: 768–69; Eyck, *Frankfurt Parliament*, 102; Mohl, *Lebenserinnerungen* 2: 31, 59, 73, 93; Wernitz, "Hermann," 31. Other prominent *Staatswissenschaftler* included Raumer from Berlin, Johann Tellkampf of Breslau, and Friedrich Wilhelm Schubert of Königsberg.

ousness of these men made them easy targets for the resentments of groups who disagreed with them.[79]

Was the failure of the Frankfurt parliament a failure of practical imagination of the kind described in these pages? Certainly the collapse of the revolution was due to a variety of factors, many beyond the control of the assembly. The sheer number and complexity of tasks that the revolutionaries faced was part of it: establishing national boundaries, placating ethnic minorities, dealing with foreign powers, maintaining authority vis-à-vis the individual states and their princes, addressing the social and economic grievances of the lower classes, establishing church-state relations—all in addition to writing a constitution. By establishing a provisional government, the Frankfurt parliament was drawn into all these conflicts; in some of these areas, particularly foreign affairs, it had little experience and less power. Dahlmann's actions during the Schleswig-Holstein crisis were central in establishing the perception of professorial incompetence.[80] Mohl, as provisional minister of justice, was energetic in suppressing the Frankfurt riots that accompanied the crisis, but at great cost to his nerves. "I realized daily more and more," he confessed, "that I was a theoretician and a doctrinaire, but not a competent statesman."[81]

On matters such as constitutional law or economic and social legislation, where the *Staatswissenschaftler* possessed some expertise, the record is more positive. True, the assembly failed to address some central questions, such as ministerial responsibility: that issue became a lightning-rod for significant ideological differences between monarchists and republicans, and was never satisfactorily resolved.[82] Out of this impasse came the famous conservative *Lückentheorie*, which held that interpreting the scope of ministerial actions was up to the government rather than parliament when the constitution was silent.[83] As is well known, Bismarck was to make effective use of this theory thirteen years later. On the whole, however, the Frankfurt constitution represented a logical and workable extension of the monarchical constitutions that had arisen in Germany since the

---

79. Beseler, *Erlebtes*, 62; Heinrich Laube, *Das erste deutsche Parlament*, 214–19. Laube, a poet of the Young Germany movement, found Hermann an easy target of satire: "An oldish man with quite old-fashioned demeanor and facial features . . . a big head with a big nose, as if made of sandstone, [he] had always looked down at the assembly with an angry expression. The majority of the house looked at him with deepest mistrust" (216).

80. Eyck, *Frankfurt Parliament*, 296; Springer, *Dahlmann*, 2: 286–88.

81. Mohl, *Lebenserinnerungen*, 2: 99. See also Siemann, *Deutsche Revolution*, 134. One of Mohl's mistakes was to order the closing of all gambling casinos in Germany—a favorite bugbear of *Polizeiwissenschaft*—an order which proved to be unpopular. See Angermann, *Mohl*, 67–68; Valentin, *Geschichte der deutschen Revolution*, 2: 323–24; Schneider, *Wirtschafts-und Sozialpolitik*, 150–54.

82. Pflanze, "Juridical and Political Responsibility," 162–82.

83. Ibid., 179. Pflanze also discusses the fate of the provisions of the Prussian constitution on ministerial responsibility (169–70).

Congress of Vienna. It did not reduce the monarch to a mere figurehead, but at the same time it opened the door to increased parliamentary power—and thus embodied the ideals of the practically oriented reformist bureaucracy.[84]

With respect to social and economic issues, the criticism of the Frankfurt parliament as being impractical is even less well founded: the representatives worked through tough issues rather than avoiding them. In this connection it is important to note that the parliamentarians saw the constitutional and economic issues as closely intertwined. When the law professor Georg Beseler of the constitutional committee argued for putting the debate on basic rights ahead of the constitution, it was in part to address "the great social movement which has gripped all of Germany."[85] And Friedrich von Rönne, chair of the economic committee, legitimated his committee's charge in similar fashion: the solution to the social question lay in the creation of favorable market conditions through the political and economic unity which a constitution would provide—rather than in enacting special provisions to protect the workers or the disadvantaged. The economic committee submitted no less than forty amendments to the drafts of basic rights and was seen as a rival to the constitutional committee.[86] There was basic agreement, however, on the need for greater uniformity of shipping on inland waterways, of railroads, customs duties, patents, post, and telegraph.

An issue which exemplified the intertwining of political and economic considerations was that of the right of citizenship and freedom of movement among the German states. It was fraught with complications. Everyone was aware that freedom of movement and the right to take up a trade were essential to a free market economy, but that dictating this principle to local communities infringed on their self-government. Moreover, it was recognized by now that local autonomy frequently meant the restriction of poor relief to local residents. The issue was linked to that of a uniform business code. The debate was thus many-sided and prolonged, crossing lines of faction.[87] Proponents as well as opponents of unrestricted freedom of movement appealed to the specter of poverty. Most of the leading *Staatswissenschaftler*, with the exception of Hildebrand, opposed a uniform code.[88] Hermann was one of its most vociferous

84. See Böckenförde, *State, Society and Liberty*, 87–114, esp. 111. Böckenförde examines the position held by Huber that German constitutional monarchy represented a distinctive type of government as opposed to a transitional form leading to democracy—and rejects it.

85. Wigard, ed. *Stenographischer Bericht*, 1: 700–701. Beseler later admitted in his memoirs that the committee did not always find the middle ground between securing rights and establishing principles of order, but that the debates on basic rights did lay the foundations for subsequent constitutions, including the Prussian (Beseler, *Erlebtes*, 62–63).

86. Noyes, *Organization and Revolution*, 249; Eyck, *Frankfurt Parliament*, 210; Beseler, *Erlebtes*, 64.

87. Wigard, ed. *Stenographischer Bericht* 1: 727 ff; Eyck, *Frankfurt Parliament*, 218–21; Walker, *Home Towns*, 369–78.

88. Wigard, ed. *Stenographischer Bericht*, 2: 1077–82.

opponents, arguing that the assembly should not be too remote from the problems faced by the people, and that conditions varied greatly from one area of the country to another. He urged instead that the assembly should issue general guidelines for residency rights rather than strict uniformity; the right to decide who votes in local affairs, for example, should remain with local governments.[89] Mohl moved that freedom of movement be restricted to those who were capable of supporting themselves.[90] In the end, however, the motion for an unrestricted freedom of movement passed by a close vote of 224–193; an amendment to adopt a uniform business code (*Gewerbeordnung*) for the Reich passed by an even narrower margin of two votes (244–242).

The events of 1848 caught liberal opinion in a process of transition on social and economic issues. It was moving away from the notion of a benevolent police state towards that of laissez-faire—a shift which at the same time narrowed the basis of liberal support among the lower classes. But the *Staatswissenschaftler* as a group did not partake of this trend to the same extent as did their former pupils. If, as Mack Walker has suggested, the majority in the assembly was ahead of its time, anticipating an industrialized society which had not yet emerged, the *Staatswissenschaftler* tended to be in touch with their time, recognizing the plight of the preindustrial workers. The flood of petitions from artisans opposing freedom of movement during the revolution tends to support this assessment. In the decade that followed, the scientists of state were to criticize the assembly for its failure to address the social question more directly.[91]

If the *Staatswissenschaftler* at Frankfurt were in touch with the realities of the moment, they did not long remain so: the rapid pace of industrialization in the 1850s and 1860s swept away the reservations about laissez-faire which they had advanced. The quickening pace of economic and social change also had an impact on the course of politics. The reaction which followed the failure of the revolution was noteworthy for its pragmatism in many respects—the conservatives largely accepted the need for constitutional government—and for its brevity. The "New Era," which was marked by the end of Friedrich Wilhelm IV's rule in Prussia in 1858 and by the unification of Italy in 1859, witnessed the resurgence of a confident liberalism which was more wary of bureaucratic intervention than before.[92] Within a few years, the remaining impediments to industrial freedom were removed in one state after another.

After 1848, the role of academic *Staatswissenschaftler* as spokespersons for liberal ideas tended to lose importance. Many of the younger advocates of political and social ideas came from outside academia. One thinks of John Prince-

89. Ibid., 1: 754, 757–58.
90. Ibid., 2: 875–76.
91. Lees, *Revolution and Reflection*, 94–103. See Walker, *Home Towns*, 384.
92. On this attitude, see Sheehan, *German Liberalism*, 109; Lees, *Revolution and Reflection*, 76.

Smith, the leader of the German Manchesterites, or Hermann Schulze-Delitzsch, the promoter of cooperative associations, or August Ludwig von Rochau, the coiner of the phrase *Realpolitik*, or Ferdinand Lassalle, the founder of the German Workingman's Association. Of the political leaders of the new Progressive party, only one, Eugen Richter, had pursued the curriculum in the sciences of state; he found it seriously deficient. Many of these new voices were those of journalists. This was especially true for the founders of the Congress of German Economists, a voluntary association that advocated liberal economic policy, in which journalists far outweighed representatives of business or academics in the leading circles.[93] Whereas scientists of state such as Mohl and Dahlmann had also written for newspapers and periodicals of wider circulation, only during this period could an aspiring professor first make a name for himself in journalism as a stepping-stone to an academic career—as happened in the cases of Albert Schäffle and Wilhelm Heinrich Riehl.

This retreat from engagement on the part of professors—to which there were of course exceptions—cannot be attributed primarily to governmental intimidation, for it was true even after the reaction of the 1850s had run its course. Moreover, there were also numerous academics in other fields who were vociferous enough in their public stands: one has only to think of the Prussian historians Droysen, Sybel, Duncker, Haüsser, and Treitschke. The change within the *Staatswissenschaften* seems rather to be linked to a diminished sense of opportunities within the field itself. Mohl's experience at Heidelberg, for example, proved to be disappointing: he found a reduced clientele compared to his earlier years at Tübingen. As he wrote to his brother Julius in 1852,

> In German state law I have about 90; in an encyclopedia of *Staatswissenschaften* 30; in my nominal subject of administrative law only 12, and those that come are asses, because history is much in the air. There is also not a single German among them, rather Serbs, Belgians, Americans, etc. What [motivates] them to participate is a complete puzzle to me.[94]

The number of law students declined drastically as part of a cyclical pattern in the late 1850s and early 1860s, even as the number of applicants to the bureaucracy remained high.[95]

These negative signs did not mean that the sciences of state were stagnating;

---

93. See Hentschel, *Deutschen Freihändler*, 38; Hamerow, *Social Foundations*, 1: 137. The moving spirit behind the Congress was Viktor Böhmert, editor of the *Bremer Handelsblatt*, who had studied under Roscher but found academic discourse to be sterile (Hentschel, 30). Other journalists who were active in the Congress were Otto Michaelis, Julius Faucher, Otto Wolff, Alexander Mayer, August Lammers, and Heinrich Oppenheim.

94. Mohl to Julius von Mohl, 20 June 1852, quoted in Angermann, *Mohl*, 72.

95. See figure 8. On applicants to the bureaucracy in Prussia, see Gillis, *Prussian Bureaucracy*, 41, 233. On the lack of opportunities, see Wagner, *Gedächtnisrede auf Hans von Mangoldt*, 30.

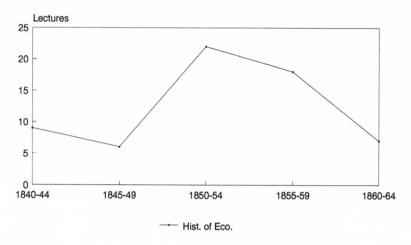

—•— Hist. of Eco.

Source: University catalogues.
See appendix

Fig. 9. Lectures in History of Economic Thought, 1840–1865

on the contrary, they were undergoing a process of intellectual stock-taking and departing from traditional patterns. One symptom was the number of new works in the 1850s and 1860s that contained no citations of other works in the field—a deviation from what had been standard practice since the eighteenth century.[96] There were other signs that the disciplines were becoming increasingly self-conscious of their own workings and history. Mohl's most important work of the period was his three-volume *History and Literature of the Sciences of State* (1855–1858); the number of lectures in the history of economic thought increased sharply (see figure 9). Naturally this reflective process took different forms in different states and institutions; the situation following the 1848 Revolution merits a survey.

In Württemberg, the political economy faculty at Tübingen fell on hard times during the 1850s. Doubtless the role the faculty members had played in fomenting the Revolution was one of the reasons, but other factors did not arise directly from the political situation. Foremost among them was the still-unresolved issue of the proper training for administrators in law. The regulation of 1844 had required candidates for the administrative career track (the *Regiminalisten*) to study *both* a complete law curriculum and the cameralist subjects, so it was not surprising that students turned away. In addition, the faculty was forced to recognize the changes in disciplinary boundaries which rendered

96. These included Lorenz von Stein's *Geschichte der sozialen Bewegungen in Frankreich*, his *System der Staatswissenschaften*, Wilhelm Heinrich Riehl's *Naturgeschichte des deutschen Volkes*, and Albert Schäffle's *Das gesellschaftliche System der menschlichen Wirtschaft*.

their offerings obsolete. Thus the chair of technology was not renewed when its holder died in 1855; Fallati's chair of statistics, political history, and international law also proved impossible to maintain for long after his death in the same year.[97]

It was perhaps more serious that the sense of common purpose within the faculty in the 1840s had been undermined. Finding a successor to Mohl had not been easy; when an appointment was finally made in 1849, it went to a person with very different ideas. This was Johann Helferich, one of the most pivotal and unsung teachers of economics in mid-century. Helferich was a student of Hermann; not himself an original thinker, he had the talent of presenting theoretical ideas so clearly and vividly "that the student assimilated them as self-evident."[98] He was also a great admirer of Thünen and was responsible for disseminating Thünen's ideas through his lectures.[99] Helferich's views on curriculum were incompatible with the encyclopedic survey. When the question of the proper training of administrators was again raised in Württemberg in 1857, Helferich delivered a ringing defense of specialization, in which he stressed *"the unity of Bildung and the mental dexterity of mastering a subject, which only the penetrating study of a single subject from all sides can give."*[100] A student who mastered a subject in this way could then read independently to acquire the technical knowledge needed to pass the state examination. An administrator did not need in-depth technical knowledge, but did have to be conversant with the law. Helferich concluded that the nucleus of administrative study should be law; "economics . . . stood far beneath the legal foundation in logical thoroughness and richness of concepts, despite the progress it has made in both respects."[101] Such a statement was tantamount to heresy in the embattled faculty, and Helferich soon left for Göttingen; he was later to become Hermann's successor in Munich.

In the late 1850s and 1860s, however, the Tübingen faculty underwent something of a revival. The conservative minister of the interior in Württemberg disagreed with Helferich's memo and in 1857 took steps to make the administrative track more attractive. This involved enabling the students to prepare for the law exam through special courses in civil and criminal law within

---

97. Born, *Geschichte der Wirtschaftswissenschaften*, 55–56. His successor, the Prussian political professor Max Duncker, was a popular lecturer, but was soon recalled to Prussia, where his loyalties lay; the next holder, Reinhold Pauli, left because he felt overburdened. On Duncker in Tübingen, see Haym, *Leben Max Dunckers*, chap. 9.

98. Brentano, *Mein Leben*, 40; cf. Knapp, *Eine Jugend*, 174–75. On Helferich's effectiveness as a teacher in Tübingen, see Fallati to Mohl, 20 Feb. 1852, UB Tübingen, Md 613, Nachlass Mohl.

99. On Helferich's virtual idolization of Thünen, see Knapp, *Grundherrschaft und Rittergut*, 140.

100. Special recommendation of Helferich, 22 Oct. 1857 (emphasis in the original), UA Tübingen, 127/59 (Regiminalwissenschaften: Generalia, 1843–1866).

101. Ibid.

the political economy faculty, as well as establishing a separate chair of state law.[102] The contours of the political economy faculty were thereby changed to emphasize the legal rather than the technical and scientific side of the sciences of state. Thus the institution became in effect a faculty of state science. Helferich's replacement, moreover, was someone who agreed to resume Mohl's subjects of politics, police science, and encylopedia in addition to economics: Albert Schäffle.[103] Schäffle also remained a political activist: he was one of the few professors who participated in the Congress of German Economists, not to mention the German Commercial Association and the Württemberg parliament. His main practical concern in the late 1850s and early 1860s was with free trade, but he defended the idea of a *grossdeutsch* customs union with Austria. This helped him eventually gain a professorship in Vienna in 1868.

The postrevolutionary reaction in Bavaria and Baden was milder than elsewhere, partly because of the enlightened character of their respective rulers, King Maximilian II and Duke Friedrich. Both had been students of Dahlmann, and both were committed to upholding their constitutions and the integrity of their parliaments—in Maximilian's case, somewhat against his conservative instincts.[104] The king, however, possessed a keen social conscience and sought to foster economic development through a separate ministry of economics. If this did not live up to expectations, it was probably because they were preempted by the cultural and educational projects that were closer to the King's heart—he once said he would rather have been a professor.[105] Maximilian sought to make Munich the cultural equal of Berlin and Vienna; to this end he pursued an active policy of recruitment of personnel for the universities, bringing them up to date with the latest trends in the humanities and natural sciences. His appointments included Heinrich von Sybel, a student of Ranke in history, and Liebig in chemistry.

In the sciences of state, the king also had his own favorite: the popular writer who had turned cultural historian and ethnographer, Wilhelm Heinrich Riehl. Riehl was the son of a minor functionary in the Rhineland, had studied to become a theologian, but became interested in society and culture through the lectures of Arndt and Dahlmann at Bonn. A gifted and prolific writer, he had made a successful career in journalism before 1848. Like many, he greeted the

102. Memo, Ministry of Churches and Schools, 6 July 1860, ibid.; Born, *Geschichte der Wirtschaftswissenschaften*, 54–55, 58.

103. Ministry to Senate, 6 July 1860, UA Tübingen, 127/35, file Schäffle.

104. On Dahlmann's influence, see Gädeke, *Riehls Gedanken*, 8; E. R. Huber, *Verfassungsgeschichte*, 3: 194. On Max's views on constitutions, see Bluntschli, *Denkwürdiges*, 2: 235.

105. On the economics ministry, see Volkert, "Bayern," *DV,* 2: 520–21; on educational policies, Laetitia Boehm, "Akademische Bildungswesen," in Spindler, ed., *Bayerischen Geschichte*, 4.2: 1020–21, 1046–51; Bluntschli, *Denkwürdiges*, 2: 122.

revolution enthusiastically, but his thinking took a sharply conservative turn in its aftermath. He concluded that the social conflicts of the day were not due to the distribution of wealth, but to the very uprooting from traditional society that the bourgeoisie had brought with it. His response to this was to employ the language of the old estates in his discussion of contemporary trends. With the help of the publisher Cotta, he embarked on a project of studying the customs and folkways by visiting the various regions of Germany. He did so with an eye to legitimizing himself in academic circles and sought to present his work as a version of state science. In a preliminary essay on "the four faculties," he criticized the traditional structure of the university for making the sciences of state a mere appendage to law, just as the natural sciences were no longer a mere part of medicine. A university which kept pace with modern developments would thus replace the law and medical faculties with those of state science and natural science respectively. Riehl's outline of the state sciences was as follows:

> The study of politics would not proceed from state law but would close with the same. It would rather proceed from a science of the people still divorced from the life of public law and from the state, i.e., with a natural history of the people.[106]

Riehl soon attracted the attention of King Max, who made him an honorary professor in 1854 and a full professor in the faculty of political economy in 1859.[107] This was against the wishes of the faculty itself, who found Riehl's researches "suitable for salon conversations" but little else; only Hermann defended Riehl's appointment.[108] In general, the faculty had lacked a clear *raison d'être* since the failure of its transformation to a polytechnical school in the 1830s.[109] When Maximilian hatched a project for a special school to train future civil servants, he favored the recommendation which stressed Roman and German legal history as the primary training rather than scientific and cameralist subjects.[110]

Such institutional questions probably had less of an impact on the intellectual life in Munich than did the informal exchanges of ideas that the king promoted. He fraternized with his professors, holding "symposia" in the castle, in

106. Riehl, *Naturgeschichte*, 1: 38.
107. For Riehl's biography, see Gädeke, *Riehls Gedanken*, 1–10.
108. Faculty circular, 16 April 1856, UA Munich M I, 1.1, vol. 2, Riehl; Hermann to faculty, 27 Feb. 1858, ibid., vol. 1; Senate, 16 Nov. 1856, Senatsakt 348.
109. Pechmann, "Staatswirtschaftliche Fakultät," 144; Boehm, "Akademische Bildungswesen," in Spindler, ed., *Bayerischen Geschichte*, 4.2: 1026. The faculty in 1855 consisted of an economist, a specialist in police science and law, an agriculturalist-botanist, two chemical technologists, a geologist, a mathematician, and a forester.
110. Gollwitzer, ed., *100 Jahre Maximilianeum*, 32–33, 57, 73.

which Riehl, Sybel, Liebig, the writer Paul Heyse, and a few officers were among the participants. The king facilitated good conversation by providing cigars, beer, and billiards.[111]

In Baden, the condition of the *Staatswissenschaften* had much to do with confessional issues, which assumed an increasing importance beginning in the 1850s. When the liberally inclined Duke Friedrich assumed his office in 1852, he encountered resistance from the local bishops, who forbade obedience to the new ruler. The tension between liberals and clericals in Baden drew the attention of all of Germany and foreshadowed the *Kulturkampf* of the 1870s.[112] The outcome was the installation of a strongly liberal cabinet in 1860, in which a number of professors had influential voices.

One of these was Mohl's successor at Heidelberg, Johann Kaspar Bluntschli. The son of a Swiss small businessman, Bluntschli had taught law at Zürich and Munich, where he had been a member of King Max's symposium. Another exception to the retreat from activism, he was one of the most prominent defenders of liberalism in this period. He coedited the influential *Deutsches Staatswörterbuch* (modeled on the Rotteck-Welcker *Staatslexikon*) beginning in 1857 and helped found the *Süddeutsche Zeitung* as an organ of liberal opinion. Under increasing pressure from Bavarian clericals, he moved to Baden in 1859, where he helped reform the administration in a way which set an an example for the rest of Germany. These reforms reflected the development of liberal thinking itself after 1848 in the direction of decentralized self-administration and bureaucratic accountability in accordance with the norms of the *Rechtsstaat*. This involved the establishment in 1863 of a new set of local administrative bodies with elected officials. In the following year, officials were made fully accountable to a new set of administrative courts on which lay persons served. The notion of accountability extended to the ministers themselves, as Bluntschli drafted a bill for impeachment proceedings (stopping short of Mohl's wish for a vote of no confidence, English style).[113] The government also introduced a ministry of economics as well as industrial freedom in 1862.[114]

These administrative reforms had repercussions on the university curriculum as well. At Bluntschli's suggestion, the law faculty petitioned in March 1864 for the formation of a separate faculty of *Staatswissenschaft* at Heidelberg, in which the state law professorships would be combined with the economic and technological ones from the philosphical faculty. The jurists noted the wide appeal of the sciences of state to non-Germans. The motion failed, however,

111. Bluntschli, *Denkwürdiges*, 2: 234.
112. E. R. Huber, *Verfassungsgeschichte*, 3: 194–98.
113. Heffter, *Deutsche Selbstverwaltung*, 417–22; Ott, "Baden," *DV,* 2: 605–8.
114. Ott, "Baden," *DV,* 2: 606.

partly because of Rau's objection, and partly because of money. After Rau's retirement, Bluntschli did succeed in establishing a joint seminar with the new economics professor, Karl Knies.[115]

Knies was yet another distinguished contributor to the sciences of state who made his career in Baden. Like his friend and mentor Hildebrand, he had been a passionate supporter of the Revolution; in the reaction that followed, he was forced to take a schoolteacher's position in Switzerland.[116] During this time he wrote the works that were the basis for his later reputation: *Statistics as an Autonomous Science* (1850), *The Railroads and Their Effects* (1853), and, most important, *Political Economy from the Standpoint of Historical Method* in the same year; these won him a professorship at Freiburg in 1855. Because of his liberal anticlerical views, he was appointed director of the office for elementary and middle schools in 1861. His planned reform of the elementary school curriculum was perceived as too anticlerical, however, and to avoid embarrassment he was made professor of *Staatswissenschaften* at Heidelberg in 1865—before Rau actually retired.[117]

Another state in which the post–1848 reaction had a tonic effect on the *Staatswissenschaften* was Austria. The Revolution itself had the effect of reopening Austria to the educational currents in the rest of Germany after years of relative isolation. Students were allowed to study outside of Austria for the first time; a separate ministry of education was formed, and the *Gymnasium* was introduced. The reaction that followed was by no means uncongenial to these reforms: rather than representing the triumph of the aristocracy, it brought back the centralizing bureaucracy. In many respects, the bureaucratic absolutism of the 1850s brought Austria to a state comparable to what other German states had achieved during the pre-March period.

This was certainly true of the universities and of the role of the sciences of state in the curriculum. The minister of education, Count Leo Thun von Hohenstein, devoted particular attention to the reform of legal studies, which had remained largely frozen since the Napoleonic era. Thun introduced the Prussian historical approach in the first two years with courses in Roman law

115. Excerpt of recommendation of law faculty, 8 March 1864, GLA, 235/29976 (Staats-u. Wirtschaftswissenschaftliche Fakultät); Rau, minority report of philosophical faculty, 29 July 1865, ibid.; Riese, *Hochschule*, 88–89.

116. Eisermann, *Grundlagen des Historismus*, 190–93.

117. Ibid., 223, 225. There is no record of faculty deliberation in the state archival file on the chair (GLA, 235/3140). According to Bluntschli, Knies was removed because he could not work with the other members of the cabinet. "Knies gave the impression of a tough, logical-sharp, somewhat doctrinaire reformer, driven by a cold passion. He reminded me of Calvin." (Bluntschli, *Denkwürdiges*, 3: 115). His student Richard T. Ely found him difficult to get to know; according to Ely, Knies felt that his contributions had not been sufficiently acknowledged by Roscher. See Ely, *Ground Under Our Feet*, 44.

and German legal history. The final two years emphasized Austrian law and retained the obligatory lectures of the pre-March period, including the sciences of state as defined by Sonnenfels (economics, police science, and finance, as well as Austrian statistics). Although the sciences of state suffered by coming at the end of this demanding curriculum—many students completed only part of it—the idea of a single training program for administrators was retained. The sciences of state and law remained integrated into a single faculty as at no other German university at the time.[118]

Given Thun's anti-Hegelian bias, the appointment of Stein to the professorship of economics at Vienna in 1855 appears surprising.[119] The reasons, however, are not difficult to find. They have to do primarily with Stein's own intellectual development since the first edition of his famous work on socialism and communism. Under the impact of the events of 1848, Stein had returned to Paris in the aftermath of the bloody June days there, and had subsequently expanded and updated the earlier work by fleshing out the broader context of modernization. The result was the work that became his masterpiece, the three-volume *History of the Social Movement in France* (1850). The conflict he had outlined in the earlier work between the contemporary commitment to personal worth on the one hand and the economic and social inequalities of class on the other now became expanded to a conflict of the very principles of state and society respectively:

> We have posited that the principle of the state is the *elevation* of all individuals to the fullest freedom, to the fullest personal development. It is further shown that the principle of society is the *subjugation* of individuals by other individuals, the completion of the individual through the dependency of the other.[120]

Society was based on interest, while the state was based on the common interest of all. Monarchy was an expression of the state as standing above the classes.[121] Moreover, Stein invested the state with a collective personality of its own. That personality had a will, expressed in its constitution and laws; the activity of the state pursuant to this was its administration.[122] It was to this

---

118. Hoke, "Österreich," *DV,* 2: 389–90; Wenger, "Stein und die Entwicklung der Verwaltungswissenschaft," 483–84; Akademischer Senat der Wiener Universität, *Geschichte der Wiener Universität,* 117.

119. The faculty had nominated Roscher as first choice and Stein as second; Rau and Hanssen were also mentioned, but Stein was the only one willing to come. See Novotny, "Lorenz von Steins Berufung nach Wien," 481. The faculty's report of 22 January 1855 is in AVA, 4258/1855, 4 Wien Jus, no. 591 (Prof. Jurid., Stein). Stein's own resumé is published in Blasius and Pankoke, *Stein,* 183–89.

120. Stein, *Geschichte der socialen Bewegung,* 1: xliii.

121. Ibid., 3: 22.

122. Ibid., 1: xxxv–xxxvi.

enlightened monarchy, particularly its administration, that one must look for the solution to the class conflicts stemming from bourgeois society. "The true, most powerful, most lasting and most loved monarchy is the monarchy of social reform," he wrote.[123]

Stein remained committed to a comprehensive field of state science, but his execution bore witness to the incompatibility of such system-building with the demands of the 1850s and 1860s. His ambitious *System of State Sciences*, begun in 1852 and based on dialectical principles, promised more than Stein himself could deliver. The work ended with the second volume on the science of society; it failed to complete the material outlined at the beginning.[124] The later ten-volume *Science of Administration* of 1866 may be viewed as the promised third part, dealing with the state proper, but it too delivered only half of what Stein had sketched.[125] Stein was continually revising and reordering his work, sometimes insisting on the tentativeness of his enterprise.[126]

These inconsistencies were undoubtedly a reason for Stein's lack of greater influence.[127] Despite his success as a lecturer and effectiveness as a journalist and consultant—which led to his being knighted in 1868—Stein was unable to create a school. As Schmoller observed as early as 1866, his ideas were more often plagiarized than quoted by others.[128] In inviting Schäffle to teach alongside Stein in 1868, the ministry noted that Stein was deficient "in the gift of making practical points of view accessible to students."[129] On Stein's legacy, Schmoller and his great opponent Karl Menger were agreed: Stein was an anachronism in the age of increasing specialization. To quote Schmoller:

> This heavy ballast of mere construction that leads to unending repetition, this unctuous and complacent bombast is unpalatable to the exact scientific method of our time. . . . [Stein] forgot that we in the sciences of state are still in the middle of learning the abc's, and that one must first understand this before one can sing of the harmony of the universe in dithyrambic verses.[130]

123. Ibid, 3: 48–49; on administration, see 1: v. For a sound interpretation of Stein's views in *Sociale Bewegung*, see Böckenförde, *State, Society, and Liberty*, 115–45.

124. Stein, *System der Staatswissenschaften*, 2: 40–49, outlines the science of society as including a discussion of classes in general as well as the particular historical "forms" of social domination. In the body of the work (428 ff), Stein announced the transition to the discussion of these "forms." That section never appeared.

125. Lindenfeld, "Polizeiwissenschaft," 156–57.

126. Stein, *System der Staatswissenschaften*, 1: x; See also Stein, *Verwaltungslehre*, 4: v–viii; Schnur, "Einleitung," 25; Menger, "Lorenz von Stein," 204.

127. Wenger, "Stein," 496; Menger, "Stein," 203; Blasius and Pankoke, *Stein*, 81–83.

128. Schmoller, *Litteraturgeschichte*, 115.

129. Recommendation of Ministry (Hasner), 26 June 1868, AVA, 5381/1868, 4 Wien Jus, (Prof. Jurid. 590, Schäffle).

130. Schmoller, *Litteraturgeschichte*, 136–37.

According to Menger, Stein was in part responsible for the mistrust of theory in the German sciences of state.[131] Yet Stein's work was to have more far-reaching effects: he was a major voice in the governmental reforms of Japan in the 1890s, and his anticipation of recent functional theories has been noted.[132]

If the cultivation of the sciences of state in South Germany continued at a diminished level, it reached a nadir in Prussia in the 1850s and 1860s. The social basis of the sciences of state—a liberal bureaucracy committed to reform—had eroded still further, thanks to the events of 1848. The revulsion against radicalism had the effect of driving many officials into the conservative camp as early as 1849.[133] The character of the reaction in the 1850s under the leadership of Otto von Manteuffel powerfully reinforced this trend. Manteuffel recognized that concessions to legal and civil equality were ultimately compatible with the domination of the traditional elites; thus Prussia learned to live with a constitution and a parliament—with the help of the three-class voting system, which increased the number of bureaucrats in the *Landtag* from 40 in 1849 to 113 in 1852.[134]

Once secure in power, Manteuffel proceeded to purge the bureaucracy of anyone suspected of political disloyalty. Although the tenure of most civil servants was guaranteed, he created a special category of "political officials" which encompassed the upper ranks of the administration. These were subject to immediate dismissal without appeal if "their behavior in or out of office showed itself to be unworthy of the esteem, respect, or confidence that their profession requires."[135] Lists were kept of officials' political leanings, and bureaucrats were expected to campaign for pro-government candidates in their districts at election time.[136] The result was a considerable narrowing of horizons: although most officials remained free of corruption and scandal, they no longer took the initiative. "We are more administered than governed," wrote Johann Gustav Droysen to Max Duncker in 1859. "The administering reaches to the high and highest positions, consumes there time and energy, hinders the collecting, the calmly ripening consideration, the grand overview."[137] For those who went along, there were rewards of status and recognition: officials and

131. Menger, "Stein," 202.

132. Schnur, "Einleitung," 21; Maluschke, "Steins Staatsformenlehre," 242. Maluschke mentions Talcott Parsons and Niklas Luhmann in particular.

133. Gillis, *Prussian Bureaucracy,* 140.

134. Ibid., 135.

135. Disciplinary law, 21 July 1852, quoted in Jeserich, "Preussen," *DV,* 2: 329. See also Gillis, *Prussian Bureaucracy,* 139.

136. Gillis, *Prussian Bureaucracy,* 150–53, 162–63.

137. Droysen, *Briefwechsel,* 2: 635.

their wives were now admitted to court, in contrast to the pre-March period.[138] In the words of the popular law professor Rudolf Gneist,

> In the formerly important and autonomous men there now developed formally two natures, the official and the private, the latter often so amiable and liberal, that some almost reconciled themselves to the system when they succeeded in being introduced to the circle of the initiated. . . . To learn how one can serve a system against one's conscience and conviction for an entire lifetime, one must be a Prussian official.[139]

It is thus not surprising that the bureaucracy obeyed orders in defiance of the law during the constitutional crisis of 1862–66.

Given this situation, it is understandable that the sciences of state languished. Even the most popular professors such as Dahlmann noticed the change: like Mohl in Heidelberg, Dahlmann saw his enrollments drop (see table 7). The crown princes of the German states who came to Bonn were advised to stay away from his lectures, and others apparently followed suit.[140] Students in general were famous for not attending lectures, because they knew they would not be tested on the sciences of state in the examination which marked the end of university study: Hanssen, who came to Berlin from Göttingen in 1860, found that something of the Hegelian style remained. "The Berliners," he wrote, "demanded . . . philosophical theoretisation, dogmas and systems, and spicy polemics."[141] The indifference of students was sometimes matched by that of the professors: in Breslau, the Professor of *Staatswissenschaft*, Johann Tellkampf, became accustomed to teaching in the summer semester only; he preferred to spend his winters in Berlin, where he was a member of the *Landtag*.[142]

The Prussian system of training civil servants put a great deal of emphasis on the apprenticeship period which followed university study; this was regarded as a more effective way of inculcating traditional values. But here also, the trainee's experience was fragmentary: it included mostly clerical work and formalities rather than observation of decision making and human interaction.[143] The main contact for most aspirants with the sciences of state came during their preparation for the second state examination, but once again

---

138. Delbrück, *Lebenserinnerungen*, 2: 142–43.

139. Gneist, "Politische Skizzen aus den Revolutionstagen 1848," quoted in Schiffer, *Gneist*, 119.

140. Springer, *Dahlmann*, 2: 381–82.

141. Hanssen, "Lebenserinnerungen," 134.

142. Memo of 10 March 1855, GPSA Dahlem, Rep. 76 Va Sect. 4 Tit. IV no. 16: 155–56 (Die Berufung des Breslauer Prof. Dr. J. T. Tellkampf . . .).

143. Richter, "Vorbildung der höheren Verwaltungsbeamten," 6–7.

Table 7 *Enrollments in Lectures in Politics under Dahlmann at Bonn, 1850–1865*

Sem.	In Politik under Dahlmann
1850–51	107
1851–52	70
1852–53	58
1854–55	54
1855–56	47
1856–57	40
1857–58	44

Source: GPSA Dahlem, Rep. 76 Va Sect. 3 Tit. VII.

superficiality prevailed: preparation frequently took place through special crash-courses, based on notebooks of previous examination questions that were color-coded according to the frequency with which they had been asked.[144] The examinations included questions on general knowledge, bespeaking a commitment to *Bildung* as well as to preprofessional education. Thus the written take-home examination for one such official consisted of three questions: one concerning the possible deficiencies in finance administration, one on tax policy for municipalities, and one on the origins of the Peloponnesian war.[145]

It is thus understandable that those who had the greatest impact on the sciences of state in the 1850s and 1860s were never professors of those subjects. One of them was the Berlin legal scholar Rudolf von Gneist, who managed to give substance to the discipline of administrative law in a way that had eluded Mohl. He did so by proceeding comparatively, beginning with a series of works on English law and gradually drawing more and more comparisons with German cases. Gneist conceptualized a trend in English history that fit the terminology which German liberals had already developed in the revolution: that of *self-government* or *self-administration*. Moreover, Gneist had a practical program: he crusaded for and to a large extent brought about a greater degree of local government in Prussia in the 1860s and 1870s, following the precedents set by Baron von Stein in the Napoleonic era.[146]

Another such figure was Ernst Engel, head of the Prussian statistical bureau after 1859. Trained as an engineer in Saxony, Engel began his administrative career as head of the Saxon statistical bureau immediately following the Revolution of 1848. In addition to such imaginative innovations as an industrial exhibition in 1850 and the invention of mortgage insurance in 1858, Engel introduced the more sophisticated Belgian model in the census of 1849 that gave his

144. Ibid., 13; Bleek, *Juristenprivileg*, 166–67.
145. Diest, *Leben eines Glücklichen*, 139–41. Cf. Richter, "Vorbildung der höheren Verwaltungsbeamten," 17–18.
146. On Gneist's achievement, see Heffter, *Deutsche Selbstverwaltung*, 379–403. According to Heffter, the Badenese reforms were quite independent of Gneist's influence (423).

occupational statistics a degree of reliability that surpassed Prussia's. In 1855 he introduced an eighteen-page questionaire on people's economic habits that was sufficiently intrusive to arouse the parliament's opposition. This led to his resignation in 1858.[147] When Dieterici, the head of the Prussian bureau, died the following year, the position was offered to Engel. Faced with a much larger operation and forced to rely on local officials who were unfamiliar with the more sophisticated techniques of data collection, Engel resolved to establish a statistical seminar for officials already in the field, which opened its doors in 1862 to eight participants.[148] He soon experienced difficulty in attracting officials away from their positions to continue training with no remuneration, and consequently expanded the membership to include advanced students at the university. His seminar soon became the training ground for a new generation of economists.[149] Its effectiveness stemmed less from its formal classes, which were taught by university professors and generally mirrored their low pedagogical standards, than from Engel's own lively and informal style and the personal interest he took in his students. In the words of one of its alumni, Georg Friedrich Knapp, "the seminar was . . . a place of stimulation, an opportunity to work, a social hub for those with similar aspirations—but also a battle cry for instruction and a new banner for research."[150] Within two years, similar seminars were established at Vienna and Jena; a third opened in Paris in 1869.

In the other North German states, the neglect of the *Staatswissenschaften* was not as serious. In Hannover, a tradition of thorough academic and practical training persisted; there are indications that students took their work more seriously in Göttingen.[151] The case of Saxony represented a variant that was closer to the South German pattern. True, the reaction after 1848 was repressive, in some ways more so than in Prussia, under the leadership of Friedrich Ferdinand von Beust, but the university of Leipzig was not easily intimidated, having traditions far older than those of Berlin. When Beust suspended freedom of assembly and press in 1850, twenty-one professors protested, among them Roscher and Biedermann. This sense of tradition also affected the teaching of

147. Seibt, "Statistik," *ENTW*, no. 37, 19–20; Hacking, "Prussian Numbers," 379.

148. Engel, *Statistische Seminar*, 14. Always the visionary, Engel hoped to expand this into an administrative academy similar to the war academy—an idea which Hanssen opposed (ibid., 44; Hanssen to Ministry, 27 Dec. 1869, GPSA Dahlem, Rep. 77 Tit. 94 no. 113, vol. 2: 19).

149. Engel, "Statistische Seminar und das Studium der Statistik," 185.

150. Knapp, *Grundherrschaft und Rittergut*, 148; on the less satisfying formal classes, see Knapp, *Eine Jugend*, 191–93; Brentano, *Mein Leben*, 42.

151. Memo to Hanssen, 5 March 1848, UA Göttingen, PA 4 V b 122, Hanssen; Hanssen to Olshausen, 14 Feb 1859, GPSA Dahlem, Rep. 76 Va Sect. 3 Tit. IV no. 40, vol. 3: 279–81 (Anstellungen, Bonn). Adolph Wagner mentioned the tradition among students of attending the lectures in economics there (Wagner, *Gedächtnissrede*, 24). On the high level of bureaucratic training in Hannover, see VfS, *Vorbildung*, 78–90.

the *Staatswissenschaften*. Ever since Pölitz, the faculty had retained the full complement of political and legal subjects along with the economic ones. In other fields as well, such as science and philosophy, Leipzig continued to attract scholars who were more than specialists.[152]

Leipzig was also the home of Wilhelm Roscher from 1848, who was arguably the most successful *Staatswissenschaftler* of his day. He embodied its tradition of breadth, teaching not only Rau's triad of theoretical economics, economic policy, and finance, but also comparative statistics, practical politics, history of political theory, and later agricultural economics and welfare policy (*Armenpolitik*). A true systematizer, though less ambitious than Stein, Roscher gradually expanded his outline of 1843 into a five-volume series: one for theoretical economics (1854), one for agriculture, one for commerce and manufacturing, one for finance, and a separate volume on welfare policy—not to mention his famous *History of Economics in Germany*. The theoretical economics was his most successful work, going through five editions in less than ten years.

If Roscher's system represented the continuity with the the earlier cameralist tradition, it nevertheless contained a major shift of emphasis. This was to move economics away from being a policy science to being a contemplative one, in which the role of the scholar was not to convey technique but to promote understanding. This did not exclude policy implications, but sought to base them on a more sophisticated foundation. "The doctrine," he wrote, "should generally not make praxis easier, like a pony, but rather make it difficult, insofar as it calls attention to thousands of considerations that are to be taken into account with every step of the legislator or state administrator."[153] In this way, economics more closely approximated the ideal of *Wissenschaftlichkeit* associated with the Humboldtian reforms: it defined the calling of a researcher as being distinct from that of a practical man of affairs. This represented a major step in the attenuation of the science of praxis.

In a very different way, the career of Bruno Hildebrand in the 1850s and 1860s illustrates the same phenomenon. A radical professor as well as a subject of one of the most repressive states, electoral Hesse, Hildebrand was forced into exile in Switzerland between 1850 and 1862. While holding professorships in Zürich and Bern, he distinguished himself as a practical organizer, helping to establish several railroad lines, a savings bank, and a fund for widows. Yet this activity was accompanied by an almost complete lack of publications. It was not until 1862, with an appointment at Jena, that he resumed the life of an active scholar. There too his contributions were in large degree organizational:

---

152. Kittel, *Universität Leipzig*, 34, 37. Examples would include Gustav Theodor Fechner, Moritz Wilhelm Drobisch, and later Wilhelm Wundt and Karl Lamprecht.

153. Roscher, *Grundriss*, v.

he distinguished himself as a seminar leader and organizer of the state statistical bureau. He founded a new journal, the *Jahrbücher für Nationalökonomie und Statistik*, where he published some further manifestos, a theory of historical stages, and several actual investigations into economic history itself. But this spurt of activity did not last beyond 1870; he soon lost interest in the journal, and as his son-in-law, Johannes Conrad, pointed out, he had already lost the ability to concentrate on reading a book from start to finish.[154] In short, Hildebrand also exemplified the increasing difficulty of combining theoretical and practical activity.

THEMES AND VARIATIONS

In the 1850s and 1860s, the language of embodiments and their variations continued to find widespread use as a substitute for clear definitions within the sciences of state and within the wider political culture. This was part of the legacy of 1848, which had thrown into sharp relief not only the power of the masses, but also the fundamental divisions among the elites on Germany's economic and political development. Those elites, however, were by no means willing to confront directly the differences that divided them; they preferred rather to mask them with a common rhetoric which perpetuated some of the hopes of 1848—probably because the potential of the masses for disruption was never far from their minds. Liberals and conservatives thus both tended to endorse the principle of the *Rechtstaat* and reject the extremes of autocratic government and popular rule.[155] Yet this rhetoric also concealed the uncertainties that both groups felt about the proper degree of change: liberals were ambivalent about how far to appeal to the *Volk*, and about the proper line between laissez-faire and state intervention; conservatives were divided on what concessions to make to parliamentarianism. The discrepancy between the reassuring rhetoric and the shifting, unstable speech acts that accompanied it was captured in 1861 by Schäffle in an allusion to the tower of Babel:

> Does not everyone mouth the same words, nationality, popularity [*Volkstümlichkeit*], reform of the state, extirpating the police state, good old law, autonomy, with the same tongues and the same language? But how confused is the structure, how they still do not understand each other, how they still mean something different by the same words . . . how they speak of freedom where there is enslavement, of the good old law of all where the privileges of old are restored under the pretext of popular freedom, of the legitimacy of nationality where other nationalities are suppressed, of people's law where it is a matter

154. Conrad, *Lebenserinnerungen*, 127; Krawehl, "*Jahrbücher*," 52–53.
155. Pflanze, "Juridical and Political Responsibility," 175–79.

of replacing an ordered and educated administration by the uneducated and disorderly rule of a thousand tyrants![156]

The same tendencies held true for learned disciplines. One instance was the new study of "culture" as a way of apprehending the *Volk.* Woodruff Smith has argued persuasively that the study of culture became an "intellectual fad" in the 1850s as an alternative to the abstract doctrines of liberal individualism.[157]

Organicism

In the sciences of state, the organic notion served a similar purpose. Never absent from those sciences in the early nineteenth century, it was ubiquitous in this period. Like "culture," it expressed the reaction to excessive abstraction which so many thinkers found at the root of the defects of the previous age. Organicism was used indiscriminately as an analogy between nature on the one hand and society and politics on the other, and as a metaphor to express the oneness of all three. These were notions which had long been a hallmark of conservative political thought; now liberals like Bluntschli embraced them with equal enthusiasm. Thus the embodiment served as another means of masking real differences of class and ideology. Yet it also perhaps served as an authentic expression of the subconscious lack of assurance with which each side faced the perplexities of the industrial age.

Certainly the powerful appeal of the organic metaphor lay partly in the linkage it provided between the sciences of state and other fields of knowledge: organicism played a central role in natural science and in religious and metaphysical thought, as well as in the sciences of society and politics. These variations were certainly well known to the *Staatswissenschaftler* and helped shape their thinking.

The links between natural science and the *Staatswissenschaften* were often personal as well as conceptual. We have noted the presence of Riehl and Liebig in King Max's "symposia." In Heidelberg, Helmholtz and Mohl belonged to an informal group of liberal professors, and Helmholtz became Mohl's son-in-law.[158] Conceptually, natural science in this period was viewed not merely as atomistic or mechanical, but increasingly as providing holistic explanations of concrete reality. The new physiology was an example of this holism, while the new thermodynamics suggested the importance of change. Stein alluded to these new trends in the introduction to his *System of State Sciences* in 1852:

156. Schäffle, "Rechtsphilosophische Zeitgedanken," 289.
157. Woodruff Smith, *Politics and the Sciences of Culture,* chap. 2, esp. 35. He views Riehl, Carl Theodor Andree, Theodor Waitz, and Rudolf Virchow as representative of the trend.
158. Angermann, *Mohl,* 73–74; Mohl, *Lebenserinnerungen,* 1: 225–26.

On all points, human knowledge begins to take on a new, more powerful shape. . . . We begin to move from the knowledge of abstract principles and concrete facts to the understanding of laws which dominate reality. In all points the mass of facts, exploited through serious and persistent experiments and experiences, is ordered into a unity in variety, into an organism.[159]

Scientific laws were also seen as compatible with historical explanation; the popularity in Germany of Thomas Henry Buckle, with his appeal to scientific laws of history, is an example.[160] Roscher characterized his own approach as the "historical or physiological method."[161] Engel had a similar view of statistics, which he characterized as "a physics and physiology of society . . . [which] mediates . . . the transition from the state and social sciences to the natural sciences."[162]

The most explicit and thorough adaptation of physiological analogies to the sciences of state was accomplished by Schäffle, who retired from the Austrian state service after serving briefly as finance minister in 1870 to become an independent scholar. This enabled him to work on his magnum opus, for which he is best remembered: the four-volume *Structure and Life of the Social Body* (1875–88). The subtitle revealed its purpose as a summa of the organicism of the period: *Encyclopedic Sketch of a Real Anatomy, Physiology, and Psychology of Human Society with Special Attention to Economics as Social Metabolism.* Schäffle was able to develop the relationships of the economic, social, and political thought of his era with contemporary philosophical and psychological thought as well as with Darwinism. Although Schäffle was fond of natural analogies and used them throughout his life, he insisted that their purpose was rhetorical rather than literal.[163]

A second associational sphere of the organic metaphor was the spiritual. If nature, society, and the state were to be viewed as an interdependent whole, then it served as evidence of God's purpose. Hence science and metaphysics were not opposed but complementary, as can be seen in the works of Gustav Theodor Fechner, Rudolf Hermann Lotze, and later Wilhelm Wundt.[164]

One of the leading purveyors of this point of view in the sciences of state was Heinrich Ahrens, a distinguished exponent of international law and state science who taught at Graz and later at Leizpig. A disciple of the idealist philospher Karl C. F. Krause, Ahrens viewed reason and nature as two distinct sources of knowledge of God's ways, which could thus be understood both

159. Stein, *System der Staatswissenschaften,* 1: vii; cf. Riehl, *Naturgeschichte,* 1: 16–17.

160. Porter, *Rise of Statistical Thinking,* 167–68.

161. Roscher, *Grundlagen der Nationalokonomie,* 55.

162. Engel, "Statistische Seminar und das Studium der Statistik," 188.

163. Schäffle, "Notwendigkeit exakt Entwickelungsgeschichtlicher Erklärung," 295.

164. See Höffding, *History of Modern Philosophy,* 2: 508–32; Merz, *History of European Thought,* 3: chap. 6; 4: chap. 12.

through philosophy and empirical knowledge.[165] This was in contrast to Hegel's monism, which Ahrens criticized for collapsing the human and divine into a single plane.[166] Nevertheless, psychology and history also gave indications of God's plan in their respective ways. Ahrens viewed history as showing the progressive merging of nations into a single humanity; he therefore favored federations of states whenever possible, which he viewed as the most appropriate expression of the collective human organism.[167]

The same metaphysics underlay Roscher's position, though it led to different conclusions. The breadth and detachment that characterized this mildmannered and tolerant soul undoubtedly stemmed from his deep-seated Lutheran piety. Roscher's theory was based on the premise that one could not fully know God's plan: "It is a major task of science to demonstrate how and why reason gradually becomes nonsense, benevolence becomes plague."[168] Thus each progressive stage of development had its inevitable dark side: industrial freedom brought factories and slums. Cultures grew, blossomed, and decayed, as Herder had claimed. Roscher's historical method contained more than a hint of disillusionment, and in this sense he spoke to the mentality of the post–1848 generation of officials—part of the same *Bildungsbürgertum* who were also turning to Schopenhauer.

A more direct link between state science and spirituality was forged by Bluntschli. His pragmatic instinct was coupled with an unquestioning religious faith that reminds one of his fictional contemporary, Johann Buddenbrook Jr. In Zürich Bluntschli had come under the influence of a religious prophet named Friedrich Rohmer, who based his mysticism on a self-styled psychology. Bluntschli attempted to apply this psychology to politics in 1844, seeking a counterpart in the state to each of Rohmer's sixteen powers of the soul.[169] Although he did not pursue this speculative attempt in later life, the influence of Rohmer remained in a more modified form; he also remained devoted to Rohmer's religious teachings, editing posthumously such works as *The Science of God* (1858).[170]

A third variation was the view that organicism was the essence of society. Stein's definition of the latter bordered on ritual incantation:

165. Ahrens, *Naturrecht*, 1: 5. This view was similar to that of Johann Friedrich Herbart, who was the preferred philosopher of the Austrian ministry of culture at this time. This did not make Ahrens a supporter of Herbart's philosophy; evidently the animosities between Kraussians and Herbartians were long-standing (ibid., 1: 193 n).

166. Ibid., 1: 187.

167. Ibid., 1: 306.

168. Roscher, *Grundriss*, v; Eisermann, *Grundlagen des Historisumus*, 123.

169. The work was *Psychologische Studien über Staat und Kirche*. See "Bluntschli," *ADB*, 47: 32; "Friedrich Rohmer," ibid., 29: 57–58. The notion easily earned Mohl's ridicule (*Geschichte und Literatur*, 1: 259) and found its way into Barnes and Becker, *Social Thought from Lore to Science*, 3: 678.

170. "Rohmer," ADB, 29: 58.

> This organic unity of human life, conditioned by the distribution of goods, regulated by the organism of labor, set in motion by the system of needs, and tied over time through the family and its law to certain families [*Geschlechter*]— is human society.[171]

It was Riehl who worked this notion out to the fullest. Organicism was at the core of his system of state sciences, which he outlined as follows:

> The first task would be to determine the organic total personality of a people on the basis of its natural ethnographic features . . . thus a general study of geography and folklore. Then would follow the study of those small groups within the people, held together by the bonds of nature and domestic life . . . the study of the family. Then would come the study of those larger organic components of the people's personality . . . in short, the study of society.[172]

His major works, written within the space of the next few years, followed this plan, though not in the order proposed: *Civil Society* (1851), *Land and People* (1854), and *The Family* (1855). He later integrated these into a into a single, multivolume work: *The Natural History of the People.*

Riehl was less interested in analogies between nature and society than in causal relationships between the two, which he pursued in two separate areas: geography and gender. The first volume of his *Natural History* explored empirically the topographical diversity of Germany and how it affected the customs and social structure of different regions; the third, devoted to the family, was based on the premise of the anatomical and physiological inequality of men and women.[173] The natural division of labor thereby dictated that politics was a male occupation, while women were the preservers of custom and tradition; the preservation of the family and household relied to a great degree on women's role and was thus crucial to Riehl's program of social reform.

For Bluntschli, as for Stein, the organic metaphor served to depict the intermediate location of the social sphere between the proper concerns of the individual and those of the state. Individuals formed the building blocks of social collectivities, which in turned form the building blocks of the body politic.

---

171. Stein, *Socialen Bewegung,* 1: xxviii. In the *Gesellschaftslehre,* Stein formulated this organicism more pretentiously as a natural law: "Every historical epoch and every people stands the higher, the more it has developed all its organic components of life completely and harmoniously in themselves. And . . . [it] follows, that a life in which either one of these elements is missing or . . . is completely suppressed, will necessarily fall ill from this lack, and just as necessarily will die from it if unaided. And this natural law we shall call the law of disease and death of the spiritual community." (*System der Staatswissenschaften,* 2: 142–43).

172. Riehl, *Naturgeschichte,* 1: 38. Stein had a similar critique of the predominant curricula in state sciences in Germany and Austria for placing law before the sciences of state; his system reversed the two, treating law as a derivative of particular economic and social presuppositions. See Stein, *Gegenwart und Zukunft,* 115–16, 323–28.

173. Riehl, *Naturgeschichte,* 3: 4–5 ("Die Familie").

Hence if classical economics dealt with the laws governing self-interest, and politics with the more complex organism of the state, the science of society occupied the space in between, dealing in "compounds" of simple elements. Bluntschli's characterization in the *Deutsches Staatswörterbuch* was typical:

> [Social science] concerns itself so to speak with the unconnected elements, which the state cannot dispense with for its existence, with the elements that join together and want to combine, sometimes in the manner of crystals that are made out of homogeneous molecules, sometimes in the manner of organic bodies whose unifying idea forms all those material parts to members of a single body. [The relation of] social science to state science is like that of organic chemistry to physiological and psychological sciences.[174]

The fourth variation was of course the state-as-organism, as can be seen from the preceding discussion. It was used to express the basic belief in the foundation of the state in natural conditions—and the corresponding relativism of political forms and values depending on those conditions. According to Bluntschli, "The natural form of the state invariably corresponds to the particularity and stage of development of the people which live in it."[175] Roscher, as we have seen, worked from the same premise, as did Heinrich von Treitschke, of whom more will be said later. Bluntschli went considerably further, however, in his use of natural analogies. He was one of the first to discuss the notion of race in politics. In the section on "human nature as the foundation of politics" he responded to the theories of Gobineau, stating that ethnic mixture was healthier than separation, though only within the white race.[176] Bluntschli also concurred with Riehl in applying distinctions of gender to politics: the state was masculine, the church feminine.[177] Finally, he propagated Rohmer's psychological theory of political parties. According to this theory, the four major parties on the political spectrum—absolutist, conservative, liberal, and radical—corresponded to four distinct personality types.[178]

Society

One of the most repeated embodiments of the 1850s and 1860s was "society," a theme which overlapped the organic metaphor but contained its own sphere of additional associations. The degree to which this unit-idea colored the thinking of the period can be seen in the number of compound words and phrases that were generated from it. From the *social question, socialism,* and *social science* of

174. Bluntschli, "Gesellschaft," *DS,* 4: 250; cf. Pankoke, *Soziale Bewegung,* 111–15 for a discussion of how these analogies moved beyond the "social physics" proposed by Comte.
175. Bluntschli, *Lehre vom modernen Staat,* 1: 117.
176. Ibid., 3: 125–26.
177. Ibid., 1: 23–24.
178. Bluntschli, "Parteien, politische," *DS,* 7: 734 ff.

the 1840s emerged *social democracy* (Stein) and *social politics* (Riehl)—all terms which dominated the vocabulary of thinkers and doers for the rest of the century and beyond.[179]

Mohl piquantly captured the mood of the postrevolutionary years in his article "Social Sciences and State Sciences" in 1851:

> The word *society* has resounded. It is uttered with profound apprehension [by some], with malicious menace by others; it serves as the catchword of dispute on the soapbox and in the tavern; powerful parties and purposes, entire theoretical structures are signified by it. In life and in science, the concept, the special existence, the need, the present and future of society come to the fore.[180]

The recognition of society was a reformulation, in the language of embodiments, of something the scientists of state had long since known: the limits of state control over the autonomous activities of individuals and groups. Now, however, the groups were more than merely autonomous—they were menacing. Given the hopes and fears that were associated with the term *society*, a scientific approach was all the more necessary. Mohl did not understate its urgency: the threat of communism was in his opinion the greatest danger to European civilization since the barbarian invasions of Rome. "The false theory of society," Mohl wrote, "can only be overcome by the true science of society."[181] As it had been earlier with Comte in France, social science was associated with social order, with the reestablishment of authority after a time of chaos.

Mohl's approach to defining the new science reflected his classificatory mentality—as well as the difficulty experienced by an older generation in accepting shifts of paradigms. Rather than changing his previous encyclopedic scheme, Mohl proposed a duplicate set of sciences of society parallel to the sciences of state, that is, separate sciences of society in general, social law, social ethics, social politics, social history, and social statistics. Economics was to be parceled among three different departments of learning: individual, social, and state—the artificiality of which he conceded four years later, when he reclassified theoretical economics as a social science.[182] In any event, this hypertrophy of categories was not in keeping with the predominant distrust of boundaries at the time, and Mohl's static scheme met with much criticism.[183] Stein and

---

179. The pervasiveness of the category is well depicted by Pankoke, *Soziale Bewegung*. See also Stein, *Socialen Bewegung*, 1: cxvii; Riehl, *Naturgeschichte*, 2: 5.

180. Mohl, "Gesellschafts-Wissenschaften," 6–7.

181. Ibid., 26.

182. Ibid., 55–57, 62; Mohl, *Geschichte und Literatur*, 1: 105.

183. Bluntschli, for example, found a separate social jurisprudence unneccesary ("Gesellschaft," *DS*, 4: 249; Angermann, *Mohl*, 369); Schäffle, "Die Konkurrenz der Organe des Staatslebens," 560; on Treitschke's polemic, see his *Gesellschaftswissenschaft*, 61–63, and Angermann, *Mohl*, 372–82. Angermann himself found Mohl's attempt to be unsuccessful (365).

Riehl both maintained, in contrast to Mohl, that the science of society was part of the sciences of state.

One variation on the idea of society was a concept taken over from natural law (and Hegel's civil society). Ever since the social contract theories of the seventeenth and eighteenth centuries, the term *society* had stood for a voluntary *association* of individuals who banded together for a common purpose. The transitional figures in linking this discourse with that of the 1850s were Ahrens and Mohl. Ahrens had stressed the multitude of empirically existing types of associations as the sources of different types of law. In addition to marriage and family, there were the wider circles of community, tribe, nation, and international federation. Moreover, Ahrens introduced a distinction between these natural human ties and more specialized types of associations with delimited purposes—such as religious, educational, artistic, or economic organizations. The laws governing each of these, Ahrens maintained, ought to be classified separately.[184] Mohl, with his predilection for classification, found Ahrens' scheme congenial and drew heavily from it.[185] For Mohl, the taxonomy of associations was the foundation for an empirical social science rather than a branch of jurisprudence. The feature that distinguished such associations from the state was that one could belong to several of them; the state, by contrast, was the organization that gave unity to the different individuals and collectives.[186] Stein also thought deeply about the nature of associations, but significantly chose to treat them as part of state science proper rather than as social science: associations expressed a degree of unified common interest rather than antagonistic self-interest—the principle which in his view set off the state from society.[187] In either case, the importance of voluntary associations, which formed part of the new meaning of self-government, was recognized by the theoreticians of the new science.

Another variation was the depiction of social classes and their changing relationships—an obvious and inescapable task of the new social science. On this matter, Stein and Riehl arrived at similar conclusions, though by different routes. For Stein, as for Marx, class distinctions were economically determined. The distribution of goods created inequalities between those who possessed property and those who relied on labor power—inequalities which in some societies led to estates or castes. Riehl consciously rejected the economic interpretation of class, and adopted—as Hegel had previously done—the term

184. Ahrens, *Naturrecht*, 1: 265–66.

185. Angermann, *Mohl*, 340–43, 353–54.

186. Mohl, "Gesellschafts-Wissenschaft," 31, 35–41. Mohl listed six characteristics of societies: they were (1) lasting, (2) of larger significance, (3) widespread, (4) compatible with membership in other groups, (5) not political, (6) did not require a formal organization.

187. Stein, *Verwaltungslehre* 1.3: 65–66.

estate to express his social categories. The decisive criteria for defining estates were custom and tradition rather than ownership or labor.[188] Riehl also polemicized against "inauthentic estates," which were characterized merely by belonging to a profession (e.g., *Gelehrtenstand, Beamtenstand*).[189] Instead he classified the estates into "the powers of social continuity"—the peasantry and the aristocracy—and "the powers of social movement"—the bourgeoisie and the "fourth estate." The latter was not simply the workers (the economic characterization), but the swelling numbers of *declassés*—those who had lost their sense of social belonging, or the anti-estate.[190] This was Riehl's reading of the modernization process. The fourth estate could include former deracinated aristocrats, peasants, and intellectuals as well as workers. In fact, it was the intellectual proletariat that set the tone for the fourth estate in Germany rather than the workers: it was they who invented the category of "worker" in Germany by extrapolating from the French situation rather than observing the variety of artisanal conditions that existed in their own country.[191]

Riehl is usually portrayed as an irreconcilable opponent of modernization; he was nevertheless not a reactionary. Like most other *Staatswissenschaftler* of his day, he valued social differentiation, and he perceived that industrialization brought its own division of labor, by which such differentiation might be preserved. Thus he suggested that the true answer to oppressive factory conditions was to establish factories modeled on the patriarchal family, and he praised Robert Owen's experiment at New Lanark as an example.[192] The aristocracy should adapt itself to modern conditions by taking the lead in industrial ownership.[193] In this way, the fourth estate could become a positive rather than a negative category.[194]

The conservative implications of such sentiments were shared by many of the *Staatswissenschaftler*. Given their concern with the social question, however, it is not surprising that social policy (*Sozialpolitik*) should be a further variation. More surprising, however, is their overall lack of concrete suggestions: the theoretical imagination was displacing the practical. This held particularly for Riehl, who announced in his volume on the family that his theory of the household (*das ganze Haus*) would contain the key to his positive social policy.[195] But this section contained no proposed solutions; Riehl rather dodged the question

188. Riehl, *Naturgeschichte*, 2: 273, 355.
189. Ibid., 2: 235–40.
190. Ibid., 2: 274–76.
191. Ibid., 2: 342–43.
192. Ibid., 2: 350.
193. Ibid., 2: 185–86 on the aristocracy.
194. Ibid., 2: 290.
195. Ibid., 3: 106–08.

by conjuring up a vision of the harmonious household of the future, in which people would make fun of the utopian schemes of past economists and statisticians, financiers and industrialists.[196] Stein, in his history of social movements, was scarcely more concrete in his notion of social monarchy.[197] His later theory of associations (*Vereinswesen*) was likewise more concerned with description than with policy-making. Mohl was the exception: he produced a fine-grained *Sozialpolitik* in 1869, evaluating the various measures that the state could take with regard to the workers and differentiating these by the types of workers affected (factory workers, agricultural day-laborers, journeymen).[198] Perhaps with a nod to Riehl, he also included a section on popular festivals and the proper attitude of the the the state towards them.[199] Most of the creative work in *Sozialpolitik*, however, was done outside the academy, by people such as Schulze-Delitzsch, Huber, and Lassalle.[200]

If one leaves out socialism and communism, one can nevertheless discern a consensus among the academic and nonacademic writers on the proper application of social science. Their sense of the validity of collectives and associations led them to endorse the rights of workers to organize for their own interest—including for many a greater share in the profits of business.[201] The right of workers to organize was recognized by that bellwether of conservative social organizations, the Central Committee for the Welfare of the Working Classes, in 1864; Schulze-Delitzsch introduced a similar motion in the Congress of German Economists the following year, arguing that unions did not violate the laws of economics, which won great approval.[202] It was Ernst Engel who presented the more radical idea of profit-sharing schemes ("industrial partnerships") to the Committee and to the Crown Prince of Prussia in 1867, with the announcement that "the social question is no longer a question; its solution has

196. Ibid., 3: 277, 282–83.

197. Lees, *Revolution and Reflection*, 168–69.

198. Mohl, *Staatsrecht, Völkerrecht und Politik*, 3: 566–604.

199. Ibid., 3: 481–508.

200. Of these, Huber had a tangiential relationship to the academic *Staatswissenschaften*. Appointed to a professorship in modern philology in Berlin for his conservative political views in the 1840s, he was isolated from the faculty; his developing views on self-help organizations after 1848 placed him at odds with the official reaction. Huber resigned in 1851 but remained active in writing on behalf of cooperatives designed to help the working class; he was a major contributor to Bluntschli's *Staatswörterbuch*. See Braunreuther, "Staatswissenschaften," 1624–31; Lees, *Revolution and Reflection*, 155–60. Huber was particularly concerned—moreso than Schulze-Delitzsch—with cooperatives to provide low-cost housing for factory workers and consumer goods at prices within their reach (ibid.), 158.

201. Mohl, *Staatsrecht, Völkerrecht und Politik*, 3: 567, 586–87, 601; Stein, *Verwaltungslehre*, 1.3: 194–96; on Schäffle, see Pankoke, *Soziale Bewegung*, 190.

202. Reulecke, "Anfänge der organisierten Sozialreform," 44; Hentschel, *Deutsche Freihändler*, 189–90.

been discovered."[203] But as with much of the *Sozialpolitik* of the period, this was merely a sketch. It was only in the 1870s that such sketches would be given substance and specificity.

Historical Method

Most of the variations on this theme consisted of elaborations of ideas put forth in the 1840s: Roscher's multivolume system, which presented a cyclical theory of stages, and Stein's *History of Social Movements in France*, which presented a narrative of modernization, were cases in point. We have already noted the increased interest in the history of economic thought as another variation.

The most significant new contribution during the 1850s and 1860s was the work of Knies. His *Political Economy from the Standpoint of Historical Method* had nothing of the convenient textbook organization to it (although his lectures at Heidelberg followed the predictable organization established by his predecessor, Rau); it was rather a series of meditations on certain economic concepts and methods—something worlds apart from Roscher's grand and orderly system.[204] Knies in fact spent much time dismantling Roscher's theory of stages and his naturalistic analogies; for Knies, to be historical meant to be context-bound. Economic facts and theories must be interpreted in the context of the place and the time period of the society or people in question, not in the light of a larger developmental scheme or timeless causal law.[205] This differentiated economics from the natural sciences; Knies was in fact an exception to the trend of viewing society in terms of naturalistic analogies. The political and social sciences, of which economics was one, constituted in his view a distinct sphere of discourse, separate from the natural sciences on the one hand and the human sciences (*Geisteswissenschaften*) on the other. The former dealt with sensorily perceivable objects and causal laws, while the latter dealt with the inward mental life of individuals and groups (e.g., in philosophy, theology, and literature). The political and social sciences, by contrast, studied the "actions or works of human beings and in the . . . states or conditions of a socialized and legally ordered life-community of many individuals or peoples."[206] This sphere was of course codetermined by nature and by internal human motives,

203. Brentano, *Mein Leben,* 44; Sheehan, *Brentano,* 17; Reulecke, "Anfänge der organisierten Sozialreform," 46.

204. Knies's lecture notes exist in the Richard T. Ely papers, LSU Library, Louisiana State University. They follow the pattern established by Rau. The book, by contrast, is divided into three main sections: "Introductory," "Economics," and "Economic Theory." "Economics" included the influence of land and the state on the economy; "Economic Theory" discussed private property, self-interest, the history of economic thought, the "law of relativity," and methods.

205. Knies, *Politische Oekonomie,* 24, 356–57. On the polemic against Roscher, see 362–64; 372–82.

206. Ibid., 6.

but was not reducible to either. In practice, this meant that economics had to be viewed in the context of natural factors (e.g., territory, climate) as well as ethical ones (religious views). Knies's work represented, in fact, the first major discussion on the differences between natural sciences and the study of the political and social world, a theme that later preoccupied philosophers such as Dilthey, Rickert, and his own student Max Weber. Knies further anticipated Weber in stressing the role of religion in shaping economic behavior.[207] His work marked a new stage in methodological self-consciousness in German economics, a work of contemplation rather than praxis.

We now turn to a survey of the individual disciplines, noting how they reflected these themes and variations.

APPLICATIONS
Economic Theory, Economic Politics, and Finance

The rapid growth of the 1850s and 1860s occasioned a lively popular interest in economics, both theoretical and practical. We have noted the founding of the Congress of German Economists in 1857 and the gap between it and the universities. Of these two discourses, the popular one was more narrow, focusing on issues that interested the middle class: industrial freedom, cooperatives, and trade policy. At the same time, the overtly socialist writers like Lassalle and Rodbertus embraced the harsher forms of classical economic theory—such as the iron law of wages—in order to frame capitalism as properly exploitative.[208] Academic economics, on the other hand, reflected the breadth and the holism of the social and political thought of the time. Economics proved to be a favorable arena for further variations on the themes of society and history.

The elision of economics and the new science of society was a recurring motif. Rodbertus attributed many of the errors of classical economic theory to its inability to view society as an organic whole.[209] Knies, in his *Political Economy*, stated at the outset that this label should be expanded to include "social economy"—a terminological change already introduced in France.[210] In exploring economic theory in the pages that followed, Knies eschewed the traditional concepts inherited from Smith and Say, but focused on two that had clear sociological implications: private property and self-interest.[211] Knies's subsequent

<hr>

207. Ibid., 110–22.

208. On Lassalle's invocation of the iron law of wages, see Hentschel, *Deutsche Freihändler*, 102. Rodbertus, however, did not accept it ("Erkenntnis unserer staatswirtschaftlichen Zustände," 69 n).

209. Rodbertus, "Zweiter und dritter Brief an Kirchmann," 382.

210. Knies, *Politische Oekonomie*, 3. In France, the term referred to the school of Le Play. See Gide and Rist, *History of Economic Doctrines*, 490.

211. Knies, *Politische Oekonomie*, 180–223; 223–53.

intellectual development, however, revealed a more analytical bent. During the late 1850s, he wrote several articles on questions such as value and credit, which contained the germinal ideas of his major later work, the three-volume *Money and Credit* of 1873–79.[212] Knies's approach to these subjects was neither primarily historical nor sociological; if there was any influence of another discipline in his mature work, it was law—quite probably reflecting his work in the joint seminar with Bluntschli.

The writer who most thoroughly worked out a sociological economics during this period was Schäffle. In 1861 he announced an "ethical-anthropological" standpoint that was similar to that of Knies. Schäffle proposed to research "not the individual or average person, but the actual, the socially and historically diverse persons."[213] In his text, *The Social System of Human Economy*, which went through three editions in the 1860s, Schäffle presented the processes of production, circulation, distribution, and consumption of goods as social processes, albeit regulated by competition; more significantly, he saw these as insufficient to explain the entire economy. One also needed a "common economy" (*Gemeinwirtschaft*) of social groups—namely the family, commune, and state. This scheme replaced the threefold classification of agriculture, manufacturing, and commerce in his text.[214] It was adopted by one the leading economists of the subsequent period, Adolph Wagner.

The interest in scientific history also had a profound effect on the theorists of this generation by turning their attention to the temporal dimension of economic relationships and to articulating laws of change. As we have already noted with Roscher and Knies, there was no sharp distinction between economic theory and history during this period—a fact which the label "older historical school" has done much to obscure. The opposition between the historical and the theoretical approaches was the product of a later decade.

The way in which temporality entered into the very definition of concepts may be illustrated by Knies's work on credit.[215] Knies took exception to the idea espoused by Rau and others that credit is based on trust; rather, it was based on time. Credit, according to Knies, was "a remunerative transaction in which the deed of one occurs in the present and the counter-deed of the other

---

212. For example, see Knies, "Die Nationalökonomische Lehre vom Werth" (1855); "Erörterungen über den Credit" (1859–60).

213. Schäffle, "Mensch und Gut in der Volkswirtschaft," 236.

214. Schäffle, *Gesellschaftliche System*, 14, 63, 335, 357, 374 ff. For a discussion of Schäffle's views, see Pankoke, *Soziale Bewegung*, 153–57.

215. Another example would be Hans von Mangoldt (1824–68), a short-lived but highly regarded theoretician. Mangoldt's formulations of economic laws were often concerned with increase and decrease over time. See Mangoldt, *Grundriss*, 20, 26, 118, 161.

occurs in the future."[216] Its conceptual opposite was a cash payment. This mode of analyzing financial transactions was to be taken up in the 1880s by the Austrian economist Eugen von Böhm-Bawerk, who had studied with Knies.

The development of theory coexisted with the interest in economic history per se, and in the final years of the period, this interest also grew and became more articulated. Instead of merely invoking historical method, the younger economists actually pursued it. A survey of the *Zeitschrift für die gesamte Staatswissenschaft* reveals a sharp increase in the number of historical articles, from six between 1850 and 1859 to fourteen between 1860 and 1864. Many of these articles were based on primary sources; among them was an extensive survey of economic views during the Reformation by the young Gustav Schmoller.[217] In 1861, the historical trend received a further boost by the return of Hildebrand from his hiatus in Switzerland. This time Hildebrand did more than turn out manifestos: he too actually turned to historical research, including a history of the German wool industry.[218] As Max Weber later pointed out, he was the only member of the "older historical school" to actually engage in such research.[219] By the 1860s, the current of historical economics had become clearly recognizable to contemporaries.[220]

The concept of value also remained central to the discussion of the period. Stein, Knies, and Schäffle all viewed value as the bridge between the static concepts of classical economics and the dynamic lawful relationships they sought to express. Building on the work of Hermann in the previous period, they tended to view value as a relational concept by which the subjective and objective factors in economic decision making could be linked. In order to serve such a function, value had to be quantitative, so that various characteristics of various goods could be compared; Schäffle criticized Hermann for not going far enough in this direction.[221] Stein devised an elaborate formula to make this point, involving the variables of material, labor, product, need, application, and consumption; the value of any one of these variables consisted in the relation of that quantity to the rest. From this, Stein derived the "laws of value alteration," that is, the cases in which any, some, or all of these variables increase or decrease.[222] Knies brought his socioeconomic perspective to bear on the same issue, stressing that needs can vary from person to person, class to

216. Knies, "Erörterungen über den Credit," 576.

217. Schmoller, "Zur Geschichte der national-ökonomischen Ansichten in Deutschland während der Reformation" (1860).

218. Hildebrand, "Zur Geschichte der deutschen woll-Industrie."

219. Max Weber, "Roscher und Knies," 2.

220. Mangoldt, "Volkswirtschaft, Volkswirtschaftslehre," *DS*, 11 (1870): 124–25. Cf. Kautz, *Die geschichtliche Entwicklung der National-Oekonomie*, 2: 685–94.

221. Schäffle, "Über den Gebrauchswert," 141.

222. Stein, *System der Staatswissenschaften*, 1: 173, 176 ff.

class, nationality to nationality. "Value," he concluded, "does not depend only on the definite quantities of given goods with definite characteristics, but on the relation of these to the concrete needs of the people."[223]

Schäffle made greater claims for the importance of the value concept, calling it "undisputedly the fundamental concept of economics. Value is the meaning of a thing for the consciousness of the ethically active subject on the whole."[224] In his textbook he assigned it the "regulating power" in the production and circulation of goods.[225] For Schäffle, value was determined by the amount of sacrifice of work or fortune a person was willing to make for a good. This is why it served as the regulator: the principle of efficiency held that the most economical action was that which obtained the most goods at the least sacrifice.[226] In this way, Schäffle formulated a functional interpretation of value that anticipated the work of widely respected economists like Leon Walras and Gustav Cassels.[227] As with Knies, Schäffle showed that the language of German economics, for all its organic associations, could be used with rigor and precision. The Austrian school of marginal economics was soon to draw from these concepts, and its birth should come as no surprise to a close reader of Stein, Knies, and Schäffle.

The academic writings in *Volkswirtschaftspolitik* reflected the change in priorities of the 1850s and 1860s from those of agriculture and manufacturing to those of commerce and banking, as seen in the main journal of the period, the *Zeitschrift für die gesamte Staatswissenschaft* (see table 8). The *Zeitschrift* also reflected the distance which the sciences of state maintained from the popular literature. One still finds in it abundant examples of the deliberative style: judicious arguments with pros and cons fully stated and weighed, substantiated with extensive and impressive statistical data. In the intense public controversies over the extension of the Prussian customs union, the *Zeitschrift* presented articles advocating both free trade and protection.[228]

One area where economists could combine their interest in theory and practice—and maintain a certain authority among the practicioners—was banking.[229] It was a topic which in this period was inseparable from monetary

223. Knies, "Lehre vom Wert," 452–53.
224. Schäffle, "Konkurrenz," 196.
225. Schäffle, *Gesellschaftliche System,* 184.
226. Ibid., 51–52, 186–87.
227. Borchhardt, "Albert Schäffle als Wirtschaftstheoretiker," 613.
228. Helferich, "Die Zölle von Colonialzucker und die Rübensteuer im Zollverein" (1852); Kries, "Soll der Zollverein wirklich zerissen werden? Eine Frage aus Preussen" (1852); Hanssen, "Die volkswirtschaftlichen Zustände des Königreichs Hannover im Hinblick auf den Anschluss desselben an den Zollverein" (1853).
229. Schumacher, "Geschichte der deutschen Bankliteratur im 19. Jahrhundert," *ENTW,* no. 7: 39.

Table 8 *Articles in the* Zeitschrift für die gesamte Staatswissenschaften, *1844–1864*

	Agricultural Policy	Trades Policy	Commercial Policy
1844–48	9	3	4
1850–54	3	4	6
1855–59	6	3	12
1860–64	2	1	9

Source: *ZGS,* 1844–1864.

theory and policy, as banknotes were an increasing form of money substitute. The robust growth of the economy created a volume of transactions which the supply of currency could not possibly meet. Moreover, the shifting supplies of precious metals—as California gold entered the European market and silver was being exported to Asia—made it difficult for the states to maintain a sound ratio of hard currency to paper. Thus the states—mostly North German— allowed the establishment of a number of banks of issue: from nine in 1851 to twenty-nine in 1857. These were private banks, subject to state regulation. But the very multiplicity of sovereign states and the lack of coordination among them led to a wildly fluctuating situation, and the ensuing glut of notes led Prussia, Saxony, and Bavaria to ban notes from other states in 1857–58. This unfortunately coincided with the deflationary effects of the 1857 crash, leading once again to a shortage of currency which particularly affected small businesses and travelers.[230] Short of the wished-for unified banking system, the practicioners were at a loss.

By this time, however, other countries had experienced banking crises and had experimented with state-regulated banknotes, drawing on different theories of economists. Most prominently, the English Bank Charter Act of 1844 followed the prescription of the Ricardian "currency theory," which held that notes were a type of money and thus mandated severe restrictions on the ratio of notes to specie. The Prussian bank of 1846 followed the opposed "banking theory," which maintained that notes were a form of credit, and thus mandated fewer restrictions on note issue and eventually none at all. Neither the English nor the Prussian method was entirely successful, and German *Staatswissenschaftler* such as Rau regarded the proliferation of banks of issue with a certain understandable reserve.[231] Baden and Württemberg did not allow banks of issue until 1870.

In 1857, however, a young economist published a dissertation at Göttingen which was to modify this opinion significantly. His name was Adolf Wagner, and his influence on German economics continued until World War I. In his

230. Hentschel, *Deutschen Freihändler,* 81–82; Delbrück, *Lebenserinnerungen,* 2: 25–35; Tilly, "Germany," 165–74, 181.

231. Born, *International Banking,* 7–9, 12; Rau, *Lehrbuch,* 6th ed., 2.2: 193.

Contributions to the Theory of Banks, Wagner explained the relevant monetary theories as well as English and Prussian precedents. His conclusions were those of the banking school As he wrote to Mohl, previous theorists had failed to take into account the new role of banks as promoters of industrial development; he defended the policy of unrestricted issue, claiming that the practical defects had come from the role of the state banks themselves.[232] Wagner held these privileged banks particularly responsible for encouraging irresponsible speculation and for the trade crises that ensued. If banks were left to their own devices, the self-corrective mechanisms of the free market would discourage such excesses. But the state banks were in a position to keep interest rates and discount rates artificially low, creating irresistable temptations among investors for quick gains.[233] Wagner described the evils of contagious speculation with a moralistic fervor that was to characterize his subsequent long career:

> The cancer of our present circumstances, the stock market game, the stock-jobbing, appear then in their most repulsive manner and form and plague all our relationships in the way that we had recently to complain of [i.e., the crash of 1857].[234]

Wagner was no less concerned about the excesses of speculative fever than other academics. This was evident in his attitudes towards the policies of private credit banks founded on the model of the French *crédit mobilier*—which accounted in fact for far more transactions than the banks of issue. Wagner, Roscher, and Schäffle shared a distrust of these institutions.[235] In this respect the gap between the economists on the one hand and the bankers and industrialists on the other was still wide. Nevertheless, the increased use of credit captured the imagination of at least one economist: Hildebrand. He gave credit an elevated status in his three-stage theory of economic development: from natural- to money- to credit-based economy. If the money economy led to concentrations of wealth and impoverishment of the workers, a credit economy would allow workers to borrow and become entrepreneurs. Because credit for Hildebrand was based on trust, it was a "spiritual and ethical power, like science . . . based on the public morality of the people. Where this is absent, neither banks nor paper credit will help."[236]

232. Wagner to Mohl, 28 Oct. 1857, in *Briefe,* 12–13.

233. Wagner, *Beiträge zur Lehre von den Banken,* 236–38.

234. Ibid., 231.

235. Schumacher, "Bankliteratur," *ENTW,* no. 7, 28. On the relative role of the various credit institutons, see Tilly, "Germany," 173, 181.

236. Hildebrand, "Natural-, Geld und Creditwirtschaft," 22–23. Hildebrand's definition of credit contrasted sharply with that of Knies, who questioned Hildebrand's notion that credit characterized a distinct future stage of history: according to Knies, it was too thoroughly interwoven in the commercial economies of the past and present (Knies, "Erörterungen über den Credit," 155, 166).

The subject of *Finanzwissenschaft* during these years also bore all the earmarks of a transitional era. There was dissatisfaction with the piecemeal discussion of state expenditures and revenues that had characterized the field from the cameralists through Rau. But the alternatives were few: Roscher and Schäffle were not to publish their treatises on the subject until the 1880s. The major contributor during this period was Stein, who sought to integrate finance into his administrative science rather than into his economics, seeing it as a function of the state rather than of society. Thus, for example, he included the subjects of tax law and the legislative process of approving budgets in *Finanzwissenschaft*.[237] Stein also extended his discussion of finance to cover local self-administration. Otherwise, his innovations were more in rearranging the elements of the older works, bringing some into prominence which had formerly been in the background. Although his work did not find widespread use, it did serve to reinforce a view of the state which departed from classical liberalism: conceiving of public finance not in terms of a power over and against the individual citizens, but as a positive force in their economy through its influence on capital formation.

> We thus say that the value of each tax policy . . . never lies in the contribution or the amount of tax, but in its capital-forming power, which it receives through its application in the administration for the tax-power [*Steuerkraft*] of the citizen and through this for the economic power of the state.[238]

Drawing on the organic metaphor, Stein redefined income as "tax-power," which was a function of individual or group productivity:

> Tax-power should bring forth tax, tax bring forth administration, administration bring forth again tax-power. We call this cycle organic, because each factor conditions the others.[239]

Thus through the use of taxes in administrative functions such as public transportation and education, the state enhanced the productivity of its members. On similar grounds, Stein accepted the notion of state debt as a dynamic factor in furthering economic development—a notion that was shared by others, though by no means universally accepted.[240]

---

237. Stein, *Finanzwissenschaft*, 1: 73–77.
238. Ibid., 1: 399. On Stein's lack of subsequent influence, see Gerlach, "Geschichte der Finanzwissenschaft . . . " *ENTW*, no. 38: 35.
239. Stein, *Finanzwissenschaft*, 1: 399.
240. Ibid., 2: 463. See also Schanz, "Öffentliches Schuldenwesen," *ENTW*, no. 40: 14–17, particularly with reference to Carl Dietzel's defense of public debt in his work of 1855 and Umpfenbach's and Mangoldt's opposition to it.

Statistics

In statistics, there was a transition away from the qualitative historical statistics of the Achenwall-Schlözer type to an increasing acceptance of mathematical techniques as represented by Adolphe Quetelet. In many ways, the Belgian statistician's views and theories were congenial to German concerns at this time. Quetelet was also deeply concerned about revolutionary unrest and viewed his science of *physique sociale* as a means to alleviate it. The predictable regularities exhibited by large numbers (e.g., patterns of births and deaths, crimes, and marriages) made it possible to talk of causal laws that related different sets of numbers to one another. Quetelet was among the first to view patterns of "pathological" phenomena such as crimes as indicative of social trends—hence the name "moral statistics," which became fashionable at mid-century. Moreover, his reforms of the Belgian statistical bureau served as a model for other states to follow. His innovations found a more receptive audience in Germany after 1848 than before, as methodological questions gained more attention. The reception of Buckle contributed as well: Buckle relied heavily on Quetelet's statistical laws as evidence for his historical determinism.[241] While German statisticians responded positively to all of these aspects of Quetelet's thought, their response was not one of mere imitation, but of transformation.

It was Knies who first raised the issue of the discrepancy between historical and mathematical statistics in 1850. With his sharp eye for methodological issues, Knies distinguished between the aims of the two types: the historical approach of Achenwall and Schlözer aimed for a picture of a *particular* state in its individuality, while the mathematical approach sought an exact demonstration of causal relationships.[242] Once again, Knies anticipated a methodological distinction that was to be promulgated by the Baden neo-Kantians at the turn of the century: the distinction between the so-called idiographic interpretation of social science and the "nomothetic" one, that is, between the presentation of concrete particulars and of general laws. Knies's critique was directed against those who confused the two: the inevitable subjectivity of the idiographic historical approach invalidated historians' claims to discovering causal laws; numbers, in contrast, provided the certificate of objectivity. Far from protesting against the quantitative approach, however, Knies claimed that German statisticians had overreacted against it.[243] Only numerical statistics could claim to be a strict science, whereas the historical approach merely transmitted

---

241. Porter, *Rise of Statistical Thinking,* 167–68. Porter dates the reception of Quetelet's ideas from the 1860s; I would place them slightly earlier, with the works of Knies and Engel.

242. Knies, *Statistik als selbständige Wissenschaft,* 81, 113.

243. Ibid., 149, 152, 160–61.

a sum of knowledge; it was better labeled as the less rigorous *Staatenkunde*.[244] By the same token, economics, as a historical science, could not be reduced to quantitative relationships, and was to be clearly distinguished from statistics.[245]

The notion of a separate quantitative statistics was slow to gain acceptance—Mohl for one vigorously rejected it. By 1867, Wagner reported in the *Deutsches Staatswörterbuch* that opinion was still deeply divided, though the quantitative view was gradually gaining ground.[246] What actually occurred was a synthesis of the new quantitative techniques and the concreteness of idiographic perspective: the German transformation of Quetelet amounted to an assimilation of some of the main features of the Achenwall-Schlözer pattern. There were two specific trends which brought about this result.

The first was the actual practice of the state statistical bureaus. The number of these bureaus was increasing dramatically: ten new ones were founded between 1841 and 1864. With the increase came improvments in technique, some of them derived from the Belgian example. These techniques were intended to increase the reliability of results. They included questioning people directly rather than working through intermediaries, as well as processing all the information in a single central office in Prussia, a change from the practices of Hoffmann's day, when the local administrators compiled the data and sent them to Berlin.[247]

These changes meant that numbers were increasingly important, but many practicing statisticians still did not see quantification as incompatible with their duty to present comprehensive pictures of their respective states—even as the range of such available data was increasing dramatically. The prime mover in this trend was Engel, a man who resembled Quetelet both in his overall vision and his administrative energy. In his view, the purpose of statistics was

> to observe and arithmetically comprehend the life of peoples and states and their component parts in their appearances, and analytically set forth the causal connection between cause and effect.[248]

When it came to working out the details of this scheme, however, Engel revealed himself as beholden to the old classificatory mentality. Regarding the task of observing phenomena, he devoted much space to determining their proper order. His schemes amounted to a recapitulation of those of Mohl's *Polizeiwissenschaft:* moving from material factors (population, economics) to cultural ones (religion, education, morality) and to those that were social and polit-

---

244. Ibid., 167, 173.
245. Knies, *Politische Oekonomie*, 469.
246. Wagner, "Statistik," *DS*, 10: 400.
247. Seibt, "Statistik," *ENTW,* no. 37, 10, 18.
248. Engel, "Statistische Seminar und das Studium," 188.

ical (classes, local and state politics and administration).[249] All this was in marked contrast to Quetelet, who focused much more on the typical person (*l'homme moyen*)—the human body as well as the person's intellectual and moral qualities. As for the quantitative side, there was no discussion of mathematical techniques themselves; Engel gave no indication of understanding the significance of statistical sampling, a principle which Quetelet had clearly grasped.[250] Rather than stressing selection, he leaned toward completeness. In his eulogy of Quetelet in 1876, Engel claimed that "not the largest, but relatively local averages constitute what is really worth knowing."[251] Given Engel's influence, it is hardly surprising that German statistics was not known for mathematics until a later day.[252] Statistics remained for Engel a science of the concrete.

A second catalyst in the German assimilation of Quetelet was the lively controversy over statistics and free will in the 1860s. This was admittedly a European phenomenon, spurred in large part by the popularity of Buckle. The prospect that all human actions were statistically predictable threatened the cherished belief in human freedom and touched a raw nerve in all countries. In Theodore Porter's words, "It is far from clear that Darwin or Comte was discussed with greater urgency during the 1860s and 1870s [than was this question]."[253] In Germany, it was Adolph Wagner who provocatively raised the issue in a lecture by presenting the following picture of an imaginary state:

> In this country a state law determines each year in advance how many couples may marry, which age groups marry each other, how many young women take old men, how many young men take old women. . . . Another law standardizes in advance the number of persons who have to end their life through suicide in the next year, and distributes this number according to a predetermined relationship among the sexes, the age and occupational groups, etc.— and finally ordains further how many from these different classes will use drowning, the rope, the pistol, the knife, poison, etc. as their means to suicide. . . . A third law of the state establishes in similar fashion how many and which crimes will be committed. . . . No state power in the world, even if it united oriental despotism with the most thorough Caesaro-Papism, would be in a position to execute such an arrangement. . . . But that which could never artificially be carried through in such a way by human will or power amaz-

249. Ibid.

250. Ibid., 191–92; Hacking, "Prussian Numbers," 383. Hacking gives a good example of Engel's lack of quantitative sophistication: like Dieterici before him, Engel assumed that if one knows the mean age of a population at a given census, one can extrapolate the mean age of death. This ignores the fact that population growth and decline are uneven over time, as in baby-booms (388–89). See also Knapp, *Eine Jugend*, 192. On Quetelet, see Kern, *Empirische Socialforschung*, 43–44.

251. Engel, "Quetelet: Ein Gedächtnisrede," quoted in Porter, *Rise of Statistical Thinking*, 180.

252. Hacking, "Prussian Numbers," 392–93.

253. Porter, *Rise of Statistical Thinking*, 164. See his thorough discussion of the controversy, 167–71; 177–92.

ingly takes place automatically as a consequence of the natural order of society.[254]

Wagner's strong statement served in effect to vaccinate German writers against this naturalistic determinism: most of the writers who addressed themselves to the issue sought to soften if not oppose Wagner's position. Wagner himself used the occasion to develop a more sophisticated view of causality: the mere occurrence of regular numbers did not explain how or why such patterns occur.[255] The most pervasive response, however, was a recourse to Kantian arguments: Free will is not arbitrary behavior but that which is in accordance with moral law. This was essentially the view of the theologian Alexander von Oettingen, who published a lengthy treatise in 1868 entitled *Moral Statistics and Christian Ethical Teaching: Attempt at a Social Ethics on an Empirical Basis.* As the title implied, Oettingen posited a lawfulness in the ethical sphere that was observable through the study of motives; a true science of statistics would encompass these as well as the social laws already established.[256] Thus the notion of different types of lawfulness tended to reinforce the goal of statistics as a complete description of human society.

The controversy over statistics and free will, occurring at the end of this period, further served to loosen the ties between natural science and social science, strengthening the autonomous status of the latter. For if moral statistics encompassed the realm of motivated, comprehensible free choice, then it deserved to be distinguished from the laws of nature, which were indifferent to human motivation. The principal catalyst in establishing this view was Gustav Rümelin, a native of Württemberg who had already achieved fame as a member of the Frankfurt Parliament and as minister of education in Württemberg before turning to statistics in his fifties. Rümelin sharply distinguished between the realm of nature, "where the individual is typical," and that of human beings, where the individual is unique, and lawfully motivated free will can operate.[257] The former admitted generalizations in the form of causal laws, whereas the latter admitted descriptions of complex collective behaviors. Rümelin conceded that such descriptions, if sufficiently refined, could eventually yield strict laws, but statistics was still far from this point; Quetelet's method of averages skipped over the empirical work that needed to be done.[258] In later years, Rümelin became increasingly skeptical of arriving at any genuine social laws.[259]

254. Wagner, *Gesetzmässigkeit*, 44–46.

255. Ibid., 66.

256. Oettingen, *Moralstatistik und die christliche Sittenlehre*, 1: 309–12. Cf. Schmoller, *Litteraturgeschichte*, 199.

257. Rümelin, "Theorie der Statistik," 653, 661, 692.

258. Rümelin, "Begriff eines socialen Gesetzes," 15.

259. Porter, *Rise of Statistical Thinking*, 185.

Taken as a whole, his writings helped establish the claim for statistics that Knies had made for economics: that it dealt with the specifically human social realm. He viewed statistics as an auxiliary science which could serve a variety of human studies, from demography to economics to politics, which fell increasingly under the rubric of social science.

Politics, Polizei, and State Law

As the unit-idea of society increasingly held sway, the canon of the sciences of state itself underwent a fundamental transformation. Those sciences which dealt with the state proper began to drift away from economics and statistics. This was a gradual process, not yet evident in the statistics on course offerings. Of the thirty-two faculty members who taught politics between 1850 and 1865, seventeen taught primarily in the *Staatswissenschaften*, while four were primarily jurists and six primarily historians.[260] The most conspicuous trend, however, particularly in northern Germany, was to follow Dahlmann's example of combining politics with history. The historians Heinrich von Sybel, Max Duncker, Georg Waitz, and later Heinrich von Treitschke all lectured on politics at various times in their careers.[261] But whereas Dahlmann had taught these subjects along with the other sciences of state, the generation of *kleindeutsch* historians that followed him severed the connection, tying politics more and more closely to history alone.[262] This was due partly to the influence of Ranke, for whom history was primarily political, and politics presupposed a thorough knowledge of history for its generalizations. According to Johann Droysen, politics was "nothing other than the present of history, but not from the standpoint of static conditions [*Zuständlichkeit*] like statistics, rather from that of the moving forces, the prevailing conditions, the indicated trends."[263] If politics tied history to the present, the Prussian historians made no effort to hide their present political concerns. Their written lecture notes, whether published or not, give only a hint of their passion, which was contagious in the lecture hall—Sybel drew over two hundred students for his *Politik* at Bonn.[264] If, paradoxically, the state

260. The figures are based on the survey of university catalogs.

261. For a brief comparative treatment, see Hübner, "Droysens Vorlesungen über die Politik," 325–30. Droysen, however, gave his lectures on politics only once, at Kiel in 1850. On Sybel, see Seier, "Sybels Vorlesung über Politik," 90–112, and Dotterweich, *Heinrich von Sybel*, esp. 132–67. Waitz's lecture outlines were published as *Grundzüge der Politik* (1862); Treitschke's were published posthumously: *Politik* (1899).

262. See Riedel, "Staatsbegriff der deutschen Geschichtsschreibung," 45, who emphasizes the continuity of this view with that of Aristotle—in contrast to the earlier abstract natural law tradition of the eighteenth century and the new separation of state and society.

263. Quoted in Hübner, "Droysens Vorlesungen über die Politik," 344.

264. Hübinger, ed. *Historische Seminar*, 121. Treitschke was a popular lecturer from the start, although his *Politik* attracted less attention at Freiburg than his historical lectures; this changed by the time he got to Berlin. See Dorpalen, *Treitschke*, 49, 83, 227.

was no longer exclusively the subject of mere *Staatswissenschaft*, it was because the word *state* had assumed the same holistic significance as the word *society:* the center of a multitude of associations, rational and irrational. Most would have agreed with Stein's formulation: If society signified plurality and self-interest, then the state signified unity and patriotism. If the science of society had the harmony of classes as its practical concern, the science of politics had the role of the nation: the agenda of German unification was never far from the surface.

The figure who extensively explored the relationship between the sciences of politics and society was Heinrich von Treitschke. Treitschke was a product of the 1850s, entering the University of Bonn in 1851. He came under Dahlmann's influence there and later turned to political economy under Roscher at Leipzig. As a *Privatdozent* at that university, he soon developed a reputation as a fiery lecturer; in 1863 he was called to Freiburg, thanks to the strong *kleindeutsch* sentiments of some of the Badenese liberals.[265] His *Habilitationsschrift*, written at the age of twenty-four in 1858, was entitled *The Science of Society: A Critical Essay.* In a none-too-careful polemic directed against Mohl, he showed how each of Mohl's social groups or associations had a political dimension to it.[266] The work was also replete with critical remarks on Riehl, Ahrens, and to a lesser extent Stein. Treitschke particularly objected to Riehl's contrasting the state as artificial to the people as natural.[267]

Treitschke did not deny the importance or the autonomy of social forces and tendencies, but claimed only that they should be studied together with politics:

> The entire science of state is socio-political; its task is to show how the idea of unity of the people realizes itself in the multitude of their special endeavours [and] . . . to show further the natural preconditions (land, location, etc.) on which society and state depend. The state is exposed to all influences of nature and society; by the same token, political relationships are mirrored even in the freest social relationships, even in so-called sociability. The difficult thing to understand about this interaction is this: one can with equal justification see the state as end and as means of society.[268]

Treitschke then proposed two ways in which the spheres of state and society might be integrated. The first was to show how the spirit of a people manifested itself in a state over time. Political history was the easy way to do this, but Treitschke suggested something more ambitious: a cultural history that would integrate all branches of human activity—as Riehl had also proposed but conceived too narrowly. The second was a more static aproach: to show how the

265. Dorpalen, *Treitschke*, 49, 79–80.
266. See Angermann, *Mohl*, 376–78 on Treitschke's reading of Mohl and the latter's response.
267. Treitschke, *Gesellschaftswissenschaft*, 66.
268. Ibid., 69–70.

state ordered, regulated, and affected these various activities. This was less ambitious, since it sought merely to describe rather than explain. It was the true mission of *Staatswissenschaft*, of which politics was the main discipline.[269] As commentators have noted, these were the two principal projects to which Treitschke devoted the remainder of his life: they bore fruit in his famous *History of Germany* and his *Politics*.

Police science was also in transition. "Police science finds itself presently in a very vacillating state," wrote the curator of the university of Bonn in a memorandum of 1858. "The goals of *Polizei* are conceived completely abstractly . . . whereby the consequences that one derives for its activity appear often to be most arbitrary, in part fantastic."[270] The discrepancies between the popular use of the term *police* and the academic content of police science had increased dramatically in the years after 1848. The pejorative phrase *police state* was taken for granted by writers like Riehl and noted by Rau and in the *Deutsches Staatswörterbuch*.[271] As a response to this, the formal definitions of *Polizei* shifted away from its purposes and towards its functions: police was viewed as the activity of commanding and compelling, a definition more in line with popular usage.[272] This did not necessarily mean that the aim of promoting the general welfare was forgotten, either by the *Staatswissenschaftler* or by the police officials themselves: the powerful commissioner of police in Berlin, Karl L. F. von Hinckeldey, was remembered both for his spy networks and his fire protection.[273] But it was the preventive or protective aspects of these activities, as distinct from positive programs to promote well-being, that were stressed: for example, ordinances to keep roads or buildings in good repair were considered to be police functions, as opposed to programs for building them. In Munich, the university lectures on "medical police" were rechristened "hygiene" in 1855, indicating that public health was to be an offshoot of natural science rather than *Polizei*.[274] For Stein, *Polizei* was "the totality of all administrative measures to be taken for the protection of the general interest."[275]

Definitional problems were nothing new to *Polizeiwissenschaft*, and they did not immediately affect its role in the curriculum. It was still a required examination subject in Bavaria and Württemberg; it became one in Hesse-Darmstadt

---

269. Ibid., 60–61, 80.

270. Curator to ministry, 28 June 1858, GPSA Dahlem, Rep. 76 Va Sect. 3 Tit. IV no. 40, vol. 3: 206 (Anstellungen, Bonn).

271. Riehl, *Naturgeschichte*, 2: 76; Rau, "Begriff und Wesen der Polizei," 607; Medicus, "Polizei," *DS*, 8: 133.

272. Medicus, "Polizei," *DS*, 8: 131; cf. Brater, "Neueren Bearbeitungen der Polizeiwissenschaft," 82; Rau, "Begriff und Wesen der Polizei," 614, 620.

273. Gillis, *Prussian Bureaucracy*, 183–85; Siemann, *Deutschlands Ruhe, Sicherheit, und Ordnung*, 343.

274. Weindling, *Health, Race, and German Politics*, 157.

275. Stein, *Verwaltungslehre* 2: 73.

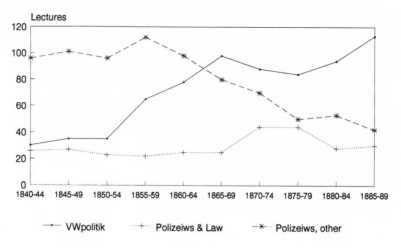

Lectures

—•— VWpolitik   ⋯+⋯ Polizeiws & Law   —*— Polizeiws, other

Source: University catalogues;
see appendix.

Fig. 10. Lectures in *Volkswirtschaftspolitik* and *Polizeiwissenschaft*, 1840–1890

in 1851 and in Baden in 1853.[276] Nevertheless, its material tended to be transformed in one of two directions. One was specialization: thanks to Rau, the economic aspects of the old police science gained increasing recognition as the separate discipline of *Volkswirtschaftspolitik*, and there was a lesser tendency to treat the other aspects separately as well (see figure 10).

The other direction was to subsume police science under a broader science of administration (*Verwaltungslehre*), of which Stein was the main author, while Schäffle followed suit.[277] Stein shifted the study of administration from a practical to a speculative and theoretical science. Not only did it include administrative law as well as *Polizei*, but it represented a clear break with the liberal notion of the *Rechtstaat:*

> The most recent period . . . has meant primarily by the so-called "Rechtstaat"
> . . . a state of affairs that contains nothing but a finished state as autonomous
> juristic personality on one side, and the free citizen on the other, so that the
> *Rechtstaat* essentially establishes only the juristic order of the relation of the
> two, the totality of the propositions concerning the inviolability of one
> through the other. This impoverished view of the state belongs however only

276. Lindenfeld, "Polizeiwissenschaft," 145. Baden's requirement had been prepared well before the revolution of 1848. See VFS, *Vorbildung zum höheren Verwaltungsdienst*, 131–33.

277. Schäffle, "Stellung der politischen Verwaltung," 235. On the dissolution of *Polizeiwissenschaft*, see Maier, *Verwaltungslehre*, 238–47.

to the most recent time, and its representative is, as is well known, Robert Mohl. But in truth the relationship is essentially different.[278]

According to Stein, the notion of the *Rechtstaat* left no room for a proper conceptualization of administration. His purpose was in large part to give the executive function its due in state law and to redress the emphasis on the legislative power in the earlier part of the century. In Stein's view, administration was the wave of the future.[279] It was based on a more intimate relation between the individual and the collective. "Domestic administration," he wrote, "is in the final analysis nothing but the great process of free devotion of the individual to the state and the giving-back to the individual through the state."[280] It was the activity of the collective personality, bound by the law, executed in ordinances. Stein's highly metaphorical language did have the advantage of flexibility: he found such collective activities not only in government administration as commonly thought of, but also in self-administration (e.g., local government) and voluntary associations. The treatises on state administrative law, local government, and associations comprised the first three volumes of Stein's system; the remaining seven concerned aspects of the old police science: population, health, education, and economics. These works were rich in erudition: drawing on Gneist's studies of England and his own on France, Stein was able to adduce a vast amount of comparative data throughout. His own historical sense enabled him to comprehend changes which had passed by the older *Polizeiwissenschaft* (for example, in the section on population, which he found no longer subject to direct administrative control).[281] At other points, however, Stein sacrificed empirical research to conceptual consistency: he insisted on imposing his distinctions between legislative and administrative power, between laws and ordinances, when there was little basis for them in fact.[282] Above all, the work was a survey of past laws and precedents rather than a genuine policy science.

Such broad-ranging speculation naturally aroused the skepticism of some legally trained minds, and this period witnessed the beginnings of the movement to detach state law from the sciences of state in order to anchor it more firmly in the methods of jurisprudence. The need for definitional clarity, which the sciences of state had formerly sought to fulfill but were now renouncing, led a new generation of jurists to an approach that became known as legal positivism. In many respects, this movement expressed a contrary impulse to

278. Stein, *Verwaltungslehre*, 2: 24.

279. Ibid., 1.1: 71, 126; 2: viii, 29. Schäffle, drawing on the ideas of Ahrens and Krause, also proposed to overcome the dichotomy between law and *Polizei*, since law ultimately served the purpose of the welfare of the society (Schäffle, "Rechtsphilosophische Gedanken," 365, 384).

280. Stein, *Verwaltungslehre*, 2: 45–46.

281. Ibid., 2: 122.

282. This was Gneist's opinion (*Rechtstaat*, 267–68).

the contextualizing aims of the sciences of society and politics: it sought to construct an internally consistent formal structure of law that would remain firm amidst the changing tides of contemporary events. There have been several attempts to explain this development in terms of ideology: it is seen either as part of the conservative reaction after 1848, by silencing any questions about the philosophical or sociological dimensions of an authoritarian state, or alternatively, as a foundation for the emerging liberalism, providing a legal base of security and consistency so that individuals and groups could better pursue their self-interest.[283] These explanations are not incompatible; they leave out, however, another important aspect, namely, the pedagogical. The study of the principles underlying a logically constructed legal system could provide a mental discipline which neither the study of comparative constitutions nor the theme-and-variation approach could deliver. This was evident also in the area of Roman law, which was taught increasingly through the "Pandects," a digest dating from Justinian that was known for its logical coherence. This bespoke a certain disillusionment of jurists with the historical school as well: instead of merely assimilating factual material from the past, they looked to extrapolations of the principles which underlay the factual law and rendered it more consistent. During the 1850s, scholars such as Carl Friedrich Gerber and Rudolph von Ihering began to extend this method of logical construction to other areas of law. In their concern for internal consistency, they sought to excise any reference to social or historical context, or to extralegal subject matter such as the *Staatswissenschaften*.[284]

Only gradually was this approach applied to state law. As with so many other trends of this period, the change involved the laying of foundations and establishment of broad outlines, the details of which were worked out only after 1866.[285] It is ironic, however, how thoroughly this transition was rooted in the prevailing organicist language of the time—with all its wooliness.[286] Thus when Gerber first addressed the subject of state law in 1852, he took the same position that Eichhorn had taken in the 1820s: that historical conditions in Germany were too unstable to allow for a valid logical construction. But much work by practicioners within the individual states on questions of state law—appearing mostly in periodicals rather than textbooks—changed the situation in the ensuing years.[287] Thus in 1865, Gerber reversed himself, claiming,

283. For the former, see Wilhelm, *Juristischen Methodenlehre*, 155–56, 159; on the latter, Oertzen, "Bedeutung C. F. v. Gerbers," 205; Bleek, *Juristenprivileg*, 300.

284. Wilhelm, *Juristischen Methodenlehre*, 88–91, 97; Böckenförde, *State, Society, and Liberty*, 12–14.

285. Stolleis, "Verwaltungsrechtswissenschaft," *DV*, 3: 86–87. The best treatment of the transition is Oertzen, *Soziale Funktion* (1974).

286. Oertzen, *Soziale Funktion*, 68–69, 114, 150–51.

287. Stolleis, *Geschichte des öffentlichen Rechts*, 2: 284–85.

> The majority of German states . . . have completed an entirely new formation in this sense of an organic peoples' state. German science views these foundations presently as worthy of an autonomous scientific view, because they are a product of the ethical power [*Kraft*] of the German people.[288]

Gerber was referring here to the fact that most German states had adopted a common form of government, namely, constitutional monarchy. Nevertheless, he took pains to distinguish the sphere of legal formalism from its organic nimbus:

> We come to the conclusion that the so-called organic and legal views of the state are related to each other as two considerations of the same object from different standpoints. The former wants to determine the natural life, the physiology, the latter the ethico-juristic content of the state . . . the one grasps the actual foundations of the law, the other the law itself.[289]

The legal system no longer needed the ethical and philosophical foundations of the sciences of state, which Gerber contemptuously dismissed as a "prologue in philosophical heaven."[290] Despite this separation, however, the organicist perspective entered into Gerber's exposition at a number of crucial points. The monarch and the estates were still the "organs" of the state. The state as a whole had a "personality" which was not simply the counterpart of the legal person of civil law, but an expression of its ethical basis in the unity of the people.[291] This notion of a single personality made it possible to draw on analogies to civil law, insofar as the subjects of civil law were individuals endowed with a personality and will. The state-personality had, however, a distinctive way of expressing its will, namely, domination. This was the fundamental principle from which the other elements of constitutional law could be derived, the logical first premise. On this basis, Gerber proceeded to retract the liberal assumptions regarding the legitimacy of the state: rights of the people were not prior to the state, but granted as a gift of the dominating sovereign in return for submission.[292] Thus despite his claim to clarity and precision, Gerber's extralegal assumptions affected his substantive conclusions. The interwoven concepts of organism, unity, will, domination, and sovereignty are revealed in the following passage:

288. Gerber, *Grundzüge des deutschen Staatsrechts*, 9–10. On the contrast to his earlier views, see Wilhelm, *Juristische Methodenlehre*, chap. 4.

289. Gerber, *Grundzüge des deutschen Staatsrechts*, 224.

290. Ibid., 238.

291. Ibid., 21 n; Stinzing and Landsberg, *Geschichte der deutschen Rechtswissenschaft*, 3.2: 827; Oertzen, *Soziale Funktion*, 175–77.

292. Gerber, *Grundzüge des deutschen Staatsrechts*, 50. See Wilhelm's exposition for greater detail, which is much more thoroughly based than Oertzen's contention that Gerber sought to make concessions to liberal thought.

The state-power [*Staatsgewalt*] is the will-power [*Willensmacht*] of a personally conceived ethical organism. It is not an artificial and mechanical combination of many individual wills, but the ethical total power of the self-conscious people. Its existence and nature is based not on an arbitrary determination and premeditated creation, but is a natural power. . . . The juristic expression of state-power is domination. This means an effective will-power for the tasks of state connection, to which the entire people in all its members are subject. Its success . . . is based on the fact that it is the highest power in the people and that the conviction of its irresistability is generally established.[293]

Gerber was trying to find the appropriate legal construction for the form of constitutional monarchy that had in fact developed in Germany. But as Peter von Oertzen has pointed out, the attempt was arbitrary: Gerber's stress on unity clashed with the mixed character of constitutional monarchies.[294]

Although Gerber distinguished his approach from that of the *Staatswissenschaftler*, his views on many substantive matters paralleled theirs; both represented a shift in opinion following 1848 in a conservative direction. For example, the contract theory of government met with their disfavor, or was viewed as obsolete.[295] Their commitment to constitutional monarchy was unshaken by the events of 1848, but they distinguished more and more sharply between constitutional and parliamentary monarchy: with the exception of Mohl, they viewed the latter as conceding too much to popular sovereignty and to the divisiveness of party rule. In short, the urge to unity underlay both the allusive associations of the *Staatswissenschaftler* and the constructive clarification of Gerber.

In sum, by the end of this period the notion of the sciences of state as a coherent intellectual field was becoming less and less meaningful. Instead, a bifurcation was taking shape which would lead to two parallel processes of articulation, by which the themes and variations of the transitional period were gradually molded into coherent systems. One of these was the elaboration of social science, drawing on methods and material from economics, history, and statistics. The other was the elaboration of legal positivism, extending the methods of civil law to state and administrative law. Moreover, the system of social science would succeed in reviving the connection between theory and practice that had been subdued in the previous generation—albeit more tenuously than had been the case before 1840. This is what we mean by a truncated revival.

293. Gerber, *Grundzüge des deutschen Staatsrechts*, 19–22.
294. Oertzen, *Soziale Funktion*, 184 ff.
295. Bluntschli, *Lehre vom modernen Staat*, 1: 338; Stein, *Verwaltungslehre*, 1.1: 297–98; Gerber, *Grundzüge des deutschen Staatsrechts*, 8n, 50 nn.

A Truncated Revival, 1866–1890: Organized Research and Charisma

The process of German unification had a mixed effect on the development of the sciences of state. On the one hand, the predominance of Prussia in the new Germany tended to reinforce the relatively cavalier treatment of the *Staatswissenschaften* that had prevailed there compared to the south. On the other hand, as unification reinforced the process of industrialization, the increasing complexity of economic and social life generated a need for more administrators and for greater specialization among them: the total number of officials increased by 24 percent between 1875 and 1881.[1] This was due in part to the superposition of a federal administration over that of the states: the imperial constitution gave the central government jurisdiction over post and telegraph, railroads, waterways and highways, weights and measures, patents and copyrights, customs, banking, citizenship and passports, press, and public health, as well as finances, foreign service, and the military—a good bit of the material of the old *Polizei*.[2]

The relationships between these changes and the intellectual developments in the sciences of state were by no means simple or clear cut. Certainly the growth of the bureaucracy did not lead to complete specialization within the disciplines. The prestige and the exalted ethos of the upper bureaucracy continued to permeate the entire hierarchy, at least until the 1890s. The self-image of the German official has been compared to that of the Anglo-American professional, in that both saw themselves as providing expertise in the service of a higher ethical contribution to society than mere market considerations would dictate.[3] In neither the Anglo-American nor German tradition was training seen to be purely specialized or technical: general education or *Bildung* was also

1. Wunder, *Geschichte der Bürokratie*, 72; Morsey, *Oberste Reichsverwaltung*, 316.

2. Morsey, "Öffentlichen Aufgaben," *DV*, 3: 129–30. This jurisdiction was not exclusive: legislative competence was shared with the states in many cases, and certain exceptions ("reserved rights"), such as Bavarian and Württemberg post and telegraph, were stipulated in the *Reich* constitution itself, a product of Bismarck's negotiations with these states for entry.

3. See Caplan, "Profession as Vocation," 166–68; McClelland, *Professionalization*, 77, 109. McClelland discusses the Anglo-American and German literature on professionalization in chapter 1.

considered essential. In the German case, the belief in the organic view of society was also characteristic of the bureaucratic ethos by the 1870s. Hence the social sciences tended to retain some of the holistic views that had dominated the previous generation.

The same political and economic conditions also contributed to the expansion of the universities and to greater opportunities for a confident new generation of *Staatswissenschaftler*. In addition, these conditions stimulated the proliferation of national organizations outside the government, such as professional associations and economic interest groups. The academic *Staatswissenschaftler* participated in this trend, developing their own organizations. As they did so, they could not completely ignore the demand for clearly spelled-out criteria of professional competence: holism could no longer be equated quite as easily with vagueness. If specialization was not always defined in terms of a strictly delimited subject area, it was at least becoming defined by specified and testable techniques. This involved a new strategy for organizing the intellectual field.

It was thus during the Bismarckian era that research in its contemporarily recognizable form emerged as the central purpose of the sciences of state. *Research* is taken here to mean the systematic acquisition of new knowledge as distinct from the ordering, synthesizing, or application of existing knowledge which had characterized the sciences of state in the past. As an intellectual strategy, it was no longer based on claims of comprehensiveness but of fruitfulness. Its goals were that of causal explanation and understanding rather than classification. The increase in knowledge which it produced has generally presupposed esoteric skills, a higher degree of methodological self-consciousness, and hence more rigorous and extended training, all of which enhanced the sense of professional identity among the practitioners. The concept of a discipline as a research program had long since been developed in areas such as philology, history, and the natural sciences—and had contributed much to the international fame of German universities. During this period it gave decisive shape to the constellation of new social sciences which centered around economics and statistics. This change gave a new and different meaning to the notion of knowledge as power. With the loss of claims to comprehensiveness, the scientists of state were giving up one of their principal sources of authority, namely, their claim to speak on the basis of a broad range of knowledge. Its place was taken by the authority of the expert. As if to compensate for this loss, experts generally amassed a more extensive power base in terms of concrete institutions from which to affect society: research institutes, seminars, and professional organizations. In the case of German social science, this power was also enhanced by the charismatic personalities of several of the leading professors, who served as concrete embodiments of an intellectual tradition. This

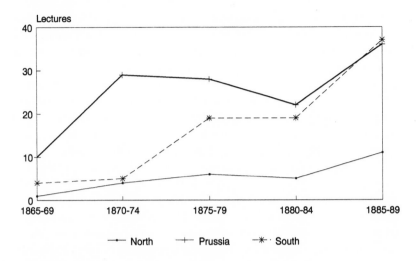

Source: University catalogues;
see appendix.

Fig. 11. Lectures in Social Policy, 1865–1890

likewise compensated for the loss of the comprehensiveness of the systems themselves. These developments would also have profound implications for the relation of theory to practice and for the metamorphosis of practical reasoning that these disciplines brought with them.

The economic circumstances that favored academic innovation also brought the social question to the fore once again. During the speculative frenzy of the early 1870s, consumers encountered higher prices that exceeded growth in personal income: the price index of private consumption increased 19 percent between 1869 and 1873, while real per capita income rose only 5.4 percent between 1866 and 1875.[4] Not surprisingly, strikes increased and socialism spread: in addition to Lassalle's German Workers Party, the Marxist Socialist party of Bebel and Liebknecht was founded in 1869. The bloody events of the Paris Commune of 1871 further focused attention on the social question. The university lectures devoted to the social question increased accordingly (see figure 11).

In fact, neither the economic atmosphere nor the dramatic events of unification seemed to have contributed to a feeling of great confidence in the new Reich itself. The initial euphoria of military victory gave way to an anxiety over the fragility of the new creation. The regional, religious, and social tensions within the nation were only too evident; in addition, the discrepancy between

4. Lütge, *Sozial-und Wirtschaftsgeschichte*, 424, 450–51.

Germany's newly found wealth and her cultural heritage struck many intellectual leaders as decadent. "It is shocking, even for the greatest optimist," lamented Treitschke in the Reichstag in 1871, "to see how indulgence, materialism, the neglect of all ideal aspects of life is spreading among the younger generation."[5] Out of this anxiety emerged the search for enemies, of which the *Kulturkampf* was the most striking example. It is hard to explain the vehemence of this campaign against Ultramontanism other than by such appeals to depth-psychology. As one might expect, the fear of socialism was another product of this mood. And one equally predictable response to this situation was a renewed impulse to promote social reform from above as a way of forestalling revolution.

Thus even as the economists were turning inward and developing their research programs, they were simultaneously reaching outward to wider audiences, founding another organization, the *Verein für Sozialpolitik*, to influence public opinion and state policy. Here too, the organization itself was a force for articulation, transforming *Sozialpolitik* from a unit-idea to a specific agenda of social research and policy recommendations.

UNIFICATION, THE TRAINING OF ADMINISTRATORS, AND THE UNIVERSITIES

Let us first examine the impact of the Prussian model on the training of administrators. Here one must begin with Bismarck, whose personality left its mark on virtually every aspect of his age. On the bureaucracy, this mark was negative: Bismarck contributed significantly to the undermining of administrative self-confidence and initiative. His dislike for bureaucratic routine dated back to an early age, as did his dislike for ideologues and academics: politically engaged professors were thus doubly suspect. In his view, officials owed their obedience to their superiors rather than to abstract principles. During the Prussian constitutional conflict of the early 1860s, Bismarck reportedly subjected about one thousand officials to reprisals for their political views.[6]

Bismarck's hostility to the bureaucracy and its role in politics was evident in his own constitutional draft for the North German Confederation of 1867, which became the basis for that of the Second Empire after 1871. That draft was largely Bismarck's own work; leading academic authorities such as Gneist and Mohl were not consulted, probably because of their vocal opposition to Bismarck prior to 1866.[7] Bismarck's version contained a provision to exclude

5. Quoted in Dorpalen, *Treitschke*, 207.
6. M. L. Anderson and Barkin, "Myth of the Puttkamer Purge," 656.
7. Gneist did not overcome his opposition to Bismarck until April of 1867 (Heffter, *Deutsche Selbstverwaltung*, 457); Mohl, who wanted to come Berlin, was denied the post of Badenese ambassador; he was made ambassador to Bavaria instead. (Mohl, *Lebenserinnerungen* 2: 307).

officials from parliament altogether. Since the constituent Reichstag which had to approve the document was still largely composed of officials—190 representatives out of 297—this provision failed.[8] The draft also contained no mention of ministerial responsibility. True, Bismarck eventually conceded this to the liberals also—albeit with typically vague phraseology—but at the price of keeping all executive functions in the hands of a single federal chancellor, rather than creating a cabinet of ministers.[9]

Such moves had the effect of increasing the vigilance of the liberals, and this found several avenues of expression. One was the formation of the National Liberal Party in October of 1867. While acknowledging Bismarck's achievement and expressing a willingness to work with him in the future, the National Liberals viewed the constitution of the North German Confederation as only the starting point of a process that would lead to greater parliamentary participation. Their platform included demands for the right to supervise the budget, the extension of ministerial responsibility, and subordination of Prussian institutions to federal ones.

A second area of liberal assertion was to push for the program of self-administration in Prussia along the lines of the Badenese reforms of the 1860s. The need for the administrative integration of the newly annexed Prussian provinces of Hannover, Frankfurt, electoral Hesse, and Schleswig-Holstein as a result of the War of 1866 provided the opportunity, and in this connection the National Liberal platform called for "the removal of the estate principle from the local, county, and provincial governments and their reform on the basis of equal rights and self-administration."[10] Gneist played an important role in persuading Bismarck that such legislation could curb the independent power of the bureaucracy and still preserve a place for de facto local aristocratic rule; Treitschke also lent support in his essays.[11] A law was eventually passed in 1872 which introduced elected representatives into the county level of government, where they served alongside appointed officials under the chairmanship of the *Landrat*.[12] The county boards also served a judicial function as well: they heard appeals on infringements of administrative law. This, plus the expanded tasks of government itself, tended to give the appointed officials more weight than the elected ones; it put a premium on professional competence, particularly in

8. E. R. Huber, *Verfassungsgeschichte*, 3: 661–62.

9. Pflanze, "Juridical and Political Responsibility," 171–72; E. R. Huber, *Verfassungsgeschichte*, 3: 658–60.

10. Treue, ed., *Deutsche Parteiprogramme*, 55. The pro-Bismarckian Free Conservatives adopted the same position, though elaborated in less detail (58).

11. Heffter, *Deutsche Selbstverwaltung*, 510. Heffter insists that Gneist's role in the process was overestimated both by contemporaries and by subsequent scholars (506, 637 ff). On Treitschke's views, see Dorpalen, *Treitschke*, 137, 146.

12. Heffter, *Deutsche Selbstverwaltung*, 512–13, 549.

administrative law.[13] This in turn affected the juristic sciences of state, by way of increasing pressure for more lectures on this subject.[14] Administrative law thus emerged as a new member of the canon during this period.

A third area in which liberals sought to assert themselves was that of training and qualifications for the bureaucracy, which of course affected the relationship between law and the *Staatswissenschaften*. This became a matter of intense controversy during the late 1860s and 1870s, because it reflected the conflicting pulls of the conservatives' desire to retain a decisive influence on the bureaucracy, the liberals' increasing demands for professional criteria, and the shifting administrative needs of the newly unified nation-state. The key to conservative influence lay in the way the Prussian system combined academic study and practical apprenticeship, allotting only three years to the former and four to the latter. It was felt that the long apprenticeship provided the opportunity to inclulcate traditional values and to weed out the candidates who did not go along with them. As we have seen, this emphasis was at the expense of taking academic study seriously: not only was it considered fashionable for students to ignore lectures and cram for examinations, but the prescribed three years at a university were frequently further abridged by the one-year military service in the reserves. These practices aroused an increasing amount of criticism from academics, both *Staatswissenschaftler* and jurists, who pointed to the contrast with other German states.[15] The indictment of the legal scholar Otto von Gierke was typical:

> If the well-known theory of the worthlessness of jurisprudence as a science is no longer loudly proclaimed in the marketplace, it has passed into the flesh and blood of a large part of the Prussian practitioners . . . What the jurist, the judge, the attorney, the administrative official has to learn, [it is said,] he learns only in life. . . . Yes—and now a counterargument is no longer possible—the Reich chancellor himself cut lectures by his own admission![16]

13. Ibid., 549, 555. The prestige of the bureaucratic model as an example for other professions in Germany was illustrated by the pattern of physicians and lawyers. In the 1870s, both groups established similar organs of self-administration (*Kammern*) to enforce professional ethics. Membership in the chambers, which were separate from the professional organizations themselves, was obligatory, so that doctors and lawyers could not escape penalties for violations. See McClelland, *Professionalization*, 83, 87.

14. Stengel, "Begriff, Umfang und System des Verwaltungsrechts," 220; Stolleis, "Verwaltungsrechtswissenschaft," *DV,* 3: 91.

15. For criticism, see Richter, "Vorbildung der höheren Verwaltungsbeamten"; Nasse, *Universitätsstudien und Staatsprüfungen;* Gierke, "Juristische Studienordnung"; Gierke and Gneist, "Gutachten," in *Verhandlungen des Vierzehnten deutschen Juristentages* (1878). Gneist also mentioned Bethmann-Hollweg, Dahn, Goeppert, Goldschmidt, Hälschner, Georg Meyer, Ortloff, Lorenz von Stein, Stinzing, and Adolph Wagner as urging reform (144).

16. Gierke, "Juristische Studienordnung," 11.

The events of unification precipitated a discussion on the issue in the Prussian legislature.[17] Since the annexations that followed the War of 1866 had led to an oversupply of officials, the Prussian government temporarily ceased training candidates altogether in 1868. But attempts in the following year to enact a new set of requirements were thwarted by Bismarck himself, who insisted that the training of administrators was a matter of governmental ordinance rather than parliamentary legislation. "Bismarck wants to have an unconditional hand in the naming of non-judicial state officials," wrote the Bonn economist and parliamentary representative Erwin Nasse to Gustav Schmoller, "and places no value whatsoever in examinations."[18] This standoff led to an eleven-year period in which administrators, in the absence of any clear regulation, were simply given the same training as judges. The regulations of 1869 for the latter did vaguely stipulate that the "foundations of the *Staatswissenschaften*" were to be included in the first examination (following the academic study).[19] By the mid–1870s, however, this situation was becoming less satisfactory. The new Reich administration was deriving most of its personnel from Prussia and had no law or ordinance of its own regulating educational qualifications.[20] Perhaps because of this need for clarification—and because of Bismarck's need for liberal cooperation in the *Kulturkampf*—the government changed its position and introduced a draft to the legislature in 1875. The most controversial issue surrounding the bill was whether the qualifications should be extended to the office of *Landrat* itself, since this was seen as the pivotal position for transmitting conservative values. This and other disputes prevented the bill from being passed until March of 1879.[21]

From the perspective of the academic *Staatswissenschaften*, the new law was no improvement over the old. It still called for three years of academic study and four years of practicum. There was no mention of extending the former or of deducting the period of military service. The first exam still only called for "foundations of the *Staatswissenschaften*," and examiners for the second exam still did not include professors from the sciences of state. In the debate, Gneist

17. On this and the following, see Bleek, *Juristenprivileg*, 170–85.

18. Nasse to Schmoller, 1 Nov. 1870, GPSA Dahlem, Rep. 92 Schmoller no. 136: 11; Bleek, *Juristenprivileg*, 173.

19. Herrfurth, ed., *Gesetz*, 23 n.

20. E. R. Huber, *Verfassungsgeschichte*, 3: 966; Jeserich, "Entwicklung des öffentlichen Dienstes," *DV*, 3: 664.

21. Herrfurth, *Gesetz*, 8–18; Bleek, *Juristenprivileg*, 177–78. The law of 1879 exempted the *Landrat* until 1884, unless a new regulation specifically governing this position could be worked out in the meantime. This was done in 1881 and provided that the *Landrat* in a specific region could substitute residency and experience in self-administration there for the examinations (Herrfurth, *Gesetz*, 79–81).

maintained that there was enough legal material to be covered, that the sciences of state were too variable in content, and that most of the examiners would not be competent to test in fields such as economics. The Catholic Center Party seconded this position, claiming that legal education, tested by impartial (i.e., nonprofessorial) examiners, was the best guarantee of fairness in the face of liberal prejudice.[22] The effect of the law was to leave the academic critics as dissatisfied as before.[23] Nevertheless, the Prussian government did issue a memo in 1883, specifying the subjects to be included under *Staatswissenschaft* as economics, finance, state law, and administrative law. According to Nasse, this did get some law students back into the lecture halls.[24] Given the lopsided balance of academic study and apprenticeship, however, the problem of enforcing these requirements remained, as did the problem of student laziness. A French observer remarked in 1885 that this was more noticeable in Germany than elsewhere, prompting the professors to renew their critiques.[25]

The debate on the Prussian law also revealed that liberals' attitudes on the proper relation of law to the sciences of state were changing. The notion that legal study provided a rigorous mental discipline that economics could not provide was increasingly accepted by the *Staatswissenschaftler* themselves. Their dissatisfaction with existing requirements was directed less to the study of law per se than to the proportion of civil to state law within it. The trend could be seen in the South German states as well. In Baden and Württemberg, where finance officials were still trained separately, the finance ministries themselves urged more legal training, noting the decline in quality of the candidates.[26] At Tübingen, the new professor of "administrative science, admnistrative law, and politics," Ludwig Jolly, declared in his inaugural lecture of 1875 the need for training in civil law for aspiring officials, largely on pedagogical grounds: knowledge in state science came from experience, not the classroom.[27] Elsewhere he pointed out the inferior social status of the administrative candidates as another argument for merging the curriculum with law.[28] In 1885, the requirements in Württemberg for administrative officials were assimilated to those for jurists,

22. Bleek, *Juristenprivileg*, 183–84; on Gneist, see VFS, *Die Vorbildung zum höheren Verwaltungsdienst*, 174–75.

23. Ibid., 159–84. See also articles by Gustav Cohn and Robert Bosse in the same volume.

24. Ibid.,, 176, 177–78; Herrfurth, *Gesetz*, 48.

25. Schmoller, review of Georges Blondel, *De L'enseignement de Droit dans les Universités allemands*, 612–14. See also VfS, *Vorbildung*, 62, 150; Clemens von Delbrück, *Ausbildung*, 14.

26. Memo of Finance Ministry 17 Nov. 1872, GLA, 235/4696, (Lehrplan für juristische Fakultäten . . .) urging a complete merging with the curricula for justice and administration; Württemberg: Ministry of Churches and Schools, 21 Dec. 1872, UA Tübingen 127/35, (Jolly), reporting the wishes of finance and interior ministries for a lecture in imperial finance law.

27. Jolly, "Ausbildung der Verwaltungsbeamten," 427, 432.

28. VFS, *Vorbildung zum höheren Verwaltungsdienst*, 121–22.

resembling the Prussian model.[29] At the same time, many legal scholars saw the need for judges to be conversant with state law and economics as well as civil law and legal history—the Congress of German Jurists passed a resolution to this effect in 1878.[30]

The most vivid expression of the will to combine law and the sciences of state occurred in the founding of the university of Strassburg in the newly acquired territory of Alsace-Lorraine. Administered by a special Reich office, the new university was to be a showplace for German scholarship at its highest level. Its organization was entrusted to a Badenese official, Franz Roggenbach, who, following the ideas proposed in Baden in the 1860s, incorporated the idea of a single faculty of law and state science into the new university. Roggenbach's original plan envisaged coordinate sections of law and state science, with ten professorships in the latter; the Reich ministry reduced this to four, for economics, statistics, administrative law, and politics, respectively.[31] The new university was to become an arena for the disputes between civil and public lawyers on the role of the *Staatswissenschaften;* as we shall see, it also at least partially fulfilled the hope for the fostering of research within the latter.

These developments inevitably had an effect on the remaining faculties of political economy; as centers for the old cameralist curriculum, they were obviously anachronistic. In 1878 the moribund faculty at Würzburg was joined to the law faculty; in 1881, the name of the Tübingen faculty was formally changed from *political economy* to *sciences of state,* reflecting its incorporation of state law.[32] Nevertheless, the old cameralist heritage survived in one field, namely forestry. This discipline had followed the path of agriculture into separate academies in midcentury. But as the influence of the natural sciences increased, reintegration into the university appeared desirable, and in Bavaria and Württemberg the political economy faculties provided a suitable place. Thus the Munich faculty gained five new professorships in forestry in 1878, and Tübingen gained two in 1881.[33] The arguments of the Munich academic senate made it clear that foresters needed an upgrading of status through general education as well as special knowledge in the sciences of state.[34]

---

29. Bleek, *Juristenprivileg,* 226; Jeserich, "Entwicklung des öffentlichen Dienstes," *DV,* 3: 665.

30. Gierke and Gneist, *Verhandlungen des vierzehnten deutschen Juristentages,* 2: 238.

31. Schmoller to Roscher, 4 June 1873, in Bierman, ed. *Briefwechsel,* 24. See also Carl Dietzel, *Strassburg als deutsche Reichsuniversität;* John Craig, *Scholarship and Nation Building,* 40, 44–45.

32. Wegele, *Geschichte der Universität Würzburg,* 2: 521–22; Born, *Geschichte der Wirtschaftswissenschaften,* 69.

33. On Tübingen, see Born, *Geschichte der Wirtschaftswissenschaften,* 58; on Munich, Pechmann, "Staatswirtschaftliche Fakultät," 147–48; Weis, "Bayerns Beitrag zur Wissenschaftsgeschichte," in Max Spindler, ed. *Handbuch der bayerischen Geschichte,* 4.2: 1058–59.

34. Report of academic senate 1 March 1873, UA Munich M I 1.1: 2 (Staatswirtschaftliche Fakultät: Organization).

Table 9 *Appointments in the Social Sciences, 1865–1890*

	Privatdozenten	Extraordinarien	Ordinarien
1865–70	6	4	5
1870–75	2	3	8
1875–80	8	3	2
1880–85	10	6	5
1885–90	7	10	6

Source: VRS (Vampola-Ringer-Sidel) Reconstitution of the Göttingen Survey [of German university-level faculty members], subject-codes 509, 527, 611–652. Available on diskette from Fritz Ringer, Department of History, University of Pittsburgh, Pittsburgh, PA, 15260.

The numbers are drawn from 81.55 percent of the total number of 168 faculty members in the social sciences (excluding anthropology) who were born after 1840 and who habilitated by 1914. Complete information on years of *Habilitation* or appointment was not available for the remaining 18.45 percent.

The contrast between the restricted place of the *Staatswissenschaften* in the Prussian curriculum and the self-confidence and broad influence of a new generation of professors—Gustav Schmoller, Lujo Brentano, and Adolph Wagner—is striking. That confidence was partially rooted in an increased sense of opportunity within the field. The expansion of the universities began during the economic boom of the late 1860s and early 1870s. The stock market crash of 1873 and the slump that followed only fueled the influx of students further—at a phenomenal rate that far exceeded the growth in population. Enrollments more than doubled, going from 14,000 in 1871–72 to 28,820 in 1889–90.[35] Recent scholars tend to agree with the analysis of the economist Johannes Conrad at the time: students sought social advancement, the prestige of *Bildung*, and an alternative to a commercial or business career during the "great depression."[36] While this growth led to overcrowding and the well-worn fear of an academic proletariat, it also helped increase the size of the faculty, which almost doubled between 1860 and 1890.[37] For economics and related fields, the opportunities were greatest in the early 1870s (see table 9).

In addition, the clientele for economics was diversifying, so that professors found themselves addressing a wider audience than that of aspiring officials. This was due in part to developments in the former cameralist areas of agriculture and technology—which led to new forms of cross-fertilization with the social sciences. In the case of agriculture, Liebig had launched a campaign in the 1860s to reform the discipline on the basis of soil chemistry and at the expense of such topics as business techniques. This involved an attack on the

35. Jarausch, *Students, Society, and Politics,* 30. See also McClelland, *State, Society, and University,* 242.

36. Conrad, *German Universities,* cited in Jarausch, *Students, Society, and Politics,* 33. See also Ringer, *Education and Society,* 52–53, 87, 89.

37. McClelland, *State, Society, and University,* 258 on faculty numbers.

separate agricultural academies and a proposal to reintegrate agriculture into the universities, which would provide an environment of ongoing research in the natural sciences. Although Liebig's ideas aroused great indignation and opposition at first, they gradually began to bear fruit. The first successful such agricultural institute was founded at Halle in 1862 under the enterprising leadership of Julius Kühn. Kühn combined Liebig's ideas and methods with a concern that future farmers get their share of *Bildung:* that combination of general and special education that would confer status and expertise on professional agriculturalists.[38] This applied to the sciences of state as well: according to Kühn, agriculturalists should hear the same economics as future administrators and businessmen.[39] Kühn's success soon provided a model for others, and most of the isolated academies were closed by 1880, replaced by university institutes.[40] In the case of technology, the process was different: rather than being reintegrated, the separate academies themselves were upgraded to university status in the form of *technische Hochschulen.* The early plans for these *Hochschulen,* as developed by the head of the Association of German Engineers, Franz Grashof, involved the same combination of general and special education that motivated Kühn.[41] Thus economics figured prominently in these plans.[42]

In the universities themselves, these expanding numbers also provided the opportunity for the proliferation of seminars. In the sciences of state, six new seminars were established in the 1870s and four in the 1880s, compared to two in the 1860s, none in the 1850s, and one in 1848 at Jena.[43] Despite the examples of the other disciplines, the notion of the seminar as a locus for ongoing research had taken hold slowly. The early ones had more restricted pedagogical aims, to give students practice in writing and speaking; in this they were probably an extension of the "drills" (*Übungen, Conversatorien, Repetitorien*) that were already widespread.[44] (see figure 12).

38. Kühn, *Studium der Landwirtschaft,* 21. On Liebig's influence and Kühn's activity, see Frauendorfer, *Ideengeschichte der Agrarwirtschaft,* 1: 451–54, 460–62.

39. Kühn, *Studium der Landwirtschaft,* 83, 87–89.

40. Von der Goltz, "Entwicklung," 90.

41. Gispen, *New Profession, Old Order,* 53, 79.

42. See, for example, excerpts from the Budget of the Interior Ministry for 1864 and 1865, GLA, 235/3131 (Lehrstellen der Landwirtschaft . . .).

43. "Staatswissenschaftliche Seminare," in *Deutschen Universitäten,* 1: 603–6.

44. Thus the Königsberg professor Ernst Glaser requested a seminar in 1856 to carry on his *Übungen* with an official name, which the ministry declined to grant. Memo of Glaser, 4 August 1856; Ministry to curator, 21 Nov. 1856, GPSA Dahlem, Rep. 76 Va Sect. 11 Tit. X no. 17, vol. 1: 12, 15 (Errichtung eines staatswirtschaftliche . . . Instituts). Later Karl Umpfenbach, also at Königsberg, viewed the name "seminar" as a status symbol which raised false expectations of academic careers in its participants (Umpfenbach to curator, 28 Feb. 1886, ibid., 37–42). For statements of goals, see Gustav Fischer, *Errichtung staatswissenschaftlicher Seminarien,* 119; Born, *Geschichte der Wirtschaftswissenschaften,* 132–33.

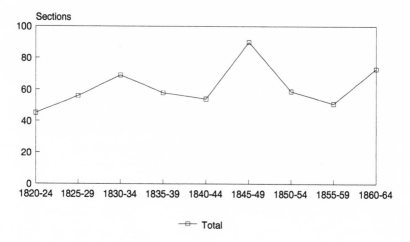

Source: University catalogues;
see appendix.

Fig. 12. Economics Drills, Recitations, and Seminars, 1820–1865

What was added was a library—a separate physical space devoted to the subject alone. This required funding and hence an autonomous institutional status.[45] The Jena seminar, like the later Knies-Bluntschli effort at Heidelberg, originally sought to encompass the breadth of the *Staatswissenschaften* by bringing together professors from the philosophy and law faculties. But this in itself was not conducive to research: it was only when the seminars began to utilize new sources of data that research arose. The first providers of such data were the statistical bureaus, which made Engel's seminar in Berlin and Hildebrand's in Jena such exciting places to be. In both cases, however, it was more the personalities of the directors and the informal atmosphere they encouraged among their students that provided the decisive stimulus to original research, rather than any specific institutional, pedagogical, or methodological innovation. Hildebrand's seminars encompassed papers and discussions on a wide variety of subjects (including a discussion of *Das Kapital* the year after it was published).[46] Only gradually did the seminars prove to be vehicles for the transformation of certain disciplines into research programs.

45. An exception was the Knies-Bluntschli seminar at Heidelberg, whose lack of physcial space helped undermine its effectiveness (Riese, *Hochschule,* 206).

46. Protokollbuch des staatsws. Seminars, 1868/69, UA Jena. Other topics for that semester covered mortgage credit institutions, gold currency, and industrial freedom. On Hildebrand's talents as a discussion leader, see Conrad, *Lebenserinnerungen,* 127–29; on Engel, see Knapp, *Grundherrschaft und Rittergut,* 147–48.

THE LEADING PERSONALITIES: SCHMOLLER,
BRENTANO, AND WAGNER

This concatenation of circumstances—sociopolitical, institutional, and personal—explains the revival of the sciences of state in the form of social science in the 1870s. They are exemplified in the life and thought of Schmoller, who was undoubtedly the central figure in the process. He also displayed most clearly the continuities of the new *Sozialpolitik* with the tradition of South German enlightened bureaucracy. For Schmoller (b. 1838) came from a line of Württembergian officials—not as highly placed as Mohl's forbears, to be sure, but dating back to the seventeenth century. His mother came from a family of academics; the decisive figure in shaping his aspirations, however, was his older brother-in-law Rümelin, from whom he derived a wide range of intellectual interests as well as his *kleindeutsch* sympathies. When he arrived at Tübingen to study, he was drawn to history rather than economics.[47] While working in the Württemberg statistical office under Rümelin in the early 1860s, he published on a wide variety of topics: the Reformation, the philosophy of Fichte, the theory of income, the Württemberg manufacturing statistics of 1861, the Franco-Prussian trade treaty—and the worker question. His pro-Prussian views were sufficient to destroy his chances in the Württemberg bureaucracy, but helped further his academic career in Prussia itself. On the basis of these publications—and the fact that he was a Lutheran—he received an appointment to a new position at Halle in 1864, largely to meet the needs of the newly arrived agricultural students.[48] His lectures indicated the direction of his interests: in addition to the standard offerings in economics, he introduced lectures on poverty and the proletariat as well as the history of the Prussian constitution and administration. His enrollment figures indicated his increasing popularity (see table 10). He was also active in local politics, serving on the city council.[49] He founded seminars at Halle, at Strassburg, where he accepted an appointment in 1872, and at Berlin, where he moved a decade later.

The synthesis of economics, history, statistics, and *Sozialpolitik* which guided Schmoller's career found expression in his *History of the German Small Trades* (*Kleingewerbe*) *in the Nineteenth Century,* published in *The Worker's Friend,* the journal

---

47. On Schmoller's early years, see Pauline Anderson, "Gustav Schmoller," in Wehler, ed., *DH,* 2: 41–42. Schmoller never studied with a member of the "older historical school," although Roscher was a mentor from the time of his first publication.

48. Biermann to Mühler 14 Feb. 1864; Anschütz, 11 Feb. 1864, UA Halle, Curatorsakten no. 332: 236–40.

49. He offered the one-hour lecture on poverty each summer from 1867 to 1872, the history four times from 1869 to 1872; enrollments in GPSA Dahlem, Rep. 76 Va Sect. 8 Tit. VII; student population in *Personalverzeichnis;* on his political activity, see Lehmann, "Nationalökonomie in Halle," 154.

Table 10 *Schmoller's Enrollments at Halle, 1865–72*

Semester	Lecture: "Poverty, Proletariat, and the Worker Question"	Total University Enrollment
1865	50	834
1867	160	840
1868	80	859
1870	70	881
1871	80	840
1872	156	1018

Sources: for Schmoller's lecture: GPSA Dahlem Rep. 76 Va Sect. 8 Tit. VII; for university enrollment, *Amtliches Verzeichnis des Personals und der Studierenden der königlichen vereinigten Friedrichs-Universität Halle-Wittenberg* (n.p.: 1865–72).

of the Organization for the Welfare of the Working Classes, in 1869. His statistical researches convinced him that industrialization was not leading to the decline of handcrafts and small businesses; instead of a simplistic class division of bourgeois and proletariat, the division of labor in fact led to a whole series of gradations.[50] The work combined scholarship and advocacy, containing an extensive documentation of the situation of the handworkers as it had developed, as well as the conclusion that the self-help programs of the cooperative movement were insufficient to relieve their plight, and that state intervention was required. For this Schmoller envisaged "something like a combination of the Württemberg Central Office [for Trade and Commerce] and the English factory inspector system."[51]

In the preface to the work, Schmoller located his effort with respect to the dominant ideological trends as he saw them:

> Unbiased research, which strives to proceed from the things themselves, free from all scholastic theories and interests, . . . will see on both sides errors on the one hand, legitimate factors on the other, and must . . . declare these openly. . . . It is not to serve the parties, but to stand above them; it has only one aim—honorably and with exertion of all its means to strive for the truth.[52]

How could one reconcile this contemplative ideal, which Schmoller inherited from Roscher and the previous generation, with the imperatives of social engagement? In an essay some years later on justice in the economy, Schmoller gave the following answer: The scholar interprets the dominant ethical and religious ideals of a particular culture or community, as given in custom and law, and asks whether existing institutions measure up to these ideals.[53] This

50. Schmoller, "Arbeiterfrage," 403, 405.
51. Schmoller, *Geschichte der deutschen Kleingewerbe*, 695, 700.
52. Ibid., xii.
53. Schmoller, "Gerechtigkeit in der Volkswirtschaft," 49.

meant that scholars should not directly enter the political fray, but rather interpret and evaluate practical affairs in their capacity *as* research scholars—with all the privileged access to truth that the term implied. Schmoller expressed this in an image he used repeatedly: "*Wissenschaft* should be like the chorus in [Greek] tragedy—it should not act itself, but, standing apart from the stage, accompany the actors by its observations, and measure their action according to the highest ideals of the time."[54] This was a new version of the practical imagination which was typical of Schmoller's generation. It was the mentality which Fritz Ringer so convincingly described as that of the "German mandarin," in which "the intellectual leaders of the cultivated elite filled the role of intermediaries between the eternal and temporal realms."[55] Note that this strategy did not involve a form of reasoning specific to practical affairs, that is, a means of deciding which course of action would more closely approximate such ideals. Although Schmoller's writings were often very rich in practical insights, they were still far from positing a specialized system of propositions which set the social sciences apart from other disciplines. Theory and practice were thus not joined by a distinctive ordering principle or methodology.[56] Rather the mandarin himself, with his superior intuitive qualities, served as the link. Although Schmoller himself did not endorse a "great man" theory of history, his strategy certainly legitimized the inspired professor as a medium between the ideal and the real.[57] This charismatic aspect was more pronounced in Schmoller's contemporaries, Lujo Brentano and Adolph Wagner.

If Schmoller's predilection for history led him to distrust any abstract theorizing, his friend Lujo Brentano strove to integrate theory as well as history with social concern. Brentano was born in 1844 to a Catholic merchant family whose name had already become famous through the romantic movement: his aunt and uncle, Bettina and Clemens Brentano, were poets. His father authored many religious pamphlets, and his older brother Franz was to achieve fame as a professor of philosophy in Vienna. Like Schmoller, Brentano was greatly influenced by an older brother-in-law, Peter Le Page Renouf, who taught at the Catholic college in Dublin. Brentano's extended visit there at age seventeen instilled in him a love for the British Isles.[58]

When Brentano returned to Germany, he studied law at Munich with the

54. Schmoller, "Zweck und Ziele des Jahrbuchs," 9.

55. Ringer, *Decline of the German Mandarins*, 113. Cf. also Schiera, *Laboratorium der bürgerlichen Welt*, 98–101, who argues that the very pursuit of disinterested research constituted a form of political expression in the context of the German sense of identity as a cultural nation. See also Jarausch, *Students, Society, and Politics*, 6–13, 167.

56. See below, p. 238.

57. On the "great man" theory, see Schmoller, "Gerechtigkeit in der Volkswirtschaft," 52–53.

58. On Brentano's youth, see Sheehan, *Career of Lujo Brentano*, chap. 1; on Franz Brentano, see Lindenfeld, *Transformation of Positivism*, 43.

idea of becoming an official. But the events of 1866 dissuaded him. His family had long been opposed to Protestant Prussian domination; as liberal Catholics, they felt doubly isolated in the face of the Prussian victory and the increasing conservatism of the papacy. According to his memoirs, Brentano had no desire to serve either the Prussian or the Bavarian state, and went to Göttingen for further study. It was then that he came under the influence of Helferich and wrote a dissertation on Thünen. The appeal of Hermann's and Helferich's economic theory and of Thünen's isolated state was doubtless strong to someone alienated from contemporary political developments, and he retained Hermann's demand-oriented theory of prices in his later lectures.[59] But he soon sought a closer connection to empirical reality, and in 1867 went from Göttingen to Berlin to enter Engel's seminar.

It was Engel—and perhaps the conditions in industrial Berlin—that kindled Brentano's interest in the social question. He was taken with Engel's scheme for profit-sharing organizations—a form of cooperatives—and returned with his teacher to England in 1868 to study the English attempts at these. While there, however, his interest turned away from cooperatives toward trade unions. They appealed to him for a variety of reasons. Given the seriousness of class antagonisms as he saw them, he began to doubt the effectiveness of cooperatives, as Schmoller had also done. Furthermore, he viewed the unions as instruments for more than mere economic gain, seeing them also as centers for the "elevation of the hygienic, intellectual, and moral state of the working class" through educational efforts.[60] Finally, he saw in the organization of unions a validation of the economic laws he had learned from Hermann and Helferich, including the notion that self-interested action could redound to the common good independently of the state. John Stuart Mill and William Thomas Thornton were making the same arguments in England at the very time of Brentano's visit, and his early work on unions reflected all these influences.[61]

Brentano's interest in the theoretical implications of unionism did not exclude an interest in history. His English acquaintances had collected much material on the old guilds in order to show the continuity between them and the unions, and Brentano's first publication was a lengthy introduction in English to a collection of historical sources on guilds. Brentano sought to portray

---

59. Brentano, lecture notes on Allgemeine Volkswirtschaftslehre (n.d.), Zweites Buch, 41–47, Bundesarchiv Koblenz, Nachlass Lujo Brentano, no. 116; Brentano also defended Hermann's theory in his trial lecture before the Berlin philosophical faculty in his *Habilitation* there in 1871 (Brentano, *Mein Leben*, 64). On Helferich's influence, see also Sheehan, *Brentano*, 13–15.

60. Brentano, *Arbeitergilden der Gegenwart*, 2: 318.

61. Ibid., 2: 201–3.

unions as successors to guilds, arguing that both were formed in periods of upheaval for self-protection of workers. The piece ended with the following exhortation: "May the English working-men, like the English barons and middle-classes in former times, be a bright example in the attainment of freedom to their brethren on the Continent!"[62] Brentano returned to Germany in 1869 to work through the material he had collected; the result was the two-volume *Arbeitergilden der Gegenwart* (*Workers' Guilds of the Present*) of 1871–72. Meanwhile, the final unification of Germany had won him over to the new Reich.

Brentano's initial English work had come to Schmoller's attention, and the two soon became close friends. There were certainly differences between them: Brentano's use of history was certainly more willful than Schmoller's, as his argument on guilds and unions demonstrated.[63] He also never put as much faith in bureaucracy: "I don't share your satisfaction in the Gneist-Sybel-Treitschkean idolization of the state," he wrote to Schmoller in 1873.[64] Nevertheless, their views overlapped considerably: both objected to an overly partisan approach to the social question, whether liberal or conservative, and viewed the Manchesterites as particularly egregious in this regard. Despite their varying commitments to theory, both believed profoundly that economics must be treated in a cultural and sociological context. Brentano labeled his approach "historical-realistic," and his lectures on economics included technology, customs, and the state as concrete conditions of the economy.[65]

The third major actor was Adolph Wagner. Wagner had already established himself as an expert on banking and finance, and had attained his cherished goal of a professorship at Berlin in 1870. Prior to this, however, he had a conversion experience. The catalyst was Rodbertus, whose piece on the credit deficiency of landowners appeared in 1868. "This work impressed me as scientific works seldom do and brought me to my 'Damascus' vis-à-vis the dominant Smithian economic theory," wrote Wagner ten years later.[66] This conversion did not happen overnight: in 1869, he opposed the Lassallean program and still saw the accumulation of private capital as the best way to uplift the working classes.[67] In a polemic against the Marxists the following year, *On the Elimination of Private Property*, Wagner acknowledged the historical contingency of private property but defended it as the most appropriate form for contemporary cir-

---

62. Brentano, *History and Development of Gilds*, cxcviii. See also Sheehan, *Brentano*, chap. 2.

63. Sheehan, *Brentano*, 37–38.

64. Brentano to Schmoller, 1 Feb. 1873, in Goetz, ed., *Briefwechsel*, 29.1: 155.

65. Brentano, lectures on Allgemeine Volkswirtschaftslehre, vol. 1, Bundesarchiv Koblenz, Nachlass Brentano, no. 116.

66. Wagner, "Einiges von und über Rodbertus-Jagetzow," 211.

67. Wagner, "Antrag Wagner zur Arbeiterfrage," 14 Feb. 1869, in *Briefe*, 72–73.

cumstances.[68] By the end of 1870, however, he could write as follows to his brother:

> Despite my polemic, according to my convictions, against the insanities of the Social Democrats, I am still inwardly closer to these socialists than to the "economists" and want to pursue studies in the history of law. For it is unmistakeable: everything culminates in a reform of the property concept.[69]

The following October, Wagner delivered a highly publicized speech on the social question to a Lutheran meeting at the Garnison Church in Berlin. He proclaimed economics to be in crisis, that it needed to become an ethical science, and acknowledged the justice of much of the socialist critique. Wagner called for a host of specific measures in that speech, including increased wages, reduction in working time, workers insurance, female- and child-labor legislation, safer factories, cheaper housing, and progressive direct taxation.[70] By November, 1872, Wagner, by his own account, was criticizing in his lectures the basic principles of the capitalist order—including personal freedom and private property—to an audience of four hundred, including many nonstudents; by March of 1873, he confessed that whereas he had formerly found socialist theory to be 95 percent false, he now found it to be 95 percent true.[71]

Wagner and Brentano were passionate men, a fact which affected the style and substance of the sciences of state. Wagner's "easily excitable temperament" was well known, and Brentano appears to have been his equal; the two managed to turn Brentano's *Habilitation* at Berlin in 1871 from a dull lecture on the wage-fund theory into something resembling a medieval disputation.[72] Both of them were extremely popular lecturers: "Brentano addressed his classes as he would have political meetings, and they responded with cheers and countercheers. Adolf Wagner shouted and stamped and shook his fists at imaginary opponents," wrote Josef Schumpeter.[73] Schmoller was calmer and more conciliatory, impressing his colleagues as polite and reserved, statesmanlike and cal-

---

68. Wittrock, *Kathedersozialisten*, 42–43.

69. Wagner to Hermann Wagner, 3 Dec. 1870, in *Briefe*, 91.

70. Wagner, *Rede über die Sociale Frage*, 30–35. Wagner's speech was followed a few weeks later by another highly publicized lecture of another economics professor, Gustav Schönberg, who called for the establishment of special offices of labor throughout the country (Wittrock, *Kathedersozialisten*, 29).

71. Wagner to Hermann Wagner, 24 Nov. 1872, 19 March 1873, in *Briefe*, 118, 120.

72. Brentano, *Mein Leben*, 63, 65 ff; on Wagner's temperament, see Hermann Wagner, "Mein Bruder Adolph," in Wagner, *Briefe* 18; Johanna Wagner and Hermann Wagner, 13 April 1866, ibid., 42–43, 98–99.

73. Schumpeter, *History of Economic Analysis*, 802; see also Sheehan, *Brentano*, 3, Lindenlaub, *Richtungskämpfe*, 136.

culating.[74] He preferred for many years to operate behind the scenes in the *Verein,* assuming its presidency only in 1890. Yet his sense of engagement was no less genuine. His desire to acknowledge all sides of an argument could easily become a rhetorical device rather than a genuine expression of impartiality: in his polemical writings during this period, he frequently began a paragraph by conceding a point to his opponent or making a qualifying statement—only by way of leading up to and reinforcing his own position.[75] In short, Schmoller was no less willing than Wagner and Brentano to attack a position he thought was wrong; all three brought tremendous personal energy and flair to the cause of social reform, thereby bringing the sciences of state to a wider public.

All three also participated in the antagonistic mood of postunification. Although the differences between Schmoller, Brentano, and Wagner were significant, they shared a common opposition to the prevailing liberal economic doctrine as expressed by the Congress of German Economists. Their increasingly open critiques were directed less to any specific liberal economic position than to its general ideological standpoint, particularly the appeal to unalterable natural laws. Even Brentano, who preserved his admiration for liberalism to a greater extent than the others, expressed this sentiment vividly:

> You, we addressed our opponents, are like the primitives with respect to lightning. Lightning strikes also by natural law. But while the civilized person makes use of this natural law to render lightning harmless by means of a lightning rod, you wait until the lightning sets your cottage afire, then fall on your knees and pray to the thunder-god: only your thunder-god is called natural law. For with the uttering of this word you regard your task in socio-political life as fulfilled.[76]

This confidence was manifest both in their popularity as lecturers and in their ability to launch the *Verein* as an organization to defend and propagate their point of view. Certainly the need to organize arose in part as a reaction to the restrictions on bureaucratic education in the *Staatswissenschaften.* The economists developed cohesion as they realized the need to defend their interests.

THE *VEREIN FÜR SOZIALPOLITIK*

The *Verein* may also be viewed as an instance of a pattern of melioristic response to industrialization on the part of cultivated elites that occurred in all major industrializing societies. Part of this pattern was the association of social reform

---

74. Hintze, "Gustav Schmoller," 527; Meinecke, "Drei Generationen," 265.

75. Seven out of the eighteen paragraphs in his opening speech to the Eisenach meeting in 1872, printed in Boese, *Geschichte,* 6–11, contain this device.

76. Brentano, *Mein Leben,* 75.

with the application of rational knowledge that merited the label of "science"—however loose the fit between theory and practice might have been. Thus two prominent organs for the dissemination of philanthropic knowledge already in existence were the British National Association for the Promotion of Social Science, founded in 1857, and the American Social Science Association, patterned after it in 1865.[77] These organizations were populated by a cross section of the upper classes, as were earlier groups in Germany, such as the Central Association for the Welfare of the Working Classes or the Economic Congress. The *Verein* was probably less influential than the British association at its height, with its thirty-one Peers and forty-eight MPs, but more influential than its American counterpart, which had practically ceased to exist in the mid–1870s due to loose organization and lack of a coherent program.[78] But the British association dissolved in the mid–1880s, while the *Verein* lasted through the Weimar Republic. Unlike the others, the *Verein* succeeded in combining the broad mission of social reform with some of the functions of a professional association for economics.

Aside from the heightened public interest in the social question, there were two specific catalysts which led to the formation of the *Verein*. The first was the issue of training Prussian administrative officials. The neglect of economics in the examinations had already brought about a common awareness among the economics professors that their interests needed defending and promoting. Erwin Nasse had protested the testing procedures in a pamphlet in 1868, and Wagner had urged economics as a subject for all law students in his inaugural lecture at Berlin in 1870. In the same year, Schmoller, Wagner, Nasse, and Engel considered sending a joint petition to the Prussian legislators and ministers to institute academic training for officials by means of a petition.[79] Nasse, however, urged the group to take more aggressive action. "The men of the ministry," he wrote to Schmoller, "are much too dulled by the debates in the legislature and in the press to react to such a small stimulus as the petition of a few professors. Whoever wants to attain something from them must make some noise, mainly in the press, and when public opinion is thereby prepared, in the legislature."[80] The week before, Brentano had written to Schmoller asking his advice on whether academics should write articles in partisan journals. Schmoller's reply indicated that he was moving in the direction of engagement. "I find," he wrote, "the previous opposition between journalistic and academic

---

77. Abrams, *Origins of British Sociology*, chap. 4; Haskell, *Emergence of Professional Social Science*, 97–98. France lacked a comparable organization; it also generally adhered to laissez-faire liberalism for a longer time and distrusted state activities. See Mitchell, *Divided Path*, 19, 315.

78. Abrams, *Origins of British Sociology*, 45; Haskell, *Emergence of Professional Social Science*, 129.

79. Wagner to Schmoller, 20 Nov. 1870, in Wagner, *Briefe*, 85–89.

80. Nasse to Schmoller, 12 Feb. 1871, GPSA Dahlem, Rep. 92 Schmoller, no. 136: 15–16.

economics to be exaggerated. . . . Both parties must encounter each other and can at times reach out to each other. . . . The German academic economists seem to me to have been too aristocratic and reserved."[81]

The second, more decisive catalyst was the debate with the Congress of German Economists, whose polemics in the press were increasingly sharp and personal against anyone who disagreed with the doctrine of free trade and the natural harmony of interests under laissez-faire. According to Schäffle, who had suffered such attacks in his brief tenure as Finance Minister in Vienna, "the Vatican dogma of infallibility . . . was child's play compared to the infallibility in the congresses of the 'economists.'"[82] As the academic economists' attacks on laissez-faire doctrine increased, a response was soon to come.

It was the journalist Heinrich Oppenheim who launched the attack on the social reformers in the *Nationalzeitung* on 7 December 1871—leading to one of the most vehement polemical battles of the century.[83] It involved the interplay of party politics, academic politics, and journalism, a combination which favored the extremists on both sides. Oppenheim accused the reformers of playing into the hands of the socialists and coined the term *Kathedersozialist* (socialist of the chair) to describe them. Several other articles followed in the next few days in other papers which questioned whether such sympathizers should hold professorial chairs and train future administrators (the appointment of the economics chair at Strassburg was about to be made).[84] Brentano's ire was aroused, and he wrote a response the same day. The tone of these pieces was moderate compared to what followed in the spring. Oppenheim had discovered Wagner's speech at the Garnison church and wrote a piece attacking it directly, claiming he attempted to "Christianize" economics; Wagner responded that this was far less dangerous than Oppenheim's "Judiasation."[85] The attacks and counterattacks continued into the summer. The term *Kathedersozialist* soon became a badge of honor for the reformers.

The battle seems to have chastised the Congress of German Economists to an extent, for they included a number of worker-oriented issues in their August meeting in Danzig (where 40 percent of the workers were on strike at the time).[86] Meanwhile, the *Kathedersozialisten* also felt the need for an organizational basis. Schmoller called a small meeting of fifteen people at Halle in July to plan

81. Schmoller to Brentano, 5 Feb. 1871, in Goetz, ed. *Briefwechsel,* 28: 329.

82. Schäffle, *Aus meinem Leben,* 1: 90; 166–67; Brentano to Schmoller, 23 Feb. 1871, in Goetz, ed. *Briefwechsel,* 28: 332–33.

83. Hentschel, *Deutschen Freihändler,* 193.

84. Wittrock, *Kathedersozialisten,* 126–28; Hentschel, *Deutschen Freihändler,* 201. On the role of the Strassburg appointment, see Wittrock, 150–52.

85. Hentschel, *Deutschen Freihändler,* 205–6. This passage of Wagner's open letter is not included in the excerpt in *Briefe* (107–8).

86. Hentschel, *Freihändler,* 209.

a larger one at Eisenach in the fall.[87] He conceived an organization that would bring together socially concerned people from academia, politics, and business.

The initial invitation to the Eisenach meeting was signed by two landowners, two industrialists, one journalist, six administrators, and twelve professors. The list reflected the composition of the Eisenach meeting and subsequent meetings of the *Verein*.[88]

The Eisenach meeting received much attention in the press. Bismarck sent his conservative friend Hermann Wagener to observe.[89] Schmoller, in his opening speech, expressed the group's idealism and teleological assumptions:

> That an ever increasing part of our people be called to partake in all the higher goods of culture, education, and prosperity; . . . this should and must be the great democratic task of our development in the best sense of the word, as it seems to be the great goal of world history on the whole.[90]

Brentano's paper made him a well-known personality overnight, admired by some, feared by others.[91] He received an appointment as *Extraordinarius* at Breslau shortly thereafter, following Schmoller's appointment to Strassburg. The following year Bismarck remarked to Schmoller that he too was a *Kathedersozialist,* but had no time yet to exercise *Sozialpolitik*—although the program which Bismarck gradually developed was very different in emphasis from the improvement of working conditions urged by the *Verein*.[92]

Gradually, members of both the *Verein* and the Congress came to realize that, whatever their ideological starting points, they could discuss and even agree on substantive issues. After a number of feelers from both sides, the two organizations agreed to hold a joint meeting in 1876; the pattern thereafter was to meet in alternate years.[93]

Even as the battles with the Manchesterites were subsiding, however, there was a final skirmish, this time between Treitschke and Schmoller. Despite his initial support of the *Verein*, Treitschke soon found its tone to be too antagonistic toward the established order, and published several critical articles in 1874–75 under the title *Socialism and Its Patrons*. Treitschke took issue with Schmoller's egalitarian tendencies. "It is by no means the task of society to draw all men to the enjoyment of all cultural goods, . . ." he wrote. "The participation of all in

87. Wagner to Schmoller, 20 May, 13 June 1872, in *Briefe* 109–10.

88. Gorges, *Sozialforschung*, 67–68, 73.

89. Pflanze, *Bismarck*, 2: 303–4; Sheehan, *Brentano*, 72.

90. Boese, *Geschichte*, 10

91. Heuss, "Lujo Brentano," in *Deutsche Gestalten*, 376.

92. Hintze, "Schmoller," 532.

93. Hentschel, *Deutschen Freihändler*, 219, 223, 229; Boese, *Geschichte*, 25–27; Gorges, *Sozialforschung*, 66.

all blessings of culture is not merely a perhaps unattainable ideal. . . . It is not an ideal at all."[94] Not only was society inherently unequal, but to expect the uplifting of the poor was to place too much emphasis on material goods. Schmoller responded that he was neither egalitarian nor materialistic; the changing laws and customs of history merely indicated that the present form of property and division of wealth was not sacrosanct.[95] Treitschke countered by accusing the historical school of economics of vagueness, lacking clear concepts of state and society.[96] While this critique anticipated the methodological debates of the next decade, it reflected more a difference in generations than in basic philosophies: Treitschke's previously articulated distrust of social science in favor of political science and political history was a way of affirming his belief in a powerful state as the embodiment of a particular social hierarchy; Schmoller's pursuit of economics and economic history rather than politics was a more innovative means of affirming the same values: the gradual leveling upward of world history did not eliminate the need for enlightened elites.

The *Verein* did develop several new ways of effectively combining theoretical and practical considerations. For each topic, they solicited recommendations from a cross section of experts—whose professional backgrounds mirrored those of the membership—and published these in advance of the meetings. These then formed the basis for specific policy resolutions, which became more and more detailed as the years went on.[97] The issues were chosen with an eye to upcoming legislative debates, and the *Verein* sent direct petitions to the Reichstag on a number of occasions. Although these petitions did not usually elicit a direct response, the *Verein*'s resolutions on the need for further factory legislation were part of a stream which eventually resulted in laws further restricting female and child labor and establishing compulsory inspection (over Bismarck's opposition) in 1878.[98] In general, the influence of the *Verein* on public policy was indirect: it shaped the thinking of the individual officials who advised and sometimes formulated governmental drafts.[99]

The *Verein* was also influential in stimulating social research in Germany. As early as 1872, aware of its need for more systematic information on factory conditions, it petitioned the Reichstag to conduct a survey, which it eventually did in 1875. Such official surveys had long since been conducted in France,

94. Treitschke, *Socialismus und seine Gönner*, 23, 24.
95. Schmoller, *Einige Grundfragen der Sozialpolitik und der Volkswirtschaftslehre*, 16–19, 44, 70 ff.
96. Treitschke, *Socialismus und seine Gönner*, 111.
97. Gorges, *Sozialforschung*, 86–87.
98. E. R. Huber, *Verfassungsgeschichte*, 4: 1205–6; Pflanze, *Bismarck*, 2: 305–10. For a precise account of the *Verein*'s impact on legislation, see Else Conrad, *Verein für Sozialpolitik*, 82–195.
99. Lindenlaub, *Richtungskämpfe*, 35–36, 141; Meinecke, "Drei Generationen," 263.

England, and Belgium, and the first effort of the new German government was modest in comparison.[100] The *Verein* was initially concerned with method, however, and devoted sessions to this in 1873 and 1877. By the 1880s, it had dropped this concern, but was conducting surveys itself. The procedures reflected the assumptions of an enlightened bureaucracy: officials and experts drew up written questionnaires and distributed them throughout the country. The questions themselves were designed to elicit qualitative rather than quantitative responses—in accordance with Schmoller's view that only the former can grasp "moral and intellectual actions."[101] This qualitative emphasis did not escape criticism, but the critics failed to alter the methodology significantly.[102]

The formation of the *Verein* may be seen as a harbinger of the broad rejection of liberalism in German politics, economics, and public opinion that began in the mid–1870s and continued to grow during the reign of Wilhelm II. This trend was ushered in by the inevitable economic crash of 1873 and was furthered by the years of intermittent recession that followed until 1896. One of the first fruits of the new economic situation was a groundswell of support for protectionism. It was an issue on which farmers and industrialists could agree, and thus paved the way for a new alignment of political interests.[103]

The economic and political changes that followed the crash of 1873 affected the *Verein* in a number of ways. First, they stimulated the members to consider other topics besides those related to workers; tax and trade issues figured increasingly as the decade wore on.[104] Second, they helped to highlight the internal divisions among the leaders—although the waning of the battle with the Manchesterites undoubtedly contributed at least as much to this. These divisions had to do mostly with their position on the degree of state intervention.[105] Brentano became more explicit in his opposition to it; in his next book on labor relations and law, he reiterated the view that the principle

100. Oberschall, *Empirical Social Research*, 19.

101. Quoted in ibid., 23. For a thorough discussion of the *Verein*'s survey methods, see Gorges, *Sozialforschung*, 104–17, 167–84.

102. A private Jewish scholar, Gottlieb Schnapper-Arndt, submitted the questionnaire on usury to a detailed examination at the 1888 meeting: the concept of usury itself was never defined, the credibility of the sources was never established, and no effort was made to arrive at quantitative results. Many respondents tacitly assumed that usury was a Jewish occupation. These criticisms were given a cool reception (Gorges, *Sozialforschung*, 177–82; Oberschall, *Empirical Social Research*, 25; on Schnapper-Arndt, see Kern, *Empirische Sozialforschung*, 59).

103. Pflanze, *Bismarck*, 2: 316; Rosenberg, "Political and Social Consequences," 46.

104. Gorges, *Sozialforschung*, 76–77.

105. This subject has been treated extensively in the secondary literature, though not always with agreement on who belonged to what faction. Thus Boese places Brentano on the left, Wagner on the right, Schmoller, Gneist, and Nasse in the middle (20–21; also Gorges, 59–60); Lindenlaub views Brentano as a liberal, Schmoller and Wagner as conservatives (86). All agree that these labels are approximate, as positions shifted over time and from issue to issue.

of self-help embodied in trade unions was most conducive to the development of freedom, "the fundamental principle of our age."[106] Wagner, at the other extreme, became more explicit in his defense of state socialism, which he conceived as the principle of planned, centrally organized economy, and which he sought to make palatable to conservatives and liberals alike.[107] Following the agreement with the Congress, Wagner resigned from the board of the *Verein* and even talked vaguely of forming a new organization for social reform.[108] He eventually gravitated to Adolf Stöcker's Christian Socialist movement and became its president in 1881.[109] Schmoller, although occupying a middle position, leaned increasingly towards Wagner, despite his disapproval of Wagner's leaving the *Verein*. This led to increased tensions with Brentano.[110]

Third, Bismarck's "change of course," involving the anti-Socialist law of 1878 and the protective tariff in 1879, led to splits within the general membership of the *Verein* which became so serious as to threaten to dissolve it. The leaders were well aware of the divisive feelings that these issues had aroused, and they consciously strove to defuse them. The tariff question could not be so easily dodged, however, and the conference of 1879 was moved from the fall to the spring to anticipate the Reichstag debate. Industrialists and merchants packed the meeting, probably viewing the *Verein's* resolution as a decisive showdown.[111] After breaking the issue down into tariffs for different types of goods, a general resolution for free trade was presented. It failed by a vote of 82 to 63.[112]

The 1879 conference marked a turning point in the history of the *Verein* and its efforts to influence policy. The presence of real differences tended to drive the *Staatswissenschaftler* away from public engagement. After a period of demoralization and indecision, the leadership proposed in 1881 no longer to vote on resolutions, that is, "to abandon agitation and adopt the exclusive task of a many-sided and thorough discussion of these issues." This proposal was passed in the following year.[113] The turning inward that ensued was reflected in the smaller size of the membership: whereas in the 1870s, it had varied between

---

106. Brentano, *Relation of Labor,* 304.

107. Wagner to the editor of the *Staatssocialist,* 20 Dec. 1877, in *Briefe,* 157–59; 15 Jan. 1878, ibid., 161–64. See also Heilmann, *Wagner,* 20–25.

108. Gorges, *Sozialforschung,* 186; Wagner to editor of *Staatssozialist* 15 Jan. 1878, in *Briefe,* 164; Held to Schmoller, 2 Jan. 1878, GPSA Dahlem, Rep. 92 Schmoller, no. 127: 52–53.

109. Barkin, *Controversy over German Industrialization,* 143; Born, *Staat und Sozialpolitik,* 57.

110. Schmoller to Brentano 13 July 1877, in Goetz, ed., *Briefwechsel,* 30: 177; 21 April 1878, ibid., 190; Brentano to Schmoller, 27 Oct. 78, ibid., 199–202; Schmoller to Brentano, 2 Nov 1878, ibid., 202–207.

111. Industrialists constituted 30 percent of the membership in 1879, whereas they had never exceeded 6 percent in previous years; merchants constituted 20 percent, compared to a previous high of 3 percent. (Gorges, *Sozialforschung,* 67–68).

112. Boese, *Geschichte,* 40.

113. Ibid., 44–45.

109 and 173, in the 1880s, it ranged from 57 to 75; whereas professors comprised 13 percent of the membership during the 1870s, they now made up 30 percent.[114]

Thus the tension between scholarship and engagement that was characteristic of Schmoller's approach resurfaced in the *Verein*. The feeling that the organization could not participate directly in policy-making without "selling out" to one side or another was not an isolated case. There was an increasingly pessimistic view among academics that their cultivated expertise was being debased by the interplay of political and economic interests.[115] Certainly the decline of cultivated men in positions of political leadership was no figment of their imagination in the Bismarckian era: the number of National Liberals in the Reichstag from the *Bildungsbürgertum* fell from 60 percent to 45 percent between 1877 and 1887.[116]

The decision to refrain from resolutions did not mean, however, that the *Verein* had given up the broader goal of influencing legislation by other means: Nasse's opening speeches at the biennial conferences made this clear.[117] Now, however, the emphasis was on investigating and uncovering issues which were not as much in the limelight—and with which legislators and officials might not have time to concern themselves—and on commenting on these in a nonpartisan manner. Most prominent among these issues was agricultural policy, which figured in each of the four meetings during the 1880s. The relevance of agriculture to contemporary concerns was clear. Not only were farmers suffering disproportionately in the "great depression" from lower prices and higher costs, but more and more were moving to the cities; as the statistics of 1892 revealed, this was the decade in which the balance between the agricultural and industrial sectors tipped in favor of the latter for the first time. The *Verein* deliberated on such issues as the optimum size of farms in a given region; the impact on this of inheritance laws; the desirability of opening new lands, primarily in the Polish areas, to small German farmers; and the dangers of usury in the countryside.[118] The concern with preserving small farmers found resonance in the larger public debate over the draft of the Reich civil law code which appeared in 1888: the *Verein's* recommendations that legal definitions of property and credit should be different for farmers were taken up by critics of the code as well as by conservative farmers' organizations.[119] On these as well

114. Gorges, *Sozialforschung*, 67–68, 156.
115. Ringer, *Decline of the German Mandarins*, 43–46; Andernach, *Einfluss der Parteien*, 69–70.
116. Sheehan, *German Liberalism*, 198.
117. Gorges, *Sozialforschung*, 153. See also Boese, *Geschichte*, 45.
118. Gorges, *Sozialforschung*, 161–64; Boese, *Geschichte*, 47–56.
119. John, *Politics and the Law*, chap. 5, passim.

as the nonagricultural topics of the 1880s, the *Verein* steered safely away from subjects that might have run it afoul of the anti-Socialist laws; it also reflected the broader tendency of academics to support Bismarck's conservative policies.[120] Schmoller's opening article in 1881 as new editor of the *Jahrbuch für Gesetzgebung, Verwaltung, und Volkswirtschaft* (*Yearbook for Legislation, Administration, and Economics*)—soon to be known as *Schmoller's Jahrbuch*—contained both the image of the scientist as the choir in Greek tragedy and a paean to Bismarck as one of history's great statesmen; it called on the political parties to unite behind the leader, while promising editorial independence.[121] In this way, the economists followed the path of the bureaucracy itself in yielding the initiative to the chancellor.

The decision to shy away from controversial issues in the 1880s meant that neither Schmoller nor the *Verein* had much say in the most significant pieces of social legislation in that decade: the programs for accident, health, and old-age insurance of 1884 and 1889. These pathbreaking laws were to a great extent Bismarck's handiwork. He saw them not only as a way of pacifying the workers to compensate for the anti-Socialist law, but also as a means of strengthening the central government. In formulating and revising his ideas, Bismarck drew from a variety of sources—industrialists, bureaucrats from the Prussian ministry of commerce, and even academics who were sympathetic to the corporatist approach. These were mainly Wagner and Schäffle. Although Bismarck at first looked to Wagner as a supporter for his programs in the press and the Prussian legislature, the outspoken professor's support proved to be a dubious blessing. Wagner as usual went his own way, departing from Bismarck's ideas on taxation; on one occasion, Bismarck privately accused him of having ruined his plans for a government tobacco monopoly.[122] Schäffle, in contrast, was invited to closer collaboration.[123] Schäffle had advocated associations based on profes-

---

120. Gorges, *Sozialforschung*, 164, 167; Lindenlaub, *Richtungskämpfe*, 153; Pflanze, *Bismarck*, 3: 27.

121. Schmoller, "Ueber Zweck und Ziele," 9, 14–17; Lindenlaub, *Richtungskämpfe*, 192. It may be said to have fulfilled this goal by not becoming a government mouthpiece.

122. Bismarck, Gespräch mit . . . John Booth, 29 Nov. 1883, in *Gesammelte Werke*, 8: 491; on the tax issue, Diktat, 13 Dec. 1882, ibid., 6c: 263–65; "Professor Wagner," wrote Bismarck to Adolf von Scholz on 24 Nov. 1882, "is clearly a brilliant speaker, but financially and politically very doubtful with his mobile income tax; landowners and homeowners who voted Conservative for him will hardly thank him if he procures for them a doubled income tax on top of the land and home tax." (ibid., 14.2: 941). On Bismarck's use of Wagner as a propagandist, see Wagner to Benndorf, 2 August 1881, in *Briefe*, 203. The correspondence between Wagner and Bismarck has not survived (ibid., 425–26), but Wagner felt that he was not consulted (Wagner to Hermann Wagner, 2 May 1881; to Stöcker, 20 June 1884, ibid., 196, 232).

123. Bismarck to Schäffle, 16 Oct. 1881 in *Gesammelte Werke* 6c: 230–31; Schäffle *Aus meinem Leben*, 2: 174, 181.

sion as the main administrative units for the health insurance system; this struck a sympathetic note with the chancellor, particularly since his original idea of a single state insurance corporation had contributed to the bill's first defeat in the Reichstag.[124] The more the government moved away from centralization towards self-administration, the greater was its success in the Reichstag, and the bill which eventually passed in 1884 multiplied the number of these units further.[125] Workers were poorly represented in these bodies, and the measures failed to wean the workers away from Social Democracy—particularly since more pressing legislation on hours and working conditions was still not included in Bismarck's program. In the long run, however, the social insurance laws probably contributed to the assimilation of the working class into the Second Empire, offsetting their lack of parliamentary power. Along with the civil legal code, Bismarck's social insurance programs were among the few institutions of the Second Empire that survived it.

Given the diversity of opinion within the *Verein*, it was not to be expected that all its members would endorse the conservative turn. Brentano in particular was disaffected by the abdication by the *Verein* of its earlier concern with workers' issues. Such concerns led to a temporary break in his friendship with Schmoller in 1887.[126] Nevertheless, Brentano also moved away from his earlier liberalism: he came to appreciate the differences between the English and German labor movements to a greater extent and began to advocate cartels as a means of controlling production and employment.[127]

In conclusion, one may view the *Verein* as part of the process of professionalization in Germany that reached a high point in the Bismarckian era. Contemporaries pointed out its resemblance to the Association of German Jurists, which had a strong academic component and had successfully shaped much legislation since the 1860s; it also resembled more remotely the Association of German Engineers, which similarly stood for engineers in the service of high-minded ideals; the ethical component was common to all three groups.[128] In the cases of both lawyers and engineers, however, separate organizations soon

124. Schäffle, *Aus meinem Leben*, 2: 146, 181; cf. E. R. Huber, *Verfassungsgeschichte*, 4: 1199; Heffter, *Deutsche Selbstverwaltung*, 687.

125. E. R. Huber, *Verfassungsgeschichte*, 4: 1201. Another crucial element was the absence of a state contribution, in contrast to the previous bills. The health insurance bill, which lacked any central agency, passed the soonest, in 1883; the old-age bill was not passed until 1889, partly because Bismarck had lost interest by that time (Heffter, *Deutsche Selbstverwaltung*, 690).

126. The occasion was the publication of a dissertation by Brentano's student Heinrich Herkner that was critical of working conditions in Alsace-Lorraine; this was highly embarrassing to the Reich government at the time, and Schmoller gave the work a harshly critical review (Craig, *Scholarship and Nation Building*, 90–92; Lindenlaub, *Richtungskämpfe*, 162).

127. Sheehan, *Brentano*, chap. 5.

128. On lawyers and engineers, see McClelland, *Professionalization*, 89, 91–92.

arose to advocate their more material interests.[129] In the case of economists, the separation of self-interest from such ethical identification did not occur: the *Verein* became a forum to promote both their social mission and their professional role. Its program coincided with the time-honored professional goals of scientists of state as trainers of officials: *Sozialpolitik* was an extension of the older *Volkswirtschaftspolitik*. Moreover, the role of the *Verein* as an organization which conducted social research powerfully bolstered the self-image and public reputation of the professors as a "community of the competent."[130] Admittedly, the prestige of the *Kathedersozialisten* often exceeded their influence: Bismarck's claiming the title for himself while opposing factory legislation is a case in point. Yet the workers' insurance laws represented a partial fulfillment of the academic reformers' agenda. The mandarin ethos of indirect influence seemed to be working.

THE ECONOMIC SCIENCES OF STATE

If the *Verein* generated a program of policy-oriented social research, the seminars within the universities tended to generate genuine schools of thought within the newly bifurcated intellectual field of the sciences of state. These schools typically involved a group of researchers that focused on a common topic under the direction of a professor. The underlying assumptions of these schools more often took the form of explanatory systems, dedicated to the understanding of a subject, rather than classificatory schemes, dedicated to the ordering thereof. The two most conspicuous examples were Schmoller's and Brentano's historical school and Carl Menger's "marginal utility" school in Austria. Wagner also developed a distinctive program that was intermediate between these two and more closely tied to the classificatory models of the past. To these we now turn.

The Historical School

Schmoller clearly viewed the call to Strassburg as an opportunity for founding a school; as he frankly told the curator,

> My hope in coming here was primarily to find in Strassburg a favorable soil, because the ample positions in the sciences of state (a professorship of Politics and Finance, of Statistics, of Administrative Law) would be encouraging for the founding of a genuine school in the sciences of state. Therein I have not been deceived.

129. The *Deutscher Anwaltverein* (1872) and the *Verein Deutscher Eisenhüttenleute* (1880; ibid., 88, 92).

130. The phrase is Haskell's, who finds this lacking in the ASSA (*Emergence of Professional Social Science,* 134). The *Verein* indeed served as the initial model for the American Economic Association, although the reformist goals were soon dropped from it (179–80, 187).

It was not, however, the candidates for the bureaucracy who made up his seminar primarily (they were immersed in law) but

> foreigners, people who want to take up the academic career, who aspire to become chamber of commerce secretaries or to places in the statistical bureau, farmers who want a doctorate on the basis of the sciences of state to teach in agricultural institutes, rich nobles . . . who think of a career as a representative . . . a school can be made of these kinds of people.[131]

Despite the opposition of many of the law professors, a separate doctorate in the sciences of state was finally established in 1880. The required subjects were economics, finance, statistics, politics, state law, and Roman civil law (the latter was dropped three years later).[132]

Although the field of the *Staatswissenschaften* was thus alive as a curricular entity, Schmoller's school centered on economic history. Unlike Hildebrand at Jena, he found it more profitable to focus the entire seminar on a single topic to promote discussion. He chose the history of the guilds in Strassburg, for which documents were available, and pursued it over several semesters, tailoring some of his lectures to the subject; he also published the most important documents. His monograph on the cloth and weaver guilds (with the help of his assistant Wilhelm Stieda) set the standard for the economic history of the time.[133]

Schmoller's immersion in historical sources qualified him for dual membership in the historical and economic communities of scholars.[134] Yet this immersion has raised the question—both in his own time and since—whether he had anything to contribute to economic theory, indeed whether his dislike of abstract thinking decisively undermined that tradition in Germany.[135] Given his

---

131. Schmoller to curator, 25 May 1874, Archives Departementales du Bas-Rhin, Strasbourg, AL 103 paq 17 no. 18: 74.

132. Schmoller to Roscher, 4 June 1873, in Roscher and Schmoller, *Briefwechsel*, 25–26; Schmoller to curator 25 May 1874, Archives Departementales, 73–74; Bestimmungen über die Erlangung des staatsws. Doktorgrads . . .; Promotionsordnung, GPSA Dahlem, Rep. 92 Schmoller, no. 6: 59–60, 219 (Strassburger Universitätsangelegenheiten); Knapp to Schmoller, 11 Jan. 1883, ibid., no. 130a: 143.

133. See Balabkins, *Not by Theory Alone*, 37; Hintze, "Schmoller," 529–30.

134. Christian Simon makes clear his role in the academic politics of history at Berlin in his *Staat und Geschichtswissenschaft*, 1: 137.

135. Balabkins's useful survey of the reviews of Schmoller's *Grundriss* reveals this (*Not by Theory Alone*, 67–76). See also Schumpeter's defense of Schmoller's theoretical contribution in "Gustav v. Schmoller und die Probleme von heute," (1926). The recent willingness to take Schmoller seriously is revealed in a spate of publications: a special section of the *Journal of Institutional and Theoretical Economics* [incorporating the *ZGS*], 144 (1988): 524–601; an issue of the *International Journal of Social Economics* 16 (1989); Schiera and Tenbruck, eds., *Gustav Schmoller e il suo tempo* (Bologna: Societa editrice il Mulino, 1989), to name a few.

pivotal position, the question bears closer examination, for Schmoller did address himself to questions of economic theory and method and thus articulated a set of guidelines for his research program.[136]

The underlying premise of Schmoller's views was that of complexity: economic phenomena could neither be explained in terms of single causal factors nor reduced to simple descriptions. "My view and disposition," wrote Schmoller in the preface to his systematic *Grundriss*, "is always to make the beginner attentive to the complicatedness and difficulty of phenomena and problems, to show him the different sides of an object."[137] This was the common assumption behind his historical researches and his attacks on laissez-faire liberalism: the reduction of human motivation to self-interest was simplistic and unrealistic. Instead, he viewed economics as involving a continual interplay between egoistic drives and cultural constraints. "Egoism in the economy," he wrote, "is like the steam in the steam engine; I know what it accomplishes only when I know the pressure under which it works. That pressure . . . always stems from the ethical cultural life; it is the pressure of the ethos on the natural drives."[138] Ethics and custom were rooted in the human psyche as much as acquisitive instinct; yet both found expression in a common set of institutions and objective cultural formations (e.g., law, religion, morality).[139] A realistic economist must thus address questions of psychology as well as history.[140]

It is instructive to compare Schmoller's methodological writings on economics with Wilhelm Dilthey's attempt to provide a philosophical foundation for the human sciences (*Geisteswissenschaften*) during the same years. Schmoller noted the affinities between the two in 1893: both were reactions to the simplifying methods of the natural sciences as applied to human society; Schmoller's ethical and cultural phenomena were essentially the same as the subject matter of the *Geisteswissenschaften* as Dilthey defined them.[141] The two also shared a common view of the psychological roots of culture and custom, as was common in the 1880s—one thinks of Wundt as well. But Schmoller never went as far in this direction as did Dilthey. He did not view introspective experience as the primary foundation of knowledge in this realm, as Dilthey proposed in 1894, but as one source among many. In calling attention also to the objective ex-

136. Most of the essays were collected in *Einige Grundfragen* in 1897—except for the review of Menger, which appeared in another collection, *Litteraturgeschichte*, 275–304.

137. Schmoller, *Grundriss*, 1: vi.

138. Schmoller, *Einige Grundfragen*, 51. See also *Grundriss*, 1: 59–60.

139. Schmoller, *Einige Grundfragen*, 44, 226; *Grundriss* 1: 48 ff.

140. See Willi Meyer, "Schmollers Research Programme," 570–80.

141. Schmoller, *Einige Grundfragen*, 279; *Grundriss*, 1: 107. Schmoller also reviewed Dilthey's first effort in this direction, the *Einleitung in die Geisteswissenschaften* of 1883 most favorably. See *Litteraturgeschichte*, 294–304.

pressions of culture, he anticipated Dilthey's more mature views.[142] In fact, Schmoller never accepted the complete assimilation of economics into the human sciences. Despite their strong affinities, economics continued to have a foot in the natural sciences inasmuch as it dealt with technology, ethnography, and demography.[143]

If Schmoller's commitment to complexity caused him to oppose classical theoretical economics, it also led him to break with the older invocations of history such as those of Roscher and Hildebrand: he went beyond them in rejecting any deterministic developmental scheme to be applied to different places and times.[144] Rather he sought to define the complex of factors which shape the economy at any particular time. He did this most effectively in his monographic studies, but a case can also be made for his replacing such developmental schemes with a set of general theoretical concepts that successfully captured the complexity of his subject matter. This was to be found in his textbook, the *Grundriss der allgemeinen Volkswirtschaftslehre*, the product of long years of labor in his later life. That work encompassed the basic natural foundations of land, population, and technology; the individual and collective actors (family, corporation, municipality, state, class, enterprise); the arrangements of circulation and distribution of wealth (trade, money, value and price, interest, banking, labor relations and institutions); and a variety of developmental phenomena (cycles and crises, class struggles, international trade relations). Given the vast amount of erudition he brought to each of these topics, it is difficult to imagine his economics as a specialized science in the usual sense. But Schmoller's purpose was not merely to be encyclopedic; it was rather to convey to the student, through all the detail, a feel for these categories as *typical* phenomena or patterns within the social sciences as they affected the economy. He defined "general economics" as a study of these typicalities, as distinct from "special economics," which dealt with particular economies of a given country or time period. Schmoller's general economics served as a midwife for sociology, so to speak: it helped move the science of society from a few rudimentary ideas to a more articulated system of topics. Schmoller was quite explicit about the overlap between his general economics and sociology. "Economics today is only a science insofar as it broadens into a theory of society and to the degree that it does so," he wrote.[145] Thus by redefining historical economics as a science of the typical

142. Schmoller, *Grundriss*, 1: 107. For an attempt to put Dilthey in the context of psychologism, see Lindenfeld, *Transformation of Positivism*, 87–88, 114.

143. Schmoller, *Einige Grundfragen*, 274; *Grundriss* 1: 108.

144. Schmoller, *Einige Grundfragen*, 52.

145. Schmoller, review of Schönberg, *Handbuch der politischen Oekonomie, SJ* 6 (1882): 1382. Schmoller was critical of Schönberg's following Rau's scheme; see also *Einige Grundfragen*, 332. On the significance of Schmoller for sociology, see Schumpeter, "Gustav v. Schmoller," 370 (although

rather than a science of the cyclical, Schmoller was able to reduce the a priori elements in his reasoning and allow empirical observation to guide his results.

Arriving at the typical involved a more varied methodological palette than had been used in the past. Schmoller defined his method as consisting of three elements: (1) empirical observation, of which the statistical and historical methods were subtypes; (2) definition and classification; and (3) causal explanation.[146] For complicated subjects like economics, observation played a greater role than in sciences which dealt with simple elements; conversely, the defining and classifying of concepts played a lesser role.[147] Schmoller recognized both the indispensability of conceptual formation and its provisionality.[148] Thus value and price theory, or a theory of historical stages, had their place in economics, provided one did not attempt to derive too much from them. If past attempts at conceptualization had proven so unfruitful, it was not because the operation itself was illegitimate, but because of the intellectual poverty of the conceptualizers: they lacked worldliness and intuitive thinking. To use his own figure of speech, "the best and sharpest millstone cannot make quality flour out of chaff."[149] Observation and classification were preliminary, however, to causal explanation, which enabled the scientist to understand typical and recurring phenomena.[150] Both induction and deduction played a role in this, and Schmoller predictably resisted the attempt to reduce one to the other; he polemicized against J. S. Mill's attempt to do so.[151] Schmoller was perfectly willing to admit the existence of causal and developmental patterns within a given cultural configuration. He opposed, however, the belief that there were ultimate causal laws in economics that transcended historical time and place.[152]

For all these innovations, the reader will recognize in the *Grundriss* certain continuities with the older *Staatswissenschaften*—the desire for exhaustiveness and completeness rather than self-imposed limitation. The linking of economics, history, statistics, and sociology represented a disciplinary complex rather than a narrow specialized field: that of social science rather than state science. And if this complex lacked the deliberate encylopedic character of its predecessor, it also lacked the clear lines delineating the various components of the

---

he does not see Schmoller's significance as a theorist as exhausted thereby); Harald Homann, "Gustav Schmoller und die 'empirische Sozialforschung,'" in Schiera and Tenbruck, eds., *Schmoller e suo Tempo*, 327–28.

146. Schmoller, *Einige Grundfragen*, 296, 305; *Grundriss*, 1: 104. Balabkins has found no less than six different methods in the *Grundriss* (63).

147. Schmoller, *Einige Grundfragen*, 299, 324.

148. Ibid., 323.

149. Ibid., 326.

150. Ibid., 327; *Grundriss*, 1: 105.

151. Schmoller, *Einige Grundfragen*, 344–48.

152. Ibid., 355–57; *Grundriss*, 1: 109.

whole. "If one contemplates the individual objects in Schmoller's scenery," wrote Schumpeter, "rather than the lines for whose sake the objects are placed, naturally one finds chaos."[153] In this breadth of scope, Schmoller remained true to his bureaucratic roots: higher officials were not to think of themselves as mere specialists, but as overseers of society in its complexity. Just as Schmoller guided the *Verein* to become a professional organization in a broader sense than usual, so he conceptualized his science as something other than a specialty in the conventional sense.

If this deliberate blurring of contours had been a necessary corrective to a liberal economics which at the popular level had become artificially simple in the 1860s and 1870s—so Max Weber credited Schmoller on the latter's 70th birthday—it simultaneously served to obscure further the relation between the two halves of Schmoller's activity, the theoretical and the practical.[154] For it was in his reformist activity, as we have seen, that he fervently expressed the belief in progress within the framework of Western history that he rejected in his methodological writings. Schmoller was certainly aware of these contradictions. The justification for engaging in practical reform—and holding the vision of progress which sustained it—stemmed, in Schmoller's view, from the fact that economics was still a most incomplete science; it was still far from delivering a set of causal explanations that would cover its vast subject matter. In the absence of these, the scholar still had to rely on subjective belief and conviction regarding the overall coherence and purpose of history and society. Economics according to Schmoller was still in Comte's second stage, the metaphysical, and was centuries away from being a truly positive science.[155] This very appeal to stages, however, invoked the view that he had elsewhere so energetically repudiated.[156] Schmoller could live with this contradiction because the borderline between empirically grounded explanation of developmental patterns on the one hand and speculative theories of history on the other was never sharply defined: there were all shades of gray in between. Thus he could point to recurring patterns of business cycles, class struggle, and international trade as being empirically well-founded typical phenomena under the specific conditions of modern Western societies.[157] But he was also willing to assert,

153. Schumpeter, "Gustav v. Schmoller," 383 n.

154. Weber's speech is quoted in Bruch, "Nationalökonomie zwischen Wissenschaft und öffentlicher Meinung," 160.

155. Schmoller, "Ueber Zweck und Ziele," 3–4; *Grundriss,* 1: 111.

156. This inconsistency was expressed by Kurt Dopfer as Schmoller's clinging to the assumption of "time symmetry," underlying cyclical and progress theories, whereas a genuinely historical theory must embrace the assumption of "time asymmetry," that is, that events will not necessarily repeat themselves with any regularity. See his "How Historical Is Schmoller's Economic Theory?," 564–65.

157. Schmoller, *Grundriss,* 2: 465–66.

albeit more tentatively, a belief in general economic progress, which improved the lot of the lower classes, as a mark of the more advanced modern nations.[158] Thus he ended his vast scholarly canvass of the *Grundriss* with the same credo which he had used to launch the *Verein für Sozialpolitik:*

> The time will come when all good and normally developed persons will understand how to combine a respectable acquisitive drive, a striving towards individuality, self-assertion, and self-affirmation with full justice and the highest sense of commonality. I hope that the path will not be as long as the one which led from the brutalities of the physical power-man to the contemporary man of culture.[159]

Schmoller never departed from the teleological assumptions of the older generation to the degree that he claimed; it is hardly surprising that the generation that lived through the disillusionments of World War I repudiated him.

Statistics

Schmoller did not forge a research program for economics singlehandedly. Statistics continued to be a vital element, embodying that same interest in the particular that had characterized it in the past and the same distrust of simplistic generalities that allied it to the historical school. The background of the leading German statisticians in the natural sciences lent substance to Schmoller's claim that the new social science was not exclusively a *Geisteswissenschaft.*

Statistics was part of the research program that developed in Strassburg, due largely to the presence of Schmoller's friend Georg Friedrich Knapp, who arrived there in 1874. While Schmoller came to economics from history, Knapp came to it from natural science. He was Liebig's nephew, and his father was a professor of chemical technology in the political economy faculty at Munich who had come there in Liebig's train. Knapp himself attended Liebig's lectures and worked in his laboratory.[160] From other members of his academic extended family he also acquired a love of literature. Although he soon discovered his lack of inclination for chemistry, he developed a command of mathematics that few of his contemporaries could match. Drawn to economics at first through Hermann and Helferich in the 1860s, he soon became disillusioned with the theoretical approach. "The virtuoso twisting of a few propositions appeared to me quite unproductive," he wrote, ". . . [and] without any value for the solving of questions."[161] He was drawn to Engel's seminar and to statistics,

---

158. Ibid., 2: 653.
159. Ibid., 2: 678.
160. Knapp, *Eine Jugend*, 43–44, 136, 147.
161. Ibid., 189–90.

where he outshone his teacher in mathematical sophistication. He soon put his abilities to use in improving the techniques for measuring changes in population and mortality rates; he was able to apply these techniques as head of the Leipzig statistical office, a post which he assumed in 1867. Although he received an academic appointment at Leipzig in 1869, he did not find there the community of scholars he sought; nor could he devote as much time to research.[162] He therefore accepted the call to Strassburg, where he remained for the rest of his career. His effectiveness as a seminar leader stemmed in large part from the personal interest he took in his students.[163]

Knapp's intellectual development may be seen as a lifelong quest to bring theory into touch with real problems and thereby to render it useful.[164] He took up the critique of Quetelet's statistical laws begun by Engel, Rümelin, and others in the controversy over free will. According to Knapp, Quetelet had been seduced by a physical analogy, namely, that of seeing the "average man" as corresponding to the "gravitational point" in the laws of physics.[165] Knapp allowed that such an analogy might be useful in describing physical characterstics such as height and weight, but not social characteristics, which change more rapidly from place to place and time to time. Anthropology, which in Knapp's view treated the physical person only, was to be sharply distinguished from the social sciences.[166]

As with Engel, the technique of sampling—and using statistics to extrapolate from samples to larger populations—seems not to have interested Knapp. He preferred the opposite approach of discovering and refining the mathematical formulas used to describe reality so that the latter's complexity could be more accurately represented. His major work in this area was in demographics. In his *Theory of Population Change*, a collection of essays published in 1874, he derived a set of formulas that could handle variable functions rather than constant ones, using differential rather than integral calculus, as had previously been the case.[167]

During the late 1870s at Strassburg, Knapp's interests began to shift from statistics to history: he dropped his regular lecture on mathematical statistics and added one on the social-political history of France and England.[168] It was

162. Knapp to Schmoller, 11 May 1874, GPSA Dahlem, Rep. 92 Schmoller, no. 130a: 2.

163. Dehio, "Knapp," 402, 405.

164. See Schumpeter's appreciation, *Ten Great Economists*, 296–97; Dehio, "Knapp," 5: 399–406.

165. Knapp, "Quetelet als Theoretiker," 111–12.

166. Ibid., 109–11. See also Porter, *Rise of Statistical Thinking*, 188–89.

167. Knapp, *Theorie des Bevölkerungs-Wechsels*, 5.

168. Knapp taught mathematical statistics four times between 1875 and 1877 and only once thereafter; he gave the history lecture five times between 1877–78 and 1883. See university catalogues.

clear that questions of contemporary *Sozialpolitik* aroused his interest. Prompted by the crisis in agriculture, he helped turn the *Verein* to that topic and began to study the background to it himself.[169] The result of his researches was a masterly historical work on what he labeled "the social question of the eighteenth century," *The Emancipation of the Peasants and the Origin of the Agricultural Workers in the Older Parts of Prussia*, published in 1887.[170] In the 1890s, Knapp was to undergo yet another metamorphosis and become a monetary theorist.

Although Knapp was not concerned with the prospects and problems associated with sampling, these were taken up by an admirer of his, another natural scientist turned statistician and economist, Wilhelm Lexis. Lexis had studied mechanics at Bonn and worked in Robert Bunsen's chemical laboratory in Heidelberg before turning to economics during an extended stay in Paris in the 1860s. He also did some of his most creative work at Strassburg, where he was Knapp's predecessor from 1872 to 1874 (he eventually landed at Göttingen).[171] Lexis was also convinced that Quetelet's assumptions about human behavior were naive, and that the diversity of conditions from one population to another (or among subgroups within a given population) made statistical generalizations across such groups extremely hazardous. A random sample drawn from different or heterogeneous populations would thus mean something different from a sample drawn from a homogeneous one. There were admittedly some types of social phenomena that were homogeneous in this sense, that is, whose components did follow normal distribution curves—his comparison of birthrates in Prussia and England on a county-by-county basis was one such instance—but fewer than the apostles of statistical determinism had thought.[172] Thus it was important for statisticians to know whether they were dealing with a homogeneous or heterogeneous group if sampling was to be used. By 1879, Lexis had come up with a mathematical technique for determining this by comparing the observed distribution in the sample with the one predicted by the probability calculus: the index of dispersion. This was taken up by the English statisticians Francis Edgeworth and Karl Pearson, assuring Lexis a leading place in the history of statistics.[173]

Like Knapp, Lexis moved on to other concerns in the 1880s and after, turning to subjects like banking, monetary theory—he became an advocate of bimetallism—and trade policy. During the Wilhelminian era he became one of

169. Boese, *Geschichte*, 35, 44.
170. Knapp, *Bauern-Befreiung*, 1: iii. Although he praised the Prussian bureaucracy for its reformist policies, he was also critical of the treatment of independent farmers, who lost rather than gained in the process (1: 322). This was the basis of the agricultural proletariat of the current day.
171. Oldenburg, "Wilhelm Lexis," 7.
172. Heiss, "Lexis," 272; Porter, *Rise of Statistical Thinking*, 243–44, 247–53.
173. Heiss, "Lexis," 273, Porter, *Rise of Statistical Thinking*, 249, 255.

the most trusted advisers to the Ministry of Culture and Education. Although he never pursued historical research, he endorsed a realistic economics based on a "versatile knowledge of actual economic states and processes," in which abstraction had a legitimate but limited place.[174]

The third major statistician, Johannes Conrad, was next to Schmoller the most successful academic organizer of research of his day. Conrad's own career illustrated the upward mobility that a newly institutionalized research program could afford and which he himself encouraged. The son of a Silesian farmer, Conrad originally wanted to study natural science and return to farming, but was prevented from doing so by a physical handicap. He eventually found his way to economics and to Hildebrand's seminar, where he distinguished himself by refuting Liebig's theory of soil depletion, based on more careful statistical studies than Liebig had done.[175] The work was representative of Conrad's strength: detailed quantitative investigations of local conditions. Thus he continued the idiographic strand of German statistics, rather than pursuing mathematical treatment as did Knapp and Lexis.

Conrad's focus on agricultural economics and policy won him a professorship at Halle to replace Schmoller in 1872, where he took over the seminar that Schmoller had just founded. Like Schmoller in Strassburg, Conrad found that most of his students were not jurists; many were agricultural students like himself. He emphasized in his first report that those who had not passed the *Abitur* were every bit as capable as those who had.[176] Unlike Schmoller, however, Conrad retained Hildebrand's method of including a variety of subjects rather than focusing on a single research topic or type of source material. "There is no alternative," he wrote, "to conforming in each case to the talent and interest of the student, and to put one's own wishes, yes even the interest of science, in the background."[177] This approach was no less successful than Schmoller's: Conrad's seminar produced thirty-one academics in the next twenty-six years, including nine Americans, not to mention directors of statistical bureaus and secretaries of economic interest groups.[178]

Conrad developed an apparatus similar to that of Schmoller: he edited both a series of scholarly publications from the seminar and a journal devoted more

174. Lexis, *Allgemeine Volkswirtschaftslehre*, 19.

175. On Conrad's early years, see his *Lebenserinnerungen*, 39–63; Diehl, "Johannes Conrad." 738–41; Lehmann, "Nationalökonomie an der Universität Halle," 167–73. Hildebrand even offered to hold the seminar in Conrad's room to accommodate him (*Lebenserinnerungen*, 62).

176. Report on the activities of the seminar in the sciences of state, 1872–73, GPSA Dahlem, Rep. 76 Va Sect. 8 Tit. X no. 43, vol. 1: 50 (Staatsws. Seminar).

177. Quoted in Kähler, "Staatswissenschaftlichen Unterricht," 170. Conrad's decision to stimulate research in others rather than produce a major work himself was again related to his handicap (*Lebenserinnerungen,* 130–31).

178. Kähler, "Staatswissenschaftlichen Unterrichts," 167 n; Diehl, "Conrad," 744.

to practical questions (*Jahrbücher für Nationalökonomie und Statistik*, following Hildebrand); he contributed to the *Verein* without being as active as others, but did serve as a token economist on the commission to revise the civil code, and edited a multivolume dictionary of the sciences of state (mostly economics) in the 1890s. His textbook, renowned for its clarity, was more popular than Schmoller's *Grundriss;* it stuck to the traditional schema of Rau. He enjoyed a reputation for nonpartisanship and independence of judgment, and he refused to take sides in the *Methodenstreit:* he recognized the contributions and limitations of both the theoretical and historical approaches. Conrad's version of a research program, producing works in such varied fields as agriculture, statistics, workers' issues, price movements, and the history of economic thought, illustrates in its own way the continuing breadth of German economics and its continuity with the *Staatswissenschaften.*

The advent of these research programs nevertheless brought about one important breach with the past, namely, in the way these scholars now viewed their own tradition. Beginning in the 1880s, there was a much greater tendency in the textbooks to denigrate the work of the early-nineteenth-century economists—with the exception of Thünen—as mere collectors of recipes rather than as creative minds. This was in marked contrast to Roscher, Knies, and even Schmoller.[179] Thus Conrad could refer to Rau and his contemporaries as lacking in originality, and the Göttingen economist Gustav Cohn could write that "while language, law, and state could attain knowledge of their own essence under the hand of historical research, the economy stuck to the delusional ideas of the eighteenth century, which transposed the historical into the natural."[180] The antagonistic discourse between Manchesterites and *Kathedersozialisten* in the press during the 1870s undoubtedly encouraged this tendency, but it is noteworthy that the further step of misinterpreting the early theoreticians as relatively unthinking advocates of laissez-faire occurred only with the firm establishment of the new paradigm of research.

Wagner and Social Economy

Although the historical-statistical approach came to dominate German economics, its influence should not be exaggerated. The view that economics

179. Roscher contrasted the "idealistic" approach with the "historical-physiological" one without mentioning any of the earlier German economists (*Grundlagen der Nationalökonomie*, 52–62); Knies explicitly warned against reducing the earlier economists to the status of unthinking dogmatists, though he found such features in the theoretical portions of Rau's work as distinct from the practical ones (*Politische Oekonomie*, 36–38); Schmoller also gave Rau credit for incorporating much from the realistic legacy of cameralism (*Grundriss*, 1: 91).

180. Cohn, *System der Nationalökonomie*, 1: 127; Conrad, *Grundriss zum Studium der politischen Oekonomie*, 1: 372. See also von Scheel, "Politische Oekonomie als Wissenschaft," 100–101.

should be based on a clearly stated set of first principles continued to be upheld by many; its most vocal spokesman came to be Adolph Wagner. He was privately expressing reservations about the usefulness of the Schmoller school and noting its cliqueishness by 1877. "I do not underestimate induction, statistical and historical research," he wrote to Wilhelm Stieda, "but I also do not overestimate it, and on the other hand do not underestimate deduction. . . . There are many roads to Rome, to scientific truth; I only claim: not only via Strassburg's guildhalls."[181] Wagner held to this pluralistic position when he actively endorsed Schmoller's appointment to Berlin despite their differences; it also characterized his approach to theory itself, which bore the stamp of Rau's classificatory all-inclusiveness.[182] Thus when Wagner undertook to revise Rau's textbook, beginning in 1873, he added still more material, attempting to incorporate recent developments in the field. Like Stein, he eventually found that this attempt at a comprehensive system outstripped his powers; it remained incomplete.[183] Nevertheless, the completed parts revealed that Wagner was rather more successful than Schmoller at integrating his own strong sociopolitical concerns into a theoretical framework, without allowing the former to dominate. "Neither communism nor free-trade optimism, but a correct middle standpoint will be represented here," he wrote, "from which the necessity in priniciple of compromises even in theory between the requirements of different economic organizational principles will be acknowledged."[184] Wagner posited several such coexisting organizational principles: (1) the private economy, based on self-interest; (2) the charitable, based on voluntary altruism; and (3) the "common," based on the good of the whole, which included the state.[185] He also proposed a "law of increasing extension of state activities," claiming that this public sector increased with economic progress.[186] These were features to be found in the work of Rodbertus and Schäffle, whom Wagner acknowledged as his closest forebears.[187] An innovative feature of Wagner's theory was an exhaustive application of these different principles to civil legal concepts of per-

181. Wagner to Stieda, 13 April 1877, in *Briefe*, 144–45.

182. Wagner had already favored Schmoller's appointment in 1879, when the ministry appointed Held (Wagner to Schmoller, 23 May 1881, in *Briefe*, 197).

183. Schumacher, "Staatswissenschaften," 147. Schumacher perceptively compared Wagner's attempt with that of Alfred Marshall in England, noting that "Marshall harvested in many respects what Adolf Wagner had sowed" (148). He attributes Marshall's success at systematic integration to his ability to leave things out—an ability which Wagner lacked.

184. Wagner, *Allgemeine oder Theoretische Volkswirtschaftslehre* 1: 141.

185. Ibid., 1: 164–65. Wagner recognized the similarity of this to Schäffle's economics system, but claimed he had arrived at it independently (ibid., 1: 156).

186. Ibid., 1: 260.

187. Wagner to Marie Rodbertus, 4 Nov. 1877, in *Briefe*, 150; Wagner to Schäffle, Feb. 1901, ibid., 351.

sonal freedom and property, indicating how these might change in an epoch of increasing state involvement.[188] Like some of the Austrian economists, he thus brought the legal and social-science systems closer together. Also, in the volumes on public finance, Wagner argued that the new epoch indicated a relatively greater emphasis on progressive taxation—amidst a great variety of alternatives derived from nine separate principles of taxation.[189]

There were signs of increasing controversy between Wagner's and Schmoller's approaches in the early 1880s. After Schmoller's arrival at Berlin, students divided into Wagnerian and Schmollerian camps.[190] The appearance of another multivolume handbook edited by the Tübingen professor Gustav Schönberg in 1882, based on Rau's classificatory principles, elicited a critical review from Schmoller, in which he affirmed the need for economics to become a broader theory of society. Wagner quickly responded. "The task of political economy," he wrote, "seems to be . . . not the transformation into a presently still unclear 'social science,' but into a true social economy [*Sozialökonomie*]."[191] But these skirmishes were soon to be overshadowed by the confrontation between the historical and the new Austrian school, which had developed a mode of theorizing at the opposite pole from Wagner's discursiveness.

Menger and the Austrian School

The Austrian school was a second economic research program that emerged in the 1870s; it was a much clearer expression of the urge to specialize than the historical school, and its staying power has been much greater. It can be traced back to the work of Carl Menger, particularly to his *Principles of Economics* of 1871, which has achieved the status of a classic.

Attempts to explain the origins and significance of Menger's ideas and those of his followers have generally taken one of two lines. The first is to place them in the context of the so-called marginal revolution, marked by the nearly simultaneous appearance of Menger's *Principles,* the *Theory of Political Economy* (1871) by William Stanley Jevons in England, and the *Elements of Pure Economics* (1874–77) by Leon Walras in Switzerland—each without knowledge of the others. According to the standard textbook accounts, the marginal revolution consisted in a shift of basic assumptions away from the genetic perspective of the labor theory of value, which traced economic growth and capital accumulation back to the labor that produced goods, to a decision-making perspective which viewed economics as a set of choices made ultimately by consumers about how

---

188. Wagner, *Volkswirtschaftslehre*, chap. 5, covering 430 pages!

189. Wagner, *Finanzwissenschaft*, 2: 228, 289–90.

190. Diehl, "Selbstdarstellung," in Meiner, ed., *VGS*, 61.

191. Wagner, review of *Handbuch der politischen Oekonomie*, 271; see also Schmoller's review of the same, *SJ* 6: 1382; also Homann, *Gesetz und Wirklichkeit in den Sozialwissenschaften*, 130–31.

to allocate a limited quantity of resources to best effect. The "neoclassical" economics that resulted went beyond the earlier school of Ricardo and Mill by explaining a greater variety of phenomena in terms of a single theory with fewer ad hoc assumptions. At the same time, the shift in perspective led to a more static approach and a relative neglect of certain topics, such as population growth.[192]

A second major way of contextualizing Menger's thought is by viewing it as a product of a specifically Austrian intellectual milieu. Menger and his followers were different from the other marginalists in that they spurned mathematical analysis. The Austrians tended to focus on the subjective aspects of the theory embodied in the term *utility*, namely, the values that different goods have in satisfying one's different needs.[193] Menger was less interested in the state of equilibrium among different allocations than in the processes by which they are chosen—and the uncertainties and errors to which they are subject.[194] Some commentators have taken this perspective further, emphasizing the differences between the Austrian and the German philosphical traditions, particularly the relative absence of Kantian and Hegelian idealism in Austrian philosophy, not to mention the lack of interest in historicism and organicism.[195]

While both of these approaches have some validity, they miss a crucial aspect of Menger's intellectual background: his roots in German theoretical economics. We have already seen examples of marginal thinking in Thünen, Hermann, Stein, Knies, and Schäffle.[196] Moreover, at the time Menger was studying in the 1860s, this German tradition had dominated the Austrian universities as well. Stein was still in Vienna, and Menger's economics professor at Prague, Peter Mischler, was likewise a German import.[197] "There is no sufficient new generation of domestic teachers [of political economy]," wrote the Austrian minister of culture and former economics professor Leopold Hasner in recommending Schäffle in 1868.[198] In addition, Menger's private reading

192. Blaug, *Economic Theory in Retrospect*, 312–14; Spiegel, *Growth of Economic Thought*, 505.

193. Boos, *Wissenschaftstheorie*, 56–58.

194. Menger, *Grundsätze*, 94–95.

195. Barry Smith, "Aristotle, Menger, Mises," in Caldwell, ed., *Menger*, 266–70, 272–79; on the Austrian value-theorists, see Fabian and Simons, "Second Austrian School," 37–102.

196. Others include Augustin Cournot (1838) and Jules Dupuis (1844) in France, R. Jennings (1855) in England, and Heinrich Hermann Gossen (1854) in Germany, whose dense mathematical treatment of marginal utility went unnoticed by the *Staatswissenschaftler* until the 1890s—although Gossen was a Prussian official himself. See Nicholas Georgescu-Roegen's introduction to Gossen's *Laws of Human Relations*, esp. li–lviii. On other early marginalists, see Spiegel, *Growth of Economic Thought*, 507–13, Blaug, *Economic Theory in Retrospect*, 319–20.

197. Streissler, "Influence of German Economics," in Caldwell, ed., *Menger*, 36–37, 60–61. Streissler traces Menger's notion of a hierarchy of goods to Mischler.

198. Recommendation of Ministry (Hasner), 26 June 1868, AVA, 5381/1868, 4 Wien Jus Prof. Jurid. 590, Schäffle.

notebooks, dating from the late 1860s, reveal an astonishing range, from economics to philosophy—including Kant and Hegel—to geography, natural science and technology, and was certainly not limited to any one country.[199] These notebooks contain extensive annotations to Rau's (German) and Kudler's (Austrian) textbooks.[200] Menger displayed this wide range of reading in the notes to the *Principles*.

It is quite clear from the *Principles* that Menger formulated his questions, delimited his area of investigation, and derived most of the concepts and laws themselves from the German tradition of economic theory. As he stated in his preface:

> It was a special pleasure to me that the field here treated, comprising the most general principles of our science, is in no small degree so truly a product of recent development in German political economy, and that the reform of the most important principles of our science here attempted is therefore built upon a foundation laid by previous work that was produced almost entirely by the industry of German scholars.[201]

The book was dedicated to Roscher, who was the author most frequently cited (17 times). The other authors most cited were Hermann (12), Smith (11), Say, Schäffle (10 each), Knies, Aristotle (9 each), Condillac (8), Rau, and Turgot (7 each).[202]

Despite his indebtedness to German economists, the originality of Menger's *Principles* is incontestable. We can point here to two fundamental differences from its German predecessors and contemporaries. The first is Menger's break with organicism and his stress on "individualism." This meant to him both a change in substance and a change in method. Menger's substantive individualism conceptualized economics as the sum of individual or group activities rather than as an organic whole; it may already be found in the 1867 notebooks:

> In each people we see numerous individual economies, which are tied to each other . . . through commerce, but which no more lose their individuality than does the physical individual by being part of a people.[203]

---

199. Menger papers, Duke University, box 1, notebooks 1–20.

200. Menger, *Carl Mengers Erster Entwurf*; Streissler, "Influence of German Economics," in Caldwell, ed., *Menger*, 35–36.

201. Menger, *Grundsätze*, xlviii; see also 70 n, 216 n.

202. Streissler, "Influence of German Economics," in Caldwell, ed., *Menger*, 34–35. Streissler demonstrates the German connection most convincingly.

203. Menger papers, box 1, notebook 9, "Theoretika," 21 Nov. 1867; cf. Menger, *Erster Entwurf*, 29.

The methodological individualism was stated succinctly in the preface:

> We will strive in the following to trace back the complicated phenomena of human economy to their simplest elements—the most accessible to sure observation—to weigh them according to their nature, and, holding on to these, to re-investigate how the more complicated economic phenomena develop lawfully from their elements. This is the method of research, which . . . is unmistakably called the natural scientific one, although . . . it is more correctly called the empirical.[204]

Much of the later *Methodenstreit* centered on the validity of these two assumptions.

Menger's second innovation, from which most of his original insights are derived, consisted of treating the standard sequence of concepts in German political economy textbooks—need, good, value (in use and exchange), elements of production (land, labor, capital), price, and money—as steps in a single rigorous argument rather than as separate topics. The focal point was the causal relationship by means of which a material object or a service satisfied a subjectively felt need. *Good* was then defined as the capacity of an object to cause such a satisfaction. An example of Menger's logical acumen was his ability to deduce the elements of production from these simple definitions: one could distinguish between goods which satisfied needs directly and those which caused other objects to do so (e.g., food versus a plow and fertilizer). The former were "goods of the first order," while the latter were "goods of a higher order," and land, labor, and capital were no more than subspecies thereof.[205] In highly developed economies, the causal chain linking these different orders of goods could become quite complicated.

A specifically *economic* relationship was one where the needs exceeded the objects, that is, where choices among a finite number of goods must be made. This put a premium on measuring and ranking them. *Value* was then defined as the subjective judgment of the relative importance of a good in an economic situation.

The marginal principle—Menger did not use the term—enabled one to determine the basic unit of value imputed to a good in an individual case: that portion of the good which met the need that could most easily be dispensed with. That principle was indeed central to Menger's argument, for it was necessary for the derivation of exchange and price. By defining such units of value, it established the boundaries beyond which exchange was no longer useful for either party, and this in turn determined the range of prices. Prices were thus derivative of value and were no more than "symptoms of the economic

---

204. Menger, *Grundsätze*, xlv.
205. Menger, *Grundsätze*, 8–9, 130, 138.

agreement [*Ausgleich*] between human economies."[206] What was important is how prices were arrived at. Finally, the exchange situation defined a specific type of good, namely commodities (*Waaren*), of which money was a subspecies to be found in particular economies at various places and times. Menger's final chapter on money dealt with these particularities, providing a historical finale to an otherwise highly theoretical treatise.

Recognition of the *Principles* was not immediate. Menger submitted the material from the last, least original chapter on money as a *Habilitationschrift* at the university of Vienna in 1871, where it was rejected. The book also received a mixed reception in the German journals, but there were enough favorable ones for Menger to resubmit the entire work to the Vienna faculty, where he was accepted as *Privatdozent* in June of 1872.

From this point on, recognition increased swiftly. The favorable academic job market brought him four offers within the next three years from Austria, Germany, and Switzerland.[207] He preferred to remain at Vienna, where he became *Extraordinarius* in 1873 and *Ordinarius* in 1879. Menger's loyalty to the Habsburg monarchy at a time when some students were swayed by pan-German sentiments was no small factor in this decision.[208] His abilities as a lecturer and his political loyalty won him an appointment in 1876 as a tutor to the Crown Prince Rudolph, to whom he became quite close. Rudolph's notes from Menger's tutorials have survived, revealing Menger's strong laissez-faire ideas on practical policy.[209] The two collaborated in an anonymous and controversial pamphlet directed against the role of the nobility in the Austrian economy—a typical liberal position in the Dual Monarchy.[210]

Menger's willingness to attack the aristocracy bespoke a certain combativeness which increased once he had established himself. It was evident in his academic politics, where he led a faction to reduce the power of the "incompetent oligarchs" in the Vienna faculty. This pitted him against Stein.[211] One such fight was over the introduction of seminars, which Menger favored.[212] Like his

206. Ibid., 172. I do not see that price is as central a concept to Menger's argument as some commentators make it out to be (e.g., Boos, *Wissenschaftstheorie*, 11, who cites Menger's outline for a later edition, or Hayek, *Grundsätze*, xvii, who sees it as his "crowning achievement").

207. Menger papers, box 21, diary transcriptions, nos. 3, 4, 6.

208. Report of Statthalterei, 30 July 1873; recommendation (Streymayr) 2 Sept. 1873, AVA, 12,506/1873, 4 Wien Jus Prof. Jurid. 589 Menger. According to McGrath, *Dionysian Art*, 36–37, Stein was popular with these students.

209. Streissler, "Carl Menger on Economic Policy: The Lectures to Crown Prince Rudolph," in Caldwell, ed., *Menger*, 110. There is no mention of the marginal principle in these notes (ibid., 127).

210. Boos, *Wissenschaftstheorie*, 34–36.

211. Menger papers, box 21, diary transcriptions, no. 7 (25 Jan., 9 June 1876).

212. Ibid., no. 7, 1874.

German colleagues, Menger also strove to increase the role of the sciences of state in the administrative curriculum. He toyed briefly with the idea of a separate faculty, but came to accept the idea of reforming the existing unified curriculum in law and state science. This idea gradually gained enough acceptance to prompt a general reform for Austria in 1886, due in part to the increasing scope of administrative law, as in Germany. Menger successfully moved the Vienna faculty to recommend that economics be taught in the first two years, thereby integrating the subjects in law and the sciences of state rather than treating them sequentially. To this end, an introductory encyclopedic survey lecture on both was also introduced.[213] Menger also unsuccessfully urged compulsory lectures in *Volkswirtschaftspolitik* and statistics for jurists and administrators alike; he also bore witness to his ideal of rigorous thinking by supporting—again without success—a compulsory lecture for all jurists and administrators on logic and psychology.[214]

Menger made clear to his students his commitment to the unified curriculum in his lectures on economics:

> Our faculty is not only one of law, but of law and the sciences of state . . . for here not only the *jurists* in the narrow sense of the word, but also those who will one day be called to participate in the *administration of the state* and the autonomous life-circles, find their highest scientific training. You are not just *jurists*, but also *cameralists*.[215]

Meanwhile, Menger had attracted two followers who, although not formally his students, adopted his approach and formed with him the core of the Austrian school. They were Eugen von Böhm-Bawerk and Friedrich von Wieser: both sons of higher officials, classmates in the famous *Schottengymnasium* and at the university (their transcripts were practically identical), and later brothers-in-law, they each expanded on an aspect of Menger's teaching and related it to a broader stream of economic thought.[216] They came to Menger in 1872 out of dissatisfaction with both classical and contemporary economics;

213. Rechts-und Staatswissenschaftliche Fakultäten, *Gutachten und Anträge*, 1, 44. On the idea of a separate faculty, see Menger papers, box 21, diary transcriptions, no. 7 (Jan. 10, 1876).

214. *Gutachten und Anträge*, 45, 51, 55–58. Austrian statistics had been part of the 1855 curriculum, in the old sense of political geography. The majority of professors wanted this replaced with more state and administrative law. But Menger urged that the lecture be revised, bringing in comparative perspectives and theory, rather than discarded (58).

215. Menger papers, box 13, lecture on economic theory, 1892–93, 24.

216. The transcripts are in UA Wien, Nationalien. They heard Schäffle in economics (1870–71) and Stein in Finance (1871) and Administrative Science (1871–72). See also Spiegel, *Growth of Economic Thought*, 537.

in 1875, Menger secured for them scholarships to study in Germany, where they spent a year in Knies's seminar at Heidelberg.[217]

Of the two, Böhm-Bawerk was more receptive to German thought, and Knies evidently made a particular impression on him; some of his most important later contributions stemmed from his seminar paper.[218] On reading Knies's treatise *Money and Credit* next to Böhm-Bawerk's works, it is difficult to deny the influence of one on the other. For one thing, Knies discussed utility with a different emphasis than Menger, stressing the objective rather than the subjective aspects—that is, the ability of a good to produce useful effects (*Nutzwirkungen*). Böhm-Bawerk appropriated this idea, giving it a more atomistic twist, talking of such effects in terms of discrete units, for which he used the term *Nutzleistung*.[219] For another thing, Knies had introduced certain legal concepts into his discussion of money and credit. Credit could be explained as a particular type of contract which transfers the use of a good or service from one party to another (e.g., a lease); specifically, credit is defined by a time-lag occuring between the act of transfer and the compensation for it.[220] Böhm-Bawerk saw this as an instance of the way legal rights function economically, leading eventually to the satisfaction of needs; it formed part of the complex of causal chains that Menger had sketched as goods of a higher order. This was the subject of Böhm-Bawerk's first major book, *Rights and Relations from the Standpoint of the Economic Theory of Goods* (1881), written just after he gained a position at Innsbruck; it used some of the same examples that Knies used.[221] Böhm-Bawerk employed a similar line of thought in his next major work, the two-volume treatise *Capital and Interest* (1884, 1889). Here he addressed a question which had been raised by the socialists' theory of surplus value: How is economic growth possible; that is, How does capital generate the additional income that is known as interest? Although Böhm-Bawerk claimed to give an original answer to this question—he spent the first volume discussing and rejecting all previous theories—that answer was also based on the notion of a time-lag between two transactions: it was a variation, in other words, of the general approach laid out by Menger and Knies.[222]

217. Menger papers, box 21, diary transcriptions, nos. 3, 9. They went on to hear Roscher and Hildebrand at Leipzig and Jena.

218. Hennings, *Austrian Theory of Value*, 104.

219. Knies, *Geld und Kredit*, 1: 90 n; Böhm-Bawerk, *Rechte und Verhältnisse*, 57–61; *Capital and Interest*, 223. The term has been translated as "material service" or "rendition of service," which severs the connection with "utility" that is clear in the original German.

220. Knies, *Geld und Kredit*, 1: 87 ff, 2.1: 6.

221. Böhm-Bawerk, *Rechte und Verhältnisse*, 47–50.

222. Böhm-Bawerk devoted much space to refuting the "use theories" of Knies and Menger (see esp. *Capital and Interest*, Book 3, chaps. 7, 9). The family resemblances, particularly with Menger,

Meanwhile, Wieser, now at Prague, was extending Menger's ideas in other ways, by drawing attention to parallels with the other marginal theorists (Jevons, Walras, Gossen). Though not as original a thinker as Böhm-Bawerk, Wieser focused on the theory of value and coined the German term *Grenznutzen* to express marginal utility. Like Böhm-Bawerk, he was willing to go beyond Menger, notably in criticizng the additive way in which his goods of a higher order combined to effect the satisfaction of needs.[223] Both he and Böhm-Bawerk drew out the implications of the marginal utility approach for the critique of socialism: if value was not merely the result of labor, and if interest was a sort of time-payment, then these features of a market economy would not simply disappear even if socialism were implemented.[224]

The Methodenstreit

During the years in which Menger was battling for a reform of the Vienna faculty, he was planning a campaign to increase the precision of German economic discourse through a methodological treatise.[225] When it eventually appeared in 1883, as *Investigations on the Method of the Social Sciences and Political Economy in Particular,* it also took the form of an attack on the historical school. It was Menger, in short, who instigated the famous *Methodenstreit.*

Menger's polemic was neither simplistic nor reductionistic: he acknowledged the legitimacy of both economic history and practical policy study in their respective spheres. But he accused the historical school of conflating these with theory, which was concerned with typical phenomena and laws. Even within the realm of theory, Menger allowed for a plurality of approaches: (1) a "realistic-empirical" direction which sought to arrive at these typical phenomena inductively—a clear nod to Brentano.[226] Such "real types," however, could never be more than approximations of the complex and irregular reality which the realists tried to describe.[227] It was therefore to be distinguished from: (2) his

---

have been recognized, as has Böhm-Bawerk's tendency to distort the writings of others. On the first, see Roger W. Garrison, "Austrian Capital Theory," in Caldwell, ed., *Menger,* 140–41; on the second, see Hennings, *Austrian Theory of Value,* 33, 200–201. Böhm-Bawerk's theory of interest was indeed original but not terribly plausible in the eyes of many subsequent economists: it was based on the assumption that people value present goods more than future ones; interest is thus the result of purchasing tomorrow's goods at today's prices. See his *Positive Theory of Capital,* 279–81; for criticism, see Spiegel, *Growth of Economic Thought,* 540–41; Blaug, *Economic Theory in Retrospect,* 314; chap. 12.

223. Wieser, *Der Natürliche Werth,* 91. He also applied the theory to production costs (166 ff).

224. Ibid., 59, 64; Böhm-Bawerk, *Positive Theory of Capital,* book 6, chap. 10.

225. Boos, *Wissenschaftstheorie,* 38–40.

226. Menger to Brentano, 13 March 1884, Bundesarchiv Koblenz, Nachlass Brentano, Briefe I/38: 87–88.

227. Menger, *Untersuchungen,* 34.

"exact" direction, which sought to define its concepts and laws as rigorously as possible. Menger emphasized not so much the deductive side of this method as the constructive one: such concepts were formed by deliberately isolating a particular aspect of reality from its empirical context without much regard for the latter. Thus Menger responded to the charge that classical economics exaggerated the role of individual self-interest by claiming that such an assumption was necessary to the construction of exact economics in the same way that the absence of friction was necessary to that of exact physics, or the assumption of pure, unadulterated elements was to exact chemistry.[228] One would no more confuse physics or chemistry with the "real-empirical" science of physiology than one would confuse exact and real social sciences. The historical school was thus at fault not only for failing to distinguish between history and theory, but for failing to distinguish between two types of theory as well.

Menger also responded to the charge that theoretical economics is ahistorical, that is, that it does not take temporal factors into account. A good realistic-empirical treatment of prices, for example, would have to account for their rise and fall, drawing on different historical examples; Menger thus in effect endorsed the type of theory that Schmoller practiced.[229] Menger was not as clear about the use of time in exact economics, but his own treatment in the *Principles* of the value of goods of a higher order in terms of their eventual effects might serve as an example. But neither of these sorts of temporal laws warranted the generalizations about laws of development that Menger associated with the historical school—in his view another illicit combination of theory and history.[230]

Menger also attacked the generalizations about economy and society based on organic analogies such as Schäffle's, and in doing so expanded his arguments beyond economics. His starting point here was his substantive individualism, that collective phenomena are products of the intentional actions of individuals and voluntary associations rather than vice versa. He called this explanation of complex social phenomena the "pragmatic" one, in contrast to the organic explanation.[231] Using an extended example of the origin of money as the product of such willed actions, he speculated that other collective phenomana such as religion, language, and law could be similarly explained.[232]

For all his differentiations, Menger's picture of the historical school contained much caricature, and Schmoller was not long in responding. Schmoller correspondingly acknowledged the legitimacy of abstract theory in principle,

228. Ibid., 41, 76.
229. Ibid, 105–10.
230. Ibid., 112–14, 126–27.
231. Ibid., 162.
232. Ibid., 180.

but the point was "to abstract correctly, so that . . . scientific truths result, not schematic phantoms or fantastic Robinsonades."[233] Economics was still too young a science, supported by too little empirical investigation, to yield the rigorous concepts and laws that Menger called for. Menger lacked a knowledge of the advances in other sciences such as psychology, linguistics, philosophy of law, and ethics that undermined his substantive individualism.[234] Schmoller concluded with a personal attack in his usual rhetorical style:

> In many details which he brings forth against the historical school of German economists, he is right; his *Investigations* . . . are a gratifying sign of the intellectual tension and the scientific differences which distinguish the contemporary German science of state. But he will not be effective as a reformer; he is rather an epigone, who, schooled exclusively in Mill's natural-scientific logic, . . . [cultivates] a corner of the great building of our science.[235]

Menger responded with a more pointed attack, *The Errors of the Historical School*, which added nothing of significance; Schmoller did not deign to respond to it.

The *Methodenstreit* was complicated and prolonged by the fact that neither all Germans nor all Austrians lined up neatly on one side or the other. Conrad was sympathetic to the Austrians without actually entering the fray; he opened the pages of the *Jahrbücher* to them.[236] Wagner and his student Heinrich Dietzel were more vocal: they took the opportunity to define their own antihistorical position and to conspicuously criticize Schmoller. Dietzel's position was basically to accept Menger's methodology of abstract construction but to reject his substantive individualism.[237] But Menger was in no mood for reconciliation. "Dietzel is wrong when he admonishes [me] to be moderate," he wrote. "What we don't gain in victory our opponents will not concede."[238] Menger's confrontational style also did not win him the unanimous approval of his Austrian colleagues and superiors.[239] This became evident when Stein retired in 1887. The

233. Schmoller, *Litteraturgeschichte*, 283.

234. Ibid., 290.

235. Ibid., 293.

236. Conrad wrote to Menger, "Theoretical investigations from you and your colleagues are especially welcome, because I regard them as indispensable for such a journal if it is to contribute the the progress of science, and I receive such [pieces] extremely seldom from German colleagues." See Conrad to Menger, 14 Sept. 1887, Menger papers, box 20 (correspondence 1885–88).

237. Heinrich Dietzel, "Beiträge zur Methodik der Wirtschaftswissenschaft," 19–20. On Wagner's position, see his "Systematische Nationalökonomie," 204.

238. Menger [to Böhm-Bawerk?], 29 July 1884, Menger papers, box 20 (correspondence 1883–84).

239. The professor of statistics at Vienna and head of the Austrian statistical bureau, Karl Theodor von Inama-Sternegg, wrote to Schmoller, "In the face of Menger's *Historismus*, I cannot restrain myself from expressing my indignation over the unqualified attacks to which you are exposed in this abusive piece." Inama to Schmoller, 4 March 1884, GPSA Dahlem, Rep. 92 Schmoller, no. 128.

ministry first made overtures to Schmoller, then to Brentano, who accepted.[240] Brentano's inaugural lecture, entitled "Classical Economics," was a veiled attack on the Austrian school along the lines of Schmoller's polemic—to Menger's evident bitterness.[241] Brentano remained in Vienna for only a year, however; he soon received a call to Leipzig—where he fired off another inaugural lecture at the Austrians.[242] Stein's position was eventually filled by one of the few Austrians who had made a successful career in Germany: the Freiburg professor Eugen von Phillipovich, who had defended Menger's abstract method there in 1886.[243] Böhm-Bawerk came to Vienna from Innsbruck in 1890 to become minister of finance; he soon received an honorary professorship as well. Wieser came in 1903 upon Menger's retirement.[244] Thus it was only gradually that Menger's school became accepted.

The *Methodenstreit*, for all its bitterness, did contribute to the heightened awareness of methodological issues in Germany which lasted well into the twentieth century, but it did not win over most Germans to the exact approach, which continued to be an Austrian specialty.[245] This can be traced in part to differences in teaching styles—particularly in the seminars, which were the most effective means of propagating a particular research program. As Schmoller had propagated a school in Strassburg by focusing on a common historical topic, so did Böhm-Bawerk in Vienna with conceptual topics. Wagner, although sympathetic to theory, took the eclectic approach, which in his hands failed to elicit the same degree of collective involvement.[246] The *Methodenstreit* also may have handicapped the development of the Austrian school insofar as it turned Menger's attention away from substantive issues to methodological ones (to the impatience of Walras).[247] Perhaps Schmoller's critique of his narrowness did nevertheless have an effect on him: in the following years, Menger's notes for a revision of the *Principles* turned increasingly towards biology, physiology, and psychology in an attempt to provide a further foundation for the subjective theory of value,[248] but he never completed the revision.

240. Brentano, *Mein Leben*, 137; Lindenlaub, *Richtungskämpfe*, 161.

241. Brentano, "Die klassische Nationalökonomie," 9, 31–32; *Mein Leben*, 142; Sheehan, *Brentano*, 97–98; on Menger's disappointment, see Philippovich to Menger, 8 August 1887, Menger papers, box 20 (correspondence 1885–88).

242. Brentano, *Ursachen der heutigen socialen Noth*, 1, 3–4, 29.

243. Biesenbach, *Nationalökonomie*, 183–85.

244. Memo, 10 Nov. 1890, AVA, 23040/1890, 4 Jus Wien Prof. Jurid. 587 Böhm-Bawerk; recommendation (Hartel), 21 July 1903, ibid., 26853/1903, Prof. Jurid. 592 Wieser.

245. Winkel, *Deutsche Nationalökonomie*, 118–19, 145–49.

246. Seager, "Economics at Berlin and Vienna," 12–14, 25–27.

247. Walras wrote to Menger, "For God's sake! Stop demanding the way in which science is done best and do it as you wish; but do it." Walras to Menger, 2 July, 1883, quoted in Boos, *Wissenschaftstheorie*, 47.

248. Boos, *Wissenschaftstheorie*, 87

The Austrian school certainly exemplified the notion of specialized science to a greater degree than did the German one. Yet the very occurence of the *Methodenstreit* indicated that both sides were becoming increasingly conscious of their identity as specialists, however differently defined. The contrast between this polemical tide and that of the 1870s was striking: the *Methodenstreit* was intramural rather than extramural. It presupposed a community of scholars within which debate could take place. Such a community had long existed, but its standards had changed from the relatively uncritical inclusiveness which characterized the classificatory ideal to the methodologically self-conscious ex-clusiveness which characterized research. By this heightened emphasis on stan-dards, economics participated in the process of professionalization that was characteristic of the 1870s and 1880s in many fields. In this sense the *Methoden-streit* and the *Verein für Sozialpolitik* were symptoms of the same underlying phenomenon. This could be seen not only in the changes in economics, but also in the political disciplines, where the same appeal to rigorous standards and scientific exclusiveness was evident in the triumph of legal positivism in state law.

THE JURISTIC SCIENCES OF STATE: STATE LAW AND ADMINISTRATIVE LAW

In a two-volume survey of academic disciplines edited by Lexis in 1893, one finds under the rubric *Staatswissenschaften* the disciplines of economics and fi-nance, economic history, and statistics (agriculture and forestry were treated as separate disciplines). The survey contained no heading for politics, much less police science. In the section on state law, there appeared the following statement:

> As in German legal science altogether, the natural-law views have been com-pletely overcome also in the area of state law. The treatment of state law is thoroughly positive on a historical foundation. Also the mixing of legal and political perspectives, still to be found in the writings of Mohl and Bluntschli, [has] been rejected by the new science: under the influence of Gerber and Laband, the treatment of state law has more and more a juristic one.[249]

The integration of state law into the the rest of jurisprudence at the level of method under the rubric of "legal positivism" was a matter of pride to the legal scholars of the Bismarckian era. It was viewed as a triumph of exact science and clear thinking at the expense of intellectual slovenliness. Its resemblances to Mengerian economics have been noted by more than one commentator.[250]

---

249. Georg Meyer, "Staats-und Verwaltungsrecht," in *Die deutschen Universitäten*, 1: 370.

250. Smend, "Einfluss der deutschen Staats- und Verwaltungsrechtslehre," 333; Wilhelm, *Juristische Methodenlehre*, 12–13.

At the same time, its tendency to exclude philosophical, ethical, political, or sociological considerations has frequently been given an ideological interpretation: that it was the perfect alibi for the educated bourgeosie who had abdicated their ethical and political responsibilities in accepting Bismarck's means of unification.[251] This charge is misleading to the extent that virtually all legal thinkers, positivist or not, supported unification.[252] But it is of course true that the events of unification had a profound effect on the sciences of state law and politics. The Prussian constitutional crisis had drawn attention to the power of parliament over the budget; the North German Confederation and later the Second Empire had raised the issue of whether Germany was a federal state or a unitary one.[253] Given the bewildering changes that had destroyed the old order of the German Confederation and delivered the Second Empire, thanks to Bismarck's maneuvering, there was a felt need to find the basis for constitutional law in more abstract principles rather than in the unpredictable political and economic circumstances of the day.[254] By the same token, the fact of unification explains the virtual standstill of the science of comparative governmental forms that went under the name of *Allgemeine Staatslehre*, or *Politik*. Treitschke's enormously popular lectures on *Politik* at Berlin were also less oriented to comparison and more to providing a foundation for patriotism. In law, the pressing need was to understand the particular state that had just been created rather than to study states in general. As Michael Stolleis has pointed out, the creative works of modern political theory have arisen in times of crisis, when the form of government was unclear or at least showed signs of toppling; now the form had been decided for Germany, the task was to understand it and to ground it in firm principle.[255]

The career of Paul Laband, who took Gerber's ideas and articulated them into a fully developed system, illustrates these trends; the clarity of his thought also sheds light on the deeper question of the ideological implications of legal positivism. Laband, a Jewish-born legal historian, had no interest in state law before 1866; as a student at Heidelberg, he had found Mohl's lectures boring. But when asked to lecture on it at Königsberg in 1868, he realized its newfound importance. His first publication addressed the controversial issue of the Prussian budget law. Laband defended Bismarck's flouting of the parliamentary majority by defining the budget as an administrative act within the limits of the

251. For a brief review, see Oertzen, *Soziale Funktion*, 321–22; John, *Politics and Law*, 90.

252. Oertzen, *Soziale Funktion*, 159.

253. Treitschke had argued for the unitary idea already in 1864; this prompted the Bavarian legal scholar Max von Seydel to argue the case for federalism. See Dorpalen, *Treitschke*, 93–98; Jellinek, "Georg Meyer," 274–75.

254. Stolleis, "Verwaltungsrechtswissenschaft," *DV,* 3: 89.

255. Stolleis, *Geschichte des öffentlichen Rechts*, 2: 423.

law rather than a legislative one; to suspend expenditures and revenue collection in the absence of parliamentary approval would mean the self-destruction of the state.[256] The success of this work brought him fame and a call to Strassburg (where he befriended Schmoller and sided with him against the civil jurists in favor of a doctorate in *Staatswissenschaften*).[257] Laband's ability to meet the needs of the legal profession in response to changing political conditions was also demonstrated in his *State Law of the German Empire* (1876–83), the first text to systematize the constitutional law of the new Reich. This work did more than any other to spread legal positivism to the next generation.[258]

Legal positivism in Laband's hands was anything but a mere description of given law. It was rather a commentary on positive law in the light of certain general assumptions. In his own words,

> The scientific task of a dogmatics of a particular positive law lies in the construction of law institutes, in tracing back the individual legal propositions to more general concepts and on the other hand the derivation of the consequences that follow from these concepts. . . . To accomplish this task there is no other means but logic.[259]

Laband carried out this process with more rigor than Gerber. There was no appeal to organicism or the unity of the people; Laband simply provided a historical introduction on the origins of the new empire. "The establishment of the North German Confederation and the expansion of the same to the German Empire appears more and more as an unalterable fact," he wrote, "to which those who find it undesirable must also accomodate."[260] At the same time, Laband made no attempt to dodge the difficulties of fitting the institutions of the Second Empire, which had been shaped by Bismarck often on the basis of political expediency, into a schema of generally accepted concepts. He wrote, for example, "the establishment of the constitutional nature of the emperorship is not without difficulty, since a federal state composed of monarchies is without precedent in history."[261] But Laband consistently steered away from the criticizing the Reich on the basis of such problems; it merely meant that his logical derivations of the given law from general principles were more complicated and ingenious. Thus the emperor was, strictly speaking, neither constitutional monarch nor president of the new federation, but one member of that federa-

---

256. Laband, *Das Budgetrecht,* 19, 77–78.

257. Laband, "Lebenserinnerungen," 62–63, 77; Schmoller to Roscher, 4 June 1873, in Roscher and Schmoller, *Briefwechsel,* 25.

258. Stolleis, "Verwaltungsrechtswissenschaft," *DV,* 3: 88.

259. Laband, *Staatsrecht des deutschen Reiches,* 1: ix.

260. Ibid., 1: v.

261. Ibid., 1: 215.

tion—the King of Prussia—who happened to have special rights.[262] The tone of this and similar arguments was consistently affirmative, and the effect was that of legitimating the new Reich.[263]

Moreover, the logical constructions that Laband distilled out of German historical practice were thoroughly authoritarian. Drawing on Gerber, he defined sovereignty as the right to dominate free persons through command and force; the basic duties of citizens, namely obedience and loyalty, were enumerated before their rights, namely the right to protection abroad and at home and the right to vote.[264] Authority was not rooted in the monarch or the people, but in the abstract juridical person of the state itself.[265] As a source of subsequent veneration for authoritarian government in Germany, this rational vision of legal positivism should not be underestimated.

Needless to say, such a vision did not pass entirely without criticism. It was no coincidence that the main spokesman for the opposition was also a leading critic of the new civil code, based on positivist principles, and a specialist in German rather than Roman law: Otto von Gierke.[266] It was also no coincidence that Gierke chose to present his objections in the journals of the *Staatswissenschaften;* he later became active in the *Verein für Sozialpolitik.* Gierke argued that to base sovereignty on domination was to place might before right; legal positivism could not do without historical and philosophical investigations in constructing its first principles.[267] Gierke did not oppose the method of construction per se, only the narrow empirical base on which it was formed. He held to the notion of the state as an organism which expressed the spirit of the people; his major systematic work was a two-volume law of associations (*Genossenschaftsrecht*). While Gierke represented a clear opposing position to that of Laband, there were numerous representatives of intermediate positions: other adherents of legal positivism found ways of softening its implications by including more historical material and teleological considerations than Laband was willing to do.[268]

262. Ibid., 1: 215–19.

263. Ibid., 1: 216, 234, 375–76; Stinzing and Landsberg, *Geschichte der deutschen Rechtswissenschaft,* 3.1: 978; Oertzen, *Soziale Funktion,* 260.

264. Laband, *Staatsrecht des deutschen Reiches,* 1: 62; 140–58.

265. Ibid., 1: 94–95.

266. On Gierke's role in the civil code controversy, see John, *Politics and Law,* 108–16.

267. Gierke, "Grundbegriffe des Staatsrechts," 183; "Labands Staatsrecht," 1114, 1118. On his involvement in the *Verein,* see Boese, *Geschichte,* 56, 62. Another sharp critic was Edgar Loening, whose objections to legal positivism echoed Schmoller's critique of Menger. See his "Die Konstruktive Methode," 541–67. According to Laband, Schmoller opposed his coming to Berlin (*Lebenserinnerungen,* 97).

268. Stolleis, *Geschichte des öffentlichen Rechts,* 2: 348–58; "Verwaltungsrechtswissenschaft," *DV,* 3: 89–90; Smend, "Einfluss der deutschen Staats-und Verwaltungsrechtslehre," 338.

The Bismarckian era also witnessed the emergence of administrative law as a separate subject. Long a subcategory of state law, it had served to depict the organizational structure of the bureaucracies in the individual states and the particular law under each ministry. After 1848, some scholars began to summarize and synthesize this material; this process accelerated in the 1880s, after the subject was included in the Prussian law for training of administrative officials of 1879.[269] Laband's strict method was of less help here, for much of the material of the new administrative tasks of the Reich had yet to be systematized before logical construction could take place. Thus the textbooks of the 1880s tended to follow the accepted schemes of the old *Polizeiwissenschaft*.[270] This was all the more true of the works that dealt with laws of individual states, which retained jurisdiction over matters of education and poor relief, as well as many aspects of public health and economic policy, including—against Bismarck's wishes—the railroads. Nevertheless, the science of administrative law probably did not have the impact of constitutional law or of economics; it lacked the theoretical relevance of the former and the practical relevance of the latter.[271] As for administrative science apart from law, it enjoyed a brief continuation in Austria following the death of Stein, but with no clear consensus on the boundaries between it and the legal disciplines. Although *Verwaltungslehre* was incorporated into the Austrian curricular revision of 1893, it declined in practice thereafter.[272]

CONCLUSION

As we have seen, the Bismarckian era witnessed the greatest discontinuities in the sciences of state since the end of the eighteenth century. Instead of a single canon embracing economics and politics that was still to be seen in Roscher and Stein, economics was now seen as the center of a new configuration of social science, while politics all but disappeared in the shadow of a new science of state law. Although there were still many continuities with the older disciplines, particularly at the level of the organization and presentation of knowledge, these were no longer seen as the main activity of science. Considerations of classification and synthesis were replaced by considerations of method. The most striking congruence between the separate developments in economics and state law were the issues of clarity and exactness as criteria of scientific

---

269. For a survey, see Stolleis, *Geschichte des öffentlichen Rechts*, 2: 394–403.

270. Stolleis, "Verwaltungsrechtswissenschaft," *DV,* 3: 94–98; Lindenfeld, "Polizeiwissenschaft," 154–56.

271. Smend, "Einfluss der deutschen Staats-und Verwaltungsrechtslehre," 341; Stolleis, *Geschichte des öffentlichen Rechts*, 2: 236, 383. Cf. Schiera, *Laboratorium der bürgerlichen Welt*, 109, for a more positive view.

272. Brauneder, "Formen und Tragweite," 264–65.

worth as opposed to realistic fidelity to a more fluid empirical subject matter: the same issues that divided Menger from Schmoller also divided Laband from Gierke. These two perspectives suggest two divergent interpretations of the intellectual field of the sciences of state during the Bismarckian era—interpretations which provide suggestive links to the larger society.

The first, propounded by Peter von Oertzen, is to view the field in terms of a changing liberalism; for if the appeal to organicism and vague boundaries had been part of conservative ideology since the days of Burke and Müller, the appeal to clarity and distinctness has been part of the liberal ethos. And if the older *Staatswissenschaften* represented a wide range of knowledge with relatively clear and static internal and external boundaries, reflecting the liberalism of the bureaucracy, then the new liberalism embraced the dynamic clash of individual and collective wills embodied in laissez-faire economics and civil law, in which scientific precision was linked to the calculability of actions and their consequences. To quote von Oertzen, "In place of 'representation' arises 'interest group', in place of state 'order' arises 'domination and organized will'; the ethical pathos of the 'citizen' [*Bürger*] is replaced by the calculation of the 'bourgeois.'"[273] This ideology obviously had a stronger appeal to the community of legal scholars, and the triumph of legal positivism in state law is thus seen by von Oertzen as an extension of principles that already dominated private law. Certainly the conceptions of private law had an increasing effect on the imagination of prominent economists, as we have seen with Wagner, Knies, and Böhm-Bawerk. And it particularly fit the Austrian school: Menger's exact science was based on just such a calculus of interests, and his own politics were unequivocally liberal. This may also help explain Menger's own sense of embattlement, since liberals in Austria were much more exposed to opposition both from the aristocracy and from the non-German nationalities than were their German counterparts.[274]

In any case, the German liberals were in a different situation, enthralled by Bismarck even as he deserted them. This is where von Oertzen's interpretation has its limits; for if the liberal assumption of a plurality of conflicting wills were consistently applied to issues of state law, it could have led legal scholars with equally impeccable logic to portray the Second Empire as a mixed constitutional monarchy with a plurality of centers of power. But it was the opposite assumption of the indivisibility of power which formed the basis for Gerber's

273. Oertzen, *Soziale Funktion*, 319. Oertzen masterfully links the change to the decline of liberalism in the 1880s.

274. One could perhaps draw an analogy between Menger's methodological crusade and another, imaginary product of a defensive Austrian liberal: the Freudian ego, which its author portrayed as an entity struggling valiantly against the powerful forces of the id and the superego in the name of reason.

and Laband's constructions. One can still support von Oertzen's contention that legal positivism fit a pattern of liberal thinking with its veneration for law and reason, while also maintaining that it was an adulterated liberalism all too willing to ally with the conservative elites—a pattern that was obviously taking place in German politics and society at the time.

This brings us to the second interpretation: the aforementioned "decline of the German mandarins" propounded by Fritz Ringer. Certainly the main features of his picture ring true: the distrust of interest-group politics, of analytical distinctions, and clear intellectual boundaries; to see oneself as the embodiment, as part of an administrative and educational elite, of a larger, intangible whole. The rejection of Menger's exact method by the majority of German economists indicated its depth and breadth.

Yet Ringer's interpretation needs to be modified in one important respect: he divided the mandarins into an "orthodox" majority and a "modernist" minority—those who sought a return to preindustrial conditions and those who reluctantly bowed to inevitable change.[275] For this generation of *Staatswissenschaftler*, the modernists clearly outnumbered the orthodox: *Sozialpolitik* represented just the sort of accommodation that Ringer describes. The tradition of practical knowledge within the sciences of state prevented these mandarins from becoming overly nostalgic.

Taken together, these interpretations point to a fundamental feature of the field in Bismarckian Germany: the coexistence of highly articulated, specialized systems of knowledge, conveyed in seminars and research programs, on the one hand, with the charismatic appeal of professors like Treitschke, Brentano, and Wagner on the other. This coexistence enables us to speak of the *Staatswissenschaften* at this time as a form of national ideology, presenting in some detail the rationalizations and justifications for German greatness and power, while at the same time providing the means for an emotional identification with the nation—enabling this elite discourse to establish contact with the broader political culture. These diverse levels of communication within the field were in some kind of equilibrium; except for the *Methodenstreit*, the internal tensions and contradictions within the ideology which we have pointed out did not serve to overwhelm or splinter the discourse. Admittedly, this brand of nationalism contained its illusions. While the seminars and research programs provided proof of Germany's eminence as a cultural leader among nations, they also masked the fact that unification had been engineered by politicians and generals whose values were at times far removed from those of the mandarins. The glories of German scholarship could at best hide the fact that the bureaucracy had lost much of its former initiative under Bismarck. Schmoller and his fellow

275. Ringer, *Decline of the German Mandarins,* 128–31.

economists could inspire students in a general way without providing the next generation of officials with a concrete sense of implementation that could rekindle that initiative.[276]

It was only after Bismarck had stepped down, however, that the tensions and contradictions within the field increased in intensity, rendering this equilibrium precarious and eventually disrupting it. This is the subject of the final chapter.

276. On the passivity of the bureaucracy, see Morsey, *Reichsverwaltung*, 322–24; Röhl, "Higher Civil Servants in Germany," 130, 132. On the broad influence of Schmoller and Wagner, see Born, *Staat und Sozialpolitik*, 44–45 nn.

❧ 6 ❧

The Wilhelminian Era, 1890–1914:
Specialization and Clarification

The Wilhelminian era poses formidable problems of interpretation for historians, occurring as it did in the shadow of the Thirty Years' Crisis that followed. This is true both for political history and for that of the *Staatswissenschaften*. In both cases, there was an undeniable increase of instability and dissension within the fields. In politics, the divisions between liberals and conservatives and between moderates and radicals on the right and the left alike have been richly documented.[1] Whether this was a temporary state of affairs that would have righted itself had the war not intervened is difficult if not impossible to say.

Within the sciences of state, one can point to three factors which eroded and eventually disrupted the equilibrium of the Bismarckian era. The first was ideological: the dominance of reformist *Sozialpolitik* came to be challenged by a growing minority of economists who favored a pro-business attitude. The second was structural: the growing numbers of students and faculty members inevitably created pressures for specialization. This did not fit well with the tradition of *Bildung* with which the educated elites continued to identify. The third was generational: while the restlessness and impatience of German youth was widespread and generally recognized, it was particularly acute in the economic and social sciences—due in no small part to the longevity of the *Kathedersozialisten* in their professorial chairs. None of these factors was strong enough to disrupt the previous equilibrium singly or immediately; indeed, the prestige of the *Kathedersozialisten* at first seemed stronger than ever. But the effects of these factors were cumulative and mutually reinforcing, and the year 1905 represented something of a turning point. The linkage between research system and charismatic embodiment which had characterized the social sciences since the 1870s was ruptured thereafter.

This situation was highly conducive to intellectual creativity—as names such as Ferdinand Tönnies, Georg Simmel, Max Weber, and Werner Sombart

---

1. Wehler *German Empire*, 244–45; Eley, *Reshaping the German Right*, 293–97, 321, 349; Chickering, *We Men Who Feel the Most German*, 283–90; Schorske, *German Social Democracy 1905–1917*, 195–96, 220–21, 252, 256.

will attest. In this era, however, such brilliance did not as a rule redound to the benefit of practical policy-making, despite some noteworthy attempts to maintain such links. Thus the tensions between theory and practice that already existed within the field of social science were magnified rather than reduced.

The *Kathedersozialisten* and Public Opinion

In 1890 Gustav Schmoller, the new president of the *Verein für Sozialpolitik,* opened its eleventh meeting with the following words:

> With this general meeting, our organization enters so to speak a new epoch of its existence . . . which lies in the circumstances of our socio-political development in general. The death of Kaiser Wilhelm and Kaiser Friedrich, the departure of our great imperial chancellor, the recently achieved conclusion of our relief fund legislation, and finally the expiration of the socialist law have created a new situation. The nation stands before the great question, whether our social politics will stick to the previous ways or enter upon new ones.[2]

Schmoller's words were truer than he knew, for 1890 marked not only a change in rulers, but in the way politics were conducted in Germany. Bismarck's resignation ushered in an era of instability and contentiousness on the domestic scene. Not least responsible for the new political instability was Wilhelm himself, who, with his inner circle of friends, effected a major shift in power from the office of chancellor to the emperor by 1897.[3] Given Wilhelm's erratic personality, governing became a process of providing buffers between the emperor, the parliament, and the various interest groups. At the same time, the 1890s witnessed a remarkable process of fermentation among the electorate. Germany's growing population and rapidly changing economy led to growth in the numbers of voters and the activities of politically oriented parties and groups. The number of voluntary associations of all sorts multiplied quickly— a phenomenon known at the time as *Vereinsmeierei*—and many of these were affiliated with one political movement or another.[4] This was true across the political spectrum—from the subculture of the Social Democrats, with its plethora of singing and gymnastic societies, to the National Liberals, whose number of associations increased from 300 to 2,207 between 1890 and 1914, and to the new organizations on the right, such as the Pan-German League and the Agrarian League.[5] All these movements exemplify Habermas's notion

2. Boese, *Geschichte,* 62.
3. Röhl, *Germany without Bismarck,* 271.
4. Chickering, *We Men,* 183.
5. On the figures, see Sheehan, *German Liberalism,* 232.

of a "structural transformation of the public sphere," insofar as the boundaries between private and public life were redrawn.[6]

In the absence of stable leadership at the top and the presence of seething popular energy at the bottom, the weaknesses of the Reich's constitution—in the words of Wolfgang Mommsen, a "system of evaded decisions"—became evident.[7] All the conflicts between interest groups and parties that Bismarck had more or less kept under control were now given full play, with little or no clear means of resolving them.

In contrast to the larger political scene, the smaller world of academic politics which affected the disciplines of the *Staatswissenschaften* was marked by continuity with the previous period: professors like Wagner, Schmoller, Conrad, and Lexis, who had achieved eminence during the years of opportunity in the 1870s, remained in their places. None of them retired before 1914.[8] Brentano made one final move in 1890 to Munich as Helferich's successor, where twice new lecture halls had to be provided to accommodate his audiences.[9] A latecomer to this circle of acknowledged leaders was the new *Ordinarius* at Leipzig in 1890, Karl Bücher, who had come to academia via journalism (he was the son of a brushmaker).[10] His historical studies on workers in antiquity, medieval Frankfurt, and the bookbinder trade soon won him the respect of his senior colleagues, gradually overcoming the stigma of having worked with a left-liberal newspaper, the *Frankfurter Zeitung*.[11] Like the others, Bücher remained throughout the period.

There was also continuity of administration in Prussia—in the person of Friedrich Althoff, the official in charge of Prussian higher education under five different ministers of instruction from 1882 to 1907. Althoff was a controversial figure in his own day and immediately following, because he stepped on some important toes (such as Brentano's and Max Weber's); subsequent historiography regarding him has tended to replicate those partisan attitudes.[12] Althoff is

---

6. Habermas, *Strukturwandel*, chaps. 5, 6, esp. his reference to a new "political-social sphere" (164, 193). Habermas views the increased scope of mass parties and the expanded activities of the state in what was formerly the private sphere (e.g., welfare legislation) as part of the same transformation.

7. See Mommsen, "Deutsche Kaiserreich," 260.

8. Lexis retired in 1914, Schmoller in 1915; Conrad died in 1915, Wagner retired in 1917, Brentano in 1918.

9. Sheehan, *Brentano*, 116.

10. On Bücher's early years, see his *Lebenserinnerungen*, passim.

11. Lindenlaub, *Richtungskämpfe*, 129–30; Bücher, *Lebenserinnerungen*, 250, 405–6.

12. Brentano, *Mein Leben*, 135, 218; Weber, *Max Weber on Universities*, 26–36; the critical emphasis is also apparent in McClelland, *State, Society, and University*, 290–99; on the positive side, see Sachse, *Friedrich Althoff*, and Bernhard vom Brocke, "Hochschul-und Wissenschaftspolitik," 9–119.

important to our study because of his close ties to certain *Staatswissenschaftler*. He began his administrative career in Alsace-Lorraine in the 1870s and became a professor of French civil law at Strassburg in 1872, where he met both Schmoller and Lexis.[13] They remained part of his informal network of confidence-men when he entered the Prussian ministry.[14] If Althoff's papers are any indication, the two of them functioned in very different ways. Schmoller advised Althoff primarily on personnel matters and was often not the only one to do so—Conrad was also called upon frequently.[15] Lexis, by contrast, was hired to draft memoranda on a great variety of subjects, from professors' salaries to grain tariffs and pharmacists.[16] Lexis's position at Göttingen suited his natural-scientific bent; he collaborated easily with the mathematician Felix Klein, Althoff's main representative for building the sciences there.[17] In general, most appointments in Prussia fit the practical-realistic notion of economics that Schmoller and Lexis stood for; but Althoff was not closed to the more philosophically oriented trends within the social sciences, as indicated by his support of Tönnies.[18]

In weighing the positive and negative sides of Althoff's tenure, one can conclude that it was indeed fortunate to have such a strong personality as an advocate and buffer for Prussian higher education, given the frequently rough-and-tumble atmosphere of Wilhelminian politics. A good illustration of what could

13. Sachse, *Friedrich Althoff,* 12–14, 47.

14. Brocke, "Hochschul-und Wissenschaftspolitik," 70, 82. Althoff took a particularly predatory attitude toward Strassburg once he entered the Prussian service, raiding its best professors whenever possible and contributing significantly to its decline as a leader in German scholarship. See Craig, *Scholarship and Nation Building,* 92–98, 161.

15. Compare the files in GPSA Dahlem, Rep. 92 Althoff: A II, no. 95, vol. 2 ("Beziehungen mit einzelnen Persönlichkeiten: Schmoller") with A I, no. 63 ("Staatswissenschaftler. Beurteilungen").

16. Ibid., A II, no. 84 (Lexis), vols. 1–3. On salaries, 1: 10, 64–68; on tariffs, 1: 42–46, 76; on pharmacists, 85–86. A memo on the Social Democrats urged the government to remain neutral in the wage disputes rather than depending on patriarchal relationships between employers and employees (ibid., 136–41). See also Lexis's memo in A I, no. 64 ("Verein für Sozialpolitik"): 33.

17. Memo of Klein, 19 Feb. 1906, ibid., A II, no. 84, vol. 3, 38–39; Manegold, *Universität,* 179, 188, 203–4.

18. This raises the question of whether Prussian academic policy favored a conservative ideological line. Lindenlaub contends that conservatives tended to be found in Prussia, liberals in other German states (*Richtungskämpfe,* 154–55). I have difficulty seeing this as an object of conscious policy. Certainly Bücher and Schulze-Gaevernitz, two "liberals," were highly regarded in Prussia in the 1890s. See Schmoller to Althoff, 21 July 1889, GPSA Dahlem, Rep. 92 Althoff, A I, no. 95, II: 59–60; Conrad to Althoff, 2 Sept 1893, A I, no. 63, 60–61; Althoff to Schulze-Gaevernitz, 2 Sept 1892, ibid., 24. Conversely, economists who befriended the workers' cause too openly had difficulty not only in Prussia—the Grand Duke of Baden was unwilling to appoint Sombart, and Herkner was regarded with suspicion in Baden in the late 1890s as well. On Sombart, see Brocke, "Werner Sombart," 29–30; Herkner, "Selbstdarstellung," in Meiner, ed., *VGS,* 96.

happen in the absence of such a personality was the Bernhard affair, which occurred in 1908, the year after Althoff retired. Under the influence of the regional administrators in Silesia and Posen, the minister of culture, Ludwig Holle, created a new professorship in Berlin for a patriotic thirty-two-year-old scholar, Ludwig Bernhard, who had written on Polish activism at the municipal level in Prussia. He did this without consulting Wagner and Schmoller or considering the traditional rights of the faculty to suggest candidates. The ensuing affair, which dragged on until 1911, provoked much protest among academics and much cynicism in the press.[19]

It is equally true, however, that Althoff's tactics were not the only means of advancing the universities to keep abreast of the changing times, as the cases of other German states demonstrated. Bavaria and Saxony increased their budgets at the same rate as Prussia between 1866 and 1914, while Baden's increase during the years of Althoff's tenure was by 133 percent, compared to Prussia's 170.8 percent.[20] Moreover, such growth occurred without tampering with the prerogatives of the faculties to nearly the same extent. Weber's famous impressionistic statement, "When I left the dominion of the Prussian educational administration for Baden I had the feeling of going into fresh air," has been confirmed by Reinhard Riese's more systematic study of Heidelberg.[21] If the professors were not always open to new disciplinary directions, they were often able to resolve conflicts in an enlightened way.[22]

Such open-mindedness was easier in years of continually expanding budgets; the fundamental fact of universities during these years was their continuing explosive growth. After a brief pause in the early 1890s, student enrollments skyrocketed again from 27,321 in 1893–94 to 60,748 in 1914. Faculty growth did not keep pace, however, going from approximately 2,300 in 1890 to over

19. Bruch, *Wissenschaft*, 130–33; E. R. Huber, *Verfassungsgeschichte*, 4: 965–70. Althoff came out of retirement to help settle it (Sachse, *Friedrich Althoff*, 193). On the influence of the Silesian and Posen *Oberpräsidenten*, see anonymous memo, n.d., GPSA Dahlem, Rep. 92 Althoff A I, no. 109, 43.

20. McClelland, *State, Society, and University*, 291, 307; Riese, *Hochschule*, 372. The absolute numbers for Prussia from 1882–1907 were: 9.6 million to 26 million marks; for Baden 1882–1908: 38,068 to 88,907 marks.

21. Weber, *On Universities*, 26; Riese, *Hochschule*, 286. See also Meinecke, *Strassburg, Freiburg, Berlin, 1901–1919*, 62.

22. Riese, *Hochschule*, 112. For example, the two faculties of state science at Tübingen and Munich both were involved in rivalries with the law faculties during this period: the Tübingen faculty wanted to monopolize appointments in state law, while the Munich faculty—composed primarily of foresters—opposed Brentano's appointment, which the law faculty supported. In both cases, the issue was resolved by the university senate in favor of the law faculties' more open-minded views. See Entscheidung des Senats, 12 June 1909, UA Tübingen 127/50; Munich: memo of pol. eco. faculty, 25 Nov. 1890; of law faculty, 30 Dec. 1890; pol. eco. faculty, 17 Jan. 1891; senate, 24 Jan. 1891, in UA München, Senatsakten 346. The jurists pointed out that they had some 300 students of economics compared to about 40 from the political economy faculty.

3,000 in 1905.[23] This increase in numbers was as powerful a force for bureau-cratization in the universities as was the personality of an Althoff.

The contrast between the unstable political environment and the stable world of academic politics created a situation which gave economists an un-equaled degree of visibility and prestige in the 1890s. "Economics," according to the reformer Friedrich Naumann, "is the main science of our age."[24] It is true that professors in many fields played an active role in influencing public opinion at this time, from petitioning the legislatures to joining the various na-tionalist organizations such as the Pan-German League—although their par-ticipation in these did not exceed those of other middle-class groups.[25] But inso-far as economic issues and *Sozialpolitik* were at the forefront of controversy, the economists had a special authority. Wilhelm had raised tremendous hopes for the peaceful integration of the working class into German society with his "new course" of 1890, promising legislation to improve working conditions; Wagner and Schmoller were in contact with officials who helped draft this legislation.[26] The philosopher Max Dessoir compared the influence of Schmoller and Wagner on the students to that of Fichte and Hegel in an earlier age, while the jurist Gustav Radbruch recollected, "we youth were in an expectant mood of being on the eve of great social upheavals, of the coming social revolution."[27] The popularity of the social question in the 1890s was borne out by enrollment figures for the university lectures devoted to the subject (see table 11).

The economists were part a reform movement that vaguely envisaged an alternative to both the Social Democrats and the right-wing nationalist groups—a mood summed up by the recurring phrase "socialism of the culti-vated."[28] "We writers and teachers are the most advanced posts of the great proletarian army and the most distrusted by the enemy," wrote Sombart to a friend.[29] Sombart's brilliant lectures on Marxism won the praise of Engels and raised hopes in some that he would become a second Lassalle; Sombart saw himself rather as the first revisionist.[30] The *Bildungsbürger* found support in phil-osophical neo-Kantianism. The Marburg professor Hermann Cohen reinter-preted the categorical imperative as the social imperative: Society should treat

23. Jarausch, *Students, Society, and Politics*, 28, 30–31; McClelland, *State, Society, and University*, 258–59.

24. Quoted in Bruch, *Wissenschaft*, 29. See also Barkin, *Controversy*, 11.

25. Bruch, *Wissenschaft*, 428–32. In his study of the Pan-German League, Roger Chickering found professors rarely in leadership roles (*We Men*, 146). On professors' effectivness as a legislative pressure group, see Bruch, *Wissenschaft*, 62–63; Barkin, *Controversy*, 7–9.

26. Bruch, *Wissenschaft*, 20, 23; Born, *Staat und Sozialpolitik*, chap. 1, esp. 44.

27. Bruch, *Wissenschaft*, 157, 158 n.

28. Ibid., 158; he identified it in three separate newspaper articles of the time.

29. Sombart to Otto Lang, 5 Oct. 1893, quoted in Mitzman, *Sociology and Estrangement*, 219.

30. Käsler, *Frühe Deutsche Soziologie*, 425; Brocke, "Sombart," 25; Lenger, *Sombart*, 83.

Table 11 *Lectures with Highest Enrollments in the Philosophical Faculty, 1885–1910*

	Bonn	Berlin	Halle
1885	Kekule: Inorganic chemistry (195)	Treitschke: Italian history (213)	Kirchhoff: On the German colonies (211)
1885–86	—	Treitschke: History and politics of European state systems (628)	Haym: History of German drama since Lessing (194)
1890	Kekule: Inorganic and experimental chemistry (156)	Wagner: The worker question (332)	Erdmann: Materialism and spiritualism (131)
1890–91	Kekule: Experimental chemistry (155)	Treitschke: State and church (898)	Haym: History of philosophy (200)
1895	Koser: History of Wars of Liberation (195)	Schmoller: The worker question (357)	Haym: Critical history of post-Hegelian philosophy (158)
1895–96	Gothein: Social question of the present (335)	Wagner: Critique of socialism (1243)	Conrad: The social question of the present (249)
1900	Gothein: Renaissance and humanism (243)	Wilamowitz: Classical historiography (370)	Riehl: Modern drama (319)
1900–01	Anschuetz: Experimental chemistry (144)	E. Schmidt: German playwrights of the nineteenth century (1226)	Stammler: Theory of the social question (241)**
1905	Adolph Weber: Social problem in the big cities (645)	Wilamowitz: Ancient Greeks (551)	Riehl: Psychology (349)
1905–06	Clemen: Monument protection and care (347)	Wagner: Development of national and world economies (883)	Stammler: Theory of the social question (398)**
1910	Clemen: History of art of Rhinelanders (624)*		Goldschmidt: On landscape painting (311)
1910–11	Clemen: Michelangelo (724)*	Wagner: Agrarian versus industrial state (1483)	Goldschmidt: Albrecht Dürer (315)

Source: GPSA Dahlem, Rep. 76 Va Sects. 2 (Berlin), 3 (Bonn), 8 (Halle), Tit. VII.

*Respectively, 1909 and 1909–10.

**Taught in law faculty but cross-listed in philosophical faculty.

its members and others as ends rather than means.[31] This use of Kant was not restricted to the ivory tower. The Social Democrat Eduard Bernstein made similar use of Kant in support of his revisionism within the party itself,[32] and the economist Gerhard von Schulze-Gävernitz, grandson of the idealistic agriculturalist of the early nineteenth century, used the same argument in trying to win over the workers from Social Democracy to the monarchy.[33]

The economists were willing to use their prestige to help shape the changing public sphere by promoting their views beyond the traditional academic channels such as the lecture hall or the scholarly journal. The Bonn professor Eberhard Gothein, for example, gave five public lectures in Düsseldorf, Elberfeld, Barmen, and Cologne within a single week in 1901.[34] Sombart depended increasingly on public lecture fees to supplement his salary as *Extraordinarius*.[35] While the channels open to professors were fewer than those of the mass movements, the universities themselves provided one such arena in the form of a multitude of student organizations. The wave of student idealism in the 1890s was marked by the spread of social-scientific student organizations, which were conceived as an alternative to the already strident anti-Semitic nationalist organizations. The first was founded in Göttingen in 1891–92; they then spread to most universities.[36] These organizations were soon tarred with the stigma of socialism, however, and an address by Bernstein to the Berlin group in 1901 did not aid the cause (there was also a minority of overtly socialist student groups that were suppressed).[37] But the idealism of students was not limited to these groups; a variety of student organizations participated in establishing instructional courses for workers in basic skills such as German and mathematics, which were estimated to have reached eleven thousand people.[38]

The economists also made extensive use of the press in propagating their views. This was particularly true of the political weeklies, such as Johannes Grunow's *Grenzboten*, Friedrich Naumann's *Hilfe*, and the "enfant terrible of the Wilhelminian journalistic scene," Maximilian Harden's *Die Zukunft*.[39] Brentano

---

31. Willey, *Back to Kant*, 112–13.

32. Gay, *Dilemma of Democratic Socialism*, 155–60.

33. Lindenlaub, *Richtungskämpfe*, 305–10; Krüger, *Nationalökonomen*, 50–57.

34. M. L. Gothein, *Eberhard Gothein*, 124.

35. Lenger, *Sombart*, 63.

36. Bruch, *Wissenschaft*, 170. Cf. Max Weber's description of the reformist idealism in Berlin in his letter to Hermann Baumgarten of 30 April 1888 in *Max Weber. Werk und Person*, 67–68.

37. Bruch, *Wissenschaft*, 172–73; Jarausch, *Students, Society, and Politics*, 356–57. On Bernstein's address, see his "Selbstdarstellung," in Meiner, ed., *VGS*, 37–39. It was this address that led to Bernstein's censure by the Social Democrats.

38. Jarausch, *Students, Society, and Politics*, 362.

39. The phrase is from Bruch, *Wissenschaft*, 233; see also 35–49, and Wagner's correspondence with Harden in Wagner, *Briefe*, 322 ff.

actually preferred these journals to scholarly ones after 1890.[40] These magazines, directed to a broad middle-class readership, took an editorial stance that was sharply critical of the extreme right-wing tendencies in Wilhelminian Germany; this was also true of the *Preussische Jahrbücher* under the historian Hans Delbrück. In them, the professors successfully attacked the legislative bills directed against the Social Democrats—now that the Kaiser had reversed his "new course"—in 1895 and 1899 (the so-called Overthrow Bill and Penitentiary Bill), and the "Lex Heinze" of 1899, designed to increase censorship.[41] All of these measures failed.

Another avenue of influence was the voluntary association. The *Verein für Sozialpolitik* was joined in 1890 by two religious groups, the People's Association for Catholic Germany and the Evangelical Social Congress. The latter was built in part on Wagner's continuing contacts with religious leaders; it also held regular meetings devoted to social reform, and by 1914 could boast a membership of almost fifteen hundred. Many contemporaries acknowledged that its agenda was shaped largely by the economists rather than by theologians.[42] In 1895 the *Verein* and the Congress cosponsored a continuing education course on *Sozialpolitik* in Berlin for 780 attendees, including 186 women (but no workers). This was but one of several such courses organized throughout Germany by different groups.[43] Eventually, in 1901, another organization was formed with the express purpose of legislative agitation on workers' issues: the Society for Social Reform, which boasted fourteen hundred members by 1912. Schmoller, Brentano, and Werner Sombart were all on its board, and its journal, *Soziale Praxis*, was edited by Schmoller's cousin, Ernst Francke.[44] Cooperation between it, the *Verein*, and the Evangelical Social Congress remained close.

From these activities emerged the hope of a new political party: Schmoller, Brentano, and Ferdinand Tönnies talked vaguely in the mid–1890s of increased political involvement in a party that would bring the educated elite and workers together.[45] The most promising initiative stemmed from the Protestant pastor Friedrich Naumann, who had been active in Adolf Stoecker's Christian Socialists but became disillusioned with Stoecker's anti-Semitic appeals. Under the influence of Brentano, Max Weber, and others, Naumann sought to combine the appeals to nationalism and socialism in the *Nationalsozialer Verein* of 1895—

40. Lindenlaub, *Richtungskämpfe*, 195; see Sheehan's bibliography, *Brentano*, 209–11, which lists articles in daily papers as well (*Münchener Allgemeine, Frankfurter Zeitung, Berliner Tagblatt*).

41. Bruch, *Wissenschaft*, 143; 153–56; 232.

42. Bruch, "Bürgerliche Sozialreform," 103–6.

43. Bruch, *Wissenschaft*, 265–66; "Bürgerliche Sozialreform," 117.

44. Bruch, *Wissenschaft*, 338–44. On the board, see Lindenlaub, *Richtungskämpfe*, 188.

45. Bruch, *Wissenschaft*, 161.

a movement which fed the expectations of students and faculty alike.[46] Prior to his cooperation with Naumann, Brentano had actually opened contacts with revisionists among the Social Democrats—to the scorn of that party's majority.[47]

It was scarcely to be expected that such activism would go unnoticed by the industrialists. In January of 1895, the industrialist and Reichstag deputy Baron Karl von Stumm-Halberg attacked the *Kathedersozialisten* for monopolizing economics and training future officials to be soft on socialism.[48] This led to a series of altercations in the daily papers between Stumm and Wagner, leading the industrialist to challenge the professor to a duel. The confrontation only served to demonstrate the strength of the economists: the students held a special gathering to honor Schmoller and Wagner, who was elected rector of the university. Wagner's speech, *Academic Economics and Socialism*, contained a ringing defense of the scientific respectability of Marx, Engels, Lassalle, and Rodbertus—as well as a rejection of their socialism as a practical doctrine.[49] Two years later, the tensions between business and labor had escalated due to the Hamburg dockworkers' strike. Three junior professors had signed a petition calling for support of the workers; during the strike, Wagner added a further provocation by addressing a meeting of Christian mineworkers' unions in the heart of the Ruhr. Criticism of the *Kathedersozialisten* mounted again in the press and the Prussian legislature, culminating in a another speech by Stumm in May calling for the cultural minister's resignation. The reaction of the students was as follows:

> A stormy honor from his great number of students greeted Professor Schmoller in the first lecture since the well known speech of Baron von Stumm in the House of Lords. A stamping of feet lasting for minutes, that repeatedly grew stronger and seemed not to want to end, gave the honored teacher to know what his students thought of Stumm's attacks.[50]

A few weeks later, Brentano wrote in the *Frankfurter Zeitung*, "The main service to the *Verein für Sozialpolitik* has . . . [been rendered by] Baron von Stumm. His attacks have affected the *Kathedersozialisten* as the socialist law did the Social Democrats."[51] Schmoller now was elected rector. Meanwhile, Schmoller, Lexis, and Ludwig Elster had been busy drafting defenses of the economists for Althoff to the effect that economists could not be reduced to any single label such

---

46. Sheehan, *Brentano*, 145–46.

47. Ibid., 135–40. On the response, see Bruch, *Wissenschaft*, 144, 164.

48. For accounts of the ensuing "Stumm Era," see Bruch, *Wissenschaft*, 145–53; Lindenlaub, *Richtungskämpfe*, 54–70.

49. Wagner, *Akademische Nationalökonomie*, 27–28.

50. *Faktotum*, 17 June 1897, 6. Copy in GPSA Dahlem, Rep. 92 Althoff A I, no. 64: 108.

51. Quoted in Lindenlaub, *Richtungskämpfe*, 77.

as *Kathedersozialisten;* this material was used by Minister of Culture Robert Bosse in defending the government.[52]

These attacks on the *Kathedersozialisten* nevertheless had the effect of making the ministry aware of the political nature of academic appointments in economics—and revealed that the influence of Schmoller and his colleagues was not unlimited. The attacks occurred in the very months that the Kaiser was toying with the idea of a coup d'etat to put down the socialist menace by military rule, and Stumm was one of his confidants.[53] The ministry could not afford to ignore the attacks and adopted a strategy of appeasement. Its major concession was to be the Lex Arons the following year, directed against socialists in academia, whatever their field (Arons was a physicist). Althoff also did appoint several economics professors whose views were known to be pro-industry. Among them were Richard Ehrenberg, a chamber of commerce secretary and brother of a distinguished Göttingen classicist. Ehrenberg had defended the entrepreneurs in the Hamburg dockworkers' strike; Althoff secured for him an *Extraordinarius* at Göttingen, where Ehrenberg hoped to attract more business funding and establish an institute.[54] Another such "punitive professor"—in the heated rhetoric of the day—was Julius Wolf, who at least possessed firmer scholarly credentials. A professor at Zürich, Wolf had published a refutation of Marxism in 1892 which had already attracted Stumm's attention.[55] Althoff placed him at Breslau, to the faculty's and Schmoller's disgruntlement, to offset the effect of the young Werner Sombart, whose Marxism was well known.[56] Both Ehrenberg and Wolf remained relative pariahs among the economists. Ehrenberg became *Ordinarius* at the isolated university of Rostock in Mecklenburg, while Wolf never developed a satisfactory following at Breslau. Both expressed their resentment by continuing to publish tirades against the *Kathedersozialisten* (e.g., Ehrenberg's book *Terrorism in Economics*). Both sought to legitimate their positions by establishing journals and appealing to "exact" methodology. Ehrenberg's attempt to get industrialists to fund an institute for him at Leipzig (allegedly through the offices of Bücher's former student and business-

52. Memo of Schmoller, 31 March 1897, GPSA Dahlem, Rep. 92 Althoff A I, no. 64 (Verein für Sozialpolitik): 6–8; of Lexis, [n.d.], 20–34; of Elster [n.d.], 39–61; Pruussen, Haus der Abgeordneten, 75. Sitzung, 4 May 1897, 2385–86. See also Wagner to Bosse, 17 May 1897, in *Briefe,* 324–25, in which Wagner claimed that his Ruhr speech had been distorted by the press.

53. Röhl, *Germany without Bismarck,* 220.

54. Manegold, *Universität,* 179.

55. Lindenlaub, *Richtungskämpfe,* 81. Ironically, Rosa Luxemburg had been one of his students.

56. Memo of phil. faculty, 26 Oct. 1897, GPSA Dahlem, Rep. 76 Va Sect. 4 Tit. IV no. 56, vol. 19: 125 (Breslau, appts.); Schmoller to Althoff. 10 July 1897, Rep. 92 Althoff, A II, no. 95, II: 106; Wolf to Althoff, 29 July 1902, ibid., no. 102, 2–5; Althoff to Schmoller, 1 August 1897, Rep. 92 Schmoller, no. 112: 80.

man Gustav Stresemann) created another scandal in 1907.[57] Schmoller reacted to Ehrenberg with condescension—"Opponents to us are still welcome, but I would like better opponents than such."[58]

The conflicts of the "Stumm era" were soon offset, however, by an issue which brought the patriotism of the professors to the fore. This was the campaign at the turn of the century to build a fleet, which the vast majority of economists enthusiastically supported. The naval campaign was part of a conscious strategy of the men around the Kaiser to rule through a supportive public opinion as an alternative to a coup.[59] The new admiral, Alfred von Tirpitz, excelled in manipulating public opinion, and he found the economists as worthy of co-opting as Stumm had found them worthy of attacking. Already in the summer of 1897, his press secretary met with Schmoller, who recommended a young economist, Ernst von Halle, to coordinate scholarly support in the naval office.[60] Tirpitz's efforts extended to influencing academic appointments: he requested the ministry of culture to establish special *Extraordinarius* positions "in the sciences of state with special consideration for naval-scientific branches thereof" in Berlin and Kiel, as well as two additional positions in the latter university, both for hand-picked people.[61] Althoff hastened to do Tirpitz's bidding, with no opposition from the Berlin faculty, who recommended von Halle.[62] Nevertheless, the desire for national harmony did not mean that the *Kathedersozialisten* were willing to surrender their identity. When it came to direct participation in the Naval League, Schmoller set conditions: the academic re-

57. Wolf's file in Althoff's papers contain copies of his hostile newspaper articles (A II, no. 102). On his lack of resonance at Breslau, see his own "Selbstdarstellung," in Meiner, ed., *VGS*, 229; 244. Ehrenberg copiously documented the Stresemann affair in *Terrorismus in der Wirtschafts-Wissenschaft*, which brought him into conflict with the ever-indignant Max Weber (120–22). Ehrenberg fixated on Thünen as his model for "exact method"—hence his journal, the *Thünen-Archiv*. By this he apparently meant empirical business history, if his study of Siemens is any indication. See *Die Unternehmungen der Brüder Siemens* (1906). Wolf also wrote a work entitled *Nationalökonomie als exakte Wissenschaft* ("Selbstdarstellung," 228).

58. quoted in Bruch, *Wissenschaft*, 299. It is instructive to contrast the situation of the German economists with respect to capitalism and socialism with that in the United States. Both countries were experiencing intense labor conflicts at the turn of the century which filtered into academic politics. But in the United States, it was the pro-labor economists who were the pariahs, as in the cases of Richard T. Ely and Edward Bemis. The occasions when economists rallied to support their members under pressure—as in the case of Edward Ross at Stanford—were exceptional. See Furner, *Advocacy and Objectivity*, chaps. 7–10.

59. Röhl, *Germany without Bismarck*, 251–52.

60. Sheehan, *Brentano*, 179.

61. Tirpitz to ministry of finance (draft), 4 Oct. 1898, GPSA Dahlem, Rep. 76 Va Sect. 9 Tit. IV no. 1, vol. 11: 160–62 (Kiel, appts.).

62. Althoff to philosophical faculty, 14 April 1899 (in margin, "immediately! even sooner!"), ibid., Sect. 2 Tit. IV no. 5, vol. 10: 49 (Berlin appts.); Dekan to ministry, 14 June 1899, 79–84.

formists were to be represented on the executive board. When the right-wing supporters balked at this, the naval office organized a separate "Free Association for Naval Lectures" for the more educated.[63] The association solicited a spectrum of academic economists from Schmoller to Ehrenberg. These lectures were remarkably free of patriotic or social Darwinist rhetoric and concentrated on the professors' own areas of competence. Thus Karl Lamprecht talked of Germany's trade in the Middle Ages, while Schmoller and Sering addressed her population growth in recent years and the changes away from free-trade policies in England; Wagner showed why Germany could afford a fleet, while the young Hermann Schumacher depicted German mercantile interests in China.[64] Schmoller's self-conscious moderation was representative:

> We neither want nor will pursue a chauvinistic world-power politics, nor come to boundless plans for naval and sea power. It is a ridiculous distortion to maintain that this is the intent of the government or the friends of the navy. Certainly there are individual German chauvinists, individual extravagant colonial fanatics and individual England-haters. . . . But these are small in number and without influence.[65]

This reasoning did not prevent Schmoller on another occasion from forecasting a German colony of 20–30 million in southern Brazil in the coming century; the example shows that the "modest goals" of the professors were often indistinguishable from those of the more radical imperialists.[66] But the difference in tone was significant: the economists were still able maintain an equilibrium between reasoned argument and patriotic enthusiasm, as they had done under Bismarck.

In any event, the naval campaign did not signify a sudden shift away from *Sozialpolitik* to *Weltpolitik*. The campaign for the fleet was concurrent with the opposition to the Penitentiary Bill and the Lex Heinze. Indeed, *Weltpolitik* was seen as reinforcing *Sozialpolitik*. "No one in the German Empire will suffer more than the working population if an unhappy catastrophe should sometime transform our dependence on the world market into an actual danger," wrote Ernst Francke, president of the Society for Social Reform. "A successful world policy and world-power policy is the indispensable correlate of an energetic continuation of *Sozialpolitik* in Germany."[67] This was also the platform of Naumann's National-Social Union. It was this perceived interconnection which helped

63. Eley, *Reshaping the German Right*, 85–88.

64. Schmoller, Sering, Wagner, eds., *Handels-und Machtpolitik* (1900).

65. Ibid., 32. Cf. the statements of Delbrück, Brentano, Paulsen, and Wenckstern opposing the Pan-German League, in Marienfeld, *Wissenschaft und Schlachtflottenbau*, 93.

66. Marienfeld, *Wissenschaft*, 32; see also Krüger, *Nationalökonomen*, 37.

67. Francke, "Weltpolitik und Sozialreform," in Schmoller and Wagner, eds., *Handels-und Machtpolitik*, 1: 114, 128.

bring the Anglophile Brentano to enter the campaign. The naval office courted Brentano via Schmoller from an early stage, for they were well aware of the need to incorporate Bavarian support.[68] Brentano and others addressed such arguments directly to the workers, much to Social Democrat Kautsky's alarm.[69] At the same time, Brentano sought to expand his contacts with England in order to soften the impact of the navy bills.[70]

The naval campaign did, however, mark a turning point in the relationship between the *Kathedersozialisten* and the public sphere—as it marked a waning of the spontaneity in the changing public sphere itself. Tirpitz's massive orchestration of public opinion foreshadowed the strategy of Bernhard von Bülow, whose influence was growing before he assumed the chancellorship in 1900. Bülow's accession was due in part to his skill in manipulating the Emperor and public opinion at the same time. His policies were formulated largely at the level of the symbolic, uniting the diverse factions and parties behind grand natonalistic ideas such as the fleet, with great reliance on managing the press. This policy was directed against the extremes on the right and left.[71] It is not surprising that support for both the more radical Pan-German and Agrarian leagues declined in favor of the Naval League in the early 1900s.[72] Similarly, hopes of a social reform party led by the educated middle classes faded; Naumann's National-Social Union sent only one representative to the Reichstag in 1903.[73] But this decline was compensated by an increased influence of the *Kathedersozialisten* in governmental circles, for Bülow's aim for a moderate center coincided with their own. Bülow enjoyed the company of professors and had a "special esteem" for Schmoller, whom he had first heard speak as a *Gymnasium* student in Halle and whom he valued for his acquaintances with a wide variety of officials.[74] A contemporary observed the similarity between Schmoller's style of science, his preference for blurred outlines, and Bülow's fluid style of politics—as, in a way, did Bülow himself:

> The words of Heraclitus, that "everything flows," are also appropriate to public matters. The epochs in the life of the state follow one another like high tide and low. This became clear to me one fine summer day, in the woods of St.

68. Sheehan, *Brentano*, 179; Bruch, *Wissenschaft*, 66–67.
69. Bruch, *Wissenschaft*, 83–88.
70. Sheehan, *Brentano*, 182–83.
71. Lerman, *Chancellor*, 25, 59.
72. Chickering, *We Men*, 213, 254 ff; Vascik, "Agrarian Conservatism," 253.
73. Bruch, *Wissenschaft*, 29–30, 186; Sheehan, *Brentano*, 145–46, 150.
74. Bülow, *Memoirs*, 1: 277: "Apart from my humble self, he was in intimate touch with Miquel and Althoff, with Thiel and Lohmann, with Klemens Delbrück and Berlepsch, with Möller and Becker, the Oberbürgermeister of Cologne; that, both on the Staatsrat and on many preparatory legal and administrative commissions and committees of enquiry, and in the Upper House where he represented the university of Berlin, he could obtain direct insight into the workings of the state.

Germain, when . . . I read the essay which Gustav Schmoller had written in October, 1880 in Strassburg and had published in the *Jahrbuch für Gesetzgebung, Verwaltung, und Volkswirtschaft.*[75]

There were good grounds for cynicism about who was manipulating whom in this relationship. According to one Marburg professor, "one brought out famous scholars like parade-horses from the stall."[76] The government's coordination of scholarly opinion on the naval issue was revived for the electoral campaign of 1907, and again in favor of an inheritance tax the following year.[77]

Nevertheless, there was unmistakable progress in labor reform during Bülow's years, thanks to his Minister of the Interior, Count Posadowsky, to whom Bülow largely delegated his social policy.[78] Posadowsky's mentality corresponded admirably to Schmoller's conception of enlightened officials who could overcome a narrowly conservative class bias.[79] Whereas Posadowsky had previously pursued infractions of the labor laws with a vengeance, the defeat of the Penitentiary Bill in 1899 (which was directed at prohibiting strikes), proved to be a turning point for him; he turned thereafter to improving working conditions. At first, these improvements were aimed at lower middle-class employees and children more than factory workers, but with the miners' strike in the Ruhr in 1905, Posadowsky promised and delivered a law that partially met the workers' demands, setting maximum hours and establishing obligatory workers' boards for miners—a very different response from the one made to the Hamburg strike eight years before.[80] Posadowsky, whom Schmoller praised as an official of "wide horizon," also sponsored state-subsidized housing and worked for a liberal-sponsored law lifting restrictions on all types of organizations, which benefited women as well as workers, and which finally passed in 1908.[81]

An ounce of practice is worth a ton of theory." See also Bruch, *Wissenschaft,* 65–66, 100; Brocke, "System Althoff," who notes Schmoller's ties with the finance minister Miquel (74).

75. Bülow, *Memoirs,* 4: 122. Bülow had already been an avid student of Roscher at Leipzig (121). See also Eugen Katz to Brentano 13 June 1906, quoted in Bruch, *Wissenschaft,* 100 n.

76. Schücking, "Nachruf auf Philipp Zorn," quoted in Bruch, *Wissenschaft,* 210.

77. Bruch, *Wissenschaft.,* 180–85; Witt, *Finanzpolitik,* 217 ff.

78. Lerman, *Chancellor,* 106–7.

79. Lindenlaub, *Richtungskämpfe,* 246–47; Bruch, *Wissenschaft,* 195; see also Schmoller, "Graf Posadowsky," 57–61.

80. E. R. Huber, *Verfassungsgeschichte,* 4: 1237–38; 1241–43; Born, *Staat und Sozialpolitik,* chap. 6. This is an aspect of governmental policy ignored by Kehr and Wehler in their emphasis on *Sammlungspolitik.*

81. Schmoller, "Posadowsky," 59; Gorges, *Sozialforschung,* 319; E. R. Huber, *Verfassungsgeschichte,* 4: 1244–45. For a discussion of German law on unions and strikes, and the positions of the economists with respect to it, see Lindenlaub, *Richtungskämpfe,* 196–239.

In sum, the Bülow years encouraged Schmoller's belief in gradual reform from above and vindicated for him the efforts of the *Verein* over the years.[82]

With this emphasis on reform from above in the 1900s came the revival of attempts to alter the education of Prussian higher officials. This was a further legacy of the Stumm era, when the issue of the nefarious influence of the *Kathedersozialisten* on young minds was raised in the Landtag.[83] To this were added the ongoing complaints about the excessively juristic training and lack of practical orientation of civil servants, which had been coming from Finance Minister Miquel and from the professoriate.[84] The result was a revival of the attempt to change Prussian curricular requirements by law—with results as paltry as in the 1870s. After two commissions studied the issue, a bill was introduced in 1902 and was not passed until 1906. Once again, the issue served as a lightning rod for partisan differences. Liberals and conservatives fought again over the right of the *Landrat* to approve candidates as a way of preserving aristocratic values (Schmoller sided with the conservatives in defending that right).[85] The left-wing liberals also objected to the financial burden that an increased length of study time would impose on the poorer students, while conservatives put little faith in university study at all. In the end, the only change in a more realistic direction was that the practicum in the administrative offices was lengthened from one year to two. The debate showed the intensity of liberal-conservative differences—which Bülow's failing strategy was also soon to demonstrate.

A more satisfying solution to the problem of the training of civil servants came in the form of greatly expanded programs of continuing education, following the precedent set by the *Verein* and the Evangelical-Social Congress. This seemed to answer the conservatives' objections that the controversial sciences of state were best left to mature officials—who had already been selected for their political reliability—rather than to impressionable university students. Although had toyed with Mohl's old idea of a separate administrative academy, and in 1900 asked Lexis to draft a memo. Meanwhile, the business community and

82. One should also mention the more exclusive *Staatswissenschaftliche Gesellschaft*, which had been meeting regularly since 1883—obviously a very different means of intellectual dissemination from the attempts to reach a broader public of the 1890s.

83. Stumm's parliamentary ally, Otto von Zedlitz-Neukirch, had proposed that this influence could be neutralized by transferring their chairs from the philosophical to the law faculties, as at Strassburg. See Lindenlaub, *Richtungskämpfe*, 69; Lindenfeld, "Education of Prussian Higher Civil Servants," 214–15.

84. Röhl, "Higher Civil Servants," 131; Dietzel, "Stud. Jur. et Cam.," 679–711; Cohn, *Staatswissenschaftliche Vorbildung*.

85. Prussia, Herrenhaus, 30 April 1903, 189; on the debate, see Lindenfeld, "Education of Prussian Higher Civil Servants," 215–19.

municipal government of Frankfurt were developing an Academy for Social and Commercial Studies, designed for merchants and industrialists as well as officials; it was one of the seeds for a new university there.[86] Perhaps taking a cue from Frankfurt, Althoff decided in 1902 to establish a quasi-independent Association for Continuing Education in the Sciences of State in Berlin—a typical example of academic-state cooperation.[87] The operation was highly successful, the number of courses increasing from 12 in 1902 to 59 in 1913, and the number of students from 43 to 504, of whom 75 percent were officials. In 1907, Ludwig Elster noted that it was like a small university. Instructors were drawn equally from the professoriate and from practicing officials themselves. The courses were not simply lectures, but included discussions and excursions to local factories (a feature which Bücher associated with a certain dilettantism).[88] In any case, the Berlin association soon found imitators, first in Cologne, then in Vienna, Mannheim, Danzig, and Königsberg.[89]

The political basis for such enlightened reformism was soon to change, however. The task of balancing the divergent forces proved to be too much for Bülow. In 1906 he realized he would have to take a harsher line towards the Social Democrats if he was to retain the Kaiser's confidence; in the following year, Posadowsky was let go.[90] Although the extremely nationalistic election campaign of 1907 proved a success for Bülow's coalition in the Reichstag, it soon foundered over an issue that proved resistant to symbolic manipulation: the reform of Reich finances. The need for higher taxes and the limited options available meant that it was impossible to avoid a clash of interests: the proposed inheritance tax was taken by the conservatives as a direct threat to the landed aristocracy. The issue became in effect a test of the effectiveness of *Sozialpolitik*. A tax on the wealthy was certainly a part of the ethical social reformist principles, clearly articulated by Adolph Wagner. This theme was used in Bülow's propaganda campaign to prepare for the bill, with von Halle once again in charge.[91] The *Kathedersozialisten* once again made speeches and wrote pamphlets. But although this campaign appears to have had a positive effect in enlightening the bureaucracy on the importance of fiscal responsibility, it failed to bring in sufficient votes in the Reichstag. With its defeat, Bülow resigned in early 1909.

86. Lindenfeld, "Education of Prussian Higher Civil Servants," 221.

87. The statutes of 1904 called for an executive committee consisting of members from the various ministries, one from the university, and one member-at-large (Schmoller). Yet when the widow of an employee asked for a pension in 1908, the directors insisted that the Association was not a state institution (ibid., 222).

88. Bücher, *Hochschulfragen*, 290–92.

89. Lindenfeld, "Education of Prussian Higher Civil Servants," 222–24.

90. Lerman, *Chancellor*, 163, 170.

91. Witt, *Finanzpolitik*, 217–21.

Under the new chancellor, Theobald von Bethmann-Hollweg, the influence of the *Kathedersozialisten* on public opinion receded markedly. Although Bethmann-Hollweg was himself a product of the upper administration, he did not maintain the informal contacts with the economists that Bülow had established.[92] Moreover, public opinion itself was becoming increasingly polarized. The second Moroccan crisis in 1911 and the Social Democratic victories in the elections of 1912 contributed to the radicalization of the right and the left. Bethmann-Hollweg did indeed react to these trends by calling for the educated elites to emphasize political education in order to wean public opinion away from the naive belief in the efficacy of force. He emphasized "foreign cultural politics" to replace the emphasis on power. His closest academic confidants were two cultural historians, Karl Lamprecht and Kurt Breysig.[93] Bethmann-Hollweg evidently had in mind both the increased study of other countries and the attempt to spread German culture abroad.[94] These initiatives were obviously far removed from the tradition of internal social reform that had been a staple of the sciences of state. Given the deteriorating international situation, it is not surprising that the chancellor did not turn to the social reformers, and that the pace of social reform slackened.[95]

At the same time, much of the decline of the *Kathedersozialisten* was due to internal pressures within the profession. It is to these changes we now turn.

STRUCTURAL AND GENERATIONAL CHANGES IN THE ACADEMIC ENVIRONMENT

Within the universities, one can speak of a process of fermentation that paralleled that in the political sphere. After a brief pause in the early 1890s, enrollments continued to skyrocket, going from 27,394 in 1893–94 to 60,748 in the summer of 1914.[96] Within the discipline of economics, these quantitative changes were accompanied by qualitative ones. The notion of a professional or "practical" economist who operated outside the state bureaucracy was emerging (although one label used to characterize it was still that of *Beamte*).[97] It referred to a growing number of consultants for interest groups and other professional associations as well as corporations and cartels, in addition to the full-time secretaries of the local and regional chambers of commerce, who often served as links between the state administration and the business community. These groups had founded their own interest group in 1901, the Association

---

92. Bruch, *Wissenschaft*, 102.
93. Ibid., 103–5.
94. Jarausch, *Students, Society, and Politics*, 223–24.
95. Born, *Staat und Sozialpolitik*, 242 ff.
96. Jarausch, *Students, Society, and Politics*, 30.
97. See VFS, *Verhandlung . . . 1907*.

Table 12 *Enrollments in Economics Seminars, 1890–1914*

	Leipzig	Berlin	Bonn	Breslau	Halle
1890	22*	118	13	32	—
1895	74	238	24	100	—
1900	156	303	14	—	—
1905	202	420	88	77	127
1910	—	488	143	160	141
1914	—	435	141	150	103

Sources: Karl Bücher, "Die vereinigten Staatswissenschaftlichen Seminare," in *Festschrift zur Feier des 500 jährigen Bestehens der Universität Leipzig*, ed. Rektor and Senat (Leipzig: Hirzel, 1909), 4: 2, 8; *Chronik der königlichen Friedrich-Wihlelms-Universität zu Berlin; Chronik der rheinischen Friedrich-Wilhelms-Universität zu Bonn; Chronik der königlichen Universität zu Breslau; Chronik der Königlichen Vereinigten Friedrichs-Universität Halle-Wittenberg*, all 1890–1914.
*Respectively, 1892/3, 1893.

of German Economists; by 1907 it had about seven hundred members; at that time it was estimated that there were between 1300 and 1400 practical economists, either employed or looking for work.[98] Naturally these people sought the knowledge and status that came from academic training, as witnessed by the swelling numbers in the economics seminars (see table 12). Many of these students no longer aspired to careers in the higher civil service or could not meet its curricular or financial requirements. In the words of one commentator, "The jurist who has failed the first or second examination tends to discover suddenly that he is splendidly suited for the career of practical economist."[99] Neither were these students particularly suited to a scholarly career, to which the seminars were designed to lead; the requirement of a dissertation and Ph.D. began to be viewed as an obstacle, and pressure mounted to establish an intermediate exam and later a degree (*Diplom*)—which was only implemented in 1923.[100] Given their increased size, the seminars themselves became less effective in propagating a specific research program. Schmoller's annual reports from his seminar, for example, indicated a greater dispersion of topics, especially after 1905, rather than the common theme which he had been able to pursue in Strassburg.[101]

The growing numbers of students naturally affected the size of the faculty, and it appears that the social sciences kept pace with overall faculty growth. According to a quantitative study by Fritz Ringer, David Vampola, and Philip Sidel of professors in all fields, the increase in social science faculty from 57 in 1890 to 113 in 1910 represented 3 percent of the total increase in both years,

98. Hermann Edwin Krueger, "Beruf des praktischen Volkswirts," 1320, 1329.

99. Ibid., 1327. See also VFS, *Verhandlungen. . . 1907*, 71.

100. VFS, *Verhandlungen . . . 1907*, 31–33, 84, 155; Lindenfeld, "Professionalization," 224.

101. Staatswissenschaftlich-statistisches Seminar, Reports *Chronik der Universität Berlin*, 1890–1912.

Table 13 *Appointments in the Social Sciences, 1885–1914*

	Privatdozenten	Extraordinarien	Ordinarien
1885–90	7	10	6
1890–95	12	13	6
1895–1900	10	9	9
1900–05	20	6	10
1905–10	22	11	6
1910–14	27	5	7

Source: VRS (Vampola-Ringer-Sidel) reconstitution of the Göttingen survey (see Table 9).

whereas the percentages in humanities, law, medicine, and theology declined slightly.[102] This study also measured the mean number of years between *Habilitation* and official appointment (as a rule to *Extraordinarius*): whereas in 1880, this waiting period in the social sciences was second longest for any field (6.8 years), by 1900 it had become second shortest (4.6 years); in 1910 it was still well below the average for all fields (5.8 compared to 8.1).[103] Although these figures include other social sciences than the ones studied here (e.g., anthropology), our extrapolation of these data for economics, statistics, sociology, and economic history reveals a great deal of mobility in these fields in the late 1880s and 1890s. A turning point came in 1900, however, as the number of new *Privatdozenten* outstripped the number of appointments at higher ranks (see table 13). One can thus speak of two generations of younger scholars in this period. The first, who entered the field in the late 1880s and 1890s, had every prospect of success. The second, who came in after 1900, were much greater in number and in a much more competitive situation.[104]

One aspect of this influx was the perception that Jews were entering the profession in disproportionate numbers. Unfortunately, information on religious background is available for only about 25 percent of the faculty in all fields, but of that fraction, the proportion of Jews was declining—from 12 percent in 1890 to 8 percent in 1900 and 1910—though it was still in excess of their proportion of the general population (1 percent).[105] While the data on the specific group of social scientists from the *Staatswissenschaften* is too fragmentary to allow generalization, it is clear that the perception of Jewishness was an important factor in the evaluation of new faculty.[106] The most conspicuous case was that of Simmel, whose father was baptized as was he, but who could never

102. Ringer, "Sociography of German Academics," 255.
103. Ibid., 264.
104. Cf D. Krüger, *Nationalökonomen*, 13–14, 246.
105. Ringer, "Sociography of German Academics," 276.
106. When Max Weber was asked by a colleague in 1907 to recommend candidates for a position in the *technische Hochschule* in Munich, he divided his list into Jewish and non-Jewish candidates. See Weber to Richard Graf Du Moulin-Eckart, 1 May 1907; 4 May 1907, in Weber, *Briefe 1906–1908*, 286–96.

escape the taint of being Jewish.[107] Schmoller's correspondence with Althoff was laced with anti-Semitic observations. His main objection to Julius Wolf was his "Jewish manner, the duplicitous careerism."[108] Schmoller and Wagner both vented their concern over Jewish penetration of German society in public.[109] It is also true, however, that such remarks appeared with much less frequency from Althoff's other correspondents. If anti-Semitism was a factor in personnel decisions, however, it was not the dominating one. The memoirs of the Zionist economist and sociologist Franz Oppenheimer, who to his own surprise was accepted by Schmoller and Wagner on the merits of his work and became a close friend of Wagner in his last years, bear eloquent testimony to this fact.[110] Schmoller could characterize Simmel in his correspondence with Knapp as "a specifically Jewish-pondering mind, shimmering in all colors, unfruitful in its pure sophistry and cleverness," while giving Simmel's *Philosophy of Money* a favorable review.[111]

The growth in professional opportunities in the late 1880s and 1890s helped to create an atmosphere of rising expectations and confidence, which fueled an extraordinary burst of creativity associated with the names of Tönnies, Simmel, Weber, and Sombart. It would be superfluous here to trace the intellectual developments of these thinkers; this work has already been done.[112] Not that these creative individuals were typical of their generation in their pattern of professional advancement. They waited far longer than usual: Tönnies remained a *Privatdozent* for 28 years, Simmel for 15, while Sombart was stalled as *Extraordinarius* for 27 years. Max Weber, whose brilliance brought him early recognition, nevertheless spent most of his career outside the lecture hall. This is some measure of their unorthodox opinions, which included but were not limited to their intellectual innovativeness. But the willingness to innovate and

107. Käsler, *Frühe deutsche Soziologie*, 380–81.

108. Schmoller to Althoff, 4 Aug 1897, GPSA Dahlem, Rep. 92 Althoff A II, no. 95, II: 109–10; cf. 8 May 1896 (ibid., 92, on Simmel); 21 Nov. 1893, (A I no. 63: 76–77, on Otto Gerlach, who was not in fact Jewish).

109. Schmoller, "Obrigkeitsstaat und Volksstaat," 426; on Wagner, see Barkin, *Controversy*, 159; Heilmann, *Wagner*, 74–79.

110. Oppenheimer, *Erlebtes, Erstrebtes, Erreichtes*, 202–6; 248. According to Oppenheimer, Wagner moved away from anti-Semitism in his later years (310).

111. Schmoller to Knapp, 11 May 94, GPSA Dahlem, Rep. 92 Schmoller no. 131b: 53–54; *SJ* 25 (1901): 799–816.

112. On Tönnies, E. G. Jacoby, *Moderne Gesellschaft im sozialwissenschaftlichen Denken von Ferdinand Tönnies* (1971). On Simmel, David Frisby, *Georg Simmel* (1984). On Weber, Marianne Weber, *Max Weber: ein Lebensbild* (1926); Arthur Mitzman, *The Iron Cage* (1969); Wolfgang Mommsen, *Max Weber und die deutsche Politik*, (2d ed., 1974); Mommsen and Jürgen Osterhammel, eds., *Max Weber and His Contemporaries* (1987). On Sombart, Friedrich Lenger, *Werner Sombart* (1994); Bernhard vom Brocke, ed., *Sombarts 'Moderner Kapitalismus'* (1987), esp. the introduction; Mitzman, *Sociology and Estrangement* (New York: Knopf, 1973), which also contains sections on Tönnies and Michels.

to question authority was a typical feature of this generation in virtually every field of endeavour. In the memoirs of one eyewitness, the moderate socialist Karl Leuthner,

> Whether we speak of literature, theater, visual art, the form and setting of domestic life, the position of women, social concepts of morality, [of] names like Nietzsche, Lombroso, Lamprecht, Harnack and the theological left . . . [there is] an almost unanimous process: an army of youth, united through a leader, a name, a program of salvation, storm against the old and want to shape a new world . . . The time was youth.[113]

While the older *Kathedersozialisten* were able to serve as heroes for the younger generation in situations of conflict with reactionaries such as Baron von Stumm, they were ultimately unable to contain this generational animus directed against themselves. The divisive effects of this on the *Verein* are well documented, particularly for the years after 1900.[114] What concerns us here is how the generational revolt was directed at many of the intellectual foundations of the elders—well before the famous value-judgment controversy of the immediate prewar years. The targets of aggression were already well established: the "illusions" of the older generation and of Wilhelmine politics and society. Thus Max Weber in his Freiburg inaugural address of 1895 already scorned the "woods-and-meadows *Sozialpolitiker* and that humanly amiable and admirable but nevertheless unspeakably Philistine tender-mindedness which believes one can substitute 'ethical' ideals for political ones."[115] In 1897, Sombart wrote more soberly, "a methodologically unobjectionable argument for the ethical standpoint from *Kathedersozialist* circles is unknown to me."[116]

It was this critique of illusion which spurred much of the younger generation's creativity. In viewing the ethical basis of *Kathedersozialismus* as a set of rose-colored spectacles, so to speak, which blurred the outlines of the conflicts they saw about them and masked the inadequacy of the accepted authority figures, they refuted not only the conciliatory reformism of the older generation but its points of vagueness and internal contradiction. In place of general phrases, they sought clarity. They turned to Kant rather than Hegel for philosopical stimulation. Yet they remained too attached to the ideals of *Bildung* to find clarity in specialization. Hence they borrowed from other disciplines such as philosophy, history, and biology in this quest. In this, they remained true to the traditions of the *Staatswissenschaften* as developed by Schmoller, and it is no coin-

---

113. Leuthner, "Einst und Jetzt," quoted in Bruch, *Wissenschaft*, 31. Cf. Schmoller's review of Sombart's *Moderne Capitalismus*, in which he compared Sombart's direction to Jugendstil, in Brocke, ed., *Sombarts 'Moderner Kapitalismus,'* 136.

114. Boese *Geschichte*, 92, 113–20, 134–37; Lindenlaub, *Richtungskämpfe*, pt. 2, chaps. 5, 6.

115. Weber, "Nationalstaat und die Volkswirtschaftspolitik," 24.

116. Ibid., 24; Sombart, "Ideale der Sozialpolitik," 16–17.

cidence that three of the most "interdisciplinary" practicioners of the social sciences in these years—Simmel, Sombart, and Kurt Breysig—had all been members of Schmoller's seminar.[117]

Thus the landscape of the intellectual field during this period reveals two contradictory tendencies: specialization within the traditional subject matter of economics on the one hand, and an interest in interdisciplinary approaches on the other. Although the first of these was more characteristic of the post–1900 cohort, while the second was more typical of the creative group of the 1890s, the two phenomena were so close in time as to overlap considerably. For purposes of exposition, we shall consider the specialization first.

SPECIALIZATION

The most striking form of specialization resulted from the growth of new centers of learning outside the universities: the privately and municipally funded commercial academies (*Handelshochschulen*) which sprouted between 1898 and 1914.[118] This was due to some obvious practical factors: businessmen and industrialists were finding that academic economics was not meeting their needs for skilled managers or entrepreneurs with educational credentials. These new institutions gradually generated a new economic discipline—business economics (*Betriebswirtschaft*, or *Privatwirtschaft*) as distinct from national economy. Its focus was to convey techniques for keeping business solvent and efficient. By 1912, two journals and four textbooks on *Privatwirtschaftslehre* had appeared.[119] Naturally this was at odds with the loftier goals of *Nationalökonomie*, which, after all, studied the good of the nation rather than of private individuals. Brentano's unkind remark, "the art of becoming rich is not the subject of political economy but of business economics," probably represented a broad prejudice on the part of university professors.[120] But such views could not be kept out of the universities indefinitely; although *Privatwirtschaftslehre* itself did not significantly enter the universities until the 1920s, a new core of academic economists had already emerged by 1910 whose pro-business orientation was more subtle than that of Ehrenberg and Wolf, and who were all the more effective for their scholarly thoroughness. This group included Adolf Weber and Ludwig Bernhard, as well as two professors from the Frankfurt Commercial Academy, Ludwig Pohle and Andreas Voigt. When Pohle assumed the editorship of Wolf's journal in 1910,

117. Lindenlaub, *Richtungskämpfe*, 315.
118. Lindenfeld, "Professionalization," 213–31.
119. Ibid., 222.
120. Brentano, *Wie Studiert man Nationalökonmie?*, 4. See also Lindenfeld, "Professionalization," 220–21.

a new level of seriousness had been attained—and with it an increased ideological diversity and tension within the profession.[121]

Within the universities, an emerging specialty within economics was economic history, as the research program of the previous decades bore fruit. The number of lectures rose from six between 1885 and 1890 to fifty-six between 1905 and 1910.[122] These figures do not mean that economic history won immediate or automatic acceptance among historians: the young *Dozenten* were on the defensive against the charge of dilettantism, and Schmoller continued to draw fire from a few orthodox historians who saw the patriotic mission of history-as-state-power being threatened by this new direction.[123] But if the personnel politics of the Berlin university are any indication, economic history won general acceptance as a subfield.[124]

Much of the specialization took place within the subdivisions of *Volkswirtschaftspolitik* (see figures 13 and 14). Yet the pattern is not one of simple proliferation, but of fluctuations which corresponded to the political controversies surrounding these areas of policy.

A comparison of these figures with those of table 11 indicates that *Sozialpolitik*, while it lost some of its popularity after the 1890s, had become a firm part of the academic curriculum. Heinrich Herkner's book, *The Worker Question*, which expanded from 286 to 1269 pages in eight editions between 1894 and 1922, probably gives a representative picture of what was taught. After portraying the development of adverse working conditions in the industrialized countries, Herkner discussed the conservative, liberal, and socialist theories on the subject, and moved on to specific measures of amelioration: legal guarantees of labor contracts, trade unions, factory legislation, social insurance, and mediation and arbitration boards. It concluded with municipal measures, private welfare institutions, and consumer cooperatives.[125] The emergence of *Sozialpolitik* was also marked by a journal devoted exclusively to it, the *Archiv für Soziale Gesetzgebung und Statistik*, founded in 1888 by the revisionist Socialist Heinrich Braun. Braun perceived the need for a journal devoted to the empirical study

121. On Pohle, Voigt, and the *Zeitschrift für Sozialwissenschaft*, see Bruch, *Wissenschaft*, 307–17, esp. 314n on their pro-industrial stance. Pohle and Voigt had been active members of the *Verein* at the beginning of the 1900s; their turn away from *Sozialpolitik* was gradual. They resigned from the *Verein* in 1907 (Boese, *Geschichte*, 125).

122. University catalogues. See appendix.

123. On the charge of dilettantism, see Sommerlad, "Über das Studium der Wirtschaftsgeschichte," 99–101. On Schmoller's critic, Georg v. Below, see Bruch, *Wissenschaft*, 307 n.

124. Simon, *Staat und Geschichtswissenschaft*, 1: 135.

125. Herkner, *Arbeiterfrage*, 4th ed. (1905). Conrad's textbook of *Volkswirtschaftspolitik* reveals a similar set of topics minus the theoretical discussion. The figures on the editions are from Herkner, "Selbstdarstellung," in Meiner, ed., *VGS*, 95.

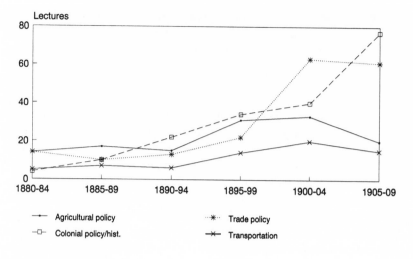

Source: University catalogues;
see appendix.

Fig. 13. Specialization in Economic Policy, 1880–1910

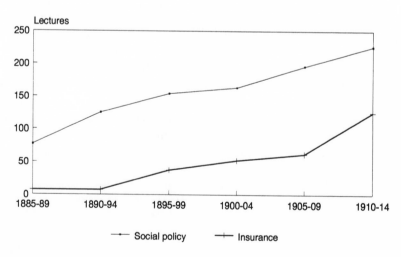

Source: University catalogues;
see appendix.
Winter semester 1914-15 not included.

Fig. 14. Lectures in Social Policy and Insurance, 1885–1914

of social conditions in order that intelligent legislation might be drafted.[126] He attracted a distinguished roster of contributors, including Sombart, Tönnies, Sydney and Beatrice Webb, Bernstein, and the feminist Lily von Gizycki, whom Braun soon married; feminism was thus understood to be part of the social question.[127] By the time Braun sold the journal in 1903 to its new editors—Max Weber, Sombart, and Edgar Jaffé—he could report that his mission had been accomplished; the new editors noted that all major countries had begun publishing labor statistics in the interim, which allowed the journal to move from an empirical to a theoretical emphasis—hence the new title, the *Archiv für Sozialwissenschaft und Sozialpolitik*.[128]

After 1900 there was a tendency to deemphasize the role of the state in solving the social question. Younger scholars such as Robert Wilbrandt and Bernhard Harms more often looked to independent cooperatives and mediation as positive measures; in 1911 a new seminar on cooperatives was founded at Halle.[129] Two years later, Max Weber's brother Alfred called for a reorientation of *Sozialpolitik*, to view "the social question of today as the question of saving the personality from absorption into the apparatus [of the state]."[130] Paradoxically, the first professorship in the *Staatswissenschaften* to be established with the help of private fortunes—those of the Jena optical manufacturer Ernst Abbe—was earmarked for *Sozialpolitik*. Abbe's father had been a spinner who had worked 15–16 hours a day, and Abbe himself had conducted an empirical study of his workers which showed them to be more productive when working 8 hours a day than the prevailing 9.[131]

Another specialty in the process of formation was insurance science. The requirements of the Bismarckian social insurance programs helped generate the need for special lectures devoted to the subject—and led to seminars in Göttingen (1895), Freiburg (1910), and Munich (1911). The Göttingen institute, under Lexis's direction, was designed to provide training for officials in both public and private sectors, while the Freiburg effort emphasized the public sector. This was a case where specialization and the interdisciplinary approach converged: the institutes brought together lectures in mathematics, economics, statistics, and law. The Munich institution was an extension of the statistical seminar.[132]

126. Heinrich Braun, "Zur Einführung," 1–2.

127. Alfred Meyer, *Feminism and Socialism*, 17–23. Conrad also included women, artisans, and the "educated proletariat" as part of the social question (*Grundriss*, 6th ed., 2: 210).

128. Braun, "Abschiedswort," vi; [M. Weber, Sombart, Jaffé], "Geleitwort der Herausgeber," v–vi.

129. Lindenlaub, *Richtungskämpfe*, 369–73. On Halle, see the university catalogues.

130. Alfred Weber, "Neuorientierung in der Sozialpolitik?" 10.

131. Oberschall, *Empirical Social Research*, 112–13. On Abbe, see Heuss, *Deutsche Gestalten*, 416.

132. On Göttingen: minutes of meeting 6 Sept. 1895, GPSA Dahlem, Rep. 76 Va Sect. 6 Tit. X no. 63, vol. 1: 2 (includes proposed curriculum); Prüfungsordnung für Versicherungsverständige,

One of the oldest divisions of *Volkswirtschaftspolitik*, namely agricultural policy, received much attention. The reasons were clear, given the agricultural crises of the 1880s and 1890s—and the noise created by the Farmers' League. There was also the perception that the reliance merely on improved techniques of fertilization to solve agricultural problems, as Liebig had urged, was no longer adequate: economic, social, and ethnic considerations were part of the picture. The leading crusader in this campaign to broaden the perception of agricultural policy had been Theodor von der Goltz, who taught agriculture at Königsberg, Jena, and Bonn. Goltz considered himself Schulze's successor in stressing the moral and ethical virtues of the farmer and the need to perpetuate them.[133] *Agrarpolitik* focused, however, on more concrete issues: farmer indebtedness and credit, land distribution, and the flight of agricultural laborers.[134] These were sensitive issues which affected a variety of conflicting interests—large landowners versus small, rural versus urban workers, and Germans versus Poles; they remained at the forefront of the *Verein*'s agenda into the early 1890s. The most famous example was the massive research project on the status of the laborers on the east Elbian estates; at issue was the massive migration of Germans from the landed estates east of the Elbe to the western industrial centers and their replacement by migrant Polish workers. Max Weber's contribution to the study in the early 1890s won him immediate renown as a scholar.[135] As is well known, Weber stressed the political as well as the economic aspects of the process. As he stated in his Freiburg inaugural speech,

> Our descendents will hold us responsible *not* for the type of economic organization that we hand down to them, but for the amount of elbow room in the world which we obtain and leave behind for them. Economic developmental processes are in the final analysis *power* struggles; . . . the science of economic policy is a *political* science" (emphasis in original).[136]

The predominant response of the *Agrarpolitiker* was a resettlement program that involved purchasing large estates and converting them into smaller farms—"inner colonization," in the words of its leading proponent, the conser-

---

85–86; on Freiburg: Bericht der rechts-und staatsws. und phil. Facultäten, 4 Nov. 1906, GLA, 235/ 7855; on Munich: Müller, ed. *Wissenschaftlichen Anstalten*, 33.

133. Wygodzinski, "Volkswirtschaftlichen Grundlagen der landwirtschaftlichen Betriebslehre," *ENTW,* no. 22: 17; see also Schumacher and Heinrich Dietzel, obituary for von der Goltz in Schumacher, *Chronik der Universität Bonn*, 1906, 2–5.

134. A good summary is Karl Grünberg, "Agrarpolitik," *ENTW,* no. 21.

135. Gorges, *Sozialforschung*, 242; Boese, *Geschichte*, 67–68.

136. Max Weber, "Nationalstaat und Volkswirtschaftspolitik," 14.

vative Max Sering.[137] Although Sering later applied such proposals to external colonization as well during World War I, he distanced himself from extreme nationalist rhetoric at the time. "The social task in Posen has been made significantly more difficult through the national-political goals that were mixed with it," he maintained in a speech honoring the Kaiser's birthday in 1892.[138] Sering's advocacy of inner colonization stemmed primarily from economic and social concerns over Germany's growing population, her consequent dependence on foreign agriculture, and the extreme class differences between large landowner and day-laborer. A shift from extensive to intensive agriculture would both lead to greater population density and increase crop yields; it would also satisfy the small farmer's demand for freedom and dignity.[139] The main object of Sering's concern was the small farmer; in this his liberal counterpart Brentano agreed. Indeed, by 1905, there seemed to be increasing agreement on this point among the ideological positions; even the socialists were giving up the position that small farms inevitably gave way to large ones.[140] The exception, of course, were the large landowners themselves, who used their influence on the bureaucracy to slow the pace of resettlement—as Sering noted with discouragement in 1912.[141]

After 1900, concern with agricultural policy was partly eclipsed by a burgeoning interest in commercial and colonial policy—again for transparent reasons. The topic of tariff protection had in fact been at the forefront of public discussion since 1890. It was inseparable from the agricultural issues in its highlighting of the conflicting interests of farmers and industrialists. Chancellor Leo Caprivi's liberal trade policies had elicited the rise of the Farmer's League, and the acrimony between agrarian protectionists and free-traders reached new heights during Bülow's first years as chancellor. Superimposed on this was the naval agitation, which reinforced the interest in international trade. Indeed, these issues were symptomatic of a broader awareness of Germany's role in a world economy which was also reflected in the universities. In addition to lectures on trade, those devoted to the economies of other countries went up from five between 1890 and 1895 to twenty-seven between 1905 and 1910. In addition to the "naval professors," economists with international contacts and expe-

137. Barkin, *Controversy,* 179–80; Boese, *Geschichte,* 68.

138. Sering, *Arbeiterfrage und Kolonisation,* 15. Sering referred to the hasty purchase of Polish estates which required much improvement before they could be redistributed.

139. Ibid., 8–10; *Verteilung des Grundbesitzes,* 29–31. On the Junkers' suspicion of Sering, see Barkin, *Controversy,* 181, who emphasizes Sering's pro-Junker statements.

140. Grünberg, "Agrarpolitik," *ENTW,* no. 21: 49–56, 63–64. For Brentano's support of intensive agriculture as a response to cheap grain from abroad, see his *Agrarpolitik,* 56–58, 133, 144.

141. Barkin, *Controversy,* 182.

rience were prized, such as Hermann Schumacher, who had spent his child-hood in Bogotá and New York as son of the German ambassador, or Karl Rathgen and Heinrich Waentig, who both spent extended time in Japan.[142] The foremost organizer in this area was Bernhard Harms, who foresook *Sozial-politik* for *Handelspolitik* when he moved from Jena to Kiel in 1908. Harms set about transforming the economics seminar there into the Institute for Sea Transport and World Economics, largely with private funding; it opened its doors in February, 1914. Meanwhile, Harms had decreed a new economic field, *Weltwirtschaft* (world economics), to complement *Privatwirtschaft* (business economics) and *Volkswirtschaft*, and launched a new journal, the *Weltwirtschaft-liches Archiv*, to bear it out. Like Braun in *Sozialpolitik*, Harms saw the need for a collecting point for data on international commerce, which had previously been lacking for Germany.[143]

No less a part of the international emphasis was the rapid expansion of lectures on colonial policy: the perceived need for Germany to catch up with Britain and France as a colonial power was widespread. In some cases, the profes-sors made no attempt to hide their patriotic zeal—the most flagrant case being that of Ernst Hasse, *Extraordinarius* for statistics at Leipzig, who became head of the Pan-German League. A historian of that movement has described him as "a man of boundless but humorless enthusiasm, volatility, and impatience."[144] Similar tones could be heard from the conservative Carl Ballod in Berlin, who ended his summary of *Kolonialpolitik* in Schmoller's *Festschrift* as follows:

> It would not only be racial and national suicide if one wants to leave the most fertile and extended areas of the globe that are at this time thinly populated exclusively to the lower colored races, but this also must lead to the decline of culture and civilization![145]

Yet aside from the spectacular growth of lectures, *Kolonialpolitik* failed to exhibit the other accoutrements of a specialty—neither journals (apart from the popu-lar *Deutsche Kolonialzeitung*) nor institutes (apart from a private one in Hamburg unconnected to a a university) emerged. The reasons were probably (1) that German scholarship was heavily indebted to French and British sources, re-flecting the relative age and strength of the respective empires themselves, and (2) that *Kolonialpolitik* drew heavily on other well-established disciplines such as geography and history, rather than having a distinct subject matter of its own.

---

142. On Schumacher, see Wendt, "Schumacher," 150–51; on Rathgen, see Gundlach, *Catolo-gus Professorum Academiae Marburgiensis*, no. 817; on Waentig, see "Tagebuch," *Chronik der Universität Halle*, 1909.

143. Harms, "Institut für Weltwirtschaft," 309–11.

144. Chickering, *We Men*, 53.

145. Ballod, "Wissenschaftlichen Ansichten über Kolonialpolitik," *ENTW*, no. 30: 11.

The Göttingen professor Gustav Cohn called it "a bundle of cut plants which have no roots."[146] Nevertheless, the sheer increase of lectures in this area attests to the breadth of academic participation in the imperialist agenda. Colonial studies also fit in with Bethmann-Hollweg's program of spreading German culture abroad; he favored "the full equality of colonial studies with other disciplines."[147] A further subdivision of *Handelspolitik* dealt with transportation issues (*Verkehrspolitik,*) which likewise blossomed at the time of public controversy over the building of the fleet and the Elbe-Weser canal, and which further divided agrarians and industrialists.[148]

It should be evident from the preceding discussion that much of the apparent specialization within *Volkswirtschaftspolitik* was more superficial than substantive. The issues raised by agricultural, commerical, colonial, and social policy were closely linked and were perceived as such by the economists themselves. Because these issues were controversial, the economists' treatment of them was never exclusively a discourse among experts, but also discourse among shapers of public opinion. Moreover, the controversies were linked to an underlying question that was also thematized: how to evaluate Germany's frenetic economic development and predict its implications. The discussion of this question, triggered by the tariff debates of the 1890s, reached a peak of intensity between 1897 and 1905 in the form of the controversy over whether Germany should be predominantly an agrarian or an industrial state.[149] Here too there was a reasonably clear division of opinion between conservatives and liberals across generational lines, with Wagner and Brentano leading their respective frays in favor of agricultural and industrial development respectively. The label fails to convey, however, the complexity of the discussion. Despite the exaggerated prophecies that accompanied such loaded issues at the beginning, both sides came to realize that the issue was one of proper balance and proportion between the two sectors.[150] The crux of the argument was how Germany's rap-

146. Cohn, *Universitätsfragen und Erinnerungen* (Stuttgart: Enke, 1913), 34; see also Günther Anton's unflattering review of German colonial literature compared to the French in *JNS* 85 (1905): 534–38.

147. Quoted in Jarausch, *Students, Society, and Politics*, 223.

148. Barkin, *Controversy,* 215–17, 222; on the implications of it and the naval campaign on transport issues, see Wiedenfeld, "Volkswirtschaftliche Einfluss der modernen Verkehrsmittel," *SF*, no. 29: 28.

149. See Barkin, *Controversy,* chaps. 4–5; Herkner, *Arbeiterfrage,* 53–96; Schmoller, *Grundriss,* 2: 645–46.

150. See Wagner's repeated protestations to this effect in his *Agrar-und Industriestaat* (9, 15, 86, 221), where he accused Brentano of oversimplifying his position. Brentano's concern with maintaining a strong agricultural sector is evident in his *Agrarpolitik* (39–40, 58, 144). Barkin's treatment emphasizes the polarizing aspects, to my mind to the point of distortion, particularly of Wagner's views. Barkin's paraphrase "that industrialism was a transitory stage that arose in response to rural overpopulation and would disappear with the recognition that the remedy created more problems

idly growing population could be sustained, and whether such rates of increase were desirable in the future. Brentano viewed export-oriented industrialization as the answer, enabling a country to sustain a much higher population density than could an agrarian society. Wagner gloomily predicted that such rapid expansion—whether of population, industry, or exports—would only lead to emigration or imperialism or both, as the example of Great Britain demonstrated. "Perhaps it is . . . the mark of a future," he wrote, "where peoples vie with each other in a 'struggle for space'. . . but the political, social, and ethical scruples regarding this path are then pushed aside."[151] When it came to agriculture, the two sides differed on what products could be profitably grown on German soil and on how much land could be converted to labor-intensive, diversified cultivation.[152] Wagner argued that grain products would remain the staple of production and deserved protection (though he did not go so far as the extremists in the Reichstag); Brentano argued that such grain prices would adversely affect the working class.[153]

Much of the debate was conducted at the level of statistics and their interpretation, and one can agree with Schmoller's assessment that the controversy had an enlightening effect.[154] It made both sides aware of how numbers could be manipulated and of the need for precision. Nevertheless, such empirical issues were not completely separable from basic differences of worldview and ideology. Conservatives and liberals did differ in their assessments of the Junkers and their role in German society. Brentano, the Webers, and Naumann on the liberal side saw them as obstacles to progress and tended to deprecate any defense of agrarian interests as supporting them; conservatives such as Wagner and Sering, although more concerned about the small farmer than the large landowner, tended to defend the Junkers when pushed into a corner. The conservatives remained pessimistic about modernization, while the liberals were optimistic; the conservatives were also less deterministic than the liberals, who tended to rest their case on the inevitability of it all. "Despite all romantic enthusiasm for land and agriculture," claimed Brentano, "people will be driven to the city and to industry. And so it will remain as long as *dira necessitas* determines the destiny of human beings."[155] Wagner countered, "We do not deny that such developments . . . have something 'natural' about them. But they are

---

than it solved" (*Controversy*, 153) seems to me incompatible with Wagner's assertions that prioritizing agriculture and industry were matters of degree.

    151. Wagner, *Agrar-und Industriestaat*, 83.

    152. Ibid., 108–10; Brentano, *Agrarpolitik*, 54–59.

    153. Brentano, *Agrarpolitik*, 59; Wagner, *Agrar-und Industriestaat*, 126.

    154. Schmoller, *Grundriss*, 2: 645. See, for example, the exchange between Alfred Weber and Ludwig Pohle, "Deutschland am Scheidewege," 1294–1305; 1701–1717.

    155. Brentano, "Über Landwirtschaft und Industrie," quoted in Herkner, *Arbeiterfrage*, 217.

on the other hand not so far removed from human will and influence through goal-directed human action or through legislative or administrative measures."[156]

The significance of such ideological differences was exaggerated, however, by the forum in which the debate was conducted, namely, the press. Wanting to remain in the public sphere, the economists interspersed their intricate assessments of facts and figures with name calling and simplification, so that the connection between economic arguments and the issues of social and political hegemony in Germany would be kept before the public eye. Indeed, the question of the appropriate forum became increasingly an issue in the debate itself. "It is the evil of small articles and occasional lectures," wrote Wagner to Brentano, "that one cannot possibly present and substantiate one's views sufficiently."[157] The liberal Alfred Weber took his conservative opponent, Ludwig Pohle, to task for mixing scientific and journalistic polemics in his book *Germany at the Crossroads*.[158]

It was this heightened consciousness of rhetoric, occurring just when Bülow's manipulation of the press was in full swing, that finally disrupted the increasingly fragile equilibrium between professional and public discourse that had held up to 1905. The scene was the *Verein* meeting of that year, which witnessed a division within the organization more serious than any since 1879. Although the split was triggered by a debate on the regulation of cartels, the crucial issue was the type of rhetoric appropriate to the *Verein*'s meetings. Naumann had called Schmoller's proposals for state regulation "nonsense" (to much applause), and Schmoller countered by calling Naumann's speech "demagoguery." The seriousness of such breaches of etiquette lay precisely in the dual role of the *Verein* as both a scholarly forum and shaper of public opinion that Schmoller had fashioned for it. Differences of opinion were allowed, even encouraged, but not in "demagogic" language—for this, Schmoller feared, could split the right wing from the left and thereby render the *Verein* ineffective.[159] Schmoller was thus faced with the same problem in the *Verein* that his friend Bülow faced in the Reichstag: that of holding together an increasingly restive coalition. Neither succeeded for long in patching over the differences. Bülow was soon faced with the *Daily Telegraph* affair in 1908, in which the Kaiser's inflammatory rhetoric had serious political consequences; Schmoller was soon faced with the even more virulent value-judgment controversy in the *Verein* in 1909 and after.

In fact, these disputes within the *Verein* served to focus the multiple disrup-

156. Wagner, *Agrar-und Industriestaat*, 29.
157. Wagner to Brentano, 20 March 1901, *Briefe*, 353.
158. A. Weber and Pohle, "Deutschland am Scheidewege," 1305.
159. Boese, *Geschichte*, 113–22, esp. 118–19; Lindenlaub, *Richtungskämpfe*, 417–18.

tive forces which had been building in intensity, such as the dissatisfaction of the business-oriented group and the impatience of the younger generation. If the former was perhaps an indication of the tendency to specialization, the latter was finding expression in the the interdisciplinary approach.

INTERDISCIPLINARY TRENDS: SOCIOLOGY, HISTORY, ANTHROPOLOGY

Much of the interchange between economics, philosophy, history, and biology took place under the umbrella term of *sociology*. While we are inclined to think of sociology as a newly emerging specialty within the field of the social sciences, this makes more sense for the 1920s than for the Wilhelminian period. With the possible exception of Tönnies, the so-called founding fathers of German sociology (Simmel, Max Weber, and Sombart) were much less goal-directed in laying the foundations for such a specialty than is usually thought. Rather than being self-conscious advocates of a particular discipline, they were drawn to a set of substantive issues and problems (such as the nature of capitalism) which were larger than could be handled by any single approach. As they worked through these issues, they gradually became aware of a greater need for clearer concepts and methods; the term *sociology* expressed the need as well as the initial tentative results. For these reasons, it had an appeal for philosophers as well as economists. The varied listings for sociology in the university catalogs reflected this unstable status (see table 14); the Berlin philosophical faculty could still refer to it in 1900 as a "playground of half-sciences"—even as it recommended Simmel for appointment as *Extraordinarius* in philosophy.[160] The founding of the German Sociological Association in 1909 admittedly marked a turning point in the institutionalization of the discipline, but the variety of positions and approaches aired in its meetings revealed how gradual the process continued to be. In short, the innovations of the 1890s and 1900s constituted a period of experimentation, resembling in some respects the 1840s and 1850s—if under the aegis of clear concepts rather than unifying symbols.[161]

160. Memo of phil. faculty, 2 Feb. 1900, GPSA Dahlem, Rep. 76 Va Sect. 2 Tit. IV no. 5, vol. 10: 331–32 (Berlin, appts.).

161. Dirk Käsler has suggested that the social background of the early sociologists helps explain the origins of that discipline. He points out that Simmel, Tönnies, Weber, and Sombart came from the commercial bourgeoisie rather than the *Bildungsbürgertum*. See Käsler, *Frühe Deutsche Soziologie*, 335 ff. According to Käsler, the conflicts between the pragmatic world of industrialists and merchants and the celebrated ideals of "culture" to which their sons aspired gave the generational conflict a particular intensity and focus for this group, which he traces in younger sociologists of the 1910s and 1920s as well. This approach is illuminating in some cases. For Sombart and Weber, their preoccupation with capitalism clearly stemmed from personal experience. But there is no indication of such conflict in Tönnies' case; on the contrary, his father agreed to support him financially in his studies at age twenty-two. (Tönnies to Paulsen, 26 Nov 1877, in Paulsen and Tönnies, *Briefwechsel*, 5). I believe Käsler goes too far in claiming that the pursuit of sociology was

Table 14 *Lectures in Sociology by Main Subject Area of Professor, 1885–1914*

	Philosophy	Ethnology	History	Economics	Other/Unknown
1885–89	3	1	9	2	5
1890–94	6	3	11	0	5
1895–99	12	3	10	2	4
1900–04	7	5	13	4	0
1905–09	13	4	6	14	3
1910–14*	4	4	9	21	1

Source: University catalogues; see appendix.
*Winter semester 1914–15 not included.

A case in point was Simmel. As a popular lecturer at Berlin who taught the subject in the 1890s, Simmel was probably the first to bring a measure of public recognition to sociology in Germany. He turned to it as a reaction to the collectivist assumptions of Social Darwinism which he had formerly held. He began instead to develop a picture of society composed of individuals—and to examine the principles for ordering relations and interactions among them. Sociology for him was to be a science of forms and abstract constructions, related to the other social sciences roughly as geometry was related to the natural sciences—though Simmel was quick to stress the limits of such analogies.[162] He had in mind such dimensions as subordination and superordination, conflict, and the conditions of group membership. But Simmel was never one to push formal or systematic thinking too far; indeed, after 1900 he moved increasingly away from sociology.[163] Although he helped found the German Sociological Association, Simmel left it in 1913 to pursue philosophical questions and finally received a professorship in philosophy at Strassburg the following year.[164]

In the very years that Simmel was turning away from sociology, Tönnies was more explicitly embracing it. His research on Hobbes and Spinoza in his early years had led to the distinction of *Gemeinschaft* and *Gesellschaft* (community and society) of 1887, which he used in two ways: (1) as an abstract typology of social and psychological relations, and (2) as the basis for a cyclical theory of history, in which *Gemeinschaft* evolved into *Gesellschaft*, both in classical antiquity and in modern times. It was only gradually that Tönnies realized that these uses were distinct, and it was after 1900 that he separated them into "pure"

---

a matter of "social climbing" (350). While it is true that *Bildung* had a higher social status than *Besitz*, it is hard to see why these intellectuals would have undergone the privation that came from their disciplinary choices if improved social status was their goal; it would have been much easier to become a specialist in economics rather than someone with a still indeterminate disciplinary affiliation.

162. Simmel, *Soziologie*, 9–12.
163. Ibid., 20–21; Frisby, *Simmel*, 31.
164. Frisby, *Simmel*, 15, 33.

and "applied" sociology.[165] He became the first president of the German Sociological Society, but assumed a professorship of sociology only in 1921, at the age of 66.

Max Weber's quest for clear concepts likewise long antedated his use of the term *sociology*—which he used sparingly and hesitatingly only after 1908.[166] As a professor of economics in the 1890s, Weber availed himself of Menger's notion of abstract concepts from the *Methodenstreit* with Schmoller. Like Menger, Weber stressed the constructive aspect of such concepts—the deliberate accentuation of certain aspects of reality at the expense of others—which he distinguished from inductive generalizations. Weber had used the concept of *homo economicus* as an example already in his Heidelberg lectures of 1898—in his own words, "a *constructed* 'economic subject' . . . as opposed to the empirical person," in which all noneconomic qualities are ignored and full knowledge of all variables and the most expedient use of resources are assumed.[167] This was an early version of what Weber later called an "ideal type" in his methodological essay of 1904. The purpose of such concepts was not to look for confirming examples within empirical reality, but rather to provide a basis for comparing and contrasting the concept with reality, thereby arriving at a more differentiated understanding of the latter. His well-documented encounters with the neo-Kantian philosopher Heinrich Rickert and the law professor Georg Jellinek broadened Weber's use of the ideal type, which he fashioned as a distinctive feature of the "cultural sciences."

Rickert also contributed the notion of "value relevance" (*Wertbezogenheit*) as defining the subject matter of these sciences: that which society perceives as important and worth knowing. One takes the trouble to construct such types in order to isolate what is meaningful and worth knowing in the empirical flow. For example, the construction of *homo economicus* in classical and Mengerian economics served as a model for purposive, calculating rationality—one of Weber's most important ideal types. One of Weber's most distinctive contributions to the task of clarification was to separate "value relevance" from "value judgments": one can empirically analyze causal relationships and make informed predictions within the sphere delimited by value-relevant concepts without commending or condemning the results from an ethical standpoint. This set Weber apart from the older generation of *Kathedersozialisten,* who had failed to make this distinction in their self-appointed capacity as transmitters of the "highest ideals."[168] Weber's methodological essay was the most pointed attempt

165. Jacoby, *Tönnies,* 80; Tönnies, "The Nature of Sociology," in *Tönnies on Sociology,* 106–7.

166. Tenbruck, "Abschied der 'Wissenschaftslehre'?" 97.

167. Weber, *Grundriss zu den Vorlesungen,* 8. See also Schön, "Gustav Schmoller und Max Weber," 60–62.

168. Weber "Objektivität," esp. 151, 157.

to correct some of the internal contradictions of social science as laid down by Schmoller; the other early attempts at formation of sociological concepts had the same effect.

The same was true of the use of *history* by the generation of the 1890s. Recall that Schmoller had denied the existence of historical laws but sanctioned the use of certain long-term interpretive schemas—without clearly defining the difference between the two. The generation of the 1890s was more explicit about these long-term schemas, emphasizing comparative morphological patterns and overarching causal explanations. A prominent example was Schmoller'student Kurt Breysig. Moving in the mid–1890s from Prussian history to comparative European history and then to universal history, Breysig's work elicited the same opposition from most historians that Karl Lamprecht's broad-ranging schemes had done a few years before. Not surprisingly, his attempt to found a seminar in comparative history at Berlin in 1907 was rejected by the faculty—but defended in a minority vote by the three *Staatswissenschaftler* Schmoller, Wagner, and Sering, who saw in this "border area between politics and economics on one side and history on the other . . . a great future" and offered Breysig a limited place in the economics seminar.[169]

More appealing was the effort to account for long-term trends through causal explanations. As in the 1840s, the rapid industrial growth at the end of the century fed the need to understand such large-scale changes through theories of modernization, in which the notion of historical stages played a prominent role. This was the period when Marx was finally assimilated into academic economic discourse.[170] It was Marx's determinism which intially appealed to Sombart, and he sought to carry that scheme further in his two-volume history, *Modern Capitalism*, in 1902, which was based on a theory of developmental stages. The capitalist stage was one of four; the others were agricultural, artisanal, and the future socialist-cooperative stage.[171] Contrasting his approach to Schmoller's, he sought "a unified ordered explanation drawn from the prevalant dominant motivations of leading economic subjects of a given epoch."[172] Yet Sombart's work was never just schematic; his ability to integrate empirical detail and generalizing frameworks gave the work lasting value.

Sombart's Marxism contained an aesthetic dimension. He likened it to naturalism in literature and *plein air* in art.[173] In the preface to *Modern Capitalism*, he claimed that the task of synthesizing explanatory theory and empirical detail

---

169. quoted in vom Brocke, *Breysig*, 98.
170. Lindenlaub, *Richtungskämpfe*, 274–91, who correctly stresses the relative neglect of Marx prior to 1890.
171. Sombart, *Moderne Kapitalismus*, 1: xxxi–ii.
172. Ibid., 1: xxi.
173. Lenger, *Sombart*, 82.

was that of an artist. "It will require an education through generations," he wrote, "before truly a race of artists [will] pursue science, before in our case an ethical economics will be superseded by an aesthetic economics."[174] Marx himself was such an artist, Sombart claimed six years later.[175] Such passages reveal another common fascination of the generation of the 1890s, reflected in their many personal links with artists and writers.[176] The pervasive influence of Nietzsche, who also held out an aesthetic ideal for society as distinct from an ethical or political one, was a related phenomenon.

These passages also help one to understand Sombart's "aristocratic turn" after 1900, when he gradually moved from historical materialism to an aggressive nationalism. There were numerous way-stations in this development—a renunciation of political involvement, an embracing of the distinction between the natural and human sciences—reflecting an intellectual restlessness similar to Simmel's.[177] After 1909, Sombart turned increasingly to distinguishing between the "heroic" capitalism of the entrepreneur and the calculating capitalism of the merchant, often Jewish.[178] He insisted that his portraits of such types were free of value judgments. "I shall adduce my proofs," he wrote in *The Jews and Modern Capitalism* (1913), "that they may be easily followed . . . by the assimilationist Jew no less than the Nationalist . . . by the anti-Semite as by his opponent."[179] Yet his use of the notion of the typical was quite different from Weber's: rather than viewing types as abstract tools with which to compare and contrast concrete reality, Sombart viewed them as essences—such as the Jewish "collective soul"—which were contained in and confirmed by that concrete reality.[180] They were the basis for filling out a picture rather than for testing the validity of causal relationships.

In any case, Marxism was not the only overarching scheme to find an audience during this period. Bücher's popular *Origins of Political Economy* presented an evolution from domestic to municipal to national economy,[181] and Tönnies originally presented his distinction of *Gemeinschaft* and *Gesellschaft* as a historical

174. Sombart, *Moderne Kapitalismus*, 1: xxx.

175. Sombart, "Karl Marx und die soziale Wissenschaft," 446.

176. Tönnies was befriended in his early years by the novelist Theodor Storm; Breysig and Sombart socialized with *Jugendstil* and expressionist artists respectively; Breysig, Simmel and Weber all had brief but intensive contacts with Stefan George and his circle. On Tönnies, see Jacoby, *Tönnies*, 2; on Breysig, Brocke, *Breysig*, 75, 159–70; on Sombart, Brocke, "Sombart," 37, Lenger, *Sombart*, 155, 174; Liebersohn, *Fate and Utopia*, 144–51; Lepenies, *Between Literature and Science*, chap. 12.

177. See Lindenlaub, *Richtungskämpfe*, 330–37; Bruch, *Wissenschaft*, 185–89; Mitzmann, *Sociology and Estrangement*, 209; Schaff, *Fleeing the Iron Cage*, 203–5.

178. Mitzman, *Sociology and Estrangement*, 208, 238.

179. Sombart, *Jews and Modern Capitalism*, 158.

180. Ibid., 253.

181. Bücher, *Entstehung der Volkswirtschaft*, 108.

morphology, seminally influenced by Marx.[182] In the 1890s, Tönnies was among the first to identify the growth of capitalism with the more general historical tendency to rationalization, that is, "to utilize and extend the calculability of events, the command of nature"—a notion which figured prominently in Weber's *Protestant Ethic and the Spirit of Capitalism* as well.[183]

The willingness of the 1890s generation to embrace such causally deterministic schemes also had political implications. It made them impatient with any attempts to "turn back the clock" in the name of preserving antiquated classes such as landowners and artisans. As already noted, Weber attacked the *Junkers* in his research on East Prussian agricultural policy in the 1890s and in his Freiburg inaugural address.[184] Sombart emphatically stated at the 1899 meeting of the *Verein* that "to want to be moral at the cost of economic progress is the beginning of the end of the whole development of civilization."[185] It was this belief in the inevitability of capitalism and the futility of conservative resistance that made Sombart and Weber allies of the liberal Brentano in the *Verein* and thus strengthened the liberal faction of that group after 1900. Indeed, it was the question of state regulation of cartels which triggered the debate that almost split the *Verein* in 1905: Schmoller's proposal to have state officials as members of cartels over a certain size aroused the scorn of younger members— in this case Max Weber and Naumann—who viewed the concentration of big business as part of the irreversible tide of modern history.[186] Such conflicts were illustrative of the general heightening of tension between the bourgeoisie and aristocracy in Germany in Wilhelminian era.

The same conditions that fostered an imaginative use of history were, incidentally, largely unfavorable to statistics. This was a period of little innovation in that field. Granted, the *Verein* continued to turn out thorough empirical studies of economic and social topics with great industry but not with great sophistication. An attempt to study worker psychology through questionnaires proved to be disappointing, both in terms of the number of responses and the level of analysis of the data.[187] An exception was Tönnies, who alternated his historical and philosophical meditations with personal interviews of some six thousand prisoners in Schleswig-Holstein from 1874 to 1913.[188] Tönnies was looking for correlations between rural and urban backgrounds and the number and types

182. Tönnies, *Gemeinschaft und Gesellschaft*, xxiii, 57, 140, 217, 219.

183. Tönnies, "Historicism, Rationalism, and the Industrial System," in *Tönnies on Sociology,* 273.

184. Weber, "Nationalstaat," 17–18.

185. VFS, *Verhandlungen . . . 1899*, quoted in Mitzman, *Sociology and Estrangement*, 157.

186. Boese, *Geschichte*, 113; Lindenlaub, *Richtungskämpfe*, 410.

187. Oberschall, *Empirical Social Research*, 130; Kern, *Empirische Sozialforschung*, 100.

188. Jacoby, *Tönnies*, 217.

of crimes committed.[189] In doing so, he devised a method which avoided the notion of the "*homme moyen*" of Quetelet, relying instead on ranking and grouping his data as a basis for comparing variables with each other.[190] Nevertheless, Tönnies criticized reliance on purely numerical statistics, claiming they made sense only to someone who knew the concrete circumstances in which they were collected. His proposed "sociography" to replace statistics amounted to a restatement of the Achenwall-Schlözer position.[191]

Another ingredient in the interdisciplinary mix was *anthropology*—or rather that amorphous set of overlapping fields known at the time as ethnology, *Völkerpsychologie*, racial hygiene, and so on, which dealt with the issues raised by social Darwinism: the collective traits of geographically delimited groups, the role of hereditary and environmental influences on them, and the means to their preservation and "improvement." These issues were of course not new to historically minded economists; Schmoller devoted an entire chapter of his *Grundriss* to the geographical conditions of the economy and another to races and peoples. His cautious pronouncement that "our knowledge of the foregoing area . . . has certainly not attained the degree of development that would be desirable for use in economic investigations . . . but nevertheless . . . is not without value and scientific meaning" may be taken as representative of his generation and the younger one as well.[192] Tönnies and Breysig both read the ethnologist Lewis Henry Morgan in their formative years; Leipzig became a center for the discussion of such issues, via an informal circle that boasted Lamprecht, Bücher, Wundt, and the geographer Gustav Ratzel as members.[193]

Social Darwinism was of course fraught with controversial political and ideological implications. These included not only the obvious issues of racism and imperialism, but also that of physical degeneration, that is, whether industrialization and urbanization were leading to the deterioration of the health and life span of the German people—as August Bebel persuasively argued in his popular book *Women under Socialism*—and in that event, how it was to be corrected. Social Darwinism was thus inseparable from the social reform movements and found expression in such causes as temperance and the fight

189. Tönnies, "The Place of Birth of Criminals," in *Tönnies on Sociology*, 241–47.

190. Jacoby, *Tönnies*, 214–18; Oberschall, *Empirical Social Research*, 51–63.

191. Tönnies, "Statistics and Sociography," in *Tönnies on Sociology*, 235, 237. Another exception was the mathematical statistician Ladislaus von Bortkiewicz, who studied with Lexis and taught at Berlin. Although he was active in the *Verein*, his mathematical writings were widely respected but little understood. See Gimbel, "Bortkiewicz," 128–31. Porter maintains that this period witnessed an increasing split between mathematical and social-scientific concerns (Porter, *Rise of Statistical Thinking*, 254).

192. Schmoller, *Grundriss*, 1: 158.

193. On Tönnies, see Jacoby, *Tönnies*, 18; on Breysig, Brocke, *Breysig*, 58–61; on the Leipzig circle, W. Smith, *Politics and the Sciences of Culture*, 208–9.

against tuberculosis.[194] Given the alarm over socialism in the late 1890s, it is not surprising that conservatives should try to channel these public health concerns away from changing the social and economic structure and toward improving the hereditary traits of the nation. Such a move was initiated by the steelmaker Friedrich Krupp, who anonymously donated a prize of thirty thousand marks for the best scientific essays on "what can we learn from the principles of evolution for the development and laws of states." The judges for the competition included the biologist Ernst Haeckel as well as the economist Conrad. The incident of the "Krupp prize"—his identity was soon revealed—only served to show how deeply divided social Darwinists were from one another; in a manner parallel to the naval campaign that was taking place at the same time, the social and biological scientists took great pains to distance themselves from the Aryan ideologues and the more zealous advocates of eugenics and to secure academic respectability for their ideas.[195] For this reason, some were drawn to sociology.

Among the leading figures who attempted to bring Darwinism to sociology were the eugenicist Alfred Ploetz and the "social hygienicist" Alfred Grotjahn. Ploetz was more cautious in public than other eugenicists and hence more effective, urging that the hereditary and social components of variation be treated as an open question. He believed that the scientific study of variation was the surest basis for a eugenics policy—and for balancing the conflicting claims of humanitarian aid and racial health.[196] If Ploetz nevertheless accentuated the hereditary side of the debate, Grotjahn took the opposite approach, emphasizing such factors as nutritional levels in the urban population. A student of Tönnies while in medical school and later a participant in Schmoller's seminar, Grotjahn had associated with reformist socialists in the 1890s and claimed to be the first medical *Kathedersozialist*.[197] Grotjahn avoided the term *race* and spoke strictly of social hygiene; he nevertheless was willing to give more authority to medical doctors in eugenic decisions than did Ploetz.[198]

The writings of the Social Darwinists had an effect on the innovative social thinkers similar to that of the neo-Kantian philosophers: they served as a stimulus to sharpen their own conceptual distinctions, in particular the difference between the biological, the psychological, and the peculiarly social aspects of their field of inquiry. Thus Max Weber, Sombart, and Edgar Jaffé, when they

194. On these interconnections, see Weindling, *Health, Race, and German Politics*, chaps. 1–3.
195. Ibid., 112–20.
196. Ibid., 123, 130–31; Ploetz, "Sozialpolitik und Rassenhygiene," 416.
197. Weindling, *Health, Race, and German Politics*, 221–22; Tutzke, *Grotjahn*, 25. Schmoller drew Grotjahn to Althoff's attention in 1903 and tried unsuccessfully to get the Berlin medical faculty to accept him as a *Privatdozent* in 1905; Grotjahn attained this position only in 1912.
198. Weindling, *Health, Race, and German Politics*, 223–24.

assumed the editorship of the *Archiv für Sozialwissenschaft und Sozialpolitik* in 1904, called special attention to "those problems . . . which are customarily labeled socio-anthropological. . . . We would like to contribute our part to overcoming in the future the dilettantish way in which these border-questions between biology and social science have previously been treated."[199] The main pathbreaker in this critical activity was undoubtedly Tönnies, who actually entered the Krupp competition and won honorable mention; at Schmoller's request, he reviewed the winning entries for the *Jahrbuch*, which resulted in a bitter polemic with the first-prize winner, Wilhelm Schallmeyer. Tönnies found Schallmeyer's leap from the physical to the sociopolitical entirely too facile, arguing that intelligent and creative minds may possibly be housed in frail and unhealthy bodies. He strongly objected to Schallmeyer's proposed prohibitions on marriage and reproduction.[200] He reiterated the irreducibility of the psychological categories of will to biological factors—as he had done in *Gemeinschaft und Gesellschaft*—and accused the Darwinists of imprecision in the way they defined the "fittest."[201] This became the basis for Tönnies's working-out of a more clearly defined level of *social* interaction as distinct from both the biological and the psychological—a level characterized by custom, ethics, law, religion, public opinion, and so on.[202] His demand for a more differentiated set of categories paralleled the critiques of Simmel and others of social psychology, particularly the assumption of *Völkerpsychologie* that each nation shared certain psychological traits.[203] Nevertheless, Tönnies was far from regarding the issue of the relationship between race and society as closed, and advocated a subdivision on sociobiology in the German Sociological Association.

THE JURISTIC SCIENCES OF STATE

These interdisciplinary explorations raised anew the question of the relationship between the ecosocial and juristic sciences of state. Was it at all meaningful on the eve of the First World War still to speak of a canon of sciences of state which spanned both sets of disciplines? As on most issues, professional opinion was divided. The belief in the old canon was still surprisingly strong, as is evident in the proposals to transfer professorial chairs in economics to the law faculties, creating in effect faculties of law and *Staatswissenschaft*, with a separate

199. [Max Weber, Sombart, Edgar Jaffé], "Geleitwort der Herausgeber," v.

200. Tönnies, "Anwendung der Deszendenztheorie," 148–50, 158, 170. On the polemic as a whole, see Jacoby, *Tönnies*, 153–55; Weindling, *Health, Race, and German Politics*, 121–22.

201. Tönnies, "Anwendung der Deszendenztheorie," 191, 248.

202. Tönnies, "Wesen der Soziologie," 350, 356, 361. Tönnies divides the purely sociological categories into social relations, social will, and social groups.

203. Simmel, "Wesen der Sozial-Psychologie," 285–86; Eulenburg, "Möglichkeit und die Aufgaben einer Socialpsychologie," 206–7. W. Smith, *Politics and the Sciences of Culture*, 127–28, makes the point that *Völkerpsychologie* was cut off from experimental psychology as well.

doctorate in the latter. On Max Weber's initiative, the University of Freiburg approved such a merger in 1896; on Althoff's initiative, the newly created University of Münster incorporated the same arrangement in 1902.[204] The movement was given a further boost in the Stumm era, when some conservative politicians believed that the pernicious influence of the *Kathedersozialisten* would be diminished if they were lodged in the legal faculty.[205] Nevertheless, the public debate revealed the divisions among the economists themselves over where their discipline belonged.[206] So did the results of an inquiry from the Prussian Ministry of Culture in 1909 on whether a gradual transition to faculties of law and state science was desirable. Of the nine Prussian universities, six of the legal faculties favored the change, compared to two of the philosophical faculties. The economists were split, with nine in favor, six opposed.[207] One group argued for the substantive unity of economics and law; the other argued for its growing affinity with history and philosophy. As the older professors retired, however, the ministry negotiated with the universities, so that by the end of the First World War, all except Berlin and Bonn had made the transition. Thus, despite the diversity of the legal sciences and the social sciences, the notion of the sciences of state as a curricular entity remained alive.

In any event, the juristic sciences of state underwent the same double process of specialization and interdisciplinary broadening as did the social. The former took place in administrative law, while general state law followed the latter course.

It was recognized at the time that administrative law had completed the transition to a full-fledged juristic discipline, moving from a classificatory to a deductive model. This was the accomplishment of Otto Mayer, a professor at Strassburg and Leipzig, whose systematic *German Administrative Law* of 1895 constituted the turning point.[208] Mayer's accomplishment was to go beyond the concrete areas of administrative activity derived from police science (e.g., health, economics, transportation, finance) to develop an organizing principle based on relations between administrator and subject (e.g., command, permission, punishment, appeal). The parallel with Gerber's and Laband's transformation of state law a generation earlier was apparent—but misleading at the level of substantive conclusions. Mayer's work was in fact part of an interna-

204. Biesenbach, *Nationalökonomie*, 213–15; Brocke, "System Althoff," 50.

205. Lindenfeld, "Education of Prussian Higher Civil Servants," 214.

206. Ibid.

207. Memos of Prussian phil. and jurist. faculties, 1909, GPSA Dahlem, Rep. 76 Va Sect. 1 Tit. III, 265, 271–396 (Spruch-Kollegien . . . sowie juristische Fakultäten uüberhaupt). The ministerial inquiry, which strongly favored the merger, may be found in UA Halle, Juristische Fakultät, Tit. II no. 8: 31–33 (Wever to curators, 1 Feb. 1909). Among the proponents were Wagner, Conrad, Lexis, and Wolf; among the opponents were Schmoller, Sering, and Dietzel.

208. Stolleis, *Geschichte des öffentlichen Rechts*, 2: 404.

tional trend, a product of an increasingly legalistic and less arbitrary administrative practice in all major European countries; Mayer himself had published a major work on French administrative law.[209] Moreover, his system was less authoritarian in its implications than Laband's: he distinguished administrative law from administrative acts as involving dual obligations of officials and subjects alike.[210] It encompassed the rights of self-administrative bodies. It was the binding nature of these rights and duties that distinguished current German administrative law from that of a police state.

The years following the appearance of Mayer's work were ones of consolidation for administrative law under the new paradigm, which appealed to practicing administrators as well as academics.[211] Under such conditions, voices for a nonjuridical administrative science were isolated.[212] One of the casualties of this arrangement was the absence of any systematic treatment of bureaucratic organization or clear overview of the spheres of competence of federal, state, and local agencies—a lack that would be sorely felt during the First World War.[213]

In state law, in contrast, the restlessness of the 1890s bred a dissatisfaction with legal positivism and the attempt to excise all sociological, psychological, and philosophical considerations from the study of the state. Indeed, jurisprudence in general held relatively little stimulation for budding social scientists in the 1890s—as shown by the case of Max Weber. Originally trained in commercial law, Weber forsook this "relatively barren province" for economics, which offered greater opportunities for political engagement.[214] But these very conditions also brought about a reversal in the thinking of some legal theorists who were open to the new impulses from the social sciences.[215] One aspect of this

209. Heyen, "Entwicklungsbedingungen," 23.
210. Otto Mayer, *Deutsches Verwaltungsrecht,* 1: 83. He also believed in the separation of powers, unlike Laband (1: 70). See Schiera, *Laboratorium,* 127–35.
211. Stolleis, "Verwaltungsrechtswissenschaft," *DV,* 3: 101; On closeness to praxis, see Stolleis, *Geschichte des öffentlichen Rechts,* 2: 405; Heyen, "Segmentation institutionelle," 208–9 (a comparative study of France and Germany).
212. One of the few was Ferdinand Schmid at Leipzig. See his inaugural lecture, "Bedeutung der Verwaltungslehre," 193–224.
213. Stolleis mentions only one such work, which appeared in 1914 ("Verwaltungsrechtswissenschaft," *DV,* 3: 101).
214. See Hennis, "A Science of Man," 28; also Scaff, *Fleeing the Iron Cage,* 26–31. Weber continued to think of jurisprudence in positivistic terms. See Rehbinder, "Recht und Rechtswissenschaft," 497–514. According to Rehbinder, "Weber . . . thoroughly misunderstood the law and jurisprudence of his time" (497).
215. For example, the "free school of law" of Hermann Kantorowicz, who presented this view at the first meeting of the German Sociological Association. See DGS, *Verhandlungen . . . 1910,* 275–335. For an overview, see Hubert Rottleuthner, "Drei Rechtssoziolgien: Eugen Ehrlich, Hugo Sinzheimer, Max Weber," 227–30.

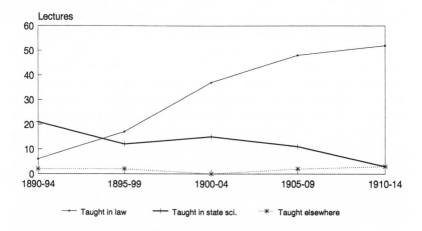

Fig. 15. Lectures in Politics and General Theory of State, 1890–1914

change was a revival of political science around 1900 in the law faculties under the title of "general theory of the state" (*allgemeine Staatslehre*)—just as the teaching of *Politik* in the philosophical faculties had reached its nadir with the death of Treitschke in 1896[216] (see figure 15) Of the new textbooks that appeared in this area, the most successful was that of the Heidelberg jurist Georg Jellinek, which went through three editions between 1900 and the War. Jellinek, an Austrian Jew whose religion prevented his advancement in Vienna, brought to Heidelberg the concern for keeping the legal and political sciences together: he insisted on retaining the Knies-Bluntschli seminar, so that his students could obtain either a Ph.D. or a Dr. Juris degree.[217]

Jellinek's achievement was to combine this concern for the social context of law with the neo-Kantian (and legal positivist) insistence on the strict separation of facts and norms. He did this by dividing his text into two major parts: the first, the social theory of the state, dealt with the essence, goals, and legitimacy of the state, which Jellinek acknowledged to be historically relative; the second, the general theory of state law, dealt with concepts that served as norms for positive law: sovereignty, constitutional structure, and forms and functions of the state. Jellinek did not dodge the question of the relation of one part to

216. Stolleis, *Geschichte des öffentlichen Rechts*, 2: 450. On the decline of politics, see Hintze, "Roschers politische Entwicklungstheorie," 3; Sombart, "Ideale der Sozialpolitik," 1. Hintze's lectures on constitutional and administrative history were seen as a substitute for Treitschke's *Politik* in the philosophical faculty (Simon, *Staat und Geschichtswissenschaft*, 1: 121).

217. Riese, *Hochschule*, 206.

the other: he viewed such norms as arising out of social practices but becoming clearly distinguishable as legal concepts over time.[218]

In elucidating this relationship, Jellinek also employed the notion of types—stemming from his close association with Rickert and Weber—although his terminology was again different from that of his contemporaries. Like Weber, Jellinek viewed the typical as a standard to which empirical phenomena could be compared. This was preeminently applicable to jurisprudence: the law provided precision with respect to individual behavior and culpability. But such standards did not imply the expectation of complete conformity. Rather, the uniqueness of individuals and their actions also played an integral part in jurisprudence—in the leeway provided in sentencing a convicted criminal, for example. So too the purpose of historical and social science was to use concepts as bases for comparison, serving as a heuristic tool for better understanding the uniqueness of an individual or of a historical situation, but not with the expectation that the individual would completely fit the concept.[219] Jellinek called these concepts "empirical types," which he distinguished from the teleological "ideal types" of ancient and medieval political theory. The latter were ideal in an evaluative sense: they claimed to be models of the "best state" and thus contained the expectation that individual citizens would conform to it. Unlike Weber, Jellinek thus used the term *ideal type* in a pejorative sense.[220]

Despite its favorable reception, Jellinek's mediating effort did not escape criticism. Its treatment of norms was insufficiently rigorous for some, while its sociology was insufficiently realistic for others.[221] Among the latter was the Freiburg law professor Richard Schmidt, who saw the need for a systematic political science that was less bound to juridical concerns. Schmidt's political science included such topics as political parties and their interaction.[222] Schmidt helped launch a new journal in 1908, the *Zeitschrift für Politik* (a preliminary title had been *Journal for Scientific Politics with Special Consideration for Parliamentary Problems*).[223] It was wide ranging and cosmopolitan, featuring reports on political developments in various parts of the world; the measure of its participation in broader cultural currents may be gauged by the credentials of Schmidt's coeditor, the conservative scholar and journalist Adolf Grabowsky, who had books

218. Jellinek, *Allgemeine Staatslehre*, 337–39.
219. Ibid., 32–33.
220. Ibid., 34–35, 139–40, 497.
221. On the former, particularly Hans Kelsen, see Stolleis, *Geschichte des öffentlichen Rechts*, 2: 451–53.
222. Richard Schmidt, "Wege und Ziele der Politik," 20. Schmidt criticized Jellinek for following the old categories (22).
223. Adolf Grabowsky to Tönnies, 18 April 1907, Tönnies Nachlass, box 56 (private letters to Tönnies).

of poetry and art criticism to his credit as well.[224] Although far from being a mainstream phenomenon, political science was thus reestablished.

The Revival of Economic Theory after 1900

The quest for clarity which underlay the interdisciplinary trends was also manifest within economics, which witnessed a revival of interest in theory after the turn of the century. One topic which elicited such interest was money. Simmel had published a *Philosophy of Money* of roughly six hundred pages in 1900, which went to a second edition in 1907. Simmel's treatment was characteristically interdisciplinary and intuitive, embracing psychology, ethics, aesthetics, and sociology, but explicitly avoiding the economic perspective.[225] Nevertheless, it spurred other, more limited investigations.[226] On the practical side, interest in money and banking had been increasing since the Bismarckian era. Lectures on the subject rose from thirty-one between 1880 and 1885 to ninety-five between 1905 and 1910.[227] This was doubtless spurred in part by the considerable currency reforms that followed unification, and in part by the controversy over the gold standard versus bimetallism which swept across Europe and the United States in the 1880s and 1890s.

This practical perspective found expression in 1903 in an equally lengthy and widely read treatise, simply called *Money*, by Karl Helfferich—an economist who would later become Treasury and Interior Minister during World War I and a leading politician in the early Weimar Republic. According to his biographer, Helfferich's policies in these capacities were based on ideas he had developed between 1894 and 1901.[228] A student of Knapp, Helfferich had already made connections with the business and banking community by the time he entered academia and had already achieved some notoriety as a representative of their interests. He had defended the gold standard against the agrarians' attempt to overthrow it in favor of bimetallism in the 1890s.[229] The treatise nevertheless stood on its own as a scholarly work. In addition to the expected historical and juridical treatment of monetary systems, it contained a lengthy theoretical analysis of the role of money in the economy and on the value of money. While it was not a radically innovative work—it fell within the conven-

---

224. On Grabowsky, see Bruch, "Kulturstaat," 86–88. Grabowsky also edited the Free Conservative journal *Das neue Deutschland,* seeking to bring the educated elite to the conservative cause by promoting cultural imperialism (Eley, *Reshaping the German Right,* 325).

225. Simmel, *Philosophie des Geldes,* vii.

226. Altmann, "Geldlehre," *ENTW,* no. 6: 28.

227. Source: University catalogues. See appendix.

228. Williamson, *Helfferich,* 19.

229. *Ibid.,* 19–23, 32–33, 36. Helfferich did his *Habilitation* at Berlin, over bimetallist Wagner's opposition.

tions of commodity theory—the influence of Simmel was still detectable. Simmel had viewed money as related to the forms of human interaction which he had developed in his previous sociological essays; money was different, however, in that it took one such form—namely exchange—and reified it into a commodity.[230] Helfferich also stressed the active role which money played in *fixing* values by the very act of facilitating exchange—as opposed to the frequently held view that money functioned as the *measure* of value which was fixed independently by market mechanisms.[231] As a medium and facilitator of exchange, money was comparable to transportation systems.[232] Because money had become such a stabilizing factor in the economy, Helfferich warned that the consequences of disruption of the monetary system would be magnified throughout the economy; in later editions, he noted that he had made these points prior to 1914.[233] In practical terms, this called for an agency to manage the money supply, which the Reichsbank had successfully provided.[234] Helfferich's proposed measures for such management undoubtedly appear timid in retrospect, given the much greater role that central banks have assumed since. But his thinking was not out of line with his own time, either in Germany or elsewhere.[235]

It was Helfferich's own teacher, Knapp, who put forth a more radical theory in 1905. His *State Theory of Money* was based on the premise that "money is a creation of the legal order; in the course of history it has assumed the most

230. Simmel, *Philosophie des Geldes,* 98, 100.

231. Helfferich, *Money,* 1: 324. The translation is based on the 1923 edition. Since Helfferich states in the text which of his views he held before the war, this edition may be taken as an indicator of his earlier positions. Cf. Ellis, *German Monetary Theory.* The influence of Simmel is neglected by Ellis, who focuses on Helfferich's criticism of Simmel for not going far enough in an idealistic direction, and misses his acknowledgment of the similarities (Ellis, 60–61; Helfferich, 2: 496–500, for critique; 1: 318, 2: 501, 505, for similarities).

232. Helfferich, *Money,* 1: 283.

233. Ibid., 2: 404, 547–48. This interpretation differs somewhat from that of Williamson, who sees Helfferich as believing that the monetary mechanisms were more reactive than active (48). But this seems to apply only to Helfferich's views regarding periods of monetary stability, such as existed before the war. It was against this backdrop of monetary stability that other factors such as trade cycles or interest rates assumed greater importance. But Helfferich never maintained that this stability was eternal; on the contrary, he stated that "changes in the value of money . . . produce conditions which create serious alterations in the distribution of income and of wealth, disturbances in the bases of all economic calculations, and accordingly in the economic life of the community" (2: 547).

234. Helfferich, *Money,* 2: 409. On the role of mismanagement in causing monetary crises, see 2: 404, 492.

235. Williamson, *Helfferich,* 46; Born, *International Banking,* 169; cf. Schumpeter, *History of Economic Analysis,* 1081, where he claims that the innovative analytical work of the period was not making its way into the textbooks and comprehensive surveys such as Helfferich's.

varied forms: a theory of money can therefore only be legal-historical."[236] This was the opposite extreme of Helfferich's commodity theory; Knapp claimed that money was essentially a means of payment, originally of debts, rather than a medium of exchange. It put Knapp in opposition to all forms of metallism, and it had the advantage of accounting for paper money and any other payment device, including transfer of funds.[237] Beyond this, it contained little in the way of explanation; Knapp did not seek to prove or derive his theory from any other premises, but simply erected a series of definitions and claims based upon his original assertion. The work may be seen primarily as an exercise in classification, an elaborate set of technical terms for different forms of payment that had occurred throughout history. As such, it was hailed at the time as providing the sort of conceptual clarity that had been lacking and thus stimulated a great deal of discussion.[238] But it erred in the opposite extreme, for Knapp's network of definitions and technical terms conveniently ruled out whole areas of inquiry that could challenge his assumptions. This was already clear at the 1909 meeting of the *Verein*, where von Wieser presented a new method for measuring fluctuations in monetary value based on the assumptions of the Austrian school. Knapp simply dismissed the suggestion as having nothing to do with the theory of monetary value.[239] For this reason, his theory was relatively barren of implications for policy-making, although it proved to be a convenient defense for advocates of inflationary policies during and after the War—and an equally convenient scapegoat for critics of those policies. [240]

A second means of reintroducing economic theory that found favor in these years was to strengthen contacts between the historical and the Austrian schools, since the latter had remained the center of theoretical work in the German-speaking world. Initiatives came from both the Austrian and German sides. Of the former, the most conspicuous example was the precocious young Joseph Schumpeter, whose later fame (like Helfferich's) rested on ideas he had already formulated by 1914, when he was thirty-one. As a student in Vienna, he had attended Böhm-Bawerk's seminar in the same semester (1905–06) as Otto Bauer and Rudolf Hilferding, two leading Marxists, as well as the marginalists Ludwig von Mises and Emil Lederer—a combination that led to some

236. Knapp, *Staatliche Theorie des Geldes*, 1.

237. Ibid., 137. Knapp qualified his original definition to include this case, by saying that any "community of payment" can establish a unit of value; the state is simply the oldest and the most ubiquitous community of payment.

238. Diehl, "Bedeutung der wissenschaftlichen Nationalökonomie," 310; Ellis, *Monetary Theory*, 12.

239. VFS, *Verhandlungen . . . 1909*, 546, 560–62, 616. Cf. Ellis, *Monetary Theory*, 38;, Schumpeter, *History of Economic Analysis*, 1090–91; Max Weber, *Wirtschaft und Gesellschaft*, 1: 140–45.

240. Ellis, *Monetary Theory*, 19.

stormy debates.[241] Yet there were other seminars at Vienna from which he could learn the historical approach, such as that of Karl T. Inama-Sternegg, a statistician and ally of Schmoller in the *Methodenstreit*.[242] Schumpeter's economic interests were remarkably catholic—he was an enthusiastic advocate of mathematical applications—and international as well: he traveled to London and Paris to meet the leading economists there, above all Walras. His first book, *The Nature and Essence of Theoretical Economics* (1908) was written with the partial purpose of shaking his German contemporaries out of their woeful ignorance.[243] Its centerpiece was an abstract model of equilibrium based on Walras, detached from all sociological and psychological considerations.[244] Schumpeter also repeatedly stressed his remoteness from practical considerations. "With the historian we can come to an understanding," he wrote, "[but] not with the politicizing theoretician. . . . He resembles Icarus."[245] This static approach was, however, soon to have a dynamic sequel: *Theory of Economic Development,* which appeared in 1912. Here Schumpeter adumbrated the ideas that later made him famous: a non-Marxist theory of capital formation and of economic cycles which emphasized the role of the entrepreneur. In a chapter deleted from later editions, Schumpeter made an express analogy between the entrepreneur and the Nietzschean artist-hero who was so popular in that day:

> There is a further analogy between that which we have presented first in the area of the economy and the processes in other areas of social life. . . . In each area there are statically disposed individuals and leaders. The first are characterized as doing essentially what they learned, operating in the conventional framework. . . . The second are characterized as seeing new things, as altering the conventional framework of their activity and the given data of their area. . . . In art, in science, in politics we observe this distinction, which appears with the same clarity everywhere.[246]

Two years later, Schumpeter's first major work of history appeared, entitled *Economic Doctrine and Method: A Historical Sketch,* in which he stressed the complementarity of historical and theoretical work.[247] It contained the bases for his later, more extensive *History of Economic Analysis.*

Schumpeter's educational mission to the Germans did not meet with immediate success, however. His abstract method was viewed with suspicion, as was his Austrian background; when a professorship to be devoted to theory opened

241. Swedberg, *Schumpeter,* 15.
242. Hardach, "Schumpeter," in Wehler, ed., *DH,* 6: 57.
243. Schumpeter, *Wesen und Hauptinhalt,* xxi.
244. Ibid., xix, 541–43.
245. Ibid., 575; cf. vii, 19.
246. Schumpeter, *Theorie der wirtschaftlichen Entwicklung,* 542–43.
247. Schumpeter, *Economic Doctrine and Method,* 159.

at Leipzig in 1916, the commission was divided on recommending him, despite endorsements from Bücher and Wundt.[248] Only in 1925 did he receive an appointment to Bonn.

A more successful effort at exporting Austrian ideas to Germany took the form of a popular textbook by the Viennese professor Eugen von Philippovich—one of the few marginalists who had also taught in Germany. His strategy to integrate the sociological and reformist perspectives of the Germans with the individualistic premises of the Austrian theory was to include a discussion of forms of economic organization along with the basic Mengerian concepts. He retained a broad approach to the subject, drawing for example on Wagner's valuable discussion of the legal bases of commercial economies.[249] In this way, the book provided a systematic presentation of a modern capitalist economy in a concrete and comprehensive social context, thus reinforcing the historical analysis of capitalism of Weber and Sombart. Philippovich also produced a companion *Volkswirtschaftspolitik* which followed the same organizational lines as the theoretical volume.

The contours of Philippovich's system resembled those of a German-initiated project, begun in 1908, which soon became a collaborative effort with the Austrians: a new systematic handbook of economics under the editorship of Max Weber (see table 15). This was the *Outline of Socio-Economics* (*Grundriss derSozialökonomik*)—the same label which Wagner had chosen to describe the field. The tortured genesis of this project was, however, a testimony to the centrifugal forces operating in the profession, not to mention the difficulties of intellectual integration. The initiative came from Paul Siebeck, publisher of the earlier *Handbook of Political Economy* edited by Schönberg, which had followed Rau's scheme. After unsuccessful attempts to recruit scholars for a new edition of this work under Harms' editorship, Siebeck approached Weber to launch a new handbook on different organizational principles, from which certain topics such as finance and administration would have to be excluded.[250] The transfer from one system to the other was, however, no easy task: it involved a lengthy legal dispute (due to claims by Schönberg's heirs) and a quarrel and nearly a duel between Weber and Harms—all of which cost Weber almost a year's work.[251] In addition, the contributors were notoriously slow in submitting their

248. Minutes of committee meeting 3 July 1916; faculty report 16 July, incl. minority report of Wilhelm Stieda, UA Leipzig, Personalakten 816 (Ludwig Pohle), 14, 23–33.

249. Philippovich, *Grundriss der Politischen Oekonomie*, 1: 15, 36, 76.

250. Winckelmann, *Max Weber's hinterlassenes Hauptwerk*, 8. On the relation of this project to Weber's posthumously published *Wirtschaft und Gesellschaft*, see also Schluchter, "'Wirtschaft und Gesellschaft'—Das Ende eines Mythos," 55–89.

251. Marianne Weber, *Max Weber*, 446–53. On the identity of Harms, see "Personenverzeichnis," in Weber, *Gesamtausgabe* abt. II, vol. 5: 734; on Tönnies' mediating role, see Jacoby, *Tönnies*, 166–67.

works, so that the first sections did not appear until 1914.[252] The Austrian contribution was strong: Weber's first choice for the theoretical section was von Wieser, whose "Social Economics" appeared in the first published volume, along with Schumpeter's aforementioned historical essay. Phillipovich also contributed an essay on the systems and ideals of economic and social policy.[253]

Weber's own contribution was to be titled "The Economy and the Social Orders and Powers." It was to include a discussion of economics and law, as well as various types of social organizations, from household economies to religious communities, along with a typology of domination. Such topics—as well as Weber's involvement in the project itself—bespoke a shift of emphasis in his own thinking away from developmental schemes (as in the *Protestant Ethic*) to comparative ones. During these years he gradually dropped the label *cultural science* from his vocabulary in favor of *sociology*, although he remained reluctant to use that name in the handbook.[254] The difficulties in completing such a comprehensive project applied no less to Weber than to the other contributors. He continued to revise his portions during the War, expanding them to include material which he felt had been incompletely covered by von Wieser and others.[255] His manuscripts—in different stages of revision—were published posthumously, edited by his wife, under the title *Economy and Society*.[256] His reputation as a sociologist stems primarily from these fragments. The incomplete status of Weber's final project was symptomatic both of his desire to achieve systematization in his later years and his inability to do so. Neither Weber's personality nor the trends towards specialization and an interdisciplinary approach favored such a project.

THE PROBLEMATIC RELATION OF THEORY TO PRACTICE

Around 1905, the younger economists of the 1890s and 1900s began to express more strongly their dissatisfaction with the vagueness that had characterized the deliberations of the *Verein*. The quest for clarity, which we have traced within the social sciences in general, was taken up increasingly in connection with specific questions of economic theory and practice. This new commitment soon became a new source of fragmentation, since the vagueness which was under attack had become a precondition of unity within the profession. The

---

252. Marianne Weber, *Max Weber*, 419.

253. Winckelmann, *Max Weber's hinterlassenes Hauptwerk*, 13.

254. Ibid., 33; Tenbruck, "Abschied der 'Wissenschaftslehre'?" 97.

255. Winckelmann, *Max Weber's hinterlassenes Hauptwerk*, 16–17, 38.

256. This was originally to be the title of the third section of the handbook, of which Weber's work, "The Economy and the Social Orders and Powers" was to be the largest portion. The other was to be Philippovich's "The Course of Development of Systems and Ideals of Economic and Social Policy." (ibid., 168–69).

inaugural address of Karl Diehl on assuming a professorship at Freiburg in 1909 may be taken as representative of this attitude:

> How frequently in the last ten years has the theme of housing and housing reform been treated! We possess an amount of factual material in detailed investigations of the housing situation in all countries. When one then approached the policy of housing reform itself, it turned out that despite all of these treatments of housing there was complete uncertainty about the actual *question* of housing. . . . Anyone who wants to pursue housing policy and therefore fight high housing prices should first of all be clear about the question: Are these high prices caused by ground rent or by high construction costs? Are the prices driven artificially high by speculation, or do they correspond to the relation between supply and demand? But such investigations are only rarely posed and shabbily treated: there exist not only differences of opinion among policy experts on these questions, but primarily—and more objectionably—there is often a lack of ability to observe and to judge clearly on these questions, *because the education to theoretical thinking was too strongly neglected* [emphasis in original].[257]

According to Heinrich Waentig at Halle, economists were responding to events rather than shaping them, while Carl Ballod at Berlin complained that German statisticians were not able to perform basic calculations.[258] Max Weber used the occasion of Schmoller's seventieth birthday in 1908 to note "that it is now perhaps high time to concentrate on the theoretical aspect," reversing the pendulum swing that Schmoller himself had started.[259] The awareness of the problem was clear to the *Verein*, which decided in 1909 to tackle a theoretical question for the first time, namely, the concept of economic productivity.[260] The site of the meeting, Vienna, offered the opportunity for fruitful exchange with the Austrian school.

This was also the meeting in which the controversy over value judgments came into the open, revealing the differences of opinion on how the gap between theory and practice should be bridged. Sombart and Weber first raised the issue, calling for the elimination of value judgments from scientific debate. This was part of their concern for greater theoretical sophistication and conceptual clarity in German economics. In Sombart's words, "As long as value judgments play a role in scientific considerations, it is impossible [to achieve] an objective agreement about anything that is; scientific knowledge, however,

257. Diehl, "Bedeutung der wissenschaftlichen Nationalökonomie," 308–9.

258. Waentig, "Gewerbepolitischen Anschauungen," *ENTW,* no. 25: 71; Ballod in VFS, *Verhandlungen . . . 1907,* 113–14; cf. Bücher's remarks, ibid., 26, and Tschuprow, "Aufgaben der Theorie der Statistik," 421.

259. Max Weber to Schmoller, 23 June 1908, quoted in Schön, "Gustav Schmoller and Max Weber," 59.

260. Boese, *Geschichte,* 133

moves to establish and objectively demonstrate that something is." He concluded, "We will not be able to discuss these [value judgments] until there is scientific proof of whether blondes or brunettes are prettier."[261] Weber, who was in particularly charismatic form at the time—"he shone and flamed," according to his wife—supported Sombart, presenting arguments he had already made when he took over the editorship of the *Archiv* four years before; he was later to expand them further.[262] Weber made it clear in his speech that he was not calling for theorizing at the expense of practice; that would go against the very mission of the *Verein*. He proposed instead several techniques of practical reasoning that were sanitized of such value judgments and which, had they been put into practice, would have gone far to relieve German economics of its self-acknowledged murkiness. These techniques consisted of (1) tracing value judgments back to their ultimate premises and asking whether these are consistent with one another; (2) studying empirically the means available to achieve the desired ends and again applying the test of consistency; and (3) looking for unintended side effects of this process and asking whether these would outweigh the benefit intended.[263]

In this sense, Weber was far from advocating a split between theorizing and practical deliberation. But he was adamant about another split: between such "objective" analysis of values-in-operation and a "subjective" projection of one's own values into the discussion in the form of ethics. This had been the besetting sin of Schmoller and his generation. Once again, Weber made it clear that he was not against scientists' personally holding such values or acting on them outside the classroom or the scientific forum. The sin was that of confusing one forum with another. As he put it in the Vienna meeting,

> The reason I am so extraordinarily strongly . . . against any mixing of that which ought to be with that which is, is not that I underestimate the former, but quite the contrary: because I cannot stand it when problems of earth-shaking significance, of the greatest idealistic implications, in a sense the highest problems that can move a human breast, here are transformed into a technical economic "productivity" question and made the object of discussion of a specialized discipline such as economics.[264]

It was this animus against trivialization and compromise that made Weber's position so difficult to accept. Many, including Schmoller and Tönnies, were inclined to agree that social scientists should be clear about their own values

---

261. VFS, *Verhandlungen . . . 1909*, 567, 572.

262. Ibid., 580–85; Max Weber, "'Objectivität,'" 148–61; "Sinn der 'Wertfreiheit,'" 475–526. On his tone and manner, see Marianne Weber, *Max Weber*, 419.

263. VFS, *Verhandlungen . . . 1909*, 582; Weber, "'Objectivität,'" 149–51; "Sinn der 'Wertfreiheit,'" 496.

264. VFS, *Verhandlungen . . . 1909*, 584.

and their implications, but they did not agree with Weber that the affirmation of such values could be—or should be—excised from this process. *Sozialpolitik* was, after all, based on the conviction that the standard of living of the workers should be improved.[265]

The controversy over value judgments was exacerbated by the imprecision with which all sides used that term. Despite the heightened concern with methodology and conceptual clarity, it remained undefined and unanalyzed.[266] Neither Weber and Sombart nor their opponents limited themselves to condemning clear-cut statements of what should or should not be. Rather, they found such judgments everywhere, masquerading behind such seemingly innocent concepts as "productivity" or even "prosperity" (*Wohlstand*); the term *value judgment* seemed at times to be synonomous with conceptual vagueness.[267] To confuse matters still further, it was also possible, in the eyes of some, for value judgments to masquerade as judgments of fact. This problem arose when, for example, the fact in question was not a momentary event but a long-term development, such as the rise of the proletariat. In the light of such long-term "facts," it was possible to say that short-term consequences "ought" to happen in a predictive sense—such as revolution or worker reforms. Thus it was possible for Brentano to claim that economics was the study of facts which warranted the judgment that workers' organizations were necessary—and for a business-oriented economist to dismiss this as utterly unscientific.[268] In other words, the quest for clarity had not reached a point of general agreement on what constituted a fact: the obscurity surrounding the status of long-term empirical trends had not been removed. And if the distinction between fact and value remained unclear, there was no hope of agreement on what the proper sphere of practical reasoning might be—as distinct from merely subjective or wishful thinking.

Thus the term *value judgment* continued to serve as a weapon in the factional

265. See Schmoller and Tönnies, "Zwei Bemerkungen über den Verein für Sozialpolitik," 4, 7; Herkner, "Der Kampf um das sittliche Werturteil," 536; Philippovich, in VFS, *Verhandlungen . . . 1909*, 611; Cohn, "Wirtschaftswissenschaft und Wirtschaftspolitik," 34–35.

266. Such analyses were in fact being conducted under the emerging banner of phenomenology by Brentano's brother Franz and his students Alexius Meinong and Edmund Husserl. Weber was certainly not oblivious to this movement in general; he turned to Husserl and to other philosophical psychologists to elucidate the notion of "understanding" (*Verstehen*) as a mode of apprehension in the social sciences, but the topic of judgment itself appears not to have interested him. See Weber, "Roscher und Knies," 107 ff, esp. 123, where he states that the *content* of a value judgment is relevant for his considerations and avoids analysis of the *act* of judgment. For background, see Lindenfeld, *Transformation*, esp. chap. 7.

267. Thus Weber: "In the concept of 'national prosperity' is obviously placed all the ethics that there is in the world." (VFS, *Verhandlungen . . . 1909*, 581).

268. Brentano, "Ueber Werturteile," 709–11; Pohle, "Gegenwärtige Krise," 85.

struggles among German social scientists in the years immediately preceding World War I. The continuing public visibility of the profession only made matters worse. Indeed, immediately following the stormy 1909 meeting of the *Verein*, Knapp expressed misgivings about the distortion of the controversy in the press.[269] By 1914, however, the leaders of the *Verein* had learned from experience; it was agreed that the full discussion of the value judgment controversy should not take place in a public meeting. An executive session was scheduled for January to deal with the matter. In preparation, written opinions were solicited but not published; in the meeting, no minutes were kept. It was noted, however, that Weber's proposals did not meet with great approval.[270]

The situation in the newly formed German Sociological Association was altogether more turbulent. There was considerable irony in this, for the founders of the association, including Tönnies and Weber, conceived it as a forum for purely theoretical discussion as distinct from the practical orientation of the *Verein*. This was incorporated into the statutes, which stated that the organization "rejects any practical goal (ethical, religious, political, aesthetic, etc.)"[271] In practice, this meant the strict exclusion of value judgments, whatever they might be. Tönnies believed that if theoretical sociology were removed from practical questions, a degree of value-free objectivity could be attained; Weber was initially enthusiastic for other reasons, viewing the new organization as an opportunity to conduct collaborative social research.[272] But since sociology was still relatively unformed, with no established traditions of discourse, the association was inevitably made up of representatives of different disciplines; indeed, this was the express purpose of the founders. The first meeting of 1910 included speakers from philosophy (Simmel), history (Ernst Troeltsch), law (Hermann Kantorowicz), and racial biology (Ploetz). Weber was particularly concerned that the natural sciences be represented, and it took some special pleading with Ploetz to get him to participate.[273] Given such a diverse constituency, the topics were correspondingly general and full of necessarily vague concepts. Sombart lectured on "technics and culture," Ploetz on "race and society," Kantorowicz on "jurisprudence and sociology." The result was that accusations of value judgments were hurled repeatedly throughout the debates from various sides. When Ploetz insisted that the term *preservation* was a value-

269. Boese, *Geschichte*, 135–36.

270. Ibid., 145, 148.

271. DGS, *Verhandlungen . . . 1910*, v.

272. Schmoller and Tönnies, "Zwei Bemerkungen," 8; on Weber, see Oberschall, *Empirical Social Research*, 142.

273. Ploetz to Beck, 26 Sept. 1910, 1 Oct. 1910; Weber to Beck, 4 Oct. 1910, Tönnies Nachlass, 61.1.1 (Akten der deutschen Gesellschaft für Soziologie, 1st Period, Briefe).

free term, and that a *vital race* could be defined as a unit of self-preservation, Weber dismissed it as as mysticism.[274] Tönnies even interrupted a discussant to reprimand him for committing a value judgment. This prompted Kantorowicz to protest:

> It is a most remarkable and unprecedented spectacle that a methodological-philosophical principle, namely, the exclusion of value judgments, can be made into a point of order of business. This is only possible in our methodological age.[275]

The second meeting of 1912 did not see much improvement. The dilemma was the same: a sufficiently broad topic was needed to attract a diverse constituency, but this vitiated any attempt at strict language rules. Tönnies had suggested the theme of "the concepts of people and nation in connection with race, state, and language." Simmel was skeptical. "It will lead to the controversy over concepts and definitions. We have suffered such controversies in sociology to the point of suffocation."[276] But Tönnies prevailed. Although the full debates of the second meeting were not published, the result was frustrating to Weber, who viewed the experiment in value-free discourse as a failure and resigned from the executive committee; in 1914 he resigned altogether.[277] Resignations were in fact frequent: Ploetz withdrew from the leadership soon after the first meeting, and Herkner and Simmel both resigned in 1913. To continue the sociobiological strand, Grotjahn agreed to join the executive committee. When Tönnies announced that eugenics and racial hygiene were off limits, however, he resigned in a huff.[278]

If the value judgments controversy did little to advance the cause of clarity within the *Verein*, it fueled the arguments of those economists who had broken with the organization. Thus Pohle, in his 1911 book *The Present Crisis in German Economics* cited a humorous definition as containing a grain of truth:

> "Political economy? What does that mean? Why, of course! It's when one measures the dimensions of workers' apartments and then says that they're too small!" Although this definition does not, to be sure, state the essence of political economy itself, it certainly does correctly grasp and express an essen-

274. DGS, *Verhandlungen . . . 1910*, 114–15, 153, 157.

275. Ibid., 314.

276. Simmel to the chair, 10 Oct. 1911; Tönnies to Beck, 5 Nov. 1911, Tönnies Nachlass, 61.1.1.

277. Max Weber to Beck, 22 Oct. 1912; 17 January 1914, Tönnies Nachlass, 61.1.1. Weber's efforts to launch a social research project on the press were jeopardized by his involvement in another libel trial involving the press. See Oberschall, *Empirical Social Research*, 143–44; Marianne Weber, *Max Weber*, 429–39.

278. Herkner to Beck, 4 July 1913; Simmel to chair, 11 Oct. 1913; Grotjahn to Beck, 8 March 1914, Tönnies Nachlass, 61.1.1.

tial tendency in the approach to economics prevailing in Germany at the present time.[279]

In 1913 Bernhard published an influential pamphlet, *Undesirable Results of German Social Legislation,* in which he detailed the excesses of bureaucratic regulation of factories and of the medical effects of social insurance in promoting such maladies as "accident neuroses."[280] Bernhard concluded that the pendulum had swung far enough. "After a noble and fruitful era of social progress, we should make all that has been gained secure and procure a breathing space for a start on the way to new fields of effort," he wrote.[281] These sentiments were echoed by the Minister of the Interior, Clemens von Delbrück, in a speech in January 1914.[282]

The deteriorating climate of opinion regarding *Sozialpolitik* had already attracted the notice of Weber and Brentano, and they sought in 1912 to create a new organization to agitate for social reform that would be independent of the *Verein.* They could not agree on a platform, however, and Brentano withdrew from the project.[283] This probably was a reflection of his general discouragement; Schmoller also had withdrawn increasingly from public life after Althoff's and Bülow's retirement. "Our younger generation does not know the feeling of solidarity which led us to fight next to each other and for each other despite all differences of opinion in the decisive battles," wrote Brentano to Schmoller.[284]

In sum, the quest for clarity enhanced greatly the theoretical imagination of German—and Western—social science, but at the expense of the practical. In this respect, it ironically represented a continuation of a split which Schmoller had already introduced when he characterized the social scientist as standing apart from action in the name of a higher truth. This could inform practice as long as the social scientist possessed the personal authority to embody the connection between the two. But as the aging founders of the *Verein* passed from the scene, they left no coherent system to replace them. The tendency to specialization was not conducive to such coherence, while the tendency to clarification in economics and sociology had not gone far enough to provide it. In its place arose a fragmentary discourse held together increasingly by abstract embodiments, such as *race* or *culture* or even *value judgment* itself. All

279. Pohle, "Gegenwärtige Krise," 103. See also Herkner, "Kampf um das sittliche Werturteil," 520–22, 542–45.
280. Bernhard, *Undesirable Results of German Social Legislation,* 57.
281. Ibid., 93.
282. Born, *Staat und Sozialpolitik,* 246.
283. Sheehan, *Brentano,* 174–75; Mommsen, *Weber,* 127–31; Jacoby, *Tönnies,* 165–66.
284. Quoted in Brentano, *Mein Leben,* 300. See also Sheehan, *Brentano,* 176; Lindenlaub, *Richtungskämpfe,* 459.

could agree that these terms were important, but not on what they meant. The goal of clarity seemed to be receding rather than advancing.

One can hazard the speculation that the situation within the profession mirrored that of Wilhelminian politics and society on the eve of the First World War. The ability to compromise among the parties, or among factions within the parties, seemed to be ebbing, leading to a feeling of frustration and impatience. *Reichsverdrossenheit*, to use Bethmann-Hollweg's oft-quoted term, was accompanied by *Fachverdrossenheit*.[285]

---

285. Bethmann-Hollweg, *Betrachtungen zum Weltkrieg*, quoted in Schorske, *German Social Democracy*, 224 nn.

Epilogue

Given the importance of economic factors in the decades of crisis that followed 1914, it is appropriate to conclude this study with a brief survey of the role which the academic sciences of state played in these events. As might be expected, the patriotic euphoria of the early war years embraced the *Staatswissenschaftler*.[1] Many economists were actively involved in what might be called the visionary aspects of German policy during these years, namely, the formulation of policies for German expansion that were to follow the military victory. Naumann coined a new slogan to express this vision, at least for many: *Mitteleuropa*, a German-dominated continental economic region. Although figures like Sering, Helfferich, and Schulze-Gävernitz continued to distance themselves from the Pan-German League and its demands for annexation, they were all the more active in drawing up plans for "peaceful penetration" of places like Poland, Belgium, the Baltic states, and Russia. These schemes included such measures as settling Germans in some Polish agricultural regions (an extension of Sering's prewar ideas), encouraging cultural divisions between the Flemish and Wallonians in Belgium, and reestablishing a German university in Latvia.[2]

Also in the realm of the visionary may be counted the belief that the wartime economy, with its increase in state controls, heralded the end of capitalism and the advent of the state socialism that Wagner and others had prophesied for years. Such beliefs, though expressed only by a minority of economists (such as Edgar Jaffé and Johann Plenge), nevertheless had a powerful effect on some Social Democrats and helped pave the way for their cooperation with the liberal parties under the Weimar Republic.[3] This was reinforced by the fact that many economists, especially the younger ones, while continuing to think of Germany's wartime and postwar policies in capitalist terms, readily acknowledged an increased role for the state. Most would probably have agreed with

1. See D. Krüger, *Nationalökonomen*, chap. 10.
2. Ibid., 180–84; Fischer, *Germany's Aims in the First World War*, 117, 169, 274–77, 483–85.
3. Krüger has documented the influence of Plenge's journal *Die Glocke* quite convincingly (*Nationalökonomen*, 229–31).

Schulze-Gävernitz's formula in the Reichstag of a "synthesis of a state-socialist and free market order."[4] Opinions varied widely, however, on the specific mix.

At the same time, the war exposed the deficiencies of the bureaucracy when it came to practical reasoning. A case in point was agricultural policy: unlike Britain and France, Germany failed to feed her civilian population during the war.[5] While some of the causes can be traced to the blockade, it is clear that an administrative failure was involved as well. The role of fertilizers in crop production was simply ignored, and the effect of price controls on the total system of prices was not understood. In 1915 the price of pork, for example, was set without a corresponding control on beef, which sent the price of beef spiraling upward.[6] This was exactly the sort of incomprehension of causal relationships of which Diehl and others had complained six years before. When such complaints surfaced during and after the war, the reason most commonly given was the primarily legal education of officials and the cavalier attitude taken toward the *Staatswissenschaften* in Prussia.[7] In addition, the separation of *Agrarpolitik* from any technical education in agriculture undoubtedly played a role.[8] In this area as in others, the lack of coordination among bureaucratic branches created further inefficiencies.[9] The crisis of the war thus brought to the surface the long-standing inadequacies of German administration and education. The consequences of these failures were significant. On the one hand, they increased the popular hatred of bureaucracy, a factor which helped foster the revolutionary mood of 1918.[10] On the other, they promoted the increased independence and power of the industrialists, who often took over the management of the economy when officials failed at their tasks.[11] Their voices on economic policy were to be heard more often after the war. Thus the decline in influence of the academic economists vis-à-vis the industrialists was further accelerated.

It would be overly simplistic to judge the contributions of economists to the war effort solely in terms of such performance. As the war lengthened and the problems of paying for it became more urgent, the emphasis on sober analysis tended to increase. To its credit, the *Verein* resolved in 1916 to tackle the central

4. Ibid., 163 (cf. 135, 152).

5. J. M. Winter, "Some Paradoxes of the First World War," 38.

6. Joe Lee, "Administrators and Agriculture," 235.

7. Jastrow, "Das Studium der Verwaltungswissenschaft nach dem Kriege," 967; comments of Minister of State Bill Drews and former Interior Minister Clemens von Delbrück, in VFS, *Reform der staatswissenschaftlichen Studien*, 369–70, 373.

8. See the comments of agriculture professor Friedrich Aereboe in VFS, *Reform der staatswissenschaftlichen Studien*, 322.

9. Winter, "Some Paradoxes of the First World War," 38.

10. Kocka, *Facing Total War*, 118, 159.

11. Ibid., 139–40; Winter, "Some Paradoxes of the First World War," 39–40.

problem of financing the war effort—at a time when many still believed that the enemy would pay. While holding an open meeting on the subject was considered too politically risky, a series of policy studies were commissioned and appeared in 1917 and 1918. Although some favored state monopolies in certain industries as the answer, the majority supported a one-time tax on personal wealth (*Vermögensabgabe*) and other indirect taxes as having the least disturbing effect on the free market. Notably absent was the inflationary solution that the government was actually pursuing.[12] Nevertheless, the study was symptomatic of the degree of illusion that still persisted within the profession; for even as most of the recommendations were in fact enacted, they proved to be woefully inadequate to meet the Reich's increasing debt—most of which was not even reflected in the ordinary budget![13]

The most striking fact about the Reich's internal fiscal and monetary policies was the discrepancy between propaganda and reality. This can be seen in the policies of the most influential economist by far, Helfferich, who served first as Secretary of the Treasury and then as Minister of the Interior from January 1915 to November of 1917. There was nothing vague about Helfferich's thinking or his style of presentation: his command of facts and figures and his ability to argue persuasively before the Reichstag rendered him indispensable to Bethmann-Hollweg and enabled him to survive briefly the chancellor's fall from power.[14] He recognized the limited ability of the Reich to levy taxes—an issue which had been fought and lost in 1909—and supported the decision to borrow via war-bond drives; indeed, he was the moving force behind the successful propaganda campaigns to float the bonds. But this source of income also enabled him to maintain a fiction of bookkeeping: by consigning military expenditures and war-bond income to "extraordinary expenses," he could ignore the alarming debits that were building up in this category while proudly maintaining that the relatively modest tax rates were more or less covering "ordinary" expenses.[15]

Helfferich was certainly not alone in engaging in such mendacity; other examples could be found in leadership circles. One of the most important in retrospect had to do with the issue of notes by Germany's banking institutions, an issue which bore directly on the inflation to come. Central to the trust in the financial stability of the Reich was the ability of subjects to redeem paper marks for gold at the Reichsbank; this too was made the object of a propaganda campaign, calling upon the German people to donate gold to the Reichsbank

12. Boese, *Geschichte*, 153–55; D. Krüger, *Nationalökonomen*, 149–52.
13. Feldman, *Great Disorder*, 40; Holtfrerich, *The German Inflation 1914–1923*, 112–13. Holtfrerich includes a perspicuous discussion of war financing in general (102–8).
14. Williamson, *Helfferich*, 152, 235–38.
15. Feldman, *Great Disorder*, 39–41.

to enable the issuance of more paper—again as a matter of patriotic duty. At the same time, however, additional loan bureaus were established in 1914 which were not subject to such redeemability requirements and whose power to issue notes was subject to the flimsiest of limitations. As the demand for currency increased, the printing presses began to turn out marks to keep up with these issues, thus undermining the Reichsbank's noble pronouncements.[16] Such policies could be and were justified in terms of the exigencies of the lengthening and expanding war effort, but they set in motion behaviors which were increasingly difficult to control after the war.

All of this reflected most adversely on the quality of economic education in Germany. The shortcomings of the economics curriculum were further exacerbated by the immediate postwar conditions. Returning veterans found economics to be one of the few fields that did not require a training program before employment. They therefore flocked to it in record numbers: enrollments increased from 3,836 in 1914 to 10,670 in 1919–20.[17] Needless to say, the quality of instruction suffered. Complaints surfaced in the 1920 study by the *Verein* on curricular reform in the sciences of state. Three large manufacturing firms in Frankfurt am Main reported that they no longer hired economists because of their lack of practical knowledge. The head of a local chamber of commerce wrote that economists were too theoretically trained.[18] The comments of the business editor of the *Frankfurter Zeitung* indicated that the problem went back before the war. He noted the "painful gaps" in knowlege of a dozen young Ph.D.'s whom he had trained in the previous twelve years. He preferred students without degrees, who were more open to learning: "Those without titles must demonstrate with solid knowledge what those with titles . . . believe they have brought with them," he wrote.[19] Clearly the crisis within the economic sciences of state on the eve of the war was having its effects.

If the main problem which economists faced immediately before 1914 was to bring their newly discovered interest in theory into contact with practical questions, the inflationary years of the early 1920s afforded them the opportunity to do so. At issue was the cause(s) of the ongoing inflation. The answers fell into one of two camps, which were recognized at the time: (1) the balance-of-payments theory, which traced the expansion of the money supply to Germany's increased foreign obligations, such as war reparations; (2) the so-called quantity theory, which treated that expansion as a causative factor of its own, which the government could take steps to correct independently of the repara-

16. Ibid., 34–35.
17. Lindenfeld, "Professionalization," 224.
18. Recommendation of Society for Economic Training in Frankfurt, in VFS, *Reform der staatswissenschaftlichen Studien*, 184–85.
19. Comments of Ernst Kahn, ibid., 160.

tions situation.[20] Such a debate was obviously fraught with political implications and was put to propagandistic use which at times deviated from the economists' own factual assessments. Thus it is not surprising to find the Reichsbank arguing along the lines of the first theory in its official reports while simultaneously urging the government to control currency emissions in its confidential ones.[21] Indeed, given the hostility to the Versailles Treaty, it is remarkable that there was any debate among German economists at all. It is true that most of the economists who had begun their careers before the war held to the balance of payments theory, while the younger ones tended to be found in the quantity-theory camp.[22] What is clear, however, is that arguments on either side could be quite sophisticated, taking into account the complex dovetailing of domestic, international, and psychological factors.[23] Neither was pure ideological window-dressing, and the gap between intricate argument and propagandistic assertion was narrowing. One confirmation of this—however cold the comfort it provided the Germans—was that the findings of an international commission of experts (including John Maynard Keynes and the Swedish economist Gustav Cassel) brought in to study the German economy in 1922 proved to be equally divided as to which factors came first.[24] Indeed, Helfferich, who became the chief architect of the stabilization which eventually occurred in 1923, had previously been a staunch advocate of the balance-of-payments theory.[25]

If such accumulating wisdom nevertheless failed to prevent the collapse of the German mark and the near-collapse of the Republic in 1923, it was due to the progression of the political and intellectual fragmentation which had begun in the prewar period. The economists now were only members of a chorus of "experts" which included industrialists, politicians, and officials, and these groups had long since lost the art of communicating with each other. If economists were short on the practical knowledge needed in industry and banking, it was no less true, as the American ambassador pointed out, that "German bankers and industrialists are mighty poor economists."[26]

---

20. For discussions, see Ellis, *German Monetary Theory*, pt. 3; Holtfrerich, *German Inflation*, 156–63; Feldman, *Great Disorder*, 385, 399 ff.

21. Holtfrerich, *German Inflation*, 164–65. After mid-1921, however, the Reichsbank abandoned such admonitions in its confidential reports as well. This was at the time of the London Ultimatum, which fixed reparations payments at 132 billion gold marks. Havenstein concluded that domestic stabilization was prohibitive under such conditions (i.e., subscribed to the balance-of-payments theory; see 166–67).

22. Ellis, *German Monetary Theory*, chaps. 13, 14. Exceptions to the first group were von Mises and Pohle, who embraced the quantity theory.

23. Ibid., 290–93; Feldman, *Great Disorder*, 399–400.

24. Feldman, *Great Disorder*, 476.

25. *Ibid.*, 708 ff; Williamson, *Helfferich*, 383–94.

26. Quoted in Feldman, *Great Disorder*, 506.

During the years of relative prosperity between 1924 and 1929, the maturing of German economics continued, and the distance between German concerns and those of other countries narrowed considerably. The focus of much attention was on business cycles, with writers like Schumpeter, Ludwig von Mises, and Friedrich Hayek making important contributions.[27] In addition, Harms's Institute for World Economics at Kiel had helped make that university a major center for cyclical analysis.[28] At the same time, however, the indigenous German tradition of holistic economics as part of a more comprehensive theory of society continued to find audiences: one of the most popular economics texts of the 1920s was that of Othmar Spann, which went through five editions between 1917 and 1929.[29] And Sombart continued to find wide acceptance even as he was increasingly isolated from professional economists.[30]

Unfortunately, the very integration into the mainstream of Western economic thought on the part of many economists did not prepare them for the Great Depression. At first, most followed the conventional wisdom of advocating deflationary policies like those of the Brüning government. As the crisis deepened, however, the tide turned—even among the liberal economists—in favor of more aggressive state intervention. The debate over the "end of capitalism" of the war years was revived, and the tone became more strident and ideological.[31] The supporters of the collective economic good as opposed to self-interest gained strength, on which Nazism naturally drew.

In its use of unifying symbols as a substitute for analysis and differentiation, the Nazi regime represented a new extreme of embodiment-type thinking in German history. Identification with the Führer as the embodiment of the German nation and the destruction of the Jews as the embodiment of all evil governed much of the regime's behavior. Within the intellectual fields, these unit-ideas served as points of gravitation, so to speak, reshaping the contours of the various systems of science and professional expertise. Strategies of racial classification were officially recognized and rewarded—as long as they conformed to Nazi ideology. Studies in recent years have demonstrated the willingness of many doctors, lawyers, anthropologists, and other highly educated men and women to participate in the regime's programs, including the most extreme acts of genocide. This willingness was obviously shaped by the perceived continuities between Nazism and earlier ideas—eugenics, the organic view of

27. Ellis, *German Monetary Theory*, pt. 4, esp. 299; Krohn, *Wirtschaftstheorien als politische Interessen*, chap. 4.

28. Krohn, *Wirtschaftstheorien als politische Interessen*, 123–28.

29. Spann, *Fundament der Volkswirtschaftslehre*, esp. 9–12.

30. Lenger, *Sombart*, 276, 322.

31. Krohn, *Wirtschaftstheorien als politische Interessen*, 142–49; D. Krüger, *Nationalökonomen*, 233 nn.

the state, a loyal administration, and the cultural uniqueness and superiority of Germany, to name a few. Certainly the sciences of state contributed their share to this body of precedents.

Yet it seems that, as a group, economists were less heavily implicated in the Nazi movement than other professional groups. This was partly because of the Nazis' own relative indifference to economics compared to racial science or even sociology. But it was also due to internal trends within the field: the continuing reaction against the historical school and the growing prestige in the 1920s of analysis rather than holism. The persistence of the Austrian school in the persons of Von Mises and Hayek throughout the upheavals of the 1920s, 1930s, and 1940s was one of the remarkable features of the field. Émigré economists such as Wilhelm Röpke helped provide a body of expertise for the social market economy which helped shape Germany's prosperity in the 1950s. Thus, while Nazism could draw on past precedents from the *Staatswissenschaften*, so too could the Federal Republic.

The broader questions of the significance of Nazism in the context of both German history and the history of modern Western civilization continue to haunt us. The notion that the Holocaust was the product of a peculiarly German set of traditions continues to find popular support in many countries. Scholarly opinion in recent years has shifted away from this interpretation— in the direction of viewing it as the product of peculiarly Western ones stemming from the Enlightenment. Thus industrialization, bureaucratic organization, and technocratic hubris are seen as what made the Holocaust and World War II so destructive. It seems safe to say, however, that while the Third Reich was not completely alien to the traditions of Germany or of the Enlightenment, it was far from the inevitable outgrowth of either. As this narrative has sought to demonstrate, modern bureaucracies are capable of a variety of strategies and mind-sets, and practical reasoning can encompass differentiated and humane responses. It is to be hoped that this story can nourish our sense of alternatives, allowing us to see "Germany" and "Enlightenment" not as embodiments, but as complex fields of thought and action.

Appendix: The Data from
University Catalogues

In a lecture entitled "The Statistical Disease," Wilhelm Heinrich Riehl warned against relying on numbers to gauge trends in higher education:

> We know quite well that some lectures stand out by the uncountable numbers of students who come regularly without being on the list, and others by the very countable numbers who stay away although they are on the list. . . . The words of our Lord Christ on the sower, who sows his seeds on all types of soil, fit here much better than any numerical statistics.[1]

Riehl's warning applies to lectures listed in catalogues as well. The mere fact of being listed did not mean that the lecture took place, or that anyone came. In flouting Riehl's advice, however, this study proceeds on the assumption that sufficiently large numbers, tablulated over sufficiently long periods of time, can offset the distortions arising from such cases. The fact that lecture titles were fairly standardized from one university to another made it feasible to convert the data into machine-readable form, enabling the use of such large numbers. While these listings do not always provide an accurate picture of what sorts of subjects students learned, they at least yield a measure of the intent of the faculty in choosing to offer them. I hope that Riehl will rest easy insofar as these statistics are used as but one source among many in tracing the changes in this field of knowledge over time.

The data were culled from a number of different sources. Foremost were the German catalogues (*Vorlesungsverzeichnisse*) in which the rubric *Staats-und Kameralwissenschaften* or some variant thereof appeared. In addition, a Latin version (*Index Lectionum*) was published in the first half of the century, which listed lectures by faculty and professor; when the German versions were missing, these served as an alternative. When neither of these were available, one could consult several literary periodicals—or in some cases their supplements (*Intelligenzblatt*)—which published the catalogues: the *Allgemeine Literatur-Zeitung*, the *Jenaische Allgemeine Literatur-Zeitung*, the *Leipziger Literatur-Zeitung* in the early part of the century, and the *Literarisches Zentralblatt für Deutschland* after 1862.[2] Finally, many of the listings for Prussia were taken from archival sources: the lists of lectures by professor at the Zentrales Staatsarchiv Merseburg (now at the Geheimes Preussisches Staatsarchiv Dahlem in Berlin). These lists also contained (*pace* Riehl) enrollment fig-

---

1. Riehl, "Die Statistische Krankheit," in *Freie Vorträge* (Stuttgart: Cotta, 1885), 2: 261.
2. A full listing of these sources may be found in Horst Walter Blanke, "Bibliographie der in periodischer Literatur abgedruckten Vorlesungsverzeichnisse deutschsprachiger Universitäten, 1700–1919," *Berichte zur Wissenschaftsgeschichte*, 6 (1983): 205–27; 10 (1987): 17–43.

ures, which are used in some of the tables.[3] Given this multiplicity, it proved possible to arrive at a nearly complete database for the years 1820–1914.[4] Of the nineteen universities charted (twenty after the founding of Strassburg in 1872), yielding 380 semester catalogues per decade (400 after 1872), only 3 catalogues were missing for the 1820s, 2 for the 1830s, 2 for the 1840s, 9 for the 1850s, and 1 for the 1870s.[5]

From these sources, lectures and seminars listed under *Kameralwissenschaften, Staatswissenschaften,* or *Staats-und Kameralwissenschaften* were noted; each title was given a different number. One source of imprecision was in minor variations of title, but these proved easy to lump together for the most part. Another, more serious problem lay in the fact that not all the sources listed lectures in the same way. When the above rubrics were not used (as in the *Indices Lectionum* and the Prussian archives), inferences were made on the bases of available *Vorlesungsverzeichnisse* within a few years before or after. Fortunately, there were enough of these extant to instill confidence that these inferences were sound. In most universities, these listings were found under the philosophical faculty; in a few cases they were included under law (for Strassburg and for Freiburg before 1843 and after 1896–97), but again the standardized nature of the titles made it easy to distinguish the material to be included.

Lectures from other rubrics were also included if they were related (e.g., lectures in statistics that were listed under history, in sociology if listed under philosophy, or politics if listed under law). For topics in state and administrative law, however, a separate category was created which contained listings at five-year intervals rather than continuously (this material is used in figure 2).

An exception was made in the case of agriculture. The numbers and variety of titles burgeoned after 1865, making the task of recording them simply unmanageable. Therefore only courses in agricultural policy (*Agrarpolitik*) were listed after that date. Also, lectures in agricultural institutes affiliated with a university were not listed, regardless of date.

The lecture titles were then classified by subject area, and the resultant taxonomical categories formed the basis for the graphs in the book. Obviously the classification process involved a certain number of subjective decisions. There were many borderline cases and titles which fit in more than one category (e.g., lectures entitled "Economics and Finance"). When entering the data on the computer, however, it became possible to cross-reference these, so that the results include both the listings in a given area (e.g., economics) and those which combine several areas (e.g., economics and finance). This will account for some discrepancies between the data published here and that published in an earlier article on *Polizeiwissenschaft* for which the numbers were tabulated manually.[6] Occasionally, and to my frustration, the titles were ambiguous in themselves. The most notable case was *Staatswirtschaft,* which was sometimes used synonymously with *Nationalökonomie* and *Volkswirtschaft* to mean "economics"; at other times it was used for

3. GPSA Dahlem, Rep. 76 Va, Sect. 2 (Berlin), 3 (Bonn), 4 (Breslau), 6 (Göttingen), 7 (Greifswald), 8 (Halle), 9 (Kiel), 11 (Königsberg), 12 (Marburg), Tit. VII, XIII in each of these.

4. The winter semester 1914–15 was not included.

5. These were: Kiel 1820, 1834, 1856, 1856–57, 1857, 1857–58, 1858; Leipzig 1835–36; Greifswald 1849, 1850, 1850–51, 1852–53, 1853; Rostock 1874; Tübingen 1822, 1823; Würzburg 1841. The University of Münster, founded in 1901, was not included.

6. Lindenfeld, "Decline of Polizeiwissenschaft," 141, 146, 152–53.

the combination of economics and finance, and in a few instances it meant finance exclusively. There was no way to judge which of these meanings was intended from the catalogues; I arbitrarily included this title with economics.

When the same title was taught by more than one professor in a given semester, each listing was counted separately. The same applied to separate sections of a seminar—these tended to proliferate as numbers grew in the early twentieth century.

The universities were also grouped into regions. Those in Prussia constituted one obvious denomination (Berlin, Bonn, Breslau, Greifswald, Halle, and Königsberg), while "North" represented non-Prussian universities in northern Germany (Giessen, Göttingen, Jena, Kiel, Leipzig, Marburg, and Rostock). In 1866, the grouping changed as Prussia acquired Göttingen, Kiel, and Marburg. "South" included Erlangen, Freiburg, Heidelberg, Munich, Tübingen, and Würzburg throughout, to which Strassburg was added in 1872.

While data were collected for both summer and winter semesters, they are grouped into years or spans of years in most of the tables. A given year refers to the summer semester of that year plus the succeeding winter semester (e.g., "1844" includes both the summer semester of 1844 and the winter semester of 1844–45).

I plan to make the data, including the taxonomy, available through the Inter-University Consortium for Political and Social Research, P.O. Box 1248, Ann Arbor, Michigan 48106–1248.

Notes on Individual Figures

Most of the listings in each category fell under certain standard lectures, but included many lectures that were given infrequently as well. The following lists indicate the titles for the standard lectures only.

Figure 1: "Encylopädie der Kameralwissenschaften," "Encylopädie der Staatswissenschaften," or combinations of both (two-year intervals.)

Figure 2: "Deutsches Staatsrecht," "Preussisches Staatsrecht," and that of other German states. Based on data at five-year intervals, listed under law and/or *Staatswissenschaften*. Combinations with other subjects not included.

Figure 3: "Politik," "Allgemeine Staatslehre," "Allgemeine Staatsrecht und Politik," "Geschichte der politischen Theorien," "Politische Geschichte der Staatenbünde," and combinations with other subjects.

Figure 4: "Nationalökonomie," "Volkswirtschaftslehre," "Staatswirtschaft," plus combinations with other subjects such as finance.

Figure 5: "Polizeiwissenschaft," "Polizeiwissenschaft-und Polizeirecht," "Sicherheitspolizei," and combinations with other subjects; does not include "Volkswirtschaftspolitik."

Figure 6: Statistics of individual states, "Statistik der deutschen Staaten," "Statistik der europäischen Staaten."

Figure 7: "Landwirtschaft," "Agrarpolitik," "Ackerbau," "Landbau," "Botanik," "Landwirtschaftliche Vermessungskunde," "Agrarische Chemie," "Viehzucht," "Forstwissenschaft," "Forstbotanik," "Forstschutz," "Forstpolizei," "Landwirtschaftliche Betriebslehre," "Bergbaukunst," "Technologie," "Spezielle Technologie," "Technische Mechanik," "Chemische Technologie." Does not include combinations with other subjects.

Figure 8: Includes all categories listed separately in figure 1.

Figure 9: "Geschichte der Nationalökonomie."

Figure 10: "Polizeiwissenschaft," "Polizeiwissenschaft und Polizeirecht," "Volkswirtschaftspolitik."

Figure 11: "Soziale Frage," "Sozialpolitik," "Gewerbliche Arbeiterfrage," "Öffentliche Armenpflege," "Sozialismus," "Individualismus und Sozialismus."

Figure 12: "Übungen," "Repetitorien," "Conversatorien," "Staatswirtschaftliche Gesellschaft."

Figure 13: "Agrarpolitik," "Handelspolitik," "Verkehrswesen," "Kolonialpolitik und Geschichte." No combinations with other subjects.

Figure 14: "Versicherungsesen," "Versicherungsmathematik," in addition to titles listed in figure 11.

Figure 15: "Politik," "Allgemeine Staatslehre."

Abbreviations

ADB	*Allgemeine deutsche Biographie*
APO	*Archiv für politische Ökonomie und Polizeiwissenschaft*
ASS	*Archiv für Sozialwissenschaft und Sozialpolitik* (including its predecessor, the *Archiv für soziale Gesetzgebung und Statistik*
AVA	Allgemeine Verwaltungs-Archiv, Austria (Vienna)
DGS	Deutsche Gesellschaft für Soziologie
DH	*Deutsche Historiker,* ed. Hans-Ulrich Wehler
DS	*Deutsches Staatswörterbuch,* ed. Johann Kaspar Bluntschli
DV	*Deutsche Verwaltungsgeschichte,* ed. Kurt G. A. Jeserich, et al.
GGA	*Göttingsche Gelehrte Anzeigen*
ENTW	*Die Entwicklung der deutschen Volkswirtschaftslehre im 19. Jahrhundert. Gustav Schmoller zum siebzigsten Geburtstag*
GLA	Generallandesarchiv, Baden (Karlsruhe)
GPSA	Geheimes Preussisches Staatsarchiv (Dahlem)
GS	*Gesammelte Schriften*
HDS	*Handwörterbuch der Staatswissenschaften*
INDU	*Die Institutionalisierung der Nationalökonomie an Deutschen Universitäten,* ed. Norbert Waszek
JNS	*Jahrbücher für Nationalökonomie und Statistik*
PA	Personalakten
SJ	*Schmollers Jahrbuch*
UA	Universitätsarchiv
UB	Universitätsbibliothek
VFS	Verein für Sozialpolitik
VGS	*Die Volkswirtschaftslehre der Gegenwart in Selbst-darstellungen,* ed. Felix Meiner
ZGS	*Zeitschrift für die Gesamte Staatswissenschaften*

Bibliography

UNPUBLISHED SOURCES

Allgemeine Verwaltungsarchiv, Vienna
  Unterrichtsministerium
  Präsidium
  Studienhofkommission
Archives Departementales du Bas-Rhin, Strasbourg
Bayerische Hauptstaatsarchiv, Munich
Bundesarchiv Koblenz
  Nachlass Lujo Brentano
  Nachlass Alfred Weber
Duke University Library, Manuscript Dept.
  Papers of Carl Menger
Geheimes Preussisches Staatsarchiv Dahlem
(formerly Zentrales Staatsarchiv Merseburg)
  Rep. 76 Va Kultusministerium. Universitäten
  Rep. 77 Tit. 94 Statistisches Seminar
  Rep. 92 Nachlass Altenstein
       Nachlass Althoff
       Nachlass Schmoller
  Rep. 120 Gewerbliches Unterrichtswesen
  Rep. 196 Verein für Sozialpolitik
Generallandesarchiv Baden, Karlsruhe
Institut für Weltwirtschaft, Kiel: Hausarchiv
Louisiana State University Library, special collections
  Papers of Richard T. Ely
Schleswig-Holsteinischen Landesbibliothek Kiel
  Nachlass Ferdinand Tönnies
  Nachlass Lorenz von Stein
Universitätsarchiv Freiburg
Universitätsarchiv Göttingen
Universitätsarchiv Halle
Universitätsarchiv Heidelberg
Universitätsarchiv Jena
Universitätsarchiv Leipzig
Universitätsarchiv München

Universitätsarchiv Tübingen
Universitätsarchiv Wien
Universitätsbibliothek Göttingen
Cod Ms G. Hanssen
Universitätsbibliothek Tübingen
Nachlass Johannes Fallati
Nachlass Friedrich Hack
Nachlass Robert v. Mohl
Nachlass Albert Schäffle
Teilnachlass Gustav Schmoller
Wirtschaftswissenschaftliche Dekanat Tübingen
Memorabilienbuch der staatswirtschaftlichen Fakultät

PUBLISHED SOURCES

Abrams, Philip. *The Origins of British Sociology 1834–1914*. Chicago: University of Chicago Press, 1968.

Achenwall, Gottfried. *Die Staatsklugheit nach ihren ersten Grundsätzen*. Göttingen: Vandenhoeck & Ruprecht, 1761.

Ahrens, Heinrich. *Naturrecht oder Philosophie des Rechts und des Staates*. 6th ed. 2 vols. 1870. Reprint, Aalen: Scientia, 1968.

Akademischer Senat der Wiener Universität. *Geschichte der Wiener Universität von 1848 bis 1898*. Vienna: Holder, 1898.

Allgemeine deutsche Biographie. 56 vols. Leipzig: Duncker & Humblot, 1875–1912.

Andernach, Norbert. *Der Einfluss der Parteien auf das Hochschulwesen in Preussen*. Göttingen: Vandenhoeck & Ruprecht, 1972.

Anderson, Margaret Lavinia, and Kenneth Barkin. "The Myth of the Puttkamer Purge and the Reality of the Kulturkampf: Some Reflections on the Historiography of Imperial Germany." *Journal of Modern History* 54 (1982): 647–86.

Angermann, Erich. *Robert von Mohl 1799–1875. Leben und Werk eines altliberalen Staatsgelehrten*. Neuwied: Luchterhand, 1962.

Anon. "Drei Neue Handbücher der Volkswirtschaftslehre." *JNS* 18 (1872): 342–45.

Anton, Günther. "Koloniale Literatur." *JNS* 84 (1905): 534–38.

Aristotle. *Nicomachean Ethics*. Translated by J. A. K. Thomson. Baltimore: Penguin, 1955.

———. *The Politics*. Translated by T. A. Sinclair. Edited by Trevor J. Saunders. Revised, Harmondsworth: Penguin, 1981.

Aubin, Gustav. "Aus der Geschichte der Universität Halle um die Wende des 18. Jahrhunderts." *Hallische Universitätsreden* 52 (1931). Halle: Max Niemeyer.

Avinieri, Shlomo. *Hegel's Theory of the Modern State*. Cambridge: Cambridge University Press, 1972.

Baker, Keith Michael. "Politics and Public Opinion under the Old Regime: Some Reflections." In *Press and Politics in Pre-Revolutionary France*. Edited by Jack Censer and Jeremy Popkin. Berkeley: University of California Press, 1987, 204–46.

Balabkins, Nicholas W. *Not by Theory Alone . . . The Economics of Gustav von Schmoller and Its Legacy to America*. Berlin: Duncker & Humblot, 1988.

Barkin, Kenneth. *The Controversy over German Industrialization, 1890–1902*. Chicago: University of Chicago Press, 1970.

Barnes, Harry Elmer, and Howard Becker. *Social Thought from Lore to Science.* 3 vols. 1938. Reprint, New York: Dover, 1961.

Bauer, E. G. Anton. *Lehrbuch des Naturrechts.* 3d ed. Göttingen: Vandenhoeck & Ruprecht, 1825.

Bazillion, Richard J. *Modernizing Germany. Karl Biedermann's Career in the Kingdom of Saxony, 1835–1901.* New York: Peter Lang, 1990.

Becher, Johann Joachim. *Politische Discurs.* 3d ed. 1688. Reprint, Glashütten: Auvermann, 1972.

Becher, Ursula. *Politische Gesellschaft. Studien zur Genese bürgerlicher Öffentlichkeit in Deutschland.* Göttingen: Vandenhoeck & Ruprecht, 1978.

Becker, Otto. *Bismarcks Ringen um Deutschlands Gestaltung.* Edited by Alexander Scharff. Heidelberg: Quelle und Meyer, 1958.

Beckert, Manfred. *Johann Beckmann.* Leipzig: Teubner, 1983.

Beckmann, Johann. *Anleitung zur Technologie,* 5th ed. Göttingen: Vandenhoeck & Ruprecht, 1802.

———. *Grundsätze der Deutschen Landwirtschaft.* 3d ed. Göttingen: Dietrich, 1783.

Behr, Wilhelm Josef. *Ueber die Notwendigkeit des Studiums der Staatslehre nebst einem vorausgeschickten Grundrisse eines Systems.* Würzburg: Rienner, 1800.

Berdahl, Robert. *The Politics of the Prussian Nobility.* Princeton: Princeton University Press, 1988.

Bernhard, Ludwig. *Undesirable Results of German Social Legislation.* Translated by Harold Villard. New York: Workmen's Compensation Publicity Bureau, 1914.

Beseler, Georg. *Erlebtes und Erstrebtes, 1809–1859.* Berlin: Wilhelm Hertz, 1884.

Bezold, Friedrich von. *Geschichte der Rheinischen Friedrich-Wilhelms-Universität.* Bonn: Marcus & Weber, 1920.

Biedermann, Karl. *Erinnerungen aus der Paulskirche.* Leipzig: Gustav Mayer, 1849.

———. *Mein Leben.* Breslau: Schottländer, 1886.

Biesenbach, Friedhelm. *Die Entwicklung der Nationalökonmie an der Universität Freiburg i. Br. 1768–1896.* Freiburg: Eberhard Albert, 1969.

Bismarck, Otto von. *Die Gesammelte Werke.* 15 vols. 1924. Reprint, Nendeln: Kraus, 1972.

Blackbourn, David. *Class, Religion, and Local Politics in Wilhelmine Germany.* New Haven: Yale University Press, 1980.

Blaich, Fritz. "Der Beitrag der Deutschen Physiokraten für die Entwicklung der Wirtschaftswissenschaft von der Kameralistik zur Nationalökonomie." In *Studien zur Entwicklung der Ökonomischen Theorie.* Edited by Harald Scherf. Berlin: Duncker & Humblot, 1983.

Blanke, Horst Walter. "Bibliographie der in periodischer Literatur abgedruckten Vorlesungsverzeichnisse Deutschsprachiger Universitäten, 1700–1919." *Berichte zur Wissenschaftsgeschichte* 6 (1983): 205–23; 10 (1987): 17–43.

Blanning, T. C. W. "The Enlightenment in Catholic Germany." In *The Enlightenment in National Context.* Edited by Roy Porter and Mikulas Teich. Cambridge: Cambrige University Press, 1981, 118–26.

———. *Reform and Revolution in Mainz, 1743–1803.* Cambridge: Cambridge University Press, 1974.

Blasius, Dirk, and Eckart Pankoke. *Lorenz von Stein.* Darmstadt: Wissenschaftliche Buchgesellschaft, 1977.

Blaug, Mark. "The Economics of Johann von Thünen." In vol. 3 of *Research in the History of Economic Thought and Methodology*. Edited by Warren J. Samuels. Greenwich, CT: Jai Press, 1985, 1–25.

———. "The German Hegemony of Location Theory: A Puzzle in the History of Economic Thought." *History of Political Economy* 11 (1979): 21–29.

———. *Economic Theory in Retrospect*. 3d ed. Cambridge: Cambridge University Press, 1978.

Bleek, Wilhelm. *Von der Kameralausbildung zum Juristenprivileg*. Berlin: Colloquium, 1972.

Blessing, Werner K. "Der Geist der Zeit Hat die Menschen Sehr Verdorben . . .: Bemerkungen zur Mentalität in Bayern um 1800." In *Reformen im Rheinbündischen Deutschland*. Edited by Eberhard Weis. Munich: Oldenbourg, 1984, 229–50.

Bluntschli, Johann Caspar. *Denkwürdiges Aus Meinem Leben*. 3 vols. Nördlingen: Beck, 1884.

———. *Lehre vom Modernen Staat*. 3 vols. 1876–1886. Reprint, Aalen Scientia, 1965.

Böckenförde, Ernst-Wolfgang. *Gesetz und Gesetzgebende Gewalt*. Berlin: Duncker & Humblot, 1958.

———. *State, Society, and Liberty*. Translated by J. A. Underwood. New York: Berg, 1991.

Bödeker, Hans Erich. "Das staatswissenschaftliche Fächersystem im 18. Jahrhundert." In *Wissenschaft im Zeitalter der Aufklärung*. Edited by Hans Erich Bödeker et al. Göttingen: Vandenhoeck & Ruprecht, 1985, 143–62.

———. "Prozesse und Strukturen politischer Bewusstseinsbildung der deutschen Aufklärung." In *Aufklärung als Politisierung—Politisierung der Aufklärung*. Edited by Hans Erich Bödeker and Ulrich Herrmann. Hamburg: Meiner, 1987, 10–31.

Böhm-Bawerk, Eugen. *Capital and Interest*. Translated by William Smart. New York: Brentano's, 1922.

———. *Positive Theory of Capital*. Translated by W. Smart. London: Macmillan, 1891.

———. *Rechte und Verhältnisse vom Standpunkte der Volkswirtschaftlichen Güterlehre*. Innsbruck: Wagner, 1881.

Boese, Franz. *Geschichte des Vereins für Sozialpolitik 1872–1932*. Berlin: Duncker & Humblot, 1939.

Bog, Ingomar. *Der Reichsmerkantilismus*. Stuttgart: Gustav Fischer, 1959.

Boldt, Hans. "Zwischen Patrimonialismus und Parlamentarismus: Zur Entwicklung vorparlamentarischer Theorien in der deutschen Staatslehre des Vormärz." In *Gesellschaft, Parlament, Regierung*. Edited by Gerhard A. Ritter. Düsseldorf: Droste, 1974, 77–100.

Boos, Margarete. *Die Wissenschaftstheorie Carl Mengers*. Vienna: Böhlau, 1986.

Borchhardt, Knut. "Albert Schäffle als Wirtschaftstheoretiker." *ZGS* 16 (1961): 610–35.

Born, Karl Erich. "Structural Changes in German Social and Economic Development at the End of the Nineteenth Century." In *Imperial Germany*. Edited by James Sheehan. New York: Franklin Watts, 1976, 16–38.

———. *Geschichte der Wirtschaftswissenschaften an der Universität Tübingen*. Tübingen: Mohr, 1967.

———. *International Banking in the Nineteenth and Twentieth Centuries*. Translated by Volker R. Berghahn. New York: St. Martin's Press, 1983.

———. *Staat und Sozialpolitik seit Bismarcks Sturz*. Wiesbaden: Steiner, 1957.

Bourdieu, Pierre. "The Intellectual Field: A World Apart." In *In Other Words*. Translated by Matthew Adamson. Stanford: Stanford University Press, 1990, 140–49.

———. "Social Space and Symbolic Power." In *In Other Words*. Translated by Matthew Adamson. Stanford: Stanford University Press, 1990, pp. 123–39.

Bowley, Marian. *Nassau Senior and Classical Economics*. New York: Kelly, 1949.

Brater, Karl. "Die Neueren Bearbeitungen der Polizeiwissenschaft." *Kritische Überschau der deutschen Gesetzgebung und Rechtwissenschaften* 5 (1857): 69–90.

Braun, Heinrich. "Zur Einführung." *ASS* 1 (1888): 1–6.

———. "Abschiedswort." *ASS* 18 (1903): v—vi.

Brauneder, Wilhelm. "Formen und Tragweite des deutschen Einflusses auf die österreichische Verwaltungsrechtswissenschaft 1850–1914." In *Wissenschaft und Recht der Verwaltung Seit dem Ancien Regime*. Edited by Erk Volkmar Heyen. Frankfurt/Main: Klostermann, 1984, 249–83.

Braunreuther, Kurt. "Die Staatswissenschaften von 1810–1860 an der Humbolt-Universität." *Zeitschrift für Geschichtswissenschaft* 8 (1960): 1604–1631.

Brentano, Lujo, *Agrarpolitik*. Stuttgart: Cotta, 1897.

———. *Die Arbeitergilden der Gegenwart*. 2 vols. Leipzig: Duncker & Humblot, 1871–72.

———. *On the History and Development of Gilds and the Origin of Trade-Unions*. 1870. Reprint, New York: Burt Franklin, 1969.

———. "Die Klassische Nationalökonomie." In *Der wirtschaftende Mensch in der Geschichte*. Leipzig: Meiner, 1923.

———. *Mein Leben im Kampf um die soziale Entwicklung Deutschlands*. Jena: Diederichs, 1931.

———. *The Relation of Labor to the Law of To-Day*. Translated by Porter Sherman. 1876. Reprint, New York: Putnam, 1891.

———. *Über die Ursachen der heutigen socialen Noth*. Leipzig: Duncker & Humblot, 1889.

———. "Ueber Werturteile in der Volkswirtschaftslehre." *ASS* 33 (1911): 695–714.

———. *Wie Studiert man Nationalökonomie?* Munich: Reinhardt, 1911.

Breysig, Kurt. "Nietzsches ethische und soziologische Anschauungen." *SJ* 20 (1896).

Brocke, Bernhard vom. "Hochschul-und Wissenschaftspolitik in Preussen und im deutschen Kaiserreich 1882–1907: Das 'System Althoff.'" In *Bildungspolitik in Preussen zur Zeit des Kaiserreichs*. Edited by Peter Baumgart. Stuttgart: Klett-Cotta, 1980, 9–118.

———. *Kurt Breysig*. Lübeck: Matthiesen, 1971.

———. "Werner Sombart 1863–1941." In *Sombarts 'Moderner Kapitalismus.'* Edited by Bernhard vom Brocke. Munich: Deutscher Taschenbuch Verlag, 1987, 11–65.

Brose, Eric Dorn. *The Politics of Technological Change in Prussia: Out of the Shadow of Antiquity, 1809–1848*. Princeton: Princeton University Press, 1993.

Bruch, Rüdiger vom. "Bürgerliche Sozialreform im deutschen Kaiserreich." In *Weder Kommunismus noch Kapitalismus*. Edited by Rüdiger vom Bruch. Munich: C. H. Beck, 1985, 61–179.

———. "Zur Historisierung der Staatswissenschaften." *Berichte zur Wissenschaftsgeschichte* 9 (1985): 131–46.

———. "Kulturstaat—Sinndeutung von Oben?" In *Kultur und Kulturwissenschaften um 1900*. Edited by Friedrich Wilhelm Graf, Gangolf Hübinger, and R. vom Bruch. Stuttgart: Steiner, 1989, 63–101.

———. "Nationalökonomie zwischen Wissenschaft und öffentlicher Meinung im Spiegel Gustav Schmollers." in *Gustav Schmoller e il suo tempo*. Edited by Pierangelo Schiera and Friedrich Tenbruck. Bologna: Societa editrice il Mulino, 1989, 153–80.

———. *Wissenschaft, Politik und öffentliche Meinung*. Husum: Matthiesen, 1980.

Brunner, Otto. "Das 'Ganze Haus' und die Alteuropäische 'Oekonomik.'" In *Neue Wege der Sozialgeschichte*. Göttingen: Vandenhoeck & Ruprecht, 1956, 33–61.

Brunschwig, Henri. *Enlightenment and Romanticism in Eighteenth-Century Prussia*. Translated by Franz Jellinek. Chicago: University of Chicago Press, 1974.

Brückner, Jutta. *Staatswissenschaften, Kameralismus und Naturrecht*. Munich: C. H. Beck, 1977.

Buchholz, Ilse. "Nachwort" to *Jung-Stillings Lebensgeschichte*, by J. H. Jung-Stilling. 1777. Reprint, Berlin: Union Verlag, 1958.

Bücher, Karl. *Die Entstehung der Volkswirtschaft*. 3d ed. Tübingen: Laupp, 1901.

———. *Hochschulfragen*. Leipzig: Wörner, 1912.

———. *Lebenserinnerungen*. Tübingen: Laupp, 1919.

Bülau, Friedrich. "Über das Formelle in den Staatswissenschaften." *Archiv für politische Ökonomie und Polizeiwissenschaft* 3 (1838): 1–17.

Bülow, Prince [Bernhard] von. *Memoirs*. 4 vols. Translated by Geoffrey Dunlop and F. A. Voight. London: Putnam, 1931–32.

Büsch, Johann Georg. "Rede in welcher Viel Böses und Wenig Gutes von der Handlungstheorie Gesagt Wird." In vol. 14 of *Johann Georg Büsch's Sämtliche Schriften*. 1772. Reprint, Vienna: Bauer, 1817, 5–34.

———. "Handlungswissenschaft." In vol. 1 of *Johann Georg Büsch's Sämtliche Schriften*. 1772. Reprint, Vienna: Bauer, 1813.

Caldwell, Bruce J., ed. *Carl Menger and His Legacy in Economics* Durham: Duke University Press, 1990.

Caplan, Jane. "Bureaucracy, Politics, and the National Socialist State." In *The Shaping of the Nazi State*. Edited by Peter Stachura. London: Croom Helm, 1978, 234–56.

———. "The Imaginary Universality of Particular Interests: the 'Tradition' of the Civil Service in German History." *Social History* 4 (1979): 299–317.

———. "Profession as Vocation: The German Civil Service." In *German Professions, 1800–1950*. Edited by Geoffrey Cocks and Konrad H. Jarausch. New York: Oxford University Press, 1990, 163–82.

Carpenter, Kenneth. *Dialogue in Political Economy*. Boston: Baker Library, Harvard School of Business Administration, 1977.

Carr, W. *Schleswig-Holstein, 1815–48: A Study in National Conflict*. Manchester: Manchester University Press, 1963.

Caspary, Anna. *Ludolf Campenhausen's Leben*. Stuttgart: Cotta, 1902.

Chickering, Roger. *We Men Who Feel the Most German*. Boston: Allen & Unwin, 1984.

Cohn, Gustav. *Georg Hanssen*. Leipzig: Duncker & Humblot, 1895.

———. *System der Nationalökonomie*. 3 vols. Stuttgart: Ferdinand Enke, 1885.

———. *Ueber die staatswissenschaftliche Vorbildung zum höheren Verwaltungsdienst in Preussen*. Berlin: Springer, 1900.

———. *Universitätsfragen und Erinnerungen*. Stuttgart: Enke, 1913.

———. "Wirtschaftswissenschaft und Wirtschaftspolitik." *ZGS* 66 (1910): 1–40, 445–61.

Coleman, D.C. "Eli Heckscher and the Idea of Mercantilism." In *Economic Thought:*

A Historical Anthology. Edited by James Gherity. New York: Random House, 1965, 43–66.

Conrad, Else. *Der Verein für Sozialpolitik.* Diss. Universität Zürich, 1906.

Conrad, Johannes. *Grundriss zum Studium der Politischen Oekonomie.* 6th ed. 3 vols. Jena: Gustav Fischer, 1907.

————. *Lebenserinnerungen.* Edited by Else Kesten-Conrad and Herbert Conrad. Halle: Unpublished ms., 1917.

Coser, Lewis A. "The Stranger in the Academy." In *George Simmel.* Edited by Lewis A. Coser. Englewood Cliffs, NJ: Prentice-Hall, 1965, 29–39.

Craig, John. *Scholarship and Nation Building.* Chicago: University of Chicago Press, 1984.

Dahlmann, Friedrich Christoph. *Die Politik.* 1835. Reprint, Frankfurt/Main: Suhrkamp, 1968.

Dehio, Ludwig. "Georg Friedrich Knapp." In vol. 5 of *Die Grossen Deutschen.* Berlin: Propyläen, 1957, 399–406.

Delbrück, Clemens von. *Die Ausbildung für die höheren Verwaltungsdienst in Preussen.* Jena: Fischer, 1917.

Delbrück, Rudolph von. *Lebenserinnerungen, 1817–1867.* 2 vols. Leipzig: Duncker & Humblot, 1905.

Demel, Walter. *Der bayerische Staatsabsolutismus 1806/08–1817.* Munich: C. H. Beck, 1983.

Denzer, Horst. *Moralphilosophie und Naturrecht bei Samuel Pufendorf.* Munich: C. H. Beck, 1972.

Deutsche Gesellschaft für Soziologie. *Verhandlungen des ersten deutschen Soziologentages . . . 1910 in Frankfurt/Main.* Tübingen: Mohr, 1911.

Deutsche Verwaltungsgeschichte. Edited by Kurt G. A. Jeserich, Hans Pohl, and Georg-Christoph von Unruh. 6 vols. Stuttgart: Deutsche Verlags-Anstalt, 1983–1988.

Die deutschen technischen Hochschulen. Munich: Verlag der Deutschen Technik, 1941.

Deutsches Staats-Wörterbuch. Edited by J. C. Bluntschli. 11 vols. Stuttgart & Leipzig: Expedition des Staats-Wörterbuchs, 1857–1870.

Dickinson, H. D. "Von Thünen's Economics." *Economic Journal* 79 (1969), 894–902.

Diefendorf, Jeffry. *Businessmen and Politics in the Rhineland, 1789–1834.* Princeton: Princeton University Press, 1980.

Diehl, Karl. "Die Bedeutung der wissenschaftlichen Nationalökonomie für die praktische Wirtschaftspolitik." *JNS* 92 (1909): 289–315.

————. "Johannes Conrad." *JNS* 104 (1913): 727–62.

Diephouse, David J. "Editor's Introduction." In *The Natural History of the German People,* by Wilhelm Heinrich Riehl. Translated by David J. Diephouse. Edited by David J. Diephouse. Lewiston, NY: Edward Mellen Press, 1991, 1–23.

Diest, Gustav von. *Aus dem Leben eines Glücklichen.* Berlin: Mittler & Sohn, 1904.

Dietzel, Carl. *Strassburg als deutsche Reichsuniversität und die Neugestaltung des juristischen und staatswissenschaftlichen Studiums.* Frankfurt: Sauerländer, 1871.

Dietzel, Heinrich. "Beiträge zur Methodik der Wirtschaftswissenschaft." *JNS* 42 (1884): 17–44, 193–259.

————. "Stud. Jur. et Cam." *JNS* 69 (1897): 679–711.

Dipper, Christof. *Die Bauernbefreiung in Deutschland 1790–1850.* Stuttgart: Kohlhammer, 1980.

Dopfer, Kurt. "How Historical Is Schmoller's Economic Theory?" *Journal of Institutional and Theoretical Economics.* 144 (1988): 552–69.

Dornreich, Julius. *Der badische Politiker Franz Josef Buss.* Diss. Freiburg. 1922.

Dorpalen, Andreas. *Heinrich von Treitschke.* New Haven: Yale University Press, 1957.

Dotterweich, Volker. *Heinrich von Sybel, Geschichtswissenschaft in Politischer Absicht (1817–1861).* Göttingen: Vandenhoeck & Ruprecht, 1978.

Droysen, Johann Gustav. *Briefwechsel.* Edited by Rudolf Hübner. 2 vols. 1927. Reprint, Osnabrück: Biblio Verlag, 1977.

Dufraisse, Roger. "L'Influence de la Politique Économique Napoléonienne sur L'Économie des États du Rheinbund." In *Reformen im Rheinbündischen Deutschland.* Edited by Eberhard Weis. Munich: Oldenbourg, 1984, 75–98.

Ebert, Kurt. *Die Grazer Juristenfakultät im Vormärz.* Graz: Leykam, 1969.

Ehrenberg, Richard. *Der Terrorismus in der Wirtschafts-Wissenschaft.* Berlin: Hobbing, 1910.

———. *Die Unternehmungen der Brüder Siemens.* Jena: Gustav Fischer, 1906.

Eiselen, Fredrich. *Die Lehre von der Volkswirtschaft in ihren allgemeinen Bedingungen und in ihrer besonderer Entwicklung.* Halle: Schwetschke, 1843.

Eisermann, Gottfried. *Die Grundlagen des Historismus in der deutschen Nationalökonomie.* Stuttgart: Enke, 1956.

Eley, Geoff. *Reshaping the German Right.* New Haven: Yale University Press, 1980.

Ellis, Howard S. *German Monetary Theory, 1905–1933.* Cambridge, MA: Harvard University Press, 1934.

Ely, Richard. *Ground Under Our Feet: An Autobiography.* New York: Macmillan, 1938.

Endres, Rudolf. "Das Armenproblem im Zeitalter des Absolutismus." In *Aufklärung, Absolutismus und Bürgertum in Deutschland.* Edited by Franklin Kopitsch. Munich: Nymphenburg, 1976, 220–45.

Engel, Ernst. "L. A. J. Quetelet: ein Gedächtnisrede." *Zeitschrift des königl. preussischen statistischen Bureaus* 11 (1871), 207–20.

———. *Das statistische Seminar des königliche preussischen statistischen Büreaus in Berlin.* Berlin: Königlichen Geheimen Ober-Hofbuchdruckerei, 1864.

———. "Das statistische Seminar und das Studium der Statistik überhaupt." *Zeitschrift des königl. preussischen statistischen Büreaus,* 11 (1871): 181–211.

Engelhardt, Ulrich. "Zum Begriff der Glückseligkeit in der kameralistischen Staatslehre des 18. Jahrhunderts (J. H. G. V. Justi)." *Zeitschrift für historische Forschung* 8 (1981): 37–79.

Die Entwicklung der deutschen Volkswirtschaftslehre im 19. Jahrhundert. Gustav Schmoller zur siebenzigsten Wiederkehr seines Geburtstages. 2 vols. Leipzig: Duncker & Humblot, 1908.

Epstein, Klaus. *The Genesis of German Conservatism.* Princeton: Princeton University Press, 1966.

Eulenburg, Franz. "Ueber die Möglichkeit und die Aufgaben einer Socialpsychologie." *SJ* 24 (1900): 201–37.

Eyck, Frank. *The Frankfurt Parliament, 1848–1849.* London: Macmillan, 1968.

Fabian, Reinhard, and Peter M. Simons. "The Second Austrian School of Value Theory." In *Austrian Economics.* Edited by Wolfgang Grassl and Barry Smith. New York: New York University Press, 1986, 37–101.

Fallati, Johannes. "Gedanken über Mittel und Wege zu Hebung der praktischen Statistik, mit besonderer Rücksicht auf Deutschland." *ZGS* 3 (1846): 496–557.

Farr, Ian. "Populism in the Countryside: Peasant Leagues in Bavaria in the 1980s." In *Society and Politics in Wilhelmine Germany.* Edited by Richard Evans. London: Croom Helm, 1978, 136–59.

Feist, Bruno. *Die Geschichte der Nationalökonomie an der Friedrichs-Universität zu Halle.* Diss. Halle, 1930.

Feldman, Gerald. *The Great Disorder.* New York: Oxford University Press. 1993.

Fisch, Stefan. *Von Kameral-Institut zur polytechnischen Schule. Studien zur Vorgeschichte der technischen Hochschule München.* Unpublished ms., 1977.

Fischer, Fritz. *Germany's Aims in the First World War.* New York: Norton, 1967.

Fischer, Gustav. *Über die Errichtung staatswissenschaftlicher Seminarien auf den deutschen Universitäten.* Jena: Mauke, 1857.

Flad, Ruth. *Studien zur politischen Begriffsbildung in Deutschland während der preussischen Reform. Der Begriff der öffentlichen Meinung bei Stein, Arndt und Humboldt.* Berlin: De Gruyter, 1929.

Foucault, Michel. "Governmentality." In *The Foucault Effect.* Edited by Graham Burchell, Colin Gordon, and Peter Miller. Chicago: University of Chicago Press, 1991, 87–104.

———. "Politics and the Study of Discourse." In *The Foucault Effect.* Edited by Graham Burchell, Colin Gordon, and Peter Miller. Chicago: University of Chicago Press, 1991, 53–72.

———. *Power/Knowledge: Selected Interviews and Other Writings, 1972–1977.* Translated and edited by Colin Gordon. New York: Pantheon, 1981.

———. *Surveiller et Punir.* Paris: Gallimard, 1975.

———. *The Order of Things.* Translated anon. 1971. Reprint, New York: Random House, Vintage, 1973.

Fraas, C. *Geschichte der Landbau-und Forstwissenschaft.* Munich: Cotta, 1865.

Frauendorfer, Sigmund. *Ideengeschichte der Agrarwirtschaft und Agrarpolitik.* 2 vols. Munich: Bayrischer Landwirtschaftsverlag, 1957–58.

Frensdorff, F. *Über das Leben und die Schriften des Nationalökonomen J. H. G. von Justi.* 1903. Reprint, Glashütten: Auvermann, 1970.

Friedenthal, Richard. *Goethe: sein Leben und seine Zeit.* Munich: Piper, 1963.

Frisby, David. *Georg Simmel.* Chichester: Ellis Horwood, 1984.

Fulda, Friedrich Karl. *Grundsätze der Ökonomisch-politischen oder Kameralwissenschaften.* Tübingen: Osiander, 1816.

———. *Systematische Abriss der sogenannten Kameralwissenschaften.* Tübingen: Heerbrandt, 1802.

Furner, Mary. *Advocacy and Objectivity.* Lexington, KY: University Press of Kentucky, 1975.

Gagliardo, John. *From Pariah to Patriot: The Changing Image of the German Peasant, 1770–1840.* Lexington, KY: University of Kentucky Press, 1969.

———. *Reich and Nation.* Bloomington: Indiana University Press, 1980.

Gall, Luther. *Benjamin Constant. Seine politische Ideenwelt und der deutsche Vormärz.* Wiesbaden: Steiner, 1963.

Gasser, Simon Peter. *Einleitung zu den oeconomischen politischen und Kameralwissenschaften . . .* Halle: Waysenhaus, 1729.

Gay, Peter. *The Dilemma of Democratic Socialism: Eduard Bernstein's Challenge to Marx.* 1952. Reprint, New York: Collier, 1962.

————. *The Enlightenment: An Interpretation.* Vol. 2. 1969. Reprint, New York: Norton, 1977.

Gädeke, Hannah. *Wilhelm Heinrich Riehls Gedanken über Volk und Staat.* Berlin: Deutscher Rechtsverlag, 1937.

Gehring, Paul. *Friedrich List. Jugend-und Reifejahre 1789–1825.* Tübingen: J. C. B. Mohr, 1964.

Georgescu-Roegen, Nicholas. "Hermann Heinrich Gossen: His Life and Work. In *The Laws of Human Relations,* by Hermann Heinrich Gossen. Translated by Rudolph C. Blitz. Cambridge, MA: MIT Press, 1983, xi—cxlv.

Gerber, Carl Friedrich von. *Grundzüge des deutschen Staatsrechts.* 3d ed. Leipzig: Tauschnitz, 1880.

Gerth, Hans. J. *Bürgerliche Intelligenz um 1800.* Göttingen: Vandenhoeck & Ruprecht, 1976.

Gide, Charles, and Charles Rist. *A History of Economic Doctrines.* Translated by R. Richards. Boston: Heath, 1915.

Gierke, Otto von. "Die Grundbegriffe des Staatsrechts und die neuesten Staatstheorien." *ZGS* 30 (1874): 153–98, 265–335.

————. "Die juristische Studienordnung." *SJ* 1 (1877): 1–32.

————. "Labands Staatsrecht und die deutschen Rechtswissenschaft." *SJ* 7 (1883): 1097–1195.

Gierke, Otto von, and Rudolph Gneist. "Gutachten über die Frage: "Ist eine gemeinsame Prüfungsordnung für Richter und Anwälte notwendig. . .?" In *Verhandlungen des Vierzehnten deutschen Juristentages.* Berlin: Guttentag, 1878, 3–24.

Gillis, John. *The Prussian Bureaucracy in Crisis, 1840–1860.* Stanford: Stanford University Press, 1971.

Gimbel, E. J. "Ladislaus V. Bortkiewicz." In vol. 2 of *International Encyclopedia of the Social Sciences.* New York: Macmillan, 1968, 128–31.

Gispen, Kees. *New Profession, Old Order: Engineers and German Society, 1815–1914.* Cambridge: Cambridge University Press, 1989.

Goerke, Heinz. "Linnaeus' German Pupils and Their Significance." In *Linnaeus: Progress and Prospects in Linnaean Research.* Edited by Gunnar Broberg. Stockholm: Almqvist & Wiksell, 1980, 233–39.

Goethe, Johann Wolfgang, Georg Sartorius, and Caroline Sartorius. *Goethes Briefwechsel mit Georg und Caroline Sartorius.* Edited by Else von Monroy. Weimar: Böhlau, 1931.

Gollwitzer, Heinz, ed. *100 Jahre Maximilianeum, 1852–1952.* Munich: Richard Pflaum, 1953.

Goltz, Theodor von der. "Die Entwicklung der höheren landwirtschaftlichen Unterrichtswesens in Deutschland und die Stellung der Akademie Poppelsdorf innerhalb Desselben." In *Festschrift zur Feier des Fünfzigjährigen Bestehens der Königlich-Preussischen Landwirtschaftliche Akademie Poppelsdorf.* Bonn: [n.p.], 1897, 83–106.

Gooch, G. P. *Germany and the French Revolution.* London: Longmans, Green & Co., 1920.

————. *History and Historians in the Nineteenth Century.* 1935. Reprint, Boston: Beacon Press, 1959.

Gordon, Colin. "Governmental Rationality: An Introduction." In *The Foucault Effect.* Edited by Graham Burchell, Colin Gordon, and Peter Miller. Chicago: University of Chicago Press, 1991, 1–51.

Gorges, Irmela. *Sozialforschung in Deutschland, 1872–1914.* 2d ed. Frankfurt/Main: Anton Hain, 1986.

Gothein, Marie Luise. *Eberhard Gothein. Ein Lebensbild.* Stuttgart: Kohlhammer, 1931.

Gray, Marion W. "Prescriptions for Productive Female Domesticity in a Transitional Era: Germany's Hausmütterliteratur, 1780–1840." *History of European Ideas* 8 (1987): 413–26.

————. "From the Household Economy to 'Rational Agriculture.'" In *In Search of a Liberal Germany.* Edited by K. H. Jarausch and L. E. Jones. Oxford: Berg, 1990, 25–54.

Gros, Karl Heinrich. *Lehrbuch des philosophischen Rechtswissenschaft oder des Naturrechts.* 3d ed. Tübingen: Cotta, 1816.

Gundlach, Fritz. *Catologus Professorum Academiae Marburgiensis, 1527–1910.* Marburg: Elvert, 1927.

Habermas, Jürgen. *Strukturwandel der Öffentlichkeit.* 2d ed. Neuwied: Luchterhand, 1965.

Hack, Friedrich. Review of *Grundsätze der Volkswirtschaftslehre,* by Carl Menger. *ZGS* 28 (1872): 183–84.

Hacking, Ian. "Prussian Numbers, 1860–1882. In vol. 1 of *The Probabalistic Revolution.* Edited by Lorenz Krüger, Lorraine J. Daston, and Michael Heidelberger. Cambridge, MA: MIT Press, 1987, 377–94.

Hagen, William W. "The Junkers' Faithless Servants: Peasant Insubordination and the Breakdown of Serfdom in Brandenburg-Prussia, 1763–1811." In *The German Peasantry.* Edited by Richard J. Evans and W. R. Lee. New York: St. Martin's Press, 1986, 71–101.

Hamerow, Theodore. *The Social Foundations of German Unification, 1858–1871.* 2 vols. Princeton: Princeton University Press, 1969.

————. *Restoration, Revolution, Reaction.* Princeton: Princeton University Press, 1958.

Hammerstein, Notker. *Aufklärung und Katholisches Reich.* Berlin: Duncker & Humblot, 1987.

————. "Reichs-Historie." In *Aufklärung und Geschichte.* Edited by Hans Erich Bödeker et al. Göttingen: Vandenhoeck & Ruprecht, 1986, 82–104.

————. *Jus und Historie.* Göttingen: Vandenhoeck & Ruprecht, 1972.

Handwörterbuch der Staatswissenschaften. 6 vols. Edited by Johannes Conrad et al. Jena: Gustav Fischer, 1890–97.

Hansen, Joseph. *Gustav von Mevissen. Ein Rheinisches Lebensbild.* Berlin: Reimer, 1906.

Hanssen, Georg. "Lebenserinnerungen des Agrarhistorikers und Nationalökonomen Georg Hanssen." Edited by H. Hanssen. *Zeitschrift der Gesellschaft für Schleswig-Holsteinische Geschichte* 40 (1910): 1–180.

————. "Das statistische Büreau der preussischen Monarchie unter Hoffmann und Dieterici." *APO* n. f., 4 (1846): 329–90.

————. "Die volkswirtschaftlichen Zustände des Königreichs Hannover im Hinblick auf den Anschluss Desselben an den Zollverein." *ZGS* 9 (1853): 379–414.

Harl, Johann Paul. *Grundlinien einer Theorie des Staates . . .* Erlangen: Palm, 1805.

Harms, Bernhard. "Das Institut für Weltwirtschaft und Seeverkehr in Kiel." In *Forschungsinstitute: Ihre Geschichte, Organisation und Ziele.* Edited by Ludolph Brauer, Adolph Mendelssohn-Bartholdy, and Adolf Meyer. Hamburg: Paul Hartung, 1930, 305–23.

Harnisch, Helmut. "Peasants and Markets: The Background to the Agrarian Reforms in Feudal Prussia East of the Elbe, 1760–1807." In *The German Peasantry.* Edited by Richard J. Evans and W. R. Lee. New York: St. Martin's Press, 1986, 37–70.

Hasek, Carl William. "The Introduction of Adam Smith's Doctrines into Germany." *Studies in History, Economics, and Public Law,* no. 117. Edited by Columbia University Faculty of Political Science. New York: Columbia University, 1925.

Haskell, Thomas. *The Emergence of Professional Social Science.* Urbana, IL: University of Illinois Press, 1977.

Hassel, G. H. *Lehrbuch der Statistik der europäischen Staaten für höhere Lerhanstalten, zugleich als Handbuch zur Selbstbelehrung.* Weimar: Verlage des Geographischen Instituts, 1822.

Hausherr, Hans. *Hardenberg. Eine Politische Biographie.* Edited by Karl Erich Born. Cologne: Böhlau, 1963.

Haym, Rudolf. *Das Leben Max Dunckers.* Berlin: Gaertner, 1891.

Heckscher, Eli. *Mercantilism.* Translated by Mendel Shapiro. 2 vols. London: Allen & Unwin, 1935.

[Heeren, Adolph], Review of Conrad Mannert, *Statistik der europäischen Staaten. GGA,* no. 84 (1806), 833–39.

———. Review of A. W. Rehberg, *Über die Staatsverwaltung deutscher Länder. GGA,* no. 131 (1807), 1298–1308.

Heffter, Heinrich. *Die deutsche Selbstverwaltung im 19. Jahrhundert.* Stuttgart: Koehler, 1950.

Hegel, G. W. F. *Philosophy of Right.* Translated by T. M. Knox. London: Oxford, 1967.

Heilmann, Martin. *Adolph Wagner—Ein deutscher Nationalökonom im Urteil der Zeit.* Frankfurt/Main: Campus, 1980.

Heiss, Klauss-Peter. "Wilhelm Lexis." In vol. 9 of *International Encyclopedia of the Social Sciences.* New York: Macmillan, 1968, 271–76.

Helferich, Johann. "Die Zölle von Colonialzucker und die Rübensteuer im Zollverein." *ZGS* 8 (1852): 70–106.

Helfferich, Karl. *Money.* Translated by Louis Infeld. 2 vols. New York: Adelphi, 1927.

Henderson, W. O. *Friedrich List, Economist and Visionary, 1789–1846.* London: Frank Cass, 1983.

———. *The Zollverein.* Chicago: Quandrangle, 1959.

Hennings, Klaus-Hinrich. *The Austrian Theory of Value and Capital: Studies in the Life and Work of Eugen von Böhm-Bawerk.* Diss. Oxon, 1972.

Hennis, Wilhelm. *Politik und praktische Philosophie.* Neuwied: Luchterhand, 1963.

———. "A Science of Man." In *Max Weber and his Contemporaries.* Edited by Wolfgang Mommsen and Jürgen Osterhammel. London: Allen & Unwin, 1987, 25–58.

Hentschel, Volker. *Die deutschen Freihändler und der volkswirtschaftliche Kongress 1858 bis 1865.* Stuttgart: Klett, 1975.

———. "Die Staatswissenschaften an den deutschen Universitäten im 18. und frühen 19. Jahrhundert." *Berichte zur Wissenschaftsgeschichte* 1 (1978): 181–200.

———. "Zwecksetzungen und Zielvorstellungen in den Wirtschafts-und Soziallehren des 18. und 19. Jahrhunderts." *Berichte zur Wissenschaftsgeschichte* 5 (1982): 107–30.

Herkner, Heinrich. "Der Kampf um das sittliche Werturteil in der Nationalökonomie." *SJ* 36 (1912): 515–55.

———. *Die Arbeiterfrage.* 4th ed. Berlin: Guttentag, 1905.

Hermann, Friedrich B. W. *Über polytechnischen Institute im Allgemeinen und über die Erweiter-*

ung der technischen Schule zu Nürnberg insbesondere. Nürnberg: Riegel und Weissner, 1826.

———. *Staatswirtschaftliche Untersuchungen.* 1st ed. Munich: Weber, 1832; 2d ed. Munich: Fleischmann, 1870.

Hermbstädt, Siegesmund. *Grundriss der Technologie.* 2d ed. Berlin: Reimer, 1830.

Herrfurth, Ludwig, ed. *Das Gesetz, betreffend die Befähigung für den höheren Verwaltungsdienst.* 3d ed. Berlin: Carl Heymanns Verlag, 1888.

Heuss, Theodor. *Deutsche Gestalten.* Stuttgart: Wunderlich, 1949.

Heyen, Erk Volkmar. "Entwicklungsbedingungen der Verwaltungsrechtswissenschaft." *Der Staat* 22 (1983): 21–32.

———. Sur la Segmentation institutionelle du Discours scientifique en Droite administrativ vers 1900." In *Formation und Transformation des Verwaltungswissens in Frankreich und Deutschland (18./19.Jh.).* Edited by Erk Volkmar Heyen. Baden-Baden: Nomos, 1989, 207–20.

Hildebrand, Bruno. "Die gegenwärtige Aufgabe der Wissenschaft der Nationalökonomie." *JNS* 1 (1863): 5–26; 137–46.

———. "Natural-, Geld-, and Creditwirtschaft." *JNS* 2 (1864): 1–24.

———. "Zur Geschichte der deutschen woll-Industrie," JNS 6 (1866): 186–254; 7 (1866): 81–153.

———. *Die Nationalökonomie der Gegenwart und Zukunft.* Frankfurt/Main: Literarische Anstalt, 1848.

———. "Die Wissenschaftliche Aufgabe der Statistik." *JNS* 6 (1866): 1–11.

Hinrichs, Carl. *Preussentum und Pietismus.* Göttingen: Vandenhoeck & Ruprecht, 1971.

Hintze, Otto. "Prussian Reform Movements Before 1806." In *The Historical Essays of Otto Hintze.* Edited by Felix Gilbert. New York: Oxford University Press, 1975, 64–87.

———. "Roschers politische Entwicklungstheorie." In *Soziologie und Geschichte.* 2d ed. Göttingen: Vandenoeck & Ruprecht, 1964, 3–45.

———. "Gustav Schmoller." In *Soziologie und Geschichte.* 2d ed. Göttingen: Vandenhoeck & Ruprecht, 1964, 519–43.

Hippel, Wolfgang von. "Zum Problem der Agrarreformen in Baden und Württemberg, 1800–1820." In *Reformen in rheinbündischen Deutschland.* Edited by Eberhard Weis. Munich: Oldenbourg, 1984, 131–49.

Hoffmann, Johann G. *Die Lehre vom Gelde als Anleitung zu gründlichen Urteilen über das Geldwesen mit besonderer Beziehung auf den preussischen Staat.* Berlin: Nicolai, 1838.

———. *Die Lehre von den Steuern.* Berlin : Nicolai, 1840.

———. *Nachricht von dem Zwecke und der Anordnung der Vorträge.* Berlin: Gädicke, 1823.

———. *Sammlung kleiner Schriften staatswirtschaftlichen Inhalts.* Berlin: Nicolai, 1843.

Hoffmann, Karl H. L. "Das Bedürfnis eigenthümlicher statistischer Grundlagen für die Wirksamkeit der innern Verwaltung . . ." *ZGS* 2 (1845): 576–96.

Holtfrerich, Carl-Ludwig. *The German Inflation, 1914–1923.* Translated by Theo Balderston. Berlin: De Gruyter, 1986.

Homann, Harald. "Gustav Schmoller und die 'Empirische Sozialforschung.'" In *Gustav Schmoller e Il Suo Tempo.* Edited by Pierangelo Schiera and Friedrich Tenbruck. Bologna: Società editrice il Mulino, 1989, 327–51.

———. *Gesetz und Wirklichkeit in den Sozialwissenschaften.* Diss. Tübingen, 1989.

Horvath, Robert A. "Statistische Deskription und Nominalistische Philosophie." In

Statistik und Staatsbeschreibung in der Neuzeit. Edited by Mohammed Rassem and Justin Stagl. Paderborn: Schönigh, 1980, 37–52.

Höffding, Harald. *A History of Modern Philosophy.* Translated by B. E. Meyer. 4 vols. 1904–1912. Reprint, New York: Dover, 1955.

Huber, Ernst Rudolf. *Deutsche Verfassungsgeschichte seit 1789.* 8 vols. Stuttgart: Kohlhammer, 1957–90.

————, ed. *Dokumente zur deutschen Verfassungsgeschichte.* 3d ed. 3 vols. Stuttgart: Kohlhammer, 1978.

Huber, Ursula. *Universität und Ministerialverwaltung.* Berlin: Duncker & Humblot, 1987.

Hübinger, Paul Egon, ed. *Das historische Seminar der reinischen Friedrich-Wilhelms-Universität zu Bonn.* Bonn: Roehrscheid, 1963.

Hübner, Rudolf. "Johann Gustav Droysens Vorlesungen über die Politik." *Zeitschrift für Politik* 10 (1917): 325–76.

Hufeland, Gottlieb. *Neue Grundlegung der Staatswirtschaftskunst durch Prüfung und Berichtigung ihrer Hauptbegriffe . . .* Giessen: Tache und Müller, 1807.

Humboldt, Wilhelm von. *The Limits to State Action.* Edited by J. W. Burrow. Cambridge: Cambridge University Press, 1969.

————. *Wilhelm von Humboldts Gesammelte Schriften.* Edited by the königlich preussischen Akademie der Wissenschaften. 15 vols. Reprint, Berlin: De Gruyter, 1968.

Iggers, George G. "The European Context of Eighteenth-Century German Enlightenment Historiography." In *Aufklärung und Geschichte.* Edited by Hans Erich Bödeker et al. Göttingen: Vandenhoeck & Ruprecht, 1986, 225–45.

Ingrao, Charles. "The Problem of 'Enlightened Absolutism' and the German States." *Journal of Modern History,* 58 (1986): 161–80.

————. *The Hessian Mercenary State.* Cambridge: Cambridge University Press, 1987.

International Journal of Social Economics 16 (1989): nos. 9–11. [special issues on Gustav Schmoller].

Jacoby, E. G. *Die moderne Gesellschaft im sozialwissenschaftlichen Denken von Ferdinand Tönnies.* Stuttgart: Ferdinand Enke Verlag, 1971.

Jakob, Ludwig Heinrich. *Einleitung in das Studium der Staatswissenschaften als Leitfaden für seine Vorlesungen ausgearbeitet.* Halle: Hemmerle und Schwetschke, 1819.

————. *Grundsätze der National-Oekonomie oder National-Wirtschaftslehre.* Halle: Russischen Verlagsbuchhandlung, 1805.

————. *Grundsätze der Policeygesetzgebung oder Policeyanstalten.* Charcow: [n.p.], 1809.

————. *Die Staatsfinanzwissenschaft.* 2d ed. Reutlingen: Mäck, 1824.

Jarausch, Konrad H. *Students, Society, and Politics in Imperial Germany.* Princeton: Princeton University Press, 1982.

Jastrow, J. "Das Studium der Verwaltungswissenschaft nach dem Kriege." *ASS* 42 (1916–17): 958–68

Jay, Martin. *Marxism and Totality.* Berkeley: University of California Press, 1984.

Jellinek, Georg. "Georg Meyer." In *Ausgewählte Schriften und Reden.* Berlin: Häring, 1911.

————. *Allgemeine Staatslehre.* Edited by Walter Jellinek. 3d ed. Berlin: Springer, 1921.

Jentzsch, Rudolf, *Der deutsch-lateinische Büchermarkt.* Leipzig: Voigtländer, 1912.

John, Michael. *Politics and the Law in Late Nineteenth-Century Germany.* Oxford: Clarendon Press, 1989.

Johnson, Douglas. *Guizot: Aspects of French History.* London: Routledge & Kegan Paul, 1963.

Jolly, Ludwig. "Zur Geschichte der Staatswissenschaftlichen Fakultät in Tübingen." *SJ* 13 (1889): 159–81.

———. "Die Ausbildung der Verwaltungsbeamten." *ZGS* 37 (1875): 420–37.

Jones, Larry Eugene, and James N. Retallack, eds. *Between Reform, Reaction, and Resistance.* Providence, RI: Berg, 1993.

Jung-Stilling, Johann Heinrich. *Die Grundlehre der Staatswirtschaft.* Marburg: Academischen Buchhandlung, 1792.

———. *Jubelrede über den Geist der Staatswirtschaft.* Mannheim: Academia, 1787.

Justi, Johann H. G. von. *Grundsätze der Policeywissenschaft.* Edited by Johann Beckmann. 3d ed. 1782. Reprint, Frankfurt/Main: Sauer & Auverman, 1969.

———. *Staatswirtschaft.* 2d ed. 2 vols. 1758. Reprint, Aalen: Scientia, 1963.

Kann, Robert A. *A History of the Habsburg Empire.* Berkeley: University of California Press, 1974.

Kant, Immanuel. *Gesammelte Schriften.* 29 vols. Edited by preussische Akademie der Wissenschaften. Berlin: Reimer; De Gruyter, 1902–1983.

Karle, Joan. *August Ludwig V. Schlözer: An Intellectual Biography.* Diss. Columbia University, 1972.

Karmarsch, Karl. *Geschichte der Technologie seit der Mitte des achtzehnten Jahrhunderts.* 1872. Reprint, New York: Johnson Reprint Co., 1965.

Kaufmann, Georg. *Geschichte der Universität Breslau, 1811-1911.* 2 vols. Breslau: Hirt, 1911.

Kautz, Julius. *Die geschichtliche Entwicklung der National-Oeknomie.* 2 vols. Vienna: Gerold's Sohn, 1860.

Kähler, Wilhelm. "Die Entwicklung des staatswissenschaftlichen Unterrichts an der Universität Halle." In *Festgabe für Johannes Conrad.* Edited by Hermann Paasche. Jena: Gustav Fischer, 1898, 115–81.

Käsler, Dirk. *Die frühe deutsche Soziologie 1909 bis 1934.* Opladen: Westdeutscher Verlag, 1984.

Keller, Richard August. *Geschichte der Universität Heidelberg.* Heidelberg: Carl Winter, 1913.

Kern, Horst. *Empirische Socialforschung.* Munich: C. H. Beck, 1982.

Kindleberger, Charles P. *A Financial History of Western Europe.* London: Allen & Unwin, 1984.

Kink, Rudolf. *Geschichte der Kaiserliche Universität Wien.* Vienna: Karl Gerold, 1854.

Kittel, Rudolf. *Die Universität Leipzig und ihre Stellung im Kulturleben.* Dresden: Helingsche Verlagsanstalt, 1924.

Klemm, Volker. "Entstehung, Grundideen und charakteristische Merkmale der Agrarwissenschaftlichen Schule A. D. Thaers." In vol. 2 of *Wissenschaftliche Schulen.* Edited by Semen R. Mikulinskij, Michail G. Jorsevskij et al. Berlin: Akademie-Verlag, 1979, 119–30.

Klemm, Volker, and Günther Meyer. *Albrecht Daniel Thaer, Pionier der Landwirtschaftwissenschaften in Deutschland.* Halle: Max Niemeyer, 1968.

Klippel, Diethelm. "Naturrecht als politische Theorie. Zur politischen Bedeutung des deutschen Naturrechts im 18. und 19. Jahrhundert." In *Aüfklarung als Politisierung—*

Politisierung der Aufklärung. Edited by Hans-Erich Bödeker and Ulrich Herrmann. Hamburg: Meiner, 1987, 267–94.

Klüber, Johann Ludwig. *Öffentliches Recht des Teutschen Bundes und der Bundesstaaten.* Frankfurt: Andrea, 1817.

Klüpfel, K. "Aus Johannes Fallatis Tagebüchern und Briefen." *Württembergische Vierteljahrshefte für Landesgeschichte* 8 (1886): 1–31.

Knapp, Georg Friedrich. *Die Bauern-Befreiung und der Ursprung der Landarbeiter in den älteren Theilen Preussens.* Leipzig: Duncker & Humblot, 1887.

———. *Grundherrschaft und Rittergut.* Leipzig: Duncker & Humblot, 1897.

———. *Eine Jugend.* Edited by Elly Heuss-Knapp. 2d ed. Stuttgart: Deutsche Verlags-Anstalt, 1947.

———. "Quetelet als Theoretiker." *JNS* 18 (1872): 89–124.

———. *Staatliche Theorie des Geldes.* Leipzig: Duncker & Humblot, 1905.

———. *Theorie des Bevölkerungs-Wechsels.* Braunschweig: Vieweg, 1874.

Knemeyer, Franz-Ludwig. *Regierungs-und Verwaltungsreformen in Deutschland zu Beginn des 19. Jahrhunderts.* Cologne: Grote, 1970.

Knies, Karl. "Erörterungen über den Credit." *ZGS* 15 (1989): 559–90.

———. *Geld und Kredit.* 2d ed. 2 vols. Berlin: Weidman, 1876–1885.

———. "Die Nationalökonomische Lehre vom Werth." *ZGS* 11 (1855): 420–75.

———. *Die politische Oekonomie vom geschichtlichen Standpuncte.* 2d ed. Braunschweig: Schwetschke, 1883.

———. *Die Statistik als selbständige Wissenschaft.* Kassel: Luckhardt, 1850.

Knudsen, Jonathan. "Liberal Politics in Berlin, 1815–48." In *In Search of a Liberal Germany.* Edited by K. H. Jarausch and L. E. Jones. Oxford: Berg, 1990, 111–32.

Kocka, Jürgen. *Facing Total War: German Society, 1914–1918.* Translated by Barbara Weinberger. Cambridge, MA: Harvard University Press, 1984.

Kolb, George. "Über die Theilbarkeit des Grundeigentums." *APO* n. f., 1 (1843): 84–116.

Kolde, Theodor. *Die Universität Erlangen unter dem Hause Wittelsbach, 1810–1910.* Erlangen: Deichert, 1910.

Koptizsch, Franklin. "Lesegesellschaften im Rahmen einer Bürgerrepublik. Zur Aufklärung in Lübeck." In *Lesegesellschaften und Bürgerliche Emanzipation.* Edited by Otto Dann. Munich: C. H. Beck, 1981, 87–102.

Koselleck, Reinhart, *Kritik und Krise.* Frankfurt/Main: Suhrkamp, 1979.

———. *Preussen zwischen Reform und Revolution.* Stuttgart: Klett, 1967.

Köpke, Rudolf. *Die Gründung der Königlichen Friedrich-Wilhelms-Universität zu Berlin.* Berlin: G. Schade, 1860.

Kraus, Christian Jacob. *Staatswirtschaft.* Edited by Hans von Auerswald. 5 vols. Königsberg: Nicolovius, 1808.

Krauth, Wolf-Hagen. *Wirtschaftstruktur und Semantik.* Berlin: Duncker & Humblot, 1984.

Krawehl, Otto-Ernst. *Die "Jahrbücher für Nationalökonomie und Statistik" unter den Herausgebern Bruno Hildebrand und Johannes Conrad (1863–1915).* Munich: Verlag Dokumentation, 1977.

Krieger, Leonard. *The German Idea of Freedom.* Chicago: University of Chicago Press, 1957.

Kries, C. G. "Soll der Zollverein wirklich zerissen werden? Eine Frage aus Preussen." *ZGS* 8 (1852): 565–609.

Krohn, Claus-Dieter. *Wirtschafttheorien als Politische Interessen: die Akademische Nationalökonomie in Deutschland, 1918–1933.* Frankfurt/Main: Campus, 1981.

Krüger, Dieter. *Nationalökonomen in Wilhelminischen Deutschland.* Göttingen: Vandenhoeck & Ruprecht, 1983.

Krueger, Hermann Edwin. "Der Beruf des praktischen Volkswirts." *SJ* 31 (1907).

Kudler, Joseph. *Die Grundlehren der Volkswirtschaft.* Vienna: Braumüller & Seidel, 1846.

Kühn, Julius. *Das Studium der Landwirtschaft an der Universität Halle.* Halle: Plötz, 1888.

Laband, Paul. *Das Budgetrecht nach den Bestimmungen des preussischen Verfassungsurkunde . . .* Berlin: Guttentag, 1871.

———. "Lebenserinnerungen." In *Abhandlungen, Beiträge, Reden und Rezensionen.* Leipzig: Zentralantiquariat der DDR, 1980, 5–112.

———. *Das Staatsrecht des deutschen Reiches.* 5th ed. 4 vols. Tübingen: Mohr, 1911.

Langewiesche, Dieter. *Liberalismus und Demokratie in Württemberg zwischen Revolution und Reichsgründung.* Dusseldorf: Droste, 1974.

Laube, Heinrich. *Das erste deutsche Parlament.* 1849. Reprint, Aalen: Scientia, 1971.

LaVopa, Anthony. *Grace, Talent, and Merit.* Cambridge: Cambridge University Press, 1986.

Lee, Joe. "Administrators and Agriculture: Aspects of German Agricultural Policy in the First World War." In *War and Economic Development: Essays in Memory of David Joslin.* Edited by J. M. Winter. Cambridge: Cambridge University Press, 1975, 229–38.

Lee, Lloyd. *The Politics of Harmony: Civil Service, Liberalism, and Social Reform in Baden, 1800–1850.* Newark, DE: University of Delaware Press, 1980.

Lees, Andrew. *Revolution and Reflection: Intellectual Change in Germany During the 1850s.* The Hague: Nijhoff, 1974.

Lehmann, Otto. "Die Nationalökonomie in der Universität Halle im 19. Jahrhundert." *Volkswirtschaftliche Literatur* 19 (1935): 1–199.

Lenger, Friedrich. *Werner Sombart, 1863–1941.* Munich: C. H. Beck, 1994.

Lenz, Friedrich. "Friedrich List und der Liberalismus." *SJ* 48 (1924): 405–37.

———. *Friedrich List's Staats und Gesellschaftslehre.* Neuwied: Luchterhand, 1967.

———. *Friedrich List. Der Mann und Seinen Werk.* Munich: Oldenbourg, 1936.

Lenz, Max. *Geschichte der königlichen Friedrich-Wilhelms-Universität zu Berlin.* 4 vols. Halle: Waisenhaus, 1910.

Lepenies, Wolfgang. *Between Literature and Science: The Rise of Sociology.* Cambridge: Cambridge University Press, 1988.

Lerman, Katherine A. *The Chancellor as Courtier: Bernhard von Bülow and the Governance of Germany.* Cambridge: Cambridge University Press, 1990.

Lexis, Wilhelm. *Allgemeine Volkswirtschaftslehre.* 2d ed. Leipzig: Teubner, 1913.

Lidtke, Vernon. *The Alternative Culture.* New York: Oxford, 1963.

Liebersohn, Harry. *Fate and Utopia in German Sociology, 1870–1923.* Cambridge: Cambridge University Press, 1988.

Liebig, Justus von. *Reden und Abhandlungen.* Heidelberg: Carl Winter, 1874.

Lindemann, Mary. *Patriots and Paupers: Hamburg, 1712–1830.* New York: Oxford University Press, 1990.

Lindenfeld, David F. "The Decline of Polizeiwissenschaft: Continuity and Change in the Study of Administration in German Universities During the Nineteenth Century." In *Formation und Transformation des Verwaltungswissens in Frankreich und Deutschland (18./19.Jh.)*. Edited by Erk Volkmar Heyen. Baden-Baden: Nomos, 1989, 141–59.

———. "The Education of Prussian Higher Civil Servants in the Staatswissenschaften, 1897–1914." In *Historische Soziologie der Rechtswissenschaft*. Edited by Erk Volkmar Heyen. Frankfurt/Main: Klostermann, 1986, 201–25.

———. "The Myth of the Older Historical School of German Economics." *Central European History* 26 (1993): 405–16.

———. "On Systems and Embodiments as Categories for Intellectual History." *History and Theory* 27 (1988): 30–50.

———. "The Professionalization of Applied Economics: German Counterparts to Business Administration." In *German Professions, 1800–1950*. Edited by Konrad Jarausch and Geoffrey Cocks. New York: Oxford University Press, 1990, 213–31.

———. "Tönnies, the Mandarins, and Materialism." *German Studies Review* 11 (1988): 57–81.

———. *The Transformation of Positivism. Alexius Meinong and European Thought, 1880–1920*. Berkeley: University of California Press, 1980.

Lindenlaub, Dieter. *Richtungskämpfe im Verein für Sozialpolitik*. Wiesbaden: Steiner, 1967.

Link, Christoph. "Johann Stephan Pütter." In *Staatsdenker im 17. und 18. Jahrundert*. Edited by Michael Stolleis. 2d ed. Frankfurt/Main: Metzner, 1987, 310–29.

List, Friedrich. "Gutachten über die Errichtung einer Staatswirtschaftlichen Fakultät." In vol. 1 of *Schriften, Reden, Briefe*. Edited by Karl Goeser and Wilhelm von Sontag. Berlin: Reimar Hobbing, 1932, 341–52.

———. *Das Nationale System der Politischen Ökonomie*. Edited by Günter Fabiunke. 1841. Reprint, Berlin: Akademie-Verlag, 1982.

Loening, Edgar. "Die konstruktive Methode auf dem Gebiete des Verwaltungsrechtes." *SJ* 11 (1887): 541–67.

Lotz, Johann F. E. *Über den Begriff der Polizei und den Umfang der Staatspolizeigewalt*. Hildburghausen: Hanisch, 1802.

———. *Revision der Grundbegriffe der Nationalwirtschaftslehre*. 4 vols. Koburg: Sinnerschen Buchhandlung, 1811–1814.

Ludewig, Johann Peter. *Die von seiner Königlichen Majestät . . . neu Angerichtete Profession in Oeconomie, Policey und Cammer-Sachen*. Halle: Neuen Buchhandlung, 1727.

Ludwig, Bernd. "Einleitung" to Kant, *Metaphysische Anfangsgründe der Rechtslehre*. Edited by Bernd Ludwig. Hamburg: Meiner, 1986, xiii–xl.

Lueder, August Ferdinand. *Kritische Geschichte der Statistik*. Göttingen: Röwer, 1817.

Luhmann, Niklas. *Soziale Systeme*. 1984. Reprint, Frankfurt/Main: Suhrkamp, 1988.

Lüdtke, Alf. "Polizeiverständnis preussicher Polizeihandbücher im 19. Jahrhundert. Zur Folgenlosigkeit akademischer Diskurse." In *Wissenschaft und Recht der Verwaltung seit dem Ancien Regime*. Edited by E. V. Heyen. Frankfurt/Main: Klostermann, 1984.

———. *"Gemeinwohl," Polizei und "Festungspraxis": Staatliche Gewaltsamkeit und innere Verwaltung in Preussen, 1815–1850*. Göttingen: Vandenhoeck & Ruprecht, 1982.

Lütge, Friedrich. *Deutsche Sozial-und Wirtschaftsgeschichte*. Berlin: Springer, 1960.

Lundgreen, Peter. "The Organization of Science and Technology in France: A German Perspective." In *The Organization of Science and Technology in France, 1808–1914*.

Edited by Robert Fox and George Weisz. Cambridge: Cambridge University Press, 1980, 311–32.

———. *Techniker in Preussen während der frühen Industrialisierung.* Berlin: Colloquium, 1975.

Mahoney, Susan K. *A Good Constitution. Social Science in Eighteenth-Century Göttingen.* Diss. University of Chicago. 1982.

Maier, Hans. "Die Lehre der Politik in den deutschen Universitäten, vornehmlich vom 16. bis 18. Jahrhundert." In *Wissenschaftliche Politik.* Edited by Dieter Oberndörfer. Freiburg: Rombach, 1962, 59–116.

———. *Die ältere Deutsche Staats-und Verwaltungslehre.* 2d ed. Munich: C. H. Beck, 1980.

Malchus, Carl August Freiherrn von. *Handbuch der Finanzwissenschaft und Finanzverwaltung.* 2 vols. Stuttgart: Cotta, 1830.

Maluschke, Günther. "Lorenz von Steins Staatsformenlehre." in *Staat und Gesellschaft. Studien über Lorenz von Stein.* Edited by Roman Schnur. Berlin: Duncker & Humblot, 1978, 223–43.

Manegold, Karl-Heinz. *Universität, Technische Hochschule und Industrie.* Berlin: Duncker & Humblot, 1970.

Mangoldt, Hans von. *Grundriss der Volkswirtschaftslehre.* Stuttgart: Engelhorn, 1963.

Marienfeld, Wolfgang. *Wissenschaft und Schlachtflottenbau in Deutschland, 1897–1906.* Beiheift of *Marine Rundschau,* 1957.

Marshall, Alfred. *Principles of Economics.* London: Macmillan, 1891.

Martitz, Ferdinand von. "Völkerrecht." In vol. 1 of *Die deutschen Universitäten.* Edited by Wilhelm Lexis. Berlin: A. Asher, 1893, 373–82.

Marx, Karl. "Über Friedrich Lists Buch 'Das Nationale System der Politischen Ökonomie.'" In *Das Nationale System der Politischen Ökonomie,* by Friedrich List. Edited by Günter Fabiunke. 1841. Reprint, Berlin: Akademie-Verlag, 1982.

Marx, Karl, and Friedrich Engels, *Die deutsche Ideologie.* Vol. 3 of *Marx-Engels Werke.* Berlin: Dietz, 1959, 9–530.

Mayer, Otto. *Deutsches Verwaltungsrecht.* 2 vols. Leizpig: Duncker & Humblot, 1895.

McClelland, Charles E. *State, Society, and University in Germany, 1700–1914.* Cambridge: Cambridge University Press, 1980.

———. *The German Experience of Professionalization.* Cambridge: Cambridge University Press, 1991.

McGrath, William J. *Dionysian Art and Populist Politics in Vienna.* New Haven: Yale University Press, 1974.

Meek, Ronald L. *Social Science and the Ignoble Savage.* Cambridge: Cambridge University Press, 1976.

Meinecke, Friedrich. "Drei Generationen deutscher Gelehrtenpolitik." *Historische Zeitschrift* 125 (1922): 248–83.

———. *Machiavellism.* Translated by Douglas Scott. 1957. Reprint, New York: Praeger, 1965.

———. *Strassburg, Freiburg, Berlin, 1901–1919.* Stuttgart: Koehler, 1949.

Meiner, Felix, ed. *Die Volkswirtschaftslehre der Gegenwart in Selbstdarstellungen.* Leipzig: Meiner, 1924.

Meitzen, August. "Georg Hanssen als Agrar-Historiker." *ZGS* 37 (1881): 371–417.

Melton, James Van Horn. *Absolutism and the Eighteenth-Century Origins of Compulsory Schooling in Prussia and Austria.* Cambridge: Cambridge University Press, 1988.

———. "From Enlightenment to Revolution: Hertzberg, Schlözer, and the Problem of Despotism in the 'Aufklärung.'" *Central European History* 12 (1979): 103–23.

Menger, Carl. *Carl Mengers erster Entwurf zu seinem Hauptwerk "Grundsätze," geschrieben als Anmerkungen zu den "Grundsätzen der Volkswirtschaftslehre" von Karl Heinrich Rau.* Tokyo: Bibliothek der Hitotsubashi Universität, 1963.

———. *Grundsätze der Volkswirtschaftslehre.* 1871. Reprint, London: London School of Economics, 1934.

———. "Lorenz von Stein." *JNS* 56 (1891): 193–209.

———. *Untersuchungen über die Methode der Socialwissenschaften.* Leipzig: Duncker & Humblot, 1883.

Meusel, Johann Georg, *Lehrbuch der Statistik.* 3d ed. Leipzig: Fritzsch, 1804.

Meyer, Alfred. *The Feminism and Socialism of Lily Braun.* Bloomington: Indiana University Press, 1985.

Meyer, Georg. "Staats-und Verwaltungsrecht." In vol. 1 of *Die deutschen Universitäten.* 2 vols. Edited by Wilhelm Lexis. Berlin: A. Asher, 1893, 362–73.

Meyer, Willi. "Schmoller's Research Programme, His Psychology, and the Autonomy of Social Sciences." *Journal of Institutional and Theoretical Economics* 144 (1988): 570–80.

Miaskowski, A. von. "Georg Hanssen, ein Nationalökonomisches Jubiläum." *SJ* 5 (1881): 837–58.

Mieck, Ilja. *Preussische Gewerbepolitik in Berlin, 1808–1844.* Berlin: De Gruyter, 1965.

Mitchell, Allan. *The Divided Path: The German Influence on Social Reform in France after 1870.* Chapel Hill: University of North Carolina Press, 1991.

Mitzman, Arthur. *Sociology and Estrangement.* New York: Knopf, 1973.

———. *The Iron Cage.* New York: Grosset & Dunlap, 1969.

Mohl, Robert von. "Über Büreaukratie." *ZGS* 3 (1846): 330–64.

———. *Encyclopädie der Staatswissenschaften.* Tübingen: Laupp, 1859.

———. "Ueber die Errichtung eigener Staatswissenschaftlicher Fakultäten." In vol. 3 of *Staatsrecht, Völkerrecht und Politik.* Tübingen: Laupp, 1869, 220–41.

———. *Die Geschichte und Literatur der Staatswissenschaften in Monographien Dargestellt.* 3 vols. Erlangen: Enke, 1855–58.

———. "Gesellschafts-Wissenschaften und Staats-Wissenschaften." *ZGS* 7 (1851): 3–71.

———. *Lebenserinnerungen.* 2 vols. Stuttgart: Deutsche Verlags-Anstalt, 1902.

———. "Literarhistorische Übersicht über die Encykopädien der Staatswissenschaften." *ZGS* 2 (1845): 423–80.

———. "Über die Nachteilen, welche wowohl den Arbeitern selbst, als dem Wohlstande und der Sicherheit der gesamten bürgerlichen Gesellschaft von dem fabrikmässigen Betriebe der Industrie Zugehen." *APO* 2 (1835): 141–203.

———. *Die Polizeiwissenschaft nach den Grundsätzen des Rechtstaates.* 1st ed. 2 vols. Tübingen: Laupp, 1832–33; 3d ed. 2 vols. Tübingen: Laupp, 1866.

———. "Das Prüfungswesen in Seinem Verhältnisse zur Bildung." In vol. 3 of *Staatsrecht, Völkerrecht, Politik.* Tübingen: Laupp, 1869, 241–67.

———. "Sorge für den Bedarf an höheren Staatsdienern." In vol. 3 of *Staatsrecht, Völkerrecht, Politik.* Tubingen: Laupp, 1869, 449–72.

———. "Sozialpolitik." In vol. 3 of *Staatsrecht, Völkerrecht, Politik.* Tübingen: Laupp, 1869, 475–660.

―――. *Staatsrecht des Königreiches Württemberg.* 2 vols. Tübingen: Laupp, 1829–31.

―――. *Die Verantwortlichkeit der Minister in Einherrschaften mit Volksvertretung.* Tübingen: Laupp, 1837.

―――. "Über die Wissenschaftliche Bildung der Beamten in den Ministerien des Innern. Mit besonderer Anwendung auf Württemberg." *ZGS* 1 (1845): 129–84.

Mohnhaupt, Heinz. "Vorstufen der Wissenschaften von 'Verwaltung' und 'Verwaltungsrecht' an der Universität Göttingen (1750–1830)." In *Formation und Transformation des Verwaltungswissens in Frankreich und Deutschland (18./19.Jh.).* Edited by Erk Volkmar Heyen. Baden-Baden: Nomos, 1989, 73–103.

Mommsen, Wolfgang. *Max Weber und die Deutsche Politik.* 2d ed. Tübingen: Mohr, 1974.

―――. "Das Deutsche Kaiserreich als System umgangener Entscheidungen." In *Vom Staat des Ancien Regime zum Modernen Parteienstaat.* Edited by Helmut Berding et al. Munich: Oldenbourg, 1978, 239–65.

Mommsen, Wolfgang, and Jürgen Osterhammel, eds. *Max Weber and His Contemporaries.* London: Allen & Unwin, 1987.

Moran, Daniel. *Toward the Century of Words: Johann Cotta and the Politics of the Public Realm in Germany, 1785–1832.* Berkeley: University of California Press, 1990.

Moraw, Peter. *Kleine Geschichte der Universität Giessen 1607–1982.* Giessen: Ferber, 1982.

Morsey, Rudolph. *Die oberste Reichsverwaltung unter Bismarck 1867–1890.* Münster: Aschendorff, 1957.

Mosse, W. E. *Jews in the German Economy: The German-Jewish Economic Elite, 1820–1935.* Oxford: Clarendon Press, 1987.

Müller, Adam. *Nationalökonomische Schriften.* Edited by Albert Josef Klein. Lörrach: Albert Kern, 1983.

Mueller, Hans-Eberhard. *Bureaucracy, Education, and Monopoly. Civil Service Reforms in Prussia and England.* Berkeley: University of California Press, 1984.

Müller, Karl Alexander von, ed. *Die wissenschaftlichen Anstalten der Ludwig-Maximilians-Universität zu München.* Munich: Oldenbourg, 1926.

Muncy, Lisbeth W. *The Junker in the Prussian Administration Under Wilhelm II, 1888–1914.* Providence: Brown University Press, 1944.

Muth, Heinrich. "Preussische Kameralstudienpläne um 1800." *Reich, Volksordnung, Lebensraum* 6 (1943): 241–317.

Nasse, Erwin. *Über Universitätsstudien und Staatsprüfungen der preussischen Verwaltungsbeamten.* Bonn: Marcus, 1868.

Nebenius, Friedrich. *Der Öffentliche Credit.* 2d ed. Karlsruhe: Marx, 1829.

―――. *Über Technische Lehranstalten . . . mit besonderer Rücksicht auf die Polytechnische Schule zu Karlsruhe.* Karlsruhe: Müller, 1833.

Neumann, Karl. *Die Lehren K. H. Rau's.* Diss. Giessen, 1927.

Novotny, Alexander. "Lorenz von Steins Berufung Nach Wien." In *Festschrift zur Feier des 200 Jährigen Bestandes des Haus-Hof-und Staatsarchivs.* Edited by Leo Santifaller. Vienna: [n.p.], 1951, 474–84.

Noyes, P. H. *Organization and Revolution: Working-Class Associations in the German Revolutions of 1848–1849.* Princeton: Princeton University Press, 1966.

O'Boyle, Leonore. "The Problem of an Excess of Educated Men in Western Europe, 1800–1850." *Journal of Modern History* 42 (1970): 471–95.

Oberkofler, Gerhard. *Studien zur Geschichte der Österreichischen Rechtswissenschaft.* Frankfurt/M: Peter Lang, 1984.

Oberschall, Anthony. *Empirical Social Research in Germany 1848–1914*. Paris: Mouton, 1965.

Oertzen, Peter von. *Die soziale Funktion des staatsrechtlichen Positivismus*. Frankfurt/Main: Suhrkamp, 1974.

———. "Die Bedeutung C. F. v. Gerbers für die deutsche Staatsrechtslehre." In *Staatsverfassung und Kirchenordnung. Festgabe für Rudolf Smend*. Göttingen: Vandenhoek & Ruprecht, 1962.

Oestreich, Gerhard. *Neostoicism and the Early Modern State*. Translated by David McLintock. Edited by H. G. Koenigsberger and Brigitta Oestreich. Cambridge: Cambridge University Press, 1982.

Oettingen, Alexander von. *Die Moralstatistik und die Christliche Sittenlehre*. Erlangen: Deichert, 1868.

Oldenburg, K. "Wilhelm Lexis." In *Chronik der Georg-August Universität zu Göttingen*. 1914, 7–10.

Oppenheimer, Franz. *Erlebtes, Erstrebtes, Erreichtes*. Düsseldorf: Melzer, 1964.

[Ordinance on Curriculum for Finance Officials]. *Grossherzogliches badisches Staats-und Regierungsblatt*, 1838, 194.

[Ordinance on Technical Instruction]. *Bayrischer Intelligenzblatt*, 20 April 1836, 510–12.

Osterloh, Karl-Heinz. *Joseph von Sonnenfels und die Österreichische Reformbewegung im Zeitalter des Aufgeklärten Absolutismus*. Lübeck: Matthiesen, 1970.

Pankoke, Eckart. *Soziale Bewegung-Soziale Frage-Soziale Politik*. Stuttgart: Klett, 1970.

Pasquino, Pasquale. "Politisches und historisches Interesse. 'Statistik' und historische Staatslehre bei Gottfried Achenwall." In *Aufklärung und Geschichte*. Edited by Hans Erich Bödeker et al. Göttingen: Vandenhoeck & Ruprecht, 1986, 144–68.

Paulsen, Friedrich. *Geschichte des gelehrten Unterrichts auf den deutschen Schulen und Universitäten* . . . 2 vols. Leipzig: Veit & Comp., 1919–1921.

Paulsen, Friedrich, and Ferdinand Tönnies. *Briefwechsel, 1876–1908*. Edited by Irma Fischer, Olaf Klose, and Eduard G. Jacoby. Kiel: Hirt, 1961.

Pechmann, Hubert von. "Geschichte der staatswirtschaftlichen Fakultät." In *Die Ludwig Maximilians Universität in ihren Fakultäten*. Edited by Letitia Boehm and Johannes Spörl. Berlin: Duncker & Humblot, 1972, 127–85.

Permaneder, Michael. *Annales Almae Literarum Universitatis Ingolstadii*. Munich: Weiss, 1859.

Pflanze, Otto. "Juridical and Political Responsibility in Nineteenth-Century Germany." In *The Responsibility of Power*. Edited by Leonard Krieger and Fritz Stern. Garden City, NY: Doubleday, 1967, 162–82.

———. *Bismarck and the Development of Germany*. 3 vols. Princeton: Princeton University Press, 1990.

Philippovich, Eugen von. *Grundriss der Politischen Oekonomie*. 4th ed. 2 vols. Tübingen: Mohr, 1901.

Ploetz, Alfred. "Sozialpolitik und Rassenhygiene in ihrem Prinzipiellen Verhältnis." *ASS* 17 (1902): 393–420.

Pohle, Ludwig. "Die gegenwärtige Krise in der deutschen Volkswirtschaftslehre . . ." *Essays in European Economic Thought*. Edited and translated by Louise Sommer. Princeton: Von Nostrand, 1960, 81–105.

Poppe, Johann. *Ausführlichere Anleitung zur Allgemeinen Technologie*. Stuttgart: Cotta, 1821.

———. *Über das Studium der Technologie*. 2nd ed. Tübingen: Hopfer de l'Orme, 1819.

Porter, Theodore M. *The Rise of Statistical Thinking, 1820–1900.* Princeton: Princeton University Press, 1986.

Pölitz, Karl H. L. *Die Staatswissenschaften im Lichte unserer Zeit.* 2d ed. 5 vols. Leipzig: Hinrich, 1827–1828.

Preradovich, Nikolaus von. *Die Führungsschichten in Österreich und Preussen, 1804–1918.* Wiesbaden: F. Steiner, 1955.

Preu, Peter. *Polizeibegriff und Staatszwecklehre.* Göttingen: Otto Schutz, 1983.

Preussen. Haus der Abgeordneten. *Stenographische Berichte,* 4 May 1897.

————. Herrenhaus. *Stenographische Berichte,* 30 April 1903.

Pütter, Johann Stephen. *Anleitung zum teutschen Staatsrechte.* Translated [from Latin] by Carl A. F. von Hohenthal. Bayreuth: Zeitungsdruckerei, 1791.

————. *Versuch einer academischen Gelehrten-Geschichte von der Georg-Augustus Universität zu Göttingen.* 2 vols. Göttingen: Vandenhoeck, 1765–1788.

Rabb, Theodore. *The Struggle for Stability in Early Modern Europe.* New York: Oxford University Press, 1975.

Radbruch, Gustav. *Rechtsphilosophie.* 4th ed. Stuttgart: Koehler, 1950.

Raeff, Marc. *The Well-Ordered Police State.* New Haven: Yale University Press, 1983.

Rau, Karl Heinrich. *Ansichten der Volkswirtschaft.* Leipzig: Goschen, 1821.

————. "Beiträge von der Verkleinerung der Landgüter." *APO* n. f. 1 (1843): 116–23.

————. "Ueber Begriff und Wesen der Polizei." *ZGS* 9 (1853): 605–25.

————. "Gedanken über die Wissenschaftliche Vorbereitung zum Administrativsache." *APO* 2 (1835): 77–91.

————. *Über die Kameralwissenschaft.* Heidelberg: Carl Winter, 1825.

————. *Lehrbuch der politischen Oekonomie.* 3 vols. 1st–4th ed. Heidelberg: Carl Winter, 1828–1860; 2nd–5th ed. Heidelberg: Winter, 1844–47; 5th–8th ed. Leipzig: Carl Winter, 1862–1868.

————. *Ueber den Luxus.* Erlangen: Heyder, 1817.

————. "Über den Nutzen, gegenwärtigen Zustand, und die neueste Literatur der Nationalökonomie." *APO* 1 (1835): 1–43.

————. Review of Friedrich List, *Das Nationale System. APO,* n. f. 1 (1843): 252–97, 349–412.

————. *Ueber das Zunftwesen und die Folgen seiner Aufhebung.* Leipzig: Goschen, 1816.

Raumer, Friedrich von. 2 vols. *Lebenserinnerungen und Briefwechsel.* Leipzig: Brockhaus, 1861.

Rechts-und Staatswissenschaftliche Fakultäten der Österreichischen Universitäten, *Gutachten und Anträge zur Reform der Juristischen Studien.* Vienna: Gorischek, 1887.

Redlich, Fritz. "Academic Education for Business." In *Steeped in Two Cultures.* New York: Harper & Row, 1971, 199–257.

Rehbinder, Manfred. "Recht und Rechtswissenschaft im Werk von Max Weber." In *Max Weber Heute: Erträge und Probleme der Forschung.* Edited by Johannes Weiss. Frankfurt/Main: Suhrkamp, 1989.

Reill, Peter. "Science and the Science of History in the Spätaufklärung." In *Aufklärung und Geschichte.* Edited by Hans Erich Bödeker et al. Göttingen: Vandenhoeck & Ruprecht, 1986, 430–51.

Reulecke, Jürgen. "Die Anfänge der organisierten Sozialreform in Deutschland." In *'Weder Kommunismus Noch Kapitalismus.'* Edited by Rüdiger vom Bruch. Munich: C. H. Beck, 1985, 21–59.

Ricardo, David. *Principles of Political Economy and Taxation*. Introduction by Donald Winch. 1817. Reprint. London: J. M. Dent & Sons, 1973.

Richter, Eugen. "Die Vorbildung der höheren Verwaltungsbeamten in Preussen." *Preussische Jahrbücher* 17 (1866): 1–19.

Riedel, Manfred. "Der Staatsbegriff der deutschen Geschichtsschreibung des 19. Jahrhunderts in seinem Verhältnis zur klassisch-politischen Philosophie." *Der Staat* 2 (1963): 41–67.

———. Einleitung to *Die Politik*, by Friedrich Christoph Dahlmann. 1835. Reprint, Frankfurt/Main: Suhrkamp, 1968, 7–31.

———. *Studien zur Hegel's Rechtsphilosophie*. Stuttgart: Klett-Cotta, 1969.

Riehl, Wilhelm Heinrich. *Die Naturgeschichte des Volkes*. 6th ed. 4 vols. Stuttgart: Cotta, 1862–69.

———. "Die Statistische Krankheit." In *Freie Vorträge*. Stuttgart: Cotta, 1885.

Riese, Reinhard. *Die Hochschule auf dem Wege zum wissenschaftlichen Grossbetrieb: die Universität Heidelberg und das badische Hochschulwesen, 1860–1914*. Stuttgart: Klett, 1977.

Ringer, Fritz. *The Decline of the German Mandarins*. Cambridge, MA: Harvard University Press, 1969.

———. *Education and Society in Modern Europe*. Bloomington: Indiana University Press, 1979.

———. *Fields of Knowledge*. Cambridge: Cambridge University Press, 1992.

———. "A Sociography of German Academics, 1863–1938." *Central European History* 25 (1993): 251–80.

Ritter, Gerhard. *Stein. Eine Politische Biographie*. 3d ed. Stuttgart: Deutsche Verlags-Anstalt, 1958.

Rodbertus, Johann Karl. "Zur Erkenntnis unserer staatswirtschaftlichen Zustände." (1842). In vol. 1 of *Gesammelte Werke und Briefe*. Edited by Th. Ramm. Osnabrück: Zeller, 1972, 33–218.

———. "Zweiter und dritter Brief an von Kirchmann . . . Zur Beleuchtung der Sozialen Frage, Teil I." In vol. 1 of *Gesammelte Werke und Briefe*. Edited by Th. Ramm. Osnabrück: Otto Zeller, 1972, 333–672.

Rohr, Donald. *The Origins of Social Liberalism in Germany*. Chicago: University of Chicago Press, 1963.

Roscher, Wilhelm. "Zur Erinnerung von Johann Georg Büsch." *ZGS* 23 (1867): 219–41.

———. *Geschichte der Nationalökonomik in Deutschland*. Munich: Oldenbourg, 1874.

———. *Grundlagen der Nationalökonomie*. 19th ed. Stuttgart: Cotta, 1888.

———. *Grundriss zu Vorlesungen über die Staatswirtschaft nach geschichtlicher Methode*. Göttingen: Dieterischen Buchhandlung, 1843.

———. *Naturgeschichte der Monarchie, Aristokratie, Demokratie*. 1892. Reprint, Meersburg: Hendel, 1933.

Roscher, Wilhelm, and Gustav Schmoller. *Briefwechsel zwischen Wilhelm Roscher und Gustav Schmoller*. Edited by W. Biermann. Greifswald: L. Bamberg, 1922.

Rosenberg, Hans. *Bureaucracy, Aristocracy, and Autocracy*. Cambridge: Harvard University Press, 1958.

Rotteck, Carl von. *Lehrbuch des Vernunftrechts und der Staatswissenschaften*. 4 vols. 1829–30. Reprint, Stuttgart: Franck; Hallberger, 1834–35.

Rotteck, Carl von, and Karl Theodor Welcker, eds. *Staatslexikon oder Encylopädie der Staatswissenschaften.* 15 vols. Altona: Hammerich, 1834–43.

Rottleuthner, Hubert. "Drei Rechtssoziolgien: Eugen Ehrlich, Hugo Sinzheimer, Max Weber." In *Historische Soziologie der Rechtswissenschaft.* Edited by Erk Volkmar Heyen. Frankfurt/Main: Klostermann, 1986, 227–52.

Röhl, John C. G. *Germany without Bismarck.* Berkeley: University of California Press, 1967.

————. "Higher Civil Servants in Germany, 1890–1900." In *Imperial Germany.* Edited by James Sheehan. New York: New Viewpoints, 1976, 129–51.

Rümelin, Gustav. "Zur Theorie der Statistik." *ZGS* 19 (1863): 653–96.

————. "Über den Begriff eines socialen Gesetzes." In *Reden und Aufsätze.* Tübingen: Laupp, 1875, 2–31.

Sachse, Arnold. *Friedrich Althoff und sein Werk.* Berlin: Mittler, 1928.

Sachsse, Christoph, and Florian Tennstedt. *Geschichte der Armenfürsorge in Deutschland.* 2 vols. Stuttgart: Kohlhammer, 1980.

Sartorius, Georg. *Abhandlungen, die Elemente des National-Reichthums und die Staatswirtschaft betreffend.* Göttingen: Röwer, 1806.

————. *Einladungs-Blätter zu Vorlesungen über die Politik während des Sommers 1793.* Göttingen: Barmeier, 1793.

————. *Handbuch der Staatswirtschaft zum Gebrauche bey Akademischen Vorlesungen.* Berlin: Unger, 1796.

————. *Von den Elementen des National-Reichthums und von der Staatswirtschaft, nach Adam Smith.* Göttingen: Röwer, 1806.

Scaff, Lawrence. *Fleeing the Iron Cage: Culture, Politics, and Modernity in the Thought of Max Weber.* Berkeley: University of California Press, 1989.

Schanz, Georg. *Die Staatswirtschaftliche Fakultät der Universität Würzburg.* Würzburg: H. Stürtz, 1911.

Schäffle, Albert. *Bau und Leben des socialen Körpers.* 4 vols. Tübingen: Laupp, 1875–1878.

————. "Über den Gebrauchswert und die Wirtschaft nach den Begriffsbestimmungen Hermanns." *ZGS* (1870): 122–79.

————. *Das gesellschaftliche System der menschlichen Wirtschaft.* 2d ed. Tübingen: Laupp, 1867.

————. "Die Konkurrenz der Organe des Staatslebens . . ." *ZGS* 18 (1862): 520–605; 20 (1864): 139–203.

————. *Aus meinem Leben.* 2 vols. Berlin: Ernst Hofmann, 1905.

————. "Mensch und Gut in der Volkswirtschaft." *Deutsche Vierteljahrschrift,* 24, no. 4 (1861): 232–307.

————. "Ueber die Notwendigkeit exakt entwickelungsgeschichtlicher Erklärung und exakt entwickelungsgesetzlicher Behandlung unsere chronischen Landwirtschaftsbedrängnis." *ZGS* 1903, 255–340, 476–552.

————. "Rechtsphilosophische Zeitgedanken über politische Bedeutung der Nationalität, historisches Recht, Autonomie und Polizeistaat." *Deutsche Vierteljahrsschrift* 24, no. 1 (1861): 288–329.

————. "Die Stellung der politischen Verwaltung im Staatsorganismus . . ." *ZGS* 27 (1871): 181–250.

Scheel, Hans von. "Die Politische Oekonomie als Wissenschaft." In vol. 1 of *Handbuch der Politischen Oekonomie*. 2d ed. Edited by Gustav Schönberg. Tübingen: Laupp, 1885, 67–106.

Schiera, Pierangelo. *Laboratorium der bürgerlichen Welt*. Frankfurt/Main: Suhrkamp, 1992.

———, and Friedrich Tenbruck, eds. *Gustav Schmoller e il suo tempo*. Bologna: Società editrice il Mulino, 1989.

Schiffer, Eugen *Rudolf von Gneist*. Berlin: Carl Heymanns, 1929.

Schissler, Hanna. "Einleitung: Preussische Finanzpolitik 1806–1820." In *Preussische Finanzpolitik, 1806–1810*. Edited by Eckart Kehr. Göttingen: Vandenhoeck & Ruprecht, 1984.

———. *Preussische Agrargesellschaft im Wandel*. Göttingen: Vandenhoeck & Ruprecht, 1978.

Schlözer, August Ludwig von. *Theorie der Statistik*. Göttingen: Vandenhoeck & Ruprecht, 1804.

———. *Weltgeschichte*. 2d ed. 1775. Reprint, Göttingen: Vandenhoeck & Ruprecht, 1792.

Schmalz, Theodor. *Handbuch der Staatswirtschaft*. Berlin: Maurer, 1808.

Schmid, Ferdinand. "Ueber die Bedeutung der Verwaltungslehre als selbständiger Wissenschaft." *ZGS* 45 (1909): 193–224.

Schmidt, Richard. "Wege und Ziele der Politik." *Zeitschrift für Politik* 1 (1908): 1–60.

Schmidt, Werner. *Lorenz von Stein*. Eckernförde: Schwensen, 1956.

Schmoller, Gustav. "Die Arbeiterfrage." *Preussische Jahrbücher* 14 (1864): 393–424, 523–47; 15 (1865): 32–63.

———. *Über einige Grundfragen der Sozialpolitik und der Volkswirtschaftslehre*. 2d ed. Leipzig: Duncker & Humblot, 1904.

———. "Die Epochen der Preussischen Finanzpolitik." *SJ* 1 (1877): 3–114.

———. "Die Gerechtigkeit in der Volkswirtschaft" *SJ* 5 (1881): 19–54.

———. *Zur Geschichte der Deutschen Kleingewerbe im 19. Jahrhundert*. 1869. Reprint, Hildesheim: Olms, 1975.

———. "Graf Posadowsky als Sozialpolitiker." In *Zwanzig Jahre Deutscher Politik*. Munich: Duncker & Humblot, 1920, 57–61.

———. *Grundriss der Allgemeinein Volkswirtschaftslehre*. 2 vols. Leipzig: Duncker & Humblot, 1900–1904.

———. *Zur Litteraturgeschichte der Staats-und Sozialwissenschaften*. 1888. Reprint, New York: Burt Franklin, 1968.

———. *The Mercantile System and Its Historical Significance*. Translated by W. J. Ashley. New York: Macmillan, 1910.

———. "Obrigkeitsstaat und Volksstaat." *SJ* 40 (1916): 2031–42.

———. Review of Georges Blondel, *De L'enseignement de Droit dans les Universités Allemands*. *SJ* 10 (1886): 612–14.

———. Review of Gustav Schönberg, ed. *Handbuch der Politischen Oekonomie*. *SJ* 6 (1882): 1379–86.

———. Review of Werner Sombart, *Der moderne Kapitalismus*. In *Sombarts 'Moderner Kapitalismus.'* Edited by Bernhard vom Brocke. Munich: Deutscher Taschenbuch Verlag, 1987, 135–46.

———. "Simmels *Philosophie des Geldes*." *SJ* 25 (1901): 799–816.

————. "Ueber Zweck und Ziele des Jahrbuchs." *SJ* 1 (1881): 1–18.

Schmoller, Gustav, and Lujo Brentano. "Der Briefwechsel Gustav Schmollers mit Lujo Brentano." Edited by Walter Goetz. *Archiv für Kulturgeschichte* 28 (1938): 316–54; 29 (1939): 147–83, 331–47; 30 (1941): 142–207.

Schmoller, Gustav, Max Sering, and Adolph Wagner, eds. *Handels-und Machtpolitik.* 2 vols. Stuttgart: Cotta, 1900.

Schmoller, Gustav, and Ferdinand Tönnies. "Zwei Bemerkungen über den Verein für Sozialpolitik." *SJ* 36 (1912): 1–9.

Schnabel, Franz. *Deutsche Geschichte im neunzehnten Jahrhundert.* 4th ed. 4 vols. Freiburg: Herder, 1948.

Schneider, Walter. *Wirtschafts-und Sozialpolitik im Frankfurter Parlament 1848–1849.* Frankfurt/Main: Frankfurter Societäts-Druckerei, 1923.

Schnur, Roman. "Einleitung." In *Staat und Gesellschaft. Studien Über Lorenz von Stein.* Edited by Roman Schnur. Berlin: Duncker & Humblot, 1978, 13–26.

Schorske, Carl E. *German Social Democracy, 1905–1917.* 1955. Reprint, New York: Harper, 1972.

Schön, Manfred. "Gustav Schmoller und Max Weber." In *Max Weber and His Contemporaries.* Edited by Wolfgang Mommsen and Jürgen Osterhammel. London: Allen & Unwin, 1987, 59–70.

Schrader, Wilhelm. *Geschichte der Friedrichs-Universität zu Halle.* 2 vols. Berlin: Dümmler, 1894.

Schröder-Lembke, Gertrud. "Englische Einflüsse auf die deutsche Gutswirtschaft im 18. Jahrhundert." *Zeitschrift für Agrargeschichte* 12 (1964): 29–36.

Schulze, Friedrich Gottlob. *Geschichtliche Mitteilung über das Akademische Studium und Leben auf dem Landwirtschaftlichen Institute zu Jena . . .* Jena: (n.p.), 1858.

Schulze, Reiner. "Polizeirecht im 18. Jahrhundert." In *Recht, Gericht, Genossenschaft und Policey.* Edited by Bernhard Diestelkamp and Gerhard Dilcher. Berlin: Erich Schmidt Verlag, 1986, 199–220.

Schumacher, Hermann. "Theodor von der Goltz." *Chronik der rheinischen Friedrich-Wilhelms-Universität Bonn,* (n.p.), 1906, 2–5.

————. "Staatswissenschaften." In *Aus fünfzig Jahren deutscher Wissenschaft. Die Entwicklung ihrer Fachgebiete in Einzeldarstellungen.* Edited by Gustav Abb. Berlin: De Gruyter, 1930, 136–58.

Schumpeter, Joseph. *Economic Doctrine and Method: A Historical Sketch.* Translated by R. Aris. London: Allen & Unwin, 1954.

————. "Gustav V. Schmoller und die Probleme von Heute." *SJ* 50 (1926): 337–88.

————. *History of Economic Analysis.* Edited by Elizabeth Boody Schumpeter. New York: Oxford University Press, 1954.

————. *Ten Great Economists from Marx to Keynes.* 1951. Reprint, New York: Oxford University Press, 1965.

————. *Theorie der wirtschaftlichen Entwicklung.* Leipzig: Duncker & Humblot, 1912.

————. *Das Wesen und Hauptinhalt der Theoretischen Nationalökonomie.* Leipzig: Duncker & Humblot, 1908.

Schüz, Karl W. *Grundsätze der National-Oeconomie.* Tübingen: Osiander, 1843.

————. "Das politische Moment in der Volkswirtschaft." *ZGS* 1 (1844): 329–49.

Seager, Henry R. "Economics at Berlin and Vienna." In *Labor and Other Economic Essays.* New York: Harper, 1931, 1–29.

Seckendorff, Veit Ludwig von. *Teutscher Fürsten Stat.* 2 vols. 1665. Reprint, Glashütten: Auvermann, 1976.

Seier, Hellmut, "Sybels Vorlesung über Politik und die Kontinuität des 'staatsbildenden Liberalismus.'" *Historische Zeitschrift* 187 (1959): 90–112.

Seifert, Arno. "Staatenkunde. Eine neue Disziplin und ihr Wissenschaftstheoretischer Ort." In *Statistik und Staatsbeschreibung in der Neuzeit.* Edited by Mohammed Rassem and Justin Stagl. Paderborn: Schönigh, 1980, 217–48.

Sering, Max. *Arbeiterfrage und Kolonisation in den östlichen Provinzen Preussens.* Berlin: Parey, 1892.

———. *Die Verteilung des Grundbestizes und die Abwanderung vom Lande.* Berlin: Parey, 1910.

Sheehan, James. *The Career of Lujo Brentano.* Chicago: University of Chicago Press, 1966.

———. *German History, 1770–1866.* Oxford: Oxford University Press; Clarendon Press, 1989.

———. *German Liberalism in the Nineteenth Century.* Chicago: University of Chicago Press, 1978.

Sieber, Eberhard. "Der politische Professor um die Mitte des 19. Jahrhunderts." In *Beiträge zur Geschichte der Universität Tübingen.* Edited by Hansmartin Decker-Hauff et al. Tübingen: Attempto, 1977, 285–306.

Siemann, Wolfram. *"Deutschlands Ruhe, Sicherheit, und Ordnung": Die Anfänge der politischen Polizei, 1806–1866.* Tübingen: Niemeyer, 1985.

———. *Die deutsche Revolution von 1848/49.* Frankfurt/Main: Suhrkamp, 1985.

———. *Die frankfurter Nationalversammlung 1848/49 zwischen demokratischen Liberalismus und konservativer Reform.* Bern: Herbert Lang, 1976.

Simmel, Georg. *Soziologie.* 3d ed. Munich: Duncker & Humblot, 1923.

———. *Philosophie des Geldes.* 3d ed. Leipzig: Duncker & Humblot, 1920.

———. "Ueber das Wesen der Sozial-Psychologie." *ASS* 26 (1908): 291–95.

Simon, Christian. *Staat und Geschichtswissenschaft in Deutschland und Frankreich, 1871–1914.* 2 vols. Bern : Peter Lang, 1988.

Small, Albion. *The Cameralists.* Chicago: University of Chicago Press, 1909.

Smend, Rudolf. "Der Einfluss der deutschen Staats-und Verwaltungsrechts-lehre des 19. Jahrhunderts auf das Leben in Verfassung und Verwaltung." In *Staatsrechtliche Abhandlungen.* Berlin: Duncker & Humblot, 1955, 326–45.

Smith, Adam. *An Inquiry Into the Nature and Causes of the Wealth of Nations.* Edited by Edwin Cannan. 1776. Reprint, Chicago: University of Chicago Press, 1976.

———. *Lectures on Justice, Police, Revenue, and Arms.* Edited by Edwin Cannan. New York: Kelly & Millman, 1956.

Smith, Woodruff. *Politics and the Sciences of Culture in Germany, 1840–1920.* New York: Oxford University Press, 1991.

Soden, Julius. *Die Nationalökonomie.* 4 vols. Vienna: Bauer, 1815.

Sombart, Werner. "Ideale der Sozialpolitik." *ASS* 10 (1897): 1–48.

———. *The Jews and Modern Capitalism.* Translated by M. Epstein. Glencoe, IL: Free Press, 1951.

———. "Karl Marx und die soziale Wissenschaft." *ASS* 26 (1908): 429–50.

———. *Der moderne Kaptalismus.* Leipzig: Duncker & Humblot, 1902.

Sommer, Louise. *Die Österreichischen Kameralisten.* 2 vols. 1920–25. Reprint, Aalen: Scientia Verlag, 1967.

Sommerlad, Theo, "Über das Studium der Wirtschaftsgeschichte." In *Festgabe für Johannes Conrad*. Edited by Hermann Paasche. Jena: Gustav Fischer, 1898, 97–111.

Sonnenfels, Joseph von. *Antrittsrede von der Unzulänglichkeit der alleinigen Erfahrung in den Geschäften der Staatswirtschaft*. Vienna: G. L. Schulz, 1764.

———. *Grundsätze der Policey, Handlung, und Finanz*. 5th ed. 3 vols. Vienna: Edlen von Kurzbeck, 1787.

Spann, Othmar. *Fundament der Volkswirtschaftslehre*. 5th ed. 1929. Reprint, Graz: Akademische Druck-u. Verlagsanstalt, 1967.

Spiegel, Henry William. *The Growth of Economic Thought*. 2d ed. Durham: Duke University Press, 1983.

Spindler, Max, ed. *Handbuch der Bayerischen Geschichte*. 4 vols. Munich: C. H. Beck, 1966–1975.

Springer, Anton. *Friedrich Christoph Dahlmann*. 2 vols. Leipzig: Hirzel, 1870–72.

[Staatswissenschaftlich-statistisches Seminar, Berlin. Reports, 1889–1912]. *Chronik der Königlichen Friedrich-Wilhelms-Universität zu Berlin*. 1889–1912.

"Staatswissenschaftliche Seminare." In vol. 2 of *Die Deutschen Universitäten*. Edited by Wilhelm Lexis. Berlin: Asher, 1893, 603–6.

Stavenhagen, Gerhard. *Geschichte der Wirtschaftstheorie*. Göttingen: Vandenhoeck & Ruprecht, 1951.

Stein, Lorenz von. *Gegenwart und Zukunft der Rechts-und Staatswissenschaft Deutschlands*. Stuttgart: Cotta, 1876.

———. *Geschichte der Socialen Bewegung in Frankreich*. 2d ed. Leipzig: Otto Wigand, 1855.

———. *Lehrbuch der Finanzwissenschaft*. 4th ed. Leipzig: Brockhaus, 1878.

———. *Der Socialismus und Communismus des heutigen Frankreichs*. Leipzig: Otto Wigand, 1842.

———. *System der Staatswissenschaften*. 2 vols. Tübingen: Cotta, 1852–56.

———. *Verwaltungslehre*. 8 vols. 1869–1884. Reprint, Aalen: Scientia, 1975.

Steinmetz, George. *Regulating the Social: The Welfare State and Local Politics in Imperial Germany*. Princeton: Princeton University Press, 1993.

Stengel, Carl von. "Begriff, Umfang und System des Verwaltungsrechts." *ZGS* 38 (1882): 219–61.

Stieda, Wilhelm. *Die Nationalökonomie als Universitätswissenschaft*. Leipzig: Teubner, 1906.

Stinzing, Roderich von and Ernst Landsberg. *Geschichte der Deutschen Rechtswissenschaft*. 3 vols. Munich: Oldenbourg, 1880–1910.

Stolleis, Michael. *Geschichte des Öffentlichen Rechts in Deutschland*. 2 vols. Munich: C. H. Beck, 1988–1992.

———. "Die 'Wiederbelebung der Verwaltungslehre' im Nationalsozialismus." In *Wissenschaft und Recht der Verwaltung Seit dem Ancien Regime*. Edited by Erk Volkmar Heyen. Frankfurt/Main: Klostermann, 1984, 147–62.

Storch, Heinrich Friedrich von. *Handbuch der National-Wirtschaftslehre*. 3 vols. Translated by Karl Heinrich Rau. Hamburg: Perthes & Besser, 1819.

Stuckenberg, J. H. W. *The Life of Immanuel Kant*. London: Macmillan, 1882.

Stützel-Prüsener, Marlies. "Die deutschen Lesegesellschaften im Zeitalter der Aufklärung." In *Lesegesellschaften und bürgerliche Emanzipation*. Edited by Otto Dann. Munich: C. H. Beck, 1981, 71–86.

Swedberg, Richard. *Schumpeter*. Princeton: Princeton University Press, 1991.

Sweet, Paul R. *Humboldt: A Biography.* 2 vols. Columbus: Ohio State University Press, 1978–80.

Szporluk, Roman. *Communism and Nationalism: Karl Marx versus Friedrich List.* New York: Oxford University Press, 1988.

"Tagebuch," *Chronik der Königlichen Vereinigten Friedrichs-Universität Halle-Wittenberg.* 1909.

Tenbruck, Friedrich. "Abschied der 'Wissenschaftslehre'?" In *Max Weber Heute: Erträge und Probleme der Forschung.* edited by Johannes Weiss. Frankfurt/Main: Suhrkamp, 1989, 90–115.

Thaer, Albrecht, *Einleitung zur Kenntniss der englischen Landwirtschaft,* 2d ed. 3 vols. Hanover: Hahn, 1801–1804.

———. *Geschichte meiner Wirtschaft zu Möglin.* Berlin: Realschulbuchhandlung, 1815.

———. *Grundsätze der rationellen Landwirtschaft.* 2d ed. 4 vols. Berlin: Realschulbuchhandlung, 1811–1812.

Thielen, Peter Gerrit. *Karl August von Hardenberg, 1750–1822: eine Biographie.* Cologne: Grote, 1967.

Thünen, Johann Heinrich von. *Der Isolierte Staat.* 3d ed. 1842–1850. Reprint, Jena: Gustav Fischer, 1930.

Tilly, Richard. "The Political Economy of Public Finance and the Industrialization of Prussia, 1815–1866." *Journal of Economic History* 26 (1966): 484–97.

———. "Germany, 1815–1870." In *Banking in the Early Stages of Industrialization.* Edited by Rondo Cameron. New York: Oxford University Press, 1967, 151–82.

Timm, Albrecht. *Kleine Geschichte der Technologie.* Stuttgart: Kohlhammer, 1964.

Titze, Hartmut. *Das Hochschulstudium in Preussen und Deutschland, 1820–1944.* Göttingen: Vandenhoeck & Ruprecht, 1987.

Toews, John. *Hegelianism: The Path Toward Dialectical Humanism, 1805–1841.* Cambridge: Cambridge University Press, 1980.

Tönnies, Ferdinand. "Die Anwendung der Deszendenztheorie auf Probleme der sozialen Entwicklung." In vol. 1 of *Soziologische Studien und Kritiken.* Jena: Gustav Fischer, 1925.

———. *Ferdinand Tönnies on Sociology: Pure, Applied, and Empirical.* Edited by Werner Cahnmann and Rudolf Heberle. Chicago: University of Chicago Press, 1971.

———. *Gemeinschaft und Gesellschaft.* 8th ed. 1935. Reprint, Darmstadt: Wissenschaftliche Buchgesellschaft, 1979.

———. "Das Wesen der Soziologie." In vol. 1 of *Soziologische Studien und Kritiken.* Jena: Gustav Fischer, 1925, pp. 350–68.

Treitschke, Heinrich von. *Die Gesellschaftswissenschaft: Ein Kritischer Versuch.* 1859. Reprint, Darmstadt: Wissenchaftliche Buchgesellschaft, 1980.

———. *Politik.* Edited by Max Cornicelius. 2 vols. Leipzig: Hirzel, 1899.

———. *Der Socialismus und seine Gönner.* Berlin: Georg Reimer, 1875.

Treue, Wilhelm. "Adam Smith in Deutschland. Zum Problem des 'Politischen Professors' zwischen 1776 und 1810." *In Deutschland und Europa. Festschrift für Hans Rothfels.* Edited by Werner Conze. Düsseldorf: Droste, 1951, 101–33.

Treue, Wolfgang, ed. *Deutsche Parteiprogramme, 1861–1954.* Göttingen: Musterschmidt, 1961.

Tribe, Keith. *Governing Economy: The Reformation of German Economic Discourse, 1750–1840.* Cambridge: Cambridge University Press, 1988.

Troitzsch, Ulrich. *Ansätze technologischen Denkens bei den Kameralisten des 17. und 18. Jahrhunderts.* Berlin: Duncker & Humblot, 1966.

Tschuprow, A. A. "Die Aufgaben der Theorie der Statistik." *SJ* 29 (1905), 421–80.

Tuck, Richard. "The 'Modern' Theory of Natural Law." In *The Languages of Political Theory in Early Modern Europe.* Edited by Anthony Pagden. Cambridge: Cambridge University Press, 1987, 99–119.

Turgot, A. R. J. "Plan for a Paper on Taxation . . ." In *The Economics of A. R. J. Turgot.* Edited by P. D. Groenewegen. The Hague: Nijhoff, 1977.

Turner, Steven. "The Prussian Professoriate and the Research Imperative, 1790–1840." In *Epistemological and Social Problems of the Sciences in the Early Nineteenth Century.* Edited by H. N. Jahnke and M. Otte. Dordrecht: Riedel, 1981, 109–21.

———. "University Reformers and Professorial Scholarship in Germany, 1760–1806." In vol. 2 of *The University and Society.* Edited by Lawrence Stone. Princeton: Princeton University Press, 1974, 495–531.

Tutzke, Dietrich. *Alfred Grotjahn.* Leipzig: Teubner, 1979.

Valera, Gabriella. "Statistik, Staatengeschichte, Geschichte im 18. Jahrhundert." In *Aufklärung und Geschichte.* Edited by Hans Erich Bödeker. Göttingen: Vandenhoeck & Ruprecht, 1986, 119–43.

Vann, James Allen. *The Making of a State: Württemberg, 1593–1793.* Ithaca: Cornell University Press, 1984.

Valentin, Veit. *Geschichte der deutschen Revolution von 1848–1849.* 2 vols. Cologne: Kiepenheuer & Witsch, 1977.

Verein für Sozialpolitik. *Die Reform der Staatswissenschaftlichen Studien.* Edited by I. Jastrow. Schriften des Vereins für Sozialpolitik. No. 160. München: Duncker & Humblot, 1920.

———. *Verhandlungen der Generalversammlung . . . 1907 (Die Berufsmässige Vorbildung der Volkswirtschaftlichen Beamten).* Schriften des Vereins für Sozialpolitik. No. 125. Leipzig: Duncker & Humblot, 1908.

———. *Verhandlungen der Generalversammlung in Wien . . . 1909.* Schriften des Vereins für Sozialpolitik. No. 132. Leipzig: Duncker & Humblot, 1910.

———. *Die Vorbildung zum höheren Verwaltungsdienst in den deutschen Staaten, Österreich, und Frankreich.* Schriften des Vereins für Sozialpolitik. No. 34. Leipzig: Duncker & Humblot, 1887.

Vierhaus, Rudolf. "Aufklärung und Reformzeit." In *Reformen in Rheinbündischen Deutschland.* Edited by Eberhard Weis. Munich: Oldenbourg, 1984, 287–301.

Vopelius, Marie-Elizabeth. *Die altliberalen Ökonomen und die Reformzeit.* Stuttgart: Gustav Fischer, 1968.

Vorstand der Staatswissenschaftlichen Gesellschaft, ed. *Hundert Jahre Staatswissenschaftliche Gesellschaft zu Berlin, 1883–1983.* Berlin: Duncker & Humblot, 1983.

Wagner, Adolph. *Agrar- und Industriestaat.* 2d ed. Jena: Gustav Fischer, 1902.

———. *Die akademische Nationalökonomie und der Socialismus.* Berlin: Becker, 1895.

———. *Allgemeine oder theoretische Volkswirtschaftslehre.* Leipzig: Carl Winter, 1876.

———. *Beiträge zur Lehre von den Banken.* Leipzig: Voss, 1857.

———. *Briefe, Dokumente, Augenzeubenberichte, 1851–1917.* Edited by Heinrich Rübner. Berlin: Duncker & Humblot, 1978.

———. "Einiges von und über Rodbertus-Jagetzow." *ZGS* 34 (1878): 199–237.

————. *Finanzwissenschaft.* 3 vols. Leipzig: Carl Winter, 1877–1889.

————. *Gedächtnisrede auf Hans von Mangoldt.* Freiburg: Poppen, 1870.

————. *Die Gesetzmässigkeit in den scheinbar willkürlichen menschlichen Handlungen vom Standpunkt der Statistik.* Hamburg: Boyes & Geisler, 1864.

————. *Rede über die sociale Frage.* Berlin: Wiegandt & Grieben, 1872.

————. Review of *Handbuch der Politischen Oekonomie.* Edited by G. Schönberg. *ZGS* 39 (1883): 258–72.

————. "Systematische Nationalökonomie." *JNS* 46 (1886): 197–252.

Waitz, Georg. *Grundzüge der Politik.* 1862. Reprint, New York: Arno, 1979.

Walker, Mack. *German Home Towns: Community, State, and Local Estate, 1648–1871* Ithaca: Cornell University Press, 1971.

————. *Johann Jakob Moser and the Holy Roman Empire of the German Nation.* Chapel Hill: University of North Carolina Press, 1981.

————. "Rights and Functions: The Social Categories of Eighteenth-Century German Jurists and Cameralists." *Journal of Modern History* 50 (1978): 234–51.

Walras, Léon. *Correspondence of Léon Walras and Related Papers.* 3 vols. Edited by William Jaffé. Amsterdam: North Holland, 1965.

Waszek, Norbert, ed. *Die Institutionalisierung der Nationalökonomie an deutschen Universitäten.* St. Katharinen: Scripta Mercaturae, 1988.

Weber, Alfred. "Neuorientierung in der Sozialpolitik?" *ASS* 36 (1913): 1–13.

Weber, Alfred, and Ludwig Pohle. "Deutschland Am Scheidewege." *SJ* 26 (1902): 1294–1305, 1701–17.

Weber, Marianne. *Max Weber: ein Lebensbild.* Tübingen: Mohr, 1926.

Weber, Max. *Briefe, 1906–1908.* Abt. 2, vol. 5 of *Gesamtausgabe.* Edited by M. Rainer Lepsius and Wolfgang Mommsen. Tübingen: Mohr, 1990.

————. *Grundriss zu den Vorlesungen Über Allgemeine "Theoretische" Nationalökonomie* [1898]. Tübingen: Mohr, 1990.

————. *Max Weber on Universities.* Translated and edited by Edward Shils. Chicago: University of Chicago Press, 1973.

————. *Max Weber. Werk und Person.* Edited by Eduard Baumgarten. Tübingen: Mohr, 1964.

————. "Der Nationalstaat und die Volkswirtschaftspolitik." In *Gesammelte Politische Schriften.* Edited by Johannes Winckelmann. 2d ed. Tübingen: Mohr, 1958, 1–25.

————. "Die 'Objektivität' sozialwissenschaftlicher und sozialpolitischer Erkenntnis." In *Gesammelte Aufsätze zur Wissenschaftslehre.* 2d ed. Tübingen: Mohr, 1951, 146–214.

————. "Roscher und Knies und die logischen Probleme der Historischen Nationalökonomie." *Gesammelte Aufsätze zur Wissenschaftslehre.* 2d ed. Tübingen: Mohr, 1951, 1–145.

"Der Sinn der 'Wertfreiheit' der soziologischen und ökonomischen Wissenschaften." *Gesammelte Aufsätze zur Wissenschaftslehre.* 2nd ed. Tübingen: Mohr, 1951, 475–526.

————. *Wirtschaft und Gesellschaft.* Edited by Johannes Winckelmann. 2 vols. 1921. Reprint, Cologne: Keipenheuer & Witsch, 1964.

[Weber, Max, Werner Sombart, and Edgar Jaffé.] "Geleitwort." *ASS* 19 (1904): i–vii.

Wegele, Franz X. *Geschichte der Universität Würzburg.* 2 vols. 1882. Reprint, Aalen: Scientia, 1969.

Wehler, Hans Ulrich. *Deutsche Gesellschaftsgeschichte.* 2 vols. Munich: C. H. Beck, 1987.

————, ed. *Deutsche Historiker.* 7 vols. Göttingen: Vandenhoek & Ruprecht, 1971–1980.

————. *The German Empire 1871–1918.* Translated by Kim Traynor. Leamington Spa: Berg Publishers, 1985.

Weindling, Paul. *Health, Race, and German Politics between National Unification and Nazism, 1870–1945.* Cambridge: Cambridge University Press, 1989.

Weis, Eberhard. "Enlightenment and Absolutism in the Holy Roman Empire: Thoughts on Enlightened Absolutism in Germany." *Journal of Modern History* 58 (1986): 181–97.

————. *Montgelas.* 2d ed. Munich: C. H. Beck, 1988.

Weisert, Hermann. *Die Verfassung der Universität Heidelberg,* Abhandlungen der Heidelberger Akademie der Wissenschaften, Phil.-hist. Klasse. Heidelberg: Carl Winter, 1974.

Wendt, Siegfried. "Schumacher." In vol. 9 of *Handwörterbuch der Sozialwissenschaften.* Stuttgart: Gustav Fischer, 1956–65, 150–51.

Wenger, Karl. "Lorenz von Stein und die Entwicklung der Verwaltungswissenschaft in Österreich." In *Staat und Gesellschaft. Studien über Lorenz von Stein.* Edited by Roman Schnur. Berlin: Duncker & Humblot, 1978, 479–501.

Wernitz, Axel. "Friedrich Benedikt Wilhelm von Hermann (1795–1868)." *Oberbayrisches Archiv* 90 (1968): 26–37.

Whaley, Joachim. "The Protestant Enlightenment in Germany." In *The Enlightenment in National Context.* Edited by Roy Porter and Mikulas Teich. Cambridge: Cambridge University Press, 1981, 106–17.

Wieser, Friedrich von. *Der Natürliche Werth.* Vienna: Hölder, 1889.

Wigard, Franz, ed. *Stenographischer Bericht über die Verhandlungen der deutschen Constituirenden Nationalversammlung.* 10 vols. Leipzig: Breitkopf und Härtel, 1848–1850.

Wilhelm, Walter. *Zur juristischen Methodenlehre im 19. Jahrhundert.* Frankfurt/Main: Klostermann, 1958.

Willey, Thomas E. *Back to Kant.* Detroit: Wayne State University Press, 1978.

Williamson, John G. *Karl Helfferich, 1872–1924.* Princeton: Princeton University Press, 1971.

Winckelmann, Johannes. *Max Weber's hinterlassenes Hauptwerk: Die Wirtschaft und die Gesellschaftlichen Ordnungen und Mächte.* Tübingen: Mohr, 1986.

Winkel, Harald. *Die deutsche Nationalökonomie im 19. Jahrhundert.* Darmstadt: Wissenschaftliche Buchgesellschaft, 1977.

Winter, J. M. "Some Paradoxes of the First World War." In *The Upheaval of War.* Edited by Richard Wall and J. M. Winter. Cambridge: Cambridge University Press, 1988, 9–42.

Witt, Peter-Christian. *Die Finanzpolitik des deutschen Reiches von 1903 bis 1913.* Lübeck: Mattheisen, 1970.

Wittrock, Gerhard. *Die Kathedersozialisten bis zur Eisenacher Versammlung.* 1939. Reprint, Vaduz: Kraus, 1965.

Wunder, Bernd. *Geschichte der Bürokratie in Deutschland.* Frankfurt/Main: Suhrkamp, 1986.

————. *Privilegierung und Disciplinierung. Die Entstehung des Berufsbeamtentums in Bayern und Württemberg (1780–1825).* Munich: Oldenbourg, 1978.

Zachariae, Karl Salomo. *Vierzig Bücher vom Staate.* 5 vols. Stuttgart and Tübingen: Cotta, 1820 (vols. 1–2); Heidelberg: Osswald, 1826 (vols. 3–5).

Zehntner, Hans. *Das Staatslexikon von Rotteck und Welcker.* 1929. Reprint, Vaduz: Topos, 1984.

Zielenziger, Kurt. *Die alten deutschen Kameralisten.* 1913. Reprint, Frankfurt/Main: Sauer & Auvermann, 1966.

Zimmermann, Gustav. *Die deutsche Polizei im neunzehnten Jahrhundert.* 2 vols. Hannover: Schlüter, 1845.

Zincke, Georg Heinrich. *Cameralisten-Bibliothek.* 2 vols. 1751. Reprint, Glashütten: Auvermann, 1973.

Index

Abbe, Ernst, 289
Abel, Carl, 99
Academy for Social and Commercial Studies,
Frankfurt, 278–79
Achenwall, Gottfried, 40, 41–42, 43, 44, 56,
84, 131–32, 302
Administration, science of, 43, 169, 200–201,
212, 260, 306
Administrative law. *See* Law, administrative
Aesthetic dimension of social science, 299–
300, 312
Aggregate national income, 121
Agrarian League (Farmers' League), 265, 290,
291
Agrarian vs. industrial state, controversy,
293–95
Agricultural economics, 78, 135–38
Agricultural institutes, 76, 134; Göttingen,
138; Greifswald, 135; Halle, 215; Jena, 135;
Möglin, 77–78, 134
Agricultural policy, 30–31, 53, 64, 127–28,
139, 230, 288, 290–91, 293–95, 324; credit,
78–79, 131; inner colonization, 290–91. *See
also* Serfdom, elimination of
Agriculture, study of, 6, 16, 22, 29–31, 76–79,
95, 96, 99, 103, 120, 133–39, 174, 214–15,
256, 324; as *Ökonomie*, 79
Ahrens, Heinrich, 177–78, 182, 198
Allgemeines Landrecht (Prussian legal code), 51,
82
Allgemeine Staatslehre. *See* Politics, science of
Altenstein, Karl v., 71
Althoff, Friedrich, 266–68, 269, 273–74, 275,
279–80, 284, 305, 321
American Social Science Assocation, 224
Analysis, as intellectual strategy, 121, 123, 136
Anthropology, and sciences of state, 302–44
Anti-Semitism, 225, 271, 272, 283–84
Archiv für Soziale Gesetzgebung und Statistik, 287

Archiv für Sozialwissenschaft und Sozialpolitik, 289,
303–4, 317
Aristotle, 2, 11, 16, 17, 18, 19, 20, 40, 115,
247
Arndt, Ernst M., 48
Assimilation, as intellectual strategy, 47, 55
Association for Continuing Education in Sci-
ences of State, 280
Association of German Economists, 281–82
Association of German Engineers, 215, 232
Associations, voluntary, 259, 265, 272. *See also*
Society, science of
Austria, curricular requirements, 69–70, 167–
68, 250, 260
Austrian school of economics, 245–56, 261,
311–14, 316, 329

Baden, curricular requirements, 68–69, 97,
122, 134, 200, 212
Ballod, Carl, 292, 316
Banking, 131, 325–26; study of, 189–91, 241,
309–10
Basedow, Johann B., 49
Bauer, Otto, 311
Bavaria, curricular requirements, 51–52, 99,
165, 199
Bebel, August, 302
Becher, Johann J., 12–13, 26, 28–29, 85
Bechstein, Johann M., 79n
Beckmann, Johann, 29–33, 34, 40, 41, 80
Bedürfnis, economic need, 35–36, 65–66
Behr, Wilhelm J., 58
Bentham, Jeremy, 115
Berg, Günther H. von, 82
Berlin, sciences of state at, 72–74, 103–9, 138,
171, 217, 244–45, 275, 280, 282, 287, 296,
299, 305
Bernhard, Ludwig, 268, 286, 321
Bernstein, Eduard, 271